PROBLEM SOLVING WITH C

JACQUELINE A. JONES & KEITH HARROW

Brooklyn College of the City University of New York

Scott/Jones Inc., Publishers
P.O. Box 696
El Granada, CA 94018
Tel: (415) 726-2436
Fax: (415)-726-4693
E-mail: scottjones2@aol.com
Web page: http://www.scottjonespub.com

PROBLEM SOLVING WITH C
by Jacqueline A. Jones and Keith Harrow

Production Management: Heather Bennett
Copy Editor: Barbara Bannon
Design and Composition: Cecelia G. Morales, Arizona Publication Service
Cover Design: Michelle Calvert and Skip Kuebel, Cyber Island Graphics
Book Manufacturing: Malloy Lithographing

TRADEMARKS

ADDITIONAL TITLES OF INTEREST FROM SCOTT/JONES

Visual Basic Programming
The Visual Basic Coursebook
Quick Start in Visual Basic
The DOS 6 Coursebook
Quick Start in DOS
by Forest Lin

The Windows Textbook
The Windows 95 Textbook
Quick Start in Windows
Short Course: Windows 95
by Stewart Venit

Modern FORTRAN 77/90, Alternate Edition
Fortran for Scientists and Engineers, Second Edition
by Gary Bronson

Assembly Language for the IBM PC Family
Quick Start in C++
by William Jones

C by Discovery, Second Edition
by L. S. Foster

Computer Architecture and Assembly Language: The MC6800
by G.M Prabhu and Charles Wright

Word Perfect 6.0a for Windows
by Rolayne Day

Visual Basic with Applications
by Mark Simkin

CONTENTS

PREFACE

TO THE STUDENT

Rather than presenting a series of polished, one-step solutions to programming problems, this text seeks to lead you through the process of analyzing problems and writing programs to solve them. You should be an active participant in this process, not a passive reader or memorizer. This is reinforced in three ways.

1. First, we've included numerous Self-Check questions throughout the text. We offer one very important piece of advice: Whenever you see a question in the text, try to answer it. If you can't think of the answer immediately, try looking back through the section until you find it. If necessary, read the entire chapter a second time. At that point, you should be able to answer almost all of the questions.

2. Second, in addition to the Self-Checks, we've included a comprehensive set of exercises at the end of each chapter. We urge you to do as many of these exercises as possible, including all of the simple ones at the beginning of each group.

3. Thrid, throughout the book, we ask you to write complete programs in a clear, consistent style. We've tried to write our own programs in this way, especially by including comments. We hope that you will strive to follow this same pattern.

FEATURES OF THIS TEXT

In glancing through the text, you may notice a variety of headlines, boxes, and graphics. These elements will help you organize your study of the C programming language and guide you in using this book as a reference tool. These features are outlined below.

CHAPTER OVERVIEW

At the beginning of each chapter, there is a list of the items covered in that chapter. The list may include the following:

SYNTAX CONCEPTS: the new features of the C language to be introduced.

PROGRAMMING CONCEPTS: the programming ideas we will discuss. (These are somewhat independent of the choice of language.)

CONTROL STRUCTURES: the features of C that allow a programmer to control the way in which a program is built up from smaller pieces.

PROBLEM-SOLVING TECHNIQUES: the general concepts of how to go about writing a program to solve a problem.

STATEMENT OF THE PROBLEM: the detailed statement of the problem to be solved.

In addition, throughout the book, there are sections of text set off from the main flow of the discussion with icons, special headings, or in boxes. These contain different types of material. Here is an explanation of each type:

STYLE WORKSHOP advises the beginning programmer on what is considered to be the better way to write a section of code. As you write more and more programs in C, you will become sensitive to issues of style.

IN DEPTH discusses topics that go somewhat beyond the scope of an introductory programming text. The material is provided for enrichment and deeper understanding, but it is not crucial to understanding the basic ideas in the course.

HIGHLIGHTS indicates one of the most important features relating to a topic. Be sure that you understand each Highlights section before you go on in the text.

 CAUTION warns that you should be especially careful when using the particular feature of the language it describes. These often list traps and pitfalls to avoid.

PROGRAM TRACE signals a step-by-step analysis of how a program works. It is most important that you understand these processes. You must be able to follow each trace in the text and be able to complete one on your own.

EXAMPLES are designed to illustrate a specific feature of the language that has just been described in the text. Some examples are quite basic, but others introduce useful applications of the new feature.

SELF-CHECK

A **Self-Check** consists of a series of questions at the end of each section of text. Some of the questions are simple and can be answered in a word or two, while others require more thought. Answers to all the Self-Checks are in the back of the book.

A general form box shows the **general form** of a C feature, as shown below.

> *general form text*

 PROGRAM LISTING

This heading usually designates the code for a solution to a problem. At least one complete solution for each program is included on the disk accompanying this textbook.

A shaded oval represents the screen and contains **output** from a section of code.

$$\boxed{\text{output}}$$

Finally, each chapter contains two sections of intensive review material:

♦ The **Summary** gives an overview of the chapter's contents. Be sure that you are comfortable with all of the points covered in each summary.

♦ The **Exercises** test your mastery of the material presented in each chapter.

TO THE INSTRUCTOR

WHAT THIS TEXT IS

This text is intended to be used in a one- or two-semester course covering introductory programming using C. No previous knowledge of mathematics or computer science is assumed, other than a familiarity with the mathematical notation used in a high-school algebra course.

Problem-Driven Pedagogy

The basic approach of the text is this: Present a real problem; interact with the student in writing a program to solve the problem; ask the student to solve a similar problem as a homework assignment.

Each chapter starts with a statement of a real problem. The major portion of the chapter is then devoted to using problem-solving techniques to develop a C program that will solve the problem. The problems are simple at first, but they reach quite a complicated level rather quickly. The first few problems involve numerical calculations, since this gives the student an easy way to check some of the results by hand. We have found that non-numerical examples used early in a text tend to be either trivial (for example, printing patterns of asterisks or a message saying "Hello") or else so concerned with analyzing details of the problem that the point of the problem is lost.

In most cases, it is simpler to work with numbers in C, especially at the beginning of the text. However, if an instructor desires to, it should be relatively easy to modify one or two of these numerical problems somewhat so that a subject area of relevance to the students is introduced. A number of the later examples are non-numerical, including a large text-processing program and a program to construct and manipulate a database.

Flexible Applications

In the same way, an instructor can easily make the problems more oriented to scientific applications, business applications, and so on. For example, instead of sorting test scores, the students can be asked to sort readings from laboratory experiments or a company's sales data. We encourage instructors to modify the problems in this way. We have purposely tried to avoid emphasizing any one particular subject area, leaving it up to the individual instructor to decide the exact orientation a class should take. The text has been used successfully in this way for a variety of introductory programming courses, both at Brooklyn College and elsewhere.

Programming Is Not a Spectator Sport

The text attempts to involve the student in writing a program, instead of just presenting a polished, one-step solution to the problem. The student is an active participant in developing the program, not a passive reader or memorizer. Self-Checks in every section ask the students to stop and test their mastery of the material they have just read.

Students are encouraged to write complete programs in a clear, consistent style. We try to set a good example by writing our own programs in this way, especially by including comments. We have found that students are incredibly imitative. Our experience shows that if students always see programs which are written in a clear, consistent way, with comments, they will strive to follow this same pattern.

As the student learns increasingly more sophisticated C constructs (**for** loops, **while** loops, **if** statements, functions, etc.), the programs become more and more complex.

Problem-Solving Techniques

Problem-solving techniques, including pseudocode and the concept of an algorithm, are introduced at the beginning of the text. Other problem-solving methods, including stepwise refinement and modular programming, are introduced a little later and then used consistently throughout the entire text. Most programs are written using a top-down approach, although the bottom-up method is also discussed.

Each chapter ends with a summary to review the new C statements and programming concepts introduced in that chapter. In addition to the numerous Self-Check questions, each chapter is followed by an exercise set, containing a minimum of 20 exercises per chapter, with many of the chapters containing 30 or more. Some of the exercises review the concepts just introduced; others further develop the ideas presented in the basic program; still others introduce entirely new problems suitable for homework assignments that are more challenging than simply modifying an existing program. An instructor can easily add to, or remove details from, any of these problems to arrive at a set of assignments that will be geared to the level and interests (scientific, business, or social sciences, for example) of a particular class. As you know, most students will benefit from doing as many of the exercises as possible in every chapter, including all of the simple ones at the beginning of each group of exercises, plus the Self-Checks.

Organization of the Text

◆ Chapter 0 introduces the idea of programming languages and provides an introduction to computer hardware and software for those students who have no prior computer experience.

◆ Chapters 1-6 develop a basic understanding of programming, including the concepts of loops, reading a set of data, stepwise refinement, functions, control structures, and so on.

◆ Chapter 7 then introduces arrays.

Chapters 0–7 form a core that can be followed by any of the remaining chapters: Chapter 8 (Pointers), Chapter 9 (Character Strings), Chapter 10 (Searching and Sorting), Chapter 11 (Structures), or Chapter 12 (various advanced topics). With a few modifications to certain sections, an instructor can use essentially any permutation of these topics, although Chapter 8 must precede Chapter 9.

Enrichment

Most chapters contain Enrichment sections. These sections contain additional material which is relevant to the topics of the chapter, but not necessary to the solution of the chapter problem or the flow of the course. These sections may be skipped at a first reading and may be covered at the instructor's discretion.

Appendices V through VII cover standard I/O streams and files, including file I/O functions; an instructor may introduce this material when the students need to send output to the printer. In particular,

Appendix V contains a very simple introduction to redirection, piping, and *fprintf*, suitable for use with Chapter 3.

CHAPTER DEPENDENCIES:

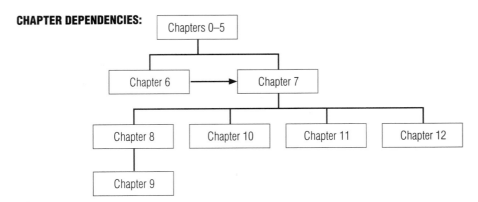

A typical course that meets for three or four hours per week should be able to cover the first nine chapters, plus two or three more. At this point, the student will have acquired basic programming skills and will be ready for a course in assembly language programming, program design and analysis, or data structures.

WHAT THIS TEXT IS NOT

The text is not meant to be an encyclopedia on C; it is not designed to teach features of DOS or Unix or some other operating system; it is not intended as a broad introduction to the field of data structures. We feel that it is impossible to cover all of these things in a single text. We have tried to give the students a solid introduction to programming, covering almost all of the basic features of C; we have touched on how a C programmer interacts with the operating system, including the use of redirection and command-line parameters; and we have included just the briefest introduction to the use of more complex data structures in C. All of these topics can be pursued in greater depth, but we leave that for other books.

DEFAULT ASSUMPTIONS

The text has been designed for use with any ANSI C compiler. In Chapter 1, there is a short introduction to running programs in DOS and in Unix. Sections in the Instructor's Resource Guide cover the use of the Turbo C++ Version 3.0 compiler running under DOS and the use of the ANSI C compiler running under Unix on a SUN Sparcstation. However, the programs have been written to minimize the special features of any one compiler. Almost all programs will run (possibly with a few minor changes) using any compiler based on ANSI C. A student using the text with some other compiler on a microcomputer, a workstation, or even a mainframe should be able to translate the programs into the appropriate C dialect quite easily.

SUPPLEMENTARY MATERIAL

The following material is provided with the text or available on request from the publisher:

♦ A 3½-inch diskette is included with every textbook. This DOS-formatted disk contains source code for at least one solution to every programming problem in the textbook, a fix for the Borland C compiler bug mentioned in Chapter 11, and answers to selected even-numbered exercises.

♦ An Instructor's Resource Guide is available from the publisher.[1] It contains a sample course syllabus, sample tests, and a sample final exam, as well as answers to selected odd-numbered exercises. In addition, it contains a section on the use of the Turbo C++ Version 3.0 compiler running under DOS on the IBM-PC and compatible machines and another section on the use of the ANSI C compiler running under Unix on a SUN Sparcstation. Adopters may reproduce the appropriate operating system information for each student in their classes.

E-MAIL ADDRESSES

Please feel free to advise the authors directly of any errors or rough spots you find in this book. Send e-mail to the following addresses:

jones@sci.brooklyn.cuny.edu   *or*   **harrow@sci.brooklyn.cuny.edu**

ACKNOWLEDGMENTS

It is a pleasure to acknowledge the assistance we have received in writing this book. First, the faculty and staff at Brooklyn College deserve our gratitude. Aaron Tenenbaum, the chair of our department, has been extremely supportive over the many years we have worked on this and other texts. Many of our colleagues at Brooklyn College have shared their expertise with us. In particular, David Arnow and Gerald Weiss served as our resident experts on C. Even though they did not always agree (with each other or with us), they have given us the benefit of their years of experience in writing real-world C code, and they helped us adjust this experience to an academic environment. Yedidyah Langsam was also very helpful in clarifying a number of issues, both language-related and pedagogic. A number of people have taught using an earlier version of this manuscript, and they have shared their experiences with us. For this, we are grateful to Chaya Gurwitz, Moshe Lowenthal, and Gerald Weiss. Eva Cogan has brought numerous errors to our attention. We would especially like to thank Annie Lee of the Brooklyn College Office of Information Technology Services; she caught many errors that would have embarrassed us if they had appeared without correction. Annie and the staff at the Brooklyn College Computer Center deserve our thanks.

A number of Brooklyn College students have assisted us in preparation of the manuscript, testing examples, and supplying answers to many of the exercises. These include: Ari Bleicher, Alex Bloch, Hong Gao, Yuriy Grager, Yevgeny Kolyakov, Henry Mok, Boris Naronov, Malky Nissenbaum, Ezhar Paz, Vitaly Shub, Yukie Tanaka, Ailian Tsui, Alex Tsymbal, and Wen Eng Yang.

We owe a tremendous debt to Dr. Barry Jacobs, a senior scientist at NASA's Goddard Space Flight Center. The problem-solving approach to programming that forms the theme of the text is based directly on his teaching method, which was inspired by the late Jack Wolfe of Brooklyn College. Nan Borreson, Publishing Relations Senior Manager at Borland International, has been extremely helpful in supplying us with information on Turbo C++. Her assistance, and that of her company, is much appreciated.

---

[1] The address and telephone number of the publisher appear on the title page.

The entire staff at Scott/Jones, Inc. publishers has been outstanding. Our copyeditor, Barbara Bannon, worked hard to clean up our text, making it shorter and clearer, and in the process catching many mistakes. The production editor, Heather Bennett, juggled draft chapters, copy edited manuscripts, galleys, and page proofs with care and good humor. For this, we give our thanks. Cathy Baehler has done an excellent proofreading job, while Skip Kueble and Michelle Calvert should be thanked for the cover. Cecelia Morales is the gifted compositor/designer who translated our drab text files into lovely pages.

We would like to acknowledge the following reviewers who have contributed many comments, criticisms, and suggestions for improvement:

Stephen Allan, Utah State University
John Ayila, San Jose State University
Jon Burgin, Texas Tech University
Thomas Byther, University of Maine
Richard Cockrum, California State Polytechnic University
Ken Collier, Northern Arizona University
Michael Gelotte, Bellevue Community College
Reza Hashemi, Howard University
Patricia Hines, Brookdale Community College
Dennis Huggins, The State University of New York at Oneonta
Stephen Leach, Florida State University
Renee McCauley, University of Southern Louisiana
Mike Pressman, C.W. Post Campus of Long Island University
James Richards, Bemidji State College
Nancy Roberts, Pennsylvania State University
Ali Salehnia, South Dakota State University
Bob Signorile, Boston College
Susan Wallace, University of North Florida.

Consulting editor Stewart Venit suggested a number of major structural changes which greatly increased the clarity and readability of the text. We are grateful to him for sharing both his technical and authorial expertise.

Our publisher, Richard Jones, deserves special thanks. Through his constant emphasis on rethinking, reorganizing, and rewriting over the past two years, he has driven us to make continual improvements in the manuscript, even after we thought we were finished. He never let us be satisfied with anything less than the best we could do. For this, we owe him a tremendous debt. If this book finds an audience, all three of us will be happy.

Naturally, we derive the greatest pleasure in thanking our families. Keith would like to thank his children, David and Jill, for letting him get to the computer every now and then, and his wife, Madeline, for accepting the countless hours spent in preparation of the book. Most of all, he would like to thank her for putting up with the boxes all over the den. Jackie would like to thank her husband, Michael Gordon, for his patience with the evenings and weekends at the computer, and for supplying take-out Chinese food.

Jacqueline A. Jones and Keith Harrow
Brooklyn, New York

INTRODUCTION

0

CONCEPTS: machine language, high-level computer languages, compiler, C programming language, parts of the computer, hardware and software, computer programs

HOW TO READ CHAPTER 0

OUTLINE:

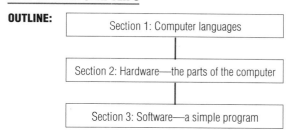

INTRODUCTION

This book tries to teach you two things, one directly and one indirectly. Its major goal is to teach you to write computer programs in a language called C. In the process, you should learn quite a bit about problem solving. This indirect effect, which is probably more beneficial than the direct one, becomes clearer as you proceed through the text.

SECTION 1 COMPUTER LANGUAGES

MACHINE LANGUAGE

Computers have had a considerable impact on our lives in the past 50 or 60 years, and this impact is bound to be even greater in the future. Therefore, it is increasingly important for a person to be able to interact with these machines. Even though computers seem to be all-knowing, the only language they "understand" is their own **machine language**. This machine language varies greatly from one computer family to another (e.g., personal computers, workstations, or large multiuser computers, called mainframes) and, to a smaller degree, among computer models within the same family. However, from a human point of view, the most striking feature about all machine languages is that they are composed solely of long strings of zeros and ones. For example, 0010101111000011 is a simple subtraction instruction in the machine language for IBM-compatible personal computers (PCs).

This format makes it quite hard for a person to learn how to use machine language. On the other hand, it is even harder for a computer to use English, French, Chinese, or another natural language with which human beings are comfortable. Natural languages, especially English, are notoriously ambiguous and imprecise. (A computer would have trouble interpreting this sentence: "I cannot recommend this applicant too highly.")

HIGH-LEVEL COMPUTER LANGUAGES

Since a computer prefers machine language, while a person wants to use a natural language, special **high-level computer languages** have been developed to bridge this communication gap. A high-level language, like C, uses English words plus symbols and numbers. It is specifically designed to be clear and precise in a way that natural languages cannot be. Although a typical high-level computer language is not as easy for a person to use as English, it is relatively simple to learn one of these languages.

COMPILATION

However, the high-level language must still be translated into machine language before the computer can understand it. This translation is done by a special computer program called a compiler. The **compiler** translates the program in two stages. First, it converts it to **assembly language**, whose instructions have a one-to-one correspondence with machine language but are easily read by humans. Then it replaces the assembly language instructions with the corresponding machine language, as shown in Figure 0-1.

At the beginning of your first course in computer programming, the compiler (the program that translates what you write into machine language) and the computer (the physical machine) probably seem almost identical. Gradually, you will learn how to distinguish the compiler's work from something done by the computer.

SOME HIGH-LEVEL LANGUAGES

There are a large number of high-level computer languages. Two of the very first, Fortran and COBOL, were developed in the 1950s and are still in use. Fortran, which stands for Formula Translation, is especially adapted to the needs of scientific computing. COBOL, which stands for COmmon Business Oriented Language, is used in business. It is readable even by someone who knows little about programming.

Some other common languages include Ada, BASIC, C, Modula-2, Pascal, and PL/I. These are general-purpose languages, used to create varied types of applications. Each has strengths and weaknesses which make it appropriate for certain tasks and not others.

FIGURE 0-1 Translation from high-level language to machine code

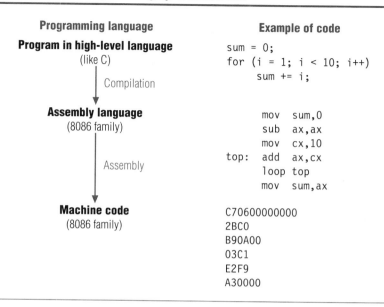

THE C PROGRAMMING LANGUAGE

The particular language used in this book is C. C was designed to be a simple, portable language that gives the programmer access to all functions of the machine. The language is portable because it works on different kinds of computers; for example, a program written on a PC can be run on a Sun workstation and vice versa. Over the past 10 to 15 years, C has become an extremely popular language for commercial and scientific use. More recently, largely because of its growing popularity in the business world, C has also been used to teach computer programming at colleges and universities. The version of C that we use is called **ANSI C**.

You will see that C has a number of powerful features. Unfortunately, these features also allow a naive programmer to go astray. As these features are introduced, we will try to explain the right way to use them and how to avoid potential pitfalls. A more detailed justification for using C is best left for a later course. For now, it is enough to say that C is relatively easy to use and widely available on a variety of personal computers and workstations. Once you know C, it is very easy to learn another language, either a simple one like BASIC or Pascal, or a more powerful one like Ada or C++.

In addition to being much easier to learn, a high-level language like C has another advantage over machine language. As we noted, a machine-language program that runs on an IBM-compatible personal computer does not work on a Sun Sparcstation or an Apple Macintosh. A

C program, however, can be used on any computer for which there is a C compiler; the compiler can translate the program into the appropriate machine language. A few minor changes may have to be made in the program, but a high-level language is much more "machine independent" than a machine-language program.

VERSIONS OF C

There are several versions of C. They differ only slightly from each other, like dialects of a natural language such as Chinese or Spanish. The version we use, called ANSI C, has been approved as the standard by the American National Standards Institute. ANSI C has been implemented on a variety of computers, including IBM-compatible personal computers (PCs), mainframes, minicomputers, and workstations.

There are a few important differences in using C on these machines, especially the details of the way the programmer interacts with the compiler and the editor used to construct the program. As the need arises, we will point out some of these differences. When we refer to C without specifying a particular version, we mean features that are common to all implementations of ANSI C. However, most of our programs, with a few exceptions noted later, run with almost no change in just about any version of C. In particular, every program has been run on at least two machines: a Sun Sparcstation running ANSI C under Unix, and an IBM PC or compatible machine running Turbo C++ (Version 3.0) under DOS.

Although technically Turbo C++ is a compiler for the language C++, we use a component of the Turbo C++ compiler corresponding to features from C. In fact, when we refer to this compiler, we abbreviate its name as Turbo C.

SELF-CHECK 0-1

1. What do we call a set of instructions telling a computer how to solve a problem?
2. What is an example of a high-level language? What about a natural language?
3. What language do we use to write our programs? Where is this language used?

SECTION 2 HARDWARE—THE PARTS OF THE COMPUTER

Before we start our discussion of programming, we need to describe the physical parts of a computer system. Two systems are shown in Figure 0-2.

The physical parts of a computer—the plastic, glass, silicon, and metal parts that compose the machine—are sometimes called the **hardware**. Whether your computer is a desktop or a laptop, old or new, it has the following essential parts (the first two are the most important):

♦ a CPU, or central processing unit, which is the brain of the computer, where all the actual computation takes place;

♦ main memory, which is short-term storage;

- an input device, most commonly a keyboard, which enables the user to type commands and information into the computer;

- an output device, usually a monitor or screen, on which the computer displays the results of its computation (a printer is also an output device, but it is not technically part of the computer); and

- long-term storage—generally a disk.

Figure 0-3 shows how all the parts work together.

FIGURE 0-2   Two computers—PC and Sparcstation

FIGURE 0-3   A computer system (arrows indicate flow of information)

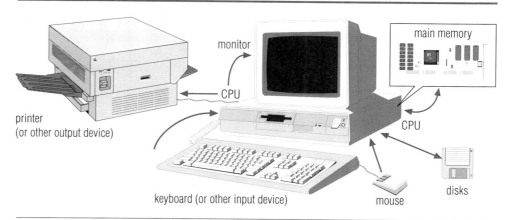

THE CENTRAL PROCESSING UNIT

The **central processing unit** (**CPU**) is the brain or heart of the computer, consisting of thousands of electronic circuits. Before the introduction of integrated circuits in the 1960s, CPUs were quite large, made up of vacuum tubes (which look like light bulbs) or transistors. However, in modern machines, including PCs and workstations, the CPU is a **micro-processor** or **chip**; in some cases, this chip is smaller than a postage stamp. The logic circuits of the computer are etched on the chip. All computation takes place in the CPU.

There are a number of different CPUs in common use today. PCs generally use chips based on the Intel 8086 architecture. There are many chips in this family: the 8086, 80286, 80386, 80486, the Pentium, and the Pentium Pro, as well as similar chips made by other companies like Cyrix, AMD, IBM, and Texas Instruments. These are called **CISC** (**Complex Instruction Set Chips**). Workstations generally use another kind of chip, called a **RISC** or **Reduced Instruction Set Chip**. Chips of this sort include Sun's various SPARC chips, NEC's MIPS chip, and the PowerPC chips produced in cooperation by IBM, Apple, and Motorola.

CPU speed is one of the most important factors in computing. It is measured in **megahertz** (**MHz**) or in **MIPS** (million instructions per second). The original IBM PC ran at 3.77 MHz, while the fastest chips at the present run at 200 MHz, with faster ones imminent. Desktop computers now can run faster than mainframe machines from just a few years ago.

MAIN MEMORY (PRIMARY STORAGE)

The main memory of the computer is second only to the CPU in importance. The CPU stores programs and data in **main memory** or **RAM** (standing for **random access memory**) while it is using them. Main memory represents information as a sequence of electrical impulses: on represents one, and off represents zero. Main memory in PCs is measured in **megabytes** (**MB** or just **M**). Currently PCs are configured with from 2 to 256MB of main memory.

The main memory of the computer stores data and instructions. The CPU fetches an instruction from the memory, interprets it, retrieves a data value from memory for the instruction to act on (if necessary), and stores a new value in memory (if appropriate). This cycle, called the **fetch-and-execute cycle**, is repeated as long as the computer is running a program (see Figure 0-4).

FIGURE 0-4   Interaction between CPU and main memory

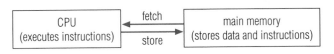

KEYBOARD

Whether you want to run a program, play a game, or write a letter, you must tell the computer what to do. The **keyboard** is the usual way to communicate with a computer, the most common **input device**. Most keyboards have a main set of keys, which look like a typewriter. In addition, they have another set, called **function keys**, usually along the top of the main keypad. These keys have special uses within various programs. Finally, most keyboards have a separate **numeric keypad** on the side, which looks like a calculator and is used to enter numeric information. Certain other keys have special uses, alone or in combination with others. On the PC keyboard, these are (CTRL), (ALT), (SHIFT), and (ESC) (see Figure 0-5). On a workstation keyboard, (ESC) and (SHIFT) are the most commonly used special keys.

MONITOR

One of the most important parts of a computer is the **monitor** or **screen**. The monitor is the primary **output device** by which the computer communicates with the user. Without the monitor, we would not know what is going on inside the computer. A program can run, but we will be unaware of whether it is operating correctly. In addition, the monitor usually displays the information we type in on the keyboard. This is called **echoing the input**. Because the input is echoed, we can check to see if we have typed what we wanted to.

Monitors are judged by their size and the quality of their image, as well as flicker and level of emissions. Although laptop computers may have tiny screens, desktop computer screens range from 14 inches (measured diagonally) to 25 inches or larger.

There are several ways to evaluate the image quality of a monitor. One is the screen **resolution**. The image on a computer screen is made up of thousands of tiny dots, called picture elements or **pixels**. The more pixels on the screen, the sharper the image. The resolution of

FIGURE 0-5   A typical PC keyboard

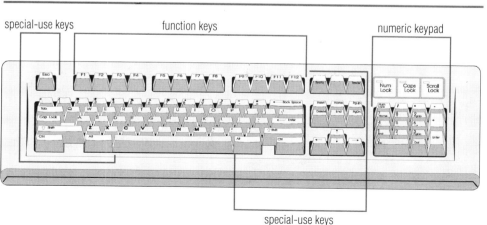

special-use keys   function keys   numeric keypad

special-use keys

screens is measured by the number of pixels across by the number down. Certain resolutions have names; for example, 640 by 480 is called VGA, and anything above that (such as 800 by 600 or 1024 by 780) is called Super VGA. Very high resolutions are used for graphics programs like computer-aided design (CAD) and computer-aided manufacturing (CAM).

Another measure of the quality of the image is the **dot pitch**, which measures the space between the pixels and determines how grainy the screen image will be. The smaller the dot pitch, the better. In addition, other factors are important in determining how much the screen flickers; a monitor with less flicker has a more stable image and is less likely to cause eyestrain.

HARD DISKS (SECONDARY STORAGE)

Main memory is volatile, which means that the information it stores disappears when the computer is turned off. Since main memory is also limited in size, computers have a secondary storage device. Typically, this is a **hard disk**. Disks store information magnetically, the same way that cassettes and videotapes do. Magnetic storage is more permanent, but it can be erased if exposed to magnetic fields. That's why it is important to back up a hard disk, either to floppy disks or magnetic tape.

The capacity of hard disks, like that of main memory, is measured in megabytes (MB). Currently, computers come with hard disks ranging from 85MB to multiples of 1 gigabyte (1000MB, which is approximately 1,000,000,000 bytes). Another important measure of a hard disk is its **access time**, which means how long it takes to retrieve information from the disk. A speedy disk has an access time of about nine milliseconds (ms) or less.

FLOPPY DISKS

Hard disks have a large capacity and speedy access time, but they are limited because they are fixed inside the machine. One way to move data from one machine to another is to copy the information to a **floppy disk** or **diskette**. You can save a file on a disk on one computer, then read the file on another. The access time for information on a floppy disk is much longer than for a hard disk, but the convenience makes up for the slowness. A floppy disk is both a storage and an input/output device.

The term *floppy disk* is more and more a misnomer since most of them aren't "floppy" anymore. The original floppy disks were 8½ inches on a side and flopped when held by the edge. Currently, the most common floppy disk is 3½ inches square and is covered in rigid plastic so that it doesn't bend at all. Nonetheless, the name *floppy* has stuck. Floppy disks also come in 5¼-inch versions, but this size is being phased out.

The measure of a floppy disk is its capacity in kilobytes (KB) or megabytes, and there are a variety of sizes:

◆   Low-density 5¼-inch disks hold 360 KB (about one-third of a megabyte).

◆   High-density 5¼-inch disks hold 1.2 MB.

◆   Low-density 3½-inch disks hold 720 KB.

◆ High-density 3½-inch disks hold 1.44 MB (this is currently the most popular size).

◆ Very high-density 3½-inch disks hold 2.88 MB.

To express the capacity of a floppy disk in more concrete terms: One 3½-inch high-density disk can hold about half of this textbook. A single high-density floppy disk can contain all of the programs you write for this book.

PRINTER

To use a computer most effectively, you usually need a number of **peripheral devices**, pieces of computer hardware which are not physically part of the computer but can be attached to it. Printers, modems, scanners, mice, and trackballs are all peripheral devices.

The most common peripheral device purchased with a computer is a printer. There are three printer types: laser, inkjet, and dot matrix. A **laser printer** puts an image on paper with a laser. These printers produce the most professional looking output, but they generally cost more than other types. At the low end of cost and quality are **dot-matrix printers**, which create an image by striking a number of pins on the paper, making letters which consist of small, visible dots. In the middle are **inkjet printers**, which squirt ink onto the page. They are rapidly replacing dot-matrix printers because their output is similar to that of laser printers, but they are priced more like dot-matrix printers.

Laser and inkjet printers can produce high-quality graphics as well as text; they have become the printers of choice in offices and homes. The most common printers use black ink, but color printers—both laser and inkjet—are becoming very popular.

MOUSE AND TRACKBALL

Almost all computers come with a **mouse**, a **trackball**, or some other **pointing device**. Most computer programs use a pointing device to supplement the keyboard. A mouse is a device about the size and shape of a bar of soap with a ball on the bottom. A trackball is usually fixed onto the keyboard and is essentially a mouse upside down, with the ball on top. Both devices have one or more buttons to press. Rotating the mouse or trackball causes an arrow to move on the screen; when the arrow points at the desired object, clicking one of the buttons controls what happens.

MODEM

A **modem** is a device which allows one computer to communicate with others through telephone lines. Most modems include a built-in fax so the computer can also communicate with fax machines. An external modem is a separate device which plugs into the back of the machine; an internal modem is a **card**, a circuit board installed inside the computer. Modems are measured by their speed, the number of bits per second (**bps**) that the computer can send over the phone lines. The slowest modems send and receive data at 300 bps, while currently the fastest ones work at 28,800 bps. A computer with a modem can connect with a university system, with the Internet, with services like CompuServe, Prodigy, America Online, and the Microsoft Network, as well as with another individual computer.

CD-ROM

Most PCs come equipped with a **CD-ROM player**. CD-ROM stands for Compact Disk—Read Only Memory. Each CD-ROM is a plastic disk, like an audio compact disk, which contains programs or images for retrieval by the computer. The information is burned into the disk in a form readable by a laser. At present, most players can only read the information on a CD-ROM without changing it (hence the name *read-only memory*), but the cost of writable optical disks is dropping rapidly, and they will probably become quite common. Each CD-ROM holds a large amount of information—as much as 600 floppy disks—which makes it a convenient way to store large programs and games.

OTHER INPUT/OUTPUT DEVICES

The most common input devices are still the keyboard and mouse, as well as the disk, but there are many others. Some of the other devices used currently are the scanner, pen, light pen, touch screen, microphone, MIDI (for input/output of music), and bar-code reader. And that list doesn't include specialized devices used in science and industry.

The computer also produces output in a number of ways. Standard output devices are the screen and the printer, as well as the disk, but computers can send output to tape drives, plotters, and speakers.

SELF-CHECK 0-2

1. What are the two most important parts of a computer system?

2. Identify three input devices and three output devices.

3. What is the unit which measures the size of memory or the hard disk of a computer?

SECTION 3 SOFTWARE—A SIMPLE PROGRAM

Now let's talk about **software**, the programs that run a computer. Software is not really tangible (although it does come stored on disks and usually comes packaged with manuals). A piece of software is a program or a collection of programs plus associated data.

A **computer program** is a series of instructions telling the computer what to do. Computers can be programmed to perform many kinds of tasks. You may have played computer games; each one is a program. Someone wrote the instructions to tell the computer how to create the sound and graphics that are part of the game. You may also have worked with word-processing programs like WordPerfect or Microsoft Word; or a spreadsheet program like Lotus 1-2-3 or Excel; or a database program like FoxPro, dBASE, or Access. In fact, if you have worked on a computer in any way, you have been using a program. These programs constitute the software used with a computer system.

This book is designed to show you how to write programs. Unfortunately, a beginning course in programming is not able to teach you everything you need to know to write a flight-simulator program with graphics, animation, sound, and color. That kind of program is usually written by a team of experts who have years of training and experience. However, each of them had to learn programming from the very beginning, as you are about to do. Don't be disappointed because the programs you learn to write are "too simple." The skills that you are building are the foundation for everything that can be done on the computer. It's like learning the alphabet and a few simple grammar rules before trying to read *Hamlet*, practicing scales before trying to play *Moonlight Sonata* on the piano, or learning how to throw before you can play a game of baseball.

Like most textbooks, we start with an extraordinarily simple program so you have a chance to see what one looks like. After this, we shift to a different approach—one which asks you to think through the process of writing the programs. In the process, you become familiar not only with programming in C but also with problem solving.

FIRST C PROGRAM

Let's look at a very simple C program. The program performs a simple task: it tells the computer to display the message, "Welcome to computer programming!", on the monitor. Here is the complete program to perform this task (the line numbers on the right are not part of the program but are used in the explanation):

💻 PROGRAM LISTING	line number
`/* display a message on the monitor */`	1
`#include <stdio.h>`	2
`main()`	3
`{`	4
`    printf("Welcome to computer programming!\n");`	5
`}`	6

That's it! If you type this program in, save it, and run it, the computer displays this message on the screen:

```
Welcome to computer programming!
```

Each time you run the program, that message appears on a new line. That's all this program does. The oval shape around the output from this program represents the computer screen. Whenever we show the output from a program, we indicate it this way.

EXPLANATION OF THE PROGRAM

Here is a brief explanation of the purpose of each line of this program.

- ♦ Line 1 is a comment to tell the reader what the program does.
- ♦ Line 2 allows the compiler to perform standard input and output functions to communicate with the outside world (e.g., to display messages on the screen or read in data from the keyboard).
- ♦ Line 3 is called the main program header. It tells the C compiler to start the main function of this program.
- ♦ Line 4 contains a left brace which introduces the action portion of the program.
- ♦ Line 5 prints the line of output on the screen.
- ♦ Finally, line 6 contains a right brace. This matches the left brace in line 4 and marks the end of the program.

That is the entire program. Most of this material appears in every program you write. Obviously, real-world programs are much longer, which means that they contain more statements between the left and right braces, but the basic format looks like this.

SELF-CHECK 0-3

1. Which punctuation marks surround the action portion of a program?
2. Which line in the program prints something on the screen?
3. What does this first program do if you run it?

SUMMARY

COMPUTER LANGUAGES

1. A computer understands only machine language, which is a set of instructions based on the binary alphabet of zeros and ones.

2. A person can communicate with a computer by writing in a high-level computer language; this is an Englishlike language which is precise and unambiguous.

3. A high-level language is translated into machine language by a program called a compiler. The process of translation is known as compilation.

4. Several high-level languages are C, C++, Pascal, BASIC, COBOL, Fortran, PL/I, Ada, Lisp, Snobol, Algol, and Modula-2. This book introduces C.

HARDWARE OR PARTS OF THE COMPUTER

5. The parts of a computer are called hardware. The brain or heart of the computer is the CPU (central processing unit).

6. Each computer also contains main memory, or RAM, which is the place where the CPU stores information while working on it.

7. Input devices are used to get information into the computer. The primary input device is the keyboard. Others are the mouse, trackball, modem, hard disk, floppy disk, CD-ROM, scanner, light pen, touch pad, and touch screen.

8. Output devices receive results of what has happened in the computer. The primary output devices are usually a monitor or screen and a printer.

9. A long-term storage device is used to preserve programs and other work for a long time. Most commonly, this is a hard or fixed disk which holds information via magnetic charges. Floppy disks can be removed and used on other machines. These long-term storage devices also serve as input/output devices.

10. A modem is a device which allows computers to communicate via phone lines.

SOFTWARE (PROGRAMS)

11. Computers are run by software or programs. A program is a series of instructions which tell the computer what to do.

12. Programs and the data they work on are stored in memory. When a computer runs a program, it fetches an instruction from memory, executes the instruction, stores the results in memory (if necessary), and repeats the process. This is known as the fetch-and-execute cycle.

13. A C program is a series of instructions written in a language called C. This program is translated into machine language before running on the computer. When the program runs, it controls the computer's actions.

FIRST C PROGRAM

1

SYNTAX CONCEPTS: comment, compiler directive, program header, variables and declaration statement, *int* data type, assignment statement, *for* loop, arithmetic operations, identifiers and keywords, *printf*, increment and decrement operators

PROGRAMMING CONCEPTS: assignment, printing, increment, looping, saving a program, compiling a program, running a program

CONTROL STRUCTURES: *for* loop, compound statement

PROBLEM-SOLVING TECHNIQUES: pseudocode, algorithms, program tracing, software development cycle

HOW TO READ CHAPTER 1

The following outline shows the order in which sections can be covered. An oval indicates an enrichment section. The last section is followed by a summary, which lists the most important points in the chapter. Then there is an extensive set of exercises.

OUTLINE:

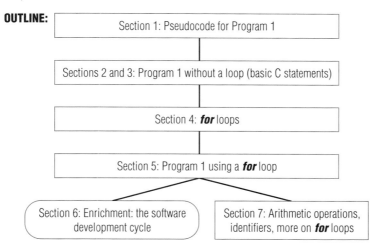

Section 1: Pseudocode for Program 1

Sections 2 and 3: Program 1 without a loop (basic C statements)

Section 4: *for* loops

Section 5: Program 1 using a *for* loop

Section 6: Enrichment: the software development cycle

Section 7: Arithmetic operations, identifiers, more on *for* loops

INTRODUCTION AND STATEMENT OF THE PROBLEM

In this chapter, we will write a complete C program to solve the problem posed below. In writing this program, we will introduce a number of C statements. Most of these statements will be used in all the programs in this book and almost all programs in the real world. We will also introduce several problem-solving techniques, including pseudocode and program tracing.

PROBLEM 1

Write a complete C program to do the following: Display a list of the numbers from 4 to 9. Next to each number, display its square—that is, the number multiplied by itself.

Let us analyze some points about this problem.

◆ First, *you* are asked to write a program. We will not present you with a finished program. Rather, we will try to lead you through the process of writing one. At first, it may be hard for you to write the program on your own. But by the second or third program (in Chapters 2 and 3), you should be able to supply many of the pieces. As we progress through the book, you should be able to write larger chunks of programs.

◆ Second, we are asking you to write a *program*. As noted in Chapter 0, a program is a set of instructions telling a computer what to do to solve a problem.

◆ Third, we want a *complete* program, not little pieces. It is necessary to get into the habit of writing complete programs because the computer insists on them.

◆ Fourth, you will write a *C* program. As we discussed in Chapter 0, there are many computer languages. We will use C, a language widely found in the academic, scientific, and commercial world.

◆ Fifth, the *output* from our first program (i.e., what is printed) should look something like this:

```
4  16
5  25
6  36
7  49
8  64
9  81
```

You should realize that in the commercial or scientific world, a computer would never be used for such a problem since a person could easily do the calculations by hand. But this is a good first problem since it illustrates many important points.

SECTION 1   A PSEUDOCODE SOLUTION TO PROBLEM 1

In this section, we will start to write a program that solves Problem 1. We will call it Program 1. (Similarly, the program we write to solve Problem 2 will be called Program 2, and so on.) This section introduces pseudocode, which is often the first step in writing a program. Pseudocode is used by most programmers to help translate from an English-language description of a problem to a program written in C.

PSEUDOCODE AS A PROBLEM-SOLVING TOOL

In our first few programs, it will be relatively easy to go directly from the English-language description of the problem to the C program. However, most actual programming problems are too long and/or complex to be translated directly. A typical problem may take one or two pages (or more) of English to describe. Most programmers find it difficult to translate directly from English to C (or Pascal or BASIC or just about any computer language).

As a problem-solving tool, programmers usually introduce at least one intermediate step between English and C. The one that we will use is called pseudocode. Pseudocode is a restatement of the problem as a list of steps, in an Englishlike format, describing what must be done to solve it. Using the pseudocode, a programmer then writes the actual program. While there are other intermediate steps between the statement of a problem and the program, pseudocode is the most commonly accepted one. Although the main use of pseudocode is to help us to translate from English to C, it is also an outline of the basic structure or logic of the program and a key part of what we will later call the documentation.

Let's give a definition: **pseudocode** consists of statements which are a combination of English and C; pseudocode is not quite C code but can easily be translated. As we shall see, pseudocode can be refined and made more precise gradually. In fact, the pseudocode used at one stage of the development process will often be a comment at the next stage.

ALGORITHM AND PSEUDOCODE FOR PROGRAM 1

To start writing the program to solve Problem 1, look at the problem statement again. Read it through carefully to make sure you understand what is being requested. Concentrate on what it asks you to compute or produce and what it asks you to do with the things you compute. Try to answer the following questions:

◆   What exactly is the program expected to do?

◆   What answers will have to be printed?

◆   How can the problem be translated from English into C?

◆   If it is too hard to translate directly, is it possible to break the problem down into simpler steps which can be translated more easily?

Let's try to develop an algorithm for solving Problem 1. An **algorithm** is the collection of thought processes which give a precise method of solving a problem. The algorithm is then expressed in pseudocode.

The problem statement says to display a list of numbers, together with their squares, starting with the number 4. *Display* means print on the screen or just print. In the algorithm, we can say, *Print the number and its square.* The problem says the numbers will go from 4 to 9. That means we will get each of these numbers, compute its square, and then print.

Here is the method we will use to solve this problem:

Start with the first number and compute its square. Print the number and its square. Then do the same for each of the other numbers.

In English, it is common to write a description like this in a paragraph; sometimes algorithms and pseudocode take this form as well. But it is usually more helpful to write pseudocode as a series of sequential steps. Here is the pseudocode for Program 1:

> *start with the number 4*
> *compute its square*
> *print the number and its square*
> *do the same for each of the other numbers from 5 to 9*

Using this pseudocode, we will write the actual C code for Program 1 in the next few sections.

SELF-CHECK 1-1

1. What is the purpose of pseudocode? What does pseudocode consist of?
2. Why don't we translate directly from the statement of the problem to C?
3. What is an algorithm?

SECTION 2   BASIC CONCEPTS OF A C PROGRAM

This section will introduce a number of features of the C language which must be included in every program, even though they do not appear in the pseudocode. In particular, we will discuss comments, the main program header, and the general outline of a C program. In the sections to follow, we will flesh out this outline and produce a complete C program to solve Problem 1.

COMMENTS AND PROGRAMMING STYLE

We will start Program 1, and every program we write, with a line that is not in the pseudocode. At the beginning of each program is a **comment** with a short description of the problem to be solved. The comment explains the program. Later we will use comments in other places as well, but for now we will simply use a single comment to describe the basic purpose of the program. The comment is not strictly necessary because a program without it is technically correct. But comments are considered the single most important part of **good programming style**. We will have much more to say about style, both in this chapter and later.

A possible comment for this program might be this:

```
/* Program prog1a.c: print the numbers from 4 to 9 and their squares */
```

The comment begins with /* and ends with */. The symbols /* and */ are called **comment delimiters** because they delimit or mark the beginning and end of the comment. Between them, we can put any message we want, including abbreviations, misspelled words, and so on. Everything between the comment delimiters is ignored by the C compiler. Note that we start the comment with the name of the program: ***prog1a.c***. This is the name of the file on the diskette accompanying this book which contains this particular program.

STYLE WORKSHOP We will usually put the main program's comment at the very top, above everything else. Notice that we are talking about comments first, which shows how important they are. We hope that if we always include comments in our programs, you will do the same.

CAUTION If, by mistake, you start a comment but forget to end it, the compiler will think the rest of your program is part of the comment. More precisely, it will skip from the beginning of the comment until either the end of the next comment or the end of the entire program, whichever comes first. Anything in between will be ignored. This usually has a catastrophic effect on your program and may cause misleading error messages. Always be sure you end each and every comment in your program.

THE PROGRAM HEADER

After the comment, we can start writing the program. The next two lines of our C program look like this:

```
#include <stdio.h>
main()
```

Any line in a program that starts with # is an instruction to the compiler, not an actual statement in the C language. The line containing *#include* tells the compiler to allow our program to perform standard input and output operations. Because these operations are so basic, this line of code will appear in all the programs we write.

The *#include* directive tells the compiler that we will be using parts of the standard function library. A **function** is a building block of a program; typically each function performs one particular task. Information about these functions is contained in a series of **header files**. In our case, we want the header file called *stdio.h* to be included in our program; *stdio* is short for standard input/output; the *.h* says this file is a header file; the pointed brackets < and > tell the compiler the exact location of this header file.

The second line after the comment, *main()*, is called the **main program header**. It tells the C compiler that we are starting to work on the **main function** of this program. Every program must have a main function since this is where the computer begins to execute the program. The parentheses [the symbols (and)] are necessary for every C function.

This is what we have so far:

```
/* Program prog1a.c: print the numbers from 4 to 9 and their squares */
#include <stdio.h>
main()
```

Every C program we write will start with a comment followed by these two lines.

THE BODY OR ACTION PORTION OF THE PROGRAM

Now we are ready to get to the **body** or **action portion** of the program. Just as an English-language paragraph is composed of sentences, a C program is made up of C statements. Inside every C main program, after the header or top line, is a set of braces ({ and }) containing a series of C statements which comprise the body; this is called the action portion of the program. In most cases, we will show only the opening brace ({), leaving the closing brace (}) for later.

However, to emphasize the structure, we have included the opening and closing braces here, using ... to indicate the missing statements. Ultimately, the body of the main program will consist of C statements derived from the pseudocode in Section 1.

THE STRUCTURE OF A C PROGRAM

Here is an outline of the structure of our C program:

```
/* Program progla.c: print the numbers from 4 to 9 and their squares */
#include <stdio.h>
main()
{
    /* action portion of the program goes here */
    ...
}
```

SELF-CHECK 1-2

1. What is the purpose of a comment? How does a comment begin and end?
2. Which line in the program is an instruction to the compiler to use standard input/output operations?
3. Which two lines will be used in all our programs?

SECTION 3   DECLARATION, ASSIGNMENT, AND PRINT STATEMENTS

In this section, we will introduce several of the most important C statements—those that allow us to declare variables, store values in these variables, and print information. Using these statements, we will be able to translate the pseudocode in Section 1 into C. This will produce a first solution to Problem 1.

VARIABLES AND DECLARATION STATEMENTS; DATA TYPE *int*

The first C statement we will introduce is called a **declaration statement**. Although it is not shown in the pseudocode, it is a crucial part of every program. The declaration tells the computer which storage locations or variables to use in the program. A **variable** is a name for a physical location within the computer that can hold one value at a time. As the name implies, a variable can change its value (e.g., from 4 to 5) as the program is running.[1] In order to decide which variables are needed to hold information, the program must be analyzed carefully. As a rule, each variable will have a single purpose in a program. You must

---

[1]A **constant** is a value that does not change; for example, 3 and 4.27 are constants. Later on we will learn how to use constants in our programs.

know what that purpose is. As you start to write a program, you will have to decide which different tasks need variables. (If you decide later that you need other variables, you can always go back and add them.)

We begin by determining what variables we need. A fairly obvious one is a variable to hold the numbers from 4 to 9. Remember that the value of a variable can change, so the same one can hold each of the numbers from 4 to 9. We can choose almost any name for a variable. Probably **numbersfrom4to9** is the most descriptive name, but we will use **number**, which is slightly shorter and almost as good. Now we need another variable to hold the value of the square of each number, and **sqnumber** is a good name.

STYLE WORKSHOP We could just as well call the variables *x* and *y*, *bob* and *charlie*, or *rate* and *time*. As long as we are consistent, there is no problem for the computer. But as one of our rules for good style, we recommend meaningful names that suggest the use of the variables; these are called **mnemonic names**. That's why we have chosen **number** and **sqnumber**. Section 7 discusses the rules for valid variable names.

In addition to the names of the variables, we have to declare to the computer what type of data to expect in these storage locations. There are several different data types in C. For now, we will distinguish between numbers with decimal points (for example, 3.1415 or −4.5) and integers (or whole numbers) such as 493 or −7. The variable **number** will always hold an integer so we will declare its data type to be **int**, which is the simplest integer data type in C. Since **sqnumber** will always hold an integer, we will give it the same data type. The complete declaration in C looks like this:

```
int number,sqnumber;
```

STYLE WORKSHOP We could declare each variable by itself in a separate statement:

`int number,sqnumber;`	*is equivalent to*	`int number;` `int sqnumber;`

In a simple program like Program 1, we prefer to combine two variables with the same data type in a single declaration.

Notice the punctuation (;) at the end of the declaration. A semicolon terminates every complete statement in C. Remember our analogy to a paragraph in English. In English, with a few exceptions, every sentence ends with a period (.). We don't use a period in C because it can be part of a number—for example, 4.50 or 3.1415. To avoid any possible confusion, a semicolon is used in C to terminate statements.

The declaration statement is the first time we have needed a semicolon. A comment does not need one since it is not a C statement. The line containing **#include** does not need one since it is a compiler directive, not a C statement. Finally, the main program header does not need one because it is not a complete C statement.

Also note that there is a blank space between **int** and **number**. You cannot put a blank space in the middle of a word (e.g., **num ber**), but between words, you need one or more spaces or some other separator such as a parenthesis, comma, or brace. Once a separator is used, any number of extra spaces can be inserted for readability.

SELF-CHECK 1-3

1.   What is the purpose of a variable?

2.   Why is *number* a better name for a variable than *numbersfrom4to9*? Why is *number* a better name than *n*?

3.   In addition to a name, what other piece of information is associated with each variable in the declaration?

REWRITING THE PSEUDOCODE

Now that we have names for the variables, we can rewrite the pseudocode using them. Rewriting and refining pseudocode as the solution to a problem is being developed is a common programming practice called **stepwise refinement** (this concept will be discussed in much more detail in Chapter 4). Typically, a programmer starts with a rough solution to the problem, then makes it more precise until everything is specified. Here is the pseudocode from Section 1, modified by the names *number* and *sqnumber*:

> *start with* number = 4
> *compute* sqnumber
> *print* number, sqnumber
> *do the same for* number = 5, 6, 7, 8, 9

STYLE WORKSHOP   To improve readability, we will write a pseudocode statement, which is a mixture of English and C, in two typefaces. The parts of the statement which make sense in C will appear in the same typeface as all our programs. However, English words and phrases which are not part of the C language will appear in italics to emphasize the difference. Any pseudocode statement which has been translated entirely into C will end in a semicolon.

ASSIGNMENT STATEMENTS

It is important to remember that a simple declaration only sets aside space for the variables. It does not give them values. (Another form of the declaration statement does give a value to a variable and will be discussed in Chapter 3.) Now let us start the actual processing by giving values to the variables. The pseudocode says to start with *number* equal to 4 so we must assign the value 4 to the variable *number*. In later programs, we will learn other ways to assign a value to a variable. One simple way is through an **assignment statement**, which computes a value and places it in a given storage location.

Since we want *number* to have the value 4, we write the following:

```
number = 4;
```

This particular assignment statement puts 4 into the storage location associated with the variable *number*. In an assignment statement, we use the symbol =, which is the **assignment operator** in C. It is imperative that you realize the difference between an assignment statement in C and an equation in mathematics. The assignment statement is to be read aloud as "*number* is set to 4" or "*number* is assigned the value 4" or "*number* takes the value 4." A sloppy way to read it is "*number* equals 4" because that confuses the assignment operator with the English word "equals."

In general, a simple assignment statement in C is interpreted as follows: Evaluate the expression on the right-hand side of the assignment operator; then put this value into the variable on the left-hand side of the assignment operator, replacing what used to be stored there.

Here is the general form of an assignment statement giving the value of the expression *expr* to the variable named *varname*:

General Form of an Assignment Statement

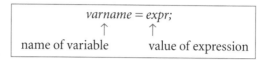

The expression *expr* on the right-hand side of the assignment statement is evaluated, and this value is stored in the variable *varname* on the left-hand side.

ARITHMETIC OPERATIONS IN ASSIGNMENT STATEMENTS

The right-hand side of an assignment statement must be a valid C expression. There are explicit rules for valid expressions. An **arithmetic expression** is one of the following: a constant (e.g., 3), a variable (e.g., *cost*), or a larger formula built from simpler expressions by arithmetic operations (e.g., *cost* + *3*).

EXAMPLE 1-1

Here is a specific example of an assignment statement which gives the value of the expression *cost* + *3* to the variable *price*:

```
price = cost + 3;
```

Assume that initially *price* holds the value 7 and *cost* holds 5. Execution of any assignment statement begins on the right-hand side. First, the expression *cost* + *3* is evaluated; in this case, the expression has the value 5 + 3 which is 8. Then this value is stored in the variable *price* on the left-hand side, replacing whatever value *price* had previously. In this example, the assignment statement gives the value 8 to *price* (erasing the 7), and *cost* remains 5.

Let's get back to the assignment statement in Program 1. Remember that we have just written

```
number = 4;
```

Easy question: What is stored in *number* after we execute the assignment statement? Answer: 4.

Harder and more important question: What is in *sqnumber*? The natural inclination is to say 4 times 4 or 16. But the correct answer is nothing, or more precisely that *sqnumber* has not yet been given a value. When *number* becomes 4, *sqnumber* is not automatically set to 16, the square of *number*. The computer does not know the relationship between **number** and **sqnumber**; the computer "knows" nothing. We said that the names of the variables could have been **bob** and **charlie**. The computer wouldn't know that **charlie** is the square of **bob**. The computer didn't read the comment or the problem description to see what we wanted to do. Remember that the purpose of the comment is to help a person looking at the program, not the computer. The program, not the problem description, is our way of telling the computer what to do.

The computer does *precisely* what you tell it to do: no more, no less. This is good news because once you learn to be perfectly precise and meticulous in spelling out your instructions, you can depend on the machine to execute them faithfully. But it is bad news because until you learn to be precise, the computer will follow your incomplete instructions to the letter without filling in the gaps. Your program may be missing a crucial step that you omitted because it was so "obvious" to you. Nothing is obvious to the computer.[2]

The variable **sqnumber** does not yet have a value; obviously, it needs one since **sqnumber** must hold the square of **number**. Another assignment statement will do the trick:

```
sqnumber = 16;
```

This is perfectly valid in C and will place 16 into **sqnumber**, but it ignores a basic purpose for using a computer—to eliminate the need for a person to do boring and repetitive work. To write this statement, we have to remember that **number** currently holds 4, we have to multiply 4 by 4, and we have to know the answer is 16. We might as well do everything by hand. A slight improvement is to remember that **sqnumber** stands for the square of **number**. We can write the assignment statement like this: **sqnumber = 4 * 4**. (The * indicates multiplication.) Even here we must keep track of the current value (4) of **number**. A better way is to let the computer keep track by writing the assignment statement like this:

```
sqnumber = number * number;
```

Let's review what this means. The assignment statement says to take the value of **number** (which is 4) and multiply it by the value of **number** (still 4). This results in 16, and 16 is put into **sqnumber**. So **number** remains 4, and **sqnumber** becomes 16.

TRACING A PROGRAM

A useful way of visualizing the execution of a program is to think of each variable as a box. The box holds the current value of the variable (remember that it can change). At the beginning of the program, immediately after the declaration, a picture would show **number** and **sqnumber** with nothing in either box, as in Figure 1-1A. Actually, something is stored there (whatever was left by the last program to use these physical storage locations), but it is

---

[2]This paragraph is in some ways the most important one in the entire book. Please read it again. Continue to read it once a week until you believe it. As you run your programs, you will begin to appreciate what it means.

garbage that is no use to our program. After the first assignment statement, we find the picture in Figure 1-1B. At our current point in the program, we have the picture in Figure 1-1C.

Keeping track of the value stored in each variable is called **tracing** or **hand simulating** a program. It is one of the most important skills for a programmer to acquire because tracing shows exactly what the computer does at each step. At the end of Section 5, we will show another way to trace a program.

DISPLAYING OUTPUT USING *printf*

Let's look back at the pseudocode. It says to print the number and its square. In general, whenever you have the computer calculate some value, it will be necessary to print the value if you want to see it. Everything described so far has gone on inside the machine. Even if you could see inside, things would happen much too fast for you to follow. Unless the computer gives you some external report of what it has done, you have no way of knowing whether the program is working. It is not necessary to print every calculation, just the ones that you want to know about. The printed or displayed results of running a program are called the **output**.

The pseudocode says, *print **number**, **sqnumber***. We can now revise it to the following, which is not quite C but very close:

print(number,sqnumber)

The simplest way to translate this into C is using ***printf***. We will use the following basic form of the ***printf***:

```
printf("%d %d\n",number,sqnumber);
```

We'll clear this up a bit before we go on. First, let's describe exactly what this ***printf*** will do. It will print the values of ***number*** and ***sqnumber***, then go to a new line. In our example, ***number*** is 4 and ***sqnumber*** is 16, so the computer displays the following line of output:

```
4 16
```

FIGURE 1-1 Successive values stored in **number** and **sqnumber**. A, after the declarations; B, after **number = 4**; C, after computing **sqnumber**.

number	*number*	*number*
–	4	4
–	–	16
sqnumber	*sqnumber*	*sqnumber*
A	B	C

FORMS OF A *printf*

There are various ways that a *printf* can appear in a program. For now, we will mention two simple forms: one that has just a **literal string** (a sequence of characters within quotation marks), and one that also has values of one or more expressions to be printed. In Chapter 2, we will see examples that combine these two forms.

General Form of a *printf* with Just a Literal String

```
printf(" ... ");
        ↑
   literal string
```

Inside the parentheses, we place a literal string. The symbols within that string are printed. This form was used in Chapter 0 for the following *printf*:

```
printf("Welcome to computer programming!\n");
```

In addition, there is a form of *printf* that will print the value of one or more expressions. This form was used earlier to print the values of ***number*** and ***sqnumber***.

General Form of a *printf* with Expressions to Be Printed

```
printf(" ... ", ... );
         ↑        ↑
control string, including    list of variables or
  conversion characters     expressions to be printed
```

This form requires a bit of explanation, which is contained in the following set of guidelines. (These guidelines apply to all forms of ***printf***.)

GUIDELINES FOR *printf*

♦ A *printf* always contains a **control string** or **format string** in quotation marks.

♦ The control string may or may not be followed by some variables or expressions whose value we want printed.

♦ Each value to be printed needs a **conversion specification** like **%d** to hold its place in the control string.

♦ This conversion specification describes the exact way the value is to be printed.

♦ When the *printf* is executed, each conversion specification is replaced by the value of the corresponding expression, then printed according to the rules in the specification.

♦ The symbols **\n** in the control string tell the machine to skip to a new line. This part of the control string affects the appearance of the output but is not displayed as part of it.

♦ With just a few other exceptions to be covered later, anything else within the control string (e.g., a word or a blank space or a punctuation symbol) will print exactly as it appears.

◆ If there are variables or expressions to be printed, commas are used to separate them from the control string and each other. Once a comma is used as a separator, it is not necessary (but it is allowed) to add blank spaces. For example, the two statements below are equivalent:

```
printf("%d %d\n",number,sqnumber);  and  printf("%d %d\n", number, sqnumber);
```

Whatever expression occurs after the control string will be evaluated and then printed according to its specification.

Now we will go through the process for the particular example in Program 1:

```
printf("%d %d\n",number,sqnumber);
```

◆ The control string for this ***printf*** is **"%d %d\n"**, and the two items to be printed are the values of the variables ***number*** and ***sqnumber***. Because these variables hold integers, the control string must contain conversion specifications for printing two integer values. This specification is **%d** (the *d* stands for decimal or digit).

◆ In addition, the control string has a single blank space between the two specifications, so the output will contain a single blank space between the two integer values.

◆ Finally, the control string ends in **\n**. The combination **\n** is considered to be a single character called the **newline character**. When this character is printed or displayed, it tells the machine that the line of output has ended. The **cursor** (this is the _ or ▮ which blinks on the screen) marks the current print position on the screen or the location of the printhead on the printer. The newline character tells the cursor to move to the beginning of a new line, and the next piece of output after **\n** begins there. (If the newline character is not included, then the next item to be printed starts on the same line—we will discuss this in more detail in Chapter 2.) Here is another view of this ***printf***:

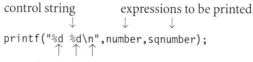

See if you can predict what will be printed by this statement, assuming that ***number*** has the value 4.

```
printf("%d\n",number+1);
```

This ***printf*** evaluates the expression ***number+1*** as 5 and then prints it. Note that the expression ***number+1*** is evaluated and printed, but the value of ***number*** remains 4. Because it is being used as part of an expression, the value of ***number*** does not change. However, the value of ***number*** would change if it were used on the left-hand side of an assignment statement.

The output from a program may be displayed on the monitor or printed on the printer. Sending output to the screen is the simplest way to print your results; this is the default output method. (**Default** means that this is what the compiler assumes you want to do if you do not instruct it otherwise.) Often it is convenient to have a **hard copy** (a printout on paper) of your results to show your output to someone else. In Chapter 3, we will discuss how to send the output to the printer. (In order to give you a way to hand in assignments, your instructor may discuss this point before Chapter 3.) For now, we are assuming that all output will go to the screen.

SELF-CHECK 1-4

1. At any one time, how many values can be stored in a single variable? Can that value change? What happens to the old value?

2. What is the purpose of a *printf*?

3. Where are the two most common places to send the output from a program? Which of these is the default method?

CHANGING THE VALUE OF A VARIABLE

After we finish printing the values of the variables, the pseudocode suggests that we should go on to 5 and 25, 6 and 36, and so on. We do not need a new variable to hold 5 (and one for 25), then another for 6, etc. As we emphasized before, a variable can have its value changed, so we can reuse *number* and *sqnumber*. We said earlier that a variable should serve one purpose in a program. Reusing *number* and *sqnumber* does not violate that rule because *number* continues to stand for a number from 4 to 9, and *sqnumber* continues to stand for its square.

A simple assignment statement, *number = 5*, seems to do what we want. Then we can use *sqnumber = number * number* and another *printf*. Here are the next three statements:

```
number = 5;
sqnumber = number * number;
printf("%d %d\n",number,sqnumber);
```

Finally, we can repeat the process with the same three steps for *number = 6, 7, 8,* and 9.

THE LAST LINE OF THE PROGRAM

After we have repeated the process for *number = 9*, there is nothing else to do in the program since the only action is to print these numbers and their squares. But don't forget that we must formally end the program; more precisely, we must close the opening brace that appeared immediately after the main program header. We do this with a line that consists of just the closing brace.

PROGRAM 1 (FIRST VERSION)

Here is what the entire program looks like using this method:

 PROGRAM LISTING

```
/* Program prog1a.c:  print the numbers from 4 to 9 and their squares */
#include <stdio.h>
main()
{
    int number,sqnumber;

    number = 4;                              /* inefficient method */
    sqnumber = number * number;
    printf("%d %d\n",number,sqnumber);
    number = 5;
    sqnumber = number * number;
    printf("%d %d\n",number,sqnumber);
    number = 6;
    sqnumber = number * number;
    printf("%d %d\n",number,sqnumber);
    number = 7;
    sqnumber = number * number;
    printf("%d %d\n",number,sqnumber);
    number = 8;
    sqnumber = number * number;
    printf("%d %d\n",number,sqnumber);
    number = 9;
    sqnumber = number * number;
    printf("%d %d\n",number,sqnumber);
}
```

STYLE WORKSHOP Observe that the pseudocode in Section 1 turned out to be similar but not identical to our final C program. In addition, comments and declarations are usually not included in pseudocode. In pseudocode, you can use any familiar mathematical symbols—for example, exponents or the square-root symbol. Most nonprogrammers find it easier to understand the pseudocode than the C program. This means that the pseudocode can guide someone who is attempting to follow the logic of the program. Often a copy is included as part of the documentation of the final program.

SELF-CHECK 1-5

1. What is the last line of every program?
2. Does the last line need a semicolon?
3. In the output, each pair of values prints on a new line because of the \n character in the control string of the *printf*. What would happen if we omitted the \n from the control string?

SECTION 4   THE *for* LOOP

In this section, we will introduce a powerful C feature called a *for* loop, that will allow us to derive a much better solution to Problem 1.

PROBLEMS WITH THE FIRST VERSION OF PROGRAM 1

The program at the end of Section 3 will work, but it is an inefficient way to solve the problem. We are doing a large amount of repetitious work. In this particular problem (the squares of the numbers from 4 to 9), the work is not too bad. But if the problem asked for the squares of the numbers from 4 to 79, or even worse, from 4 to 179, the size of our program would increase tremendously, even though the problem descriptions are almost identical. We need to get the computer to do this boring, repetitious work. Computers don't hate repetition. In a sense, they like nothing better than to do the same thing over and over.

INCREMENTING THE VALUE OF A VARIABLE

One way to change the value of *number* is to put a series of explicit values into the variable, as we've done, but that method is inefficient. A more subtle method is available, one that illustrates the difference between assignment and equality. When we go from 4 to 5, 5 to 6, or 6 to 7, we simply add 1 to the old value of *number* to get the new value. This is called **incrementing** the value of *number*. We can tell the computer to increment or add 1 for us.

To tell the computer to add 1 to the previous value, we use an assignment statement. To the left of the assignment operator is the variable *number*, which is to receive a new value. To the right of the assignment operator is the old value of *number* plus 1. So in C we write the following:

```
number = number + 1;
```

Remember how to read this. It does not say that *number* is equal to *number* plus 1, which is certainly ridiculous. Rather, it says that the new value assigned to *number* is the old value plus 1. The evaluation of an assignment statement starts with the expression on the right-hand side.

◆   In this case, the expression *number + 1* tells the computer to go to the storage location *number*, find the value stored there, add 1 to it, and compute the sum.

◆   Then the assignment statement says to store that value in the variable on the left-hand side. In this case, the assignment statement says to put the computed value into storage location *number*.

The fact that the same storage location *number* is used twice is purely coincidental from the computer's point of view, although to us it is the whole point of the statement since it has the effect of adding 1 to the value stored in *number*.

If *number* used to hold 4, then after executing this statement, it will hold 5. The 4 is erased; 5 is stored in place of it. If 4 is erased, that is not tragic because we have already used the 4 to obtain a value for *sqnumber*, and we have printed both values.

Here are the C statements that we have been talking about. Can you predict what will be printed by them?

```
number = 4;
sqnumber = number * number;
printf("%d %d\n",number,sqnumber);
number = number + 1;                         /* number is incremented */
sqnumber = number * number;
printf("%d %d\n",number,sqnumber);
```

These statements will print the following two lines of output:

```
4 16
5 25
```

We could continue to increment *number* in this way, going from 5 to 6, and so on, but we leave that for an exercise (see Exercise 13). Instead, we will introduce the concept of a loop, then use that concept in C.

REPEATING A SERIES OF INSTRUCTIONS; USING A LOOP

Instead of incrementing *number* as shown above, we can find an even better way to do it. This way of changing the value of *number* incorporates the idea of incrementing as part of a larger structure. Look back at these three lines of our program for a moment:

```
number = 4;
sqnumber = number * number;
printf("%d %d\n",number,sqnumber);
```

Concentrate on the second and third lines. When we executed them, *number* had the value 4 and *sqnumber* became 16. But if you think about it, these two lines would work just as well for other values. If *number* were 12, lines two and three would set *sqnumber* to 12 times 12 = 144 and print 12 144. If *number* were 15, 15 and 225 (its square) would print. More to the point, if *number* were 5, we would print 5 25, which is just what we want printed next. If a little later *number* became 6, we would print 6 36. In fact, this is the main reason why we wrote the second line as *sqnumber = number * number*, rather than simply using *sqnumber = 4 * 4*.

To get the computer to keep coming back to lines two and three, each time with a new value for *number*, involves the concept of a **loop**, one of the most powerful features of any programming language. A loop gives us the ability to write a statement once but have the computer execute it over and over. In this program, we want to increase *number* to 5, then go back and do lines two and three again. As we noted above, one way to get *number* to 5 is to say this:

```
number = number + 1;
```

But that by itself will not help to get *number* to be 6, 7, 8, and 9.

A better method is available, one that illustrates the power of a language like C. Instead of adding 1 ourselves and keeping track of how many times to repeat the calculations, we can let the computer do it. C has a special kind of statement, called a ***for* loop**, that allows us to increment the value of a variable and repeat a group of instructions which can use the value of that variable. Looking ahead a bit, we will include the lines that compute ***sqnumber*** and then print in a ***for*** loop; the ***for*** loop will increment the value of ***number*** to get a new value and then repeat the process. This will ensure that these two lines are executed for several different values of ***number***. Among other things, the ***for*** loop will automatically do the incrementing and repeating for us.

REFINING THE PSEUDOCODE

Now let's return to the pseudocode we developed in Section 1. In that pseudocode, we treated the number 4 separately, then said to repeat the same thing for the other numbers from 5 to 9. There is another way to say this in pseudocode which treats all of the numbers from 4 to 9 in the same way. This method is exceptionally useful because it leads us into a ***for*** loop structure. Here is a version of the pseudocode for Program 1 that uses this new method:

> *for each number from 4 to 9, do the following:*
> *compute the square of that number*
> *print the number and its square*

Recall that pseudocode can be refined so that it becomes closer to actual C code. Now that we have names for the variables, and we know a bit more about C, we can refine this pseudocode. From Section 3, we know how to translate the second and third lines into C. In the display below, the top line is still pseudocode, but the second and third lines are the C statements we want to repeat for different values of ***number***:

> *for each value of* number *from 4 to 9, do the following:*
> ```
> sqnumber = number * number;
> printf("%d %d\n",number,sqnumber);
> ```

This pseudocode will ultimately become the ***for*** loop we use in Program 1.[3]

SELF-CHECK 1-6

1. What does incrementing a variable mean? What statement can we use to add 1 to the value of a variable named *x*?

2. What arithmetic operations are the symbols + and * used for?

3. What do we call a series of statements that are written once but executed several times?

---

[3]Anytime the problem statement says to repeat something for a number of values, it makes sense to consider a loop.

A SIMPLE EXAMPLE OF A *for* LOOP

Before we include one in Program 1, let's look at a few simple examples of the way to use a *for* loop in C. We will assume that all the variables (in this first case, just *i*) have been declared to have data type *int*.

EXAMPLE 1-3 Here is an example of a simple *for* loop that will print the numbers from 1 to 5 (the comments on the right are to you; you should not put them in your programs):

```
for (i = 1; i <= 5; i = i + 1)          /* header of the loop */
    printf("%d\n",i);                   /* body of the loop   */
```

The top line is sometimes called the **header** of the *for* loop. Note that the header does not end in a semicolon because by itself it is not a complete C statement, just as the header of a main program is not one. The header is always followed by something called the **body of the loop**. The header together with the body is a complete C statement.

This simple *for* loop starts by giving an initial value to a variable (in our example, *i*), which we will call the **index** or **control variable**. The process of giving a variable an initial value is called **initialization**, and we say that *i* is initialized to 1. The *for* loop tells the computer to repeat the body of the loop, which in our example contains a single instruction [*printf(...)*], for several values of *i*. In this case, it will execute the *printf* for *i* = 1, 2, 3, 4, and 5.

Let's go through this in a little more detail. The *for* loop header specifies three things, separated by semicolons: what initial value to use, what test determines whether or not the loop should continue, and how the loop control variable should change (in this case, increment) each time through the body of the loop. Here is a diagram of these features in our example:

```
              initial value                    increment
                   ↓                                ↓
for loop header:     for (i = 1; i <= 5; i = i + 1)
                                   ↑
                   test whether to continue the loop
```

In this example, the initial value for *i* is 1. The test to determine whether to continue is to see if *i* is less than or equal to 5. The statement *i = i + 1* means that at the end of each pass through the body of the loop, the control variable *i* will increase by 1 until it reaches 6 (and this value causes the test controlling the loop to become false). Note that all of this information is contained in the header of the *for* loop.

After the *for* loop header comes the body of the loop. We are allowed to specify one statement that will be executed each time through the body. In this case, the one statement is the *printf*. To summarize, each time through the body of the loop, the current value of *i* is used in the *printf*. Then the new value of *i*, which is obtained by adding 1 to the previous one, is used to test the condition controlling the loop.

 CAUTION Even though the increment step (*i = i + 1*) is contained in the header, it is not executed until after the body of the loop.

TRACING THE *for* LOOP

Now let's go step by step through the *for* loop.

PROGRAM TRACE

◆ The variable *i* starts at 1, which is immediately compared to the final value of 5. Since 1 is less than or equal to 5, the program enters the body of the loop and executes the *printf* instruction. Naturally, the *printf* instruction prints the value 1. This completes the first pass through the body of the *for* loop.

◆ Then we increment *i* by 1 to 2 and compare this new value to 5. Since 2 is less than or equal to 5, we execute the body of the loop. This time the *printf* prints 2 on a new line. This completes the second pass.

◆ Then *i* increases to 3, which is less than or equal to the limiting value of the control variable (5), so we print 3.

◆ Similarly, *i* increases to 4, and we print 4.

◆ Then *i* increases to 5, which is also allowed since we test whether the current value is less than *or equal to* the final one. The *printf* prints 5.

◆ Then *i* increases to 6. At this point, the condition *i* <= *5* is no longer true. Therefore, we do not enter the body of the loop with *i* having the value 6. Instead, the *for* loop is completed, and we continue with the next statement. In our example, since the body of the loop consists of a statement to print the value of *i*, the entire *for* loop prints the values 1, 2, 3, 4, and 5, each on a separate line.

A *for* LOOP USING A COMPOUND STATEMENT

Let's look at a slightly more complicated example, which is very close to what we want to do in Problem 1. In this example, we will do two things inside the body of the *for* loop.

EXAMPLE 1-4

Let's write a loop to compute the expression *i* * *i*, which we will store in a variable called *sq*, then print both *i* and *sq*. (Once again, assume that the variables are declared to have data type *int*.)

```
for (i = 1; i <= 5; i = i + 1) {
    sq = i * i;
    printf("%d %d\n",i,sq);
}
```

We will not trace this *for* loop in detail because it is so close to the one that will be used in Program 1. However, note several things about the way it looks. First, there is a pair of braces: { and }. We also used an opening brace at the start of the action portion of the program, immediately after the main program header, and a closing brace to end the entire program. The symbol just before a closing brace is a semicolon, but the brace should not be followed by a semicolon.

In general, a pair of braces is used in C whenever we want to execute a series of statements where normally just one is allowed. This entire group, called a **compound statement**, can then be treated as a single statement. In particular, after the header in a *for* loop, we are allowed to execute only a single statement.

STYLE WORKSHOP Note that the opening brace is on the same line as the *for* loop header, and the closing brace is directly underneath the word *for*. The statements inside the body of the loop are indented. Aligning and indenting like this are not technically necessary, but they make a program much more readable. In Section 6, we will talk more about what you can do to make programs readable.

 CAUTION If the header of a *for* loop is followed by a semicolon, then the *for* loop has no body, and the program continues with the next statement.

EXAMPLE 1-5 Consider the following loop, which has a semicolon after the header:

```
for (i = 1; i <= 5; i = i + 1);                    /* incorrect */
    printf("hello\n");
```

Because of the semicolon, the body of the loop is considered to be a null statement and does nothing for each value of *i* from 1 to 5. The loop increments and tests *i* five times, then prints "hello" once. This is probably not what the programmer had in mind.

SELF-CHECK 1-7

1. How many component statements does a *for* loop header contain? What is the purpose of each component?

2. How many statements can appear in the body of a *for* loop? Is there a way to get around this restriction?

3. In Example 1-5, what does the compiler consider to be the body of the *for* loop? What does the compiler consider to be the statement following the *for* loop? Does the compiler care that this statement has been indented?

SECTION 5 A BETTER VERSION OF PROGRAM 1

In this section, we will use the *for* loop from Section 4 to provide a better version of Program 1. We will rewrite the entire program with a *for* loop and then trace it to make sure it works.

USING A *for* LOOP IN PROGRAM 1

Now that we have seen how a *for* loop can repeat a series of steps, let's return to **number** and **sqnumber**. In Program 1, we want to repeat a series of statements (computing **sqnumber**, then printing **number** and **sqnumber**) for several values of **number**. We can write this in C with a *for* loop using the values of **number** from 4 to 9, going up by 1 each time. The *for* loop will look like this:

```
for (number = 4; number <= 9; number = number + 1)  {
    sqnumber = number * number;
    printf("%d %d\n",number,sqnumber);
}
```

Even before we trace how it works, you should be able to guess what the loop does. It repeats the statements inside the body of the loop for **number** = 4, 5, 6, 7, 8, and 9, exactly what we want.

PROGRAM 1 (SECOND VERSION)

We will repeat the entire program here in exactly the form that you would use to type it into the computer. This entire program is on the disk that came with your book, in a file called *prog1b.c*. If you printed the program, it would look just like this. Such a printout is called a **program listing**. In addition, we have shown the output. If you compiled and then ran the program (see Section 6 for a quick overview), the output would look just like this. Be sure that you understand the difference between the program listing and the output. In most cases, you will need a copy of both if you are giving the program to someone else (e.g., to an instructor to be graded).

🖥 PROGRAM LISTING

```
/* Program prog1b.c:  print the numbers from 4 to 9 and their squares */
#include <stdio.h>
main()
{
    int number,sqnumber;

    for (number = 4; number <= 9; number = number + 1)  {
        sqnumber = number * number;
        printf("%d %d\n",number,sqnumber);
    }
}
```

OUTPUT

```
4  16
5  25
6  36
7  49
8  64
9  81
```

PROGRAM TRACE Now let's trace exactly what happens as this program is executed.

♦ When the *for* loop statement is executed, *number* starts off with the value 4 (what is in *sqnumber* at this point?).

♦ Since this value is less than or equal to the limiting or final value of *number* (in this case, 9), we can execute the body of the loop.

♦ Inside the opening bracket for the body of the loop, *sqnumber* is set to *number* * *number*, which in this case is 4 * 4 = 16. The *printf* prints the values 4 and 16.

So far, this is exactly what we had before we introduced the *for* loop, but now the computer will increment the value of *number* each time through the loop.

♦ When we reach the closing bracket, the program automatically goes back to the loop header, where *number* increases by 1, making it equal to 5.

♦ Since 5 is less than or equal to the limiting value of 9, we execute the body of the loop.

♦ This time, *sqnumber* is set to 5 * 5 = 25. The *printf* prints 5 and 25 on a new line.

♦ Then *number* increases by 1 again, so that it now has a value of 6.

♦ The body of the loop is executed, *sqnumber* is set to 6 * 6 = 36, and 6 and 36 are printed.

♦ When *number* is 7 and 8, we print 7 49 and 8 64.

♦ After printing, we go back to the header, where *number* increases to 9.

♦ Since 9 is less than or equal to 9, we execute the body of the loop once again.

♦ This time *sqnumber* is set to 9 * 9 = 81, and the values 9 81 are printed.

♦ When *number* increases to 10, the condition controlling the loop is false.

♦ Therefore, we do not enter the body of the loop again. Instead, we continue with the next statement in the program.

In Section 7, we will talk more about *for* loops, which we will use in almost all of our later programs. For now, you only need to understand the trace that we have just given.

You should appreciate the control that a *for* loop gives us. The series of instructions inside the body of the loop is written only once but executed several times. A large part of the power of a computer comes from the ability to repeat a calculation for different values. Each instruction appears just once in the program but can be executed 6 or 100 or any number of times.

TWO WAYS TO TRACE A PROGRAM

Trace this example through again until you are completely convinced that it works. Do this on all of your programs before you run them. You will be amazed at how many errors can be caught (and then corrected). In fact, short of actually running the program, there is no better way to see if it is correct.

As you do the trace, do not attempt to keep track of the values of the variables in your head. Instead, do one of two things. You can draw a box for every variable and at each step use it to hold the current value (see Figure 1-1, page 25). This is how the computer actually works since it keeps track of only the current value of a variable.

The other method of tracing is to draw a series of columns down a page, one column per variable. At the top of the column, put the name of the variable. Underneath the name, keep a record of what is stored in the variable by writing down each new value assigned (see Figure 1-2). The advantage of this method is that you have a complete record of the program trace.

You are welcome to use whichever method of tracing you prefer, but you should definitely use pencil and paper, rather than just your memory.

SECTION 6 ENRICHMENT: RUNNING A C PROGRAM, SOFTWARE DEVELOPMENT CYCLE

Now that we have given a complete C program, we will describe how to run it on an actual computer. We will also describe the parts of the software development cycle.

CAUTION The details of how to do this may vary greatly from computer to computer, and even from one computer center using a particular computer to another one. Be sure to find out the precise rules that govern your installation. If you are using this text in class, your instructor will probably distribute these rules.

We will assume that you are using C on a personal computer or workstation. Typically, a person communicates with a personal computer through a keyboard and monitor with programs and data stored on either a hard or a floppy disk. All of the programs in this text have been run on a Sun Sparcstation using ANSI C and also on a personal computer using the Turbo C compiler, which is a component of the Turbo C++ Version 3.0 compiler.

FIGURE 1-2 Another method of tracing a program

number	sqnumber	
–	–	initially
4	–	after the *for* loop header sets *number* to 4
4	16	after computing *sqnumber* the first time
5	16	after incrementing *number* to a new value
5	25	after computing *sqnumber* with the new value for *number*
6	25	
6	36	...
7	36	
7	49	
8	49	
8	64	
9	64	
9	81	after computing *sqnumber* with the final value for *number*
10	81	at the end of the *for* loop (note that *number* increases to 10, but we do not use this value to compute *sqnumber*)

ENTERING A PROGRAM WITH A TEXT EDITOR

The first step is to enter your program into the computer using the keyboard and monitor. You must use a text-editing system to enter the program. There are a large number of text editors; in fact, this book was written using many different systems.

Turbo C comes with a built-in editor that is very easy to use. Unix comes with a built-in editor called *vi*; unfortunately, *vi* is not so easy to use. However, most Unix installations have some other editor that can also be used to type in a program. From now on, we will assume that you are using one of these editors to write your programs.

TYPING A C PROGRAM

A program consists of a series of lines. A **line** is a group of characters ended by hitting the ⟨RETURN⟩ or ⟨ENTER⟩ key. Each statement of your C program should start on its own line. If a statement is too long, it can continue on the next line. Simply stop at some convenient point (not in the middle of something—try to do it after a blank or comma) and put the rest of the statement on the next line; indent the second line to make it easier to read. If the statement requires a semicolon at the end, it goes after the entire statement, not at the end of the first line. When the computer reads the first line, it will know that the statement is not finished and continue reading. When the computer sees the semicolon, it will know the statement is complete.

You will rarely have to continue onto a new line because most C statements fit comfortably on a single line. However, in certain circumstances, you should purposely spread a statement out over several lines for readability. For example, technically a *for* loop is a single statement, but you should always separate the body from the header by putting each on a new line.

Actually, C allows you more freedom in entering text than we have implied. Each statement does not have to start on a new line. (However, a program is usually much more readable if it does.) Two or more C statements can be put on the same line, separated by a semicolon.

STYLE WORKSHOP You will save room if you put two or more statements on a line, but, in the long run, you will cause yourself grief because it will be much harder to get your programs to work if they are difficult to read. Furthermore, you will probably make more typing errors, and each error may be harder to locate and correct on a line with two or three statements. Therefore, we recommend that you put one statement per line.

The only exception is that two small assignment statements can often be put on the same line without any confusion. For example, if *x* and *y* are both to be set to 0, then most people won't mind if you write the statements like this:

```
x = 0;    y = 0;
```

Observe that each statement ends in a semicolon. Obviously, the semicolons are crucial in telling the compiler where one statement ends and the next one starts. In fact, with the proper use of semicolons, you can put any number of C statements on the same line; however, the *#include* directive must appear on its own line.

Here is another version of Program 1, rewritten with no extra spaces. Note that the comment has also been eliminated.

```
#include<stdio.h>
main() {int number,sqnumber;for(number=4;number<=9;number=number+1){sqnumber=
number*number;printf("%d %d\n",number,sqnumber);}}
```

Although the program is perfectly valid from the compiler's point of view, it is essentially unreadable by a person. As a general rule, you should never combine a large statement with anything else since a person is likely to overlook any smaller statements. For example, it is easy to lose the assignment statement in this line:

```
printf("help is close, so keep hanging on\n"); x = 0;
```

INDENTING STYLE

A C statement can appear anywhere on a line, but you should follow a consistent set of guidelines when typing your program. Here are the rules that we will follow:

♦   We will start the first comment, describing what the program does, in column 1.

♦   The lines specifying the include file(s) to be used with a program will also start in column 1, as will the line containing *main()*.

♦   The opening brace and the closing brace at the end of the program will be in column 1.

♦   Inside the action portion of a program, we will indent all statements five spaces. Some C programmers use the TAB key to indent. Depending on the system you are using, this will indent up to eight spaces, which may be too much.

♦   In addition, we will indent the statements in the body of a *for* loop five spaces. Once again, you can use the TAB key.

♦   If the body of the loop is a compound statement, the closing brace will appear directly underneath *for*. Because the body of the loop has been indented, there will be nothing in the direct line between the closing brace and *for*.

Here is a sketch of this indenting style (other rules will be given later):

```
col. 1
↓
#include <stdio.h>
main()
{
     int ...

     for ( ... )
col. 6↓    ...
     }    ↑col. 11
}
```

STYLE WORKSHOP   While indenting is not strictly necessary, it will make your program much more readable and is considered an important aspect of good programming style. Please follow these rules or some other easy-to-read method. Above all, be consistent. Indent all statements in a loop one tab position, for instance; don't indent some but not others. You should not indent too much because statements will be hard to read when they seem to run off the right-hand side of the screen. The time you spend getting your program to look nice is an excellent investment.

SAVING, COMPILING, AND RUNNING A PROGRAM

After you have finished typing your C program, *you must save it before doing anything else*. In fact, you may wish to save your program several times while you are writing, just in case something happens. Saving allows you to work on your program later if it needs revision.

When you are typing the program, it is stored in the memory of the computer in RAM; as we noted in Chapter 0, things in RAM are stored by electric current, and they disappear when the flow is disturbed. If someone pulled out the plug of your computer, or if a lightning storm knocked out your power, or even if the machine had some mechanical glitch, you might lose all the material you had just typed in. In addition, an error in the program might cause the system to crash.

For all these reasons, it is important to save your program. **Saving** means copying the program from the memory of the machine (its short-term memory, to use a human term) to a disk (its long-term memory). Once you have saved your program to a disk, you can re-use it, change it, or carry it from one machine to another (if it is on a floppy disk).

The method you will use to save your program depends on the system. We'll tell you how to do it with the two editors we have used to test the programs in this book: the Turbo C editor and the *vi* editor found on all Unix systems. If you are using one of these two systems, read the relevant sections below. If you are using some other system, your instructor will probably give you directions.

SAVING A PROGRAM IN THE TURBO C EDITOR

♦ Press the F2 function key to save your program and stay in the Turbo C editor.

♦ If you have not previously saved or named your program, a **Save File As** window will pop up, and you will be asked to type in a name for your program. Type in a name (up to eight characters starting with a letter), followed immediately by the extension *.c*. For example, type ***prog2.c*** or ***program2.c***. The extension tells the compiler that this is a C program. Then press ENTER, and your program will be saved under that name.

♦ If you have already named your program, it will automatically be saved. The editor will display a "Saving" message in the lower left corner of the screen, but it may flash by so quickly that you can't read it.

SAVING A PROGRAM IN UNIX *vi*

♦ Press *:w* (colon, followed by w). This will save the program under the name you gave it when you entered *vi* and leave you in the editor.

or

♦ Press ESC and then either ***ZZ*** or ***:wq*** (colon, followed by wq). Either of these commands will save the program under the name you gave it when you entered *vi* and terminate your *vi* session, returning you to the Unix prompt.

On either system, the best way to prevent problems is to follow this rule: **Always Save Your Program Before Running It**. If something goes wrong, at least you won't have to worry about losing your work.

COMPILING A PROGRAM

Once your program has been saved, you are ready to compile and then run it. When you compile your program, you are invoking the compiler, a special program that will translate your program into machine language. The method you will use is again system dependent. Here is how to do it in Turbo C and in ANSI C running under Unix.

COMPILING A PROGRAM USING TURBO C

From the Turbo editor:

◆   Press ⎡ALT⎤-⎡F9⎤ (hold the ⎡ALT⎤ key, then press the ⎡F9⎤ function key).

From the command line:

◆   At the DOS prompt, type *tcc*, followed by the name of your program. If your program is named *prog1.c*, you would type the following:

```
tcc prog1.c
```

COMPILING A PROGRAM USING ANSI C RUNNING UNDER UNIX

At the command prompt, type *acc*, followed by the name of your program. If your program is named *prog1.c*, you would type the following:

```
acc prog1.c
```

ERROR CORRECTION AND RECOMPILATION

During compilation, the compiler may find errors which make it unable to translate your program. A large part of the software development process is finding and correcting errors; this process, known as **debugging a program**, is discussed in more detail in Chapter 2. Look carefully at the error messages, which will identify the type of error and the line number where it occurred; you should easily be able to see what is wrong most of the time. If not, ask your instructor for assistance. (However, if there are many errors, some of the error messages may be misleading. In that case, concentrate on fixing the first few.) Correct the errors using your editor and then recompile the program. Continue this cycle until your program compiles with no errors. Don't be discouraged if this process takes quite a while. No one always writes error-free code; your goal should be to find and correct most errors before you compile the program, and to correct the others carefully without making more.

RUNNING A PROGRAM (PROGRAM EXECUTION)

Once your program has compiled successfully, a copy in machine language is stored on the disk. Now you can **execute** or **run** your program, which means to let the instructions you wrote actually control the machine. Once more, the method to run your program is system dependent. Here is how to do it in Turbo C and ANSI C running under Unix.

RUNNING A PROGRAM USING TURBO C

From the Turbo editor:

◆   Press CTRL-F9 (hold the CTRL key, then press the F9 function key).

This key sequence will actually compile and run your program in sequence, so you may decide to use it directly instead of starting with ALT-F9. If there are errors, the process will stop after compilation; otherwise, it will continue and also run your program. (If the program has already been compiled and no changes have been made, pressing CTRL-F9 will run it again without recompiling.)

From the command line:

◆   Type the name of the program without an extension. In DOS, if your original file was named ***prog1.c***, the compilation process produces an executable file with the name ***prog1.exe***. To run this program, type the following:

```
prog1
```

RUNNING A PROGRAM USING ANSI C RUNNING UNDER UNIX

In Unix, the compilation process produces an executable file with the name ***a.out***. To run the program, type the following:

```
a.out
```

VIEWING THE OUTPUT

The output will normally appear on the screen as a result of running your program. In Unix, or from the command line in DOS, you will immediately see the output on the screen. However, if you ran your program from within the Turbo C editor, you will be returned to the editor after the output scrolls quickly across the screen. From the Turbo C editor, you can view the output again by pressing ALT-F5 (the ALT key, followed by the F5 function key) to get to the User screen. When you are finished viewing your output, press any key to return to the editor.

SELF-CHECK 1-8

1. If you are using C on a Unix system, what is the name of a common text editor? If you are using Turbo C, where will you find a text editor?

2. If a statement continues for more than one line, how does the compiler know that it is not finished at the end of the first line?

3. What is the difference between compiling and running a program?

SOFTWARE DEVELOPMENT CYCLE

Suppose you look at your output, and it is wrong. The computer didn't make a mistake; you did. You have to figure out what is wrong with your program, correct the error, and go through the process we've outlined again until the output is correct.

Writing computer programs (also called software) is often a lengthy process. Multimillion dollar companies that write software go through the same process, called the **software development cycle**, that you must when creating a program. Let's look at some of the steps in the process; you will become more familiar with them as you go along.

The process starts with a statement of the problem.

◆ Sometimes the problem statement is not perfectly clear, and you will need to check with the person who wrote it (for now, your instructor) to determine exactly what is required.

◆ You must analyze the problem statement, determining what the program is to do, what input it gets, what output it produces, and what process will get from the input to the output. Be sure you understand all these things before you go on.

◆ You then need to write pseudocode for the program.

◆ Next you will write the program from the pseudocode.

◆ After typing in, editing, and saving the program, you will compile it. There will probably be errors, and you must correct them and recompile the program.

◆ Once the program compiles correctly, you will run it. There may be errors in the output, which means there are errors in the program. You must correct the errors and recompile the program.

As your programs get more complicated, you will need to do program testing. This involves running the same program with different data until you are certain that it works in all cases.

Once the program and its output are correct, you will submit it to the person who requested it. You may find that the program does not meet the specifications (in other words, it doesn't work in all cases, or it does something other than what it is supposed to do, or the output isn't readable). In that case, you may have to make further modifications and go through the process again until the program is satisfactory.

Now you are ready to run your first program. Good luck!

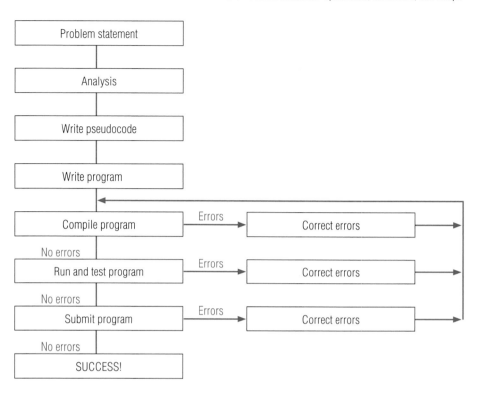

SELF-CHECK 1-9

1. What are the steps in the software development cycle?
2. Which steps have we done for you in Program 1?
3. Which will you have to do on your own?

SECTION 7 MORE DETAILS: ARITHMETIC OPERATIONS, IDENTIFIERS, *for* LOOPS

In this section, we will go into a little more depth on some topics introduced earlier in this chapter.

ARITHMETIC OPERATIONS IN C

We have been using the words "operator" and "operation," and it might be helpful to explain their meaning in C. An **operation** is a way of combining objects, usually one or two at a time, to form something new; the **operator** is the symbolic representation of the operation. For example, addition is an operation, and the operator + represents addition in C. The objects are normally numbers or characters, but they can also be other things, as we will see later. The simplest operations are those that work with numbers. We will call these **arithmetic operations**.

A number of arithmetic operations are available in C. Addition and multiplication are two simple ones that have been used in Program 1, with + used for addition and * for multiplication. Even though many symbols can be used in arithmetic or algebra to denote multiplication [e.g., we can use $a \times b$, $a \cdot b$, ab, or $a(b)$], an asterisk, as in $a * b$, is the only way to indicate multiplication in C. Subtraction is also easy, just $a - b$.

Division in arithmetic is normally $\frac{a}{b}$ or $a \div b$, but in C, division is indicated by a slash (/). More precisely, a/b means a divided by b. Here are some examples:

◆ If a is 10 and b is 5, then a/b is 2.

◆ If a is 11 and b is 4, then a/b is 2 (the fractional part of the answer is lost).

◆ If a is 10, then $a/4$. is 2.5 (in this case, the entire answer is kept).

◆ If a is 4, then $10.0/a$ is 2.5 (the entire answer is kept).

◆ If $dist$ is 3.6 and $hours$ is 2.4 (in the next chapter, we will discuss how variables can hold such values), then $dist/hours$ is 1.5.

In these examples, the result of division, called the quotient, is sometimes an integer and sometimes not. If either (or both) operand is not an integer (e.g., 10.6/2.3, 10.6/2, or even 10/2.0), the division will be performed the way it is in arithmetic, and the quotient will have decimal places. However, if one integer is divided by another, C uses **integer division** to find the quotient. This value is always an integer since any fractional part of the quotient is chopped off.

Because the fractional part of the answer is lost in integer division, C has a **modulus** or **remainder operator**, denoted by %, that will give the remainder when one integer is divided by another. For example, if c is 10 and d is 6, then $c \% d$ is 4. As another example, 26 % 5 is 1. Also 5 % 6 is 5. In general, $x \% y$ gives the remainder when x is divided by y. (The calculations can be tricky if one or both of the values is negative. See Exercise 11 for more details.) Of course, for both of these operations (/ and %), it is understood that the second operand cannot be 0 to avoid the obvious problem of dividing by 0.

Table 1.1 summarizes these operations. Note that arithmetic operators can be surrounded by any number of blanks (including none, as in $y+z$). In our programs, we will usually include a single blank on each side if it improves readability.

TABLE 1.1 Arithmetic Operations in Arithmetic and C

Operation	Arithmetic	C	Other C Examples	
Addition	$a + b$	$a + b$	$age+1$	$sum + tax$
Subtraction	$a - b$	$a - b$	$10-rate$	$ht - wt$
Multiplication	$a \cdot b$, ab, $a(b)$	$a * b$	$2*pay$	$mass * veloc$
Division	$a \div b$ or $\frac{a}{b}$			
quotient		a/b	$age/12$	$dist / hours$
remainder (or modulus)		$a \% b$	$value \% 10$	$months \% yrs$

In Chapter 2, we will add several other arithmetic operations to this list. We will also study further properties, including how to combine them to form complex expressions.

SELF-CHECK 1-10

1. What is the result of each of these division operations?

    a. 6/3   c. 5/6   e. 6/4.
    b. 6/4   d. 199/100   f. 199/100.

2. What is the result of these operations?

    a. 6 % 3   c. 5 % 6   e. 200 % 100
    b. 6 % 4   d. 199 % 100   f. 201 % 100

IDENTIFIERS

An **identifier** is a name for a variable or function. In C, the following characters are valid as part of an identifier name:

◆ letters, either lowercase or uppercase;

◆ the digits 0–9; and

◆ the underbar symbol (_).

An identifier name is a series of one or more valid characters. The first character must be a letter or the underbar symbol, but the remainder can be letters, digits, or underbars. Any other symbols are illegal in an identifier name.

We will usually not use underbars unless the name is long, and the underbar improves readability (e.g., ***largest_grade***). Unfortunately, the various versions of C differ in the rest of the rules for a valid identifier name.[4]

You are allowed to use any combination of capital and lowercase letters in a C program. In fact, a single identifier name can contain a mixture of the two (e.g., ***Rate***). However, please note the following warning!

CAUTION Unlike most other languages, the C compiler distinguishes between capital and lowercase letters, so ***RATE***, ***rate***, and ***Rate*** do *not* refer to the same identifier. Technically you can use all of these in your program, and they will be considered different. Obviously, this can lead to a tremendous amount of confusion. Later in this section, we will recommend how to use capital and lowercase letters to eliminate confusion.

---

[4]Certain versions of C restrict identifiers to just 8 characters; others allow them to be any size. For example, in Turbo C, the name of an identifier can be any size, but only the first 31 characters determine if two identifiers are identical (see Exercise 10). In general, we will use large names (but not 31 characters!) when it is convenient.

EXAMPLE 1-6   Here are some valid names:

a, a1, sales1995, rate, sumoftestgrades, r2d2, student_avg, PI

Here are some invalid ones, with the reason in parentheses:

new sum	(a blank in the middle)
test-grade	(a minus sign in the middle)
96sales	(a digit as the first symbol instead of a letter)
entry#	(an illegal symbol, the #, in the name)

KEYWORDS

There are three general categories of identifiers in C: keywords, standard identifiers, and pro-grammer-defined identifiers. Let's go through these one by one. Certain words in a C program must be used in specific places and have a particular meaning in that context. For example, here are two words that appeared in our first program: *int* and *for*. These special words are called **keywords**, which means that they cannot be used by the programmer in any other way. For example, in our program, we could not use a variable named *int* or *for*. Appendix I con-tains a complete list of the keywords in ANSI C. Other versions of C may have slightly different lists of keywords, and some implementations have added a few.

STANDARD IDENTIFIERS

Other words have a special meaning in the language, but a programmer is allowed to over-ride it by using them as the names of variables or in other places. These words are called **standard identifiers**. In almost all cases, standard identifiers are names of functions in the standard library (see Chapter 2, Section 5 and Appendix IV), but there are a few others.

Standard identifiers have their predeclared meaning unless the programmer explicitly uses their name for some other purpose in the program. For example, *printf* is not a key-word, but it does have a special meaning. A programmer could declare a variable with the name *printf*, and this new meaning would take precedence over its predeclared meaning. (This means that *printf* could no longer be used to print a line of output.) A programmer could use the name *printf* for some other purpose, but it is hard to imagine what is gained. Therefore, we recommend that you do not use standard identifiers for anything other than their intended purpose unless you have a compelling reason.

PROGRAMMER-DEFINED IDENTIFIERS

All other identifiers are **programmer** or **user defined**. For these identifiers, the user must give an explicit declaration. The programmer-defined identifiers we used in our first pro-gram are *number* and *sqnumber*.

The same identifier cannot have two meanings in any one main program or function (we will talk more about functions later). For example, if a variable is named *query*, then nothing else in the main program can have that name. If a standard identifier such as ***printf*** is adopted as a programmer-defined name, it is not possible to use its predeclared meaning.

STYLE WORKSHOP In this text, we will use certain conventions to write identifiers. Keywords and standard identifiers will always be written in lowercase letters (e.g., ***int*** or ***printf***). Programmer-defined identifiers will also be written in lowercase letters (e.g., ***number*** or ***sqnumber***). Capitals will be reserved for a special purpose, to be explained later.

In a program or display, we will use a special typeface for keywords, standard identifiers, and programmer-defined identifiers. In the body of the text, identifiers will be written in bold italics. For example, we would write ***number*** = ***number*** + ***1*** in the middle of a paragraph.

When you are typing your program, everything that you enter must be in the same typeface.[5] You may wish to adopt conventions of capitalization or naming which improve readability. The most important advice is to be consistent.

SELF-CHECK 1-11

1. What are the rules for a valid identifier name?

2. What are the differences among keywords, standard identifiers, and programmer-defined identifiers? Give an example of each in Program 1.

3. Are programmer-defined identifiers usually written using uppercase or lowercase letters?

A *for* LOOP USING DECREMENT

As a way of introducing the additional power of a ***for*** loop, let's try one modification of Program 1. If we want the table of values for ***number*** and ***sqnumber*** to be printed out in reverse order, from 9 81 at the top to 4 16 at the bottom, there are many ways to do this. Most of them are too advanced for this chapter. However, there is a simple modification (called a **decrement** rather than an increment) to the ***for*** loop that will accomplish this.

To decrement using a ***for*** loop, start the control variable at a higher value than the final one. In addition, change the condition that controls when to execute the body of the loop. (Execute the body of the loop if the control variable is greater than or equal to the final value.) Finally, rather than incrementing the control variable each time through the loop, decrement instead. No changes are made in the body of the loop. All we have to do is change the ***for*** loop header. In particular, the statement ***number*** = ***number*** - ***1*** will cause the value of ***number*** to decrease each time through the loop. The new ***for*** loop will execute for ***number*** having the values 9, 8, 7, 6, 5, and 4. After the value 4 has been processed, ***number*** will decrease to 3; the test condition will now be false, and the loop will terminate. Of course, we should also alter the comment at the top of the program to indicate the change in order.

---

[5]If you are using a word processing program such as WordPerfect or Microsoft Word, which includes italics, boldface, and underlining, *do not use these special features*. They will confuse the compiler. Instead, save the program in a form called DOS or ASCII text.

EXAMPLE 1-7   Here is the complete program using a decrement loop. We will not bother tracing this version (which we will call *prog1c.c*), although you may find it useful to do that yourself.

```
/* Program prog1c.c: print the numbers from 9 to 4 and their squares */
#include <stdio.h>
main()
{
    int number,sqnumber;

    for (number = 9; number >= 4; number = number - 1)  {
        sqnumber = number * number;
        printf("%d %d\n",number,sqnumber);
    }
}
```

MORE EXAMPLES OF *for* LOOP HEADERS

Two special cases of *for* loop headers are worth noting. If we use the type of loop discussed in this chapter, and if the starting value is the same as the last value to be processed, the body of the *for* loop will be executed only once, with the control variable having that common value.

EXAMPLE 1-8   The loops shown below will both print the number 5.

```
for (i = 5; i <= 5; i = i + 1)          for (i = 5; i >= 5; i = i - 1)
    printf("%d\n",i);                       printf("%d\n",i);
```

If the test controlling the loop is false initially, then the body of the loop will not be executed at all.

EXAMPLE 1-9   The loops shown below do not print anything since neither *printf* will ever be executed. (See if you can predict what value *i* will have when each loop ends.)

```
for (i = 6; i <= 5; i = i + 1)          for (i = 5; i >= 6; i = i - 1)
    printf("%d\n",i);                       printf("%d\n",i);
```

The header of a *for* loop can be more complicated than the ones we have used so far. Consider the following example:

EXAMPLE 1-10   We can have a *for* loop that looks like this:

```
for (i = 1, j = 7; i <= j; i = i + 3, j = j + 1)
    printf("%d %d\n",i,j);
```

The header has two initialization statements, separated by a comma, plus two increment statements, also separated by a comma. This loop starts by performing both initializations; then the values of *i* and *j* are compared. If the value of *i* is less than or equal to the value of *j*, the body of the loop is executed, and both increments are done. The test controlling the loop determines whether to execute the body again. If the body is executed, the increments, the test, and so on will follow.

In the body of the loop above, the following pairs of values of *i* and *j* will be printed:

```
1  7
4  8
7  9
10  10
```

Then *i* will increment to 13, and *j* will become 11. These values of *i* and *j* will cause the loop to terminate because *i* is not less than or equal to *j*.

THE GENERAL FORM OF A *for* LOOP HEADER

C has an even more general form of *for* loop header. In this general form, the initialization and update steps (note that we call it update—more on this below) can consist of any number of individual C statements, separated by commas. However, there must still be just one test controlling the loop.

General Form of a *for* Loop

```
for (initialization statement(s); controlling condition; update statement(s))
       body of the loop
```

Let's describe how this general form is executed.

◆ First, all of the initialization statements are performed. In case there are two or more initialization (or update) statements, they are performed from left to right.

◆ Then the controlling condition is checked. If it is true, the statement(s) in the body of the loop are executed.

◆ After the body of the loop, all of the update statements are executed, and the controlling condition is checked again. If the condition is true, the body of the loop is executed again, the update statements are executed, the condition is checked again, and so on.

The loop continues as long as the condition is true. The loop will terminate when the controlling condition becomes false.

In the general form of the *for* loop header, we use the term *update statements*, rather than *increment statements*. Statements which change things from one pass to another are not limited to increments or decrements. They can, in fact, be any C statements whatsoever.

SHORTHAND FOR INCREMENTS: ++ AND ––

Because increment statements are so common, C has a shorthand form that is almost always used. In the line below, the statement on the right is an abbreviation for the statement on the left.

```
i = i + 1;      can be replaced by      i++;
```

Actually, the abbreviated form becomes much more useful if the name of the variable is large, rather than very short like *i*. For example, compare these two statements:

```
verylongname = verylongname + 1;     compared to     verylongname++;
```

Another advantage of this form comes when it is used as part of larger C constructs. In later chapters, we will see how to use the increment operator in these situations.

EXAMPLE 1-11

As a simple example, we will show how to use the increment operator in a *for* loop header:

```
for (number = 4; number <= 9; number++)
```

In the same way, subtracting one from a variable can be abbreviated by using the decrement operator --. For example, these two statements are equivalent:

```
number = number - 1;     and   number--;
```

EXAMPLE 1-12

Once again, here is an example using a *for* loop header:

```
for (number = 9; number >= 4; number--)
```

Finally, the increment and decrement operators can also appear to the left of the variable name. In the case of a simple assignment statement (e.g., as part of a *for* loop header), these three statements have the same meaning:

```
i++;     ++i;     i = i + 1;
```

However, as we will see in Chapter 12, if the increment or decrement operator is used as part of a larger expression, there can be differences in meaning. We will avoid using *++i* and *--i* in larger expressions until we can explain these differences.

SELF-CHECK 1-12

1. In a decrement version of a *for* loop, what happens to the control variable each time through the body of the loop?

2. How many statements are allowed to appear in the initialization or update portion of a *for* loop header? How many are allowed in the test portion?

3. What does the statement *i++* mean? What does *++i* mean? What about *i--*?

SUMMARY

BASIC CONCEPTS

1. The computer programs in this text are written in the language called C. Several versions of C are available. The version used in this text is ANSI Standard C. Two compilers were used to test all programs: Turbo C++ Version 3.0 for the IBM-compatible personal computer, and ANSI C running under Unix on a Sun Sparcstation.

2. Comments should be used to explain (to a person, not the computer) what the program is designed to do. Comments are ignored by the compiler but are printed with the program. The symbols /* and */ are comment delimiters. Every program should have a comment at the top explaining what the program does.

3. The line below, called a compiler directive, is usually included at the beginning of every C program:

```
#include <stdio.h>
```

This directive, although not strictly a part of the C language, allows the program to access information about certain functions from the standard library. The header file *stdio.h* contains information about the *printf* function. A compiler directive must start in column 1, and it cannot be followed by anything else on the same line.

4. A C program is composed of individual C statements. The first line of C code in a program, sometimes called the main program header, is

```
main()
```

5. Each complete C statement (except for comments and directives, which are not technically C statements) must end in a semicolon. If a statement is too long to fit on a single line, it can be continued on the next line, with a semicolon at the end of the entire statement.

6. For clarity, each statement should start on a new line. Actually, two or more statements can be put on a single line, separated by a semicolon. However, a program will normally be more readable and easier to understand if no more than one statement is on any line. Consistent use of indentation and alignment also makes a program more readable.

PSEUDOCODE AND ALGORITHMS

7. Pseudocode, consisting of statements which are a mixture of English and C code, is an intermediate step in writing a program. Pseudocode is an aid in writing the program and also a guide to following it once it is written.

8. Pseudocode comes from the English-language description of a program. Then the C program is written from the pseudocode. This two-step process is almost always easier than going directly from English to C.

9. Standard mathematical notation is allowed in pseudocode, including exponents, the symbol for square root, and so on. These must all be translated into C when the program is written.

10. An algorithm is a step-by-step explanation of a process that is precise enough to be expressed in pseudocode and then developed into a program.

IDENTIFIERS

11. Almost any combination of letters and digits (starting with a letter or underbar) that fits on a single line is a valid identifier name; certain versions of C have further restrictions—for example, on the length of the name. Capital and lowercase letters can both be used in an identifier name. However, the compiler will consider an uppercase letter to be distinct from the corresponding lowercase one. For example, *alpha* and *Alpha* are two different identifiers. For consistency, we will use only lowercase for variable names.

12. A number of identifiers (e.g., *for* and *int*) have special meanings in C. These are called keywords and should always be used with their intended meaning.

13. Other identifiers (e.g., *printf*) have a predeclared or standard meaning, but a programmer can override it by using them in some other way. However, it is recommended that a programmer use these identifiers only in the standard way.

14. An identifier that is neither a keyword nor a standard identifier is called a programmer-defined identifier.

FORMAT OF A C PROGRAM

15. The header or top line of a program is followed by a series of declarations, which tell the compiler which programmer-defined identifiers are being used. The declarations are followed by the main body of the program. The declarations and main body form the action portion of the program. The entire action portion is surrounded by a pair of braces ({ and }).

16. Here is a diagram of the form that a C program should follow:

`/* ... */`	comment describing the job of the program
`#include ...`	reference to functions from the standard library
`main()`	main program header
`{`	start of the action portion of the program
`int ...;`	declarations
`...`	statements to accomplish the program's task
`}`	end of the main program

VARIABLES, ASSIGNMENT STATEMENTS, AND ARITHMETIC OPERATIONS

17. A variable is a type of identifier that holds information during the execution of a program. Every variable in C must be declared explicitly by associating the name of the identifier with a data type. The simplest data type is *int*, short for integer, which allows a variable to hold integer values only. Here is a declaration for two integer variables named *alpha* and *beta*:

```
int alpha,beta;
```

18. A variable does not have a value until the computer is told explicitly to put something into that storage location, typically through an assignment statement. An assignment statement has this general form:

```
varname = expr;
```

This is executed by evaluating the expression (*expr*) on the right-hand side of the assignment symbol (=) and then assigning this value to the variable (*varname*) on the left-hand side.

19. The standard arithmetic operations of addition (+), subtraction (−), and multiplication (∗) are available in C. Several types of division are also available. The symbol / is used to divide one number by another. For example, 7/2 is 3; 7/2. is 3.5. The modulus or remainder operator % recovers the remainder when one integer is divided by another; $x \% y$ gives the remainder when x is divided by y (e.g., 7 % 2 is 1).

printf

20. A *printf* can be used to print the value of one or more variables. For example, the line below will print the value of x, one space, and then the value of y. The output statement after the *printf* will print on a new line because of the newline character (*n*).

```
printf("%d %d\n",x,y);
```

LOOPS

21. Statements are normally executed sequentially. However, a loop can modify this order. In general, a loop contains a series of statements that are written once but can be executed repeatedly.

22. A common programming technique is incrementing a variable, which means to increase its value (usually, but not always, by 1). Incrementing allows us to get the next in a series of values as we progress through a loop. The general form of an increment to the variable *varname* by *increment_value* is:

```
varname = varname + increment_value;
```

23. C has a number of different loop structures. The one that is used first in the text is a *for* loop, which allows a series of instructions to be executed a specified number of times.

24. One simple form of a *for* loop is the following:

```
for (index = start; index <= limit; index = index + 1)
    statement;
```

Here *index* is used as the control variable or *for* loop index; *start* is the starting or initial value for *index*; *limit* is the final or limiting value for *index*; *statement* is a single C statement. Each time through the body of the loop, the value of the control variable is increased by 1. The body of the loop consists of one single statement, but this can be modified by using a compound statement.

25. This *for* loop is executed as follows: *index* is initialized to *start* and compared to *limit*. If *index* is less than or equal to *limit*, then the one statement constituting the body of the loop is executed with *index* equal to *start*. Each time the body of the loop is completed, *index* is incremented by 1, and the process is repeated. That is, the new value for *index* is tested against *limit*; if it is less than or equal to *limit*, then the body is executed again. The loop continues until the condition controlling it is false (in this case, when *index* is not less than or equal to *limit*). When that occurs, the *for* loop is terminated, the body of the loop is not entered, and the next statement in the program is executed.

26. Some variations are allowed in the general form of a *for* loop. For example, by using a compound statement, which consists of a pair of braces around a group of statements, a programmer can include any number of C statements in the body of the loop. In the example below, *statement-1*, *statement-2*, ..., *statement-n* will be done each time the body of the loop is executed.

```
for (index = start; index <= limit; index = index + 1)  {
    statement-1;
    statement-2;
    ...
    statement-n;
}
```

27. The general form of a *for* loop allows any number of initialization statements, one controlling condition, and any number of update statements:

```
for (initialization statement(s); controlling condition; update statement(s))
    body of the loop
```

First, all of the initialization statements are performed. Then the controlling condition is checked. If it is true, the statement(s) in the body of the loop are executed. Finally, all of the update statements are executed, and the controlling condition is checked again. The loop continues as long as the condition is true. The loop terminates when the controlling condition becomes false.

SOFTWARE DEVELOPMENT CYCLE: SAVING, COMPILING, AND RUNNING A PROGRAM

28. As part of the software development cycle, a programmer must do the following: analyze a problem, come up with an algorithm and express it in pseudocode, and write a program to translate the pseudocode into a programming language. The program should then be typed in, saved, compiled, run, and tested. The details of how to do these steps vary from system to system.

INCREMENT AND DECREMENT OPERATORS

29. Because increment and decrement statements are so common, C has shorthand operators that are often used. The statements on the right are an abbreviation for the ones on the left.

```
number = number + 1;    becomes    number++;
number = number - 1;    becomes    number--;
```

30. The increment and decrement operators can be used in a *for* loop header. For example, here is another way to write the header in paragraph 26:

```
for (index = start; index <= limit; index++)
```

This form will be used in almost all our later programs.

EXERCISES

For each exercise, assume that all variables have been declared to have data type *int*. If you are asked to write a program, be sure to include comments. In the exercises, when we give a complete C program, we usually omit comments.

TRACING EXERCISES

1. For each of the following series of C statements, trace what happens as the section of code is run. That is, show what value is stored in each variable as each step is executed. You can use either of the tracing methods in Section 5.

a.
```
y = 2;
x = y + 1;
y = y + 1;
x = 4;
```

b.
```
numb = 5;
cbnumb = numb * numb * numb;
sqnumb = numb * numb;
```

c.
```
w = 6;
w = w + 1;
q = 2 * w;
```

d.
```
rate = 7;
time = 5;
junk = rate - time;
dist = rate * time;
```

e.
```
for (x = 6; x <= 10; x = x + 1)
    y = x * 2;
y = 13;
```

f.
```
s = 0;
for (i = 1; i <= 5; i = i + 1)
    s = s + i;
```

2. For each of the following C programs, show what is printed.

a.
```
#include <stdio.h>
main()
{
    int x,y;

    y = 2;
    x = y + 1;
    printf("%d %d\n",x,y);
    y = y + 2;
    x = 5;
    printf("%d %d\n",x,y);
}
```

b.
```
#include <stdio.h>
main()
{
    int numb,cbnumb;

    numb = 4;
    cbnumb = numb * numb * numb;
    printf("%d %d %d\n",numb,
            cbnumb,numb*numb);
}
```

c.
```
#include <stdio.h>
main()
{
    int w,q;

    w = 6;
    w = w + 3;
    q = 4 * w;
    printf("%d %d\n",w,q);
}
```

d.
```
#include <stdio.h>
main()
{
    int rate,time,dist,junk;

    rate = 7;
    time = 3;
    junk = rate + time;
    dist = rate * time;
    printf("%d %d %d %d\n",rate,
            time,junk,dist);
}
```

e.
```
#include <stdio.h>
main()
{
    int x,y;

    for (x = 6; x <= 10; x++)  {
        y = x * 5;
        printf("%d %d\n",x,y);
    }
    x = 8;
    printf("%d %d\n",x,y);
}
```

f.
```
#include <stdio.h>
main()
{
    int i,s;

    s = 0;
    for (i = 1; i <= 7; i++)
        s = s + i;
    printf("%d\n",s);
}
```

3. a. The traces in Exercise 1(a) through (d) are much shorter than those for parts (e) and (f). Why is this true? [*Suggestion:* What new instruction is used in parts (e) and (f)?]

   b. In Exercise 1(b), would it be legal to write either *cbnumb = numb * numb* or *sqnumb = numb * numb * numb*? If so, is it a good idea? If it is illegal, explain why.

4. Assume that the variables *x*, *y*, *z*, and *w* of type *int* have the values shown below (for each part of this exercise, start from these initial values). As each step is executed, show what is stored in each variable.

   x = 7; y = 6; z = 1; w = 4;

a. `z = x / y;` b. `x = y / w;` c. `x = x + 1;` d. `w = y - w;`
    `w = x % y;`   `z = y % w;`   `y = x + 1;`   `z = y / x;`
                                      `z = x * y;`

5. Each part of this question contains two similar series of statements. However, there is a significant difference in each part between the two series. Trace each part step by step and show what is printed. Be sure that you understand the difference between (1) and (2) in each part.

a. (1) `numb = 9;`   (2) `numb = 9;`
        `printf("%d\n",2 * numb);`   `numb = 2 * numb;`
        `printf("%d\n",numb);`   `printf("%d\n",numb);`

b. (1) `numb = 3;`   (2) `numb = 3;`
        `printf("%d\n",numb);`   `numb = numb + 1;`
        `numb = numb + 1;`   `printf("%d\n",numb);`

c. (1) `x = 5;`   (2) `x = 5;`
        `x = x + 1;`   `y = x;`
        `y = x;`   `x = x + 1;`
        `printf("%d %d\n",x,y);`   `printf("%d %d\n",x,y);`

6. Show what is printed by each of the following *for* loops.

a. `for (i = 1; i <= 8; i++)  {`   b. `for (i = 8; i >= 1; i--)  {`
        `k = 9 - i;`   `k = i;`
        `m = 2 * k;`   `m = 2 * k;`
        `printf("%d %d %d\n",i,k,m);`   `printf("%d %d %d\n",i,k,m);`
    `}`   `}`

ANALYSIS EXERCISES

7. Here is a list of possible names for variables in C. Which are legal names for your particular compiler? Which are illegal names? If a name is illegal, explain why (e.g., it starts with an illegal character).

a. *beginend*   n. *fore*
b. *space1999*   o. *zyxwvutsrqponmlkjihgfedcba*
c. *1999_space*   p. *upto*
d. *p qrs*   q. *downto*
e. *IBM*   r. *legal*
f. *i.b.m.*   s. *legal?*
g. *iNtEL*   t. *#1*
h. *5*   u. *number1*
i. *one_2*   v. *_a*
j. *2one*   w. *a_*
k. *help+me*   x. *FOR*
l. *abc...xyz* (with ... in the name) y. *1x*
m. *for*   z. *x1*

8. Here is the final version of Program 1 from Section 5. The numbers to the left of the statements are for our discussion only, to make it easier to refer to individual statements. They

are not part of the C program and should not be included when you type the program. Answer the questions below the program.

```
1.   /* Program prog1b.c:  print the numbers from 4 to 9 and their squares */
2.   #include <stdio.h>
3.   main()
4.   {
5.        int number,sqnumber;
6.
7.        for (number = 4; number <= 9; number = number + 1)  {
8.             sqnumber = number * number;
9.             printf("%d %d\n",number,sqnumber);
10.       }
11.  }
```

a. Line 1 is a comment. What is its purpose?

b. Line 2 says that we want to include something in our program. What will we include? Why do we want to include it?

c. Line 3 is called the main program header. What does it tell the compiler?

d. Line 4 consists of a single piece of punctuation, the opening brace ({). What does this symbol mean?

e. Line 5 is a declaration, which sets aside space for the variables (whose names are?) and tells what type of information they will hold (what type?).

f. Line 6 is blank. Why is it included?

g. Line 7 sets up a *for* loop, which will process successive values of ***number*** from 4 to 9. What is the control variable of this loop? The initial value? What is the condition used to control the loop? What is the last or limiting value to be processed? What does the control variable increase by each time? Line 7 does not end in a semicolon since the statement is not yet complete (why not?). What does the opening brace at the end of this line indicate to the compiler?

h. How many things do we want to do in the body of the loop? Lines 8 and 9 contain the statements that are to be executed each time through the body of the *for* loop. What type of statement is line 8? What value does it give to ***sqnumber***?

i. What is the purpose of line 9? What does it print? What is the string inside quotation marks called? What does ***%d*** mean? What is the purpose of the ***\n*** character?

j. Line 10 uses a closing brace (}) to indicate the end of the series of statements that we want to include inside the body of the *for* loop. What is the brace aligned under? Why doesn't this line end in a semicolon?

k. Line 11 also consists of a closing brace. What other symbol is this closing brace matched with? What line is that symbol on? What is the purpose of line 11?

9. When the program below was compiled, there was an error message. What was the error message? How should the program be fixed to correct this error?

```
#include <stdio.h>
main()
{
     int Numb;

     numb = 1;
}
```

10. In Section 7, we described rules used by a compiler to determine if two identifier names are identical. Decide if each of the following possible names for variables is valid on your system. Also determine if two or more of these names will be considered identical by your compiler.

    a. *xxxxxxxxxxxxxxxxxxxxxxxxx* (writing *x* 25 times)
    b. *xxxxxxxxxxxxxxxxxxxxxxxxxxxxxxxxxxx* (writing *x* 35 times)
    c. *xxxxx...xxxx* (writing *x* 75 times)
    d. *xxxxx...xxxx* (writing *x* 150 times)

11. In most cases, the operations of / and % are used with positive integers. However, they are defined for negative values as well. Make up a series of little programs that allow you to discover the rules your compiler follows for negative values. For example, write a program that determines the value of –1 % 5, 9 / –2, –7 % –3, or –5 / 4. Construct a chart summarizing the rules. (*Warning:* The rules may vary slightly from one C compiler to another. Therefore, most programmers avoid using these special cases in a program that may eventually run on some other compiler.)

12. The program below has many errors in it. Try to find and correct all of them. Some of them are foolish, like leaving off a semicolon. Others are things like misspelled words, and so on. When you think you have found all the errors, run the program to see if you missed any. An error in a program is called a *bug*. Getting a program to work correctly by making sure there are no mistakes in it is called *debugging*. You will learn much more about debugging as you write more programs.

```
/* comant is ok {;
#includ <stdio>;
main
{
    ints x,y;

    x + 1 = 4;
    y = y + 1;
    x = 3y + 5x
    printf(x,y)
```

EXERCISES TO MODIFY PROGRAM 1

13. In Section 3, we gave a version of Program 1 which did not use a *for* loop; in this version, we explicitly assigned the values 4, 5, 6, 7, 8, and 9 to **number**. In Section 4, we started to write another version of Program 1 which did not use a *for* loop; in this version, we incremented **number** to hold each of the values from 4 to 9.

    a. Finish writing this version of Program 1.
    b. Assume that we want the squares of the numbers from 4 to 59. How many more statements are needed? Assume that we continue to write the program using one of the versions without a *for* loop.
    c. Repeat part (b) with the assumption that the program will print the squares of the numbers from 4 to 159, instead of 4 to 59.
    d. What can you conclude about the power of a *for* loop?

14. In this and the next few exercises, we will modify the *for* loop version of Program 1. The first modification is very simple. We put the **sqnumber = number * number** statement after

the ***printf.*** Rewrite the program with this modification. Then describe what happens if we run the new program. (*Suggestion:* The program runs, but the answers are very strange.)

15. Show how to modify Program 1 so that it prints the squares (only the squares, not the numbers themselves) of all the numbers from 1 to 12. The new program should print

> 1 4 9 16 25 ... 144

16. Modify Program 1 so that it prints the numbers from 4 to 9, together with each number's square and cube. For example, it starts by printing

> 4 16 64

17. Modify Program 1 so that it prints the numbers from 4 to 9, together with the square of the number, the cube of the number, two times the number, and three times the number.

18. Modify Program 1 so that it prints the even numbers from 4 to 20 and their squares—i.e., 4 16, 6 36, 8 64, up to 20 400. (*Suggestion:* If the variable *i* increases by 1, then *2 * i* increases by 2. Or, as an alternative, as part of the ***for*** loop header, you can have *i* itself increase by 2.)

19. Modify the program from Exercise 18 so that it prints the even numbers from 4 to 20 and their squares, and then the odd numbers from 5 to 19 and their cubes. (*Suggestion:* Use two loops, one for each part.)

20. Modify Program 1 so that it prints the numbers from 4 to 9 and their squares, except that the square is printed only for numbers greater than 5. The output should be

> 4 5 6 36 7 49 ...

Note that 4 and 5 print, but their squares do not. (*Suggestion:* Treat 4 and 5 separately outside of a loop.)

PROGRAMMING PROJECTS

21. Write a program that prints all of the numbers less than 2000 that are evenly divisible by 10. The first few numbers are 10 20 30 ....

22. Write a program that prints all of the numbers that are evenly divisible by 10. Of course, you won't be able to find all of them, but see how many you can print before there is a problem.

23. a. Without using a loop, write a program that prints your name twice and has three blank lines between the two lines of output.
    b. Repeat part (a), but this time write your name 5 times.
    c. Repeat part (a), but this time write your name 100 times. Does it make sense not to use a loop for this version?

24. Write a program that prints the numbers from 1 to 100 with five values per line, two blank spaces between values. The last few lines will look like this:

> 91 92 93 94 95
> 96 97 98 99 100

25. a. A computer programmer wants to give her boyfriend several pieces of candy every day during June, starting with six on the first day and increasing by five more pieces each day. Write a program that prints the days of the month (the numbers from 1 to 30), together with the number of pieces of candy to be given on that day.

   b. Modify the program from part (a) so that it begins with *start* pieces of candy on the first day and goes up by *increase* number of pieces per day; you will give *start* and *increase* values at the beginning of the program.

26. Go through the earlier exercises that ask you to write programs. Solve each exercise by first writing pseudocode, then writing the program from the pseudocode. If you have already written programs for some of these exercises, compare how easy it was to write the original programs with how easy it is to write them from pseudocode. What conclusions can you draw?

EVALUATING AN EXPRESSION

2

SYNTAX CONCEPTS: *double*, *float*, and *char* data types; printing messages, arithmetic precedence rules, *if* statement, relational operators, compound assignment operators, scientific notation, standard library of functions

PROGRAMMING CONCEPTS: evaluating an expression, branching, creating readable output

CONTROL STRUCTURES: *if* statement

PROBLEM-SOLVING TECHNIQUES: debugging

HOW TO READ CHAPTER 2

OUTLINE:

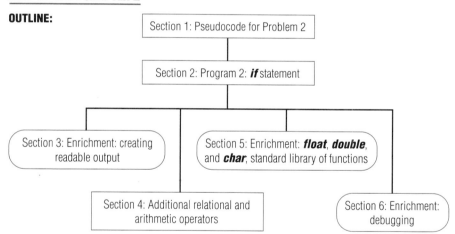

Section 1: Pseudocode for Problem 2

Section 2: Program 2: *if* statement

Section 3: Enrichment: creating readable output

Section 5: Enrichment: *float*, *double*, and *char*; standard library of functions

Section 4: Additional relational and arithmetic operators

Section 6: Enrichment: debugging

INTRODUCTION

This chapter shows how to write a program to evaluate a complex mathematical expression. In the process, it presents C's precedence rules. It introduces the idea of branching—executing one statement or another, depending on the value of an expression—and discusses relational operators. Chapter 2 also uses real numbers (types **double** and **float**), scientific notation, and the standard library of functions. It discusses how to create readable output and introduces debugging. In the process of writing Program 2, we reiterate and consolidate ideas introduced in Chapter 1.

STATEMENT OF THE PROBLEM

Our second problem starts with a story. At University A, sections of a certain class fill very quickly because of the popularity of Professor B. To determine if a student can enter a closed section, the professor uses the student's grade point average (which we will call **gpa**) to evaluate a complicated mathematical formula, which we will signify by **result = formula(gpa)**. If the value of the formula is high enough, the student gets into the section. However, the professor dislikes tedious mathematical calculations so the student must go to the registrar's office.

Until recently, the registrar asked for the student's **gpa**, plugged it into the formula **result = formula(gpa)**, then said either "Congratulations" or "Sorry." Because of the large number of students involved, the registrar has become increasingly busy and has decided to computerize part of the process (in the exercises, you will be asked to program other parts as well) by constructing a chart showing various values for the grade point average and the formula. This way, when a student comes in, the registrar can simply look up the average in the table and find the correct answer to the formula instead of recomputing it each time.

PROBLEM 2

Write a complete C program to produce a table for the registrar's formula, starting at **gpa** = 0.00 and going up to **gpa** = 4.00, increasing by 0.50 each time.

$$result = \frac{gpa^3 + 7gpa - 1}{gpa^2 - \dfrac{gpa + 5}{3}}$$

Next to each value of **result** that is greater than or equal to 0, print the message "Admit".

If you don't know how to evaluate the formula, don't worry. The computer will do that task for you. All you have to do is write the formula in a form that the computer can understand.

Keep in mind that the story is whimsical. We are simply trying to describe a problem that lets us introduce the question of evaluating a formula in C.

SECTION 1 PSEUDOCODE FOR PROBLEM 2

STARTING THE PROGRAM

Just as in Chapter 1, we are to write a complete C program to solve this problem. This time the calculations are more complex, and it is more reasonable to do them on a computer. However, as before, we will not start writing code immediately. Instead, we will think through the problem and devise pseudocode for the solution. First, we will analyze the statement of the problem and determine what the program has to do and what output it produces. It's easier to start with the output.

The problem statement says to produce a table of values. This clearly implies that we want to print some results. The formula in the problem computes a relationship between each value of **gpa** and **result**: For each value of **gpa**, the formula produces a value for **result**. To create a table, we should print both values. Analyzing the output this way gives us two lines of pseudocode:

> *compute* result = *the formula applied to* gpa
> *print* gpa,result

Notice that we haven't gone into the details of how to write the formula in C. The pseudocode doesn't need to be carried to that level since it is just an outline of what we plan to do.

These two lines of pseudocode are sufficient for one value of **gpa**, but the problem statement says to compute **result** for a number of values, starting at 0.00 and ending at 4.00, increasing each time by 0.50. This suggests that we need a loop structure, which leads to the next version of the pseudocode:

> *for values of* gpa *from 0.00 to 4.00, increasing by 0.50*
>   *compute* result = *the formula applied to* gpa
>   *print* gpa,result

The last part of the problem statement says to print a message next to each value of **result** that is greater than or equal to 0. Let's try to make this more precise. After printing each set of **gpa** and **result** values, we want to determine if **result** is greater than or equal to 0. If it is, we want to print the word "Admit" and continue processing with the next value of **gpa**. If **result** is less than 0, we will just continue processing. Let's write a question as part of our pseudocode, using the mathematical symbol for "greater than or equal to":

> *for values of* gpa *from 0.00 to 4.00, increasing by 0.50*
>   *compute* result = *the formula applied to* gpa
>   *print* gpa,result
>   *is* result $\geq$ *0?*
>   *print* "Admit"

That's it. It almost looks like a C program already, largely because of the indenting. It is customary and helpful when writing pseudocode to indent as you would in a program. Then it is clear how the parts of the pseudocode go together in the translation.

WRITING PROGRAM 2: THE _if_ STATEMENT

STARTING THE PROGRAM

Now that we've written the pseudocode, let's start on the C code. The first few lines are not shown in the pseudocode since it deals only with the action part of the program. These lines are exactly the same as for our first program, except for the comment.

```
/* Program prog2a.c:                                        */
/* creates a table to evaluate a formula based on values of */
/* gpa in the range from gpa = 0.00 to 4.00 in units of 0.50 */
#include <stdio.h>
main()
{
```

STYLE WORKSHOP Note that the comment is too long to fit on one line so we break it up into three smaller comments. This is done for readability only. We could also have written it in either of these ways:

```
/* Program prog2a.c:
   creates a table to evaluate a formula based on values of
   gpa in the range from gpa = 0.00 to 4.00 in units of 0.50 */
```

or

```
/*
 * Program prog2a.c:
 * creates a table to evaluate a formula based on values of
 * gpa in the range from gpa = 0.00 to 4.00 in units of 0.50
 */
```

This last format is especially good when a comment is very long. It is widespread in C and is the format we most often use in this textbook.

NEW DATA TYPE: _double_

Now we need a declaration of the variables and their data types. We have already decided to use **gpa** and **result** for the names of the variables.

Next let's see what kind of values **gpa** and **result** hold in this program. The index **gpa** starts at 0.00, then becomes 0.50, 1.00, 1.50, ..., 3.50, 4.00. Some of these values can be represented as integers, but others cannot. Therefore, **gpa** cannot have data type **int**. To allow for the decimal places, we will declare **gpa** to have data type **double**. This data type allows **gpa** to hold a real number, one that may contain decimal places. Clearly the result of the formula (the value stored in **result**) will not be an integer in all cases, so we will give **result** data type **double** as well. Here is the declaration:

```
double gpa,result;
```

SETTING UP THE *for* LOOP FOR PROGRAM 2

The pseudocode makes it obvious that we want to use a *for* loop in this program. The initial value we want is 0.00, the final value is 4.00, and the increment is 0.50. Since we want *gpa* to start at 0.00, we initialize it in the header:

```
for (gpa = 0.00; ... ; ...)
```

The *for* loop should use all values of *gpa* up to and including 4.00, so we can continue the *for* loop header with the following condition:

```
for (gpa = 0.00; gpa <= 4.00; ... )
```

Finally, the pseudocode says that we want to increment the value of *gpa* by 0.50 each time, so we complete the *for* loop header like this:

```
for (gpa = 0.00; gpa <= 4.00; gpa = gpa + 0.50)
    compute result = the formula applied to gpa
    print gpa,result
    is result ≥ 0?
        print "Admit"
```

THE BODY OF THE LOOP

Since we must give *result* a value and also do some printing, the loop body will consist of several statements and should be surrounded by a pair of braces. Inside the loop, the variable *result* should be set to whatever the formula determines is a given value of *gpa*. For now, we will simply write the assignment statement as *result* = *formula*, where *formula* stands for the C translation of the formula. Since the details of this translation are tricky, we will come back to it later.

STYLE WORKSHOP Don't think that this is a poor way to program. It is very common to sketch the basic outline of a program or part of one, then fill in the details later. Chapter 4 discusses this idea further.

PRINTING *double* VALUES

After computing *result*, the pseudocode says to print *gpa* and *result*. An interesting issue arises. Since *gpa* and *result* are not integer values, we can't use *%d* to print them. Instead, we use *%f*, which specifies to print a real number in decimal notation. We can use the following line to print the values of *gpa* and *result*, with each pair of values on a new line:

```
printf("%f    %f\n",gpa,result);
```

The three blanks in the control string cause three spaces to print between the numeric values. There will be no blanks between the items unless we specifically enter them. Assuming that *gpa* has the value 1.0 and *result* has the value 6.5 (this is a value selected at random, not the correct one when *gpa* is 1.0), the following prints:

```
1.000000    6.500000
```

Notice that the *%f* conversion specification causes real numbers to print in decimal format with six decimal places.

THE LOOP SO FAR

Let's look at the loop so far:

```
for (gpa = 0.00; gpa <= 4.00; gpa = gpa + 0.50) {
    result = formula;
    printf("%f    %f\n",gpa,result);
    is result ≥ 0?
        print "Admit"
}
```

SELF-CHECK 2-1

1. Could the variables *gpa* and *result* instead be called *number* and *sqnumber*?

2. Why can't we increment by writing *gpa++*? (*Hint*: What does the *++* operator do?)

3. What prints from the following *printf* if *num1* has the value 2.5 and *num2* has the value –4.76?

```
printf("%f %f\n",num1,num2);
```

MAKING DECISIONS USING A CONDITIONAL OR *if* STATEMENT

The pseudocode says to print the word "Admit" whenever the value of *result* is positive or zero. If *result* is less than 0, we don't want to print. In either case, we want to continue processing with the next value of *gpa*. In C, a **conditional** or *if* statement is used to ask a question or make a decision, and *printf* is used to print a message. The pseudocode easily translates to the following C code:

```
if (result >= 0)
    printf(" Admit\n");
```

Let's first look at the *if* statement. Up until now, all our programs have been written so that each statement executes each time the program runs. Most programs, however, need more than that. A conditional or *if* statement allows a program to **branch**, which means to allow the path of execution to go in one of two directions, depending on a specific condition. Some statements will be executed, and others will not, depending on the condition's value.

In a conditional statement, the keyword *if* is followed by some condition (which must be in parentheses) that evaluates to either true or false. Usually, the condition compares two items using a **relational operator**; in the example, that operator is >= (with no space between the two symbols), which means greater than or equal to.

◆ If the condition is true, we execute the line that follows [in our case, ***printf(" Admit\n")***], and continue processing.

```
result = 3.0;
if (result >= 0)
        printf(" Admit\n");
next_stmt;
```

◆ If the condition is false, we simply skip that statement and "fall through" to the next instruction.

```
result = -1.0;
if (result >= 0)

        printf(" Admit\n");


next_stmt;
```

In the example above, if **result** is greater than or equal to 0, we print the word "Admit," but if **result** is less than 0, we don't. Instead, we proceed to the next statement, which in Program 2 is the loop header.

General Form of an *if* Statement

`if (cond)`	`/* no semicolon here */`
`    stmt-1;`	`/* end of if statement */`
`stmt-2;`	`/* next statement */`

In general, the keyword ***if*** is followed by a condition (*cond*) in parentheses. As shown in Figure 2-1, *cond* is evaluated; if it is true, we execute *stmt-1*; if *cond* is false, we skip *stmt-1*. In either case, we continue with *stmt-2*, which follows the *if* statement.

FIGURE 2-1 Flow of control using an ***if*** statement

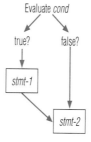

CAUTION Do not put a semicolon after the *if* condition since the *if* statement is not yet complete. Here is an example of the error:

```
if (cond);
    stmt-1;
stmt-2;
```

If by accident you put a semicolon after the *if* condition, the *if* statement terminates. The condition is tested, but nothing happens, and *stmt-1* is executed in all cases.

STYLE WORKSHOP It is considered good style in C to put the *if* condition on one line and the statement to be executed, *stmt-1*, on the next line, indented several spaces or one tab position.

PRINTING MESSAGES

Now let's look at *printf* more carefully. In Chapter 1, we used *printf* to print the values of variables. However, *printf* can do much more. We can print a message, which is simply any combination of allowed symbols, by enclosing it in quotation marks in the control string of a *printf*. A string of characters in quotation marks is called a **literal** or **literal string**.

EXAMPLE 2-1 What happens if we write this?

```
printf("help");
```

Because the word "help" is in quotation marks, the following prints on the screen:

```
help
```

The *printf* prints the word "help", not the value of a variable called **help**. Notice that the message is part of the control string and thus does not need a conversion specification.

EXAMPLE 2-2 What will be printed by the following *printf*?

```
printf("I am a college freshman\n");
```

It will print the following:

```
I am a college freshman
```

Then the cursor will move to a new line. The quotation marks and the \n will *not* print.

The line ***printf(" Admit\n")*** prints the word "Admit", preceded by a space, and then goes to a new line. In Section 3, we will explore further ways to use messages to enhance the appearance of the output from this program.

CAUTION Before going on, be sure that you understand the difference in C between ***printf("gpa")***, which prints "gpa", a string consisting of the three letters g-p-a, and ***printf("%f",gpa)***, which prints the value of the variable ***gpa***.

TRACING PROGRAM 2

Let's look at the entire loop to verify that it works.

```
for (gpa = 0.00; gpa <= 4.00; gpa = gpa + 0.50) {
    result = formula;
    printf("%f    %f\n",gpa,result);
    if (result >= 0)
        printf(" Admit\n");
}
```

PROGRAM TRACE

◆   Initially, **gpa** gets the value 0.00. This value is less than or equal to 4.00, and we enter the body of the loop. The value 0.00 is used to compute a value for **result**, and we print **gpa** and **result**. Then we test to see if the value computed for **result** is greater than or equal to 0. If it is, we print "Admit"; otherwise we skip that line.

◆   In either case, we return to the header of the **for** loop, where we increment the value of **gpa** by 0.50 to 0.50 and then test the new value against 4.00. Since **gpa** is less than or equal to 4.00, we enter the body of the loop. There we compute a new value of **result**, print, test it, and again return to the loop header to increment **gpa**, this time to 1.00.

◆   Eventually, we print 4.00 ... (where ... is the value of **result** when **gpa** = 4.00) and check the value of **result**. Then **gpa** increases to 4.50, which is greater than 4.00, so we fall out of the loop.

ENDING THE PROGRAM

After the loop, we could just end the program with a closing brace. But let's print a message that the table is finished:

```
    printf("The table is finished\n");
}
```

This message, called a **trailer message**, is helpful to both the programmer and the user. It signals to the programmer that the program has run to completion and has not become stuck in the middle. To the user, it signals that the output is finished and no pages are missing.

SELF-CHECK 2-2

1.   What is the difference between the output of the two **printf** statements in this program sequence?

```
int help;

help = 3;
printf("%d",help);
printf("help");
```

2.   What is the purpose of an *if* statement?

3.   What is wrong with the following *if* statement?

```
if x < 7
    printf("less");
```

WRITING THE FORMULA IN C

Our program is almost complete, but we still have a major omission: we have not expressed the formula in C. Using the symbols for arithmetic operations from Chapter 1, Section 7, we can produce a first approximation of the correct formula. Recall that the formula looks like this:

$$result = \frac{gpa^3 + 7gpa - 1}{gpa^2 - \dfrac{gpa + 5}{3}}$$

By a straightforward translation, this becomes in C:

```
result = gpa * gpa * gpa + 7 * gpa - 1 / gpa * gpa - gpa + 5 / 3;
                                                       /* incorrect */
```

PRECEDENCE: THE ORDER OF OPERATIONS

This is not, however, a correct translation because it ignores precedence of operations, the order in which arithmetic operations are performed. For example, in the original mathematical formula, the entire numerator is divided by the entire denominator; division is the last step. But in the C formula as written, the + between *gpa* and 5 is the last step (you will see why shortly). We want to instruct the computer to execute operations in the correct order.

To do this, we have to determine what order C uses if we do not specify the precedence—that is, the natural order of operations in C. Table 2.1 summarizes the precedence of basic arithmetic operations in C.

EXAMPLE 2-3   In what order are the following C expressions evaluated?

    A. a * 3 - b
    B. x + 1 / 2

In expression A, multiplication is done before subtraction:

```
a * 3 - b
  ↑     ↑
  1     2
```

TABLE 2.1 The Arithmetic Precedence Rules[1]

higher precedence (done first)	* / %
lower precedence (done last)	+ −

---

[1]These rules are identical to the ones for arithmetic (e.g., $2 + 3 \times 4$ is $2 + 12 = 14$). In arithmetic, however, the meaning is usually made clear by the way we write the formula: for example, in the expression $3 - 2x$, we know to multiply 2 by x before subtracting.

In expression B, division is done before addition:

$$x + 1 / 2$$
$$\quad\quad \uparrow \quad \uparrow$$
$$\quad\quad 2 \quad 1$$

C has two uses for the minus sign, as does standard arithmetic. One use is subtraction (e.g., 5 – 3). The other is **unary minus** (e.g., –7), so called because it has one operand. Similarly, C has two uses for the plus sign. There is addition, and there is **unary plus** (e.g., +7). Unary minus (sometimes called negation) and unary plus have precedence over all other arithmetic operators.

EXAMPLE 2-4

What is the value of this expression?

6 * –4

It evaluates to –24. The 4 is negated, then multiplied by 6.

ASSOCIATIVITY

There is another concept, called **associativity**, that accompanies precedence. Associativity determines which has priority if two operators with the same precedence are next to each other.

◆   For the binary operators (*, /, %, +, and –), associativity is left to right.

◆   For the unary operators (unary minus, unary plus, ++, and --), associativity is right to left.

In an expression like *a / b * c* or *a – b + c*, where both operations have the same precedence, the one on the left has priority over the one on the right because of associativity.

EXAMPLE 2-5

Evaluate the following program sequence:

```
int a,b,c,ans;

a = 3;
b = 4;
c = 24;
ans = c / b * a;
```

In this case, first *c* is divided by *b* to yield 6; this value is multiplied by *a* to give 18. The value 18 is assigned to *ans*.

THE C ARITHMETIC PRECEDENCE RULES

Table 2.2 summarizes the arithmetic precedence rules in C. Example 2-6 shows an expression where both precedence and associativity rules are used.

TABLE 2.2 The C Arithmetic Precedence Rules

		Associativity
highest precedence (done first)	unary minus unary plus ++ --	right to left
	* / %	left to right
lowest precedence (done last)	+ −	left to right
	Operators on the same line have the same precedence	

EXAMPLE 2-6 $5 - 3 + 2 * 6 / 2$ evaluates to 8 in the order shown:

$$5 - 3 + \quad 12 \quad / 2 =$$
$$5 - 3 + \quad 6 \quad =$$
$$2 \quad + \quad 6 \quad = 8$$

If the precedence rules do not correspond to the order in which we want things to be done, the way to override them in C is the same as in arithmetic—use parentheses. We can write $y = a / (b + 3)$ in order to add before dividing.[2]

EXAMPLE 2-7   x * 2 + 1   says to multiply *x* by 2, then add 1.

x * (2 + 1)   says to add 2 + 1, getting 3, then multiply by *x*.

Inside a pair of parentheses, the same precedence rules apply.

EXAMPLE 2-8   How do we evaluate this C expression?

5 * (3 + 4 / y)

The first operation performed is division, followed by addition. Once the expression inside the parentheses has been evaluated, multiplication is done.

SELF-CHECK 2-3

1. What does "precedence of operations" mean?
2. What happens if two operations with the same precedence occur next to each other in an expression?
3. How can you override the normal order of precedence?

---

[2]Parentheses can be inserted even if they are not needed, such as in $(a * b) + 7$ instead of $a * b + 7$.

APPLYING THE RULES TO PROGRAM 2

Now let's return to our formula. We wrote it as

```
result = gpa * gpa * gpa + 7 * gpa - 1 / gpa * gpa - gpa + 5 / 3;
                                                    /* incorrect */
```

In Exercise 4, you are asked to trace the precise order in which this is evaluated in C and the sequence in which the original mathematical formula would be evaluated. It should be clear that they are not the same.

As a first step to correcting this problem, we can put parentheses around the numerator and denominator:

```
result = (gpa * gpa * gpa + 7 * gpa - 1) / (gpa * gpa - gpa + 5 / 3);
                                                    /* incorrect */
```

This will guarantee that division is performed last. Curiously, despite the length of this expression, this simple use of parentheses is almost enough. You should verify that the numerator is correct, but the denominator must be fixed. We want **gpa + 5** to be divided by 3, not just 5 divided by 3, so we need another pair of parentheses around **gpa + 5**. No other parentheses are needed since the operations are now in the correct sequence. Here is the correct C translation:

```
result = (gpa * gpa * gpa + 7 * gpa - 1) / (gpa * gpa - (gpa + 5) / 3);
                                                    /* correct */
```

STYLE WORKSHOP We really shouldn't say that this is *the* correct translation because many others are equally valid. For example, another correct formula comes from adding extra parentheses within the existing ones, making the numerator into this: ***((gpa * gpa * gpa) + (7 * gpa) – 1)***, and so on. In fact, we could put in so many parentheses that there would be no need to remember the precedence rules, but this isn't a good idea. First, the extra parentheses make the formula hard to read. Second, if you are not careful, you may put in an extra (or), or leave one out. Any of these mistakes will cause an error in your program. Use parentheses only when you must—when you want to override the normal rules of precedence. Of course, if you are in doubt, an extra pair in the right place (always a pair) won't hurt.

We could also have omitted all the blank spaces in the C version of the formula, but it would be much harder to read. We often insert extra blanks in C statements for readability. We have inserted some extra blank lines into the final version of the program for the same reason.

We can now substitute our C statement for the one that reads ***result** = formula* to get an almost complete version of Program 2.

PROGRAM 2 WITH THE FORMULA

Program 2 with the complete formula is on the following page.

🖳 PROGRAM LISTING

```c
/*
 * Program prog2a.c:
 * creates a table to evaluate a formula based on values of
 * gpa in the range from gpa = 0.00 to 4.00 in units of 0.50
 */
#include <stdio.h>
main()
{
    double gpa,result;

    for (gpa = 0.00; gpa <= 4.00; gpa = gpa + 0.50) {
        result = (gpa * gpa * gpa + 7 * gpa - 1) / (gpa * gpa - (gpa + 5) / 3);
        printf("%f    %f\n",gpa,result);
        if (result >= 0)
            printf(" Admit\n");
    }
    printf("The table is finished\n");
}
```

Although it appears that we are finished with Program 2, we can still make improvements. To see why, let's take a look at the output.

FIGURE 2-2 Output from Program 2 (Version **_prog2a.c_**)

```
0.000000    0.600000
  Admit
0.500000    -1.657895
1.000000    -7.000000
1.500000    154.500000
  Admit
2.000000    12.600000
  Admit
2.500000    8.566667
  Admit
3.000000    7.421052
  Admit
3.500000    7.048673
  Admit
4.000000    7.000000
  Admit
The table is finished
```

OUTPUT FROM PROGRAM 2 SO FAR

Figure 2-2 shows the output from this version of Program 2 (*prog2a.c*). If you can't tell what it means, that is probably because we haven't labeled or identified the output. Another problem is that the word "Admit" appears on a separate line from the result to which it refers. We will fix some other problems in the next section.

SELF-CHECK 2-4

1. In what order will the operations in each of the following C expressions be evaluated? What will the value of each expression be if $p = 4$, $q = 7$, $r = 3$, and $s = 5$?

    a. (p − q) + (r − s)   b. p − (q + r) * s

2. Which is a correct C translation of the right-hand side of the following equation? If more than one is correct, which is preferred?

$$y = \frac{p + q * r - s}{p + q}$$

    a. (p + q) * (r -s) / (p + q)   d. ((p + (q * r) - s)) / (p + q)
    b. ((p + q) * (r - s)) / p + q   e. p + (q * r) - s / p + q
    c. (p + q * r - s)/(p + q)   f. (p + q * r - s) / p + q

SECTION 3   ## ENRICHMENT: CREATING READABLE OUTPUT

Even though we have written the last line and the formula, we are not quite finished with Program 2. One thing a programmer must always consider is the readability of the output. The output from our program is messy and unclear, but we can fix it by improving the printing. We will identify the columns in the output, put a heading on the table, fix the position of the word "Admit", and put in blank lines that will make the output clear to the person who uses the program.

PRINTING MESSAGES TOGETHER WITH VALUES

The output from this program is a little confusing. In Program 1, it was easy to see that the value of **sqnumber** was the square of **number**, but it is more difficult to see the correspondence between **gpa** and **result**. It would be clearer to have next to each number an indication of what it represents. For example, "gpa = 0.000000 result = 0.600000" is more readable than just "0.000000 0.600000". To print the messages "gpa =" and "result =" to the left of the numbers, insert these words and symbols into the control string of the **printf**. Let's see how this works.

THE *printf* CONTROL STRING AND CONVERSION SPECIFICATIONS

Suppose you want to print a line which is a combination of messages and the values of variables. Let's look at the control string used to print the values of **number** and **sqnumber** in

Program 1. It was **"%d %d\n"**. Now that you have seen more examples of strings (such as "Admit" or "The table is finished"), that first string should look similar: it is a sequence of characters surrounded by quotation marks. By now, of course, you know that the string **"%d %d\n"** is not printed exactly as it appears.

The major difference is the % symbol, which tells the compiler that what follows is a conversion specification. A conversion specification tells *printf* how to convert and format the value for printing. The computer doesn't print the % symbol or the characters immediately following it. Instead, it looks at the list of variables or expressions following the control string, takes the next item which has not already printed, and prints it using the specified format. In effect, the value of the item is substituted for the conversion specification in the control string. If the value of **number** is 4, and **sqnumber** is 16, 4 is substituted for the first **%d** and 16 for the second one as the string is printed.

If we added words or blanks to the control string, they would be printed, just like the blank between the first and second **%d**. To print "number = 4   sqnumber = 16", we could insert the messages "number = " and "sqnumber = " into the control string:

```
printf("number = %d    sqnumber = %d\n",number,sqnumber);
```

The computer would make the same substitutions as before—putting in the value of **number** for the first **%d** and the value of **sqnumber** for the second one. Then it would print the resulting string:

```
number = 4      sqnumber = 16
```

STYLE WORKSHOP Note that we usually include blanks in messages to separate the words from the surrounding values. We insert as many blanks at the end (or the beginning) of the message as needed to make the final output easy to read.

Now let's apply this technique to Program 2. The conversion specification is different, but otherwise all we change are the names. So our new *printf* is this:

```
printf("gpa = %f    result = %f\n",gpa,result);
```

On the output screen, the message inside the quotation marks appears exactly as it did in the *printf*, with the value of **gpa** substituted for the first **%f** and the value of **result** substituted for the second one. The first line of output looks like this:

```
gpa = 0.000000    result = 0.600000
```

If we change the *printf* in **prog2a.c** to what is above and leave everything else exactly the same, the output is like Figure 2-3. This is certainly an improvement over just printing numerical values for **gpa** and **result**. We should always label our output so that the user knows what has been printed.

FIGURE 2-3 Output from Program 2 with messages

```
gpa = 0.000000    result = 0.600000
  Admit
gpa = 0.500000    result = -1.657895
gpa = 1.000000    result = -7.000000
gpa = 1.500000    result = 154.500000
  Admit
gpa = 2.000000    result = 12.600000
  Admit
gpa = 2.500000    result = 8.566667
  Admit
gpa = 3.000000    result = 7.421052
  Admit
gpa = 3.500000    result = 7.048673
  Admit
gpa = 4.000000    result = 7.000000
  Admit
The table is finished
```

SUMMARY OF *printf*

Table 2.3 summarizes the action of *printf*.

TABLE 2.3 Action of *printf*

```
int     num;
double  x;
num = 14;
x = 22.6;
```

Statement	Result
printf("help");	help
printf("%d",num);	14
printf("14");	14
printf(14);	compilation error
printf("%d",14);	14
printf("%f is the answer",x);	22.600000 is the answer
printf("%d is less than %f",num,x);	14 is less than 22.600000
printf("stop here");	stop here
printf("go\non\n");	go
	on
	▊ (cursor position)

PRINTING A HEADING ON THE OUTPUT

Let's go further in improving the output. So that the user knows what this table is, we'll print a message at the very start, saying that this is a table of function values. For clarity, we want to leave a blank line before printing the first values of **gpa** and **result**. All it takes is this:

```
printf("Table of Function Values\n\n");
```

STYLE WORKSHOP Printing a heading on the output is good programming style and is necessary even if there is already a comment saying the same thing. The comment is associated with the listing of the program, while the heading goes with the output.

We have seen that a ***printf after*** the loop [***printf("The table is finished")***] prints once, after the loop is completed. A ***printf inside*** the loop [***printf("gpa = ...")***] prints each time the loop is executed. Obviously, a ***printf before*** a loop prints once before the loop begins. This is what we want, a message that appears as the first line of the output. Let's insert the new ***printf*** right after the declaration:

```
double gpa,result;

printf("Table of Function Values\n\n");
for (gpa = 0.00; gpa <= 4.00; gpa = gpa + 0.50) {
        result = (gpa * gpa * gpa + 7 * gpa - 1) / (gpa * gpa - (gpa + 5) / 3);
        printf("gpa = %f    result = %f\n",gpa,result);
        if (result >= 0)
            printf(" Admit\n");
}
```

USING THE NEWLINE CHARACTER

DOUBLE SPACING

There is something special about the heading we just wrote:

```
printf("Table of Function Values\n\n");
```

There are two newline characters at the end of the string. This is one method of printing a blank line or double spacing. Each newline character makes the cursor go to the beginning of a new line. Since this ***printf*** has two newline characters, the cursor goes to the beginning of a new line twice, thus skipping a line.

STAYING ON THE SAME LINE

Sometimes the question is not how to go to a new line, but how to stay on the same one. One problem with the output from this program is that the word "Admit" appears on the line below the values associated with it. Our first set of values printed like this:

```
gpa = 0.000000 result = 0.600000
Admit
```

This happened because we put **\n** at the end of the control string in this **printf**:

```
printf("gpa = %f    result = %f\n",gpa,result);
```

To tell the computer to stay on the same line after printing, omit **\n** from the control string. After the computer finishes the line of output, the cursor remains ready to print again on the same line.

One last modification: After we make this change, the line **printf("Admit\n")** causes a problem. It will only start a new line in the output if the word "Admit" is printed. We want each set of values to start on a new line even if "Admit" is not printed. To solve this problem, we begin by removing the newline character from **printf("Admit")**.

STARTING ON A NEW LINE

The instruction **printf("\n")** alone moves the cursor to the beginning of a new line. By placing this statement at the bottom of the loop, we ensure that our output has one line for each value of **gpa**, regardless of whether the word "Admit" prints. Here is what the section of code looks like with this change:

```
for (gpa = 0.00; gpa <= 4.00; gpa = gpa + 0.50) {
    result = (gpa * gpa * gpa + 7 * gpa - 1) / (gpa * gpa - (gpa + 5) / 3);
    printf("gpa = %f    result = %f",gpa,result);
    if (result >= 0)
        printf(" Admit");
    printf("\n");
}
```

The last **printf** in the loop sends the cursor to a new line before returning to the top of the loop.

We can also use the newline character to improve the line spacing, this time outside the loop. The trailer message "The table is finished" prints right under the values above it; it would look nicer to skip a line before printing it. We can do it in either of two ways. One is to include another **printf("\n")** between the **for** loop and the final **printf**:

```
printf("\n");
printf("The table is finished\n");
```

A better way, however, is to combine these two lines into one:

```
printf("\nThe table is finished\n");
```

This revised **printf** causes the cursor to move to a new line before printing the message and again afterward.

COLUMN HEADINGS

Let's make one further modification. Instead of having messages and values printed across the page, we can make a neat table of **gpa** and **result** values and messages. In fact, we can make column headings for the table, eliminating the need for the messages "gpa = " and " result = " in each *printf.*

Column headings should be printed once—before the loop starts but after the message announcing the table. Here are *printf* statements for the headings, including some blank lines to improve readability:

```
printf("Table of Function Values\n\n");
printf("Grade Point Average   Value of Formula   Status\n\n");
```

The extra blanks in the headings space the words across the page.

STYLE WORKSHOP It is much more informative to have column headings reading "Grade Point Average" and "Value of Formula" rather than "gpa" and "result". In fact, printing a heading that describes the variable is usually better than printing the variable's name.

Now, inside the loop, we can print several lines of output with these statements:

```
printf("          %f               %f",gpa,result);
if (result >= 0)
      printf("        Admit");
printf("\n");
```

Note that we no longer print "gpa = " or "result = " each time through the loop. Instead, the numerical values should be aligned under the appropriate headings. We will also have, on some of these lines, the word "Admit" in the column headed "Status".

To ensure that the values print out neatly aligned under their headings, we have added a number of blanks in the *printf* which prints the values of *gpa* and *result* and the one which prints the message "Admit".

SELF-CHECK 2-5

1. What is the difference between the comment at the beginning of the program and the heading printed with the table? Who will see the comment? Who will see the heading?

2. What is the advantage of column headings over messages printed with the output values?

3. How can you go to a new line before printing a message?

PROGRAM 2 WITH PRINTING CHANGES

Let's take a look at the whole program with all the printing changes we have made: a title on the output, column headings, neatly spaced columns, and the word "Admit" on the correct lines.

🖥 PROGRAM LISTING

```
/*
 * Program prog2b.c:
 * creates a table to evaluate a formula based on values of
 * gpa in the range from gpa = 0.00 to 4.00 in units of 0.50
 */
#include <stdio.h>
main()
{
    double gpa,result;

    printf("Table of Function Values\n\n");
    printf("Grade Point Average   Value of Formula   Status\n\n");
    for (gpa = 0.00; gpa <= 4.00; gpa = gpa + 0.50) {
        result = (gpa * gpa * gpa + 7 * gpa - 1) / (gpa * gpa - (gpa + 5) / 3);
        printf("        %f              %f",gpa,result);
        if (result >= 0)
            printf("        Admit");
        printf("\n");
    }
    printf("\nThe table is finished\n");
}
```

OUTPUT FROM PROGRAM 2 SO FAR

Figure 2-4 shows the complete output from *prog2b.c* (the appearance is still odd, but we'll take care of that in the next version).

FIGURE 2-4   Output from Program 2 (Version *prog2b.c*)

```
Table of Function Values

Grade Point Average   Value of Formula   Status
        0.000000            0.600000      Admit
        0.500000           -1.657895
        1.000000           -7.000000
        1.500000          154.500000        Admit
        2.000000           12.600000        Admit
        2.500000            8.566667      Admit
        3.000000            7.421052      Admit
        3.500000            7.048673      Admit
        4.000000            7.000000      Admit

 The table is finished
```

THE TAB CHARACTER

Now let's resolve the final problem in the appearance of the output. Because the values of *result* printed with different lengths, the column of "Admit" messages is not aligned. Inserting blanks in the string won't help because the number of blanks needs to vary. However, another useful feature of *printf* can create neat columns. Just as \n is the newline character when inserted into the control string, \t is the **tab character**. Inserting \t into the string causes the cursor to tab to the next position before printing. This feature is very useful for aligning output in columns.

Here's how we can use it in Program 2. Instead of putting eight blanks in the string before the word "Admit" (that would look like this: "   Admit"), type the following:

```
printf("\tAdmit");
```

Each time this line is executed, the cursor moves from one to eight spaces to the right before printing, since tab positions are eight characters apart. Each occurrence of the word prints in an aligned column on the screen or paper. In the final version of Program 2, we have used tabs to align the output. Sometimes we needed more than one tab to align the values under the headings. To see if you understand how tabs work, figure out what is printed by the following:

```
printf("\tFirst\tSecond\tThird\nFourth");
```

It prints

```
        First   Second  Third
   Fourth
```

COMPLETE PROGRAM 2 AND OUTPUT

Here is the final version of Program 2 with the formula and all the printing improvements:

 PROGRAM LISTING

```c
/*
 * Program prog2c.c:
 * creates a table to evaluate a formula based on values of
 * gpa in the range from gpa = 0.00 to 4.00 in units of 0.50
 */
#include <stdio.h>
main()
{
    double gpa,result;

    printf("\t\tTable of Function Values\n\n");
    printf("Grade Point Average\tValue of Formula\tStatus\n\n");
```

```
    for (gpa = 0.00; gpa <= 4.00; gpa = gpa + 0.50) {
        result = (gpa * gpa * gpa + 7 * gpa - 1) / (gpa * gpa - (gpa + 5) / 3);
        printf("%f\t\t%f",gpa,result);
        if (result >= 0)
            printf("\t\tAdmit");
        printf("\n");
    }
    printf("\nThe table is finished\n");
}
```

Figure 2-5 shows the output from ***prog2c.c***. Notice how it is now neatly aligned in columns.[3]

ESCAPE SEQUENCES

The computer uses the \ symbol to distinguish between the *t* that is the tab character and one that might occur anywhere in the string. The symbol \ is called the **escape character** and tells the computer to treat the next character as special. (We call a sequence like **\n** an **escape sequence**.) We can use the escape character to tell the computer to print characters

FIGURE 2-5 Output from Program 2 (Version ***prog2c.c***)

```
              Table of Function Values


   Grade Point Average      Value of Formula         Status


      0.000000                 0.600000           Admit
      0.500000                -1.657895
      1.000000                -7.000000
      1.500000               154.500000             Admit
      2.000000                12.600000             Admit
      2.500000                 8.566667             Admit
      3.000000                 7.421052             Admit
      3.500000                 7.048673             Admit
      4.000000                 7.000000             Admit

   The table is finished
```

---

[3]In Chapter 3, we will see how to improve the appearance of output further.

TABLE 2.4 Common Escape Sequences in C

\n	the newline character
\t	the tab character
\b	the backspace character
\"	double quote
\\	backslash
\%	the percent sign
\0	null character
\a	BEL (makes an audible signal)
\f	formfeed (new page on printer)
\r	carriage return character

which otherwise would be unprintable, like %, ", and \ itself. To print any of these special formatting characters, simply precede it with a backslash. Here is an example:

```
printf("\% \\ \"\n");
```

The cursor goes to a new line after the program prints the following:

```
%   \   "
```

Table 2.4 shows the escape sequences commonly used in C. Here is an example using some of the escape sequences:

```
printf("\n\t\"Table of Function Values\"");
```

This prints the following in the ninth position of a new line:

```
"Table of Function Values"
```

CONVERSION SPECIFICATIONS AND CONVERSION CHARACTERS

While we are discussing items that go in the control string for *printf*, let's quickly review conversion specifications. A conversion specification consists of the % symbol followed by a conversion character, which is a single character like *d*.[4] Table 2.5 summarizes the most common conversion characters.

TABLE 2.5 Most Common Conversion Characters for *printf*

Data Type	Conversion Character
int	d
float	e or f
double	e or f
char	c

---

[4]There may be other items between the % symbol and the conversion character. In this way, a conversion specification can supply a number of formatting options, as we will see in Chapter 3.

SELF-CHECK 2-6

1. What is an escape sequence?
2. What symbol introduces an escape sequence?
3. What symbol introduces a conversion specification?

SECTION 4 ## RELATIONAL OPERATORS, COMPOUND ASSIGNMENT OPERATORS

In a condition, values are compared using relational operators. In this section, we introduce all the remaining relational operators and discuss their precedence. In addition, we introduce several new operators.

RELATIONAL OPERATORS

We used an *if* statement in Program 2 to determine whether to print the word "Admit". In that case, we wanted to print the message under these circumstances:

```
if (result >= 0) ...
```

The operator >= means greater than or equal to. To print the message if **result** is less than or equal to 0, we use the operator <=.

```
if (result <= 0) ...
```

A number of operators can be used to represent the relationship between values; they are called relational operators. Table 2.6 shows the ones available in C.

Two of these may surprise you. First, the operator to test equality, called the **logical equals operator**, is ==. This is not the same as the = used in mathematics to compare two values. It is different because C uses the = symbol for assignment. Certain computer languages (for example, BASIC and PL/I) use the same symbol ("=") for both operations. Someone using such a language must carefully distinguish between the two meanings in a given situation.

Second, the != operator is also different from the symbol used in mathematics (≠). In C, you can think of ! as standing for not, so != is "not equal."

TABLE 2.6 The Relational Operators

Symbol	Meaning	Example
<	less than	a < b
>	greater than	num > 4
<=	less than or equal to	x <= 12
>=	greater than or equal to	result >= 3.5
==	equal to	sqnumber == 16
!=	not equal to	answer != 7

These relational operators can be used wherever your program requires a condition. Obviously, an *if* statement uses a condition, but there is another one in Program 2 (and also in Program 1). Let's look again at the *for* loop headers:

```
for (number = 4; number <= 9; number++)        (from Example 1-11)
for (number = 9; number >= 4; number--)         (from Example 1-12)
for (gpa = 0.0; gpa <= 4.0; gpa = gpa + 0.50)   (from Program 2)
```

Right in the middle of each *for* loop header is a condition—the one that determines whether or not we are finished executing the loop. Although conditions using <= or < are probably the most common in *for* loops, others are also possible. Some are explored in the exercises.

INCREMENT AND DECREMENT OPERATORS

These *for* loop headers give us the perfect opportunity to explore other operators in C. Let's look at the third part of the header, the increment. Chapter 1 introduced the increment operator ++, used in *number++* to increase the value of *number* by 1. An expression like *number++* can be used in the header of a *for* loop or as a separate statement. In Chapter 1, we also introduced the decrement operator, --, used in the second *for* loop above to decrement *number*. The ++ and -- are unary operators, with the same precedence as unary minus and unary plus and the same associativity, right to left. Because their use can be complex, we will employ these operators for now only in simple increment and decrement statements and *for* loop headers.

CAUTION It is not possible to increment or decrement an expression or a constant. Both of the following examples are illegal in C:

```
(x + y)++;                    /* illegal */
4--;                          /* illegal */
```

Only a variable can be incremented or decremented.

COMPOUND ASSIGNMENT OPERATORS: +=, −=, *=, /=, %=

The loop header from Program 2 does not use ++; we cannot increment *gpa* with the ++ operator because ++ always increments by 1, and we need to increase *gpa* by 0.50. However, using another operator, we can replace *gpa = gpa + 0.50* with the following:

```
gpa += 0.50;
```

The += is a **compound assignment operator** which combines addition and assignment. The operator says to take the value to its right and add it to the value of the variable to the left. This is exactly the same as **gpa = gpa + 0.50**. The **for** loop header for Program 2 could be rewritten this way:

```
for (gpa = 0.0; gpa <= 4.0; gpa += 0.50)
```

STYLE WORKSHOP Since we can also use the += operator to increment by 1, we have four equivalent statements:

```
number = number + 1;
number += 1;
number++;
++number;
```

Experienced C programmers usually use **number++** (except when other factors require **++number**).

Let's look at a few more examples using the += operator.

EXAMPLE 2-9   We can write a **for** loop to print all the numbers between 10 and 500 which are divisible by 10.

```
for (number = 10; number <= 500; number += 10)
     printf("%d\n",number);
```

EXAMPLE 2-10   Here is a loop to add 6 to each value of **result** computed by the formula in Program 2.

```
for (gpa = 0.0; gpa <= 4.0; gpa += 0.50) {
     result = formula;
     result += 6;
     ...
}
```

It should be noted that += is not the only compound assignment operator in C. There are similar operators for subtraction (-=), multiplication (*=), division (/=), and remainder (%=). Addition and subtraction are by far the most common. All have the same precedence as the assignment operator, which is lower than any arithmetic or relational operator. All assignment operators associate right to left.

From here on, we will use the ++ , --, +=, and -= operators quite regularly since they are standard in C.[5]

MORE ON THE C ARITHMETIC PRECEDENCE RULES

Table 2.7 expands Table 2.2 by summarizing the arithmetic precedence rules for all the operators seen so far.

---

[5]You may be using a compiler called C++ to run your C programs. The C++ compiler was developed later and includes more features; what does its name suggest?

TABLE 2.7 Precedence of Arithmetic, Assignment, and Relational Operators

		Associativity
highest precedence (done first)	− (unary) + (unary) ++ −−	right to left
	* / %	left to right
	+ −	left to right
	< <= > >=	left to right
	== !=	left to right
lowest precedence (done last)	= += −= *= /= %=	right to left

SELF-CHECK 2-7

1. What relational operator represents each of the following?

   a. greater than   c. less than

   b. not equal to   d. greater than or equal to

2. What is wrong with this **if** statement? (*Note*: This statement will *not* generate an error message; in Chapter 12, you will see why.)

   ```
   if (x = 4)
       printf("%d",x);
   ```

3. Write each of the following using the new operators if possible:

   a. `sum = sum + num;`   d. `numleft = numleft - 1;`

   b. `count = count + 1;`   e. `avg = num / count;`

   c. `result = result % 4;`   f. `result = result * 2;`

SECTION 5   **ENRICHMENT: TYPES *float*, *double*, AND *char*; STANDARD LIBRARY OF FUNCTIONS**

DATA TYPES *float* AND *double*; REPRESENTING REAL NUMBERS

In C, **double** is the primary data type for real numbers. This data type permits decimal places; in addition, it can represent numbers that are extremely large or small. ANSI C relies on the individual compiler and its implementation on a specific machine to determine the limits of data types. The range of numbers that can be represented by data type **int** is relatively small; type **long int** (usually abbreviated as **long**) has a larger range of integers.[6]

In contrast, a variable with data type **double** can store a much wider range of values. The exact range varies from compiler to compiler, but almost all allow numbers like positive or negative values ranging from 1.0×10^{-30} to 1.0×10^{30}, from infinitesimal to enormous. Exercise 17 asks you to determine the range of data types **int** and **double** on your own system.

---

[6]For example, in Turbo C, the largest integer is 32,767, and the range is −32,768 to +32,767 (32,767 is exactly $2^{15} − 1$). In ANSI C on a Sun workstation, an integer has a range of approximately −two billion to +two billion ($\pm 2^{31} − 1$). This is also the size of type **long int** on a PC. On a Sun, type **long int** is much larger ($\pm 2^{63} − 1$).

STYLE WORKSHOP C has another data type, *float*, which can also hold floating point numbers but in a smaller range. Although our numbers fit comfortably into variables of type *float*, we always use the larger type *double* as is commonly done in C for efficiency.

SCIENTIFIC NOTATION

Real numbers—data types *double* and *float*—are stored as **floating point numbers** in a computer. Floating point notation is something like **scientific notation**, which allows a real number to be stored by representing its significant digits times a power of 10. A wide range of values can be stored with only a few digits.

For example, the number 16 can be represented in scientific notation as 1.600000×10^1 or 160.0000×10^{-1}. The computer uses a form like the first representation, with one digit to the left of the decimal place and six to the right, plus an exponent to the base 10. It is called **normalized form**.

The computer stores the **mantissa** of a real number (for 16, the mantissa is 1.600000) plus the **exponent** to the base 10 (for 16, the exponent is 1; see Figure 2-6). The mantissa stores the significant digits of the number, represented with one digit to the left of the decimal point; the exponent tells how far, and in which direction, the decimal point should move (float) to get to the actual value.

To get from 1.600000e+01 to the actual value, move the decimal point one position to the right, producing 16.00000. To get from 5.000000e–01 to the actual value, move the decimal point one position to the left, producing .500000.

A real number can be printed in scientific notation by using the **%e** conversion specification (see Figure 2-6). Example 2-11 shows how numbers are printed with the **%e** specification.

EXAMPLE 2-11   Suppose we have the following:

```
double num;

num = 16.0;
printf("%e",num);
```

In this case, *num* prints as 1.600000e+01, which is read as 1.6 times 10 to the first power. If *num* had the value .50, it would print as 5.000000e–01, which is read as 5 times 10 to the –1 power.

FIGURE 2-6   Type *double*: *A*, as printed with *%e*; *B*, internal representation.

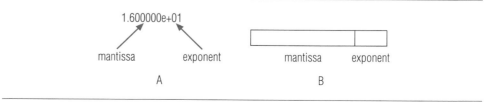

A programmer can use any of the equivalent forms of scientific notation. For example, we can write **num** = 16.0 or **num** = 1.6e+01, or **num** = 1.600000e+01. We can even write **num** = 16, assigning the integer 16 to a variable with data type **double**. It is also legal to assign a real number to a variable of type **int**, but any decimal portion is lost. Example 2-12 shows what happens.

EXAMPLE 2-12   Suppose that we assign real number **num** to **answer**, an integer variable:

```
double num;
int    answer;

num = 1.6;
answer = num;
printf("num is %f and answer is %d\n",num,answer);
```

This prints the following:

```
num is 1.600000 and answer is 1
```

MIXED-MODE ARITHMETIC

An expression which applies an operator to two operands of the same type produces a result of that same type. For example, applying an operator to two values of type **int** produces an **int** result, while two values of type **double** produce a **double** result. In C, it is also possible to perform arithmetic on different types. This is called **mixed-mode arithmetic**. Whenever an operator is applied to two operands of different types, such as **int** and **double**, C uses its rule of automatic type conversion to change the value of the more restrictive type (**int**) into the less restrictive one (**double**) for the duration of the operation. From most to least restrictive type, the order is **char** to **int** to **float** to **double** to **long double**.

SELF-CHECK 2-8

1. What two data types in C represent real numbers? Which one is used in this text?

2. Show three different ways to write the number 254.75 in scientific notation.

3. Which representation of 254.75 results if the number is printed with conversion specification **%e**? **%f**?

STANDARD LIBRARY OF FUNCTIONS

In addition to the five standard arithmetic operations (+, −, *, /, and %), C offers simple methods to perform other mathematical operations. These methods save a lot of programmer time; instead, the computer does most of the work. For example, it is common to need the square root of a number. C has a function called **sqrt** that automatically finds the square root.

EXAMPLE 2-13   What value is given to the variable *root*?

```
double w,root;

w = 12;
root = sqrt(w + 7);
```

The expression *sqrt(w + 7)* finds the square root of *w + 7*. Since *w* has the value 12, the *sqrt* function finds the square root of 19 (which is 4.36) and assigns it to *root*.

The function *sqrt* is called a **library function** because its instructions are stored in a library. The collection of these functions is called the **standard library of functions** or the C library.

The expression which invokes a function from the standard library is known as the **call to the function** or a **function call**. Typically, a function call specifies two things: the name of the function and the value or values on which it should operate, as shown in Figure 2-7.

A call to a library function can be placed on the right-hand side of an assignment statement, in a *printf*, or anywhere that an expression can occur. For example, here are some C statements that use library functions (we will explain *ceil* and *floor* in a moment):

```
a = sqrt(b);
printf("%d",ceil(realnum));
z = x + floor(w);
```

In addition to *sqrt*, there are many other library functions. A useful one is *abs*. The expression *abs(x)* finds the absolute value of the integer *x*, which in mathematics is written |*x*|. A call to *abs* always returns a positive or 0 answer.

EXAMPLE 2-14
```
abs(4)      = 4
abs(-4)     = 4
abs(-4.34)  = 4  (won't give the correct answer of 4.34)
```

For numbers with type *float* or *double*, a corresponding function, *fabs*, computes the absolute value of a floating point number.

```
fabs(-4.34) = 4.34
```

The library contains trigonometric functions such as *sin*, *cos*, and *tan* to find the sine, cosine, and tangent of an angle that is measured in radians, and *floor* and *ceil*, which convert a

FIGURE 2-7   A call to a library function

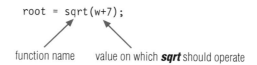

```
root = sqrt(w+7);
```
function name   value on which **sqrt** should operate

float or *double* value to the next lower or higher integer. (The *floor* function is not actually necessary since assigning *double* to an integer automatically cuts off the decimal places.)

EXAMPLE 2-15

```
int bot,top;

bot = floor(4.78);          /* same as bot = 4.78 */
top = ceil(9.8);
```

The variable *bot* gets the value 4; the variable *top* gets the value 10.

Another useful numeric task, related to *floor* and *ceil*, is rounding. C does not have a library function to round a number to the closest integer; however, the simple addition in Example 2-16 does the trick.

EXAMPLE 2-16

To round a real number to the closest integer, you can write this:

```
int     intnum;
double  realnum;
...
intnum = realnum + .5;
```

If the fractional part of *realnum* is less than .5, then adding .5 to it does not affect the integer part. For example, if *realnum* is 3.4, adding .5 gives 3.9; the 3 remains the same. Assigning the result to an integer truncates the fractional part so that *intnum* gets the value 3. If, on the other hand, the fractional part of *realnum* is greater than or equal to .5, adding .5 to it raises the number to the next integer. For example, if *realnum* is 3.6, adding .5 produces 4.1, and the assignment gives *intnum* the truncated value 4.

To use any of the library functions which work with floating point numbers (essentially all but *abs* and an integer version of *sqrt*), *#include <math.h>* has to be inserted at the beginning of your program. Notice that each *#include* directive must appear on its own line; it cannot be combined with anything else.[7]

```
#include <stdio.h>
#include <math.h>
main()
...
```

OTHER C LIBRARY FUNCTIONS: *printf*

The C library contains functions for more than mathematical tasks. We have been using the library function *printf* in every program so far. Each time we use *printf* in a program, we are calling the function *printf* and telling it what to print.

---

[7]This new line tells the compiler to include a file with information about the math library functions. If you try to use these functions without including this line, you will either get an error message or a very strange result (your program may say that *sqrt(7)* is –32712).

As the need arises and in the exercises, we will introduce other library functions. In Chapter 3, we introduce the *scanf* function. In Chapter 5, we learn how to write our own functions.

DATA TYPE *char*

You may have noticed a new data type in Table 2.5. It is *char*, which stands for character. A variable of this data type can hold any one character (e.g., 'a' or ' ' or '?'). A character is essentially anything that can be typed—a number, letter, space, period, or symbol. Appendix II contains a list of all the printable characters that can be used in C. Note that values of type *char* are enclosed in single quotation marks, while strings are enclosed in double quotation marks. Example 2-17 shows the declaration for a variable *letter* of type *char* and some statements using *char* variables and values:

EXAMPLE 2-17

```
char letter;

letter = 'a';
if (letter != 'b')
    printf("letter has the value %c\n",letter);
```

Since *letter* is not equal to 'b', this example prints the following:

```
letter has the value a
```

Data type *char* is actually a subset of type *int*. Each *char* value has a number associated with it, called its **ASCII value**; the ASCII values for characters range from 0 to 255. We could change the declaration in Example 2-17 to the following without altering our code:

```
int letter;
```

In fact, as you will see in Chapter 9 when we discuss the function *getchar*, this declaration is sometimes preferred for variables holding *char* data.

For a while, we use characters only as part of strings to be printed. A variable of type *char* by itself is not very useful (it can hold only one character). In addition, working with strings in C requires more complicated programming.

SELF-CHECK 2-9

1. What does the *sqrt* function do?

2. What is the purpose of the line *#include <math.h>*?

3. What data type would you use to hold each of the following?

    a. the distance from the sun to the earth   c. the value of pi
    b. a letter grade (A, C, etc.)   d. your total SAT score

SECTION 6   ENRICHMENT: DEBUGGING

This section introduces an important problem-solving technique called debugging. An error in a program is often called a **bug**. **Debugging** is the process of finding and removing errors from a program without creating new ones. Since a program rarely works perfectly the first time it is run, debugging is one of the most important programming skills. The various types of errors that a program might have include compilation, execution, and logic errors.

COMPILATION ERRORS

A **compilation error** is one caught by the compiler while it is translating your program into machine language before running it. Compilation errors caused by mistakes in the syntax or form of a statement are called **syntax errors**. These errors are caught in the first phase of compilation. Here are some examples of syntax errors with the particular mistake identified in parentheses:

```
fir(i = 1; i< 5; i++)   (misspelled keyword)
a = (b + 1/3;           (missing right parenthesis)
x + 3 = 5;              (expression on the left of an assignment statement)
x = 5                   (missing semicolon)
```

Errors discovered in the second phase of compilation are called **linker errors**. This phase is handled by the linker, the program that connects your program with the standard

FIGURE 2-8   A sample program (***prob2err.c***) with compilation errors

```
   /*
    * Program prog2err.c:
    * creates a table to evaluate a formula based on values of
    * gpa in the range from gpa = 0.00 to 4.00 in units of 0.50
    */
   #include <stdio.h>
   main()
   {
        double gpa,result;

1.      print("Table of Function Values\n\n");
        printf("Grade Point Average   Value of Formula    Status\n\n");
        for (gpa = 0.00; gpa <= 4.00; gpa = gpa + 0.50) {
2.          result = gpa * gpa * gpa + 7 * gpa - 1) / (gpa * gpa - (gpa + 5) / 3);
3.          printf("\t%f\t%f",GPA,result);
            if (result >= 0)
                  printf("\tAdmit");
4.          printf("\n")
        }
        printf("\nThe table is finished\n");
   }
```

libraries. If you use a library function, the compiler looks for it in the standard library during the link phase of compilation. If it doesn't find the function (either it doesn't exist or you have misspelled its name), the linker gives you an error message. Here is an example of a linker error:

```
print("%d",num);
```
(The linker tries to find function ***print***, which doesn't exist; ***printf*** is misspelled.)

Figure 2-8 shows a program with several errors. Some lines are numbered so that we can refer to specific errors as we discuss the kinds of messages they generate. If your program has a compilation error, the compiler will indicate the type. The compiler finds several different types of compilation errors in this program.

1. a misspelled identifier (***print*** instead of ***printf***)

2. a missing left parenthesis before the first ***gpa***

3. an identifier in the wrong case (***GPA*** instead of ***gpa)***

4. a missing semicolon at the end

Sometimes the compiler cannot figure out what the programmer intended. For example, if a parenthesis is missing in an expression, the compiler doesn't know where it should go. One compiler misinterpreted the missing opening parenthesis in the formula above as a missing semicolon, but making the suggested correction results in a different error. Correcting errors without careful thought can cause serious problems in the program. Be sure to determine what is really wrong before you fix an error and rerun the program.

The compiler may also generate warnings, which are normally less serious than errors. Some (but not all) warnings can be ignored, but this is not a good habit to get into.

After reading the error messages, correct the mistakes and recompile the program. When all errors have been removed, save the program or the changes will be lost.

EXECUTION ERRORS

The next kind of error, an **execution error**, is not caught by the compiler. Instead, it is detected once the program is running, which is why it is sometimes called a **run-time error**. As an example, suppose that your program attempts to divide by a variable whose value is zero. The compiler will not object to this expression, but the computer will be unable to execute it. Your program will normally stop at the error and display an error message.

While compilation errors are often only typing mistakes, execution errors can be much more serious and require careful thought to correct. If the error is very serious, the machine may "hang" completely; you won't get an error message, nor will you be able to get out of C or into the editor—you may not be able to do anything but shut off the machine. If this happens, don't panic; there are solutions. To avoid disaster, follow the rule we stated in Chapter 1:

Always Save Your Program Before Running It.

LOGIC ERRORS

The last type of error, a logic error, is the hardest to catch. Each individual statement in a program may be valid in C and thus acceptable to the compiler. The program may run without causing any execution errors, but the answers may be wrong. This type of error is called a **logic error**. A logic error may be something simple—for example, initializing a variable to 1 instead of 0, or multiplying by 2 instead of 3, or using an incorrect formula—but it can also be a basic mistake in the logic of the program. Such a mistake is hard to find and correct, since it won't generate an error message. The programmer has to catch logic errors by critically examining the output and testing the program on all possible sets of data.

Be aware, too, that many statements that look like compilation errors are actually valid C statements. For example, the statement below is not a compilation error, although someone probably used the wrong symbol for assignment:

```
x == x + 3;
```

Unfortunately, this is a valid statement in C, even though it does not assign a value to *x*. In Chapter 12, we will see what this statement actually does.

HOW TO DEBUG A PROGRAM

To debug a program, first check for compilation or execution errors, perhaps compounded by inappropriate "corrections" by the compiler. Second, verify that the program you actually ran matches what you want it to be; that is, make sure that you have not made any typing errors.

If these two steps do not produce any explanations for the problem, trace the program step by step once again (you should have done that first before you ran it). As we did in Chapter 1 (see figures 1-1 and 1-2), have a box or position for each variable and be careful to use the current value of that variable at all times. Make sure that you go step by step; do not skip or add anything. In almost all cases, a detailed trace will locate the problem.

Finally, the best way to eliminate a bug is not to include it in the first place. Theoretically, at least, if a program is written correctly the first time, there is no need to debug it. What this means is that you should be extremely careful in planning your original solution to the problem, writing the program, and hand simulating it before you run it. If this is done, and the rules for good style are followed, most mistakes will be caught before they do any damage.

To be honest, we must admit that debugging is really an art, not a science. Most programmers develop their own approach to it, just as they develop their own programming style. Later on, we will suggest some things to make debugging easier. (Exercise 28 gives you practice in finding errors of all three types.)

SELF-CHECK 2-10

1. What is a compilation error? Give three examples.

2. What is an execution error? Give an example.

3. What is a bug? What is debugging?

SUMMARY

EVALUATING AN EXPRESSION

1. A C program can evaluate a complicated mathematical expression, as shown in the sample problem in the text. The programmer does not have to be able to evaluate the expression by hand but only express it in C.

DATA TYPES: *float*, *double*, AND *char*

2. A variable declared to have data type *double* or *float* can store numbers with decimal places, or, more generally, numbers in scientific notation. The exact range depends on the compiler, but it almost surely can hold positive or negative values from 1×10^{-30} to 1×10^{30}.

3. A variable declared to have data type *float* or *double* can be assigned a value in any format: an integer value, a real number in decimal format (1., .1, or 0.1) or a value in scientific notation. A real number can be expressed using either an exponent or a decimal point or both (314e–2 or 3.14 or 31.4e–1).

4. A variable with data type *float* or *double* is printed by the computer in one of two ways, depending on the conversion specification. If the conversion specification is *%f*, the number prints in decimal notation with six decimal places. If the conversion specification is *%e*, the number prints in scientific notation in normalized form, with one digit to the left of the decimal point and six digits to the right, plus an exponent. For example, the value 16.23 prints as 16.230000 with the *%f* format and as 1.623000e+01 with the *%e* format (or 1.623000E+01 with the *%E* format). These values are interpreted as 1.623 times 10 to the first power.

5. A variable with type *char* can hold a single character, like 'a' or '*'. It is possible to use variables and values of type *char* in conditions and assignment statements. To print a value of type *char* with *printf*, use conversion specification *%c*.

CONDITIONAL OR *if* STATEMENTS

6. A conditional or *if* statement makes a decision. The general form of a conditional statement (where *cond* is a condition that evaluates to true or false and *stmt-1* is any C statement) is

   if *(cond)*
       stmt-1;

   If *cond* is true, then *stmt-1* is executed. If *cond* is false, then *stmt-1* is skipped.

7. In a condition, items are compared using a relational operator like <, >, <=, >=, ==, or !=. To test for equality in a condition, use the logical equals operator (==), not the assignment symbol (=). To test for inequality, use !=.

PRINTING MESSAGES USING *printf*

8. The *printf* function can be used to print a message. Putting the message inside quotation marks creates a literal string [e.g., *printf("help")*].

9. The general form of a call to *printf* is this:

   printf(*control-string,variable-list*);

   The *control-string* portion can consist of conversion specifications (like *%d* and *%f*), escape sequences (like \n and \t), and messages (words and punctuation). The *variable-list* portion contains one variable or expression for each conversion specification.

10. Messages and values can be combined in the output string printed by *printf*. In addition, escape sequences like **\n** (newline) and **\t** (tab) can be included in the control string to shape the appearance of the output. A control string used to print both messages and values is written with conversion specifications in place of the variables whose values are to be printed; the list of the variables or expressions follows the string. When *printf* is executed, the variables' values are substituted for the conversion specifications in left to right order.

11. Here is an example:

```
int     first;
double second;
...
printf("first number = %d, and second number = %f\n",first,second);
```

When this is printed, *first*'s value is substituted for **%d** and the value of *second* is substituted for **%f**. The line of output is printed, and then the cursor goes to a new line. For example, if *first* has the value 12 and *second* has the value 86.35, the statement prints the following:

```
first number = 12, and second number = 86.350000
```

12. A blank line is produced in the output by using *printf* with a control string consisting only of "**\n**". Double or triple spacing, indenting, and printing in columns is done by judicious placement of \n and \t characters.

13. The escape character \ can be used to print control characters like %, ", and \; simply place the \ character immediately in front of the control character to be printed. The combined symbol (e.g., \") is called an escape sequence.

COMPOUND ASSIGNMENT OPERATORS

14. C has compound assignment operators, which do arithmetic and assignment in one operation. These operators are +=, −=, *=, /=, and %=. For example, to add 3 to *y* and store the result in *y*, simply say *y += 3*. The compound addition and subtraction operators are more commonly used than the others.

PRECEDENCE OF OPERATIONS

15. The C arithmetic precedence rules determine the order in which arithmetic operations are performed in an expression. Operations with higher precedence or priority are done before those with lower precedence.

16. Unary minus, ++, and −− have the highest precedence, then multiplication and the two division operations (/ and %), then addition and subtraction, then the relational operators. The assignment operators have lowest precedence. Parentheses can override these rules.

17. When operators of equal precedence occur next to each other in the same expression, the operation to be performed first is determined by associativity. Arithmetic operators (*, /, %, +, and −) associate left to right. The unary operators (−, +, ++, and −−) and the assignment operators (=, +=, −=, *=, /=, and %=) associate right to left. Parentheses can override these rules.

FUNCTIONS FROM THE STANDARD LIBRARY

18. C has a number of standard or library functions to compute many mathematical functions. These include **sqrt** for square root and **abs** for absolute value. In addition, there are trigonometric functions, like **sin**, **cos**, **tan**, and others. Most mathematical functions cannot be used without adding the line **#include <math.h>** at the beginning of the program.

19. The expression that invokes a standard function is known as the call to the function. The call specifies the name of the function as well as the value(s) on which the function should operate.

20. The **printf** "statement" that we have been using since Chapter 1 is actually a call to the library function **printf**.

DEBUGGING

21. A mistake in a program is called a bug. The process of eliminating mistakes so that a program runs correctly is called debugging. Debugging is one of the most important skills for a programmer because very few programs work perfectly the first time they run.

22. A compilation error is one that is caught by the compiler before a program runs. Many compilation errors are simple typing mistakes—misspelling a keyword or omitting required punctuation. The programmer must always correct a compilation error before rerunning the program.

23. Some compilation errors show up as linker errors. For example, a linker error occurs if you misspell the name of a library function like **printf**. Some C compilers also produce warnings, which are not as serious as errors. Some warnings can even be ignored.

24. An execution error is caught not during compilation but while the program is running. For example, an attempt to divide by 0 causes an execution error.

25. A logic error is a mistake that is not caught during either compilation or execution but that causes wrong answers. A logic error may be something simple, such as a typing mistake that creates a valid statement but yields incorrect answers. It can also be caused by an error in the basic logic of a program.

EXERCISES

TRACING EXERCISES

1. Trace each of the following C programs step by step. Show exactly what each program prints.

   a.
   ```c
   #include <stdio.h>
   main()
   {
       int p,b;

       for (b = 2; b <= 6; b++) {
           p = 2 * b + 3;
           printf("%d %d\n",b,p);
       }
   }
   ```

b.
```c
#include <stdio.h>
main()
{
      int x,y;

      for (x = 15, y = 4; x >= 0; x -= y, y += 3)
            printf("%d %d\n",x,y);
}
```

c.
```c
#include <stdio.h>
main()
{
      int s,t;

      t = 0;
      for (s = 8; s >= 4; s -= 3) {
            if (s > t)
                  t += 3;
            if (s <= t)
                  s += 2;
            printf("%d %d\n",s,t);
      }
}
```

d.
```c
#include <stdio.h>
main()
{
      int x,y,z;

      x = -3;
      y = 1;
      z = 2;
      if (abs(x + z) > abs(y))
            printf("yes");
      if (abs(x) + abs(z) > abs(y))
            printf("no");
      printf("maybe");
}
```

e.
```c
#include <stdio.h>
#include <math.h>
main()
{
      double b;
      int    a;

      printf("number\tsquare root\n");
      for (a = 0; a <= 6; a++) {
            b = sqrt(a);
            printf("%d\t%f\n",a,b);
      }
}
```

f.
```c
#include <stdio.h>
main()
{
      int    c;
      double d;

      printf("numb\trecip");
      printf("\tcheck\n");
      for (c = 1; c <= 8; c++) {
            d = 1.0 / c;
            printf("%d\t%f\t%f\n",
                  c,d,c*d);
      }
}
```

g.
```c
#include <stdio.h>
main()
{
      double n,v;

      for (n = .4; n < 3.6; n++) {
            v = n * .5 + 1.7;
            printf("%f %f\n",n,v);
      }
}
```

h.
```c
#include <stdio.h>
main()
{
      double x;

      for (x = 17.5; x >= .5;
            x -= 4.5)
            printf("%e\n",x);
}
```

2. For each of the following series of C statements, try to describe in words what is accomplished (the larger of *x* and *y* is put into *max* and then *max* is printed; or *x* is multiplied over and over by 2 until it is more than 30, etc.). For parts (a) through (c), (f), and (g), assume that *x* and *y* have been given certain values. All variables have data type *int*.

a.
```
if (x > y)
      max = x;
if (x <= y)
      max = y;
printf("%d",max);
```

b.
```
if (x > y)
      ans = x;
if (x < y)
      ans = y;
if (x == y)
      ans = 1;
```

c.
```
hold = 5;
if (x == y)
      hold = x;
if (x < y)
      hold = y;
```

d.
```
for (x = 1; x < 100; x *= 2)
      if (x < 50)
            x *= 2;
```

e.
```
for (x = 0; x < 15; x += 4)
      if (x == 8)
            printf("%d",x);
```

f.
```
for (x = 0; x < 15;) {
      x = x + y;
      if (x < y)
            x = y;
}
```

g.
```
if (x == y)
      printf("%d",x);
if (x != y)
      printf("%d",y);
```

h.
```
for (x = 0; x <= 6; x++) {
      y = x + 4;
      if (y == 10)
            printf("done");
}
```

3. For each of the following C statements, show the exact order in which the operations are performed. Assume that all variables have data type *double* and these are the initial values: *a* = 5, *b* = 6, *c* = 3, *d* = 2, and *e* = 2. Where necessary, use the results of previous statements to provide values for the variables.

```
f = -a + b * c / 3 * d + e;
g = -a + b * c / (3 * d) + e;
h = 4 * (a - 1) * (c / (b * d));
i = 4 * a - 2 * c / b * d;
p = -a - b + c * d;
b = -(a - b + c) * d;
r = -b - p + 5;
s = 2 * b / c + 3;
t = 2 * (b / c) + 3;
u = (2 * b) / c + 3;
v = 2 * b / (c + 3);
w = b * (d + 2) / c;
x = 8 * s - t;
y = 100 * v + 10 * w - u;
```

4. a. Here is the original C translation of the formula used in Problem 2:

   `result = gpa * gpa * gpa + 7 * gpa - 1 / gpa * gpa - gpa + 5 / 3;`

   Show step by step the order of operations that would be followed to evaluate the formula as written. Is this a correct C translation of the mathematical formula for Problem 2?

   b. Here is the final C translation of the formula:

   `result = (gpa * gpa * gpa + 7 * gpa - 1) / (gpa * gpa - (gpa + 5) / 3);`

   Show the order of operations step by step. Is this a correct C translation?

MISCELLANEOUS EXERCISES

5. What is the purpose of a trailer message?

6. Which operation has higher precedence, addition or multiplication?

7. In what order will the operations in each of the following expressions be evaluated? What is the value of each expression if $p = 4, q = 7, r = 3$, and $s = 5$?

   a. `p - (q + r) - s`   f. `p + q * r - s`
   b. `q % p + r + 5`   g. `p - q + r - s`
   c. `p - q + r * s`   h. `q % p - r + 5`
   d. `q % (p - r) + 5`   i. `p * q + r * s`
   e. `p + q + r + s`   j. `s / r + q / p`

8. Which is a correct C translation of the right-hand side of the following equation? If more than one is correct, which is preferred?

$$y = \frac{(p+q) \times r - s}{p+q}$$

   a. `(p + q) * r - s / p + q`   d. `(p + q * r - s) / (p + q)`
   b. `((p + q) * (r - s)) / (p + q)`   e. `((p + q) * r - s) / (p + q)`
   c. `((p + q * r) - s) / (p + q)`   f. `(((p + q) * r) - s) / (p + q)`

9. Translate each of these mathematical formulas into C. Try to use parentheses only when necessary.

   a. $x = \dfrac{-b + \sqrt{b^2 - 4ac}}{2a}$

   b. $x = \dfrac{1 - x}{2 - x}$

   c. $z = x^2 + 3y$

   d. $p = |b - r| - |r + b|$

   e. $e = mc^2$

   f. $c = 2t^3 / 8x$

   g. The area, a, of a trapezoid is one half the height, h, times the sum of the bases, $b1$ and $b2$.

   h. k is the sine of angle a plus the cosine of angle b plus the tangent of angle c.

10. Here are some numbers in decimal notation. Show how they would be printed from a variable with data type **double** using the conversion specification **%e**. That is, show how to

write the numbers in normalized form for floating point numbers. Then show how each would be printed using the conversion specification *%f*.

a. 42
b. –6.8
c. 0.1

d. 371
e. 6174.55
f. 0.0999

g. –0.00008
h. 1000

11. Here are some numbers in floating point notation that have not been normalized. Rewrite them in normalized form.

a. 234.56700000e+00
b. 0.36472e+04
c. 10.20900e–02

d. –66.7788e+01
e. 0.0001e+01
f. 6.0e+05

12. Show a format combining variables, newline characters, and tabs that will produce the output in each part. Assume that all numbers are printed from variables specified in the following declaration, where *a* = 10, *b* = 20, *c* = 30, and *d* = 40.

```
int a,b,c,d;
```

a. 10 20 30 40
b. 10 20
    30 40
c. 10 20
    (blank line)
    30
    40

d. 10
    20
    30
    40
e. 10   20   30   (one tab position apart)
    40

13. Show what is printed by each of the following calls to *printf*:

a. `printf("The cat\n stepped over\n the jam closet\n");`
b. `printf("\n\nTADA\n\n");`
c. `printf("\"\%\n");`
d. `num = 5;`
    `printf("%d\%\n",num);`
e. `printf("\"Big deal,\" she said.\n");`
f. `x = 3;`
    `y = 4;`
    `printf("%d\t%d\n",x,y);`

14. Because of the relationship between data types *char* and *int*, using *%c* to print a *char* value prints a character, while *%d* prints the corresponding ASCII value. For example, *printf("%c %c",'a',97)* prints "a a", while *printf("%d %d",'a',97)* prints "97 97".

Using a *for* loop, print all the numbers from 0 to 255, both in integer and character format. (*Warning:* Some of these may produce odd results, since they are interpreted as printer control characters.)

15. In each of the following parts, write one or more calls to *printf* to produce the output. Use an integer variable named *number* to hold the value 23.

a. `Maria Lopez`
    `23 West Fourth St.`
    `New York NY 10011`

b. Maria Lopez, 23 West Fourth St., New York NY 10011

c. Lopez, Maria, age 23
   West Fourth St., New York NY 10011

16. Each of the following program segments is preceded by a comment that describes what we would like to accomplish. Try to use these data values to see if the segment works in all cases. If it does not work, explain exactly what happens and show how to amend it so it does work.

a.
```
/* set z to the square root of w */
    int    w;
    double z;
    z = 0.5 * w;
```
(try $w = 4, w = 8$)

b.
```
/* if x is negative, print the word negative */
/* otherwise print non-negative            */
    int x;
    if (x < 0)
        printf("negative");
    if (x > 0)
        printf("non-negative");
```
(try $x = -2, x = 0, x = 5$)

c.
```
/* add 4 to x if x is negative; otherwise add 2 */
    int x;
    if (x < 0)
        x = x + 4;
    if (x >= 0)
        x = x + 2;
```
(try $x = -6, x = -2, x = 0, x = 3$)

d.
```
/* if x is larger than 12, print x; otherwise print 12 */
    int x,ans;
    ans = 12;
    if (x > 12)
        ans = x;
    printf("%d",ans);
```
(try $x = 5, x = 12, x = 20$)

e.
```
/* find the smallest integer whose */
/* square is greater than y        */
    int number,test,y;
    test = 0;
    for (number = 1; test <= y; number++)
        test = number * number;
    printf("%d is the smallest\n",number-1);
```
(try $y = 4, y = 5, y = 26$)

17. Write a program which tests the limits of data types *int, float,* and ***double*** on your system. [*Suggestion:* Use a loop to print out successively larger (and smaller) values until you find one that is nonsense; for example, it may change its sign from positive to negative. Narrow in on the exact value that is the limit in each direction.] Your C compiler comes with a file, called ***limits.h,*** which defines the limits of each data type on your system. You may want to look at it.

18. a. Write a program which prints your name, then two blank lines, then your name, etc., a total of 4 times. Write the program two ways: using a series of calls to *printf*, and using a *for* loop to repeat a series of instructions 4 times.
    b. Repeat part (a) but have your name print 10 times.
    c. Repeat part (a) but have your name print 100 times.
    d. Which part(s) of this exercise are you willing to do? Which part(s) don't you want to do? Why? What can you conclude about the power of the *for* loop?

19. In Program 2, *result* and *gpa* were declared to have data type *double*. Was this actually necessary? What would happen if *result* or *gpa* had data type *int*? To test your answer, run three new versions of Program 2: one in which *result* has data type *int*, and *gpa* has data type *double*; one in which *result* has data type *double*, and *gpa* has data type *int*; and one in which they both have data type *int*. Do all of these work?

MODIFYING AND EXTENDING PROGRAM 2

20. The registrar with whom we began this chapter has been told more precisely how to evaluate a student's enrollment status. If the formula results in a positive value, the student should be allowed to enroll; if the value is negative, the student should be turned away; if the value is 0, the student must see the professor personally. Modify Program 2 so that it prints an appropriate message ("Accepted", "Rejected", or "See professor") next to each *result* value.

21. Assume that the registrar's instructions in Exercise 20 are not good enough. Modify the program to shift the cutoff point. It should print "Accepted" if the value of the formula is greater than 5, "Rejected" if it is less than 5, and "See professor" if it is exactly 5. Then modify it again so that 10 is the cutoff. Finally, have –5 as the cutoff point.

22. Most students coming to the registrar will not have a grade point average (*gpa*) that is exactly 2.00 or 2.50 or something similar. Modify Program 2 so that it can handle other values of *gpa*. Do this by using the *gpa* value in the table as the center of a range. For example, all values of the average from 0.00 to 0.24 are covered by the entry for 0.00; values from 0.25 to 0.74 are covered by the entry for 0.50, etc. To do this, modify the printout so that next to each *gpa* average is the range of values it covers. For example,

```
Average      Range Covered   Value of Formula
0.000000     0.00 - 0.24     0.600000
0.500000     0.25 - 0.74     -1.657895
```

23. Modify Program 2 so that it keeps track of (a) the lowest value of *result* ever obtained by the formula, and (b) the *gpa* value which led to the lowest result. There are two ways to interpret this. First, it can mean the smallest absolute value so that, for example, 0.23 is lower than –2.17. It can also mean that all negative values are lower than all positive ones. Write two programs, one for each interpretation.

24. One exercise in Chapter 1 asked you to rewrite Program 1 without a loop by using each value of *number* explicitly. This is also possible in Program 2, but it is much more tedious. Describe how to do it and explain why it is much worse in Program 2.

DEBUGGING EXERCISES

25. The following **if** statement does not generate an error message. Nonetheless, it is probably not what the programmer wants. Can you figure out what the statement does? What is wrong with it if the intention is to print the word "less" if *x* is less than 7?

```
if (x < 7);
     printf("less");
```

26. What is wrong with the following **if** statement? Will it generate an error message?

```
if (x < 7)
     printf("x is greater than 7");
```

27. Exercise 12 in Chapter 1 asked you to find and correct a number of errors in a program. Go back to that program and determine the type (compilation, execution, or logic) of each error. In some cases, this distinction is not clear-cut. See if you can find any errors that can be interpreted as either compilation or logic.

28. The following program has many bugs in it. Try to find them and identify the type (compilation, execution, or logic) of each error.

```
/* do various calculations, including
finding the perimeter of a rectangle *)

include studio.h;
mane{}
        integer x;
        y:  double;
        int perimeter;length;width;
    {
        x == 4.0;
        y = .5 * 3 \ (x - 4);
        if x = 5
            print("%d",'five')
        2y = x + (5 + 4 % 3;
        perimeter = length + width * 2;
        printf(perimeter,length,width\n)
    };
```

29. Write a program that uses the library function **sqrt** but omits the **#include <math.h>** directive. Test it by finding **sqrt(4)**, **sqrt(9)**, and then **sqrt(7)** and **sqrt(8)**. What happens?

PROGRAMMING PROJECTS

30. Write a program that prints a table of the numbers from 1 to 30, together with the square, cube, and square root of each. Include appropriate column headings.

31. a. Write a program that prints a table of the angles from 0 to 180 degrees, together with the radian measurement, the sine, and the cosine of each angle. Recall that 180 degrees is equal to pi radians. Give pi the value 3.14159 and use the library functions **sin** and **cos**.

    b. Modify the program from part (a) so that it also prints the tangent of each angle.

32. Write a program that prints a table of numbers from 1 to 50. Next to each number should be the logarithm to the base **e** (natural log) of the number and **e** raised to the number as exponent. Use the library functions **log** (for natural log) and **exp** (for **e** raised to the number as exponent).

33. Write a program that prints two conversion tables to change temperatures in Fahrenheit (**F**) to temperatures in Celsius (**C**) and vice versa. One formula is $F = (9/5)C + 32$. (What is the other formula?) One table should list the Fahrenheit values from −50 to 250 in steps of 10, together with the Celsius equivalent. The other should list Celsius values from −50 to 150 in steps of 5, together with the Fahrenheit equivalents.

34. Write a program that finds and prints the values of **ans** for values of **num** from 1 to 6 in increments of .25 (1, 1.25, 1.50,...), based on the following formula:

$$ans = \frac{(num + 2)^2 - |num - 7|}{\dfrac{(num + 3)}{14}}$$

35. Write a program that finds and prints the values of **result** for all even values of **y** from 2 to 16, using the following formula:

$$result = \frac{sqrt(y - 1) + (y + 4)^3}{y - \dfrac{1}{y}}$$

READING A SET OF DATA

3

SYNTAX CONCEPTS: *while* loop, *scanf*, field width, *if-else* statement, conditional operator (?:)

PROGRAMMING CONCEPTS: reading data, interactive data entry, using a trailer value, counting, structured read loop, selecting one of two alternatives

CONTROL STRUCTURES: *while* loop, *if-else* statement, conditional expression

HOW TO READ CHAPTER 3

OUTLINE:

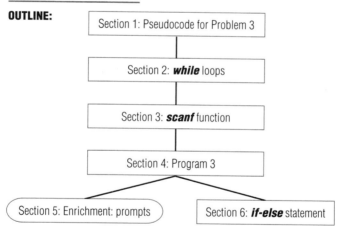

Section 1: Pseudocode for Problem 3

Section 2: *while* loops

Section 3: *scanf* function

Section 4: Program 3

Section 5: Enrichment: prompts

Section 6: *if-else* statement

INTRODUCTION AND STATEMENT OF THE PROBLEM

INTRODUCTION

Our programs so far have been unrealistic, not just because they are too simple but also because each program is completely self-contained; all the information needed to solve the problem is already known. The first program had built into it the starting point (4), the ending point (9), and the operation to perform (squaring). The second program knew the starting (0) and ending (4) points, the increment (0.50), and the formula to use (**result** = ...). Nothing further had to be supplied to either one.

A program being totally self-contained may seem like an advantage, but it is really a fault. Programs 1 and 2 each work for a single, specific problem with a specific set of values; however, neither works for a general set of problems or even another set of values. A more realistic (and more useful) program would allow some values to be specified as the program is running. This gives it much more flexibility because many different types of problems can be handled.

The simplest way of entering data is to type values into the computer as the program requests them. This process, which is the focus of this chapter, is called **reading in data**. We will explain how to enter data from the keyboard and, in the process, introduce the concept of interactive data entry. The new values specified as the program is executing are called **input data**, or just input or data. The ability to read in data adds immeasurably to the power and usefulness of a computer. Another method of entering data is to set up an external file (when you are using a personal computer, the file is usually stored on a floppy or hard disk) and have the computer read from that file. We explain how to do this in Appendices V and VI.

STATEMENT OF THE PROBLEM

PROBLEM 3

Write a complete C program to do the following: Read in data about an employee of a company. The data will contain the employee's ID number, hours worked in a week, and rate of pay per hour. Compute the employee's pay for the week, which is equal to hours times rate. Print the relevant information about this employee. Then repeat the same steps for the other employees until all have been processed. Count the number of employees processed and print the total at the end.

Two typical groups of data might be the following:

```
1234    35      14.20
2345    11.3    5.87
```

Note that the same payroll program can work for many different employees. To stay flexible, we will not specify the particular values for the ID number, hours, and rate within the program. That would limit us to just one employee.

SECTION 1   PSEUDOCODE FOR PROBLEM 3

TRANSLATING THE PROBLEM STATEMENT

According to the description of the problem, we want to read in data containing an employee's ID number, hours worked, and rate of pay. Reading in data means getting information from outside the program during execution. In the case of interactive data entry, the information is typed in from the keyboard. Sometimes we use the phrase "reading a value into a variable" because reading in data lets us give values to variables while the program is running. We have already learned one way of giving a value to a variable—the assignment statement; reading in a value is another. With an obvious choice of names for the variables, we can write the following in pseudocode:

read id
read hours
read rate

We are also told to compute the employee's pay for the week. We could write this in pseudocode as *compute **pay***, but it is simple enough to put directly in C:

pay = hours * rate;[1]

Next, we print the information about the employee:

print relevant information

Finally, we must count the employee:

count this employee

This ends what is to be done for one employee. Then the problem statement says to do the same for the other employees. Remember from Chapter 1 that anytime an action must be repeated numerous times, it makes sense to use a loop. After the loop terminates, we will print the total number of employees.

Putting all this together, here is the first version of the pseudocode for this problem:

do the following for each employee
    read id
    read hours
    read rate
    pay = hours * rate;
    print relevant information
    count this employee
print total number of employees

STYLE WORKSHOP In the pseudocode, we indicate the statements that are part of the body of the loop by indenting them a few spaces. Aligning the pseudocode statements makes it easy to see exactly which ones are included in the loop; this indenting takes the place of the pair of braces that sets off the body of the loop in C.

While this is not the final pseudocode version of this program, it will get us started. We will begin to write Program 3 and refine the pseudocode as we go along.

SELF-CHECK 3-1

1. Why is it helpful to align pseudocode statements?

2. What is input data? What is the purpose of reading in data?

3. What wording in a problem statement signals that we should use a loop?

---

[1]In pseudocode, we can use × or * for multiplication. Since pseudocode is for our convenience, we can use whatever symbols are most natural. In this case, we have used an actual C statement.

SECTION 2 **THE** *while* **LOOP**

In this section, we refine the pseudocode from Section 1. We also introduce an important new control structure, called a *while* loop, together with a trailer value (also called a flag or sentinel value) used when reading in data.

USING A LOOP IN PROGRAM 3

Once we have written the pseudocode, we should not rush into writing the program but should further refine the pseudocode. We can then see whether we have all the tools we need to write the code. In this case, we might consider whether the *for* loop structure we have introduced is adequate for this problem.

Unlike the loops in programs 1 and 2, the loop in Program 3 doesn't seem to have a starting point, stopping point, or increment value. All the pseudocode says is *do the following for each employee*. We could number the employees and use a *for* loop; however, that would violate the spirit of what we want to do, which is to read in employee information until we get to the end of the list. Fortunately, C has another type of loop, called a *while* **loop**, that will work perfectly here.

THE *while* LOOP

The *while* loop allows us to continue processing (looping), depending upon a condition whose value usually changes within the loop. It specifies no increment value but continues as long as the condition is true. Example 3-1 shows a very simple *while* loop.

EXAMPLE 3-1

```
num = 0;
limit = 10;
while (num < limit)
      num++;
```

This loop requires initial values for *num* and *limit*. As long as *num* is less than *limit*, the loop body will be executed. In this case, the loop executes ten times, with *num* having the values 0, 1, ..., 9; when *num* becomes 10, the condition *num* < *limit* is false, and the loop terminates.

The General Form of the *while* **Loop**

```
while (cond)        /* header of the loop */
      body of the loop   /* body of the loop */
```

The top line of the *while* loop, called the header, contains the keyword *while*, followed by a condition in parentheses; *cond* is any condition that evaluates to true or false; *body of the loop* is a single C statement. If more than one statement is to be executed in the body, the next format must be used.

The General Form of a *while* Loop with a Compound Statement

```
while (cond) {
    stmt-1;
    stmt-2;                          /* body of the loop */
    ...
    stmt-n;
}
```

The braces are used the same way they were in a ***for*** loop because the body of this ***while*** loop is a compound statement. A semicolon is not necessary following the closing brace.

 CAUTION Do not place a semicolon after the condition:

```
while (num < limit);
    num++;
```

If you do, the loop terminates at the semicolon, and the body of the loop contains nothing. This may cause an infinite loop during execution.

HOW A *while* LOOP WORKS

The body of the loop is executed until the condition becomes false. Each time through the loop, including the first, the condition is evaluated.

♦ If the condition is false, the body of the loop is skipped, and the statement after the body is executed.

♦ If the condition is true, the body of the loop is executed. When the computer reaches the end of the body, it goes back to the header and evaluates the condition again.

Because the condition is at the top of the loop, if it is false immediately, the body of the loop is never executed. If the condition is always true, the loop executes forever. A loop that continues forever is called an **infinite loop**. (Exercise 47 discusses infinite loops in more detail.) Table 3.1 illustrates what happens under various conditions.

TABLE 3.1 Results of *while* Condition Values

Value of the *while* Condition	Result
true	execute body of loop
false	skip body of loop
never true	never enter body of loop
never false	infinite loop

ANOTHER EXAMPLE OF A *while* LOOP

Let's look at an example with a compound statement.

EXAMPLE 3-2   Assume that we want to print all the powers of 2 less than 1000. When we fall out of the loop, we want to print a message and continue with another part of the program. Here is a *while* loop to accomplish this task:

```
power = 1;                              /* this is the first power of 2 */
while (power < 1000) {
      printf("%d\n",power);
      power *= 2;
}
printf("These are all the powers of 2 less than 1000\n");
```

Initially, *power* is given the value 1; the *while* condition *(power < 1000)* is true so we enter the body of the loop, where we print 1, which is the first power of 2 (2^0). We multiply *power* by 2, giving it the new value of 2 (remember that *power *= 2* is shorthand for *power = power * 2*). After the body of the loop executes, we go back to the header, where we test the condition again. Since *power* is still less than 1000, we enter the body of the loop again, print 2, and compute the new value 4 for *power*.

This series of actions—printing the old value, computing a new value, and testing the condition—is repeated until *power* gets the value 1024. This time when we test the condition *(power < 1000)*, it is false, and we fall out of the loop. The output from this section of code looks like this:

```
1
2
4
8
16
32
64
128
256
512
These are all the powers of 2 less than 1000
```

USING A *while* LOOP IN PROGRAM 3; A TRAILER OR PHONY DATA VALUE

The pseudocode for Program 3 says, *do the following for each employee;* clearly this means to use a *while* loop. Unfortunately, the pseudocode has a fatal flaw: there is no way to stop the looping process; we have an infinite loop! We need to stop looping when there are no more employees, and we run out of data.

We have to find a way to tell the computer that we have run out of data. A person would see that there are no values left, but a computer doesn't notice things. It doesn't know which employee is the last one.

There are many ways to do this, but the one that we will use is called a **trailer,** a **sentinel,** a **flag,** or more picturesquely, a **phony data value.** As the name suggests, our last value will not contain real employee information. Instead, it will signal to the computer that the set of data is complete.[2]

The last or phony value does not look different from the others but will be treated in a special way by our program. When the program reads this data value, it will halt instead of processing the value. Picking a phony value is difficult because it must be one which can't possibly occur in the set of data. We might use an employee who has worked 0 hours, or one whose rate of pay is 0, but it is conceivable that these values could occur. It is safer to use a phony ID number as our signal; even then, a number like 9999 or 0000 might be an actual ID. The trailer value must be something, such as a negative number, that can't possibly occur. Let's use –1111 as our signal in Program 3.

Now we must express the phony value to signal the end of the data in pseudocode. We must test each value of *id* which has been read in to see if it is –1111. The best place to test the *id* value is before computing the pay for an employee so that we don't waste time with a phony employee. We must insert a question into the pseudocode to represent this test. Let's insert the test in the header of the loop, as shown in this revised pseudocode:

> *while* id *is not equal to –1111*
>   *read* id
>   *read* hours
>   *read* rate
>   pay = hours * rate;
>   *print relevant information*
>   *count this employee*
> *print total number of employees*

This version of the pseudocode is quite close to C. We certainly could write the program from this, but first we will learn more about reading in data.

SELF-CHECK 3-2

1. What value of the condition in the *while* loop header
   a. causes the body of the *while* loop to be executed?
   b. causes the *while* loop to terminate?
2. a. What happens if the condition of a *while* loop is initially false?
   b. What happens if the condition of a *while* loop never becomes false?
3. What is the purpose of a trailer value?

---

[2]A trailer is an older technique, no longer used by professional programmers except under very specific circumstances; however, it is a simple introductory method. In Chapter 5, we introduce *EOF*, which is a more common method of handling the end of a data set.

SECTION 3 ◆ READING DATA—*scanf*

INTERACTIVE DATA ENTRY

Data read by a program can come from two places: the keyboard or a data file. Initially, our programs will read data from the keyboard, entered by **interactive data entry**, so called because the user interacts with the computer. The programmer writes the program so that the computer asks for data when it is ready to read. After the user types in the requested data values, the computer reads them and then goes ahead with the program.

USING *scanf*

According to the pseudocode, the program starts by reading in the ID number, hours, and rate of pay for each employee. However, we need a way to read in data in C.

The first technique we will introduce to read in values is *scanf*. Like *printf*, *scanf* is a function from the standard library. A call to *scanf* specifies the variable for which it is to read in a value. The symbol & must be placed in front of the variable name to get a new value using *scanf*.

We can refine the pseudocode from Section 1 to say the following (in a moment, we will discuss the control string that replaces the ellipses):

```
scanf(...,&id)
scanf(...,&hours)
scanf(...,&rate)
```

When the machine executes a call to *scanf*, it pauses, waiting for a value. Once the user types one in, followed by (ENTER), the program resumes; *scanf* reads the value and copies it into the specified variable.

A call to *scanf* does four things:

◆ reads in a value;

◆ interprets it according to the conversion specification in the control string;

◆ stores the value in the specified variable; and

◆ returns to the program the number of values read in, or **EOF** if it is unsuccessful. (We will discuss this feature of *scanf* in Chapter 5.)

The new value read in by *scanf* replaces any previous one the variable has had. In that sense, a call to *scanf* is similar to an assignment statement.

EXAMPLE 3-3

Assume we want to read an integer into the variable **num** and then print out this value. The following code will do it:

```
int num;

scanf("%d",&num);
printf("%d",num);
```

FIGURE 3-1   Effect of the call to *scanf* in Example 3-3

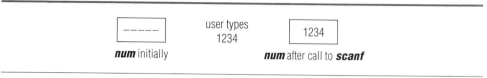

THE AMPERSAND (&)

The variable *num* is preceded by the ampersand symbol (&); in Chapter 8, we will discuss what this means. For now, know that this symbol tells the computer to put the value into the variable. If you omit the ampersand, the program compiles without error; however, the variable missing the & does not get a new value, and there may be an execution error.

GENERAL FORM OF A CALL TO *scanf*

Like *printf*, a call to *scanf* uses a control string and a list of variables. Each item in the variable list is associated with a conversion specification in the control string. Most of the conversion specifications are the same as for a call to *printf* (see Table 3.2 for a list).

The General Form of a Call to *scanf*

> scanf(*control string, variable list*);
>
> *control string* = one or more format specifications
> *variable list* = one or more variable names, each preceded by &

CONVERSION SPECIFICATIONS

Some of the conversion specifications used in the control string for *scanf* and *printf* are shown in Table 3.2. Note the difference for type *double*.

TABLE 3.2   Conversion Specifications for *scanf* and *printf*

Data Type	Specification for *scanf*	Specification for *printf*
int	%d	%d
float	%e or %f	%e or %f
double	%le or %lf	%e or %f
char	%c	%c

The first character in the specification for a variable of type *double* is a lowercase letter *l*, not a 1; *%lf* stands for "long float." Regardless of whether you type in an integer, a decimal number, or a number in scientific notation, *%lf* (or *%le*, which does exactly the same thing) tells the computer to convert that value into type *double*.

EXAMPLE 3-4

Let's read in the length and width of a rectangular room and then compute and print the area. The dimensions of the room may not be integers, so the variables must have type *float* or *double*; let's use *double*:

```
double length,width,area;

scanf("%lf",&length);
scanf("%lf",&width);
area = length * width;
printf("%f",area);
```

Assume we type in 14.5 for the length and 12.4 for the width. The first call to *scanf* reads 14.5, and this value is stored in *length*. The second reads 12.4, and this value is stored in *width*. The value 179.8 is computed, stored in *area*, and then printed. Notice that the conversion specification for each call to *scanf* is *%lf* since the variables have type *double*.

IN DEPTH

A call to *scanf* uses *%lf* to specify type *double* and *%f* for *float* because *scanf* needs information about the type of the variable to help interpret the incoming data value. The *printf* function, on the other hand, can use *%f* for both *float* and *double* because it prints these types the same way.

READING IN MULTIPLE DATA VALUES

As the general form makes clear, it is possible to read in more than one data value in a single call to *scanf*. A call that reads three integer values into the variables *first*, *second*, and *third* looks like this:

```
int first,second,third;

scanf("%d %d %d",&first,&second,&third);
```

The blanks between the two conversion specifications in the control string are not important when reading numbers (though they are when reading characters). You can put any number of blanks between the formats (including none), and *scanf* works the same way. To enter the data for this call to *scanf*, the user types three separate values, followed by ENTER. The data values themselves may be separated by any number of blanks, tabs, or newline characters but not by commas.

STYLE WORKSHOP It is good practice to read in only one value with each call to *scanf*. Reading in multiple values should be avoided in interactive programming because it works badly with prompts, which we will discuss below.

MATCHING THE DATA TO THE VARIABLES

There are some key points to remember when using a call to *scanf* to read in data. First, the order in which values are entered is important. For example, take these calls to *scanf*:

```
int    intnum;
double realnum;

scanf("%d",&intnum);
scanf("%lf",&realnum);
```

If the calls to *scanf* are done in this order, the first value entered should be an integer and is read into *intnum*, and the next value should be in numeric format, either integer or real, and is read into *realnum*. If the user enters 7 and 3.6, they will be stored as shown in Figure 3-2.

Simple conversions from integer to real can be made and vice versa. For example, if 7 is read into a variable of type *double*, then it will be stored as 7.0000. However, if you attempt to read 3.6 into an integer variable, *scanf* will stop reading at the decimal point and store the value 3 in *intnum*. The rest will be read into *realnum*. Figure 3-3 shows the effect of typing in 3.6 for these calls to *scanf* (the user won't get a chance to type in 7).

DATA ENTRY FORMAT

When numeric data is entered from the keyboard, the values can appear in free format. That means they can be on any line, in any position, separated by blanks, tabs, or newline characters (activated by pressing (ENTER)). When reading into a numeric variable, *scanf* skips all tabs, blanks, and newline characters (these are called **whitespace characters**) until it finds a value. In other words, *scanf* waits for a value to be entered and stops the program, even if you press (SPACE), (ENTER), or (TAB) instead of entering a value.

However, letters are non-whitespace characters! If you type a string of letters instead of a number, *scanf* attempts to read the first one, is unable to convert it, and fails to give the variable a new value. It remains ready to read at the first letter of the string. This is illustrated in Figure 3-4.

FIGURE 3-2   Reading values into two variables

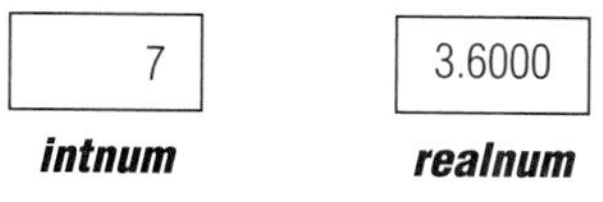

7	3.6000
intnum	*realnum*

FIGURE 3-3   Reading in values in the wrong order

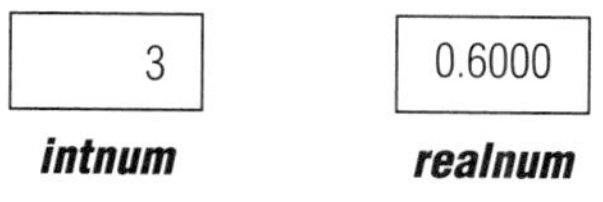

3	0.6000
intnum	*realnum*

FIGURE 3-4 *scanf* and whitespace characters

---

scanf("%d,&num);

[TAB]   [TAB][TAB][ENTER]   [ENTER]

       [TAB]   [TAB]   [TAB]   [ENTER]

7[ENTER]   abc[ENTER]

This sequence results in **num** getting the value 7.   This sequence results in **num** keeping its old value.

WHY READ IN DATA?

Before concluding, we need to make sure you understand why we read data into a program. Running a C program once or even two or three times takes only a few seconds. Because of this, some students don't appreciate why reading in data is such a powerful tool. Instead of using *scanf* to read a value into a variable, they write assignment statements. When they have different data, they change the values on the right-hand side of each assignment statement and rerun the program. They don't understand what is wrong with their technique.

As you write more programs, the answer will become clear. First of all, each time you change the statements, you must recompile the program before you run it. In contrast, if you read in data, you can simply run the same program. When you are writing a small program, you do not mind the extra compilation time. However, as your programs get longer, compilation takes more time, especially in other languages which are not so speedy.

Worse, every time you change a program, you introduce the possibility of mistakes, either through the change you make or as a side effect (accidentally erasing a line or even a single character). The last thing an experienced programmer wants to do is alter a working program.

Another important factor is the way your program will be used. Right now, you are the writer and the user of the program. If you need to change the data, you know exactly what to do. But in another environment, the programs you write will be used by others who won't know how to change your program. In fact, if you write a program for someone else, you may not even want to give them the C code for security reasons—you may not want them to know how the code works or have them mess up your program. To prevent them from seeing or changing the code, you can give them a previously compiled version of the program. Computer games and word processing programs are distributed this way. All the user does is run the program.

Then there are issues about the amount of data that a program requires and the way the sets of data are used. If you run a program two or three times using different data values, you may not find it a chore to change the values for each run (a **run** is a single execution of the program). However, suppose you are running Program 3 for a large company with 500 employees. You wouldn't want to change the program code, enter new values, and rerun the program 500 times. Allowing the program to read in data values as it needs them saves the user an enormous amount of time.

Finally, the results from your program may depend upon more than one set of data values. For example in Program 3, we count the number of employees. We can do this only if we read in the data; if we were to run the program once for each employee, the count would remain at 1. For all these reasons, reading in data is one of the most important features of any programming language.

SELF-CHECK 3-3

1. What is the purpose of a call to *scanf*?

2. What is wrong with each of the following calls to *scanf*? Assume *num* has type *int* and *realnum* has type *double*.

   a.   `scanf("%d",num);`   b.   `scanf("%f",&realnum);`

3. Give several reasons for reading data into a program.

SECTION 4   # WRITING PROGRAM 3

In this section, we use the pseudocode and the topics introduced in the last few sections to write Program 3.

PROGRAM HEADER

Let's take another look at the pseudocode, revised to include *scanf*.

while id *is not equal to –1111*
    `scanf(...,&id)`
    `scanf(...,&hours)`
    `scanf(...,&rate)`
    `pay = hours * rate;`
    print relevant information
    count this employee
print total number of employees

Looking at the pseudocode, we know how to translate everything into C. Here are the first few lines:

```
/*
 * Program prog3a.c:
 * payroll program which reads in an ID number, hours worked,
 * and rate of pay, and computes the weekly pay,
 * using interactive data entry
 */
#include <stdio.h>
main()
{
```

DECLARING THE VARIABLES

Let's see what variables we have to declare. Even though the pseudocode does not explicitly say to declare variables, we can see which were used: *id*, *hours*, *rate*, *pay*, and a variable to count employees. We'll start with *id*. Assuming that the employees' ID numbers are integers, rather than decimal numbers, we use the following declaration:

```
int id;
```

In contrast, the variables *hours*, *rate*, and *pay* will not be integers in all cases because that means ignoring all the decimal positions. Certainly someone who has a pay rate of $3.75 an hour doesn't want to lose 75 cents! We will declare these variables to have data type *double*.

```
double hours,rate,pay;
```

We are also asked to count the number of employees. An appropriate name for this variable might be *numemps*. Since the number of employees is not going to have decimal places, it makes sense to use data type *int* for *numemps*, so we use the following declaration:

```
int numemps;
```

Here is the complete declaration for this program:

```
int     id,numemps;
double hours,rate,pay;
```

STYLE WORKSHOP Note that we have combined the variables of type *int* and put them on a different line from the variables of type *double*. Using different lines is very helpful in making the declaration part of the program more readable. While you may put two or more variables of the same type on one line, always put variables of different types on separate lines.

Some people like to put variables on separate lines so they can add comments about how the variables are used. Although we won't do this, you may want to in your programs. You should be giving your variables names which are descriptive of their purpose anyway.

USING A *while* LOOP TO READ IN THE DATA

Now let's translate our loop header into C. We want to repeat the body of the loop *while id is not equal to –1111*. When *id* is equal to –1111, we want to fall out of the loop. Translated into C, the header becomes the following:

```
while (id != -1111)
```

Then, since all the indented statements are part of the loop body, it should be obvious that we need a pair of braces. Here is the code so far:

```
while (id != -1111) {
    scanf(...,&id)
    scanf(...,&hours)
    scanf(...,&rate)
    pay = hours * rate;
```

> *print relevant information*
> *count this employee*
> }
> *print total number of employees*

You may have noticed that there is going to be a problem testing the condition; we will come back to it after discussing how this loop works.

READING IN THE DATA

Inside the loop, we must read in the data, starting with the ID number and followed by the hours and rate of pay of each employee. Here are the calls to *scanf* we use to read in *id*, *hours*, and *rate*:

```
scanf("%d",&id);
scanf("%lf",&hours);
scanf("%lf",&rate);
```

Suppose that we type in 1234 for *id*, 35 for *hours*, and 14.20 for *rate*. The first call to *scanf* reads 1234 and stores it in *id*. The second reads 35 and stores it in *hours*. The third reads 14.20 and stores it in *rate*, as shown in Figure 3-5.

COMPUTING THE EMPLOYEE'S PAY AND PRINTING THE RESULTS

The next step in the pseudocode is to compute the pay. The pseudocode for this statement is identical to the C code. We compute *pay* as follows:

```
pay = hours * rate;
```

Next, we print the information about this employee. Up till now, we have been vague on exactly what should be printed. Now we must be a little more specific. We will certainly print the employee's pay, but we also need to identify the person. At a minimum, then, we should print *id* and *pay*. However, it makes the job of checking our program much easier if we also print *hours* and *rate*. Then a few simple cases can be checked by hand to verify accuracy. We should also include some messages to make the output more readable. We may decide we would like to print results that look like this:

```
Employee 1234 worked 35.0 hours at a rate of $14.20, earning $497.00
```

FIGURE 3-5   Values read in by *scanf*

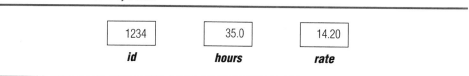

| 1234 | | 35.0 | | 14.20 |
| *id* | | *hours* | | *rate* |

We won't worry about all the details of printing this until later. For now, this is a rough approximation. In the control string of **printf**, we use just **%f** (not **%lf**) to print a variable of type **double**. Let's use this:

```
printf("Employee %d worked %f hours at a rate of $%f, earning $%f\n\n",
       id,hours,rate,pay);
```

FIXING THE FATAL FLAW

Let's look at what we have so far:

```
while (id != -1111) {                              /* incomplete */
    scanf("%d",&id);
    scanf("%lf",&hours);
    scanf("%lf",&rate);
    pay = hours * rate;
    printf("Employee %d worked %f hours at a rate of $%f, earning $%f\n\n",
           id,hours,rate,pay);
    count this employee
}
print total number of employees
```

As we mentioned, there is one big problem with this version of the program. The very first line asks us to compare the value of **id** with –1111, but we haven't given **id** a value yet. It only gets its value inside the body of the loop, after the condition in the header has been tested. However, we shouldn't test the value of a variable before it has been initialized. Instead, the simplest thing to do is read **id** outside the loop, before the test, and read **hours** and **rate** inside the loop (if **id** is not equal to –1111). Here is a revised version:

```
scanf("%d",&id);                                   /* incomplete */
while (id != -1111) {
    scanf("%lf",&hours);
    scanf("%lf",&rate);
    pay = hours * rate;
    printf("Employee %d worked %f hours at a rate of $%f, earning $%f\n\n",
           id,hours,rate,pay);
    count this employee
}
print total number of employees
```

We aren't done yet. Now that we have moved **scanf("%d",&id)** outside the loop, this program won't let us read in the ID number for any employee but the first. Trace through the indented statements, those which form the body of the loop; there isn't any place where we read in an ID number. You may think we can use the **scanf("%d",&id)** that comes before the loop. However, when we return to the top of a loop, we start at the header; we never repeat lines that come before the beginning. Therefore, **id** will continue to have the same value, and the loop will be infinite.

One solution is to insert another call to *scanf* which reads the ID number of each employee after the first. We can't put it together with the calls to *scanf* that read *hours* and *rate* because then the program would try to read in the ID number of the first employee a second time. The only place to put it is at the end of the body of the loop after processing the first employee completely, including counting that person. At that point, we are ready to start reading in data for the next employee.

```
scanf("%d",&id);
while (id != -1111) {
     scanf("%lf",&hours);
     scanf("%lf",&rate);
     pay = hours * rate;
     printf("Employee %d worked %f hours at a rate of $%f, earning $%f\n\n",
            id,hours,rate,pay);
     count this employee
     scanf("%d",&id);
}
print total number of employees
```

TRACING THE STRUCTURED READ LOOP

The type of loop that reads data once outside the loop and again inside at the bottom is called a **structured read loop**. In this type of loop, once we have read in each ID value, the next action is to check if this is the last (or phony) piece of data. In this case, the variable *id* is checked to see whether it holds –1111. If the first value read into *id* is –1111, we will never enter the body of the loop but skip to the statements that follow; if the value read into *id* is not –1111, the body of the loop will execute. In the exercises and later chapters, we will explore more reasons for using a structured read loop.

PROGRAM TRACE   Let's trace this loop with the following three ID numbers (plus associated data):

> 1234
>
> 2345
>
> –1111

◆   In response to the first *scanf("%d",&id)*, the user types in 1234.

◆   This value is placed in *id* and compared to –1111.

◆   Since it is not equal to –1111, the computer enters the body of the loop, where the user is prompted to enter values for *hours* and *rate*.

◆   Next the program computes *pay*, prints the values and messages specified in the call to *printf*, and counts the employee. This finishes the first employee.

◆   In response to the *scanf("%d",&id)* at the bottom of the loop, the user types in 2345.

◆   This gives *id* a new value, which is tested when the computer checks the condition in the loop header.

◆   Since the new value of *id* is not –1111, the computer again enters the body of the loop to read and process this employee's information. It computes and prints *pay* and counts this employee. This finishes the second person.

◆ Then the program asks for an ID number for the next employee. This time the user enters –1111.

◆ When the computer tests this value in the loop header, the condition *(id != –1111)* is false, the loop terminates, and the program prints the number of employees processed. The program does not read in *hours* and *rate* nor compute *pay* for the phony employee.

ALL OVER BUT THE COUNTING: COUNTING THE NUMBER OF EMPLOYEES

There is one last piece of pseudocode. The problem says to count each employee as the pay is processed and print the total number at the end. Let's develop an algorithm for counting a series of items.

We must have a variable whose value represents the number of items (in this case, employees) we are counting. The variable *numemps* has already been declared for this purpose.

◆ At the beginning of the program, before the loop, no employees have been processed. This tells us to initialize *numemps* to 0 before the loop.

◆ We should increment the value of *numemps* by one each time through the loop, after processing an employee. That should happen after we complete the printing, but before we read in the next ID.

An Algorithm for Counting

To count something, initialize a variable to 0. Each time the event happens, increment that variable by one. At the end, the variable holds the number of times the counted event happened.

```
count = 0;
while ( ... ) {
        /* event happens */
        ...
        count++;
}
```

When the event occurs once each time through a loop, initialize the counting variable to 0 outside the loop and increment it by one each time through. When the loop terminates, the variable has the count of the times through the loop, which is also the number of times the counted event happened.

Based on the algorithm, we can translate *count one more employee* in Problem 3 into the following:

```
numemps = 0;            /* initial value */
...
for each employee ...
        numemps++;       /* increment each time through the loop */
```

Doing this in Program 3 gives us the following:

```
numemps = 0;
scanf("%d",&id);
while (id != -1111) {
     scanf("%lf",&hours);
     scanf("%lf",&rate);
     pay = hours * rate;
     printf("Employee %d worked %f hours at a rate of $%f, earning $%f\n\n",
          id,hours,rate,pay);
     numemps++;
     scanf("%d",&id);
}
```
print total number of employees

After the **while** loop has processed all the employees, we should print the final value of **numemps**, together with an appropriate message. The final line of pseudocode translates as follows:

```
printf("We have processed %d employees\n",numemps);
```

INITIALIZATION IN THE DECLARATION

There is a handy modification of the way we have declared and initialized **numemps**. Instead of writing the declaration and the initialization separately, we can put the initial value in the declaration:

```
int    id,numemps = 0;
```

This combined statement gives the value of 0 only to **numemps**, not to **id**. If a variable is initialized in the declaration, the assigned value is just a starting one. The variable's value can still change during the program.

(ALMOST) COMPLETE PROGRAM 3

Here is our complete program, **prog3a.c**, now that we have translated all the pseudocode:

🖳 PROGRAM LISTING

```
/*
 * Program prog3a.c:
 * payroll program which reads in an ID number, hours worked,
 * and rate of pay, and computes the weekly pay,
 * using interactive data entry
 */
```
(continued)

(continued)

```c
#include <stdio.h>
main()
{
    int    id,numemps = 0;
    double hours,rate,pay;

    scanf("%d",&id);
    while (id != -1111) {
        scanf("%lf",&hours);
        scanf("%lf",&rate);
        pay = hours * rate;
        printf("Employee %d worked %f hours at a rate of $%f, earning $%f\n\n",
               id,hours,rate,pay);
        numemps++;
        scanf("%d",&id);
    }
    printf("We have processed %d employees\n",numemps);
}
```

Having assembled the parts, we have a working program that reads in the data, computes the pay, and prints out the results. In fact, you may want to run the program at this point to see how it works. Figure 3-6 shows what appears on the screen after running the program for the two employees listed in the statement of the problem. As you can see, there are still a few issues to resolve, which we will discuss in Section 5.

FIGURE 3-6   Output from ***prog3a.c*** for original two employees

```
1234
35
14.20
Employee 1234 worked 35.000000 hours at a rate of $14.200000, earning $497.000000

2345
11.3
5.87
Employee 2345 worked 11.300000 hours at a rate of $5.870000, earning $66.330000

-1111
We have processed 2 employees
```

SELF-CHECK 3-4

1. When computing **pay**, does it make any difference if we use **rate** * **hours** instead of **hours** * **rate**?

2. In a structured read loop, which reads a value once before the loop and once at the end, why is testing the value the next action after reading?

3. Why do we start counting the number of employees at 0? Can you think of a circumstance where you might begin counting at another value, say 10?

SECTION 5 — ENRICHMENT: IMPROVING THE INPUT/OUTPUT—PROMPTS AND PRINTING

This section introduces prompts for interactive data entry. In addition, it explains field width and decimal precision for printing values of type **double**. These are enhancements to the basic program in Section 4.

PROMPTS AND INTERACTIVE DATA ENTRY

If you ran the program from Section 4, you may have noticed something strange. When you run the program in this form, the computer doesn't tell you when to type in the data or which piece of data to type in at any given point. It's hard to know when the machine is ready for the data.

Actually, there is a small indication. When the computer executes a call to **scanf**, the cursor appears on the screen. The presence of the cursor is the only signal that the computer is waiting for you to type in data. The program does not continue until you do. However, even if you know what the cursor means, you may not remember which value is needed at that moment. More importantly, some other person may be running your program, and that person won't have a clue what to do.

To make it easier for the user, the computer should issue a **prompt**, which is a request for information. The prompt appears on the screen as the result of a call to **printf** in your program. The user's response is to type in the data. What the user types in is read right from the keyboard into the variable mentioned in the call to **scanf**. You can think of this format as question and answer: The computer asks a question, and the user provides the answer.

Let's begin with a simple example:

EXAMPLE 3-5   Suppose you want to write a program that reads in a number (to be stored in **number**) and prints out its square (**sqnumber**). You first have to write a prompt to tell the user to enter a number to be squared:

```
printf("Please enter a number> ");
```

Then you include the statements to read that number, square it, and write the results on the screen.

```
printf("Please enter a number> ");
scanf("%d",&number);
sqnumber = number * number;
printf("The square of %d is %d",number,sqnumber);
```

As a result of running this code, the following prompt appears on the screen, followed on the same line by the cursor (indicated by the box in the display):

```
Please enter a number> ▮
```

As the input value is typed, it appears immediately after the prompt on the same line. At this point, if the user types in 5 and then presses ⌐ENTER⌐, **number** will hold 5, and **sqnumber** will later be set to 25.

USING PROMPTS IN PROGRAM 3

Now let's see where we need to add prompts to Program 3. We have to put one in before each call to **scanf**. As a first step, use the following simple prompts (the first one is also used with the call to **scanf** at the bottom of the loop):

```
printf("Enter the employee's ID number> ");
scanf("%d",&id);
...
printf("Enter the hours worked> ");
scanf("%lf",&hours);
printf("Enter the rate of pay> ");
scanf("%lf",&rate);
```

Each prompt appears on the screen directly before the cursor. The prompt gives the user information about which data value to enter for the input statement that follows. We have ended each prompt with a right arrow and a blank; the arrow is meant to focus the user's attention, and the blank separates the data value from the prompt for easy reading. There are other possible formats.

STYLE WORKSHOP Some people prefer to write prompts ending in \n:

```
printf("Please enter a number:\n");
scanf("%d",&number);
```

After this code runs, the following prompt appears on the screen:

```
Please enter a number:
▮
```

Because the prompt ends with the newline character, the cursor appears at the beginning of the *next* line. This can be a useful format, especially if the value the user is to enter is quite long. You can also use this format to display an entire screen of information and request a response at the bottom (we will use this idea later). Use whichever format seems appropriate for the situation.

IMPROVING THE PROMPTS

We need to consider whether these prompts are adequate. They do tell the user when to enter data, but they don't give enough information about the basic nature of the program and how it runs. The following set of messages, inserted at the beginning of the program, solves the problem:

```
printf("This program computes an employee's pay.\n");
printf("Enter the ID number, hours worked, and rate of pay.\n");
printf("First, enter the employee's ID number.\n");
printf("To stop, enter -1111 as the employee's ID number> ");
```

STYLE WORKSHOP If typing a long prompt seems like a pain, remember that someone using an interactive program probably doesn't have a printout or program listing. There are no comments to explain the program to the user. One complaint people have about programs they purchase is that they are too hard to use. You should try to make every program you write easy to use.

Notice that the first three lines are not really prompts but informational messages. We terminate them with the newline character. The last line before the user enters the ID number is a true prompt and does not end in *n*; this is so that the user enters the data value on the same line as the prompt.

SELF-CHECK 3-5

1. Why does the person entering data need explanatory messages and prompts?

2. What happens if you put in a call to *scanf* but forget to put a call to *printf* preceding it?

3. What happens if you put in a call to *printf* as a prompt but forget to put a call to *scanf* following it?

PRINTING NUMBERS NEATLY: FIELD WIDTH AND DECIMAL PRECISION

We are not quite finished. We still have to take care of some of the printing details. According to our payroll report, employee 1234 is about to get a paycheck for $497.000000. This format is not going to make employee 1234 (or his bank) happy. (Of course, it is better than a paycheck for $4.970000e+02, the result of printing *pay* using *%e*. Imagine going into a bank with that check!) Fortunately, C can print real numbers in our more familiar notation.

A real number with the specifier *%f* prints in **fixed point notation**. This means that the decimal point is fixed where we would normally place it in ordinary decimal notation. However, the computer automatically prints the number with six decimal places (six digits following the decimal point). We need some way to tell it to print with only two decimal places.

To print a value occupying a specific number of print positions, we define its **field width**, how many spaces it should occupy in the output. Typically, field width is used to print real numbers, although it also works for integer values. Field width is indicated by a decimal number, like 4.2, inserted after the % symbol. The first part of the number specifies the actual width of the field or total number of positions the number occupies, including a place for the decimal point. The second part is called the **decimal precision** and tells how many of the digits follow the decimal point; this number can be greater than the default value of 6. Often the entire number is called the **format**. Note that the number indicating decimal precision can be used alone to print a number in fixed point notation without specifying a field width.

EXAMPLE 3-6

Suppose we want to print the variable *num* in six columns with two decimal places. Here is the declaration:

```
double num = 143.67;
```

The following *printf* with the format 6.2 does what we want:

```
printf("num has the value %6.2f",num);
```

The field width of 6 following the % tells the computer to print the value of *num* in six spaces, aligned along the right side of the field. The decimal precision of 2 tells it to print two of the digits after the decimal point. This line prints the following:

```
num has the value 143.67
```

EXAMPLE 3-7

Suppose *hours* has the value 26.5. How will it print with the formats in these calls to *printf*?

```
printf("%5.1f",hours);
printf("%.1f",hours);
```

The first format causes *hours* to be printed in five columns with one digit after the decimal point. Since this value requires only four columns, it prints with one space before the 2:

```
26.5
```

The second format (which omits the field width but retains the decimal point and the decimal precision value) prints *hours* in as many columns as required with one decimal digit:

```
26.5
```

Since the decimal place is obtained by rounding the remaining decimal positions, if *hours* has the value 15.36, a 4.1 field width causes it to print

```
15.4
```

Table 3.3 shows some other examples of using field widths. An integer is used as the field width to print a variable of type *int*; for example, to print the integer variable *id* right aligned in a seven-column field, we can use this line:

```
printf("%7d",id);
```

TABLE 3.3   Examples of Using Field Widths

```
double num = 32.678;
```

Format	Output	Comment
printf("%e",num);	3.267800e+01	
printf("%f",num);	32.678000	
printf("%E",num);	3.267800E+01	
printf("%7.3f",num);	32.678	leading space
printf("%4.1f",num);	32.7	rounds
printf("%4.0f",num);	33	rounds to an integer
printf("%.2f",num);	32.68	field width omitted
printf("%5.3f",num);	32.678	adjusts despite too-small format
printf("%1.1f",num);	32.7	adjusts despite too-small format

STYLE WORKSHOP   Since C prints integer values in a readable form, it is normally not necessary to use field width. However, sometimes field width is used to arrange integer values in columns or provide additional spaces before the printed value.

LEFT AND RIGHT ALIGNMENT

Once you have defined a field width, you can also specify whether you want the value left or right aligned within its field. Left aligned means starting in the far left position in the field; right aligned means ending in the far right position. Without field width, values are automatically printed in the next position available. With field width, values are automatically right aligned. However, by inserting a – flag between the % character and the field width, you can specify that the values should be left aligned. Example 3-8 illustrates the use of the – flag:

EXAMPLE 3-8

```
for (i = 99; i < 102; i++)
    printf("%5d %c",i,'a');
```

This code prints the following:

```
   99 a
  100 a
  101 a
```

```
for (i = 99; i < 102; i++)
    printf("%-5d %c",i,'a');
```

This code prints the following:

```
99    a
100   a
101   a
```

FORMATTING OUTPUT FOR PROGRAM 3

Returning to Program 3, let's figure out what format we should use to print **rate** if we want values like 12.36. We want **rate** to have a total of four digits, two of them after the decimal point. Allowing one space for the decimal point, here is the format:

```
printf("%5.2f",rate);
```

If **rate** has the value 12.36, this will print it.

Similarly, **pay** should be printed with two decimal places and a total of six digits, which requires seven spaces; this format allows for values up to $9999.99. The final version of the call to **printf** looks like this:

```
printf("Employee %d worked %4.1f hours at a rate of $%5.2f, earning $%7.2f\n\n",
        id,hours,rate,pay);
```

Suppose **id** has the value 4444, **hours** has the value 15.3, and **rate** has the value 12.36. Be sure that you understand why this call to **printf** prints the following:

```
Employee 4444 worked 15.3 hours at a rate of $12.36, earning $ 189.11
```

If you are getting nervous about all these details, realize that making a mistake in assigning the field width does not cause an error or print a misleading answer. Fortunately, C automatically makes adjustments to preserve the value as closely as possible. The computer may adjust the field width to the exact size of the number, pad the number with zeros to make it longer, or truncate or round the number on the right to make it shorter.

SELF-CHECK 3-6

1. What conversion specification should be used to print each of the following values exactly as shown?

    a. 13.5   b. −452.67

2. What conversion specification should be used to print each of the following in ordinary decimal notation with no leading blanks or trailing zeros?

    a. 7.624500e+01   b. −2.987650e−01

SPLITTING A CALL TO *printf*

We have one last thing before we display the entire program. The call to **printf** we have just created barely fits on the screen. In fact, we have broken it into two lines already. When we put the first line into a C program with appropriate indenting, it is going to run off the edge of the screen; when we print it, the line will run over onto the next one, ruining the careful indenting. The program will still compile and run, but it is hard to read, on screen and on paper.

When a line is too long to fit, it makes sense to break it up:

```
printf("Employee %d worked %4.1f hours at a rate of $%5.2f, earning $%7.2f\n\n",
        id,hours,rate,pay);
```

We have split the line carefully, after one of the commas that separate the elements. If we want to split it up further, the biggest part remaining is the control string, and splitting a string across two lines is a compilation error in C.

The best solution is to divide the call to ***printf*** into two or more individual calls. Here is one possible way:

```
printf("Employee %d worked %4.1f hours",id,hours);
printf(" at a rate of $%5.2f, earning $%7.2f\n\n",rate,pay);
```

The output from these two calls to ***printf*** looks exactly like output from the previous, unsplit call. Since we didn't end the first of the two calls to ***printf*** with \n, the second call starts its output on the same line. Whenever a long call to ***scanf*** or ***printf*** won't fit on the screen, break it up like this.

COMPLETE PROGRAM 3

Now we really are finished. We can rewrite the entire program with field widths and the full set of prompts:

🖥 PROGRAM LISTING

```
/*
 * Program prog3b.c:
 * payroll program which reads in an ID number, hours worked,
 * and rate of pay, and computes the weekly pay,
 * using interactive data entry
 */
#include <stdio.h>
main()
{
    int    id,numemps = 0;
    double hours,rate,pay;

    printf("This program computes an employee's pay.\n");
    printf("Enter the ID number, hours worked, and rate of pay.\n");
    printf("First, enter the employee's ID number.\n");
    printf("To stop, enter -1111 as the employee's ID number> ");
    scanf("%d",&id);

    /* continue until user enters -1111 */
    while (id != -1111) {
        printf("Enter the hours worked> ");
        scanf("%lf",&hours);
        printf("Enter the rate of pay> ");
```

(continued)

(*continued*)

```
                  scanf("%lf",&rate);
                  pay = hours * rate;
                  printf("Employee %d worked %4.1f hours",id,hours);
                  printf(" at a rate of $%5.2f, earning $%7.2f\n\n",rate,pay);
                  numemps++;
                  printf("Enter an ID number; enter -1111 to stop> ");
                  scanf("%d",&id);
             }
             printf("We have processed %d employees\n",numemps);
        }
```

TRACING PROGRAM 3

Before we run this final version of the program, we should trace it just to make sure. This should be done with every program you write.

For simplicity, assume that the set of data consists of the two groups discussed before and a phony ID number, where each individual value is entered in response to a prompt. Here are the three sets of values:

1234	35	14.20
2345	11.3	5.87
−1111		

PROGRAM TRACE Now let's trace our program on this set of data.

◆ The program begins by setting ***numemps*** to 0, prints some introductory messages, and continues by prompting the user to enter an ID number.

◆ The user types 1234, which is read from the keyboard, and ***id*** gets this value. Then ***id*** is compared to −1111. The two numbers are not equal so we enter the body of the loop.

◆ Inside the loop, the computer again prompts the user to enter two more values and reads these values, one into ***hours*** and one into ***rate***. We find these values stored in the variables:

1234	35.0	14.20
id	***hours***	***rate***

The variable ***pay*** has no value yet because we did not read anything into it, and we have not yet computed its value. Then ***pay*** is calculated as 35.0 × 14.20 and set to 497.00. We print the following:

```
Employee 1234 worked 35.0 hours at a rate of $14.20, earning $ 497.00
```

Then we increment ***numemps*** to 1, indicating that we have processed one employee.

◆ Next, after again prompting the user, we read in another employee's ID number, giving ***id*** the value 2345. We return to the loop header, where we find that the value for ***id*** is not equal to −1111.

◆   We enter the body of the loop and read in two more data values, setting the variables to the following:

| 2345 | 11.3 | 5.87 |
| *id* | *hours* | *rate* |

Again we compute **pay**, which is now $11.3 \times 5.87 = 66.33$. The printout looks like this:

```
Employee 2345 worked 11.3 hours at a rate of $ 5.87, earning $   66.33
```

The computer again increments **numemps**, making it equal to 2.

◆   Then we prompt for and read in the third (and last) ID number, making **id** hold the value −1111. We return to the loop header.

◆   This time when we compare, we find that **id** is equal to −1111 so we fall out of the loop. We never read in values for **hours** and **rate** or compute the **pay** for the phony employee, nor do we count that person. When we fall out of the loop, we print the final count of employees:

```
We have processed 2 employees
```

Then we end the program.

In our trace, we analyzed three employees. We could, of course, process many more; we could also run the program many times with different data values; this is the flexibility built into a program which reads in data. This completes Program 3.

SELF-CHECK 3-7

1.   What happens in Program 3 if the user types in −1111 as the first ID number?

2.   Why didn't we read in a value for **pay**?

3.   What is the potential hazard of changing a working program?

YUCKY OUTPUT

When you run this program, you will discover that the output is messy. Now that we have interactive data entry, all sorts of things are competing for space on the screen: prompts, the data typed in by the user, and the output. The output for **prog3b.c** looks like Figure 3-7 (and may be worse if there are other things there before we run the program).

STYLE WORKSHOP   To most experienced programmers, this output is unattractive and almost unreadable. More importantly, consider what will happen if there are more than two employees: the information will scroll off the top of the screen. We won't be able to look at all the output at the end of the program or print it, either. What we really want is a neatly printed payroll report with just the computed results, without prompts and data, but we won't get it from this version of the program.

FIGURE 3-7 Screen output for **prog3b.c**

```
This program computes an employee's pay.
Enter the ID number, hours worked, and rate of pay.
First, enter the employee's ID number.
To stop, enter -1111 as the employee's ID number> 1234
Enter the hours worked> 35
Enter the rate of pay> 14.20
Employee 1234 worked 35.0 hours at a rate of $14.20, earning $ 497.00

Enter an ID number; enter -1111 to stop> 2345
Enter the hours worked> 11.3
Enter the rate of pay> 5.87
Employee 2345 worked 11.3 hours at a rate of $ 5.86, earning $ 66.33

Enter an ID number; enter -1111 to stop> -1111
We have processed 2 employees
```

REDIRECTION AND PIPING OF OUTPUT

There is a simple solution to the first part of the problem—the fact that the output is hard to read or print because it scrolls off the screen. We can send all the output directly to the printer using **redirection** (in DOS and Unix) or **piping** (in Unix). The details of how to do this are discussed in Appendix V.

OOPS—WHERE ARE THE PROMPTS?

Unfortunately, redirecting output solves some problems but creates another. You won't lose any of the output, even if there is too much to fit on a single screen. Also the output will be neat and free of other messages left on the screen before you ran this program. However, the prompts are sent to the printer with the rest of the output. This is bad for two reasons: first, the prompts are worthless to the user if they go to the printer and not to the screen (they aren't available as a guide to enter data values); second, the prompts will still be mixed in with the results of the program. A solution to this problem is discussed in Appendix V.

STYLE WORKSHOP The format in which we have displayed the output is not as easy to read as one aligned in columns with headings, like the results of Program 2. The output from our payroll program would be much easier to read if it looked like Figure 3-8.

You should begin to experiment with ways to produce neat, clean output from a program, utilizing tabs, blanks, and field widths to create columns and headings. Exercise 34 asks you to rewrite Program 3 to produce the output shown in Figure 3-8. Be aware that you must eliminate the prompts to make the output this neat.

FIGURE 3-8 Suggested improved output from Program 3

```
                        Payroll Report

     Emp. ID          Hours Worked        Pay Rate           Pay

      1234                35.0              14.20           497.00
      2345                11.3               5.86            66.33

    We have processed 2 employees
```

SECTION 6 THE *if-else* STATEMENT AND THE CONDITIONAL OPERATOR

There is a very powerful C feature that we did not need in Program 3 which is helpful in modifying the basic program—for example, if we want to pay overtime to an employee who works more than 40 hours in a week or compute tax to be withheld.

CHOOSING ONE OF TWO ALTERNATIVES

Before we show how to use the new feature, let's investigate the alternative. Consider this problem: We want to find the larger of x and y, put it in *max*, and print it. Figure 3-9 diagrams the problem.

How can we translate this into C? The program should determine which path to follow, execute the appropriate statement, and finally link up the two paths to print.

FIGURE 3-9 Diagram to find the larger of *x* and *y*

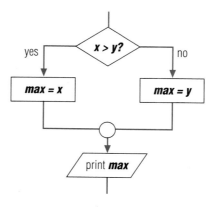

TWO POSSIBLE SOLUTIONS

First, we can initially assume that one case holds (that *y* is larger); if this is wrong, we'll make a modification.

```
max = y;
if (x > y)
     max = x;
printf("%d",max);
```

To see if this works, we don't have to try all possible combinations of *x* and *y*. We can test a representative sample of cases. In this example, there are two cases: *x* > *y* and *x* <= *y*. If we want to be meticulous, we can split this into three cases: *x* > *y*, *x* < *y*, and *x* = *y*.

PROGRAM TRACE Let's make up data to test these three cases, say *x* = 5 and *y* = 3; *x* = 4 and *y* = 6; and *x* = 7 and *y* = 7.

♦ If *x* = 5 and *y* = 3, we start by setting **max** to 3. The **if** condition is true so **max** is reset to 5, and this value prints.

♦ If *x* = 4 and *y* = 6, **max** starts at 6. The **if** condition is false; we skip the **max** = **x** statement and print 6.

♦ If *x* = 7 and *y* = 7, **max** starts at 7; we skip the **max** = **x** statement and print 7.

All possible paths work correctly, which means that this is a correct translation, except that it is doing wasted work, since **max** is initially set to *y* even if it should be *x*. This solution also doesn't match the diagram, which says to choose one thing or the other.

Let's try another method. If the answer to the question is true (if *x* > *y*), we set **max** to *x*. If it's false, or more precisely if the reverse is true (if *x* <= *y*), we set **max** to *y*.

```
if (x > y)
     max = x;
if (x <= y)
     max = y;
printf("%d",max);
```

We leave it to you to verify that this translation works in all cases for this problem. (It won't work if the first path modifies the outcome of the original question.) We are also asking two questions while the diagram says to ask only one, so again the C code does not match the diagram.

THE *if-else* STATEMENT

Our final method of translating the diagram works in all cases, does not use any extraneous statements, is more efficient, and is much closer to the spirit of the original diagram, which says to ask a question and then do one thing or another, but not both. Neither of the previous methods followed this basic outline, but the **if-else** statement does. The **if-else** statement provides two paths and allows us to execute exactly one of them, depending on the value of the condition. Example 3-9 is a solution using *if-else*. Note the indenting, which is not absolutely necessary but improves readability.

EXAMPLE 3-9   Here is the preferred solution to the problem of finding the larger of *x* and *y*:

```
if (x > y)
      max = x;
else
      max = y;
printf("%d",max);
```

PROGRAM TRACE

◆   If *x* = 5 and *y* = 3, the *if* condition is true; we execute the statement after the condition and set *max* to 5. The *else* statement is skipped when the condition is true. The call to *printf* prints 5.

◆   If *x* = 4 and *y* = 6, the *if* condition is false; as usual we skip the statement after the condition. However, now we do execute the *else* statement, which sets *max* to 6. The call to *printf* prints 6.

◆   If *x* = 7 and *y* = 7, the *if* condition is false; we skip the statement after the condition; the *else* statement sets *max* to 7. The call to *printf* prints 7.

All three cases give the correct answer, so this method works.

STYLE WORKSHOP This choice of one of two alternatives is extremely common in programming. The *if-else* statement is considered the best way to translate this choice into C. Among other things, it is more efficient: it does not waste time making extra assignments or unnecessary comparisons. You should, however, appreciate the diverse ways C can translate this relatively simple diagram. As we go on, we will find that our major concern is not finding one way to do something but choosing among many methods.

THE GENERAL FORM OF *if-else*

Figure 3-10 diagrams the general form of the *if-else* statement. This translates into C as follows on the next page.

FIGURE 3-10   Diagram of *if-else*

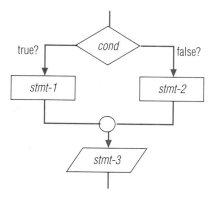

The General Form of *if-else*

```
if (cond)
     stmt-1;
else
     stmt-2;
stmt-3;
```

If *cond* is true, do *stmt-1*; if *cond* is false, do *stmt-2*. In all cases, do *stmt-3*.

STYLE WORKSHOP This format for the *if-else* statement is the most commonly used: indent the statement after the condition five spaces (or one tab position) and align the word *else* under the word *if*. Although you may see other formats, we consider this to be better C style.

EXECUTING MORE THAN ONE INSTRUCTION IN AN *if* STATEMENT

We often want to do two or more things if the condition is true or if it's false. Suppose we want to find both the larger and smaller of *x* and *y* from Example 3-9, putting the larger in *max* and the smaller in *min*. Figure 3-11 illustrates the problem.

Unfortunately, the rule we have been following limits us to executing a single statement in case the *if* condition is true and another in case it's false. Fortunately, we can modify this rule to execute more than one instruction.

USING A PAIR OF BRACES AS PART OF A CONDITIONAL STATEMENT

We faced an analogous problem earlier when we wanted to include more than one statement in the body of a *for* or *while* loop. As usual, C uses a pair of braces to solve this problem. If either part of the *if-else* statement is a compound statement, braces must surround it.

FIGURE 3-11   Diagram to find the larger and smaller of *x* and *y*

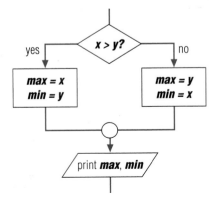

By inserting a pair of braces in an *if* statement, we can execute a compound statement on either path. If we employ this new construction, we can find values for the larger and smaller by using one *if-else* statement, as shown in Example 3-10.

EXAMPLE 3-10   This section of code uses compound statements to find both the larger and smaller of *x* and *y*.

```
if (x > y)  {
    max = x;
    min = y;
}
else  {
    max = y;
    min = x;
}
printf("max = %d and min = %d",max,min);
```

The General Form of *if-else* with Compound Statements

```
if (cond) {
        stmt-1;
        stmt-2;
        ...
}
else {
        stmt-3;
        stmt-4;
        ...
}
```

STYLE WORKSHOP We prefer this style of indenting. However, some C programmers like to align the braces in one of these ways:

```
if (cond) {                 if (cond)
    stmt-1;                 {
    stmt-2;                     stmt-1;
} else  {                       stmt-2;
    stmt-3;                 }
    stmt-4;                 else
}                           {
                                stmt-3;
                                stmt-4;
                            }
```

Most C programmers tend to be ardent advocates of one style of indenting and/or placement of braces. Your instructor may prefer a style different from ours. It is important to be consistent in whatever style you use.

REORGANIZING THE *if-else*

Statements which appear in both clauses of an *if-else* do not belong in either. These statements will be executed on each branch of the *if-else*; therefore, they should either precede or follow the entire construct. Example 3-11 illustrates this point.

EXAMPLE 3-11   The following *if-else* statement has identical statements in both clauses:

```
if (x > y) {
    printf("%d %d\n",x,y);
    max = x;
    min = y;
    printf("larger is %d and smaller is %d\n",max,min");
}
else {
    printf("%d %d\n",x,y);
    min = x;
    max = y;
    printf("larger is %d and smaller is %d\n",max,min");
}
```

The identical statements should be moved out of the *if-else*; depending on the context, they can be moved prior to or after the *if-else*, as shown here:

```
printf("%d %d\n",x,y);
if (x > y) {
    max = x;
    min = y;
}
else {
    min = x;
    max = y;
}
printf("larger is %d and smaller is %d\n",max,min");
```

USING *if-else* TO MODIFY PROGRAM 3

Let's practice the *if-else* statement by modifying Program 3 to perform an additional task. Rather than simply computing an employee's pay, let's also figure the tax. The tax rate is not flat but has two levels. For employees who earn less than $300 a week, the tax is 15 percent; for all other employees, it is 28 percent. The net pay is the pay minus the tax.

Obviously, we should compute the tax after computing *pay*. Fifteen percent of *pay* is *0.15 * pay*, and 28 percent is *0.28 * pay*. We want to subtract the appropriate amount from the employee's pay for withholding tax, so we add two new variables: *tax* and *netpay*. The variable *tax* stores the amount to withhold; *netpay* is the employee's weekly pay after taxes. A new test determines which value to store in *tax*; then we subtract *tax* from *pay* to get *netpay*.

```
double tax,netpay;
...
pay = hours * rate;
if (pay < 300)
      tax = 0.15 * pay;
else
      tax = 0.28 * pay;
netpay = pay - tax;
```

We can insert these new statements into the version of Program 3 from Section 5 to produce a complete program that computes *netpay* and *tax* and prints both. Notice that we now double-space after printing *tax* and *netpay* so that the program skips an extra line between employees.

🖥 PROGRAM LISTING

```
/*
 * Program prog3c.c:
 * payroll program which reads in an ID number, hours worked,
 * and rate of pay, and computes the weekly pay, after taxes,
 * using interactive data entry
 */
#include <stdio.h>
main()
{
    int    id,numemps = 0;
    double hours,rate,pay;
    double tax,netpay;

    printf("This program computes an employee's pay.\n");
    printf("Enter the ID number, hours worked, and rate of pay.\n");
    printf("First, enter the employee's ID number.\n");
    printf("To stop, enter -1111 as the employee's ID number> ");
    scanf("%d",&id);

    /* continue until user enters -1111 */
    while (id != -1111) {
        printf("Enter the hours worked> ");
        scanf("%lf",&hours);
        printf("Enter the rate of pay> ");
        scanf("%lf",&rate);
```

(continued)

(*continued*)

```
        pay = hours * rate;
        if (pay < 300)
            tax = 0.15 * pay;
        else
            tax = 0.28 * pay;
        netpay = pay - tax;
        printf("Employee %d worked %4.1f hours",id,hours);
        printf(" at a rate of $%5.2f, earning $%7.2f\n",rate,pay);
        printf("tax withheld was $%7.2f, leaving net pay of $%7.2f\n\n",
               tax,netpay);
        numemps++;
        printf("Enter an ID number; enter -1111 to stop> ");
        scanf("%d",&id);
    }
    printf("We have processed %d employees\n",numemps);
}
```

SELF-CHECK 3-8

1. What is printed by the following?

```
x = 10;
if (x < 8)
    y = x + 3;
else
    y = x - 2;
printf("y = %d",y);
```

2. What is wrong with this *if-else* statement? Fix the errors.

```
if (x < y);
    z = x + 1
else
    z = x + 2;
```

3. What is the value of *num* at the end of this *if-else* statement?

```
int y = 4;

if (y >= 7)
    num = 12;
else
    num = 18;
```

THE CONDITIONAL (?:) OPERATOR

C has another operator which is useful in selecting one of two alternatives. It is the **conditional operator**, whose symbol is ?: (a question mark, followed by a colon). Let's use the conditional operator to assign the larger of *x* and *y* to *max*. Here is how we did it at the beginning of this section using *if-else*:

```
if (x > y)
      max = x;
else
      max = y;
```

The conditional operator allows us to write this as a single assignment statement which gives *max* a value using a **conditional expression** as its right-hand side:

```
max = x > y  ?  x : y;
```

Let's take a closer look.

◆ The conditional expression begins with the condition *x > y*, the same as in the *if* statement above, and with the same meaning: to test the relationship between *x* and *y*.

◆ The condition is followed by the ? symbol [you can think of *x > y*? as saying *if (x > y)*].

◆ The ? symbol is followed by two possible values for the expression, separated by a colon.

  ◆ To the left of the colon is the value of the expression if the condition is true.
  ◆ To the right of the colon is the value of the expression if the condition is false.

◆ After the entire expression is evaluated, its value will be assigned to *max*.

PROGRAM TRACE

◆ If *x* is 9 and *y* is 5, the condition is true, the expression gets the value 9, and *max* is assigned that value.

◆ If *x* is 12 and *y* is 23, the condition is false, the expression gets the value 23, and *max* is assigned that value.

◆ If *x* and *y* are both 10, the condition is false, the expression gets the value of *y* or 10, and *max* is assigned that value.

It is not necessary to assign the result of the conditional operator to a variable. We can put an expression involving the conditional operator anywhere we would use any other expression. The following statement simply prints the result which we assigned to *max* in the last example:

```
printf("the larger number is %d\n", x > y ? x : y);
```

General Form of the Conditional Expression

> *expr1 ? expr2 : expr3*

expr1 is a condition that evaluates to true or false

```
if  expr1 is true
```
   expr2 is the value of the conditional expression
```
else
```
   expr3 is the value of the conditional expression

USING A CONDITIONAL EXPRESSION IN PROGRAM 3

Let's use a conditional expression to compute *tax* in *prog3c.c*. This is more complicated than our *max* example. We want to replace the *if-else* statement that computes *tax*:

```
if (pay < 300)
    tax = 0.15 * pay;
else
    tax = 0.28 * pay;
```

The following conditional expression does the same thing as this *if-else*:

```
tax = pay < 300  ?  0.15 * pay  :  0.28 * pay;
```

If this is hard to read, we can use parentheses to make it clearer:

```
tax = (pay < 300)  ?  (0.15 * pay)  :  (0.28 * pay);
```

This statement says that if *pay* is less than 300, the value of the expression is *0.15 * pay*. If *pay* is greater than or equal to 300, the value of the expression is *0.28 * pay*. In either case, the value of the expression is assigned to *tax*.

STYLE WORKSHOP The conditional expression has several advantages over the *if-else* format. It is more versatile because it can be used as part of another expression. Also, as seen above, the conditional expression emphasizes that we are assigning a value to *tax* (or to *max*), whereas the *if-else* obscures this. On the other hand, we can execute more than one statement in each branch of an *if-else*, which gives it more power.

SELF-CHECK 3-9

1. Does the result of a conditional expression have to be assigned to a variable?

2. a. What is to the left of the ? symbol in a conditional expression?
   b. What is to the left of the : symbol in a conditional expression?
   c. What is to the right of the : symbol in a conditional expression?

3. What is the value of each of the following conditional expressions?

   a. `3 > 4 ? 9 : 10;`   b. `9 < 11 ? 0 : 1;`   c. `8 == 8 ? 1 : 0;`

SUMMARY

THE *while* LOOP

1. A *while* loop can be used as an alternative to a *for* loop. A *while* loop allows a program to repeat a series of statements without specifying an exact initial value or increment.

2. Here is the general form of a *while*, where *cond* is a condition that evaluates to either true or false. If only one statement is included in the body of the loop, the { and } lines can be eliminated.

```
while (cond) {
    stmt-1;
    stmt-2;
    ...
    stmt-n;
}
```

3. The **while** loop is executed as follows: The condition *cond* is evaluated. If it is true, the body of the loop is executed. Then *cond* is evaluated again, and the process is repeated. The body of the loop is executed each time the condition is true. If the condition becomes false, the loop is terminated, the body is not executed, and the program goes on to the statement after the loop.

4. If the condition of a **while** loop is never true, the loop is never entered. If the condition of a **while** loop never becomes false, the loop never terminates. This is called an infinite loop.

READING DATA

5. As a C program is executing, it can read values from a set of data. The same program can be run with different data, leading to much more flexibility.

6. The set of data is the group of values that is input into a specific program. It is not part of the C program but is input as requested from outside while the program is running. In our first few programs, we will enter data from the keyboard. This is called interactive data entry.

7. A phony value or piece of data (sometimes called a sentinel or trailer) indicates the end of a set of data. This phony piece of data has a value which signals that it is the last one. For example, a phony value for **id** marks the end of data in Program 3.

USING *scanf*

8. Using a call to **scanf**, a program can read data values for one or more variables from the keyboard. By reading in values, a program becomes much more useful because it can be run on many different sets of data without changes or recompiling.

9. A call to **scanf**, like one to **printf**, uses a control string to tell the computer how to interpret the value to be read. The control string contains one conversion specification for each variable whose value is read. These conversion specifications are the same as for **printf** with one exception: The format for **double** is **%le** or **%lf** for **scanf**, but **%e** or **%f** for **printf**.

10. The order of values in the data must match the order of the variables in the call(s) to **scanf**. It is best to use a separate call to **scanf** for each variable.

11. Values entered as data may be separated by blanks, tabs, or newline characters. The **scanf** function reads past all these characters while trying to find a value for a numeric variable. The program does not continue until each variable in the list has been given a value.

PROMPTS

12. A prompt is a message displayed on the screen as the result of a call to **printf**. The prompt tells the user when to enter a data value. Here is an example of a prompt, followed by a call to **scanf**:

```
printf("Enter a number> ");
scanf("%d",&number);
```

With this prompt, the user enters the data value on the same line.

Here is a prompt using \n that moves the cursor to the next line before the user enters data:

```
printf("Enter a number:\n");
scanf("%d",&number);
```

STRUCTURED READ LOOP

13. A structured read loop reads in data while testing for a final value. The general form of a structured read loop is shown below, where *cond* is a condition that depends upon the value read in by the **scanf** function.

```
scanf("%d",&id);
while (cond) {
      /* process ID */
      ...
      scanf("%d",&id);
}
```

CONVERSION SPECIFICATIONS AND FIELD WIDTHS

14. A **float** or **double** value can be printed with a **%e**, **%f**, or **%E** conversion specification. Using **%e** causes the number to be printed in scientific notation with seven digits, one to the left of the decimal point and six decimal digits, plus e and the exponent. Using **%f** causes the number to be printed in decimal notation with six decimal places. Specification **%E** prints exactly like **%e**, except the exponent symbol is *E*.

15. Field width specifies the number of spaces to use to print a numeric value. The field width is a number following the % in the conversion specification. A decimal number like 3.1 specifies the field width (the total number of spaces), followed by the decimal precision (the number of decimal positions). The field width includes one space for the decimal point.

16. The value to be printed is rounded to the nearest decimal place. If the field width is too small, the results are adjusted to ensure precision. To print **realnum** with the value 35.76 in normal decimal format, we would use the field width 5.2:

```
printf("realnum=%5.2f",realnum);
```

output:

```
realnum=35.76
```

17. The field width for a variable of type **int** is specified as an integer, representing the number of spaces within which the number should be right aligned. The field width of four in the following example causes the value 9 to print with three spaces in front of it.

```
num = 9;
printf("num=%4d",num);
```

output:

```
num=   9
```

18. The – flag, inserted between the % operator and the field width, is used to left-align a value in its field. Consider these two examples:

```
num = 9;
num2 = 10;
printf("num=%4d num2=%4d",num,num2);
```

output:

```
num=   9 num2=  10
```

```
printf("num=%-4d num2=%-4d",num,num2);
```

output:

```
num=9    num2=10
```

THE *if-else* STATEMENT

19. The *if-else* construction can select one of two alternatives. The general form is

```
if (cond)
      stmt-1;
else
      stmt-2;
```

If *cond* is true, then *stmt-1* is executed; if *cond* is false, then *stmt-2* is executed instead. One of the two (but never both) statements is executed each time the *if* statement is encountered.

20. In general, C allows only a single statement to be executed on either path through a conditional statement. However, by using a pair of braces (a compound statement), a programmer can include as many statements as necessary on either path. Here is an example with two statements in one case and three in the other:

```
if (condition)   {
        st-1;
        st-2;
}
```

```
else  {
        st-3;
        st-4;
        st-5;
}
```

If *condition* evaluates to true, *st-1* and *st-2* are executed; if *condition* evaluates to false, *st-3*, *st-4*, and *st-5* are executed.

THE CONDITIONAL OPERATOR

21. The conditional (?:) operator is another method of selecting one of two alternatives and is used in a conditional expression. The general form of the conditional expression is

cond ? true option : false option

If *cond* is true, the conditional expression has the value of *true option*; otherwise, it has the value of *false option*. A conditional expression can be used anywhere any other expression is valid; the resulting value can be assigned to a variable or simply printed. Here are two examples:

```
y = a < b ? a : b;
```

```
printf(a < b ? "a is less" :
        "a is equal or greater");
```

EXERCISES

TRACING EXERCISES

1. Show exactly what is printed by each program.

    a.
    ```
    #include <stdio.h>
    main()
    {
        int p,q=2;

        printf("q  p\n");
        while (q <= 6) {
            p = 2 * q + 3;
            printf("%d  %d\n",q,p);
            q +=2;
        }
    }
    ```

    b.
    ```
    #include <stdio.h>
    main()
    {
        int x=15,y=4;

        printf("x  y\n");
        while (x >= 0) {
            x = x - y;
            y = y + 3;
        }
        printf("%d  %d\n",x,y);
    }
    ```

c.
```c
#include <stdio.h>
main()
{
    int s=8,t=0;

    while (s >= 4) {
        if (s > t)
            t += 3;
        if (s <= t)
            s += 2;
        printf("%d %d\n",s,t);
        s -= 3;
        printf("%d %d\n",s,t);
    }
}
```

d.
```c
#include <stdio.h>
main()
{
    int x=-3,y=1,z=2;

    while (x < z) {
        if (abs(x + z) > abs(y))
            printf("yes");
        if (abs(x) + abs(z)
                > abs(y))
            printf("no");
        printf("maybe");
        x++;
        z--;
    }
}
```

e.
```c
#include <stdio.h>
#include <math.h>
main()
{
    double b;
    int    a=0;

    printf("number ");
    printf("square root\n");
    while (a <= 6) {
        b = sqrt(a);
        printf("%d %f\n",a,b);
        a += 1;
    }
}
```

f.
```c
#include <stdio.h>
main()
{
    int    c=1;
    double d;

    printf("number  reciprocal");
    printf("check\n");
    while (c <= 8) {
        d = 1.0 / c;
        printf("%d %f %f\n",c,
                d,c*d);
        c += 1;
    }
}
```

2.   What is the value of **ans** at the end of the following *if-else* statement?

```c
num1 = 12;
num2 = 14;
if (num1 + 3 < num2 - 2)
    ans = num1 - 9;
else
    ans = num1 + num2;
```

3. What is printed by the following section of code?

```
int num=9,x=12;

if (num >= x) {
    num = x;
    x = num - 2;
}
else {
    x = num;
    num += 3;
}
printf("num = %d and x = %d\n",num,x);
```

4. What is wrong with the following loop?

```
x = 4;
while (x < 5);
    printf("%d ",x);
```

5. a. When reading data, which of the two—*printf* or *scanf*—causes a message to appear on the screen?
   b. Which of the two causes the computer to stop and wait for the user to type in a value?
   c. Which of the two lines below could be eliminated? Why?

```
printf("Enter a number\n");
scanf("%d",&num);
```

6. A program is said to be **user friendly** if it is easy to understand and use. What techniques help to make a program user friendly?

7. What is wrong with the following *if-else* statement? Note that it is not a simple syntax error—it *will* compile. Fix the error.

```
if (x = y)
    z = x + 1;
else
    z = x + 2;
```

8. Suppose we have the following *if-else* statement. If the code prior to it gives values only to *x* and *y*, can we rely on *p* or *z* having a value (other than garbage) in the call to *printf*?

```
if (x < y)
    p = x;
else
    z = x;
printf("%d  %d",p,z);
```

9. For each of the following series of C statements, try to describe in words what is accomplished (the larger of *x* and *y* is put into *max*, and then *max* is printed; or *x* is multiplied over and over by 2 until it is more than 30). For parts (a) through (c), (f), and (g), assume that *x* and *y* have already been given values. All variables have data type *int*.

a.
```
if (x > y)
      max = x;
else
      max = y;
printf("%d",max);
```

b.
```
if (x > y)
      ans = x;
else
      ans = y;
if (x == y)
      ans = 1;
```

c.
```
hold = 5;
if (x == y)
      hold = x;
else
      hold = y;
```

d.
```
x = 1;
while (x < 100) {
      if (x < 50)
          x *= 2;
      x *= 2;
}
```

e.
```
x = 0;
while (x < 15) {
      x = x + 4;
      if (x == 8)
            printf("%d",x);
}
```

f.
```
x = 0;
while (x < 15) {
      x = x + y;
      if (x < y)
          x = y;
}
```

g.
```
if (x == y)
      printf("%d",x);
else
      printf("%d",y);
```

h.
```
x = 0;
while (x <= 6) {
      y = x + 4;
      if (y == 10)
            printf("done");
      x += 1;
}
```

10. The segment below is designed to subtract 5 from the larger of the two numbers, *x* and *y*, and also add 5 to the smaller.

a. Does the segment accomplish this task in all cases? For example, what happens if *x* is 5 and *y* is 6? What if *x* is 6 and *y* is 5?

b. Rewrite the segment so that it does work in all cases. (*Hint:* You may want to use one or more pairs of braces.)

```
int x,y;
    ...
if (x > y)
      x -= 5;
else
      y -= 5;
if (x > y)
      y += 5;
else
      x += 5;
    ...
```

11. The following program segment is preceded by a comment that describes the goal. Try to use the data to see if the segment works in all cases. If it does not, explain exactly what happens and show how to amend it so that it does always work.

```
/*
 * find the smallest integer whose
 * square is greater than y
 */
#include <stdio.h>
main()
{
    int number=0,test=0,y;

    while (test <= y) {
        number++;
        test = number + number;
    }
    printf("%d is the smallest",number)
}
```
(try $y = 4$, $y = 5$, $y = 26$)

12. Trace step by step the execution of the following program as it reads in the data. Assume that the user types in these values as requested:

5   7   –3   4   10   –1   7   0

```
#include <stdio.h>
main()
{
    int x;

    printf("Please enter a number> ");
    scanf("%d",&x);
    while (x != 0) {
        if (x < 0)
            printf("\tnegative\n");
        if (x > 0)
            printf("\tpositive\n");
        if (x > 5)
            printf("\tmore\n");
        else
            printf("\tless\n");
        printf("Please enter another number> ");
        scanf("%d",&x);
    }
}
```

13. Trace step by step the execution of the program below. Assume that the user types in these values as requested:

```
10  -1     -1  -7     0  -1     4  14     4  6     13  5     9  0     42  42
```

```c
#include <stdio.h>
main()
{
    int x,y;

    printf("Please enter an integer> ");
    scanf("%d",&x);
    printf("Please enter another integer> ");
    scanf("%d",&y);
    while (x != y) {
        printf("%d %d",x,y);
        if (x > y)
            printf("\tx\n");
        else
            printf("\ty\n");
        printf("Please enter two more integers> ");
        scanf("%d",&x);
        scanf("%d",&y);
    }
    printf("\nFinished\n");
}
```

14. Assume that the user types in consecutive numbers, starting from 1, as data for each of the following programs. Trace step by step what is in the variables *x*, *y*, and *z* as each program is executed.

a.
```c
#include <stdio.h>
main()
{
    int x,y,z;

    printf("Enter a number");
    scanf("%d",&x);
    while (x < 6) {
        printf("Enter 2 numbers> ");
        scanf("%d",&y);
        scanf("%d",&z);
        printf("%d %d\n",y,z);
        printf("Enter 2 numbers> ");
        scanf("%d",&z);
        scanf("%d",&x);
        printf("%d %d\n",z,x);
        printf("%d\n",x);
    }
    printf("Enter a number> ");
    scanf("%d",&y);
    printf("%d\n",y);
```

```
                  printf("Enter 3 numbers> ");
                  scanf("%d",&x);
                  scanf("%d",&y);
                  scanf("%d",&z);
                  printf("%d %d %d\n",x,y,z);
          }
  b.   #include <stdio.h>
       main()
       {
             int i,x,y,z;

             for (i = 1; i <= 3; i++) {
                  printf("Enter 3 numbers");
                  scanf("%d",&x);
                  scanf("%d",&y);
                  scanf("%d",&z);
                  printf("%d %d %d\n",x,y,z);
                  printf("Enter 2 numbers");
                  scanf("%d",&y);
                  scanf("%d",&z);
             }
             printf("%d %d\n",y,z);
       }
```

15. Assume that the user enters the data values below as needed. Trace step by step the values that are read into the variables *a*, *b*, *c*, and *d*. Show exactly what is printed by this program.

```
#include <stdio.h>
main()
{
     double a,b,c;
     int    d;

     printf("Enter the first line of numbers> ");
     scanf("%lf %lf %lf %d",&a,&b,&c,&d);
     printf("%5.2f %5.2f %5.2f %5d\n",a,b,c,d);
     printf("Enter the second line of numbers> ");
     scanf("%lf",&a);
     printf("Enter the third line of numbers> ");
     scanf("%lf %lf %lf",&a,&b,&c);
     printf("%7.2f %5.2f %6.1f %5d\n",a,b,c,d);
     printf("Enter the fourth line of numbers> ");
     scanf("%lf %lf %d",&b,&c,&d);
     printf("\n%7.2f %6.2f %4.1f %4d\n",a,b,c,d);
}

     1.35  2.1  -9.2  13
     15
     123.45  0  678
     12.39  -5  5
```

16. a. Assume that the declaration for variable *c* in Exercise 15 is changed from type **double** to **int** (and the conversion specifications are changed as well). Does this affect the execution of the program? How does it affect the values printed out?

 b. Assume that all four variables are declared to have data type **double**. What effect does this have on the printout?

 c. Assume that by mistake the last line is typed as 12.39 –55, with no space between the two 5s. How does this affect the program?

17. Determine the correct field width and decimal precision needed to print each of the following numbers in the format shown.

 a. 276.345   g. 567.3
 b. –8314.5678   h. 493.888
 c. 52.676   i. –9.4
 d. –.00003   j. –19.6475
 e. .000076   k. –203.2
 f. 1.14151617

 Write a program to test whether your answers are correct.

18. Here are some possible values of a variable **num** with type **double**. For each, write a call to **printf** with a field width and decimal precision that produce the following formats:

 a. 42   e. 6174.55
 b. –6.8   f. 0.0999
 c. 0.1   g. –0.00008
 d. 371.00   h. 1000.056

19. What conversion specification should be used to print each of the following so that their exact value appears in ordinary decimal notation, with no leading blanks or trailing zeros?

 a. –1.898000e+02   b. 4.506700e–02   c. 8.345678e+04

QUESTIONS ABOUT AND MODIFICATIONS TO PROGRAM 3

20. In Program 3, why don't we read in the pay for each employee?

21. a. Why isn't 0000 or 9999 a good trailer value for Problem 3?

 b. Instead of using a trailer value, why don't we just set up a **for** loop to read in 25 employees? Or 15?

22. What happens in Program 3 if the user forgets to enter –1111 as the last ID number and instead enters 1111?

23. Here is a poor solution to fixing the flaw in the first version of the loop used to solve Problem 3. What is wrong with this solution? If you cannot see what's wrong, the questions below will help you.

```
id = 0000;
while (id != -1111) {
    scanf("%d",&id);
    scanf("%lf",&hours);
    scanf("%lf",&rate);
```

```
        pay = hours * rate;
        printf("Employee %d worked %f hours at a rate of $%f, earning $%f\n\n",
            id,hours,rate,pay);
```
count this employee

```
    }
```
print total number of employees

a. To use this solution, how many employees would there have to be, at a minimum?
b. If we used this format, how much information would have to be provided for the phony employee?
c. If we used this format, what information would be printed for the phony employee?

24. In Program 3, we said that we needed to provide a phony value only for *id*, not for *hours* and *rate*, since we used three different calls to *scanf* to read in the data. However, if we use a single call to *scanf* to read in all three values at once, then we should provide phony values for *hours* and *rate* as well. Why? Show how to do this. Indicate the changes that are necessary in the pseudocode and then in the program.

25. Modify Program 3 so that, after reading the last piece of data, it prints a message at the end indicating that the payroll is completed. *(Suggestion:* First, figure out how to modify the pseudocode; then implement the modifications in a new program.)

26. Modify Program 3 so that, in addition to computing each employee's pay, it also prints a summary at the end. This summary should print after it reads the last value and should include the total number of employees, the total number of hours worked, and the total amount of pay. Print this information several lines below the output for the final employee.

27. a. Modify Program 3 so that, after reading in the phony value, it prints out the ID number of the employee with the highest pay rate. *(Suggestion:* Have the program keep track of the highest rate of pay as it goes along and change this value when appropriate.)
     b. Modify the program from part (a) to keep track also of the employee working the most hours and the one with highest weekly pay. Print this information at the end.

28. Modify Program 3 so that each employee is paid overtime for any hours above 40. Overtime is one-and-a-half times the normal rate. For example, if an employee earning $5.00 per hour works 48 hours, the first 40 are paid at $5.00, and the extra 8 hours are paid at $5.00 × 1.5 = $7.50 per hour.

29. Modify Program 3 so that social security and state income taxes are withheld from each employee's pay. Assume that the social security tax is 9 percent of weekly pay, and that state income tax is $10.00 if the pay is less than $100.00 (with the exception given below) and $20.00 if the pay is $100.00 or more. However, the state tax is never more than the base pay minus social security tax (if the base pay is $5.00, the social security tax is $0.45, and the state income tax is $5.00 − 0.45 = $4.55, not $10.00). Print each employee's base pay, taxes, and net pay after taxes.

30. Modify Program 3 so that it reads in a fourth piece of information for each employee, either the number 1, meaning "union," or the number 0, meaning "nonunion." Use this information to determine the employee's union dues, which are 10 percent of the pay for members and 0 for nonunion workers. Print each employee's union status, dues, and net pay after dues.

31. Modify the preceding program to include the overtime rate for hours above 40 for union members only. Nonunion workers will be paid at their standard rate regardless of the number of hours.

32. Modify Program 3 so that it reads in a fourth piece of information for each employee, an integer representing the number of dependents. An employee will pay a state tax of 10 percent on the modified pay, which is the base pay minus ten times the number of dependents. The state tax should be 0 for an employee whose modified pay is negative (if the base pay is $35.00, and there are four dependents). For each employee, print the number of dependents, the modified pay, and the state tax.

33. In Program 3, we wrote the prompts using calls to *printf* without \n so that the data value typed in by the user appeared on the same line. As we noted, another common technique is to use calls to *printf* with \n for the prompts. What effect does this have? Rewrite Program 3 using \n for each prompt and run the new program to check your answer.

34. Modify Program 3 so that it produces output in columns with headings, as shown in Figure 3-8.

35. Modify Program 3 so that it reads in two initials (*first* and *last*) to identify each employee, rather than an ID number. What can you use as a phony value? Should you test *first* or *last*?

MODIFICATIONS OF OTHER PROGRAMS

36. a. Write a complete C program to do the following: The program will read in a number such as 3.10 or 2.50, which represents a student's grade point average (*gpa*). Using this *gpa*, the program will calculate the corresponding value of the registrar's formula given in Chapter 2. The program will print the student's *gpa* and the value of the formula.

    b. Modify this program so that, after finishing with the first student, it reads in a new value of *gpa* for another student. Compute the formula for this *gpa* and print the results. Repeat this process until the program reads in a negative *gpa* value (−2.35). This negative value will signal that the set of data is complete.

37. a. Modify your program for Chapter 2, Exercise 22, so that, after printing the table of interval values for *gpa* (e.g., 3.25 to 3.74 covered by 3.50), your program reads in a value for *gpa* from the data. The program should determine which line of the table applies (e.g., if *gpa* is 3.47, the program should print "Use the 3.50 value in the table above."). Repeat this process for a series of numbers.

    b. Compare the method used in part (a) of this exercise to the one in Exercise 36(b). What are the advantages and disadvantages of the two approaches? Which is better to use if the formula is relatively simple (*result = gpa * 3 + 5*)? Which would be better on an extremely complex formula that is difficult to compute? What if you expect one or two students? What if you expect several thousand?

38. Modify Program 2 so that it keeps track of how many formula values are positive, how many are negative, and how many are zero. After the last line of the table, print the number of each type found.

39. Modify Program 2 so that it keeps track of (a) the highest value of *result* ever obtained by the formula, and (b) the *gpa* value which led to the highest outcome. After printing the last line of the table, print these *gpa* and *result* values.

40. a. Modify Program 2 so that the values print in floating point notation but right aligned in their columns.
    b. Modify Program 2 so that the formula values print in fixed point notation with two decimal places.

41. Modify Program 2 so that it uses a *while* instead of a *for* loop. Which version is clearer?

42. Modify programs 1 and 2 to make them interactive. What data will you ask the user to enter? What prompts will you need?

43. Go through the exercises in chapters 1 and 2 that ask you to write programs. In each case, if it makes sense, rewrite the program so that it is interactive. What data will you ask the user to enter? What prompts will you need?

MISCELLANEOUS EXERCISES

44. Why is it a disadvantage for a program to be completely self-contained?

45. In Section 4, we said that the variable **count** will *always* contain the number of employees. This statement about **count** is an example of a **loop invariant**, an assertion which is always true when the condition in the loop is tested; it is also true after the loop has terminated. Here is a loop, followed by some examples of loop invariants:

```
sum = 0;
i = 0;
while (i <= 100) {
      i++;
      sum += i;
}
printf("i = %d and sum = %d",i,sum);
```

(1) *i <= sum*
(2) *sum >= 0*
(3) *i* is equal to the number of times we have processed the loop body
(4) *sum* is equal to the sum of the *i* values processed so far $(0 + 1 + ... + i)$

Trace the following loops; which of the statements that follow are loop invariants for that loop?

a.
```
y = 1;
x = 0;
while (x < 10) {
      x += 2;
      y *= x;
}
printf("%d %d",x,y);
```

(1) *x* is equal to 10
(2) *x < 10*
(3) *x* is not equal to *y*

(4) *x < y*
(5) *x* is even
(6) *y* is even

b.
```
x = 0;
y = 1;
while (x != 16) {
      x++;
      y *= 2;
}
printf("%d %d",x,y);
```

(1) $x < 16$

(2) x is not equal to 16

(3) x is not equal to y

(4) $x < y$

(5) x is odd

(6) y is even

(7) $y = x^2$

(8) $y = 2^x$

(9) $y < 32767$

46. In Section 6, we introduced the *if-else* construction and diagrammed the flow of control using a **flowchart**, a picture describing the flow of statements in a program. Like pseudocode, a flowchart is another intermediate step to translate the English statement of the problem into C. The main advantage of a flowchart is that many people can follow a picture or diagram better than a verbal description of a problem. Most people nowadays use pseudocode instead of flowcharts, but there are occasions, like showing the flow of a nested *if* statement (see Chapter 6), where a flowchart can be helpful. Unfortunately, in some cases, flowcharts actually obscure what is happening in the program, which is why they have lost popularity.

The flowchart in Section 6 used only a few of the common symbols. Figure 3-12 shows some of the available ones. Figure 3-13 is a flowchart for Program 3, first version, using these symbols. Notice that the flowchart does not include declarations or comments.

a. Draw a flowchart for Program 1. (This is obviously not the normal order; you write the program from the flowchart, not vice versa.)

b. Draw a flowchart for Program 2.

c. Draw a flowchart for Program 3 (the last version).

FIGURE 3-12   Flowchart symbols

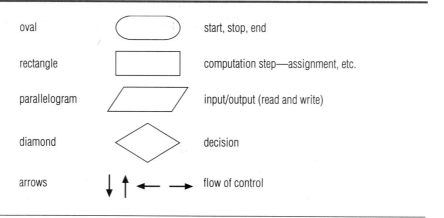

oval	start, stop, end
rectangle	computation step—assignment, etc.
parallelogram	input/output (read and write)
diamond	decision
arrows	flow of control

FIGURE 3-13   Flowchart for Program 3 (first version)

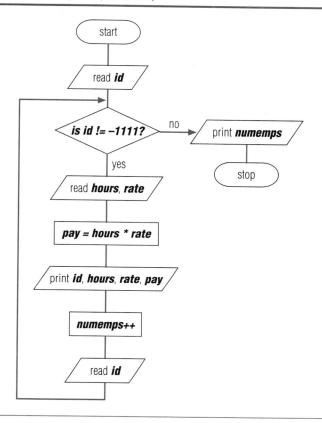

d.   Draw flowcharts for the programs shown in exercises 1 through 3, and 9 through 15. Which C constructs are difficult to represent in a flowchart?

e.   Write pseudocode for each of these programs and compare it with the flowchart. In each case, which is easier to follow?

47.   If you are in an infinite loop that contains calls to **printf**, you will know because you will see lines and lines of output; if you are in an infinite loop without any calls to **printf**, you may just see a frozen screen. Write a simple program that contains an infinite loop (a program containing the loop below will do the trick).

```
i = 0;
while (1 == 1) {
    i++;
    printf("%d\n",i);
}
```

Then run the program and see what happens. Try to break out of the loop. Now remove the call to *printf* and see what happens. Again, try to break out of the loop. Did you know what was wrong when the infinite loop occurred?

48. Anything that can be done with a *for* loop can also be done using a *while* loop and vice versa. In fact, some programmers prefer to use a *while* loop whenever a series of steps must be repeated. For example, the *for* loop on the left (which executes the body of the loop ten times, for *i* having values from 1 to 10) can be replaced by the *while* loop on the right.

```
for (i = 1; i <= 10; i++) {          i = 1;
    body of the loop                 while (i <= 10) {
}                                        body of the loop
                                         i++;
                                     }
```

a. Show how we could have used a *for* loop in Program 3.
b. Go through the earlier exercises which asked you to use *while* loops and show how to solve them using *for* loops.
c. Show that anything that can be done with a *for* loop can be done with a *while* loop and vice versa.

PROGRAMMING PROJECTS

49. Write a complete C program to do the following: Use a *while* loop to read in a series of numbers and print each number with its square and its cube. Put column headings on the output. Let 0 indicate the end of the input data. (Be careful of the limit on data type *int* in Turbo C; some squares or cubes may require a data type that can hold larger values.)

50. Write a complete C program to do the following: Read in a series of positive numbers and print each number with its square and its square root. Put column headings on the output and format the square roots to have four decimal places. Let any negative number signal the end of the input data.

51. Write a complete C program to do the following: Read in a series of positive and negative values. Print the numbers and their absolute values. Put column headings on the output. Let 0 indicate the end of the input data.

52. A prime number is one which has no divisors but itself and 1. Write a complete C program to read in a series of numbers and determine if each is prime. If it is, print "Prime"; otherwise, print a list of its divisors.

53. Write a complete C program to do the following: Read in information about the customers of the Handy Hardware Company. For each one, the data consists of a customer number, the current dollar amount of orders placed, and the current dollar amount of orders paid for. For each customer, compute the balance due. If the amount is negative, print a message saying, "Credit." If the amount is positive, print a message saying, "Amount owed." Consider a 0 balance positive.

When you have read in the information about all the customers, print the company totals: total dollar amount of orders placed, total dollar amount of orders paid for, and total balance due the company. (Should all three be computed the same way?)

54. Write a complete C program to do the following: Read in information about the students in the graduating class at Science Tech. For each one, there is a student ID number and a grade point average in the range of 0.00 to 4.00. Your program should determine whether each student can graduate and if it is with honors. Print each student's ID number and grade point average. If the grade point average is 2.0 or better, print "Graduate" next it. If it is less than 2.0, print "Sorry". If it is 3.5 or better, print "Honors" next to the word "Graduate".

    After processing all the students, print four totals: the total number of students, the number graduating, the number graduating with honors, and the number who are not graduating. (Do all of these totals have to be summed?)

55. Write a complete C program to do the following: Read in a series of numbers, each of which can contain decimal places. Print each number as it is read in. Determine whether each number is positive, negative, or zero, and print "positive," "negative," or "zero" next to it. Keep track of how many numbers are positive, negative, and zero and print these counts at the end, together with appropriate messages. Since all numbers are acceptable, pick any one you wish to signal the end of the data.

56. Write a C program, including comments, to compute statistics for how students did on an exam. The program should compute various things about a student and print them. It should repeat the process for each new student until the entire set of data has been completed.

    a. The program reads in the ID number of a student [see step (g) below] and then the number of right answers and the number of wrong answers. (The total number of questions on the test is 50.) For example, the program could read in the following:

        1234   20   5   (ID number 1234 has 20 right and 5 wrong)

    b. The program computes and prints the total number of questions answered plus the number omitted (which is simply 50 minus the number answered). The number right plus the number wrong will never be more than 50 [see optional (a) on page 168].

    c. The program computes the student's correct answer percentage, which is a decimal value between 0 and 1. The correct answer percentage is the number of right answers divided by the number of questions answered. [The student always answers at least one question—see optional (b).] For the data values shown for ID number 1234 above, the correct answer percentage is 20 / 25 = 0.800. The program should print this out as shown, with three decimal places.

    d. The program also assigns the student a numerical grade on the exam. The numerical grade is the number of right answers times 2 (ignoring the wrong answers). For example, ID number 1234 got a numerical grade of 40 on the exam (20 right × 2). The program prints the student's grade.

    e. The program determines if the student had more right than wrong answers, the same number of each, or more wrong than right answers. It prints an appropriate message.

    f. The program determines if the student omitted ten or more questions. It prints a message with this information.

    g. Then the program skips a few lines and repeats the entire process for the next student until the last one is finished. (You must decide how to recognize the last student.)

    h. At that point, the program prints the total number of students in the class (you must keep track of this) and stops.

Data: Be sure to read in data for at least 12 students. Make sure that you have at least 2 with the same number right and wrong, at least 2 with more wrong than right, and at least 2 with more right than wrong. Include a student with all wrong answers and one with all right answers. Have some students who don't omit anything and some who omit almost all the questions.

Output: Here is a complete set of output for two typical students:

```
id 1234

12 right     13 wrong

total answered 25

number omitted is 25

grade is 24

more wrong than right

correct answer pct. is 0.480

10 or more omitted
```

```
id 7890

30 right      15 wrong

total answered 45

number omitted is 5

grade is 60

more right than wrong

correct answer pct. is 0.667

less than 10 omitted
```

Optionals:

a. If a student answered more than 50 questions, print an error message, skip the rest of the processing, and go on to the next student.
b. Make sure that you do not divide by 0 if the student answered no questions (everything was omitted). Print a special message and go on to the next student.
c. Keep track of the student with the best correct answer percentage and the one with the highest grade. (These do not have to be the same—to test, make sure they are different.) Print these out at the end.

57. Write a complete C program, including comments, to compute a weekly payroll. The program reads in information for each of the employees of a company and then prints the results. After processing the last person, the program prints the total number of employees. The program does the following for each employee:

a. First, it reads in the data values for this employee. Each employee has a three-digit identification number (an integer from 100 to 999), hours worked, rate of pay, and union status (1 if the employee is in the union, 0 if not). For example, here are data values for two typical workers:

123	46	6.50	1	(ID number 123 is in the union)
456	32.12	3	0	(ID number 456 is nonunion)

b. The program computes the weekly pay, which comes from the following formula (this includes an overtime bonus of time and a half for each hour over 40):

    if hours are less than 40, weekly pay is hours times rate

    but

    if hours are 40 or more, weekly pay is 40 times the rate plus
    the number of overtime hours times 1.5 times the rate

    For example, ID number 123 would get $40 * 6.50 + 6 * 1.5 * 6.50$.
    ID number 456 would get $32.12 * 3$.

c. The program computes the union dues, which are 10 percent of the weekly pay for union members, and $5 ($5, not 5 percent) for nonunion employees. [You can assume that the only values for union status are 1 (union) and 0 (nonunion). See optional (b) below.]

d. The program computes net pay, which is weekly pay minus union dues.

e. The program prints all of the data values read in and the words "Union" or "Nonunion," plus each item that has been computed (weekly pay, union dues, net pay). Make sure that all money amounts have exactly two decimal places. You can put dollar signs in, but it is not necessary.

f. Then the program skips three lines and goes to the next employee.

After the last person has been read, the program prints the total number of employees who have been processed. (This count should not include a phony employee used to end the set of data.)

Your program must determine when the last employee has been read. Explain how to do this in a comment.

Data: Have at least ten employees. Make sure that at least four are union and four are not. Make at least four work overtime and four not (and cover all possible combinations).

Make sure that most of your values are integers (so that you can check the calculations by hand) but that a few have decimal places (e.g., 6.50 per hour or 30.5 hours).

Output : Here is a sample set of output for one employee (messages can vary):

```
employee 123 worked   46.0 hours   at  6.50 per hour    union member
weekly pay   318.50      union dues   31.85      net pay  286.65
```

Optionals:

a. Determine the total weekly payroll (for all employees added together). Print this at the end.

b. If a person's union status is not one of the allowed values (union or nonunion), print an error message. Do not subtract anything for union dues.

58. Write a complete C program, including comments, to compute baseball statistics. The program computes various things about a team and prints everything out. Then it repeats the process for each new team until the entire set of data has been completed.

a. The program reads in the ID number of a team [see step (e) below]. It reads in the number of wins and the number of losses. For example, it could read in the following:

1234 5 7   (team 1234 has 5 wins and 7 losses)

b. The program computes (and prints) the total number of games played, which is simply the number of wins plus the number of losses. If the total is exactly 20, the program prints a message saying the season is finished. If the total is less, the program prints how many games are left. No team has played more than 20 games. For example, for the team above, the total number of games played is 12, and there are 8 games left (20 – 12).

c. The program computes the team's winning percentage, which is a decimal value between 0 and 1. The winning percentage is the number of games won divided by games played. For the team above, the winning percentage is 5 / 12 = 0.41667. The program prints this out as shown, with exactly five decimal places.

d. The program computes how much the team is above or below 0.50000. This is defined as follows:

If the team has won more games than it has lost (or if these are equal), the amount above 0.50000 is the number of wins minus the number of losses. Otherwise, the amount below 0.50000 is the number of losses minus the number of wins. This value should be printed with an appropriate message (saying if this is games above or below 0.50000).

For example, the team above is 2 games below 0.50000 (5 is less than 7, and 7 − 5 = 2).

e. Then the program skips a few lines of output and repeats the entire process for the next team until it reaches the last one. (You must decide how to recognize the last team.) At that point, print the total number of teams in the league and stop.

Data: Be sure to read in data for about eight to ten teams. Make sure that at least three teams have completed their season and three have not. Have at least two teams with more wins than losses, one with an even record, and two with more losses.

Output: Here is a complete set of output for a typical team:

```
team 9867
4 wins    16 losses
total number of games played is 20
the season is finished
the winning percentage is 0.20000
the team is 12 games below 0.50000
```

Optionals:

a. Compute the team's record if it wins all of the remaining games (give the winning percentage and games above/below 0.50000) and the record if it loses all of them.

b. Keep track of the team with the best winning percentage and the one which is the most games above 0.50000. Print these out at the end.

59. Write a program that assigns a student a letter grade based upon exam marks.

First, read in the student's ID number. This should be an integer. Then read in the student's exam marks (since they can have decimal places, e.g., 87.5, the marks must be declared as ***double***). Use a trailer value to indicate the end of the grades (−1 is a good value for this trailer) to allow a student to have taken an arbitrary number of exams.

Once the grades have been read in, calculate the student's average (the sum of the exams divided by the number). Finally, based upon the average, assign a letter grade using the standard grading scale:

90 and above A
80 and above B
70 and above C
60 and above D
below 60   F

Your program should print out the student ID number, the number of exams taken and their marks, the average, and the final grade. Try to make the output readable; for example:

```
Grade report for student 122


4 exams taken:


Exam: 90
Exam: 93.5
Exam: 86
Exam: 84
----------------
Student's average is 88.125
Grade is B
```

Run this program for several students, making sure that your data values produce at least one with each grade from A through F.

60. You have just been hired as director of programming at the TooHeavy Hauling Company. Your first assignment is to write a program that calculates shipping information for the company and reports the results to the dispatcher.

The program reads in a sequence of truck shipment orders. Each order consists of three carton weights (all shipments consist of exactly three containers). Assign a truck category to the shipment based upon its total weight, according to the following table.

Category	Weight Limit	Shipping Cost
1	2,000 lbs	$50
2	5,500 lbs	$100
3	10,000 lbs	$135
4	14,000 lbs	$200

If no truck is capable of carrying the shipment (its total weight exceeds the maximum load), issue a message to the dispatcher (see the Output section). Use a trailer value of −1 to indicate the end of the set of data.

Test Data: Use the following test data:

200	300	400
1000	1	1000
1000	900	0
1000	1000	100
2000	2000	1600
2000	2000	1500
3000	3000	3000
3400	3400	3400
3334	3333	3333
4000	4000	5500

(continued)

(*continued*)

5000	5000	5000
4000	5000	5000
0	0	0
1	2	3
9000	5000	0
5000	1	9000
−1		

Output: The output serves as a report to the company's shipping dispatcher, who is required to sign off on each shipment prior to loading and dispatching the truck. All data should be printed: the individual and total weights, the resulting category (or an error message if the shipment is too large), and the shipping cost. The total number of shipments should appear at the end.

Optionals:

a. Assign to each shipment an identification number, beginning with 1. Print this number with the other information about the shipment.

b. Print the total cost for all shipments at the end of the report.

c. Assume trucks can travel 500 miles per day. Add another piece of data to each shipment order—the distance. Using the shipping cost as a daily rate, calculate and output the total for each shipment. (You have to modify the input data by adding the distance; leave the rest the same.)

d. Allow an arbitrary number of containers per shipment (you need a second trailer value and have to modify the format of your data).

e. If the shipment is heavier than the maximum weight, rather than issuing an error message, break it up into two or more shipments.

SUMMATION, STEPWISE REFINEMENT, AND NESTED LOOPS

SYNTAX CONCEPTS: defining a constant, nested loops

PROGRAMMING CONCEPTS: summing a series of terms, using a constant, reading a limit value, programming style

CONTROL STRUCTURES: nested loop

PROBLEM-SOLVING TECHNIQUES: stepwise refinement, top-down programming, structured programming

HOW TO READ CHAPTER 4

Chapter 5, Section 3 depends upon the material in sections 2 and 3; Chapter 5, Section 6 depends upon the material in Section 4.

OUTLINE:

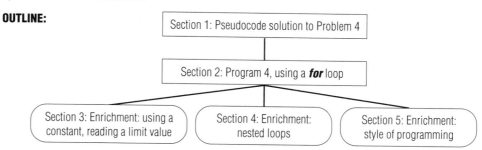

INTRODUCTION AND STATEMENT OF THE PROBLEM

This chapter introduces several key ideas. We solve a rather straightforward problem—finding the sum of the squares of the numbers from 1 to 30. This method of summing will be employed in later problems. Even more important are the programming and problem-solving techniques discussed in this chapter. The most essential is a method of attacking a problem called stepwise refinement or top-down programming. Most people working in the field agree that this method, possibly combined with others discussed later, offers the best approach to solving complex problems. After solving Problem 4, we introduce the nested **for** loop.

PROBLEM 4

The Sultan of RedValley has decided to give his daughter, who was born on the last day of June, a special birthday gift. On the first day of June, he will give her 1 (1 times 1) diamond; on the second day, he will give her 4 (2 times 2) diamonds; and so on, until the last day of June, when he will give her 30 times 30 diamonds. The sultan has asked you to determine the total number of diamonds. Write a C program to find the number.

SECTION 1   PSEUDOCODE FOR PROBLEM 4

In this section, we will develop an algorithm and a pseudocode solution to Problem 4. Much more important than the pseudocode is the method used to develop it. This method, called **top-down programming** or **stepwise refinement**, is perhaps the single most important problem-solving tool.

FIRST APPROXIMATION, USING PSEUDOCODE

The number of diamonds the sultan needs is 1^2 for the first day, 2^2 for the second day, to 30^2 for the last day. The total number is equal to the sum of the squares of the numbers from 1 to 30 (the sum of the first 30 squares). Therefore, the program must compute $1^2 + 2^2 + 3^2 + ... + 29^2 + 30^2$.

The first version of the pseudocode for Problem 4 is

find the sum of the first 30 squares
print the sum

THE METHOD OF STEPWISE REFINEMENT

Some people would argue that this pseudocode is slightly silly. They are right, but it does have a purpose. It gives us a starting point for the method of stepwise refinement.

We take this first crude pseudocode and break it up into individual steps. Once the sum has been computed, printing is easy. (Simple steps like this can be put aside while we refine the more complicated ones.) The only line we must refine is the computation itself (*find the sum of the first 30 squares*).

To compute the sum of the first 30 squares, we need an algorithm for summing a series of terms. A simpleminded approach is the following:

sumofthesquares = 1 * 1 + 2 * 2 + 3 * 3 + ... + 30 * 30;

Before we dismiss it, let's analyze this. First, we can't use the ellipsis (...) in C; a person knows how to fill in the dots, but the computer doesn't.

We could write out each of the 30 terms explicitly, but that has us doing most of the work and is certainly not the best method of solving the problem. We want to find a way to instruct the computer to generate and add the terms (first 1 * 1, then 2 * 2, etc.) without our having to write each one out individually.

DEVELOPING AN ALGORITHM FOR FINDING THE SUM OF A SERIES OF SQUARES

There is a simple algorithm for adding a series of terms. In our particular case, assume that we have already computed the sum of the first 29 squares. If we have this number, to get the sum of the first 30 squares, we can add 30 squared (30 * 30) to it:

the sum of the first 30 squares $=$ *the sum of the first 29 squares* $+$ 30^2

We still have a problem: to compute the sum of the first 29 squares. If we have the sum of the first 28 squares, we can get the sum of the first 29 squares by adding 29 * 29.

the sum of the first 29 squares $=$ *the sum of the first 28 squares* $+$ 29^2

Continuing this way, we eventually have

the sum of the first 2 squares $=$ *the sum of the first 1 squares* $+$ 2^2
the sum of the first 1 squares $=$ *the sum of the first 0 squares* $+$ 1^2

Finally, the sum of the first 0 squares is 0, of course:

the sum of the first 0 squares $=$ 0

Once we have this place to start, we can compute the sum of the first 1 squares, the sum of the first 2 squares, ..., the sum of the first 30 squares by using these formulas. Notice the order in which we add terms. We start from 0, then add 1 squared, then 2 squared, ..., then add 30 squared, even though the formulas started at 30 squared and went down.

Algorithm for Finding the Sum of a Series of Terms

To find the sum of a series of terms: Start a sum at 0. At each step, add one new term (in our case, first 1 squared, then 2 squared, ..., then 30 squared) to the sum of the terms already processed.

The method of adding a new term to an existing sum is a generalization of the relatively simple incrementing we used in earlier chapters. For example, in Chapter 2, we repeatedly added 0.5 to the old value of **gpa** to process values from 0 to 4.0; in Chapter 3, we repeatedly added 1 to the old value of **numemp** to count the number of employees. In this chapter, we are using a variable to hold the sum of an entire series of terms and repeatedly adding a new term to the sum. In later programs, we will use this same idea in many other situations.

FURTHER REFINEMENTS OF THE PSEUDOCODE

Let's be more precise about our algorithm. In other words, let's *refine* the solution further. Start by initializing a variable called ***sum*** to 0. At each step, add a new term to the running sum of what has been added so far. Here is the pseudocode for adding a series of terms and printing the sum:

```
sum = 0;
for each item from the first to the last
        compute a new term and add it to sum
        get the next item
print the sum
```

It is clear we have made significant progress. What does each new term look like? The first is 1 squared, the second is 2 squared, and the last is 30 squared. In general, each term is the next integer squared. This suggests that we use a variable *item* to represent the integer we are up to and *item* ∗ *item* as our new term. (Be sure you understand the difference between the counter *item* and the term *item* ∗ *item*.) The key step is to add the next term to the running sum of the squares so far. To express this, use the following statement:

```
sum = sum + item * item;
```

Before the first new term is added, initialize *item* to 1. Before each term is added to *sum*, test to see if another term should be added. To do this, ask if *item* is less than or equal to 30. If it is not, then we have summed all the terms and are ready to print the value of *sum*. This is leading us in a natural way toward a *for* loop. Recall that in a *for* loop, initialization, comparison, and incrementing are all specified in the header.

FINAL PSEUDOCODE AND REVIEW OF THE METHOD

Putting all the pieces together, we get our next refinement of the pseudocode:

```
sum = 0;
```
for each value of item *from 1 to 30*
```
        sum = sum + item * item;
```
print the sum

The phrasing for the header of the loop has changed slightly in each refinement of the pseudocode as the *for* loop structure emerged. In this section of pseudocode, we have a starting value for *item* (1), a limiting value (30), and a method for changing *item* each time through the loop. Therefore, we use *item* as the control variable or index of the loop. If we use a *for* loop, we do not need a separate step to initialize *item*; we do not need a separate step to compare *item* to the limit; and we do not need a separate step to increment *item* by 1. All these things are taken care of automatically. We make the *for* loop explicit in the next version.

```
sum = 0;
for (item = 1; item <= 30; item++)
        sum = sum + item * item;
```
print the sum

By this point, the last line, which you should certainly know how to translate into C, is the only one left in pseudocode. This means that we can write the C program from the pseudocode.

NOTE

All our previous programs have used some type of loop. However, this program is the first in which the loop as a single unit has a distinct purpose. In earlier programs, each pass through the loop accomplished something, and the loop repeated this series of calculations for different values. In this program, the entire loop computes a single value.

HIGHLIGHTS

Here is a summary of stepwise refinement:

◆ Start from a rough solution to the problem which has certain steps still vague.
◆ Ignore the clear steps and concentrate on the vague ones, breaking each down into further steps and making it more precise as you go.
◆ Continue the process for each new step until everything is clear.

As we have seen, pseudocode fits very nicely with stepwise refinement. Pseudocode can be refined and made more precise in a step-by-step fashion until all of it has been translated into C. In addition, the pseudocode used at one stage of the development process often serves as a comment at the next stage.

SELF-CHECK 4-1

1. In using stepwise refinement to write a program, what purpose does a rough solution to the problem serve? How do we refine that rough solution?
2. In order to sum a series of terms, what value initializes the variable which holds the sum? If we have to form a product of terms, to what value should that product be initialized?

SECTION 2 PROGRAM 4 (FIRST VERSION)

WRITING THE PROGRAM FROM THE PSEUDOCODE

It is time to write the program from the pseudocode. Theoretically, we could use any version, but it is clearly better to use the final refinement. If we have followed stepwise refinement, this last step of writing the program should be extremely easy because the pseudocode is so precise. As usual, the first few lines are standard, although they do not appear in the pseudocode.

```
/*
 * Program prog4a.c:
 * find the sum of the first 30 squares
 */
#include <stdio.h>
main()
{
```

Next is the declaration of variables. From the pseudocode, we see that ***item*** and ***sum*** must be declared. We know that each holds only integer values. In addition, we can see that ***sum*** is initialized to 0 in the first line of code. Thus, we can use the following declaration statement and also take care of initialization:

```
int item, sum = 0;
```

After the declaration is the action portion of the program. We write it from the last refinement of the pseudocode from Section 1.

```
for (item = 1; item <= 30; item++)
    sum += item * item;
printf("%d\n",sum);
```

Because the body of the *for* loop is a single assignment statement, it is not necessary to use another set of braces inside the loop. We have used the compound assignment operator += (see Chapter 2, Section 4) to simplify the assignment statement. If you recall, *sum += item * item* means that the new value for *sum* is set to the old value plus the term *item * item*.

Once we leave the *for* loop, *sum* holds the sum of the first 30 squares. At that point, all we have to do to is print the final answer. In the pseudocode, we simply printed *sum*. However, in the C program, we print a message with the value of *sum*. It is perfectly reasonable to make minor changes like this in the final program. Here is the *printf* we use:

```
printf("%d is the sum of the first 30 squares\n",sum);
```

COMPLETE PROGRAM 4 (FIRST VERSION)

Here is the complete program:

PROGRAM LISTING

```
/*
 * Program prog4a.c
 * find the sum of the first 30 squares
 */
#include <stdio.h>
main()
{
    int item,sum = 0;

    for (item = 1; item <= 30; item++)
        sum += item * item;
    printf("%d is the sum of the first 30 squares\n",sum);
}
```

TRACE OF PROGRAM 4

The program was quite simple once we refined the problem. Let's trace the program to make sure it is correct.

PROGRAM TRACE

◆ The variable *sum* is initialized to 0. When the *for* loop starts, *item* is given the value 1. Inside the loop, *item* *
item = 1 * 1 is added to *sum*, making it 0 + 1 = 1.

◆ Then *item* is increased by 1 to 2. This time through the loop, 2 * 2 = 4 is added to *sum*, giving 1 + 4 = 5.

◆ Then *item* increases to 3; we add 3 * 3 to *sum*, and so on.

◆ Eventually, *item* increases to 30, and we add 30 * 30 = 900 to *sum*, giving a total of 9455.[1]

◆ W e i n cr e a se *item* to 31, making the condition controlling the loop false.

◆ The loop ends, and we continue with the next statement in the program, which is the *printf*. This displays
the following line of output:

```
9455 is the sum of the first 30 squares
```

SELF-CHECK 4-2

1. When we translate pseudocode from the stepwise-refinement process into C, which
refinement(s) can be used?

2. Which refinement should be used?

3. In Program 4, why does each variable hold only integer values?

| SECTION 3 | **ENRICHMENT: OTHER VERSIONS OF PROGRAM 4—DEFINING A CONSTANT, READING DATA** |

In this section, we will give two other versions of Program 4 that make the program more
useful. One version introduces a constant and uses it to control the *for* loop. The other version reads in a data value to control the loop.

MODIFYING THE PROGRAM FOR A DIFFERENT NUMBER OF SQUARES

Although the program in Section 2 seems to work perfectly, there are certainly ways to
modify and improve it. What if the sultan's friends want to use the program? For example,
the Sultan of Swat might have a child who was born on May 27; he would need the sum of
the first 27 squares. We could not use Program 4 as currently written to compute that sum
since it works only for the first 30 squares.

We can modify the program to work for the first 27 squares by making a few simple
changes. The most obvious one is the limiting value in the *for* loop, which must be changed
from 30 to 27. A less obvious, but still important, change is the message at the end of the
program. Since we are computing the sum of the first 27 squares, we don't want a message say-

---

[1] See Exercise 16 for a simple way to compute the sum of the first 30 squares and check the answer from the program.

ing this is the sum of the first 30 squares. Similarly, we should change the comment at the top of the program.

Once we make these changes, the new version of the program (which we will call *prog4b.c*) looks like this:

```
/*
 * Program prog4b.c:
 * find the sum of the first 27 squares
 */
#include <stdio.h>
main()
{
    int item,sum = 0;

    for (item = 1; item <= 27; item++)
        sum += item * item;
    printf("%d is the sum of the first 27 squares\n",sum);
}
```

DEFINING A CONSTANT

This way of modifying the program is not bad, but other ways are considered more "elegant." The new methods also introduce some important C features.

It would be nice to isolate the material that is being changed (the number of squares we want to sum) from the rest of the program, which essentially stays the same. Rather than making a series of changes throughout the program, with the possibility of forgetting one or more, we would like to restrict what must be modified to just one portion.

There are many ways to do this, but one of the simplest introduces a **constant identifier** or just a **constant**. A constant identifier is like a variable because a constant is also an identifier that has a value; however, while the value of a variable can change in a program, the value of a constant is fixed. To use a constant in this program, we simply replace 30 or 27 or 35 or another particular value by a constant which we call *NUMBERTOSUM*. The definition for this constant gives it a value that can be used anywhere in the program. If we decide to change this value, we need only alter the definition for the constant.

STYLE WORKSHOP By convention, C programmers usually use capitals for the name of a constant; this distinguishes constants from variables, which typically have lowercase letters. Recall our discussion in Chapter 1, Section 2 about being consistent with identifier names.

General Form of a Constant Definition

The general form of a constant definition is this:

```
#define  name  value
```

Every time *name* occurs in a program, it is replaced by *value*.

EXAMPLE 4-1   The following program segment defines a constant called ***LIMIT*** and uses it in several comparisons:

```
#include <stdio.h>
#define LIMIT 50
main()
{
    int a,b;
    ...
    if (a > LIMIT)
        ...
    if (b > LIMIT)
        ...
}
```

When this program is compiled, every occurrence of ***LIMIT*** in the body of the program is replaced by the value 50. However, if ***LIMIT*** occurs as part of a larger word (***LIMITATION***) or in a literal string [e.g., ***printf("you reached the LIMIT")***], it will *not* be replaced.

USING A CONSTANT AS A LIMIT VALUE IN PROGRAM 4

In Program 4, we want to use the constant ***NUMBERTOSUM*** to stand for the number of squares to be summed. If we want to compute the sum of the first 30 squares, the definition for the constant ***NUMBERTOSUM*** is this:

```
#define NUMBERTOSUM 30
```

If we want to sum 27 squares, the definition is this:

```
#define NUMBERTOSUM 27
```

Any number of squares can be handled by using an appropriate constant—by changing the value after the identifier ***NUMBERTOSUM***.

Notice that the constant definition starts with a # sign, which is also used in specifying an include file. In fact, the definition of a constant is a compiler directive, just like ***#include***. Before the compiler translates the program into machine language, the preprocessor searches and physically replaces the identifier ***NUMBERTOSUM*** by the value 27 everywhere it occurs. However, when you look at the C source code, you still see the identifier, not the constant value.

In the rest of the program, we use ***NUMBERTOSUM*** instead of a particular value, say 30 or 27, as the limit of the *for* loop. In the same way, we can replace the ***printf*** at the end of the program by a slightly longer one which uses the value of the constant ***NUMBERTOSUM*** to produce a message indicating how many squares we have summed. In the ***printf*** below, the constant ***NUMBERTOSUM*** uses the format specification ***%d*** because we want its value to print as an integer.

```
printf("%d is the sum of the first %d squares\n",sum,NUMBERTOSUM);
```

As a simple example, if **NUMBERTOSUM** has the value 3, the sum of the first three squares is $1 + 4 + 9 = 14$. The **printf** produces a line of output which looks like this:

```
14 is the sum of the first 3 squares
```

SECOND VERSION OF PROGRAM 4 (USING A CONSTANT)

Here is the complete new version of the program (which we will call **prog4c.c**). Notice that we also changed the comment at the beginning.

 PROGRAM LISTING

```
/*
 * Program prog4c.c:
 * compute the sum of the first NUMBERTOSUM squares
 * with NUMBERTOSUM defined as a constant
 */
#include <stdio.h>
#define NUMBERTOSUM 30
main()
{
    int item,sum = 0;

    for (item = 1; item <= NUMBERTOSUM; item++)
        sum += item * item;
    printf("%d is the sum of the first %d squares\n",sum,NUMBERTOSUM);
}
```

If we decide to modify the program to handle the sum of the first 27 or 15 squares, all we need to change is the definition of the constant. Note that the value of a constant is fixed for each particular run of a program. However, we can change its value, recompile the program, and then rerun it with the new value.

Before we finish, we must note one restriction on the program. As we mentioned earlier, some versions of C have a limit of 32,767 on the value stored in a variable whose data type is **int**; in these versions, there is a limit on the number of squares that can be summed (see Exercise 14 for more details).

SELF-CHECK 4-3

1. What technique makes a constant identifier name look different from a variable identifier name?

2. What is the major advantage of using a constant in a program?

3. If we are using a constant, how can it be changed to some other value? Why is it necessary to recompile the program after changing the value of a constant?

READING THE NUMBER OF SQUARES FROM A LINE OF DATA

Actually, the program we have just presented is still too limited because the constant must be specified in advance. We must know which particular value the sultan wants to use as the number of squares to be summed. Once the program is written, it cannot be used for any other calculation without modifying it each time. As you write more programs, you will learn to appreciate the point we made at the end of Chapter 3: the last thing a programmer wants to do is modify a working program every time it runs. Anytime you change a program, even in the most elementary way, you introduce the possibility of an error.

As we noted in Chapter 3, a program can be made more flexible by reading in values (input data) as it is running. In this program, we can specify the number of squares to be summed as a variable (which we call *numbertosum*—note the lowercase letters since it is now a variable) rather than a constant. The same program, without any change whatsoever, can then sum any number of squares by reading in a data value for the variable *numbertosum* and letting this value control the *for* loop.

Let's make this idea more precise. First, we must declare *numbertosum* to be a variable with data type *int* rather than a constant. We must use a *scanf* to read in a value for the new variable *numbertosum*. As you know by now, whenever we ask the user to supply some data, there should be a prompt. We should print a message asking the program user to type in a number. The following two lines do these things:

```
printf("type in the number of squares to be summed> ");
scanf("%d",&numbertosum);
```

The changes for the rest of the program are shown below.

THIRD VERSION OF PROGRAM 4 (USING A LIMIT VALUE READ FROM A LINE OF DATA)

Here is the entire program (which we will call *prog4d.c*), rewritten so that it reads in a limit value:

🖥 PROGRAM LISTING

```
/*
 * Program prog4d.c:
 * compute the sum of the first numbertosum squares
 * with numbertosum read from a line of data
 */
#include <stdio.h>
main()
{
```
(continued)

(*continued*)

```
    int item,sum = 0;
    int numbertosum;

    printf("type in the number of squares to be summed> ");
    scanf("%d",&numbertosum);
    for (item = 1; item <= numbertosum; item++)
        sum += item * item;
    printf("%d is the sum of the first %d squares\n",sum,numbertosum);
}
```

Note that this version can be used to find the sum of any number of squares (within the limits of the value we can store in **sum**). The program doesn't have to be changed to find any particular number of squares. All we need to do is read this particular number in as a data value.

SELF-CHECK 4-4

1. What is the advantage of reading in a limit value as data? Will the program have to be changed if we want to use a different limit value?

2. If the limit value is read in, is it necessary to recompile the program each time we use a different data value?

3. If not, what has to be done to have the program read in a new data value?

SECTION 4 ## ENRICHMENT: USING A NESTED LOOP

To give us more practice with loops, this section focuses on one long example—a program to construct a multiplication table. As we develop and refine the pseudocode for this program, we will continue to use stepwise refinement. The solution will also introduce the nested *for* loop construction.

EXAMPLE 4-2

Write a program to produce a multiplication table that covers the numbers from 1 to 10. For example, one row of the table will show 3, followed by the first ten multiples of 3 (3 6 ... 27 30); another row will show 8, followed by the multiples of 8 (8 16 ... 72 80), and so on. Here are a few rows from the table:

1	1	2	3	4	5	6	7	8	9	10
2	2	4	6	8	10	12	14	16	18	20
3	3	6	9	12	15	18	21	24	27	30

FIRST VERSION OF THE PSEUDOCODE

Recall that stepwise refinement starts from a rough pseudocode solution, refines those pieces which are not precise, and continues until it is easy to translate everything into C. Here is a very rough solution to the problem:

> *print the headings at the top of the page*
> *construct each row of the multiplication table*
> *print the table*

REFINEMENT OF THE FIRST VERSION

This first approximation is oversimplified but provides a place to start. We need to elaborate on the top line *(print the headings at the top of the page)* and discuss how to print the table, but the most important thing is the middle statement *(construct each row of the multiplication table)* so we refine it next. Each row of the multiplication table consists of the multiples of a given number, for example, 3, which we will call the multiplicand. For each multiplicand ***m1*** from 1 to 10, we need a set of the multiples of ***m1***; more precisely, we need ***m1*** times each multiplier from 1 to 10—***m1*** times 1, ***m1*** times 2, ..., ***m1*** times 10. Using this idea, here is a refined pseudocode solution:

> *print the headings at the top of the page*
> *for each multiplicand* m1 *from 1 to 10*
>   *print a line of output showing*
>   m1 *times each multiplier from 1 to 10*

FORMAT OF THE OUTPUT

Now let's be precise about the format of the output. On the top of the page, we want to print headings. They consist of a message saying this is a multiplication table, an *X* standing for multiply, plus column headings of the multipliers from 1 to 10. Our answers will appear under them. For example, in row three (which contains the multiples of 3), the fifth column has the value 15 (which is 3×5). Here is the last version of the pseudocode:

> *print a line introducing the table*
> *print a line of multipliers from 1 to 10*
> *for each multiplicand* m1 *from 1 to 10*
>   *start a new line of output by printing* m1
>   *for each multiplier* m2 *from 1 to 10*
>   *print* m1 * m2 *under the heading for* m2

STARTING THE PROGRAM

To start, on the next page is the main comment which explains the purpose of the program, followed by the program header.

```
/*
 * Program mult.c:
 * construct a multiplication table,
 * showing the first 10 multiples of the numbers from 1 to 10
 */
#include <stdio.h>
main()
```

Now we must write the body of the program. From the pseudocode, we see that we need to declare two variables, *m1* and *m2*, of data type *int*. The declaration is followed by the calls to *printf* needed for the first few lines of output. (See Exercise 13 for a way to print the last line of the heading using a *for* loop.)

```
{
    int m1,m2;

    printf("This is a Multiplication Table, from 1 to 10\n");
    printf("\n");
    printf("  X    1    2    3    4    5    6    7    8    9   10\n");
```

The calls to *printf* produce the following lines of output:

```
This is a Multiplication Table, from 1 to 10

  X    1    2    3    4    5    6    7    8    9    10
```

PRINTING A ROW OF THE MULTIPLICATION TABLE FOR EACH MULTIPLICAND

Now we are ready to start producing the values in the chart. The next part of the pseudocode starts like this:

for each multiplicand m1 *from 1 to 10*

It is logical to use a *for* loop, with *m1* as the index, to translate this into C.

```
    for (m1 = 1; m1 <= 10; m1++)
```

Within the body of this loop, we want to start a new line of output by printing the value of *m1* on the left.

```
    printf("\n");
    printf("%3d",m1);
```

This should be followed by the multiples of *m1* (for each multiplier *m2* from 1 to 10). Each multiple should be aligned under its corresponding column heading.

When we printed the column headings, we mentioned each value from 1 to 10 explicitly in the call to *printf*. But now, to handle all the multipliers, we use another *for* loop. This second *for* loop has a second variable, called *m2*, as its index.

```
    for (m2 = 1; m2 <= 10; m2++)
        printf("%5d",m1 * m2);
printf("\n");
```

To handle the alignment, we print each multiple using a field width of five (see Chapter 3, Section 5). To make sure that each row of the multiplication table starts on a new line, we include *printf("\n")* as the first item within the body of the *m1* loop. The first time through the *m1* loop, this skips a line after the heading; on each succeeding pass, it inserts a blank line between rows of the chart to produce double spacing. We also include *printf("\n")* as the last item within the body of the *m1* loop. On each pass, this terminates the entire line of multiples of *m1*. Once the *m1* loop has been completed, we can end the entire program.

COMPLETE PROGRAM

Let's take a look at the entire program:

PROGRAM LISTING

```
/*
 * Program mult.c:
 * construct a multiplication table,
 * showing the first 10 multiples of the numbers from 1 to 10
 */
#include <stdio.h>
main()
{
    int m1,m2;

    printf("This is a Multiplication Table, from 1 to 10\n");
    printf("\n");
    printf("  X    1    2    3    4    5    6    7    8    9   10\n");
    /* nested loop to print the table */
    for (m1 = 1; m1 <= 10; m1++)  {
        printf("\n");
        printf("%3d",m1);
        for (m2 = 1; m2 <= 10; m2++)
            printf("%5d",m1 * m2);
        printf("\n");
    }
}
```

NESTED *for* LOOP

Note that we have one *for* loop contained within another. This construction is called a **nested *for* loop**. One *for* loop uses *m1* as its control variable, and the other has *m2*. The *for* loop for *m2* is completely contained within the one for *m1*, forming a nested loop. In this case, the body of the *m2* loop is a single statement. The body of the *m1* loop contains a number of statements which are inside the *m1* loop but before the *m2* loop; it contains the entire *m2* loop; and it contains a statement which is inside the *m1* loop but after the end of the *m2* loop (see Figure 4-1). When the program runs, the inner or *m2* loop will be executed completely every time we pass through the body of the outer or *m1* loop.

NOTE

When we discussed Program 4, we remarked that the *for* loop computed a single value. Similarly, we can analyze the loops in this program. The inner loop computes a row of the multiplication table. The outer loop repeats this process for a series of values. The nested loop as a whole computes a single object—a complete multiplication table.

TRACING THE PROGRAM

In order to study a nested loop, we will trace the entire program.

PROGRAM TRACE First, the computer prints the headings before either loop begins.

◆ The *m1* loop starts by setting *m1* to 1. Inside the body of the *m1* loop, we skip a line, then print the value of *m1* (1), ready to continue printing on the same line.

◆ At this point, the *m2* loop begins with *m2* initialized to 1. Inside the *m2* loop, we print 1 (since $1 * 1 = 1$).

◆ Then *m2* is incremented to 2 (with *m1* still at 1). On the same line, we print 2 ($1 * 2 = 2$).

◆ Then *m2* is incremented to 3, we print 3, and so on.

◆ Eventually, *m2* becomes 10, and we print 10. When *m2* becomes 11, the condition *m2 <= 10* is false, and the *m2* loop is completed.

The next statement to execute is *printf("\n")*, which ends this line of output. At this point, we have completed one entire pass through the *m1* loop and printed a line corresponding to the multiplication table for the multiplicand 1.

◆ We now start the next pass through the *m1* loop, this time with *m1* equal to 2. The first thing we do is skip a line because of the *printf("\n")* statement, which starts the body of the *m1* loop.

◆ Then we start a new *m2* loop, with *m2* beginning again at 1. Inside this *m2* loop, we run through all values of *m2*, from 1 to 10, each time printing the value of the multiplicand *m1* (which is 2) times the current value of *m2*.

FIGURE 4-1 A nested *for* loop

```
for (m1 = 1; ...) {
    ...
    for (m2 = 1; ...)
        printf(...);
    ...
}
```
m2 loop   *m1* loop

◆ Eventually, *m2* becomes 10, and we print 20. When *m2* becomes 11, the condition *m2<= 10* is false, terminating the *m2* loop.

After the *m2* loop, we execute the *printf("\n")* statement, which ends this line of output. It also completes the second pass through the *m1* loop and prints a multiplication table for the multiplicand 2, listing all the multiples from 2 * 1 to 2 * 10.

Similarly, we will have a pass through the outer loop for each remaining value of *m1*, first printing the multiples of 3, then those of 4, and finally the multiples of 10. Let's pick up the trace here: For the last multiple to be printed, *m2* also has the value 10, and we print 100. Then *m2* is incremented to 11, so we fall out of the *m2* loop. But then *m1* is incremented to 11, and the condition *m1 <= 10* is also false, so we fall out of the entire nested loop.

OUTPUT FROM THE PROGRAM

The output from this program looks like this:

```
This is a Multiplication Table, from 1 to 10

   X    1    2    3    4    5    6    7    8    9   10

   1    1    2    3    4    5    6    7    8    9   10

   2    2    4    6    8   10   12   14   16   18   20

   3    3    6    9   12   15   18   21   24   27   30

   4    4    8   12   16   20   24   28   32   36   40

   5    5   10   15   20   25   30   35   40   45   50

   6    6   12   18   24   30   36   42   48   54   60

   7    7   14   21   28   35   42   49   56   63   70

   8    8   16   24   32   40   48   56   64   72   80

   9    9   18   27   36   45   54   63   72   81   90

  10   10   20   30   40   50   60   70   80   90  100
```

SELF-CHECK 4-5

1. In a nested *for* loop, can the same control variable be used for both loops? Should it be used for both loops?

2. In this program, what is the body of the *m1* loop?

3. What is the body of the *m2* loop?

MORE ON THE NESTED *for* LOOP CONSTRUCTION

We have seen that one *for* loop can appear within the body of another, producing a nested construction. There are many ways to include statements within a nested loop. Let's investigate a number of possible positions where statements can appear and discuss how many times each statement is executed. The exact position of a particular statement will, of course, depend upon its role in a program.

STATEMENTS NOT INSIDE THE NESTED LOOP

In a nested loop, the inner loop is executed one complete time for each pass through the outer loop. Statements before the start of a nested *for* loop are executed once, before the entire nested loop begins; statements after the end of the loop are executed once, after the loop ends (see Figure 4-2).

As an example, we can print a heading at the start of the output and a second message after a computation is completed.

EXAMPLE 4-3 In the following code, each message prints one time, regardless of what statements appear within the loops. (In this example, we are assuming the *j* loop is the only statement within the body of the *i* loop; therefore, the *i* loop does not need braces.)

```
printf("this heading appears before the nested loop output");
for (i = 1; i <= 5; i++)
    for (j = 1; j <= 4; j++)

        ...
printf("this message appears after the nested loop output");
```

FIGURE 4-2   Statements before or after a nested *for* loop

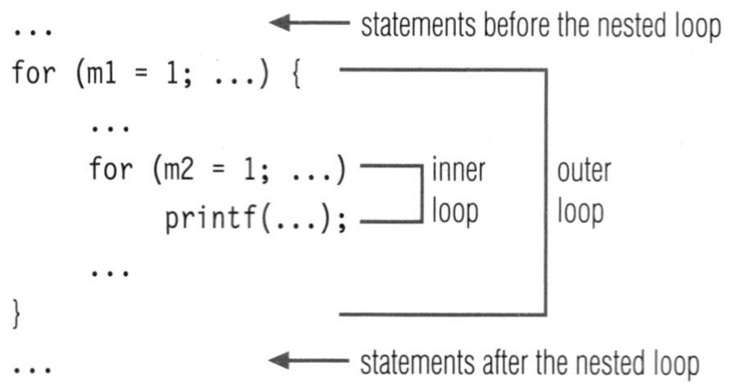

STATEMENTS BETWEEN THE TWO LOOPS

Any statement that comes before the inner loop starts or after it ends (like the ***printf*** in Example 4-4) is executed once for each pass through the outer loop. This includes the inner loop, which is executed completely each time through the outer loop (see Figure 4-3).

EXAMPLE 4-4

Here is an example that prints a blank line before the inner loop begins. The blank line is printed each time we go through the body of the outer (or *i*) loop; in this case, it prints five times. The entire inner (or *j*) loop executes five times, once for each value of *i*.

```
for (i = 1; i <= 5; i++)  {
    printf("\n");
    for (j = 1; j <= 4; j++)
        ...
}
```

STATEMENTS INSIDE BOTH LOOPS

A statement inside the body of the inner loop (which is also inside the outer loop) is executed on each pass through the inner loop. The number of times this statement executes is equal to the number of passes through the outer loop times the number of passes through the inner loop (see Figure 4-4). As an example, program ***mult.c*** has a statement which multiplies both ***for*** loop indices to produce an element of the multiplication chart. This statement is executed 100 (10×10) times.

FIGURE 4-3 Statements between the loops of a nested ***for*** loop

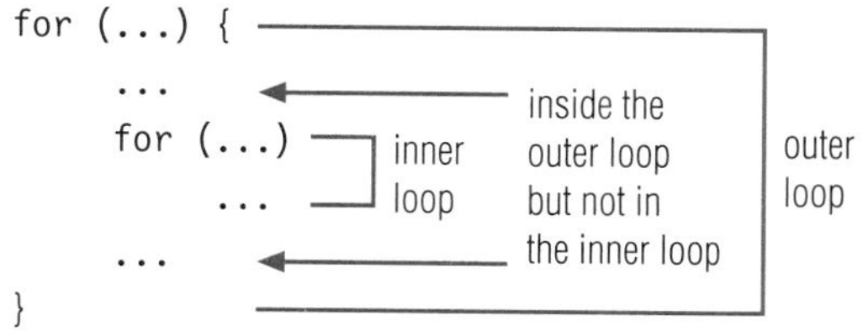

FIGURE 4-4 Statements inside both loops of a nested ***for*** loop

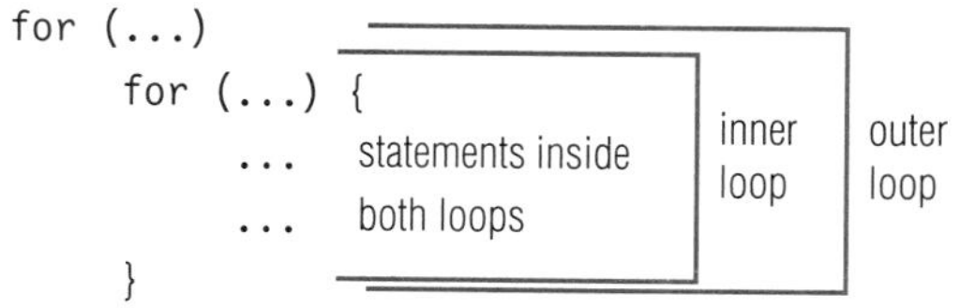

EXAMPLE 4-5

Here is an example showing a call to *printf* inside the inner loop. This statement is executed 5 * 4 = 20 times.

```
for (i = 1; i <= 5; i++)
    for (j = 1; j <= 4; j++)
        printf(...);
```

Finally, a *while* loop can replace either or both of the *for* loops in a nested loop (see Exercise 11).

SELF-CHECK 4-6

1. In Example 4-4, show exactly what value *i* has each time the call to *printf* is executed.

2. In Example 4-5, show exactly what values *i* and *j* have each time the call to *printf* is executed.

3. In a nested *for* loop, what happens after the condition controlling the inner loop becomes false? What happens after the condition controlling the outer loop becomes false?

SECTION 5   **ENRICHMENT: RECOMMENDATIONS ON STYLE; STRUCTURED PROGRAMMING**

In earlier chapters, we made some recommendations on style of programming. This section will summarize previous points and add new ideas. The general set of rules that we follow is called **structured programming**.

Originally, structured programming referred to the use of certain control structures and the avoidance of others (notably, the *goto* statement, which is discussed briefly in Chapter 6, Section 7). Structured programming emphasized these three control structures:

◆ sequence—executing statements in order;

◆ selection—choosing one of two alternatives; and

◆ iteration—repeating a series of instructions.

Nowadays, almost all programmers use preferred control structures, and the term *structured programming* usually refers to the style issues discussed in this section.

COMMENTS

Let's start by reviewing things we did to make program **mult.c** more readable. First, we included comments. It is better to include a few large comments rather than a bunch of short ones; a comment for every single C statement is counterproductive. For example, the lines below do not require comments; those shown are superfluous and make the program harder to read.

```
x = 0;        /* set x to 0 */
y = 1;        /* set y to 1 */
z = x + y;    /* add x and y together */
```

There should always be a comment at the beginning to describe the purpose of the program. After that point, include a comment if you think it will help a person reading the program to understand something. For example, in program *mult.c*, we put a comment before the nested loop. Because this program is so short, it is not necessary to include additional comments; in other programs, however, we might decide to include more. For example, if we were doing something complicated in the middle of a program, we would include a comment to explain the method, or if the program had a nested loop which needed more explanation, we would include a comment.

STYLE WORKSHOP Here are three suggestions on where to use comments:

◆ at the beginning of a program;

◆ at the start of each major unit of a program (a nested loop as in *mult.c* or a function as discussed in the next chapter); or

◆ whenever it is helpful to explain a technique or method.

Regardless of where a comment is located, several things make it more readable. A large comment can be placed on two or more lines instead of one long line, and the comment can be written in a way that draws attention to it. The object is to make the comment more visible to a person glancing over the program. Obviously, you should make sure your comment says something worthwhile.[2]

MNEMONIC NAMES

In our first few programs, we were careful to use meaningful or mnemonic names for identifiers. For example, in Program 1, we called the variables **number** and **sqnumber**; in Program 2, we used **gpa** and **result** rather than simply **x** and **y**; in Program 3, we chose **hours**, **rate**, and **pay**. In *mult.c*, **m1** and **m2**, although not as mnemonic as some of our other choices, were enough to describe the purpose of the variables. As an additional aid to the reader, the comment at the top of the main program or a function can list each variable and its use, or this can be done in the declaration statement.

EXAMPLE 4-6 We can use the following declaration in *mult.c*:

```
int m1;                    /* the multiplicand, numbers from 1 to 10 */
int m2;                    /* the multiplier, numbers from 1 to 10   */
```

These comments reinforce a point we made in Chapter 1. Every variable in a program should serve a specific purpose. Mentioning this purpose in a comment helps you understand the variable's role in your program. Of course, these detailed comments should supplement, rather than replace, mnemonic names. Don't use sloppy names like **x** and **y** just because you have comments explaining their roles.

---

[2]It should be possible to read only the comments and get some understanding of how the program works; it should also be possible to read the program without the comments getting in the way.

Some programmers prefer to be consistent in their variable names. For example, they may always use *i* or *j* as the index of a *for* loop (or *chr* as the name of a variable which holds characters), even though these are not very useful names. This is largely a matter of taste, and you can experiment as you develop your own programming style.

SPACING AND INDENTATION

The physical layout of a program is important for clarity. Remember our previous warning against writing more than one statement per line. The only possible exception (and this should be avoided) is two or more very short assignment statements on the same line. In addition, we suggest that you purposely include blank lines in your program to separate and draw attention to things. For example, a comment could be surrounded by blank space to set it off from code. Any statement or group of statements (declarations) can be accented this way. Blank lines are ignored by the compiler but are very helpful to the reader.

Statements in a program should be indented consistently. For example, the statements inside a *for* or a *while* loop should be indented. If a program uses the *if-else* construction, the keywords *if* and *else* should be aligned, and so on.

Although the advantage in following these rules is slight in a short program, a large program written this way is much easier to follow. The precise details of where to put a blank line and how to align statements are not important. What is important is clarity.

READABLE OUTPUT

Often a programmer devotes a lot of time to making sure that a program works perfectly but forgets about the output. Most people look at the output, not the program. No matter how clear the code is, if the output is a meaningless stream of numbers, the program is useless.

In addition to a comment inside the program, be sure to include headings or messages in the output to explain the various values. For example, if a program finds the sum of the first 30 squares, this should be mentioned in the output. If the program computes an employee's weekly pay, this fact should be part of the output. If a program evaluates a mathematical formula, it should print a message saying this. (Perhaps even the formula can be printed if it is relevant to the results.) Some programmers go to the opposite extreme and print everything (even a copy of the prompts requesting interactive input or output). This makes it hard for the reader to see what is important, but it is better to have an extra line of output than omit a necessary one.

DEBUG PRINTOUT

In Chapter 2, Section 6, we gave some recommendations on debugging a program. There is an important concept, called **debug printout**, that we did not mention at that time. If a program is not working, it is helpful to insert a few extra print statements at key points. These extra output statements give the programmer further information about executing the program—the values of intermediate calculations, the status of loop control variables, or the results of function calls.

In the multiplication table program, suppose we want to make sure that all possible multiplications are being produced. It may be helpful to print the values of *m1* and *m2* inside the nested *for* loop.

EXAMPLE 4-7 Here is some code that includes debug printout:

```
/* nested loop to print the table */
for (m1 = 1; m1 <= 10; m1++)  {
    printf("\n");
    printf("%3d",m1);
    for (m2 = 1; m2 <= 10; m2++)  {
        printf("m1 and m2 are: %d %d",m1,m2);        /* debug printout */
        printf("%5d",m1 * m2);
    }
    printf("\n");
}
```

Let's consider one last example from Program 4 (calculating the sum of the squares of the numbers from 1 to 30). To check that the calculation is correct, we can print the value of *sum* each time through the loop instead of just once at the end.

EXAMPLE 4-8 Here is the *for* loop from the first version of Program 4 rewritten with the extra debug printout statements:

```
printf("before the loop\n");
for (item = 1; item <= 30; item++)  {
    sum += item * item;
    printf("after %d terms, the sum is %d\n",item,sum);
}
printf("\n\nafter the loop the final sum is %d\n",sum);
```

These suggestions show that debug printout gives the programmer extra information to eliminate programming bugs. In most cases, the more debug printout you include, the easier it is to locate a bug. Of course, you usually remove the statements that generate the debug printout once the error has been found and corrected. Or you may decide to include the "quick and dirty" debug printout statements, cleaned up a little, as part of the final output from the program.

AVOID CLEVER CODE

In the 1950s and 1960s, when computing was still in its infancy, programmers vied with each other to produce "clever code" to solve a problem in a tricky or unexpected way. Believe it or not, a program incomprehensible to anyone else was considered to be "better" than an easily understood one.

As the field has matured, this attitude has been replaced by an emphasis on readability and clarity. However, some programmers, especially if they are trying to impress someone, still use a tricky or clever style.

EXAMPLE 4-9   Can you figure out what the code below is designed to do?

```
int x,y,z,w;
...
if (x > y)
      z = 0;
else
      z = y - x;
w = x + z;
```

It computes the larger of the two numbers x and y. See if you can determine how.

Naturally, a program using tricks like this is almost impossible to debug or modify by anyone other than the original programmer (even he or she may not remember how things work after a period of time).

STYLE WORKSHOP Avoid tricks. If you have two ways of doing something, a clear, but slightly less efficient, method and a tricky one, it is almost always better to use the clear version. A programmer's time is much more valuable than a machine's.

DOCUMENTATION

A program written in a good style is still almost worthless unless people can use it. The information required to use a program is called **documentation**. In the business or commercial world, a program is not considered complete until it has documentation. The following information should be included in a program's documentation:

◆   a statement of what problem the program is designed to solve;

◆   pseudocode (or some other outline of how the program works);

◆   a listing of the program, including a good set of comments;

◆   a set of instructions with any special information needed to run the program (e.g., a special format for the data); and

◆   a complete set of test cases (trying all possible paths in the program), together with sample output.

STYLE WORKSHOP As programs grow larger and larger, documentation becomes even more crucial. These rules for developing good programming style are by no means complete. There is no universal agreement in the field of programming on what constitutes good style, just as there is none in English. However, most programmers would agree with our recommendations. There is another advantage to following these rules on style: A program which obeys them is almost always easier to debug than one that doesn't follow consistent rules.

SELF-CHECK 4-7

1.   What is structured programming?

2.   What things improve the physical appearance of a program?

3.   What are the major parts of the documentation accompanying a program?

SUMMARY

STEPWISE REFINEMENT AND TOP-DOWN PROGRAMMING

1. Stepwise refinement and top-down programming are useful in solving a complex problem. Stepwise refinement starts with pseudocode that may be only a rough approximation of the final solution of the problem. Any steps that are vague are subdivided and made more precise as the solution is refined. This process is repeated until all steps are clear and can be translated easily into C.

2. When refining the solution to a problem by top-down programming, questions of detail can be postponed until overall structural decisions have been resolved. Pseudocode shows the successive refinements.

SUMMING A SERIES OF TERMS

3. A series of values or terms of a formula can be added together by the following algorithm: *Initialize a sum to 0; each time through a loop, add a new term to the sum; repeat the loop until all terms have been added to the running total. At the end of the loop, this total is the sum of the entire series of terms.*

4. In previous chapters, the purpose of a loop has been to repeat a series of calculations several times. In Program 4, the entire **for** loop has a single purpose—to compute the sum of a series of terms. Similarly, in **mult.c**, the purpose of the nested loop is to compute a multiplication table.

CONSTANTS

5. The value of a variable can change as a program is executing. However, the value of a constant is fixed by a definition. The general form of the definition for a constant is

   `#define name value`

6. The compiler replaces every occurrence of the identifier *name* with the value *value*. For example, in the program using these constant definitions, every occurrence of **NUMB** is replaced by the value 7, while **EPSILON** is replaced by 0.00001.

   ```
   #define NUMB 7
   #define EPSILON 0.00001
   ```

READING IN A LIMIT VALUE

7. The limit value controlling the number of times a **for** loop is executed can be read in from a set of data. Reading various values in (as opposed to using a constant to control the loop) gives the program more flexibility because the same program can be used to compute several different results.

NESTED *for* LOOPS

8. One **for** loop can be completely contained or nested within another. Each pass through the outer loop leads to a complete execution of the inner loop. When the program finishes a complete pass through the inner loop, it starts a second pass through the outer loop, and so on. This process continues until completion of the last pass through the outer loop.

9. Any statement that appears before the nested loop begins or after it ends is executed once. Any statement which is inside the outer loop but not contained in the inner loop is executed once for each pass through the outer loop. Any statement which is inside the inner loop is executed once for each pass through the inner loop. The entire inner loop is executed once for each pass through the outer loop.

10. This example illustrates some of these ideas:

```
int count;
int i,j;

printf("counts for each pass\n");
for (i = 1; i <= 10; i++)  {
    count = 0;
    for (j = 1; j <= 5; j++)
        count++;
```
```
    printf("%d for pass %d\n",count,i);
}
printf("finished processing\n");
```

The first and last calls to *printf* are done once; the initialization of **count** and the printout of **count** and *i* are each done ten times; the increment of **count** is done 10 * 5 = 50 times.

STRUCTURED PROGRAMMING

11. Structured programming is the name of the currently accepted style of programming. Structured programming encourages the use of comments, meaningful identifier names, consistent spacing, readable output, and proper documentation. It discourages tricky code.

12. Comments are perhaps the single most important aspect of good style. They help someone to read the program. A person should be able to read the comments without getting bogged down in the details of a program and read the program without being annoyed by the comments.

13. Any good program must be accompanied by documentation explaining its use. This documentation can include a statement of the problem, pseudocode, a program listing with comments, a set of instructions for using the program, and sample output from a complete set of test data.

EXERCISES

TRACING EXERCISES

1. For each of these program segments, show what is printed. All variables have data type *int*.

   Answer part (c) three times. First, assume that the set of data consists of the two numbers 3 5; then answer the question assuming that the set of data is 1 6; then assume it is 5 5.

   a.
   ```
   sum = 0;
   for (i = 1; i<= 10; i++)
       sum += i;
   printf("the sum is %d\n",sum);
   ```

   b.
   ```
   count = 0;
   for (i = 1; i <= 10; i++)
       count++;
   printf("the count is %d\n", count);
   ```

   c.
   ```
   scanf("%d %d",&a,&b);
   sum = 0;
   for (i = a; i <= b; i++)
       sum += i;
   printf("from %d to %d the sum is %d\n",a,b,sum);
   ```

2. Show exactly what is printed by the following program segment. All variables have data type *int*.

   ```
   sign = 1;
   sum1 = 0;
   sum2 = 0;
   for (i = 1; i <= 7; i++)  {
   ```

```
        sum1 -= sign * i;
        sum2 += sign * i * i;
        sign *= -1;
        printf("%d  %d  %d  %d\n",i,sum1,sum2,sign);
    }
    printf("at the end %d  %d  %d  %d\n",i,sum1,sum2,sign);
```

3. Show what is printed by the following program:

```
#include <stdio.h>
main()
{
    int k,sign = 1,x = 5,y = 1;

    for (k = 1; k <= 5; k++)  {
        x = y - sign * y;
        y++;
        sign *= -1;
        printf("%d  %d  %d  %d\n",k,x,y,sign);
    }
    printf("%d  %d  %d  %d\n",k,x,y,sign);
}
```

4. Show what is printed by each of the following:

    a.
```
    int i,j,n;
      ...
    for (i = 1; i <= 4; i++)
        for (j = 1; j <= 3; j++) {
            n = 10 * i + j;
            printf("%d %d %d\n",i,j,n);
        }
    printf("done\n");
```

    b.
```
    int i,j,n;
      ...
    for (i = 1; i <= 4; i++)  {
        for (j = 1; j <= 3; j++)  {
            n = 10 * i + j;
            printf("%d %d %d",i,j,n);
        }
        printf("\n\n");
    }
    printf("done\n");
```

5. Show what is printed by the following program:

```
#include <stdio.h>
#define LIMIT 10
main()
{
    int i,j,sum;
```

(continued)

(*continued*)

```
for (i = 1; i <= LIMIT; i++)  {
    sum = 0;
    for (j = 1; j <= i; j++)
        sum += j;
    printf("When i equals %d, the sum is %d\n",i,sum);
}
}
```

On the line defining the constant **LIMIT**, replace 10 by each of the following and repeat the program:

a.   5   b.   7   c.   11   d.   12

6. What is a good name for a variable whose purpose is to

   a.   hold the numbers from 1 to 100?
   b.   count how many negative numbers are read in?
   c.   hold a four-digit student ID number?
   d.   hold the average of a series of test scores?
   e.   hold the sales of a company for January?

7. In each of the following, what is wrong with the indenting and aligning? Fix each one.

   a. ```
for (i = 1; i <= 4; i++)
    sum = ...
    printf(...);
```
   b.  ```
for (i = 1; i <= 4; i++)
    sum = ...
    printf(...);
```

   c. ```
if (hours < 40) pay = hours * rate;
    else pay = hours * rate + (hours - 40) * rate * 0.5;
```

   d.  ```
for (row = 1; row <= 5; row++)  {
col = 1;
while (col <= 4)  {
printf("%d %d\n",row,col);
col++;
}
}
```

   e. ```
if (x < 0) printf("yes\n"); else printf("no\n");
```

## MODIFICATIONS OF PROGRAM 4

8.  a.   Write a loop to find the sum of the numbers from 1 to 100.
    b.   Write a loop to find the sum of the even numbers from 10 to 200.
    c.   Write a loop to find the sum of the cubes of the numbers from 1 to 10.

9.  Rewrite the loops in Exercise 8 using constants to control them.

10. There is still some trouble with the solution to Problem 4 at the end of Section 3. Assume that we want to compute the sum of the first 7 squares, the sum of the first 5 squares, the sum of the first 27 squares, and the sum of the first 8 squares. It seems that we have to run the program four times, each one with a new value for the number of squares (*n*) to be summed. However, there is a better solution.
```

Modify the program so that, after reading and processing completely one particular value for **n**, it reads another number representing a new value for **n** and starts all over again. For example, the set of data may contain 8 12 7. This directs the program to read 8 into **n** and find the sum of the first 8 squares; then the program goes back to the beginning (you must decide where), reads 12, and computes the sum of the first 12 squares; then it reads 7 and repeats the entire process for the first 7 squares. (If one of the **n** values you use is greater than 40, see Exercise 15.)

You must also provide a way to detect the end of data (perhaps a trailer value such as −1). Note that this program contains two loops, one within the other. The inner loop finds the sum of the first **n** squares; the outer loop processes several values of **n**.

11. Rewrite Program 4 using a **while** instead of a **for** loop. Rewrite Program 4 without using any loops (by taking care of each number individually). Compare the three versions. Which is the easiest to understand? Which is the longest? Which is the easiest to modify?

12. Repeat Exercise 11 for the multiplication table program in Section 4. That is, compare the original version using one **for** loop inside another to versions which use a **while** loop for the inner, outer, or both loops.

13. Modify the column headings in the multiplication table program so that the list of multipliers from 1 to 10 is printed with a **for** loop instead of by mentioning each number explicitly.

ANALYSIS EXERCISES

14. In arithmetic, the sum of a series of integer terms is always an integer, regardless of how many terms are added together. In C, this may not always be true because of the restrictions on the size of a variable of type **int**. (This value depends upon your particular compiler.)

   a. If you sum the first 20 squares, will each term be less than the maximum integer value? Will the sum of the terms be less than this maximum?

   b. If you sum the first 30 squares, will each term be less than the maximum? Will the sum of the terms be less?

   c. If you sum the first 5000 squares, will each term be less than the maximum? Will the sum of the terms be less?

   d. See if you can determine the maximum number of squares that can be summed before the sum is more than the maximum integer value. (*Suggestion:* Write a program to solve this problem.)

   e. See if you can determine the largest number whose square is less than the maximum. Why is this much easier than part (d)?

15. In addition to data type **int**, C has two other integer data types called **long int** (abbreviated as **long**) and **short int** (abbreviated as **short**).

   a. On your system, what is the largest value that can be stored in a variable of type **long**? Repeat Exercise 14 for a variable of this data type.

   b. Do the same for type **short**.

16. There is a simple mathematical formula to check the calculations obtained by the versions of Program 4 in this chapter. The sum of the first **n** squares is given by the expression:

$$1^2 + 2^2 + \ldots + n^2 = n * (n + 1) * (2 * n + 1) / 6$$

For example, if **n** is 2, then $1 * 1 + 2 * 2 = 5$, and $2 * 3 * 5 / 6 = 5$ as well.

Modify the version of the program at the end of Section 3 (*prog4c.c*) so that it computes a check on the sum. After adding up the first *n* squares, the program should set a variable called *check* to *n * (n+1) * (2n+1) / 6*. The program should then compare *sum* to *check* and print a message explaining whether they agree. [*Warning:* If you are computing the sum of a large number of squares (e.g., *n* > 40), the variables *sum* and *check* may hold values larger than the maximum (see Exercise 14). Therefore, you may want to change these variables to data type *long* or *double* rather than *int*.]

17. This exercise explores what can occur in a nested *for* loop when both loops use the same name for the loop control variable. In each part, show what is printed by inserting the nested *for* loop into the basic program below. Then rewrite each part so that the inner loop uses a new control variable, *j*. (What else must be done to the program?)

```
#include <stdio.h>
main()
{
    int i;

    /* insert nested for loop here */

}
```

a.   ```
for (i = 1; i <= 5; i++)
    for (i = 1; i <= 5; i++)
        printf("i is: %d\n",i);
```

b.   ```
for (i = 1; i <= 5; i++)
    for (i = 4; i <= 7; i++)
        printf("i is: %d\n",i);
```

c.   ```
for (i = 4; i <= 7; i++)
    for (i = 1; i <= 5; i++)
        printf("i is: %d\n",i);
```

## PROGRAMMING PROJECTS

18. a.   Write a program to do the following: Read in a series of numbers from a set of data. Print each number as you read it in. When the sum of the numbers becomes 100 or more, print a message saying that a total of 100 has been reached and stop processing. However, if you read in the number 17 before reaching 100, print a message giving the sum so far and terminate the program at that point.

   b.   Modify the program from part (a) so that it also prints the number of values used to obtain the sum. Do this for either case—whether or not you actually reach 100.

19. Write a program which reads in a number *n* from the data, then computes the sum of the first *n* integers—that is, $1 + 2 + ... + n$. As a check, this sum should be *n(n+1)/2*. After processing the first value of *n*, the program should go back to read in a new value and repeat the calculation. Repeat the entire process until the set of data is exhausted.

20. Write a program that reads in a number *n* from the data, then computes the sum of the first *n* cubes, $1^3 + 2^3 + ... + n^3$. Continue the processing until the set of data is exhausted. As a check, the sum should be *(n * (n+1)/2)²*. (Also see Exercise 14.)
```

21. Write a program that reads in two numbers, *n* and *k*, from the data, then computes the sum of the first *n* powers of *k*. For example, if *k* is 2, it computes the sum of the first *n* squares, but if *k* is 3, it computes the sum of the first *n* cubes. Is there a simple check for this problem?

22. Write a program that reads in *n* from the data, then computes the sum of the first *n* even numbers and the sum of the first *n* odd numbers. For example, if *n* is 3, then it computes $2 + 4 + 6 = 12$ as the sum of the first three even numbers, and $1 + 3 + 5 = 9$ as the sum of the first three odd numbers. The checks are *n * (n+1)* for the sum of the first *n* even numbers, and *n * n* for the sum of the first *n* odd numbers. Repeat the calculations for a series of values of *n*.

    Here is a possible method: In the program, use two separate loops, one for even numbers and the other for odd. In each loop, you have to be careful to skip over odd when adding even (and even when adding odd).

23. Write a program to read in two numbers, *x* and *n*, and then compute the sum of this geometric progression:

    $$1 + x + x^2 + x^3 + \ldots + x^n$$

    For example, if *n* is 3 and *x* is 5, then the program computes $1 + 5 + 25 + 125$. Print *x*, *n*, the sum, and the check given here, together with appropriate messages. The check for the sum is

    $$\frac{x^{n+1} - 1}{x - 1} \qquad \text{(the check cannot be used if } x \text{ is 1)}$$

    Repeat the process for a series of numbers.

24. Modify the program from Exercise 23 to do some error checking. For example, the formula does not make sense for negative exponents—if *n* is less than 0. Have your program print an error message if *n* < 0, then go back and read in the next pair of numbers without computing the sum. Are any values of *x* also illegal? If so, test for them, too.

25. a. Introduce error checking into some of the earlier exercises. For example, if we are computing the sum of the first *n* cubes, what constitutes bad data? If you find bad data, print a message, then go on to the next value.

    b. Do the same for some of the exercises from Chapter 3. (What would be bad data in a payroll program?)

26. a. Write a program to do the following: For each number *n* from 1 to 40, find the sum of the squares of the numbers from 1 to *n*. That is, compute *1*1 + ... + n*n* (see Exercise 16 for a way to check this calculation).

    b. Modify your program from part (a) so that it computes the sum of the cubes of the numbers from 1 to *n*. (Exercise 20 has a check.)

27. The Fibonacci series consists of the numbers 1, 1, 2, 3, 5, 8, 13, ... The first two terms are both 1; thereafter, each term is the sum of the two previous terms ($8 = 3 + 5, 13 = 5 + 8$).

    Write a program to read in a value *n*, then compute and print the values of the first *n* terms of the Fibonacci series. (*Suggestion:* You have to keep track of the last term and the next-to-last term and update them at the appropriate time.)

28. The factorial of a number *n*, written *n!*, is defined as follows:

    n! = 1 * 2 * ... * (n - 1) * n   (and 0! = 1)

    For example, $5! = 1 * 2 * 3 * 4 * 5 = 120$; $3! = 1 * 2 * 3 = 6$.

a. Write a program to do the following: Read in a number *n*, then compute *n!*. [*Suggestion:* Use a *for* loop to compute the product (just as we used a *for* loop to compute a sum) with an appropriate initialization and multiplication step.]

b. Write a program that computes a table of the numbers from 1 to *n*, together with the factorial of each number. For example, if *n* is 7, then it should print (each pair on a new line)

1	1	2	2	3	6	4	24	5	120	6	720	7	5040

c. Modify your program from part (a) so that it reads in a series of values for *n* and computes *n!* for each value (use a negative value as a trailer).

29. Compare the efficiency of the programs from Exercise 28, parts (b) and (c). (First, you have to specify some way of measuring program efficiency. For example, you can see which program executes fewer instructions.) If you want to compute a large number of consecutive factorial values, which is the more efficient method? If you only want one or two widely spaced factorial values, which is more efficient?

30. a. One of the sultan's friends, the Lord of Flatbush, is relatively poor. He has only 1000 diamonds to give to his child. Write a program which determines the maximum number of days on which the Lord of Flatbush can distribute diamonds (assuming that he gives 1 * 1 on the first day, 2 * 2 on the second day, and so on).

b. Write a program which starts by asking the Lord of Flatbush exactly how many diamonds he has. Then the program determines how many days he can distribute them.

31. The Sultan of RedValley wants to give his son, who was born on the last day of April, a special birthday present, lasting through the entire month. On the first day, he wants to give his son one diamond. On the second day, two diamonds, then four on the next day, and so on. Each day he gives twice as many diamonds as the day before.

a. Write a program to print the number of diamonds given on each day in April. (*Suggestion:* Can a variable of type *int* hold the number of diamonds? See exercises 14 and 15.)

b. Modify the program from part (a) so that, on each day, it also prints the total number of diamonds given so far.

32. Combine the program from Exercise 31 with the original one for Problem 4. On each day of the month, print how many diamonds the son is getting, how many the daughter is getting, and the total number received by each child so far.

33. This exercise asks you to write a series of programs to help a scientist analyze the results of some laboratory experiments.

a. The first program should do the following: Read in ten values, each representing the weight of a mouse in grams (e.g., 145.34 or 421.23). Find the average of the ten readings.

b. Modify the program from part (a) so that it reads in two values for each mouse, the weights before and after it is fed a special diet. For each mouse, find how much weight it has gained or lost. Find the average weight before and after the diet.

c. Modify the program from part (b) so that it also prints how many mice gained weight, how many lost weight, and how many stayed the same.

34. Modify the program from Exercise 33 part (c) so that the experiment is repeated for a series of mice (not necessarily ten) until a negative value is entered for a weight. For example, if the experiment has been conducted on eight mice, there will be a total of 16 weight readings, followed by a negative value to signal the end of the set of data.

35. a. Modify the program from Exercise 33 part (c) so that the experiment is repeated for five groups of mice with ten readings in each group. After processing each group of ten, print what is requested in Exercise 33. After processing all five groups, print the overall average, plus the total number of mice which gained weight, the total number which lost weight, and the total number which stayed the same.

   b. The program in part (a) uses five groups of ten readings. Modify it to read in groups of ten until a negative value is entered for the first weight in the group. At that point, print the totals.

36. A team of social scientists conducts an experiment in which they ask a group of 100 people to estimate the average family income in their community. Write a program to analyze the results of the survey. First, read in a value representing the actual average family income in the community (e.g., 23456.67). Then read in a series of 100 values, representing the estimates. For each estimate, compute how far it is either above or below the actual value. Compute the average of the estimates. Compute how far the average is from the actual value.

37. Modify the program from Exercise 36 so that it also determines which estimate is closest to the average and which one is farthest. (*Hint:* To do this, you need an algorithm to determine the largest or smallest value in a group of numbers.)

FUNCTIONS

SYNTAX CONCEPTS: functions, parameters, function definition, ***return*** statement, function declaration or prototype, type ***void***, parameters which are pointers

PROGRAMMING CONCEPTS: driver program

CONTROL STRUCTURES: function call and return, void function, parameterless function

PROBLEM-SOLVING TECHNIQUES: using functions, shifting details to functions, modular programming, *I-P-O* comments

HOW TO READ CHAPTER 5

Sections 1, 2, and 4 are the crucial ones in this chapter. It is possible to cover any of sections 4 to 8 without doing Section 3. The material on parameters which are pointers in Section 8 appears again in Chapter 8, where it is explained more fully.

OUTLINE:

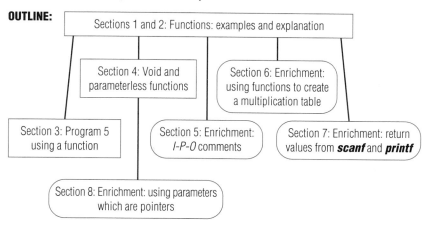

INTRODUCTION AND STATEMENT OF THE PROBLEM

The problem for this chapter should look familiar since Problem 5 is identical to the last version of Problem 4 in Chapter 4. Instead of concentrating on a new problem, we are purposely spending most of this chapter introducing an extremely powerful C feature, called a function subprogram or just a function. Then we will use a function to solve Problem 5. A number of other sections supply more details about functions and how to use them.

PROBLEM 5

Write a C program to read in a data value **n**. Then find the sum of the squares of the numbers from 1 to **n** (the sum of the first **n** squares). Print the sum of the squares.

SECTION 1 FUNCTION SUBPROGRAMS

This section introduces perhaps the single most important feature of the C language: functions. This feature is used over and over in later programs. In Section 1, we begin by reviewing and expanding our knowledge of standard library functions like *sqrt*.

THE CONCEPT OF A FUNCTION (MODULE)

In Chapter 4, we gave a number of versions or modifications of Program 4. In this chapter, there is one last modification: rewriting the program (now called Program 5) using a **function** or a **function subprogram**.[1] Before we actually rewrite Program 5, we need to discuss functions.

Each version of Program 4 centered around a series of instructions to calculate the sum of a given number of squares. A series of instructions with one specific purpose is called a **module**. A module can be written directly in the main program, as in Chapter 4, but there is another method. We can write a function that consists of the module. Then, in the main body of the program, a single instruction (known as the **call to the function**) utilizes this function in a particular situation.

Another example is the portion of Program 3 which computes and prints payroll information for a single employee. The details of the payroll calculation (base pay, taxes, etc.) could be computed in one module, and the details of the printout handled in another. The main body of the program would contain a call to the calculation function and one to the printout function (see Figure 5-1).

The concept of using modules is actually very widespread. Just about any large program can be broken up into a series of well-defined tasks or modules. Then a separate function can be written for each. After you have written a few larger programs, you will find they tend to use the same little pieces over again. For example, once you have written a module to read in a set of data, this module can be saved for reuse in other programs. If you have a module to print the results of a series of calculations, you may be able to reuse it, too. A large program can be divided into a series of reusable modules (this process is called **modularization**). Instead of starting from scratch to solve each problem, the programmer can plug in one or more previously written modules. In a business or commercial environment, once a program has been broken down, different programmers can work on separate modules, then combine their little pieces to solve the entire problem. The actual implementation of these ideas about separate compilation is beyond your current programming abilities (it is usually covered in a second programming course), but you can start to think in these terms.

---

[1]The word **subroutine** or simply **routine** is sometimes used as a synonym for subprogram or function. Some languages divide subprograms into two categories: functions and subroutines (as in Fortran) or functions and procedures (as in Pascal). But in C, all subprograms are functions.

FIGURE 5-1 Using functions in Program 3

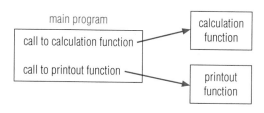

We already introduced the concept of a module with library functions like *sqrt*. We don't know what the statements inside the *sqrt* module look like—we just issue a call to tell *sqrt* what to work on. For example, we could write the following in a main program:

```
y = sqrt(w);
```

This call tells the *sqrt* function to find the square root of *w*, storing the answer in the variable *y*.

ADVANTAGES OF FUNCTIONS

There are two main advantages to using a function. First, we can separate the mechanics of a function from its particular use in a larger program. For instance, in the example above, the main program does not have to specify the individual steps in finding the square root. It simply issues a call to the *sqrt* function. In that call, the main program has to specify the value for which it wants to find the square root. This extra information sent to the function is called a **parameter** (in the example, it is *w*).

Figure 5-2 shows another example; in this one, a function performs the command to shop. The extra information, which is substituted for the blanks in the function, is the type of shopping to do.

This makes it possible for us to concentrate on the main program without having to worry about details contained in the function. As you can guess, this ties in well with top-down programming and stepwise refinement stressed in Chapter 4. Instead of refining a particular calculation or module down to the last detail in a main program, we indicate the call to

FIGURE 5-2 Using a function to shop

the function but leave the specifics for that function. A person who wants just an overview looks at the main program; to see the details, the person looks at the function.

Another advantage is that the set of instructions specifying the task performed by the function is written just once but can be used any number of times. For example, we can compute the square root of *w* and then the square root of *z + 27* simply by issuing two calls with different values for the parameter sent to the function.

To summarize:

◆ A function gives the computer a set of instructions that can be used again with different values.
◆ Once the pattern or function is specified, one single statement calls it in a given situation; to apply it three times takes three calls.
◆ To use a function to perform a particular task:
  1. Write a function which contains the instructions to perform the task.
  2. Every time you want to perform the task on actual parameter value(s), call the function with the value(s) specified.

SELF-CHECK 5-1

1. What is a call to a function? What is a parameter?
2. How many times is the code for a function written? How many times can it be called?
3. What are the two main advantages of using a function?

USING THE LIBRARY FUNCTION *sqrt*

We begin our discussion by looking at the library function **sqrt**. Recall from Chapter 2 what a library function is. The pattern or set of instructions for the function is already in the standard library available to the C compiler. To use one of these library functions, we just issue a call.

Assume that we have this main program:[2]

```
/* main program which calls the library function sqrt */
#include <stdio.h>
#include <math.h>
main()
{
    double w,y;

    w = 16.0;
    y = sqrt(w);
    printf("%f\n",y);
}
```

[2]Note the third line; if you have forgotten what it means, see Chapter 2, Section 5.

The first assignment statement gives *w* the value 16.0. In the next line, this value is sent to the function *sqrt*. While *sqrt* is working, the main program is waiting for an answer to be computed. (It resumes execution after *sqrt* computes this answer and sends it back.) The function uses some process to find the square root of the number sent to it. In this case, it finds the square root of 16.0, which is 4.0, and then sends the answer back to the main program to be put into the variable *y*. At that point, the main program resumes execution, prints the value stored in *y*, and stops.

THE FUNCTION *sqrt*

Let's look more carefully at *sqrt* itself.

EXAMPLE 5-1   This is roughly what the function *sqrt* looks like:

```
/*
 * function to find the square
 *    root of the parameter x
 */
double sqrt(double x)                               /* function header */
{
       compute the square root of x
       return the value computed
}
```

Notice the "scaffolding" surrounding the actual instructions to find the square root. This scaffolding or "shell" is necessary in every function.

WHAT'S OLD?

There are many features of the function that are familiar to us:

♦   The first two lines are comments; every function should have a comment describing what task it is designed to accomplish.

♦   The comment is followed by a line called the **function header**. Among other things, the header specifies the identifier (*sqrt*) that is used to call the function from the main program. Identifier names for functions are lowercase like variable identifiers. The function header, just like the main program header, does not end in a semicolon.

♦   Just as in a main program, the function has a pair of braces surrounding the instructions to perform its task.

WHAT'S NEW?

In addition to these familiar features, there are several new ones.

♦   The header starts with a data type, which indicates the type of answer returned by the function; in this case, the answer returned has type *double*.

- Then comes the name of the function, *sqrt*.
- This is followed by a set of parentheses, associating a data type with a name: the data type *double* is associated with the name *x*.
- Within the body of the function, a value is computed.
- The final statement of the function, called a ***return* statement**, returns this value to the program that called the function.

The value returned should match the data type (*double*) in the function header for the answer. As it is translating the function, the compiler can verify that these things match. This verification of consistency is called **type checking**. (When the compiler is translating the main program's call to the function, it can often perform additional type checking. See the information below on function prototypes.)

FUNCTION TERMINOLOGY

When a function is called, the value of the variable in the parentheses [*w* in the call *y* = *sqrt*(*w*)] is matched up with the variable in the parentheses in the function header (*x* in the function header for *sqrt*). So *x* actually gets the value of *w*. The name *x* in the function is simply a place holder for the value that we want the square root of, in our case, *w*.

- This place holder *x* is called a **formal** or **dummy parameter** of the function. The word *dummy* is more descriptive of its role as a place holder, but *formal parameter* is the more common term.
- The object that we want to find the square root of (*w* or *x3* or *alpha*) is called the **actual** or **real parameter**; sometimes it is called an **argument**.

The names of the formal and actual parameters do not have to match exactly, although, if by chance they do, there is no problem. On the other hand, the data types for both parameters (e.g., *int* or *double*) must match, with a few minor exceptions discussed later. In the main program, we use the actual name of the parameter, but in the function, we use only the formal parameter name (see Figure 5-3).

FIGURE 5-3   Names for parameters

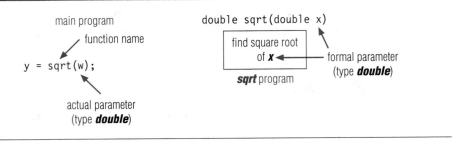

CAUTION In the function, you should not refer to the name of an actual parameter. Similarly, in the main program, you should not refer to the name of a formal parameter.

If you wonder why the variable isn't called **w** inside the function, remember that this particular library function was written quite a while ago. The person writing it didn't know that we wanted to find the square root of a variable called **w**. What's more, we can use **sqrt** to find the square root of many different things, such as **sqrt(w)**, **sqrt(x3)**, or **sqrt(alpha)**. There is no possible way for the function's name for the object always to be the same as the one in our program; whatever name we use is replaced by the name in the function. In fact, one of the great virtues of a function is this flexibility in names.

Notice that the value sent to the function (**w** or **alpha**) and the one expected by the function (**x**) both have data type **double**. Also the value computed by the function has the same data type as the variable in the main program that holds the answer (**y** or **beta**). In general, the formal and actual parameters should match; in addition, if the function returns a value of a certain type, the main program should store the answer in a variable of that same type.

STYLE WORKSHOP In many cases, an integer value (or a value of type **float**) can be matched to a formal parameter of type **double**. However, this is not considered good style. We recommend that the types of the actual and formal parameters match.

TRACING A CALL TO THE FUNCTION *sqrt*

Let's trace an example to see what happens during execution of the program. Here's the entire main program, including two calls to the function:

```
/* main program which calls the library function sqrt */
#include <stdio.h>
#include <math.h>
main()
{
    double w,y,alpha,beta;

    w = 16.0;
    y = sqrt(w);                        /* first call to the function */
    printf("%f\n",y);
    alpha = 2.56;
    beta = sqrt(alpha);                 /* second call to the function */
    ...
}
```

PROGRAM TRACE

◆ Execution begins in the main program. First, **w** is assigned the value 16.0.

◆ The value of **w** is sent to the function **sqrt**. The main program temporarily stops, and the function begins to execute. The first step of every function call is to match the value of the formal and actual parameters.

◆ In the function, the formal parameter *x* starts out with the value of the actual parameter *w*. The instructions that find the square root of *x* find the square root of the value stored in *w*.

◆ Since *w* (and thus *x*) has the value 16.0, the value computed by *sqrt* is 4.0.

◆ When the function executes the **return** statement, it stops execution, returns a value, and passes control to the main program. The function always returns to the point where it was called.

◆ When we get back to the main program, the answer returned by the function is assigned to the variable *y* and printed.

◆ The main program then assigns 2.56 to *alpha* and calls the function a second time, with *alpha* as the parameter.

◆ For this call, the value of *alpha* is stored in *x*. The function finds the square root of 2.56, which is 1.6, and returns this value to the main program. Once again, the function returns to the point where it was called.

◆ The main program stores the returned value in *beta* and continues.

HIGHLIGHTS

The same function, *sqrt*, can be used for 2 or 8 or even 200 calls, each of which finds the square root of a single value. In every case, the function keeps track of what to work on, what statement to return to, and where to place the answer. The function always returns to the point where it was called.

PARAMETER TRANSMISSION BY VALUE

We should emphasize one other point made previously. During execution of the program, the function is sent the *value* of the actual parameter, and this value is placed in the formal parameter. This method of sending a parameter to a function is called **passing a parameter by value** or **parameter transmission by value**. In C, all parameters are passed by value.[3]

 CAUTION Because all parameters are passed by value, if there is a change in the formal parameter inside the function, the value of the corresponding actual parameter does not change (see Figure 5-4).

FIGURE 5-4 Communication between function and main program

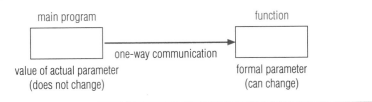

[3]Right now, this may not seem important, but in Section 8 and Chapter 8, we see the implications.

SELF-CHECK 5-2

1. What is an actual parameter in a main program? What is a formal parameter in a function?

2. If a function is called several times, where does it return?

3. In the function call below, which standard function is being called? What is the name of the actual parameter? Where is the answer stored?

```
z = ceil(v);
```

SECTION 2 PROGRAMMER-DEFINED FUNCTIONS

In this section, we learn how to write our own functions instead of relying upon standard functions. Many examples of programmer-defined functions are included, introducing a number of concepts. This is one of the longest sections in the text and one of the most important.

A SIMPLE EXAMPLE OF A PROGRAMMER-DEFINED FUNCTION: THE FUNCTION *triple*

As we have mentioned, there are many other library functions besides *sqrt*. However, there are jobs for which no built-in function is available, such as finding the sum of a number of squares. For this, we have to write our own **programmer-defined function**. To use a library function, all we need to do is call it at the appropriate place in a main program. However, we must write a programmer-defined function in addition to calling it.

EXAMPLE 5-2

As our first example of a programmer-defined function, let's write a function called **triple** that takes an integer and triples it. This is too simple to be a useful function (in fact, the function shell is much larger than the actual instructions), but it is a good first example.

Let's start by giving the function header. The function header must contain the name of the function, the name and type of each formal parameter, and the type of answer to be returned. The function header does not end in a semicolon. Here is a comment describing the job of the function, plus the function header for **triple**:

```
/*
 * function to return three
 * times the parameter numb
 */
int triple(int numb)                      /* function header */
```

After the header, and surrounded by a pair of braces, is the body of the function, which in this case is a single line.

```
{
    return 3 * numb;
}
```

This statement computes the value of **3 * numb** and then returns it to the program that calls the function.

The **return** statement is the logical end of the function, the last statement to be executed. In addition, a **return** statement is usually the last statement before the closing brace of a function. For clarity, some programmers put parentheses around the value to be returned. In that case, the **return** statement looks like this:

```
return (3 * numb);
```

We do not use this form in our programs, but you may want to.

Here is the entire function:

```
/*
 * function to return three
 * times the parameter numb
 */
int triple(int numb)                              /* function header */
{
        return 3 * numb;
}
```

The code for the function above is called the **function definition** because it defines to the compiler what this function means. This explains why the function header does not end in a semicolon, since it is just part of the function definition.

PROGRAM TRACE Here is a main program which contains a number of calls to **triple**. Note that all of the variables have data type **int** to be consistent with the formal parameter and the answer returned by the function. In this program, an extra line appears just above the main program header. This line, called the function prototype, is discussed next.

```
/* main program to test triple */
#include <stdio.h>
int triple(int);                                  /* function prototype */
main()
{
    int a,b,c,numb;

    a = 5;
    b = triple(a);                                /* first call */
    printf("original value and its triple: %d %d\n",a,b);

    numb = 2;
    c = triple(numb);                             /* second call */
    printf("original value and its triple: %d %d\n",numb,c);

    numb = triple(a - 1);                         /* third call */
    printf("original value and its triple: %d %d\n",a - 1,numb);
    printf("the variable is still: %d\n",a);

    c = triple(4);                                /* fourth call */
    printf("if the value is the constant 4, triple it is %d\n",c);

    printf("if the value is %d, triple it is %d\n",a,triple(a));    /* last call */
}
```

Note that the main program calls the function several times. However, *triple* never gets confused about which call it is on or where to return the answer.

◆   The main program starts by giving a value to the variable *a*. For the first call to the function [*b* = *triple(a)*], the main program sends *a* as the actual parameter (see Figure 5-5A).

◆   In *triple*, the formal parameter *numb* is given the value of the actual parameter *a*. The formal parameter is multiplied by 3, giving 3 ∗ 5 = 15.

◆   This is returned to the main program and put into the variable *b* (see Figure 5-5B). The first line printed is this:

```
original value and its triple: 5 15
```

Notice that the value of the actual parameter *a* has not changed, but the value of *b* has changed to reflect the answer returned by the function.

The second call [*c* = *triple(numb)*] is a little different. The actual parameter is called *numb*, and the formal parameter is also *numb*, which is fine. The main program's variable *numb* is definitely not the same storage location as *numb* in the function.

◆   The actual parameter *numb* in the main program is set to 2, so that value is given to the formal parameter *numb* inside the function.

◆   This value is tripled to 6, which is returned to the main program and put into the variable *c*. The second line printed is this:

```
original value and its triple: 2 6
```

It is not significant that the formal and actual parameters have the same name. Whatever the name of the actual parameter, its *value* is sent to the formal parameter in the function.

FIGURE 5-5   Call to the function *triple*

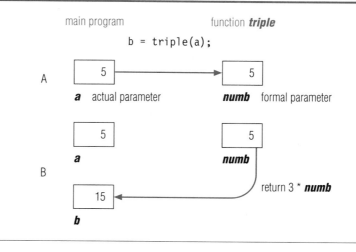

The third call [*numb = triple (a − 1)*] is trickier. First, note that the actual parameter does not have to be a variable. The actual parameter can be an expression which is evaluated to obtain a value; this value is then sent to the function as the value for the formal parameter.

◆ In this case, we are sending the value of *a − 1,* which is 5 − 1 = 4, to the function. Inside *triple*, the formal parameter *numb* has the value 4. This is tripled, giving 12.

◆ Then 12 is sent back to the main program and stored in *numb*. The printout looks like this:

```
original value and its triple: 4 12
the variable is still 5
```

As can be seen from the printout, the value of *a* has not changed. Sending *a − 1* to the function does not change the original value. Note that the identifier *numb* in the main program is definitely not the same as *numb* in the function. The *numb* inside *triple* is the name of the formal parameter every time the function is called. The *numb* in the main program is the name of a variable whose role can change. For the previous call to *triple*, *numb* in the main program served as the actual parameter; for this call, *numb* holds the value returned by the function.

For the fourth call [*c = triple(4)*], the actual parameter sent to the function is the constant 4. The function expects to receive a parameter of type *int*, and a constant value is perfectly acceptable.

◆ The constant value is sent to the function and matched to the formal parameter. Inside the function, the formal parameter *numb* has the value 4. This is tripled, giving 12, which is sent back to the main program and stored in *c*. The printout looks like this:

```
if the value is the constant 4, triple it is 12
```

Finally, the last call [*printf(...,triple(a))*] shows that the answer returned by a function can be printed directly without being stored.

◆ The value of the actual parameter (5) is sent to the function. This is tripled to give 15.

◆ The value 15 is returned and used in the *printf*. This line prints the following:

```
if the value is 5, triple it is 15
```

Here is the entire output from this program:

```
original value and its triple: 5 15
original value and its triple: 2 6
original value and its triple: 4 12
the variable is still 5
if the value is the constant 4, triple it is 12
if the value is 5, triple it is 15
```

SELF-CHECK 5-3

1. What type of answer does the function *triple* return?

2. What name are we using for the formal parameter? What is its data type?

3. For each call to *triple*, identify the actual parameter and its data type.

TYPE CHECKING AND THE FUNCTION PROTOTYPE

Earlier, we mentioned that the compiler can do some type checking when it is translating a function. In addition, the compiler should check for consistency when it is translating the main program. For example, if the function expects to receive one formal parameter of type *double*, the compiler should make sure that the main program sends such a value; if the answer returned by the function has type *double*, the compiler should make sure that the main program expects that.

Inside the function, the compiler can do type checking based on the function header. However, because of the order in which items appear in a program, the compiler may not have seen the function header at the point when the main program calls the function. ANSI C has a feature, called a **function prototype**, which gives the compiler all the information it needs to perform type checking in the main program. The function prototype, also called the **function declaration,** contains the type of answer returned by the function and the name of the function, plus the number and type of the parameters.

In our programmer-defined function *triple*, the type of answer returned is *int*, the name of the function is *triple*, there is one parameter, and its data type is also *int*. Thus, the function prototype for *triple* looks like this:

```
return type   data type for parameter
    ↓             ↓
int triple(int);                                /* function prototype */
         ↑
function name
```

If we include this function prototype, the compiler knows exactly what to expect when we call *triple* from the main program:

- ♦ The function returns an answer of type *int*.
- ♦ The name of the function is *triple*.
- ♦ The function expects to receive one parameter of type *int*.

In general, whenever it calls a function, the program should have access to the function prototype.

HEADER FILES AND LOCATION OF FUNCTION PROTOTYPES

The function prototype must appear before the call to the function. There is some flexibility, but we recommend that the prototype go just above the header of the main program. This puts the function prototype directly beneath the line containing *#include <stdio.h>* (and any other lines referring to functions from the standard library).

When using a programmer-defined function, it is the programmer's responsibility to include the function prototype explicitly. In the case of a library function, the function prototype is contained in a header file. Typically, a programmer inserts a header file into a program by using an *#include* directive. The directive *#include <stdio.h>* tells the preprocessor to include the header file *stdio.h* at this point in the program.

A header file contains function prototypes for a series of functions. The header files *stdio.h* and *math.h* contain function prototypes for the functions in these two portions of the standard library. For example, in the *math.h* header file, the function prototype for *sqrt* looks like this:

```
double sqrt(double);                        /* function prototype */
```

Note that we don't have to write this line explicitly. By using the compiler directive *#include <math.h>*, it is as if we have this function prototype, plus many others, in our program. Similarly, the *stdio.h* header file contains function prototypes for the most important functions related to input/output operations—for example, *printf* and *scanf*. By including the compiler directives for these header files, we allow our programs to use the appropriate library functions.

The header files for *stdio.h* and *math.h* are always placed at the beginning, above the main program, so that the prototypes they contain can be accessed from anywhere. Placing the prototype for a programmer-defined function directly beneath these header files puts it in the same position as the prototypes for the functions from the C library. By the time the main program calls the function, the prototype must have been seen. Therefore, the main program and any other functions in the file can access the function correctly.

Here is another main program that calls the function *triple*, highlighting the function prototype:

```
/* main program to test triple */
#include <stdio.h>
int triple(int);                            /* function prototype */
main()
{
    int a,b,c,numb;

    a = 5;
    b = triple(a);
    ...
}
```

HIGHLIGHTS

If the compiler sees the function header before the call to the function, it can do type checking to verify that the function is being called correctly. However, in many cases, it is not possible for the compiler to see the header first. In these cases, the same information is provided by the function prototype.

In general, the information from the function prototype and the function header should match.

ALTERNATE FORM OF THE FUNCTION PROTOTYPE

The function prototype that we gave above for *triple* can be modified so that it is almost identical to the function header. Here is the modified form:

return type   data type for parameter
    ↓   ↓

```
int triple(int numb);                              /* function prototype */
```
    ↑   ↑

function name   parameter name

This form gives a name, in addition to a data type, to the function's parameter. In this case, the name in the prototype matches the formal parameter name in the function header, but that is not necessary. Actually, any name can be used (or no name at all). For example, we can use either of these function prototypes:

```
int triple(int y);      or      int triple(int z);
```

The name (either **y** or **z**) that appears after the type is a dummy name and is ignored by the compiler. The important point is the type: **int**. Some programmers think it is a good idea to include a dummy name matching the one in the function header. If you do this, the function prototype and the function header will be almost identical, except that the function prototype ends in a semicolon because it is a complete C statement. (You can think of it as declaring the function, just as a variable is declared.)

STYLE WORKSHOP In the rest of this chapter, we show how to write function prototypes both with and without dummy names. However, when we give an example of a main program calling a function, we usually do not include dummy names. You can include them in your own programs.

CAUTION When you are using certain C compilers, it is possible to omit the function prototype, but we strongly recommend that you *always* include it. Some library functions (e.g., *sqrt*) do not work correctly if the header file containing their prototypes is not included. In addition, the compiler does less type checking on a function call. Similarly, some programmer-defined functions may not work correctly and/or some mistakes in parameter matching will not be caught if function prototypes are omitted.

SELF-CHECK 5-4

1. What is the purpose of a function prototype?
2. What information is contained in the function prototype?
3. How does a function prototype differ from a function header?

THE USE OF LOCAL VARIABLES WITHIN A FUNCTION: THE FUNCTION *sign*

Our next example is more realistic and introduces local variables, an important feature of functions.

EXAMPLE 5-3A Let's write a function called **sign** that does the following: Given a real number x, if x is 0, the function returns 0; if x is positive, it returns 1; if x is negative, it returns –1. This is called the **signum** or **sign function** since it tells us the sign (but not the value) of the original number.

```
/* return the sign of the parameter x: +1, 0, or -1 */
int sign(double x)
{
    int answer;

    if (x == 0)
        answer = 0;
    if (x > 0)
        answer = 1;
    if (x < 0)
        answer = -1;
    return answer;
}
```

Before we trace any calls to the function, notice that a variable (*answer*) is declared within the function. Such a variable is called a **local variable** of the function. Each time the function is called, it has a new temporary storage location with this name.

In this function, *answer* holds the value that is eventually returned. The function can be written without a local variable, but we are purposely writing it this way to illustrate the concept. Notice also that even though the formal parameter *x* has data type *double*, the local variable *answer* and the value returned by the function both have data type *int* (see Figure 5-6). The function prototype for this function can look like either of these:

```
int sign(double);     or     int sign(double x);
```

Here is a main program containing a series of calls to the function *sign*. In each case, the actual parameter sent to *sign* has data type *double* to match the formal parameter *x* within the function. However, the answer returned is stored by the main program in a variable of data type *int* to match the type of value returned by the function.

```
/* main program to test double */
#include <stdio.h>
int sign(double);                          /* function prototype */
main()
{
    double x,y,z;
    int    a,b,c,d;

    x = 5.4;
    a = sign(x);                           /* a gets the value 1 */
    y = 0;
    b = sign(y);                           /* b gets the value 0 */
    z = 7.8976;
    c = sign(z - 9);                       /* c gets the value -1 */
    d = sign(-5);                          /* d gets the value -1 */
    printf("the answers are %d %d %d %d\n",a,b,c,d);
}
```

STYLE WORKSHOP We could eliminate the main program's use of the function *sign* by replacing each function call by the three *if* statements in the body of the function. However, that would make the main program longer and more involved.

FIGURE 5-6 Call to the function **sign**

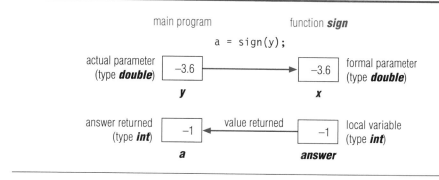

PROGRAM TRACE Let's see what is printed by this series of calls. In each case, we list the appropriate part of the main program and discuss what happens on that call.

◆ Let's start with the first call to the function:

```
x = 5.4;
a = sign(x);
```

In the main program, *x* is set to 5.4. This variable *x* is the actual parameter for the first call to **sign**. Inside **sign**, the formal parameter *x* is given the value 5.4. (Note that *x* in **sign** is not the same as in the main program, even though for this call they are matched.) The first **if** condition is false, but the second **if** is true, so **answer** is set to 1; the third **if** is also false. The value of **answer** is then returned to the main program and stored in the variable *a*.

◆ Now let's look at the second call:

```
y = 0;
b = sign(y);
```

In the main program, *y* is assigned the value 0; for this call to **sign**, the formal parameter *x* is given the value 0. This time, **answer** gets the value 0, which is returned to the main program, where it is stored in *b*.

◆ For the third call:

```
z = 7.8976;
c = sign(z - 9);
```

In the main program, *z* – **9** has the value 7.8976 – 9 = –1.1024; this is the value of the actual parameter that is sent to the function. The function computes a value of –1 for **answer** and returns this to be stored in *c*.

◆ Finally, the last call consists of the following line:

```
d = sign(-5);
```

This time the actual parameter is the integer constant –5. This is converted into a value of type **double** and sent to the function. The function computes a value of –1 and returns this to the main program to be stored in *d*.

   The printout is the following:

```
the answers are 1 0 -1 -1
```

🛑 **CAUTION** A function is always allowed to refer to its formal parameters. For example, *triple* refers to *numb*, and *sign* refers to *x*. In addition, if the function declares one or more local variables, it can refer to them. For example, *sign* refers to *answer*. However, a function cannot refer to any variables which are declared in the main program.

Similarly, a local variable declared within a function can be used only within that function. It is impossible for the main program to reference a function's local variable. In fact, a local variable can have the same name as a variable within the main program. When the function is executing, a reference to that name means the variable declared in the function; when the main program is operating, a reference to that name means the variable declared in the main program.

STYLE WORKSHOP To avoid confusion, some people like to use names for local variables that differ from those in the main program. In this chapter, we try to avoid repeating names, but in later chapters, we use whatever is the best name.

FORMAL PARAMETER AS A LOCAL VARIABLE

It is sometimes useful to view the formal parameter in a function as a local variable. The matchup of actual and formal parameters can then be interpreted as an assignment statement which is executed just before the function starts. For example, consider the function *sign* from Example 5-3. The formal parameter inside *sign* is called *x*. That example has a main program containing several calls to the function. For the last function call, the actual parameter is the constant –5. Therefore, we can view the following assignment as occurring just before the function starts to execute:

```
x = -5;
```

In general, if the actual parameter is the expression *expr*, and the formal parameter is called *param*, then the matchup can be interpreted as follows:

```
param = expr;
```

Note that *expr* gives a starting value to *param*, but they are in fact separate storage locations. If the formal parameter *param* changes inside the function, the corresponding actual parameter in the main program does not.

🛑 **CAUTION** Since a formal parameter in a function is similar to a local variable, the function cannot have a local variable and a formal parameter with the same name.

USING MULTIPLE *return* STATEMENTS

There are many other ways to write the body of the function *sign*. As we mentioned earlier, you can avoid the local variable *answer*. As soon as you determine a value for the function, you can return it. This method is illustrated in the following example:

EXAMPLE 5-3B

```
/* return the sign of the parameter x: +1, 0, or -1 */
int sign(double x)
{
```

```
            if (x == 0)
                return 0;
            if (x > 0)
                return 1;
            if (x < 0)
                return -1;
        }
```

A function can return only one value. Therefore, this function seems to be illegal because of the three **return** statements. However, the function is valid because only one statement is used on any one call to **sign**. Since only one of the three **if** conditions is true for each **x** value, only one value is returned by the function. As soon as that particular value is found, the function stops execution and returns to the main program. In other words, the last statement executed in the function will be one of these three **if** statements, depending upon the particular value stored in **x**. In fact, if we reach the third **if**, its question must be true. Therefore, the third **if** can be replaced by the following:

```
    return -1;
```

STYLE WORKSHOP Many people avoid multiple **return** statements. They think it is better to have one way to enter a function (at the top), and one way to exit (via a single **return** statement at the bottom). On the other hand, some people prefer multiple **return** statements to avoid extra local variables. You should be comfortable with both techniques.

SELF-CHECK 5-5

1. What is a local variable? Can a main program refer to a function's local variable?

2. Can a function have more than one **return** statement? Can a function return more than one value on a single call?

3. In the function **sign**, why can only one of the three **if** statements be true on any one call to the function?

A FUNCTION WITH SEVERAL PARAMETERS: THE FUNCTION *max3*

Our next example of a function has three parameters. Of course, no matter how many parameters are sent by a main program to a function, it still computes a single answer.

EXAMPLE 5-4   Assume that we have three integers and want to find the largest. We write a function called **max3** with three parameters. The header for the function mentions each of these parameters, giving it a name and data type. The code for the function is tricky, so we have included some helpful comments. The first **if** statement determines the larger of the first two formal parameters, **a** and **b**. The second **if** statement compares this value to **c**; the larger must be the largest parameter. If you do not see why this is true, trace a few examples before going on.

```
/*
 * function to find the largest
 * of three integers a, b, and c
 */
int max3(int a, int b, int c)
{
     int maxsofar;

     /* first find the larger of a and b */
     if (a >= b)
          maxsofar = a;
     else
          maxsofar = b;

     /* now compare the larger of a and b to c */
     if (maxsofar < c)
          maxsofar = c;
     return maxsofar;
}
```

Just as the header mentions three parameters, so, too, does the function prototype. We can use either of these forms:

```
int max3(int, int, int);      or      int max3(int a, int b, int c);
```

Now we can analyze some calls to **max3** from a main program, starting with this one:

```
/* main program to test max3 */
#include <stdio.h>
int max3(int, int, int);                              /* function prototype */
main()
{
     int ans,x,y,z;

     x = 3;
     y = 5;
     z = 7;
     ans = max3(x,y,z);
     ...
}
```

PROGRAM TRACE

◆ For this first call, the formal and actual parameters are matched in the order in which they are specified: *x* to *a*, *y* to *b*, *z* to *c*. Inside the function, *a* gets the value 3, *b* gets the value 5, and *c* gets the value 7 (see Figure 5-7).

◆ The first *if* condition is false, so the local variable **maxsofar** is set to 5 (the value of *b*). The second *if* condition is false, so the local variable **maxsofar** is assigned 7 (the value of *c*).

◆ This value is returned to the main program, the function stops execution, and the main program resumes. Back in the main program, **ans** is given the value 7, which is the correct answer for the maximum of 3, 5, and 7.

FIGURE 5-7 Association of actual and formal parameters for a call to **max3**

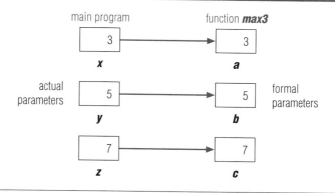

A MORE COMPLICATED FUNCTION CALL

Our next call reiterates several points. First, the answer returned from a function can be part of an expression or printed. Second, the actual parameter can be a constant or even an expression; in fact, as this example shows, it can be an expression whose value depends upon the value returned by a call to another function. Here is another example of how a main program can call the function **max3**:

```
/* main program to test max3 */
#include <stdio.h>
int max3(int, int, int);                    /* function prototype */
main()
{
    int p,q;

    p = 10;
    q = -7;
    printf("%d\n",max3(p + 2, 12, abs(q)) * 3);
}
```

PROGRAM TRACE A complicated expression like the one inside the **printf** is evaluated from the inside out, so the last thing to be done is the multiplication by 3. Note that the call to **max3** has three arguments or parameters (see Figure 5-8).

◆ The first actual parameter is the expression **p + 2,** which has the value 12; this is sent to **max3** as the value of the first formal parameter, **a**.

◆ The second actual parameter is the constant 12; this becomes the value of the second formal parameter, **b**.

◆ The third argument to **max3** is actually a call to a library function, **abs**. The expression **abs(q)** computes the absolute value of –7. This is evaluated to 7, then sent to **max3** as the value for the third formal parameter, **c**.

◆ The function **max3** finds the largest of 12, 12, and 7, which is 12. The main program multiplies the returned answer by 3 to get 36, then prints this value without storing the result anywhere.

FIGURE 5-8 Association of actual and formal parameters for a call to **max3**

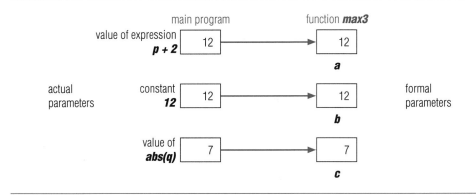

STYLE WORKSHOP Note that to evaluate this one **printf** in the main program, we executed calls to both **abs** and **max3**. Even though this is perfectly legal in C, it is not considered good style. In many cases, it is helpful to break a complicated expression into smaller pieces by adding extra variables to hold the intermediate results.

SELF-CHECK 5-6

1. Is a function allowed to have more than one parameter? If so, in what order are the formal and actual parameters matched?

2. If a call to function **f1** contains a call to function **f2**, which call is executed first?

3. What is printed by the following **printf**, assuming that **x** has the value 5?

    ```
    printf("%d",7 + abs(x - 6));
    ```

SECTION 3 PROGRAM 5; LOCATION OF FUNCTIONS

In this section, we use the ideas from Section 2 to write a function version of Program 5. This is the first programmer-defined function to use a **for** loop. We also discuss where to place a function in relation to the main program.

USING A *for* LOOP IN A FUNCTION

We have seen a variety of programmer-defined functions, but so far they have accomplished simple tasks. One important reason is that they have not used **for** or **while** loops. Now we are ready to use a loop in a function. In fact, we are ready to write the function to solve Problem 5: to find the sum of a series of squares.

EXAMPLE 5-5 We will write a function called **sumofsquares** that receives one parameter **n**; this parameter represents the number of squares that we want to sum. Inside the function, **n** controls the **for** loop.

The function also has two local variables, *i* and **sum**. The function finds the sum of the first *n* squares; that is, it computes $1^2 + 2^2 + ... + n^2$. This sum is returned as the value of the function *sumofsquares*.

In the function header, the data type for both the formal parameter and the answer returned is *int*. The body of the function uses the same instructions as the program at the end of Chapter 4, Section 3, substituting *n* for **numbertosum** and returning the answer just before ending the function. Here is the complete function:

```
/*
 * find the sum of the first n squares:
 *  1*1 + 2*2 + ... + n*n
 */
int sumofsquares(int n)                          /* function header */
{
    int item,sum=0;

    for (item = 1; item <= n; item++)
        sum += item * item;
    return sum;
}
```

USING THE FUNCTION *sumofsquares* IN PROGRAM 5

Now let's see how Program 5 uses the function *sumofsquares*. Assume that the main program has already stored a value in **numbertosum**. The main program that calls the function *sumofsquares* to sum the first **numbertosum** squares looks like this:

```
/*
 * Program prog5.c:
 * compute the sum of numbertosum squares
 * with numbertosum read from a line of data
 * using a function to sum the squares
 */
#include <stdio.h>
int sumofsquares(int);                           /* function prototype */
main()
{
    int numbertosum,answer;

    printf("type in the number of squares to be summed> ");
    scanf("%d",&numbertosum);
    answer = sumofsquares(numbertosum);
    printf("%d is the sum of the first %d squares\n",answer,numbertosum);
}
```

Notice that the main program's job is simpler when we write the module that does the actual summing as a function. Of course, the original main program in Program 4 was rather elementary, so the difference between the original and the function version is not that dramatic. In a larger program, with many functions, the savings are significant.

PROGRAM TRACE

◆ Assume that the main program has read in a value of 10 for the variable **numbertosum**. This is the value of the actual parameter for the call to the function. Inside the function, the formal parameter **n** also has the value 10.

◆ The body of the function sums the first **n** (ten) squares, giving 385.

◆ This value is returned to the main program as the value of the function. It is assigned to the variable **answer**. Then the **printf** prints this line:

```
385 is the sum of the first 10 squares
```

◆ If the main program had stored 5 as the value of **numbertosum**, this same series of instructions would have computed the sum of the first five squares. The output from the **printf** would look like this:

```
55 is the sum of the first 5 squares
```

LOCATION OF FUNCTIONS

There is one last ingredient in our formula for how to use a function: the placement of the function definition in relation to the main program. For simplicity, we will discuss the case of a main program and one function called **func**. There are a number of ways to arrange them.

One possibility is to place the entire function first, followed by the entire main program. In this case, the definition of the function appears before the main program's call to the function. Therefore, by the time the compiler reaches the call, it knows what to expect (see Figure 5-9).

FIGURE 5-9 File **method1.c** containing a function followed by a main program

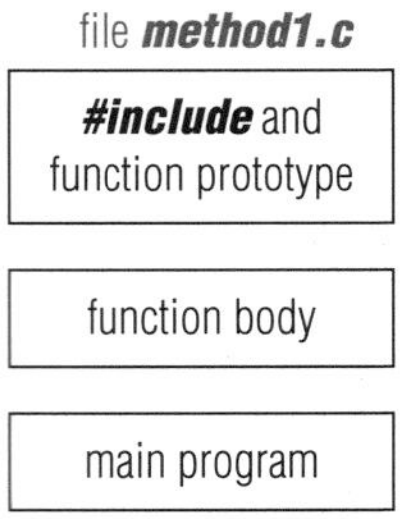

file **method1.c**

#include and function prototype

function body

main program

STYLE WORKSHOP In this case, because of the location of the function, the function prototype can be omitted, but we don't recommend it. Almost all C programmers recognize the value of a prototype. It is considered poor style to omit a function prototype, even if it is not technically necessary.

Another possible order is to have the main program first, followed by the function. Even though the function header comes *after* the main program, the function prototype appears *before* the call to the function. As long as the compiler sees the function prototype before the call to the function, it can still do type checking (see Figure 5-10). In both of these situations, the main program and the function are separate pieces in the same file.

A third possibility (called **separate compilation**) puts the function in one file and the main program in another and compiles them separately (see Figure 5-11). This is the way library functions are used. For example, the C standard library contains many functions which have been compiled into machine language. A main program, sitting in its own file, can be compiled so that it accesses these library functions.[4] It can also access other user-defined functions that have been separately compiled. This method is extremely common in real-world applications.

FIGURE 5-10   File ***method2.c*** containing a main program followed by a function

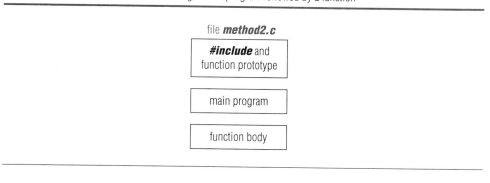

FIGURE 5-11   File ***method3m.c*** containing a main program and a separate file, ***method3f.c***, containing a function

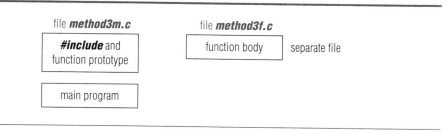

[4]In order to use this method, the file containing the main program must be linked together with the function file, and a few other lines must be included.

STYLE WORKSHOP The decision whether to put the function above or below the main program is a matter of taste. We put the function below (Figure 5-10), but you may decide that you like the other way better. It is not a good idea to mix the two methods; if you have more than one function, put all of them above the main program or below it.

Wherever you put the function, the computer knows to start execution in the main program. And in either case, the only way to execute a function is to call it. If a function is included in a file with a main program but never called, it will never be executed. If it is called ten times, it will be executed ten times.

SELF-CHECK 5-7

1. What are the various options for placing a function in relation to the main program?
2. In each case, where should the function prototype appear?
3. Which method is used for library functions?

COMPLETE PROGRAM 5

Here is complete Program 5, including the function prototype, the main program which contains the call to the function, and the function definition:

🖳 PROGRAM LISTING

```
/*
 * Program prog5.c:
 * compute the sum of numbertosum squares
 * with numbertosum read from a line of data
 * using a function to sum the squares
 */
#include <stdio.h>
int sumofsquares(int);                          /* function prototype */
main()
{
    int numbertosum,answer;

    printf("type in the number of squares to be summed> ");
    scanf("%d",&numbertosum);
    answer = sumofsquares(numbertosum);
    printf("%d is the sum of the first %d squares\n",answer,numbertosum);
}
```

```
/*
 * find the sum of the first n squares:
 *   1*1 + 2*2 + ... + n*n
 */
int sumofsquares(int n)                          /* function header */
{
     int i,sum=0;

     for (item = 1; item <= n; item++)
          sum += item * item;
     return sum;
}
```

FUNCTIONS AS MODULES

If you go through a detailed trace of this program, you see how many statements are actually executed by a single call to ***sumofsquares***. Notice how much easier this makes tracing the main program. If you are sure the function ***sumofsquares*** is working correctly, you can be confident the answer returned is right without analyzing it. Presumably, you have already done many separate tests of the function.[5] Testing it can be carried out independently of a particular main program's task.

This point becomes especially important as your programs get larger. To test a function, you can construct a main program which does nothing except call the function. This main program should consist of declarations and initializations of variables, calls to the function, and printouts of the results. As an example, look at our first programmer-defined function, ***triple***. We gave a number of calls to ***triple*** from a main program, testing various cases. In another example, we tested the function ***sign*** by giving a series of calls from a main program, including tests of all possible paths (with the parameter positive, negative, or 0) within the function. It is important to be thorough in testing the function.

Such a main program is called a **driver program** since it drives the function. We included a driver program for each function discussed in this section. See the main programs used to test the functions from examples 5-2, 5-3, and 5-4.

HIGHLIGHTS

A function can be tested by itself until we believe that it works, and then it can be trusted as a step in a larger process. This is usually much easier than trying to test a large program all at once.

So far, the task of each function we have written has been to compute and return only one value. However, functions in C are allowed to be more general than this, and there are examples later in this chapter. For example, in Section 4 we learn how to write a function

---

[5]In addition, there is a formula to check the sum of the first ***n*** squares. See Chapter 4, Exercise 16.

which prints a series of output headings; in Chapter 7, we will write a function to read in a series of data values and another to find their average.

SELF-CHECK 5-8

1. How do we test a function module?

2. What is a driver program?

3. Is it sufficient to run the function on just one or two sets of values? What must be done to make sure that a function is working correctly?

SECTION 4   VOID AND PARAMETERLESS FUNCTIONS

This section introduces a void function—one which does not return a value. We will also talk about a parameterless function; this type does not receive any parameters when it is called.

A FUNCTION THAT DOES NOT RETURN A VALUE: A VOID FUNCTION

In Section 6, we will discuss how to use a function for the multiplication problem from Chapter 4 (Example 4-2). Before we do that, consider whether a function can print a line of output which is a series of numbers (a row in a multiplication table). The basic purpose of each function so far is to compute and return one answer. What answer is returned when a list of numbers is printed?

A function which prints a list doesn't return a value. However, a function can perform one or more actions (including printing) without returning a particular value. This type is called a **void function** and is perfect for the task we have in mind. We should emphasize that void functions truly are functions. The basic purpose of a function is to perform a well-defined task. Void functions do just that.

VOID FUNCTION HEADER AND RETURN

The first line or header of a void function differs only slightly from the first line of one returning a value. At the beginning of the usual function header is the data type for the answer to be returned; in a void function, the data type is replaced by the keyword *void* because no explicit value is returned. Here is an example of a header for a function *func* which receives two *int* parameters, *x* and *y*:

STYLE WORKSHOP Many compilers allow **void** to be omitted from the header. In this case, we can use the following header:

```
func(int x, int y)                              /* function header */
```

Even if your compiler is one of these, it is better style to include **void** to help someone looking at the program. In addition, if **void** is omitted, the meaning of the header is slightly different (see Exercise 21).

There is one other distinctive feature of a void function. The functions discussed earlier used a **return** statement to return a value. In a void function, no value is returned. To indicate that control should return to the main program, use the keyword **return**, then end the function with the closing brace.

```
        return;
    }
```

STYLE WORKSHOP The word **return** can be omitted in a void function. The closing brace then ends the function. However, it is better style to mark the end of the function with a **return** statement.

A SIMPLE EXAMPLE OF A VOID FUNCTION: *printmaxmin*

Assume that we want to write a function which finds and prints both the larger and the smaller of two values, **a** and **b**, with identifying labels. In this case, we don't want to return anything, but we do want to print two things: the values of the larger and the smaller.

EXAMPLE 5-6

Let's use **printmaxmin** as the name of the function. If we start with **a** = 3 and **b** = 5, the function should print 5 as the maximum and 3 as the minimum; if **a** = 7 and **b** = 2, then **printmaxmin** should print 7 as the larger and 2 as the smaller. If the two values are equal, we don't care which is selected as the larger or the smaller.

In our function, let's call the formal parameters **x** and **y** and assume that we are working with integers. In the body of the function, we want to compare **x** and **y** to see which is larger. If **x** is larger, we want to print a message stating this; if not, we want to print a different message. Here is the entire function:

```
/*
 *  finds and prints both the larger
 *  and the smaller of x and y
 */
void printmaxmin(int x, int y)
{
    if (x > y)
        printf("%d is the larger   %d is the smaller\n",x,y);
    else
        printf("%d is the larger   %d is the smaller\n",y,x);
    return;
}
```

VOID FUNCTION PROTOTYPE AND CALL

The function prototype for a void function can look just like the function header with the addition of a semicolon. Or we can omit the names of the parameters. Here is a version of the function prototype for **printmaxmin** which does that:

```
void printmaxmin(int, int);                    /* function prototype */
```

To call a void function, write its name, together with the list of arguments. Since a void function does not return a value, we cannot include its call as part of an expression (on the right-hand side of an assignment statement or in a call to **printf**). The only way to call a void function is to write the function name, followed by the list of parameters.

In Section 3, we mentioned that a function which returns a value can be tested separately by using a driver program. A void function can also be tested as a separate module. Usually, this is very easy because there is no answer to be returned.

EXAMPLE 5-6
(continued)

Here is an example of a driver program that calls **printmaxmin**:

```
/* driver program to test printmaxmin */
#include <stdio.h>
void printmaxmin(int, int);
main()
{
    int a,b;

    a = 5;
    b = 3;
    printmaxmin(a,b);
    ...
}
```

PROGRAM TRACE Now we will trace this call to **printmaxmin**. Execution begins in the main program, with **a** set to 5 and **b** to 3. For this call, **a** and **b** are the actual parameters, which are matched to the formal parameters, **x** and **y**. Thus, **x** holds 5 and **y** holds 3. Inside the function, the **if** condition is true so we print the following (from the first **printf**):

```
5 is the larger   3 is the smaller
```

Then we execute the **return** statement in the function. This returns control to the main program, ending the function. Note that no value is returned to the main program. When the function returns control, the main program resumes execution, as shown by the ... above.

SELF-CHECK 5-9

1. What is a void function?
2. What is omitted in the header of a void function? What is omitted at the end of it?
3. What does the function prototype for a void function look like?

A COMPLETE PROGRAM CONTAINING A VOID FUNCTION

Now that we have written a void function, we have to determine where to place it in a complete program. The rules described in Section 3 also apply here—a void function can be included either before or after the main program.

EXAMPLE 5-6 (continued)

Here is a sketch of a complete program, including a main program which calls the void function *printmaxmin*:

```
/* ... */
#include <stdio.h>
void printmaxmin(int, int);
main()
{
    int a,b;

    a = 5;
    b = 3;
    printmaxmin(a,b);
}

/* ... */
void printmaxmin(int x, int y)
{
    if (x > y)
        printf("%d is the larger    %d is the smaller\n",x,y);
    else
        printf("%d is the larger    %d is the smaller\n",y,x);
    return;
}
```

PARAMETERLESS VOID FUNCTIONS

A certain type of void function, called a **parameterless void function**, does not receive any parameters. Such a void function cannot communicate with the main program (except by a method we will introduce later). Therefore, it has to perform entirely on its own.

The header of a parameterless void function uses the keyword *void* in two places: at the beginning to indicate that there is no answer to return, and inside the parentheses to show that there are no parameters. The header for a function named *func* looks like this:

```
void
return    indicates
type      no parameters
  ↓          ↓
void func(void)                                        /* function header */
       ↑
 function name
```

The function header can also omit the keyword *void* from the parentheses. Here is a header for *func* with this abbreviated format:

```
void func()                                    /* function header */
```

STYLE WORKSHOP Although the format which omits the second *void* is shorter, the original one is preferred. In the original format, *void* occurs in two places, signifying that the function does not return an answer and does not expect to receive any parameters. If that format is used for the header and function prototype, the compiler will make sure that each call to the function sends no parameters to the function and does not expect an answer to be returned. But if we omit *void* from within the parentheses in both the header and the prototype, the compiler may not perform this type checking. This could cause all sorts of errors (see Exercise 21).

EXAMPLE 5-7   As an example of a void parameterless function, assume that we have a program which generates a lot of output in a table. It has four columns, headed "Year," "Sales," "Expenses," and "Profits." Each heading should have ten blank columns between it and the next one. There should be a line of output at the top, saying, "Sales Data for the Past 15 Years."

We want to write a function *printheadings* to print these headings. Obviously, *printheadings* should not be written as a function which returns an answer. In addition, *printheadings* does not need any parameters.

Here is one version of *printheadings* (recall the use of \t to insert a tab):

```
/*
 *  prints headings for a table
 */
void printheadings(void)
{
    printf("\n\t\tSales Data for the Past 15 Years\n\n");
    printf("\tYear          Sales          Expenses          Profits\n");
    return;
}
```

This function prints these lines of output:

```
              Sales Data for the Past 15 Years


     Year          Sales          Expenses          Profits
```

Let's see how a main program uses the void function *printheadings*. Here is a driver program, including the function prototype and the call to the function:

```
/* driver program to test printheadings */
#include <stdio.h>
void printheadings(void);
main()
{
    printheadings();
}

/* printheadings goes here */
   . . .
```

Note that the driver program does not have to declare any variables or print any results. In fact, the only thing it does is call the void function! For the call, we write the name of the function, followed by a pair of parentheses with nothing inside (do not put the keyword *void* here), followed by a semicolon.

FUNCTIONS THAT HAVE NO PARAMETERS BUT RETURN AN ANSWER

It is also possible to write a function that has no parameters but returns an answer. For such a parameterless function, the function call looks like this (where *varname* is the name of a variable holding the result of the function call, and *func* is the name of the function):

```
varname = func();
```

As an example, we can write a parameterless function *randomnumber* which generates a random number. To assign a random number to the variable *x*, we call the function like this:

```
x = randomnumber();
```

This function does not receive any parameters, but it does return an answer. (In fact, C does have a function to compute random numbers; its name is *rand*. See Exercise 32.)

SELF-CHECK 5-10

1. In the function header, how do we indicate that a function receives no parameters?
2. In the call to the function, how do we indicate that the function receives no parameters?
3. Can a function with no parameters return an answer?

THE MAIN PROGRAM AS A VOID, PARAMETERLESS FUNCTION

It may have occurred to you that we have been using a void, parameterless function already: *main*, the main program. As we have mentioned, a main program is a function, although a special one.

In our programs, since *main* doesn't return an answer, it is a void function. Although we have not done so, the main program can get parameters, called **command-line arguments** or **command-line parameters** (see Appendix VI). In our examples, *main* has been a void, parameterless function. However, we usually omit the keyword *void* from the main program header, so *main* doesn't look like the void functions in this section.

Those of you using Turbo C (and some other compilers) have probably been getting warnings, saying, "Function doesn't return a value." That's because, without *void*, this compiler expects a value to be returned by the main function. To avoid the warning, use a main program header that looks like this (or add a *return* statement before the closing brace of the main program):

```
void main()                                    /* main program header */
```

The Turbo C++ manual shows a different header. If the main program is not receiving command-line arguments (it has no parameters), the manual uses this header:

```
int main(void)
```

This gives the main program the ability to return an answer, using a ***return*** statement. If you use this header, the main program can include the following statement just before it ends:

```
return 0;
```

SUMMARY ON THE USE OF VOID FUNCTIONS

Let's summarize our discussion of void functions versus those that return an answer. Either type of function performs a well-defined task. Either type can receive parameters, declare local variables, and be tested with a driver program. The only difference between them is that a void function does not return an answer.

To determine which type of function to use in a given situation, remember this: Any function is designed for a single task. If that task is to compute an answer and send it back to the program which called the function, write the function that way. If the job can be accomplished without returning an answer, use a void function, as we did in the programs using ***printmaxmin*** and ***printheadings***.

SELF-CHECK 5-11

1. In each of these cases, would you use a void function or one that returns a single answer?

    a.   Compute which of the three parameters to the function is the largest.
    b.   Print which of the three parameters to the function is the largest.
    c.   Print a long series of instructions to the person using the program.
    d.   Read in a value ***n***, then print your name ***n*** times.

2. For each of these functions, give a function header.

3. Can the ***main*** function receive parameters? If so, what are they called?

SECTION 5 ENRICHMENT: INPUT-PROCESS-OUTPUT (*I-P-O*) COMMENTS

In this section, we introduce a more detailed type of comment which helps the programmer work with functions in a systematic way. The comment focuses on three main features of a function: the input, the process to be carried out, and the output.

INPUT-PROCESS-OUTPUT (*I-P-O*) COMMENTS

It is usually quite easy to write simple functions from the English-language description. However, for a more complex function, we should organize our thoughts more systematically.

In analyzing a function, either a main program or any other function, there are three important ideas:

◆ the **input** to the function—the things it receives from the outside world;

◆ the **process** taking place in the function—how it accomplishes its task; and

◆ the **output** from the function—the way it communicates with the outside world.

One of the first goals of solving a problem is understanding these three aspects. Then it is relatively easy for you to write the function. On the other hand, if you are confused about one or more of these points, you will become even more confused as you try to write the function.

There is a method, called *I-P-O* comments, which emphasizes these three features of a function: *I* (input), *P* (process), and *O* (output). Each function's comment defines what the function's inputs are, outlines how the function processes the data values, and describes what the function's results or output will be. In addition to organizing our thoughts, this is an excellent comment since it emphasizes the task of the function and the way in which it interacts with the outside world.

Let's go through these aspects, then look at a specific example.

◆ *I* stands for the input to the function. For the examples in this chapter, input means the parameters sent to the function from the calling program. However, in more complicated functions, it can mean additional things. For example, a function can ask the user to type in values. In general, *I* is all the information the function needs to do its job.

◆ *P* stands for process, the actual work of the function. This usually entails computing one specific value, which is returned to the calling program. In general, *P* is what is performed by the function.

◆ *O* stands for output. At the simplest level, a function outputs by sending an answer to the calling program. A function can also send output directly to the screen or the printer. In general, *O* is all the ways the function communicates with the rest of the program and the outside world.

Now let's consider a specific example by looking at the function *sumofsquares* that we used in Program 5. Let's write a function to receive one parameter value (*n*) and compute the sum of the first *n* squares. As a first step, start with this analysis:

Input: the parameter value *n*—the number of squares

Process: compute the sum of the first *n* squares

Output: return the sum of squares to the calling program

Now translate this into C. The process step is simply the set of instructions used earlier to compute the sum of the first *n* squares in the main program. The output step returns this sum to the calling program. The input step is done automatically through the matchup of actual and formal parameters. Thus, we are led almost immediately to the version of the function in Section 3. As we noted, the analysis can be kept as a comment since it concisely summarizes the function's task. The complete function with the new comment is on the next page.

```
/*
 *  Function sumofsquares:
 *  Input:
 *     the parameter value n--the number
 *     of squares to be summed
 *  Process:
 *     finds the sum of the first n squares:
 *     1*1 + 2*2 + ... + n*n
 *  Output:
 *     returns the sum of the first n squares
 */
int sumofsquares(int n)
{
    int i,sum;

    sum = 0;
    for (i = 1; i <= n; i++)
        sum += i * i;
    return sum;

}
```

We will continue to use Input-Process-Output (*I-P-O*) comments in our later programs. Try to use them in your own programs as well. By following this format, you will be sure that you can describe these three main features in a function. Note that the comment is spread out over several lines. This draws the reader's attention to it.

SELF-CHECK 5-12

1. In an *I-P-O* comment, what does the *I* stand for? What are the possible forms that input to a function can take?

2. What does the *P* stand for?

3. What does the *O* stand for? What are the possible forms of output from a function?

SECTION 6 **ENRICHMENT: USING FUNCTIONS TO PRODUCE A MULTIPLICATION TABLE**

In this section, we show how to use functions to construct a multiplication table (see Example 4-2). A void function prints the first ten multiples of a given number. Then another void function produces a set of headings.

PSEUDOCODE FOR PRODUCING A MULTIPLICATION TABLE

Let's go back to an intermediate version of the pseudocode for this problem, which we developed in Chapter 4, Section 4.

print the headings at the top of the page
for each multiplicand m1 *from 1 to 10*
    print a line of output showing
        m1 *times each multiplier from 1 to 10*

Printing headings is a well-defined task which can be accomplished by a void function without cluttering up the main program. (In fact, one of our examples in Section 4 was a void function to print headings.) We will call this function **printheadings**. Since **printheadings** is a parameterless void function, the main program's call to the function is simply **printheadings()**. In top-down fashion, we will give the details of the function later.

Our pseudocode for the main program now looks like this:

```
printheadings();
for each multiplicand m1 from 1 to 10
    print a line of output showing
        m1 times each multiplier from 1 to 10
```

In Example 4-2, we refined this pseudocode in the main program. Here we use a void function to accomplish the task. Let's call this function **printrow**. It needs a parameter, **m1**, because it has to know for which number to construct the row of the multiplication table. Therefore, the main program's call to the function is **printrow(m1)**. The next version of the main program looks like this:

```
printheadings();
for each multiplicand m1 from 1 to 10
        printrow(m1);
```

Of course, the middle line can be implemented as a **for** loop. Here is the complete action portion of the main program:

```
printheadings();
for (m1 = 1; m1 <= 10; m1++)
        printrow(m1);
```

Notice how simple this main program is. Before we celebrate, we should remember that we also need to include the main program header, comments, declarations, etc. Even more importantly, we must still write the two functions, **printheadings** and **printrow**. To continue our top-down approach, first complete the main program, then write the functions.

THE MAIN PROGRAM

We can copy most of the initial portion of the main program from the original version. The only differences are the modified comment and declaration: the main program declares just one variable (**m1**) instead of two (what happened to **m2**?). The action portion is now the call to **printheadings** and the **for** loop containing the call to **printrow**. Here is the entire main program (which we call **multfunc.c**):

```
/*
 * Program multfunc.c:
 * construct a set of multiplication tables,
 * showing the multiples of the numbers from 1 to 10
 * using two functions: to print headings and tables
 */
```

(continued)

(continued)

```
#include <stdio.h>
main()
{
    int m1;

    printheadings();
    for (m1 = 1; m1 <= 10; m1++)
        printrow(m1);
}

/* the two functions go here */
```

This completes the main program. Next, we write the two functions.

THE FUNCTION *printheadings*

We start with **printheadings**. (You may want to look at the similar function in Example 5-7 in Section 4.) As usual, the function begins with a header and a comment (note that we are using the *I-P-O* comment format from Section 5.) The calls to **printf** for the headings are exactly the same as those in our first version of the program.

```
/*
 * Function printheadings:
 * Input:
 *    none
 * Process:
 *    prints headings to be used at the
 *    top of a multiplication chart
 * Output:
 *    prints several lines of headings
 */
void printheadings(void)
{
    printf("This is a Multiplication Table, from 1 to 10\n");
    printf("  X    1    2    3    4    5    6    7    8    9   10\n");
    return;
}
```

THE FUNCTION *printrow*

The function **printrow** is more complicated. For the formal parameter within the function, we can use the same name as the main program, **m1**. The function's comment and header look like this:

```
/*
 * Function printrow:
 * Input:
 *    the parameter m1 tells which table to produce
```

```
 * Process:
 *    produces a multiplication table for m1
 *    this contains the first 10 multiples of m1
 * Output:
 *    prints the multiplication table
 */
void printrow(int m1)
```

Within the body of the void function, we need all the statements to print a multiplication table. The table consists of the value of *m1* on the left, followed by its first ten multiples spread out to align under the column headings. To accomplish this, we need a local variable to represent the numbers from 1 to 10 by which *m1* is multiplied. To be consistent with Example 4-2, *m2* can be the name of this local variable. We now have the following:

```
{
    int m2;

    printf("\n");
    printf("%3d",m1);
    for (m2 = 1; m2 <= 10; m2++)
        printf("%5d",m1 * m2);
    printf("\n");
    return;
}
```

COMPLETE PROGRAM *multfunc.c* USING TWO FUNCTIONS

Now all we need to do is combine the main program and the two functions. As usual, the functions come after the main program. It does not matter which function comes first, but, for clarity, we can put them in the order called: *printheadings* and then *printrow*.

🖳 PROGRAM LISTING

```
/* Program multfunc.c */
#include <stdio.h>
void printheadings(void);
void printrow(int m1);
main()
{
    int m1;

    printheadings();
    for (m1 = 1; m1 <= 10; m1++)
        printrow(m1);
}

/* ... */
void printheadings(void)
{
    printf("This is a Multiplication Table, from 1 to 10\n");
```

(continued)

(continued)

```
        printf("  X        1    2    3    4    5    6    7    8    9   10\n");
        return;
}

/* ... */
void printrow(int m1)
{
        int m2;

        printf("\n");
        printf("%3d",m1);
        for (m2 = 1; m2 <= 10; m2++)
            printf("%5d",m1 * m2);
        printf("\n");
        return;
}
```

TRACING PROGRAM *multfunc.c*

A trace of this program is similar to the one for the original multiplication table in Chapter 4, Section 4, with only a few extra details because of the function calls.

PROGRAM TRACE   As usual, execution begins in the main program.

◆   The first thing the main program does is call the void function **printheadings**.

◆   At this point, the main program suspends execution, and control shifts to **printheadings**, which simply prints some headings.

◆   Then the function returns control to the main program, which sets up a **for** loop, with **m1** going from 1 to 10. For the first pass through this loop, **m1** has the value 1.

◆   The main program calls the function **printrow**, with **m1** as the actual parameter.

◆   The main program stops processing, and **printrow** takes over. In **printrow**, the formal parameter is also called **m1**. The function **printrow** prints a line containing the multiples of **m1** from **m1 * 1** to **m1 * 10.** In this case, we get multiples of 1.

◆   When the function finishes, it returns control to the main program, which increments **m1** to 2.

◆   The main program calls the function **printrow** again, with **m1** having the value 2, and so on.

◆   Eventually, the main program increments **m1** to 10 and sends this value to the function, which prints the multiples of 10 from 10 * 1 to 10 * 10. Then **printrow** returns control to the main program.

◆   The main program terminates the **for** loop and ends.

The output, some printed by **printheadings** and some by each call to **printrow**, is identical to that shown in Chapter 4.

COMPARISON WITH THE EARLIER VERSION, *mult.c,* FROM CHAPTER 4, SECTION 4

This is a good time to reflect on using functions to solve this problem. On one level, the function version is much longer than the original. However, on a deeper level, once you understand void functions, the new version is easier to follow because the main program has been freed of most of the details. Each individual function is straightforward, and it is clear how both of them interact with the main program. Thus, instead of one complicated main program with a nested loop structure, you have one simple main program and two simple functions.[6]

In a case where the original program is not long or complicated, this approach may not be useful, but, for more complex problems, it clearly is. (See Exercise 18 for another way to use functions in this program and a comparison of all three versions.)

EFFICIENCY CONSIDERATIONS

There is one additional consideration: the question of **efficiency**. Both versions include essentially the same arithmetic calculations and print statements. The major difference is the number of function calls since there is a large amount of overhead every time a function is called. In the original version, *mult.c*, since all work is done in the main program, there are no function calls (except for ones to *printf*). In the function version, *multfunc.c*, the main program calls *printheadings* once and *printrow* 10 times, for a total of 11 function calls. Using this criterion, the second version is much less efficient.

As important as efficiency is, clarity and simplicity are even more vital in a student environment. You must weigh all the factors and decide what to do in each situation.

SELF-CHECK 5-13

1. Why does the function *printheadings* receive no parameters?
2. Why does the function *printrow* receive one parameter?
3. What is wrong with the following call to *printrow* (*z* is a variable of data type *int*)?

```
z = printrow(m1);
```

SECTION 7 ## ENRICHMENT: CALLS TO *printf* AND *scanf*: SIDE EFFECTS VERSUS RETURN VALUES

CALLING THE FUNCTIONS *printf* AND *scanf*

This is a good time to comment on an anomalous situation regarding the functions *printf* and *scanf*. Although we have underplayed it to this point, *printf* and *scanf* are functions in the standard library. As we noted in Section 2, their prototypes are found in the header file *stdio.h*.

---

[6]In general, our goal should be to develop a main program which is as simple as possible, with the details supplied in the functions. Someone who is not concerned with the details can concentrate on the main program; someone who needs to know more can study the individual functions.

Here is a typical use of *printf* and *scanf*:

```
int val;

scanf("%d",&val);
printf("the value read in is %d\n",val);
```

These statements read a value into the variable *val*, then print it. Let's concentrate on how this code looks. Consider the calls to the functions *scanf* and *printf*. We write the name of the function, followed by a list of parameters. Therefore, each function is called as if it is a void function. Even though *scanf* and *printf* are not void functions, this is a simple way to visualize their actions.

When a function returns a value, we usually include the function call as part of a larger expression. For example, the call can appear on the right-hand side of an assignment statement, as shown here for the function *sqrt*:

```
y = sqrt(x);
```

As an alternative, the value returned can be printed directly, as in this statement:

```
printf("%f",sqrt(x));
```

In addition to using a function's return value, the function call can stand by itself, as if the function is void. For the function *sqrt*, the call would look like this:

```
sqrt(x);
```

This is a valid C statement but doesn't accomplish much. The value of *x* is sent to the function *sqrt*, which computes the square root and returns this value. Because the value returned is not part of a larger expression, nothing is done with it.

However, if the function being called has a side effect, it may be reasonable to have the function call stand by itself. This side effect is sometimes considered to be the major effect of a call to such a function.

Let's look more carefully at the two functions, *scanf* and *printf*, to see what happens when they are called. For *scanf*, the side effect of a call is that a value is read into a variable. In the case of *printf*, the side effect is that output is printed. Because of the way we use these functions, we lose sight of what is really happening and consider these side effects to be the direct results of the function calls. Therefore, we say that a call to *scanf* reads in data and a call to *printf* prints output.[7] However, these two functions do return values. Let's look at them one by one.

RETURN VALUE OF A CALL TO THE *printf* FUNCTION

The *printf* function returns the number of characters printed unless an error occurs, when it returns a negative value. For example, consider the following call to *printf*:

---

[7]Ignoring the value returned is called **casting** a function as a void function. In effect, we tell the compiler to treat the function as if it is void.

```
int val;

scanf("%d",&val);
printf("the value read in is %d\n",val);
```

This call prints 22 characters (this includes the newline character, **\n**), plus the number of digits in the value read in. If **val** is 89, the call to **printf** prints 24 characters, and the **printf** function returns the value 24; if **val** is 7, the call prints 23 characters, and the function returns the value 23. To demonstrate this, we can modify the call slightly, as shown in Example 5-8.

EXAMPLE 5-8

```
int val,count;

scanf("%d",&val);
count = printf("the value read in is %d\n",val);
printf("the first call to printf printed %d characters\n",count);
```

If we run this bit of code and **val** is 89, the output is the following:

```
the value read in is 89
the first call to printf printed 24 characters
```

STYLE WORKSHOP It is rare for an error to occur during printing with **printf**. Therefore, the value returned by a call to **printf** is almost always the number of characters printed. There are a few cases when this number is useful, but generally we can ignore the value returned by a call to **printf**.

RETURN VALUE OF A CALL TO THE *scanf* FUNCTION

Now let's look at a call to **scanf**. This function works by reading in characters, converting them to values of the right type, and storing these values in the appropriate variables. The conversion process depends upon the specifications in the control string.

A call to the **scanf** function returns the number of successful conversions (this can be 0); if there are not enough characters in the input stream to give values to all of the variables, **scanf** returns a signal that the end of the file has been reached (this is the constant **EOF**).[8] Unless the data values have been used up, a call to **scanf** returns the number of variables that receive values.

Let's look at an example that uses the return value from **scanf** to determine the end of a set of input. Here **scanf** reads a value into a single variable in accord with our earlier recommendation.

---

[8]The value **EOF** is defined in the header file **stdio.h**.

EXAMPLE 5-9

```
int val,num;

num = scanf("%d",&val);
while (num == 1) {
    printf("the value read in is %d\n",val);
    num = scanf("%d",&val);
}
```

Note that the value returned by the call to *scanf* is stored in *num* and then controls the *while* loop.

◆ If the call to *scanf* returns 1, there is a successful conversion. In this case, a value is read into *val* and can be printed in the body of the loop.

◆ If the condition controlling it is not true, the loop terminates. In this case, there are two possibilities:

1. The call to *scanf* returns *EOF*, which means there was no value to read in. The user entered an end-of-file signal—either CTRL-D in Unix or CTRL-Z in DOS—in an interactive environment; or the file contained no more values (in the case of input redirection or reading from an external file). In either case, the *scanf* function translates this signal into the value *EOF*, and the loop terminates.

2. The user entered a value which could not be converted into an integer (e.g., the user entered the character *a*). In that case, the call to *scanf* returns 0 to be stored in *num*, meaning no values have been converted. If this occurs, the loop terminates.

Therefore, as long as the user continues to enter valid data values, this loop prints them out; when the user indicates the end of the set of data (or types an illegal value), the loop terminates.

STYLE WORKSHOP Some programmers test every call to *scanf* to make sure that successful conversions have taken place. From a software-engineering point of view, this verification of input is crucial. Because we have just introduced functions and return values, we have not tested the value returned by *scanf* up till now. However, we will do so in later programs, and you are urged to do the same.

SELF-CHECK 5-14

1. What value is returned by each of these calls to *printf*?

   a. `printf("Hello World");`   b. `printf("Hello World\n");`

2. What are the values returned by each of the following calls to *scanf*? (Variables *n1* and *n2* have type *int*.) Explain why you cannot be sure what value is actually returned.

   a. `scanf("%d",&n1);`   b. `scanf("%d %d",&n1,&n2);`

SECTION 8 **ENRICHMENT: A FIRST LOOK AT PARAMETERS WHICH ARE POINTERS**

This section introduces one last feature related to functions and parameter transmission. This material will be covered in more detail in Chapter 8, Section 2.

A FUNCTION THAT CHANGES TWO OR MORE VARIABLES

In sections 1 and 2, we discussed functions which compute and return a single value. In Section 4, we discussed void functions, which do not return any answer. Sometimes it is convenient to write a function which computes more than one answer. To do this, we need to discuss how a function can change values in the program which calls it. By using parameters which are pointers, a function can change the value stored at one or more of the actual arguments in the program which calls that function. In a sense, this gives the function the ability to return any number of values.

NOTE

In this section, we concentrate on two concrete examples of how to accomplish this task. In Chapter 8, after we have discussed pointers, we can explain what actually occurs.

THE FUNCTION *findmaxmin*

Assume we want to modify the function ***printmaxmin*** from Example 5-6 in Section 4 so that the main program knows both the larger and smaller of the two values. As a first step, we give a slightly modified version of the original function. (This version stores the larger and smaller in local variables ***max*** and ***min*** and prints them.)

```
/* ... */
void printmaxmin(int x, int y)
{
    int max,min;

    if (x > y)  {
        max = x;
        min = y;
    }
    else  {
        max = y;
        min = x;
    }
    printf("max = %d and min = %d",max,min);
    return;
}
```

Printing the answer in the function solves the problem of ***printmaxmin*** but doesn't let the main program know which is larger and which smaller. To do this, the two values have to be sent from the function to the main program.

We use a new function, called ***findmaxmin***, to find the larger and smaller of two numbers and store them in locations which are parameters to the function. After the call to the function is complete, the main program can access the values stored there. Example 5-10 shows how to write the function ***findmaxmin***.

EXAMPLE 5-10 The function *findmaxmin* receives four parameters. Two of them, *x* and *y*, are the same as before, values for which we want to find the maximum and minimum. The two new formal parameters, *max* and *min*, are used by the function to reference the maximum and minimum of the original values received from the main program. Here is the new function header, showing the four parameters and their data types:

```
void findmaxmin(int x, int y, int *max, int *min)
```

Most of the new function can be the same as *printmaxmin*. However, to allow the calling function to access the new values computed in *findmaxmin*, we must replace the variables *max* and *min* by **max* and **min*. (In Chapter 8, we explain exactly what the * means.)

```
{
    if (x > y)  {
        *max = x;
        *min = y;
    }
    else  {
        *max = y;
        *min = x;
    }
    return;
}
```

This code sets **max* to the larger of *x* and *y* and **min* to the smaller. Then the function returns to the calling program without returning an explicit value. However, it communicates with the calling program by changing the values stored in two of the actual parameters.

THE COMPLETE FUNCTION *findmaxmin*

We will rewrite the entire function *findmaxmin* at this point, giving both the header and the body.

```
/*
 * Function findmaxmin:
 * Input:
 *    x and y will have values to compare
 *    max and min point to locations that
 *    will be assigned values in the function
 * Process:
 *    the function stores the larger of x and y
 *    in *max; it also stores the smaller in *min
 * Output:
 *    the locations max and min point to will get values
 */
```

```
void findmaxmin(int x, int y, int *max, int *min)
{
    if (x > y)  {
        *max = x;
        *min = y;
    }
    else  {
        *max = y;
        *min = x;
    }
    return;
}
```

CALLING THE FUNCTION *findmaxmin*: USE OF THE & OPERATOR

To show how to call this function from a main program, we can use the following driver program:

```
/*
 * driver program to test findmaxmin
 */
#include <stdio.h>
void findmaxmin(int, int, int *, int *);
main()
{
    int a=1,b=2,larger,smaller;

    findmaxmin(a,b,&larger,&smaller);
    printf("the larger is %d    and the smaller is %d\n",larger,smaller);
}
```

The actual parameters in the main program are matched to the formal parameters in the function in the usual way: *a* to *x*, *b* to *y*, *&larger* to *max*, and *&smaller* to *min*. However, you should note the use of the ampersand (&) in front of *larger* and *smaller*. The & tells the function where the main program's variables *larger* and *smaller* are stored so that it can change their values. By using ampersands, we are sending the locations, not the values, of *larger* and *smaller* to the function. Here & is used as it is in a call to the *scanf* function. (The use of & is discussed in Chapter 8.)

Before the function starts, *a* and *b* have the values 1 and 2. The variables *larger* and *smaller* do not have initial values because they will be given values in the function.

Inside the function, the formal parameter *x* has the value 1 (since *x* holds the value of *a*), and the formal parameter *y* has the value 2 (since *y* holds the value of *b*); in the same way, *max* holds the value of *&larger*, and *min* holds the value of *&smaller* (see Figure 5-12).

FIGURE 5-12 Association of actual and formal parameters for a call to *findmaxmin*

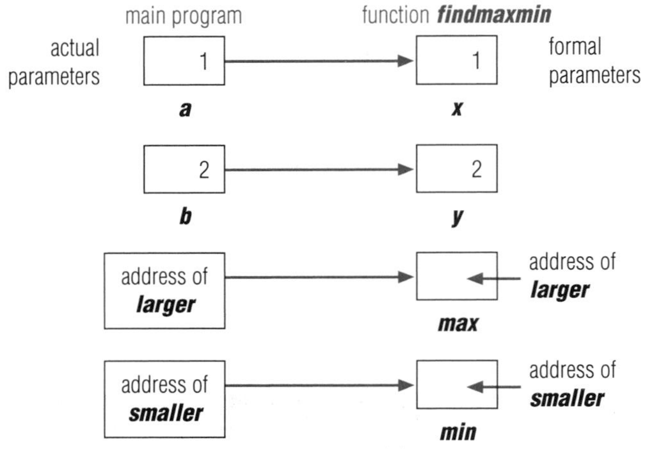

PROGRAM TRACE Now we can trace how the function works.

◆ Since the *if* condition is false, we execute the compound statement from the *else* statement, setting *max* to 2 and *min* to 1.

◆ This means that the values stored at the locations of the matching actual parameters (*larger* and *smaller*) are set to 2 and 1. Anything that happens to *max* and *min* also happens to the corresponding variables in the main program since they are the same storage locations.

◆ When we return to the main program, *larger* (matched with *max*) has the value 2, and *smaller* (matched with *min*) has the value 1. The printout, which comes from the main program, not the function, says

```
the larger is 2   and the smaller is 1
```

THE FUNCTION *setto7*

Let's look at another example of a function that changes more than one variable in the main program. Example 5-11 shows a function that receives three parameters, setting the value pointed to by each of them to 7.

EXAMPLE 5-11

```
/*
 * Function setto7:
 * Input:
 *    three parameters: x,y,z
 * Process:
 *    sets the value stored at each
 *    actual parameter to 7
```

```
 * Output
 *    returns the new values by way of the parameters
 */
void setto7(int *x, int *y, int *z)
{
    *x = 7;
    *y = 7;
    *z = 7;
    return;
}
```

Here is a driver program which calls **setto7**:

```
/*
 * driver program to test setto7
 */
#include <stdio.h>
void setto7(int *, int *, int *);
main()
{
    int a=5, b=1, c=10;

    printf("the original values are: %d %d %d\n",a,b,c);
    setto7(&a,&b,&c);
    printf("the new values are: %d %d %d\n",a,b,c);
}
```

The output from this program is the following:

```
the original values are: 5 1 10
the new values are: 7 7 7
```

Note that the actual parameters in the main program all have ampersands in the call to the function. Similarly, the formal parameters in the function all have asterisks. This is how the function matches the formal and actual parameters, *&a* to *x,* and so on.

USING A PARAMETER WHICH IS A POINTER

A formal parameter which has an asterisk is a pointer. It holds the address or location of the corresponding actual parameter. Modifying the value pointed to by the formal parameter allows the function indirectly to modify the value stored at the corresponding address. Let's go over the steps to use a parameter which is a pointer in a function.

◆   The formal parameter in the function header (or the function prototype) has a data type which includes an asterisk—*int *x.*

♦ In the body of the function, this parameter is used with the ∗—for example, ∗***x*** can appear on the left-hand side of an assignment statement.

♦ The corresponding actual argument in the main program includes an ampersand—***&a.***

♦ After the function returns control to the main program, the variable ***a*** holds the new value placed there by the function.

SELF-CHECK 5-15

1. Why can't the function ***findmaxmin*** return both the larger and smaller values?

2. In the function header for ***findmaxmin***, why don't the first two parameters have an ∗ between the data type and the name?

3. Give the header for a function ***settolarger***, which receives the addresses of two parameters, ***x*** and ***y***. For example, we can call the function by sending it the addresses of variables ***a*** and ***b***.

SUMMARY

BASIC FUNCTION CONCEPTS

1. A module is a series of instructions that performs a specific task. A module that performs a calculation directly in a main program can be replaced by two things: (1) a general set of instructions describing how to perform that calculation; and (2) the details of which values (called parameters) should be used for a particular calculation. In order to perform a calculation, the program applies the general set of instructions to a specific group of parameter values.

2. The general set of instructions is called a function or a function definition. Each group of parameter values is specified in a call to the function. Once a function has been defined, it can be called any number of times with a new set of parameters each time.

3. Standard or library functions are supplied as part of the C standard library. Most library functions compute a specific value; for example, ***sqrt*** computes a square root, and ***abs*** calculates an absolute value.

4. Besides using library functions, a person writing a C program can include additional programmer-defined functions. Each programmer-defined function should be designed to perform a single task.

5. Here is the sequence of events in a call to a function. The main program temporarily suspends execution, and the function begins. The main program usually sends some particular value(s) to the function. Each value is called an actual or real parameter (or argument) in the main program; it is matched to a formal or dummy parameter inside the function. In C, all parameters are passed by value.

6. One type of function uses the parameter value(s) to compute a single answer; this answer is sent back as the value returned by the function. For example, the library function ***sqrt*** computes and returns the square root of whatever parameter value it receives. This type of function can have any fixed number (0, 1, 2, ...) of parameters but returns precisely one answer.

FUNCTION HEADER AND DECLARATION OF LOCAL VARIABLES

7. The top line of a function is called the function header. It includes the type of answer returned by the function and the name of the function, plus the name and data type of each formal parameter. Here is an example:

```
double sample(int x, double y)
```

The name of the function is *sample*; it has two formal parameters. One, *x*, has data type *int*; the other, *y*, has data type *double*. The function returns an answer of type *double*.

8. The function header is followed by the declaration of any local variables used in the function. A local variable declared in a function has no relationship to any other variable, even one with the same name, in the main program. Just as in a main program, a pair of braces surrounds the local variable declarations and the actual instructions to perform the function.

9. Here is an example of a complete function definition, including the declaration of a local variable, *z*, within it:

```
double sample(int x, double y)
{
    double z;

    z = x + y;
    return z;
}
```

The function *sample* adds together the values of the two parameters, then returns that sum.

FUNCTION CALL AND RETURN

10. Here is an example of a call from a main program to the function *sample*:

```
#include <stdio.h>
double sample(int, double);
main()
{
    int    a;
    double b,c;
    ...
    c = sample(a,b);
    ...
}
```

A call from the main program to the function consists of the name of the function, followed by the actual parameter(s) in parentheses. For the call above, the variables *a* and *b* in the main program are actual parameters which match formal parameters *x* and *y* inside the function; *c* holds the answer returned by the function.

11. The function returns an answer through a *return* statement. Back in the calling program, the returned answer can be stored directly in another variable, appear as part of an expression, or be printed by a call to *printf*. In fact, the answer returned by one function can be sent to another as an actual parameter.

12. The function *sample* returns the value stored in *z* by the following statement:

```
return z;
```

When the main program calls *sample*, the answer returned is stored in the variable *c*.

PARAMETER TRANSMISSION AND TYPE CHECKING

13. When the function is called, the value of each actual parameter is copied into the corresponding formal parameter in the function. This is called parameter transmission by value. The actual parameters need not be variables; they can be expressions such as *2 * a + b* or constants like –6.

14. The overall task of this type of function is to compute a particular value consistent with the data type mentioned in the function header. The function always returns this value to the point at which it was called.

15. Verification that values have the correct data types is called type checking. The compiler performs type checking as it translates the function into machine language.

FUNCTION PROTOTYPES

16. When a function is called, the compiler can perform additional type checking. For example, it can verify that the parameters being sent to the function match what is expected. To do this, the compiler needs access to the function declaration or prototype while it is translating the program into machine language.

17. One way to give the compiler access to the function prototype is to have it at the top of a file which contains the main program. This is the way that function prototypes for the standard library functions work. For example, *stdio.h* contains a number of function prototypes for input/output functions; *math.h* contains a number of function prototypes for mathematical functions.

18. If the function being called is programmer defined, the function prototype should be explicit. The function prototype can look like a function header, or it can omit the names of the parameters. Because it is a complete C statement, the function prototype ends in a semicolon. Here is a function prototype for the function *sample*:

```
double sample(int, double);
```

ADVANTAGES OF FUNCTIONS

19. One major advantage of using functions is the ability to test and debug each one independently. Once a function has been thoroughly debugged, it can be trusted as a module of a larger program. For example, if a main program calls a function, each can be tested and debugged separately until they seem to work, then joined to form a complete program.

VOID FUNCTIONS

20. Certain tasks that a function can perform (e.g., to print a list of numbers) have no obvious answer to return. A special type of function, called a void function, can be used. A void function does not return an explicit value but executes a task (e.g., printing the results of some calculations).

21. The header of a void function replaces the initial data type for the answer returned with the keyword *void* to indicate that no value is returned. In a void function, the entire *return* statement can be omitted, or the keyword *return* (with no value) can be used. Here is an outline of a void function, *proc1*, that receives two parameters, *a* of type *int* and *b* of type *double*:

```
void proc1(int a, double b)
{
    ...
    return;
}
```

22. The call consists of the name of the void function, followed by the name(s) of the actual parameter(s). Here is an example of a call to the void function *proc1*, sending two actual parameters, *x* and *y*:

```
int    x;
double y;

proc1(x,y);
```

23. Here is the function prototype for the void function **proc1**, showing that it receives one parameter of type **int** and one of type **double**:

```
void proc1(int, double);
```

PARAMETERLESS FUNCTIONS

24. A function that receives no parameters is called a parameterless function. It has to be relatively self-contained since it cannot communicate by way of parameters. A parameterless function can return an answer or be void.

25. A main program can be viewed as a parameterless void function. In our examples so far, **main** has not been sent any parameters, but it is possible to send them. In addition, **main** has not returned an answer (making it void), but it can return a value.

26. The function header for a parameterless void function called **sub** looks like this:

```
void sub(void)
```

The call to the void function looks like this:

```
sub();
```

The function prototype looks like this:

```
void sub(void);
```

27. In this example, one or more uses of the keyword **void** can be eliminated, but there are slight changes in the meaning. Using the keyword is recommended.

I-P-O COMMENTS

28. Input-Process-Output (*I-P-O*) analysis is a guide to organizing a programmer's thoughts in writing a function. *I* stands for input, the various pieces of information a function needs to do its job. *P* stands for process, the task accomplished by the function. *O* stands for output, the way the function communicates its results. The *I-P-O* analysis can also serve as a comment for the function.

RETURN VALUES FROM *scanf* AND *printf*

29. Although **scanf** and **printf** are often treated like void functions, each one does return a value. A call to the function **printf** returns the number of characters printed by that call. A call to the function **scanf** returns the number of data values successfully converted. If there are not enough data values for each variable sent as a parameter to **scanf**, the end-of-file signal, **EOF**, is returned.

USING A PARAMETER WHICH IS A POINTER IN A FUNCTION

30. A function can use a parameter which is a pointer to modify one or more arguments in the calling function. Here is a function which has three such parameters:

```
void initialize(int *p, int *q, int *r)
{
    *p = 0;
    *q = 0;
    *r = 0;
    return;
}
```

31. Here is a main program that uses the function *initialize*:

```
#include <stdio.h>
void initialize(int *,int *,int *);
main()
{
    int a = 5, b = 3, c = 9;

    printf("the original values are: %d, %d, and %d\n",a,b,c);
    initialize(&a,&b,&c);
    printf("the new values are: %d, %d, and %d\n",a,b,c);
}
```

The main program sends the locations *(&a, &b, and &c)* of three variables as parameters to the function. The function has the effect of setting the value stored at each location to 0. The main program prints the following:

```
the original values are: 5, 3, and 9
the new values are: 0, 0, and 0
```

EXERCISES

TRACING EXERCISES

1. Show what is printed by the following program, which calls a function *func*.

```
#include <stdio.h>
int func(int, int, int);
main()
{
    int a,b,c,d;

    a = 5;  b = 4;  c = 2;
    d = func(a,b,c);
    printf("%d %d %d gives an answer of %d\n",a,b,c,d);
    a = func(b,c,d);
    printf("%d %d %d gives an answer of %d\n",b,c,d,a);
}

int func(int x, int y, int z)
{
    int w;

    w = x + y;
    if (y < z + 1)
        w++;
    return w;
}
```

2. Show what is printed by the following program, which calls a function ***powers***. Describe in words what the function ***powers*** does. Why is the answer returned by it given data type ***double*** rather than ***int***?

```c
#include <stdio.h>
double powers(int);
main()
{
    int    e;
    double f;

    e = 3;
    f = powers(e);
    printf("%d terms give a sum of %f\n",e, f);
    e = 5;
    f = powers(e);
    printf("%d terms give a sum of %f\n",e, f);
    e = 7;
    f = powers(e);
    printf("%d terms give a sum of %f\n",e, f);
}

double powers(int n)
{
    int    i;
    double sum;

    sum = 0;
    for (i = 1; i <= n; i++)
        sum += i*i*i*i;
    return sum;
}
```

3. Show what is printed by the following program, which calls a function ***eq2***. Describe in words what the function ***eq2*** does.

```c
#include <stdio.h>
int eq2(int, int, int);
main()
{
    int p = 4, q = 5, r = 7;

    if (eq2(p,q,r) == 1)
        printf("%d %d %d gives a true answer\n",p,q,r);
    else
        printf("%d %d %d gives a false answer\n",p,q,r);

    printf("%d %d %d",p+3,q-1,r);
    if (eq2(p+3,q-1,r) == 1)
        printf(" returns true\n");
    else
        printf(" returns false");
```

(*continued*)

(*continued*)
```
            printf("%d %d %d",p,4,q-1);
            printf(" gives an answer of %d\n",eq2(p,4,q-1));
    }

    int eq2(int a, int b,int c)
    {
        int ans = 0;

        if (a == b)
            ans = 1;
        if (a == c)
            ans = 1;
        if (b == c)
            ans = 1;
        return ans;
    }
```

4. For each of the functions in exercises 1 to 3, identify the formal parameters and local variables. For each call to a function, identify the actual parameters. Explain the matchup of formal and actual parameters.

5. Describe what is printed by this program.

```
#include <stdio.h>
double harmonic(int);
main()
{
    double sum50,sum100;

    sum50 = harmonic(50);
    sum100 = harmonic(100);
    printf("sum of 50 terms %f\n",sum50);
    printf("sum of 100 terms %f\n",sum100);
}

double harmonic(int n)
{
    int    i;
    double sum=0;

    for (i = 1; i <= n; i++)
        sum = sum + 1.0 / i;
    return sum;
}
```

6. Show what is printed by the following program.

```
#include <stdio.h>
void printlines(int);
main()
```

```
{
     int num=5;

     printlines(num);
     num = 3;
     printlines(num);
}

void printlines(int k)
{
     int i;

     for (i = 0; i < k; i++)
          printf("hello\n");
     return;
}
```

7. a. Show what is printed by the following program.

```
#include <stdio.h>
void printeach(int,int);
main()
{
     int a = 4, b = 10;

     printeach(a,b);
}

void printeach(int x, int y)
{
     int i;

     printf("here is a list of the numbers in between %d and %d\n",x,y);
     for (i = x; i <= y; i++)
          printf("%d\n",i);
     return;
}
```

b. Show what is printed when *a* is initialized to 4 and *b* to 3.

8. Show what is printed by the following program. Assume that the user types in the number 1, then the number 2, and finally, the number 5.

```
#include <stdio.h>
void printmenu(void);
main()
{
     int num;

     printmenu();
     scanf("%d",&num);
     if (num == 1)
          printf("Hello");
```
(continued)

(continued)

```
        else
            printf("Goodbye");
    }

    void printmenu(void)
    {
        printf("type 1 if you want me to say Hello\n\n");
        printf("type 2 if you want me to say Goodbye\n\n");
        return;
    }
```

9. a. Give the function prototype for a function named *func1* that receives one parameter of type *int* and computes an answer of type *int*.

   b. Give the function prototype for a function named *func2* that receives one parameter of type *double* and computes an answer of type *char*.

MODIFICATIONS OF EARLIER FUNCTIONS AND PROGRAMS

10. This call to *printf* contains a call to the function *max3*:

    ```
    printf("%d\n",max3(p + 2, 12, abs(q)) * 3);
    ```

    Show how to break the expression being printed into smaller pieces, using extra variables to hold the intermediate results.

11. a. Show how to rewrite the function *sign* using the conditional (?:) operator from Chapter 3, Section 6.

    b. Do the same for the function *max3*.

12. Does it make sense to rewrite Program 1 (the squares of the numbers from 4 to 9) using a function? Explain.

13. Write a void function, *evalformula*, to evaluate the formula in Program 2. The function is sent the value for *gpa* and computes the value for *result*, using the formula in Problem 2. In addition, the function handles all the output associated with printing this value of *gpa* and *result*. Show how the main program calls the function.

14. Rewrite the payroll program from Chapter 3, using a function to compute the employee's pay for the week. You must decide exactly what parameter(s) to send to the function.

15. Write a void function, *printprompts*, to print the prompts in Program 3. The function should print a series of messages asking the user to type in the three pieces of data requested for each employee.

16. Program 5 used a function called *sumofsquares* to compute and return the sum of the squares from 1 to a given number. The main program then printed the sum. Show how to change *sumofsquares* into a void function to compute and print the sum of the squares. What changes have to be made to the main program?

17. a. Write a program to do the following: For each number *n* from 1 to 15, the main program calls a function to find the sum of the squares of the numbers from 1 to *n*.

    b. Modify your program so that the function computes the sum of the cubes of the numbers from 1 to *n*.

18. a.   In Section 6, the function **printrow** prints one row of a multiplication table. Show how to write a function, called **multtable**, which prints an entire multiplication table. (*Suggestion*: This function should contain a nested loop.) Show how the main program has to change to use this function.

    b.   Compare this version of the multiplication table program to the original one from Chapter 4 and the one in Section 6.

19. Modify the function **printheadings** from Section 6 so that it prints the column headings appropriate for a multiplication chart that goes from 1 to 8.

20. Modify the function **printheadings** from Section 6 so that it prints the column headings appropriate for a multiplication chart that goes from 1 to **LIMIT**, where **LIMIT** is a constant defined in the main program (**LIMIT** is never more than 10). For example, if **LIMIT** is 8, the function prints the headings from 1 to 8. (*Suggestion*: You may want to use a **for** loop to print the headings instead of mentioning each number.)

ANALYSIS EXERCISES

21. This exercise explores what happens when the keyword **void** is omitted from the header of either a void or parameterless function. In each case, run a driver program to test this function. See if the compiler issues an error message or warning.

    a.   Take a void, parameterless function (e.g., the function **printheadings** from Section 4). Write the function as shown in the text—include the keyword **void** as the return type and use **void** to indicate that the function does not receive parameters.

    b.   Modify the function header and prototype so that the return type **void** is omitted (but keep **void** within the parentheses for the parameter list). See if the compiler issues an error message or warning.

    c.   Modify the function header and prototype so that the return type is **void** but do not put **void** inside the parentheses surrounding the parameter list. See if the compiler issues an error message or warning.

    d.   Make the change described in part (c). In addition, in the call to the function, send one parameter—for example, a constant.

PROGRAMMING PROJECTS

22. Many of the programming projects in Chapter 4 can be rewritten with functions instead of doing the work directly in the main program. Show how to rewrite some of these projects using functions. In each exercise you rewrite, decide exactly what parameter(s) to send to the function and what type of answer the function returns. In some exercises, include more than one function. For example, in Exercise 4-24, one function can do error checking, and one can perform calculations.

23. This and the next few exercises explore some ways to determine if one number is divisible by another.

    a.   What is the value of 7 % 2? Of 6 % 2? Of 5 % 2? In general, if **number** has type **int**, what is the value of **number % 2** if **number** holds an even number? What if **number** holds an odd number?

b. Write a function, called *iseven*, which receives one parameter *x* and uses the % operator to determine whether *x* is divisible by 2.

c. Rewrite the function from part (b) using truncation on integer division. [*Hint*: What is 2 * (7 / 2)? What is 2 * (8 / 2)?]

d. Write a function *isdivisby3* to determine whether its parameter *x* is divisible by 3. Write two versions of your function: one using % and one with truncation on integer division.

24. Write a function *isdivisby* which receives two parameters: *number* and *divisor*. The function determines whether *divisor* is a divisor of *number*. For example, the function returns the following values:

a. If *number* is 4 and *divisor* is 3, the function returns 0.

b. If *number* is 12 and *divisor* is 3, the function returns 1.

c. If *number* is 12 and *divisor* is 5, the function returns 0.

(*Suggestion*: You can use either truncation on integer division or the % operator. See Exercise 23.)

25. a. Write a function *printalldivisors* to receive one parameter, an integer *number*. The function prints all the divisors of *number*. For example, if *number* holds 15, the function prints a line of output that looks like this:

```
Divisors of 15      1   3   5   15
```

[*Suggestion*: Exercises 23 and 24 discuss several ways to determine whether a given integer divides another. You can set up a loop using one of these methods to test the possible divisors of *number* (what is the largest possible divisor?).]

b. Using the function *printalldivisors*, write a program to print each number from 1 to 40, followed by a list of its divisors.

```
Divisors of 1       1
Divisors of 2       1   2
Divisors of 3       1   3
    ...
Divisors of 40      1   2   4   5   8   10  20  40
```

26. a. Write a function to find the sum of the proper divisors of a given number *n*. The proper divisors of *n* are the numbers less than *n* that divide it evenly; they do not include *n* itself. For example, if *n* is 12, then the sum of the proper divisors is $1 + 2 + 3 + 4 + 6 = 16$. Write a main program that tests the function by reading in various values for *n* and finding the sum of the proper divisors.

b. A number is called perfect if it is equal to the sum of its proper divisors. For example, 6 is equal to the sum of its divisors, $1 + 2 + 3$. A number is deficient if it is greater than the sum of its proper divisors (9 is greater than $1 + 3$). A number is abundant if it is less than the sum of its proper divisors (12 is less than $1 + 2 + 3 + 4 + 6$). Modify your program from part (a) so that it prints the appropriate message ("Perfect," "Abundant," or "Deficient") for each number *n*.

c. Modify your program from part (b) so that it computes how many numbers from 100 to 200 are perfect, how many are deficient, and how many are abundant. Print these totals after processing the last number.

27. A number greater than 1 is prime if its only divisors are 1 and itself. For example, the only divisors of 2 are 1 and 2, so 2 is prime. The number 9 has 3 as a divisor, so it is not prime.

    a. Use the program from Exercise 26 (a) to determine whether a number is prime. (*Hint*: What is the sum of the divisors for a prime number?)
    b. Another way to determine whether a number is prime is to test whether it has any proper divisors greater than 1. If it has none, it is prime. (*Hint*: A simple way to test this is to set a flag or switch to 0 before a *for* loop that processes every possible divisor. Reset the flag to 1 if you find a divisor. If the flag is still 0 at the end of the loop, what does this imply?)

28. The method of testing for divisors in Exercise 27 is extremely inefficient. This exercise discusses several improvements.

    a. Modify the program so that it does not test whether 1 is a divisor of the number (1 must be a divisor—why?).
    b. Modify the program so that it never tests a possible divisor that is greater than the original value of **number**. Why?
    c. Modify the program so that it never tests a possible divisor that is greater than half the original value of **number**. What is the only divisor larger than half the value of **number** that divides it?
    d. Modify the program so that it never tests a possible divisor that is greater than the square root of **number**. For example, if **number** is 105, it never tests a possible divisor greater than 10. If you do this, you must print two divisors each time an exact one is found. (Why?) For example, when you find that 3 divides 105, you must also print that 35 divides it.
    e. Compare the original program to the improved versions. Which improvement do you think is the "best?" Why?

29. The factorial of a number **n**, written **n!**, is defined as follows:

    n! = 1 * 2 * ... * (n - 1) * n   (and 0! = 1)

    For example, $5! = 1 * 2 * 3 * 4 * 5 = 120; 3! = 1 * 2 * 3 = 6.$

    a. Write a program to do the following: Read in a number **n**, then use a function to compute **n!**. (*Suggestion*: Use a *for* loop to compute the product with an appropriate initialization and multiplication step.)
    b. Write a program that computes a table of the numbers from 1 to **n**, together with the factorial of each number. (Do not use a function for this version.) For example, if **n** is 7, it should print (each pair on a new line):

1	1	2	2	3	6	4	24	5	120	6	720	7	5040

    c. Modify your program from part (a) so that it reads in a series of values for **n** and computes **n!** for each value (use a negative value as a trailer).

30. Compare the efficiency of the programs from Exercise 29. (First, you have to specify a way of measuring program efficiency. For example, you can see which program executes fewer instructions.) If you want to compute a large number of consecutive factorial values, which is the more efficient method? If you only want one or two widely spaced factorial values, which is more efficient?

31. Although C does not contain an exponentiation operator (an operator to compute x^y), it does have a standard library function, called **pow**, to compute exponents. Several other computer languages, such as Pascal, do not have any direct way to compute exponents. This exercise explores two possible ways to calculate exponents in these languages.

    a.   If the exponent y is a positive integer, then exponentiation can be viewed as repeated multiplication. For example, x^3 is x multiplied by itself three times.

        Write a C function that accepts two parameters: a real number **x** and a nonnegative integer **y**. It computes x^y, using a loop for repeated multiplications. In the main program which calls this function, compare the answer to the result from the **pow** function. (The prototypes for **pow** and the functions **exp** and **log** below are all in **math.h**.)

    b.   In case **y** is not a positive integer, the method in part (a) cannot be used (why?). However, we can use the following identity:

$$x^y = e^{y \log x} \qquad \text{(assuming } x > 0)$$

        Here e is the base of the natural logarithm system and $\log x$ is the logarithm of x to the base e (the exponent to which e must be raised to get x). You can use the standard library functions **exp** and **log** to evaluate the right-hand side (see Chapter 2).

        Write a C function to accept two real parameters, **x** and **y**. It computes x^y, using the formula above. Are there any limitations on the parameters to this function?

32. C has a library function, **rand** (the function prototype is located in **stdlib.h**), which generates random numbers. If **n** has type **int**, the function call below stores a nonnegative integer value, chosen "at random," in **n**.

```
n = rand();
```

    a.   Using **rand**, write a program to generate a list of ten random numbers.

    b.   Run the program from part (a) a second and third time. What happens?

    c.   Add the statements below before you generate the first random number (where ... represents some integer value).

```
intval = ...;
srand(intval);
```

        This is a call to the parameterless void function **srand**, using **intval** as a seed to start the process.

        Now run the program several times. What happens? Try changing the value assigned to **intval**. At this point, you may want to read the documentation your compiler has on the **rand** function.

    d.   How do you generate random numbers in the range from 1 to 6? (*Hint*: You want random values, but you don't want any of them to be 0 or larger than 6.)

    e.   How do you generate random numbers in the range from 10 to 20? From **start** to **finish**?

33. a.   Using the ideas in Exercise 32, write a program to simulate tossing a die 100 times, counting how many of the tosses are even numbers. (A die is a cube with the numbers from 1 to 6 written on it.) Then repeat the program using a 1000 tosses.

    b.   Write a program to simulate tossing a pair of dice 100 times. For example, one toss might give 5 on the first die and 3 on the second; the sum of the dice values for this toss is 8. Count how many of the sums add up to each number from 2 to 12. Then repeat the program using 1000 tosses.

34. Write a complete C program to do the following: The main program reads in three bowling scores, *score1*, *score2*, and *score3*. It then calls a series of functions to process these scores.

     The main program calls a function *validgroup* to determine if this set of three values forms a valid group. The function *validgroup* receives the three scores as parameters. For the group to be valid, each number must be in the range from 0 to 300 (the possible scores in a bowling game). If the group is valid, the function prints a message saying so. If one or more of the numbers is negative or greater than 300, the function prints an overall message that the group is invalid. In addition, for each invalid value, the function prints the score and a message. If the group is not valid, the main program skips processing and simply goes on to the next group of three values.

     If the group is valid, the main program calls a function *onegamescore*, sending it one parameter, the value *score1*. This value is an integer from 0 to 300 (how can we be sure of this?). The function converts the score into a rating, using the following system: 250 to 300 is a professional game; 200 to 249 is an excellent game; 140 to 199 is a very good game; 100 to 139 is a good game; 50 to 99 is a poor game; below 50 is a horrible game. The function prints a message with the original score and the bowler's rating. Then the main program repeats this process for *score2* and *score3*.

     Next, the main program calls a function *avg3scores*, sending it three parameters: the three scores. The function *avg3scores* finds the average (as an integer) of the three scores and sends it back. The main program prints the average. Finally, the main program calls *onegamescore* again, sending it the resulting average from the function *avg3scores*. The main program then prints three blank lines.

     Then the main program goes on to the next group of three values. When the main program runs out of groups (your program must determine this), it prints the final values of three counters it has been keeping track of: the total number of groups processed, the number of valid groups, and the number of invalid groups.

35. Write a complete C program to simulate the playing of a game of dice. The program does the following:

     a. The main program calls a void function named *introduction* to print a description of what the program does at the top of the first output page. This function is not sent any parameters and does not return a value.

     b. Then the main program asks the user to type in two integer values in the range from 1 to 6. The main program reads the two integers into variables called *die1* and *die2* and prints the numbers.

     c. The main program sends these two integer values to a function named *findoutcome*. The function determines the result of using these two numbers according to this scheme:

        (1) If the numbers add up to 7 or 11, the player wins, and the function indicates this.
        (2) If the numbers add up to 2 or 12, the player loses, and the function indicates this.
        (3) If the numbers add up to anything else, the player continues, and the function indicates this.

     d. When the function returns to the main program, it prints an appropriate message, describing which of the three cases applies in this situation.

e.   If the player won or lost, the main program goes back to step (b) to read in two more integers and repeat the process.

If the player continues, the main program calls a function *continueplay* and sends it the sum of *die1* and *die2*. For example, if *die1* is 4 and *die2* is 5, the main program sends the value 9 as a parameter to the function *continueplay*.

f.   The function *continueplay* asks the player to enter two more integers from 1 to 6. The function determines which of the following applies:

(1) If these two integers add up to 7, the player loses.
(2) If the two integers add up to the value sent to *continueplay*, the player wins.
(3) If they add up to anything else, the game continues.

Eventually, the player either wins or loses. Whatever the result, the function prints the two numbers read in each time and the result of this roll of the dice. When the game is over, the function returns to the main program with the outcome (either a loss or a win); the main program continues with the next set of two numbers from step (b).

g.   At step (b), if the user types in a special combination (you must determine what this combination is and explain it to the person using the program), the program goes to step (h).

h.   At the end, print how many games were won and how many lost.

Type in a total of about ten games. Have one where the player wins immediately with 7, one where the player wins with 11, a loss with 2, a loss with 12, and have five or six games which continue. If the game continues, make sure that the player wins some and loses some. The output of your program should allow someone to follow the game. Each function should have a good comment explaining two things: what parameter(s) the function receives and what it does.

36. Write a complete C program to do the following: The main program reads in three values, representing three exam grades.

The main program calls a function *validgroup* to determine if this set of three values forms a valid group (each value is between 0 and 100). The function sends a signal back to the main program, saying whether this group is valid.

If the group is not valid, the main program skips processing and simply goes on to the next group of three values.

If the group is valid, the main program calls a function *lettergrade*, sending it one parameter. This function translates the number into a character, representing the letter grade (90 and above is an A, in the 80s is a B, and so on). The main program prints the result of the function call and repeats this process for all three of the grades.

Then the main program calls a function *avggrades*, sending it three parameters: the three grades. The function finds the average of the three grades and sends it back. The function returns the average as an integer, ignoring any decimal places (87.67 becomes 87).

The main program calls *lettergrade* again, sending it the results of *avggrades*. The main program prints the result of this call to the function with a message saying this is the overall average.

Finally, the main program goes on to the next group of three values until it runs out of groups. At that point, it prints the final values of three counters it has been keeping track of: the total number of groups processed, the number of valid groups, and the number of invalid groups.

MORE ON CONTROL STRUCTURES

SYNTAX CONCEPTS: *do-while* loop, nested *if*, *switch*, *break*, *continue*, *exit*, logical operators

PROGRAMMING CONCEPTS: one function calling another, user-response method for signaling the end of a set of data

CONTROL STRUCTURES: *do-while* loop, one function calling another, nested *if*, *switch*, *break*, *continue*, *exit*, short-circuit evaluation

PROBLEM-SOLVING TECHNIQUES: defensive programming, error checking, program testing

HOW TO READ CHAPTER 6

The first five sections completely develop the solution to Problem 6. The remaining three sections discuss additional control structures in C. It is possible to cover sections 6 to 8 without first doing sections 1 through 5.

OUTLINE:

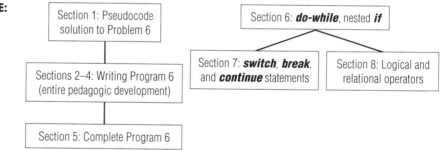

INTRODUCTION AND STATEMENT OF THE PROBLEM

This chapter solves a simple problem: Given a month and a day within that month (e.g., 6 20, standing for June 20), determine which season of the year (winter, spring, summer, or fall) and which week of the month (1, 2, ..., 5) that date is in. We will continue to use top-down programming and stepwise refinement. A number of important C constructions are introduced, including extensive use of nested *if* and *if-else* statements, logical and relational operators, *do-while* loops, and *switch* statements. These new features dramatically increase the complexity of available control structures and allow use of a wide variety of new techniques in our programs.

PROBLEM 6   Write a C program that reads in two integer values, standing for a month (from 1 to 12) and a day within the month. The program classifies these two pieces of data into the season the month is in and the week of the month the day is in. The program prints the name of the month, the day, and the results of the classification process. The program continues to read month-day combinations until the entire set of data has been processed.

Assume that winter consists of three months: 12 (December), 1 (January), and 2 (February); spring comprises three months: 3 (March), 4 (April), and 5 (May); the same holds for summer and fall. Also assume that all months have exactly 31 days, that the first four weeks in each month have 7 days each, and that week five covers days 29, 30, and 31.

The output from the program looks like this (note the format, especially the name of the month):

```
month 5 is May          spring is the season    1 is the week number for day 1

month 6 is June         summer is the season    3 is the week number for day 20

month 11 is November    fall is the season      2 is the week number for day 14
```

The statement of the problem does not discuss what to do if a piece of data is not in the right form (for example, 0 is an illegal value for the day). We will write Program 6 so that it catches many errors of this type, but Exercise 36 discusses other ways to process bad data. In addition, exercises 34 and 35 modify the assumptions about the number of days in each month and months in each season.

SECTION 1   PSEUDOCODE FOR PROBLEM 6

In this section, we develop a pseudocode solution to Problem 6. As usual, we start with rough pseudocode, then refine it into a version that translates more readily into C.

FIRST PSEUDOCODE SOLUTION TO PROBLEM 6

Here is our rough version of the pseudocode for Program 6:

> *read a month and day*
> *classify the month and day*
> *print the results*
> *repeat the above while there is more data to process*

STYLE WORKSHOP   In the last line of the pseudocode, we do not specify how to test whether there is more data to process. Such a test has to be incorporated into the final C program. Notice that the test is at the bottom of the loop, not the top.

NEXT REFINEMENT: A FUNCTION TO CLASSIFY THE MONTH AND DAY

Clearly, the next step is to work on the line, *classify the month and day*. First, we give names to the pieces of data read in; **month** and **day** are the obvious choices. It should be clear that each part of the classification process (a month into a season and a day into a week) is fairly involved. As we have learned, it is better not to include all these details in the main program. We will have the main program call a function to perform the classification process, sending *month* and *day* as parameters to the function. This function will classify *month* into one of four seasons and *day* into one of five weeks and print the results. The name *classify* is appropriate for the function.

Here is the next version of the pseudocode for the main program:

> *read* month *and* day
> *call a function* classify *to do the classification*
>   *and print the results*
> *repeat the above while there is more data to process*

PSEUDOCODE FOR THE FUNCTION *classify*

Our next step continues the top-down approach by translating the task of the function *classify* into detailed pseudocode. Inside the function, we must classify the month into a season and the day into a week. For these two subtasks, we assume that values are already stored in *month* and *day*. Since we have divided the job of *classify* into two subtasks, it seems better to use a separate function for each one. Each function works on one piece of data at a time so it needs just one parameter. In other words, *classify* calls a function to classify *month* into one of four seasons and another function to classify *day* into one of five weeks. In addition, we print the results of the calls. Let's use *whichseason* and *whichweek* as the names for these two new functions.

We can now give pseudocode for the function *classify* (which is sent two parameters—*month* and *day*):

> *call a function* whichseason *to classify* month *into one of four seasons*
> *call a function* whichweek *to classify* day *into one of five weeks*
> *print the results of the function calls*

Let's look at the format of the output. Earlier, we indicated that a typical line of output looks like this:

```
month 11 is November      fall is the season      2 is the week number for day 14
```

This line of output is constructed by all the functions working together. It contains the original data values (11 and 14), the name of the month (November) corresponding to value 11, and the values computed by the two functions (fall and week 2).

Let's concentrate on this last part of the output. When the functions *whichseason* and *whichweek* compute their answers, they should both print them out. The function *whichseason* prints the season corresponding to the month, and the function *whichweek* prints a week number from 1 to 5. For now, we are ignoring how to print the name of the month. We will solve this problem when we write the C code for the function *classify* in Section 3.

PSEUDOCODE FOR THE FUNCTION *whichseason*

Here is a rough version of the pseudocode for **whichseason** (which is sent one parameter—
month):

> *classify* month *into one of four seasons*
> *print the answer*
> *return control to the* classify *function*

This can be made more precise. We can classify **month** into a particular season by comparing the number read in with the values associated with the seasons. For example, if we
read 12 (December) as the value for **month**, we can classify it as winter; if we read 4 (April), we
can classify it as spring. We could do this classification with 12 separate **if** statements, 1 for
each month. [For example, **if (month == 1)....**] However, it is more efficient to test the months
three at a time. We now have the following refinement of the pseudocode for **whichseason**:

> if month *is 12, 1, or 2*
>   *the season is winter*
> if month *is 3, 4, or 5*
>   *the season is spring*
> if month *is 6, 7, or 8*
>   *the season is summer*
> if month *is 9, 10, or 11*
>   *the season is fall*
> *print the answer*
> *return control to the* classify *function*

PSEUDOCODE FOR THE FUNCTION *whichweek*

Similarly, we must specify pseudocode for **whichweek** (which is sent one parameter—**day**).
Here is the first rough version:

> *classify* day *into one of five weeks*
> *print the answer*
> *return control to the* classify *function*

Once again, this can be made more precise by listing the values for **day** that correspond
to each week and comparing the particular value in **day** with them. For example, if **day** has
the value 25, it is between 22 and 28—in week 4; if **day** has the value 5, we can classify it as
week 1. We could use 31 separate **if** statements, but that would be ludicrous. Here is a better
method (others are discussed in Exercise 39):

> if day *is between 1 and 7*
>   *the week is 1*
> if day *is between 8 and 14*
>   *the week is 2*
> if day *is between 15 and 21*

> *the week is 3*
> if day *is between 22 and 28*
> *the week is 4*
> if day *is 29, 30, or 31*
> *the week is 5*
> *print the answer*
> *return control to the* classify *function*

PUTTING IT ALL TOGETHER

The pseudocode for these two subtasks can be inserted into the pseudocode for the main program, replacing the call to **classify**. However, as we have discussed, it is better not to clutter up a main program. As an alternative, we can insert the pseudocode for the functions **whichseason** and **whichweek** into the pseudocode for **classify**, replacing the calls to the two functions. In sections 3 and 4, instead of either of these methods, we work directly with the various pieces of pseudocode, writing each as a function.

HIGHLIGHTS

Inside a loop (which continues until the user decides to stop), the main program reads in a value for a month and a day and sends these values to a function, **classify**. Then **classify** sends the month to one function to be classified into a season and the day to another to be classified into a week.

ADVANTAGES OF OUR APPROACH

There are several advantages of dividing up the work. First, it simplifies the main program. As a general rule, as much of the work as possible should be shifted out of the main program and into the functions. In the same way, this division of work simplifies and clarifies the job of **classify**. Each function—including **classify**, **whichseason**, and **whichweek**—has a single well-defined task. This makes testing and debugging easier, as we will discuss in Section 5. Finally, if a function has a single task, it is easier to reuse in another situation.

SELF-CHECK 6-1

1. What is the purpose of the function **classify**?

2. What is the purpose of the function **whichseason**? What is the purpose of the function **whichweek**?

3. Why is it better to use several functions rather than do everything in the main program?

SECTION 2 ## THE MAIN PROGRAM; USING A *do-while* LOOP AND THE USER-RESPONSE METHOD

In this section, we evolve the C code for the main program from the pseudocode. When we translate the pseudocode into C, we introduce two additional features: a new type of loop (a **do-while** loop) and a new way to detect the end of a set of data (the user-response method).

TRANSLATING PSEUDOCODE FOR THE MAIN PROGRAM INTO C

Here is the main program's pseudocode:

> *read* month *and* day
> *call a function* classify *to do the classification*
>   *and print the results*
> *repeat the above while there is more data to process*

Following our top-down approach, we begin the C program with the main program, then write any needed functions. As usual, the main program starts with a comment and the header:

```
/*
 * Program prog6.c:
 * classify a month-day combination
 * in terms of seasons and weeks
 */
#include <stdio.h>
main()
```

Let's assume the main program interactively asks the user to type in the data (first the number of a month, then a day within that month), reads this information, then calls the function *classify* to perform the classification. We've already decided that *classify* needs two parameters—the month-day combination. It also prints the results of the classification. Since the function *classify* handles the printing, the main program does not have to receive an answer from it. Therefore, *classify* is a void function, and the call to *classify* from the main program looks like this: *classify*(*month*,*day*).

This is what we have so far for the action portion of the main program:

> *ask the user to enter values for month and day*
> ```
> scanf("%d",&month);
> scanf("%d",&day);
> /*
>  * call a function to classify the month-day
>  * pair and print the results
>  */
> classify(month,day);
> ```
> *repeat the above while there is more data to process*

DECLARATION OF THE VARIABLES IN THE MAIN PROGRAM

We can flesh this out with declarations for the variables and specific details of the interactive input.

```
        {
            int month,day;

            printf("\nType in the number of a month");
            printf(" from 1 (January) to 12 (December)> ");
            scanf("%d",&month);
            printf("\nType in a date within the month, from 1 to 31> ");
            scanf("%d",&day);
            /*
             * call a function to classify the month-day
             * pair and print the results
             */
            classify(month,day);
```

DETECTING THE END OF THE SET OF DATA: USER-RESPONSE METHOD

Let's continue working on the main program. We must make sure there is a way for the program to end—to detect the end of the set of data. Here is a new method which enables the user to stop the program at any time. After we finish processing a particular **month-day** pair, we can ask the user the following question: "Do you want to continue?" If the user types in the letter *y* (which is stored as a single character: '*y*'), we want to repeat the process by reading in a new **month-day** pair and calling the **classify** function; if the user answers *n*, we stop. This is not quite the same as the trailer-value method, although the two are similar. (See Exercise 37 for a comparison.) To give the user this control, we can issue a prompt, asking whether to continue. Then we can read the user's response into a variable called **answer**.

The variable **answer** has type **char** (we use format specification **%c** to read it in) since the values we are interested in are '*y*' and '*n*'. Note that we print two blank lines to separate one group of input values from the next.

```
        printf("\n\nType y to continue; n to stop> ");
        scanf(" %c",&answer);
```

CAUTION Because of the strange way character input is treated by the **scanf** function, we add a space *before* the format specification **%c**. This space matches the carriage return (or newline character) that follows the integer previously read in. If the space is omitted, the newline character is read in as the value of **answer**. When we read in a numeric value, we do not have to allow for the newline character, but when we read in a character value, we must. This is discussed further in Chapter 9 with data type **char**.

Here is what we have so far; the last two statements are still pseudocode:

```
        {
            int   month;
            int   day;
            char  answer;
```

(continued)

(continued)

```
        printf("\nType in the number of a month");
        printf(" from 1 (January) to 12 (December) > ");
        scanf("%d",&month);
        printf("\nType in a date within the month, from 1 to 31> ");
        scanf("%d",&day);
        /*
         * call a function to classify the month-day
         * pair and print the results
         */
        classify(month,day);

        printf("\n\nType y to continue; n to stop> ");
        scanf(" %c",&answer);
```

if answer is 'y' repeat the process given above
if answer is 'n' stop

```
    }
```

SELF-CHECK 6-2

1. Why is the function *classify* called as a void function?

2. How can we print two blank lines before a prompt?

3. How can we employ the answer typed in by the user to control a program?

WHAT TYPE OF LOOP TO USE IN PROGRAM 6

Although we have not shown an explicit loop in the pseudocode, it is clear that the right way to implement this in C is to use one; however, we do not know in advance how many times to repeat the loop. In fact, we are giving the user the power to end the loop at any time. Therefore, we shouldn't use a *for* loop.

What about a *while* loop? When using a *while* loop, it is sometimes necessary to repeat a statement in two places—once outside the loop, just to get things going, then again at the bottom of the body so that things can continue. This is necessary because the condition in the *while* loop is tested before the loop is executed for the first time and again before each successive pass. In Program 6, the condition to test involves the user's response (stored in *answer*) and is something like this: *while (answer == 'y')*. But before the loop is executed the first time, *answer* does not have a value since the user has not yet responded to any question. In a case like this, the condition controlling a loop should not be tested the very first time; it makes more sense to test it after the body of the loop has been executed, to determine whether to continue.

As an alternative, we can use a ***while*** loop in which we set ***answer*** to '*y*' before the loop is executed the first time. However, this method is awkward in comparison to the new technique we are introducing.

A *do-while* LOOP

Fortunately, C has another loop, **a *do-while* loop,** that is perfect for this situation. The overall structure of the main program says to repeat a series of steps as long as a particular event occurs—the user's typing *y* in response to the prompt. A ***do-while*** loop works the way we want because the test is at the bottom of the loop.

The general form of a ***do-while*** loop looks like this (*cond* is a condition that evaluates to either true or false):

General Form of a *do-while* Loop

```
do
        body of the loop
while (cond);
```

Let's go through this step by step. First, the body of the loop is executed no matter what the value of *cond* happens to be at this point. When the last line is reached, the condition *cond* is evaluated. If *cond* is true, the body of the loop is executed again, and the condition is retested. (Just as in a ***while*** loop, the condition in a ***do-while*** loop usually depends on things that are changing in the body.) If *cond* is false, the body is not executed again, the loop terminates, and the next statement in the program executes.

The body of a ***do-while*** loop consists of a single statement. As usual, this restriction can be overcome by using a pair of braces to surround a series of statements.

STYLE WORKSHOP In a ***for*** or a ***while*** loop, if the body of the loop consists of just one statement, we do not enclose it in a pair of braces. In a ***do-while*** loop, even if the body of the loop consists of just one statement, some people recommend turning it into a compound statement with a pair of braces. This is done for clarity.

USING A *do-while* LOOP IN PROGRAM 6

Let's see how to use a ***do-while*** loop in Program 6. We want to repeat a series of statements as long as ***answer*** has the value '*y*'. Since once the ***do-while*** loop is finished we want to end the main program, the loop is followed by the line containing the closing brace. Here is what we have for the main program:

```
/*
 * Program prog6.c:
 * classify a month-day combination
 * in terms of seasons and weeks
 */
```

(continued)

(continued)

```c
#include <stdio.h>
main()
{
    int  month;
    int  day;
    char answer;

    do  {
        printf("\nType in the number of a month");
        printf(" from 1 (January) to 12 (December) > ");
        scanf("%d",&month);
        printf("\nType in a date within the month, from 1 to 31> ");
        scanf("%d",&day);
        /*
         * call a function to classify the month-day
         * pair and print the results
         */
        classify(month,day);
        printf("\n\nType y to continue; n to stop> ");
        scanf(" %c",&answer);
    }  while (answer == 'y');
}
```

PROGRAM TRACE Let's trace a few examples to see how the main program works.

◆ The user enters 5 1 (May 1, the birthday of one of the authors) in response to the first two prompts.

◆ The main program calls the **classify** function, which says that the month is in the spring and the day is in week number 1. Then **classify** returns control to the main program.

◆ A prompt then asks whether the user wants to continue. The user enters *y*. Since the **do-while** condition is true, the program repeats the body of the loop.

◆ The user enters the next **month-day** pair as 6 20 (June 20, the birthday of the other author).

◆ In the functions, this is classified as summer and week number 3, and control returns to the main program.

◆ Then the user types *n* in response to the prompt (we have run out of authors). Now the **do-while** condition is false, the loop terminates, and the program continues with the next step.

We have not yet given function prototypes for either **classify**, which is called directly by the main program, or the other functions called by **classify**. Once we have written all the functions, the prototypes will be shown in the final version of Program 6.

SELF-CHECK 6-3

1. In a **do-while** loop, when is the test controlling the loop made?

2. How many statements can appear in the body of a **do-while** loop?

3. Is it necessary to enclose the body of the loop in a pair of braces?

THE FUNCTION *classify*

DEFENSIVE PROGRAMMING AND ERROR CHECKING

Before we start the function *classify*, there is an important point about the correct way to write a program. The statement of Problem 6 does not say what to do if the user enters an illegal data value (e.g., 15 for *month*). We could just ignore the issue, saying that the user is at fault if bad data causes a problem. A more responsible attitude assumes that the user sometimes makes data-entry errors and provides a way to catch them. In this way, the program protects itself against illegal values. This is called **defensive programming** by analogy with defensive driving. When we write the function, we will embellish the pseudocode so *classify* can do error checking by catching bad data values and printing appropriate messages.

THE FUNCTION *classify*

Here is the pseudocode for *classify* from Section 1:

> *call a function* whichseason *to classify* month *into one of four seasons*
> *call a function* whichweek *to classify* day *into one of five weeks*
> *print the results of the function calls*

As we already decided, *classify* is a void function with two formal parameters. Because *day* and *month* are so descriptive, let's continue to use them as the formal parameters in *classify*. Here is the function header, together with an Input-Process-Output comment describing *classify*:

```
/*
 * Function classify:
 * Input:
 *   month--a number specifying a month in the year
 *   day--a number specifying a day in the month
 * Process:
 *   calls a function to determine which season
 *   (winter, spring, summer, fall) month is in
 *   calls a function to determine which week of
 *   the month (1-5) day is in
 * Output:
 *   prints the results of the classification
 */
void classify(int month, int day)
```

According to the process description, *classify* does two separate things: determines which season *month* belongs to and which week *day* belongs to. We already decided to do each in a separate function. Then *classify* prints the results.

ONE FUNCTION CALLING ANOTHER

A function (such as *classify*) is allowed to call another (such as *whichseason* or *whichweek*). This procedure is very common in a large program. In Program 6, the main program calls *classify*, which calls the other functions.

◆ In general, the function that issues a call is known as the **calling function**; the one named in the call is the **called function**.

◆ For the first call, the main program is the calling function, and *classify* is the called function.

◆ Later when *classify* calls *whichseason*, *classify* is the calling function, and *whichseason* is the called function.

Note that each function returns control to its own calling function.

There is another job for *classify* that we ignored in writing the pseudocode. Each month is represented by an integer from 1 to 12, but we want to print the name of the month rather than the number. The program has to translate the number into a name to print the month correctly.

We can do this translation in *classify* or *whichseason*, but we will write another function called *translate*. To be precise, we send *translate* the number corresponding to a month, and it prints the name of the month without returning anything to *classify*.

The printout from *translate* is followed by printout from *whichseason* and *whichweek*. Together the functions print a line of output like this:

```
month 5 is May       spring is the season    1 is the week number for day 1
```

HANDLING ILLEGAL DATA VALUES

Now let's discuss how to handle bad data. What if the value of *month* is 0 or negative or greater than 12? We can write *classify* so that, if it detects bad data, it does not send the illegal value of *month* to either *translate* or *whichseason*. (Later we will handle a bad value for *day*.) Here is some pseudocode that does what we want:

```
if (month < 1 or month > 12)
    printf("%d is not a valid value for the month",month);
else
    call the functions translate and whichseason
```

THE LOGICAL OPERATOR ||

In the pseudocode, we have used the word *or*, which corresponds to a **logical operation** in C. These logical operations are discussed more fully in Section 8. The meaning of the logical operation "or" in C is identical to English: one or the other (or both). In C, the symbol or logical operator for or is ||.

In addition, we have to write the calls to *translate* and *whichseason*. Since they are both void functions, the calls from *classify* look like this:

```
translate(month);
whichseason(month);
```

Let's put this together to get the first part of the function *classify*:

```
if (month < 1 || month > 12)
    printf("\n%d is not a valid value for the month",month);
else  {
    translate(month);
    whichseason(month);
}
```

CALLING THE FUNCTION *whichweek*

The call from *classify* to *whichweek* is similar. If the value for *day* is less than 1 or greater than 31, *classify* prints an error message and does not call *whichweek*. If the value for *day* is in the right range, *classify* calls the function *whichweek*. The call to *whichweek* is followed by the *return* statement and the closing brace:

```
if (day < 1 || day > 31)
    printf("\n%d is an illegal value for the day",day);
else
    whichweek(day);
return;
}
```

THE ENTIRE FUNCTION *classify*

Here is the function *classify*:

```
/* ... */
void classify(int month, int day)
{
    if (month < 1 || month > 12)
        printf("\n%d is not a valid value for the month",month);
    else  {
        translate(month);
        whichseason(month);
    }

    if (day < 1 || day > 31)
        printf("\n%d is an illegal value for the day",day);
    else
        whichweek(day);
    return;
}
```

SELF-CHECK 6-4

1. When function **f1** calls function **f2**, which is the calling function? Which is the called function?

2. If function **f1** calls function **f2**, and function **f2** calls function **f3**, when **f3** finishes, where does it return control?

3. What symbol is used for the logical operation or?

SECTION 4 THE REMAINING FUNCTIONS

In this section, we finish the functions for Program 6. (In Section 6, we discuss several other ways to write them.)

THE FUNCTION *translate*

First, let's write the function **translate**, which receives as a parameter a number representing a month. Recall that **translate** simply changes the number into a name to be printed. We will continue to use **month** as the name of the parameter. Here are the comment and function header:

```
/*
 * Function translate:
 * Input:
 *    month--a number specifying a month in the year
 * Process:
 *    translates the number of the month into a
 *    name for the month (e.g., 3 into March)
 * Output:
 *    prints the name associated with month
 */
void translate(int month)
```

The body of translate is straightforward, consisting of a number of **if** statements, one for each month from 1 to 12.

```
{
    printf("\nmonth %d is ",month);
    if (month == 1)
        printf("January");
    if (month == 2)
        printf("February");
    if (month == 3)
        printf("March");
```

```
    if (month == 4)
        printf("April");
    if (month == 5)
        printf("May");
    if (month == 6)
        printf("June");
    if (month == 7)
        printf("July");
    if (month == 8)
        printf("August");
    if (month == 9)
        printf("September");
    if (month == 10)
        printf("October");
    if (month == 11)
        printf("November");
    if (month == 12)
        printf("December");
    return;
}
```

THE FUNCTION *whichseason*

Next is the function **whichseason**, which receives one parameter called **month**. Here is the pseudocode from Section 1:

classify month *into one of four seasons*
print the answer
return control to the classify *function*

First come the comment and header for the function **whichseason**:

```
/*
 * Function whichseason:
 * Input:
 *   month--a number specifying a month in the year
 * Process:
 *   determines which season month is in
 *   (winter, spring, summer, fall)
 *   assume winter is December, January, February
 *   (make similar assumptions for the other seasons)
 * Output:
 *   prints the name of the season
 */
void whichseason(int month)
```

In Section 1, we also had a more detailed version of the pseudocode for this particular task:

```
if month is 12, 1, or 2
      the season is winter
if month is 3, 4, or 5
      the season is spring
if month is 6, 7, or 8
      the season is summer
if month is 9, 10, or 11
      the season is fall
print the answer
return control to the classify function
```

Naturally, it is easier to write the function with this detailed pseudocode. We start by comparing the value of **month** to the three months classified as winter: 12, 1, and 2 (December, January, and February). If the value of **month** is equal to any of them, the function **whichseason** should print "winter is the season". In order to generate the correct output format, we start each message with a tab character (**\t**). Here is an attempt to write the first part of the body:

```
{
    if (month == 12 || 1 || 2)                              /* incorrect */
        printf("\twinter is the season");
```

Unfortunately, as written, this is not correct.[1] In English, we can say, "if month is 12 or 1 or 2 ...," but this doesn't work in C. We have to be more explicit by saying **if (month == 12 || month == 1 || month == 2)**. Here is the correct version of the first **if** statement:

```
if (month == 12 || month == 1 || month == 2)
    printf("\twinter is the season");
```

In case the first **if** condition is not true, we must determine whether **month** is one of the three months in the spring:

```
if (month == 3 || month == 4 || month == 5)
    printf("\tspring is the season");
```

Similarly, we check for summer and fall. Then we can end the function. Here is the rest of the code:

```
    if (month == 6 || month == 7 || month == 8)
        printf("\tsummer is the season");
    if (month == 9 || month == 10 || month == 11)
        printf("\tfall is the season");
    return;
}
```

---

[1]The details are discussed in Section 8.

If the value for **month** is not in the range from 1 to 12, **classify** does not call **whichseason** so it is not necessary to check for bad values.

CAUTION You may be tempted to use an **else** statement instead of the last **if**, since it seems clear that if the month is not in the winter, spring, or summer, it must be in the fall. However, doing this in a naive way does not work. We discuss the correct way to use an **else** in Section 6.

OUTLINE OF THE ENTIRE FUNCTION *whichseason*

Here is an outline of the function **whichseason**:

```
/* ... */
void whichseason(int month)
{
    if (month == ...)
        printf("\twinter is the season");
    if (month == ...)
        printf("\tspring is the season");
    ...
    return;
}
```

THE FUNCTION *whichweek*

Now we can start work on the last function, **whichweek**, which receives one parameter called **day**. Here is the pseudocode for the function **whichweek** from Section 1:

classify day *into one of five weeks*
print the answer
return control to the classify *function*

The function **whichweek** is simpler than **whichseason** because we are working with consecutive integers. As usual, before we start to translate the pseudocode into C, we need the function header and introductory comment:

```
/*
 * Function whichweek:
 * Input:
 *   day--a number specifying a day in the month
 * Process:
 *   determines which week of the month (1-5) day is in
 *   assume each week (except the fifth) has 7 days
 * Output:
 *   prints the week within the month
 */
void whichweek(int day)
```

Once again, recall that we also had a more detailed version of this pseudocode:

if day *is between 1 and 7*
    the week is 1
if day *is between 8 and 14*
    the week is 2
if day *is between 15 and 21*
    the week is 3
if day *is between 22 and 28*
    the week is 4
if day *is 29, 30, or 31*
    the week is 5
print the answer
return control to the classify *function*

THE LOGICAL OPERATOR &&

To determine the number of the week that **day** is in, we use a method similar to the one in **whichseason**. We ask a series of questions, each of which selects one possible value for the function to print. For example, if the value in **day** is more than 7 and less than or equal to 14, **day** is in week 2. This introduces another of the logical operations. Here is a pseudocode statement which takes care of this:

```
if (day > 7 and day <= 14)
    printf("\t2 is the week number for day %d",day);
```

We say this is pseudocode because we still have to translate the word *and*. As you may guess, it corresponds to the logical operation "and" in C. The operator for and is **&&**. In English we can say, "if day is between 8 and 14," but C must be more specific. The C statement to do this is the following:

```
if (day > 7 && day <= 14)
    printf("\t2 is the week number for day %d",day);
```

Here is the entire body of the function:

```
{
    if (day <= 7)
        printf("\t1 is the week number for day %d",day);
    if (day > 7 && day <= 14)
        printf("\t2 is the week number for day %d",day);
    if (day > 14 && day <= 21)
        printf("\t3 is the week number for day %d",day);
    if (day > 21 && day <= 28)
        printf("\t4 is the week number for day %d",day);
    if (day > 28)
        printf("\t5 is the week number for day %d",day);
    return;
}
```

Because bad data is taken care of in *classify*, we have simplified the first and last *if* conditions. For the first condition, we do not have to ask whether *day* is greater than 0; in order for us to reach *whichweek*, that must be true. Similarly, in the last condition, we do not have to ask whether *day* is less than or equal to 31.

This completes the functions *whichweek* and *classify* and the entire program. The only thing we have to do is put the little pieces together to form Program 6 in the next section.

SELF-CHECK 6-5

1. What is the purpose of the tab character *t*?

2. What symbol is used for the logical operation and?

3. What is bad data for the functions *translate* and *whichseason*? How about the function *whichweek*?

SECTION 5 **ENTIRE PROGRAM 6**

In this section, we combine the pieces of C code to form Program 6. In addition, we include the function prototypes and discuss how to test the program.

LOCATION OF FUNCTION PROTOTYPES

The function *classify* is called from the main program. The functions *translate*, *whichseason*, and *whichweek* are called from *classify*. If we include function prototypes in the appropriate place, all four functions can appear before or after the main program.

Here are the function prototypes for all the functions in Program 6:

```
void classify(int,int);
void translate(int);
void whichseason(int);
void whichweek(int);
```

STYLE WORKSHOP In Chapter 5, we said it is better to put the function prototypes before the beginning of the main program, together with the line containing *#include <stdio.h>*, which can also be viewed as a collection of function prototypes. One advantage of this placement is illustrated by Program 6, where three of the four functions are called by *classify*, not the main program. In such a case, it is not appropriate for the main program to contain the prototypes. If the prototypes appear at the top of the file, any function (main program or other function) which appears later can access them. The function definitions can follow the body of the main program.

OUTLINE OF PROGRAM 6

On the next page, we have the outline for Program 6. All comments have been eliminated to simplify the format, but some explanations are on the right.

```
#include <stdio.h>

void classify(int, int);
void translate(int);
void whichseason(int);
void whichweek(int);
```

prototypes for the functions used in Program 6

```
main()
```

header for the main program

```
{
      int  month,day;
      char answer;
```

main program declarations

```
      ...
```

call to ***classify***

```
}
```

end of the main program

```
void classify(int month,int day)
```

header for the function ***classify***

```
{
      ...
}
```

calls to the other functions

```
void translate(int month)
{
      ...
}
```

header for the function ***translate***

```
void whichseason(int month);
{
      ...
}
```

header for the function ***whichseason***

```
void whichweek(int);
{
   ...
}
```

header for the function ***whichweek***

TESTING THE FUNCTIONS AND THE ENTIRE PROGRAM

Earlier, we traced two examples, 5 1 and 6 20 (May 1 and June 20), to show that the program is working correctly, but we should include representative data values to test all lines of code. This means we need at least one month from each season and one day from each week. It is also important to test the lines of code which catch errors. For example, we need a value of ***day*** less than 1 and one greater than 31, and a value of ***month*** less than 1 and one greater than 12. We should also test the boundary conditions: ***day*** having the values 1 and 31, ***month*** being 1 and 12.

In Chapter 5, we discussed how to test a function using a driver program that is less complex than the main one. In Program 6, the main program is already so simple that only two things can simplify it: removing the loop and assigning values to *day* and ***month*** instead of reading them in. The function ***classify*** is more complicated since it calls the other three functions. We can test these by assigning values in ***classify*** and calling each function individually.

After running the program on a thorough series of test cases, we can be fairly confident that all the functions are working correctly. At this point, we can start testing the full version of the main program, especially the ***do-while*** loop; for example, we can test what happens if the user does not answer either *y* or *n* to the question about continuing. When we have tested all the pieces, we can be confident the entire program is working correctly.

SELF-CHECK 6-6

1. When a program is being checked, can each function be tested alone?

2. Is it necessary to test a program with bad data or only data that is correct?

3. Can we assume a user always follows directions when typing in data?

PROGRAM 6

Here is the entire program for Problem 6:

 PROGRAM LISTING

```
/*
 * Program prog6.c:
 * classify a month-day combination
 * in terms of seasons and weeks
 */
#include <stdio.h>
void classify(int, int);
void translate(int);
void whichseason(int);
void whichweek(int);
main()
{
    int  month,day;
    char answer;

    do  {
        printf("\nType in the number of a month");
        printf(" from 1 (January) to 12 (December) >");
        scanf("%d",&month);
        printf("\nType in a date within the month, from 1 to 31> ");
        scanf("%d",&day);
```
(continued)

(continued)

```
        /*
         * call a function to classify the month-day
         * pair and print the results
         */
        classify(month,day);
        printf("\n\nType y to continue; n to stop> ");
        scanf(" %c",&answer);
    }  while (answer == 'y');
}


/*
 * Function classify:
 * Input:
 *    month--a number specifying a month in the year
 *    day--a number specifying a day in the month
 * Process:
 *    calls a function to determine the name of
 *    the season month is in
 *    calls a function to determine which season
 *    month is in (winter, spring, summer, fall)
 *    calls a function to determine which week
 *    of the month (1-5) day is in
 *    illegal data values for month or day
 *    will be caught
 * Output:
 *    prints the results of the classification
 *    prints an error message if either
 *    month or day has an illegal value
 */
void classify(int month, int day)
{
    if (month < 1 || month > 12)
        printf("\n%d is not a valid value for the month",month);
    else  {
        translate(month);
        whichseason(month);
    }

    if (day < 1) || (day > 31)
        printf("\n%d is an illegal value for the day",day);
    else
        whichweek(day);
    return;
}
```

```
/*
 * Function translate:
 * Input:
 *   month--a number specifying a month in the year
 * Process:
 *   translates the number of the month into a
 *   name for the month (e.g., 3 into March)
 * Output:
 *   prints the name associated with month
 */
void translate(int month)
{
    printf("\nmonth %d is ",month);
    if (month == 1)
        printf("January");
    if (month == 2)
        printf("February");
    if (month == 3)
        printf("March");
    if (month == 4)
        printf("April");
    if (month == 5)
        printf("May");
    if (month == 6)
        printf("June");
    if (month == 7)
        printf("July");
    if (month == 8)
        printf("August");
    if (month == 9)
        printf("September");
    if (month == 10)
        printf("October");
    if (month == 11)
        printf("November");
    if (month == 12)
        printf("December");
    return;
}

/*
 * Function whichseason:
 * Input:
 *   month--a number specifying a month in the year
 * Process:
 *   determines which season month is in
 *   (winter, spring, summer, fall)
 *   assume winter is December, January, February
```

(continued)

(continued)

```
 *    (make similar assumptions for the other seasons)
 *    illegal data values for month will be caught
 * Output:
 *    prints the name of the season
 */
void whichseason(int month)
{
    if (month == 12 || month == 1 || month == 2)
        printf("\twinter is the season");
    if (month == 3 || month == 4 || month == 5)
        printf("\tspring is the season");
    if (month == 6 || month == 7 || month == 8)
        printf("\tsummer is the season");
    if (month == 9 || month == 10 || month == 11)
        printf("\tfall is the season");
    return;
}


/*
 * Function whichweek:
 * Input:
 *    day--a number specifying a day in the month
 * Process:
 *    determines which week of the month (1-5) day is in
 *    assume each week (except the fifth) has 7 days
 * Output:
 *    prints the week within the month
 */
void whichweek(int day)
{
    if (day <= 7)
        printf("\t1 is the week number for day %d",day);
    if (day > 7 && day <= 14)
        printf("\t2 is the week number for day %d",day);
    if (day > 14 && day <= 21)
        printf("\t3 is the week number for day %d",day);
    if (day > 21 && day <= 28)
        printf("\t4 is the week number for day %d",day);
    if (day > 28)
        printf("\t5 is the week number for day %d",day);
    return;
}
```

STYLE WORKSHOP Program 6 is a long program and contains a series of functions which add to its size. If we did all the work in the main program, the overall program would be shorter, but it would probably be much harder to debug and modify. In most cases, it pays to divide the work up into smaller modules, writing each as a function, then combining them to form the complete program.

SECTION 6 ## MORE ON *do-while* LOOPS; NESTED *if* STATEMENT

In the next two sections, we discuss a number of ways that C directs the flow of control in a program. We begin by comparing *while* and *do-while* loops. Then we introduce a more generalized version of the *if-else* statement called a nested *if* statement.

COMPARING *while* AND *do-while* LOOPS

Let's start by comparing *while* and *do-while* loops. There is really just one important difference. In a *while* loop, the condition controlling the loop is tested at the top in the loop header; therefore, the test is made as soon as the loop begins. In a *do-while* loop, the condition is tested at the bottom; therefore, the test is made after the loop has executed the first time. In a *while* loop, if the condition controlling the loop is false initially, the body is never executed. In a *do-while* loop, even if the condition controlling the loop is false the first time, the body of the loop has already been executed once at that point. As a result, the body of a *do-while* loop is always executed at least once, but the body of a *while* loop may be skipped completely.

Figure 6-1A gives the general form for a *do-while* loop, and Figure 6-1B gives the one for a *while* loop. Study these pictures until the difference between the two loops is clear. (Actually, anything that can be done with one type of loop can also be done with the other, with appropriate modifications. See Exercise 17.)

General Form for a *do-while* Loop versus a *while* Loop

```
do                                        while (cond)
        body of the loop                          body of the loop
while (cond)
```

SELECTING ONE FROM A SERIES OF ALTERNATIVES

Two other C control structures are often useful, especially when a programmer must select from a large series of alternatives, as we did with *whichweek* and *whichseason*. One of these

FIGURE 6-1 *A*, general form for a *do-while* loop; *B*, general form for a *while* loop.

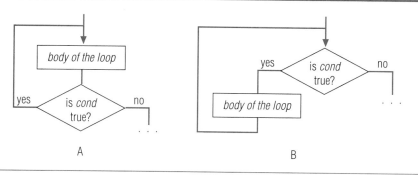

is called a nested *if* construction; the other is a **switch** statement. Let's begin with the nested *if*. (It may be helpful to review Chapter 3, Section 6 on the basic *if-else* construction.)

Assume that we have a situation with three mutually exclusive outcomes (see Figure 6-2). More precisely, assume that it is impossible for *cond-1* and *cond-2* to be true at the same time. If *cond-1* is true, *st-1* should be executed; if *cond-2* is true, *st-2* should be executed; if neither condition is true, *st-3* should be executed. We can interpret "neither condition is true" as *cond-1* and *cond-2* are false; we will call this *cond-3*. Thus, *cond-1, cond-2,* and *cond-3* are mutually exclusive.

To make things more concrete, here is a specific example with actual conditions. Everything also holds for the general situation of two conditions.

EXAMPLE 6-1

Let's assume that we are testing the value stored in variable *x*. Let *cond-1* be *(x > 0)*, and let *cond-2* be *(x == 0)*; then *cond-3* is *(x < 0)*.

Given Figure 6-2 to translate into C, the first idea that occurs to most people is the following C code:

```
if (x > 0)
    st-1;
if (x == 0)
    st-2;
if (x < 0)
    st-3;
```

In most cases, this works out. However, there is a special circumstance in which it does not work. (What if the action taken in *st-1* or *st-2* affects a later condition? For example, suppose *st-1* is something like this: *x = x – 1*. See Exercise 19.)

Although this code usually works, let's look at a possible shortcut: Instead of explicitly testing whether or not *cond-3* is true, we use an **else** statement on the second *if*.

FIGURE 6-2 Selecting one of three alternatives

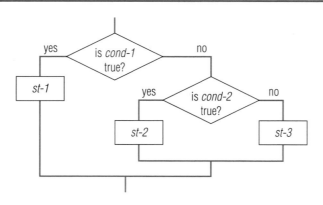

```
if (x > 0)                              /* there is a logical error here */
     st-1;
if (x == 0)
     st-2;
else
     st-3;
```

Does this shortcut work? Let's trace an example. There are three cases to consider, corresponding to the three possible outcomes. Assume first that x is –7; then the condition $(x < 0)$ is true (and the other two false). According to the example, we should execute st-3. Let's see if the C code works. Since the condition $(x > 0)$ is false, we don't execute st-1; the condition $(x == 0)$ is also false, so we don't execute st-2; the **else** statement directs us to execute st-3, which is fine.

Now assume that x is 0; then the condition $(x == 0)$ is true (and the other conditions are false). According to the example, we should execute st-2. Let's see if that works. The first **if** condition is false, the second **if** condition is true, so we execute st-2; because of the **else** statement, we skip st-3.

So far, the C code has been right in two cases; now we check the third. Assume that x is 7; then $(x > 0)$ is the only condition that is true. According to the example, we should execute st-1. When we try it out, unfortunately the program does not stop after testing the first condition. Instead, it goes on to ask the second question: Is $(x == 0)$ true? Since it is not, we skip st-2, but because of the **else** statement, we execute st-3. Therefore, the C code is not a correct translation of Figure 6-2 because we have executed both st-1 and st-3.

The problem is that in Figure 6-2, if the first alternative is true, we don't even bother to ask about the second and third. But in this C code, regardless of the outcome of the first **if**, we ask the second question.

THE NESTED **if** CONSTRUCTION

To specify that we want to execute st-1 or test $(x == 0)$ but not both, we can use a **nested if-else** (sometimes called a **nested if**) construction.[2] Here is an example:[3]

```
if (x > 0)
     st-1;
else
     if (x == 0)
          st-2;
     else
          st-3;
```

---

[2]Some people reserve the term *nested if* for a situation in which the second *if* occurs on the true branch of the first *if* and the term *cascading if* for one where the second *if* occurs on the false branch. We use nested *if* for any structure that contains one *if* inside another.

[3]The indentation improves clarity but is not strictly necessary. Another indentation pattern is shown later.

TABLE 6.1   Cases for Figure 6-2

(x > 0)	(x == 0)	Figure 6-2	C
true	–	st-1	st-1
false	true	st-2	st-2
false	false	st-3	st-3

The entire second *if* statement [*if (x == 0) ... st-3*] is now the *else* statement of the first *if*. When the first *if* condition is true, we execute *st-1* and skip the *else* statement; we don't test *(x == 0)*. But when the first *if* condition is false, we use the second *if* to choose between *st-2* and *st-3*. In this case, if *(x > 0)* is false, we do test *(x == 0)*.

Let's verify that this is a correct C translation of Figure 6-2. Table 6.1 summarizes the various cases to consider. The top line reads as follows: If *(x > 0)* is true [regardless of the outcome of *(x == 0)*], we execute *st-1*; the other lines explain the alternatives. Since Figure 6-2 matches C in every case (would it be enough to match in all but one?), the translation is correct.

ADVANTAGES OF THE NESTED *if* VERSION

The nested *if* method is preferable to the one involving three *if* statements for reasons of correctness as well as efficiency and flexibility. First, as we saw, there are special circumstances in which the three-*if* method does not give the correct answer. In addition, the nested *if* construction is much closer to the spirit of the original diagram, which contains two questions, not three. The three-*if* method assumes that the two conditions *cond-1* and *cond-2* can never be true at the same time, while the nested *if* method does not have to make this assumption.

The nested *if* method is also simpler. When a series of *if* statements is replaced by a nested *if*, the individual conditions to be tested can sometimes be simplified.

EXAMPLE 6-2A
(original indenting style)

For example, a nested *if* version of the ***whichweek*** function looks like this:

```
if (day <= 7)
    return 1;
else
    if (day <= 14)
        return 2;
    else
        if (day <= 21)
            return 3;
        else
            if (day <= 28)
                return 4;
            else
                return 5;
```

The **if** conditions have been simplified. For example, the second condition to be tested is now simply **if (day <= 14)**. We don't have to say **if (day > 7 && day <= 14)** because if we reach this point in the nested **if** structure, the condition **(day > 7)** must be true (Exercise 18 has a similar example). In addition, the last possible value to return (in this case, 5) does not need to be preceded by an **if** condition. If we reach this point, 5 must be the correct value.

Finally, the nested **if** version is more efficient. In the three-**if** version, all the conditions must always be tested; in the nested **if** version, when the first condition is true, the second **if** can be skipped completely. When there are more than three choices (four in the **whichseason** function, and five in the **whichweek** function), the savings in time can be substantial when a nested **if** is used.

One other point: The order in which we place the conditions to be tested in a nested **if** is sometimes significant since the first condition is always tested, whereas some of the others may be skipped (see Exercise 21).

CASCADING *if*, OTHER INDENTING STYLES IN A NESTED *if*

Unfortunately, a nested **if** covering more than three cases often has a major disadvantage. The various **if** conditions and **else** statements start shifting to the right, as we saw in Example 6-2A. This is especially serious if the conditions to be tested are complicated. Even if the structure looks good on the screen, when it is printed, the code wraps around from one line to the next, making the overall program listing hard to follow. A nested **if** that continues to have **else if ... else if** is called a **cascading if** and often makes the program difficult to read.

There is an alternative which most programmers choose. Instead of continuing to indent each succeeding **if** and **else**, put **else if (...)** on a single line and start each one under the original **if**. Example 6-2B shows how to rewrite Example 6-2A using this format.

EXAMPLE 6-2B
(preferred
indenting style)

```
if (day <= 7)
    return 1;
else if (day <= 14)
    return 2;
else if (day <= 21)
    return 3;
else if (day <= 28)
    return 4;
else
    return 5;
```

Note that the entire structure fits compactly on the screen (and the printed page), and the various conditions are neatly aligned. Most programmers consider this version significantly easier to read than the other one. When there are three or more **if** statements, we follow this format.

STYLE WORKSHOP In Example 6-2, we have four *if* statements (with five alternatives), which makes the original version cascade to the right. If there are just two *if* statements (with three alternatives), the cascade is not too pronounced, and the program may be quite readable, as in the example on the bottom of page 297. If there are only two *if* statements (three alternatives), you may prefer to follow the fully indented style.

OTHER EXAMPLES OF A NESTED *if* CONSTRUCTION

A nested *if* construction can be used for other situations as well. Figure 6-3 is a slight modification of Figure 6-2. The C translation is shown in Example 6-3; we leave it to you to construct a table proving that it works (see Exercise 7).

EXAMPLE 6-3

```
if (cond-1)
        if (cond-2)
                st-1;
        else
                st-2;
else
        st-3;
```

Finally, here is a complicated example that illustrates the use of pairs of braces to execute more than one instruction when the *if* condition is either true or false. See Figure 6-4.

EXAMPLE 6-4

Figure 6-4 translates into C as follows:

```
if (cond-1)  {
        st-1;
        if (cond-2)  {
                st-2;
                st-3;
        }
        else
                st-4;
}
else  {
        if (cond-3)
                st-5;
        else  {
                st-6;
                st-7;
                st-8;
        }
        st-9;
}
st-10;
```

FIGURE 6-3   Example 6-3: another way of selecting one of three alternatives

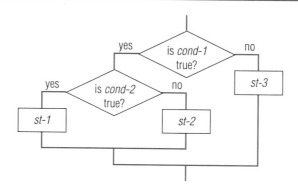

FIGURE 6-4   Example 6-4: a complex example of selecting alternatives

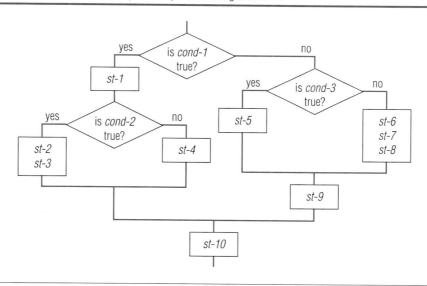

STYLE WORKSHOP   As the complexity of this example suggests, it is easy to go astray in a series of nested ***if*** statements and pairs of braces. Proper indenting and aligning help avoid this problem. Above all, be sure that every opening brace has a matching closing brace.

THE USE OF A NULL *else*

There is one more special case of a nested-***if*** to discuss. First, look back at Figure 6-3, in which the second condition is tested in case the first condition is true. Note that there are two conditions and two ***else*** statements.

FIGURE 6-5 Two options for nested *if*

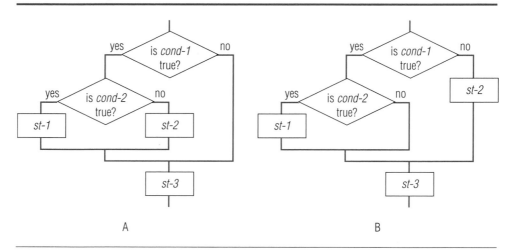

A   B

Now assume that you are given the two options in Figure 6-5. When trying to translate either into C, your first attempt may be this:

```
if (cond-1)
        if (cond-2)
            st-1;
? ←else→ ?
        st-2;
st-3;
```

We have put two question marks into the C code to indicate two possible places to place the keyword ***else***. It is not clear whether the ***else*** is associated with the first or the second ***if***. In translating Figure 6-3, where there were two ***else*** statements, it was clear which ***else*** went with which ***if***. But there are two options in Figure 6-5, and it is unclear which one this code represents.

C uses the following rule to resolve this problem: An ***else*** statement is associated with the closest preceding unmatched ***if***. Using this rule, the compiler determines that the ***else*** statement goes with ***if*** (*cond-2*).

EXAMPLE 6-5

Here is the code rewritten, with proper indenting and aligning for human readers:

```
if (cond-1)
        if (cond-2)
                st-1;
        else
                st-2;
st-3;
```

Thus, part A of Figure 6-5 is correctly translated by the C code. If you want to represent Figure 6-5B, there are several ways to do so. The problem cannot be solved by indenting and aligning (putting the word *else* directly under the first *if*) because the compiler ignores indenting. One solution which does work is using a second *else*. Nothing should appear in this second *else* statement since there are no instructions to be executed on that particular path. This is translated into C by *else;* with no statement following. This construction is called a **null** *else*. You can think of a null *else* as an *else* followed by a **null statement**, which is just a semicolon.

EXAMPLE 6-6

Let's see how to use a null *else* to represent Figure 6-5B. We can use the following C code:

```
if (cond-1)
    if (cond-2)
        st-1;
    else;
else
    st-2;
st-3;
```

EXAMPLE 6-7

We can also use a null *else* to represent Figure 6-5A:

```
if (cond-1)
    if (cond-2)
        st-1;
    else
        st-2;
else;
st-3;
```

Although the original C code is a translation of this situation, a null *else* construction is useful for clarity.

Another way to force the correct matchup of *if* and *else* is by using a pair of braces to associate the statements. This is shown in Example 6-8.

EXAMPLE 6-8

```
if (cond-1)  {
    if (cond-2)
        st-1;
}
else
    st-2;
st-3;
```

SELF-CHECK 6-7

1. In a nested-*if*, when both conditions are true, which condition has preference?
2. In order to select one from four alternatives, how many individual *if* statements are needed? In a nested-*if* version, how many conditions have to be tested?
3. Which option, Figure 6-5A or 6-5B, is translated by the code in Example 6-8?

SECTION 7 | **MORE CONTROL STRUCTURES: *switch, break*, AND *continue* STATEMENTS; *exit* FUNCTION**

THE *switch* STATEMENT

C has another method of selecting one from a series of alternatives that is sometimes preferable to the nested *if* construction. It is called a ***switch* statement** and can be thought of as a question with any number of possible outcomes, not just the two in an ***if-else*** statement.

General Form of a *switch* Statement

The basic form of the *switch* statement follows (this form does not include a ***default*** clause):

```
switch (selector)   {
  case value-1:
        st-1;                   /* group-1 */
        st-2;
        ...
        break;
  case value-2:                 /* group-2 */
        st-3;
        ...
        break;
    ...
  case value-n:                 /* group-n */
        ...
}
```

The value (*value-1*, *value-2*, ..., *value-n*) of the integer expression *selector* determines which group of statements to begin executing. Once a group is chosen, statements in that and succeeding groups are executed until the end of the ***switch*** statement or execution of a ***break*** **statement**. At that point, the ***switch*** statement is complete, and execution continues with the statement after the closing brace. (In this example, because each group has a ***break*** statement, we do not automatically fall through into the next group.)

Now let's go through this basic form in more detail.

◆ The various values that *selector* can assume are listed as *value-1*, *value-2*, and so on. These values must be constants, not expressions or variables.

◆ If the value of *selector* is *value-1*, the group containing *st-1*, *st-2*, ..., *break* is executed.

◆ If the value of *selector* is *value-2*, the group containing *st-3*, ..., *break* is executed.

◆ In each group, because of the *break*, the rest of the alternatives are skipped.

◆ If *selector* has a value that is not listed, the *switch* statement does nothing, and processing continues after the closing brace. (This assumes there is no *default* clause, which is discussed later.)

◆ If we don't want to take any action when a given alternative occurs, we can use a null statement—just a semicolon.

A SIMPLE EXAMPLE OF A *switch* STATEMENT

Before we talk more about restrictions and special cases, let's look at a specific example.

EXAMPLE 6-9   Assume that we want to determine whether a given number (stored in **anynumber**) is a multiple of 3, 1 more than a multiple of 3, or 1 less than a multiple of 3. Also assume that **anynumber** has a value to begin with. In the code below, note that **remainder** has type **int**; in fact, the only values it can have are 0, 1, and 2 because of the way the modulus or remainder operator % works. Therefore, we can use **remainder** as the expression to be tested.

```
int anynumber,remainder;

...
remainder = anynumber % 3;
switch (remainder)  {
  case 0:
        printf("%d is a multiple of 3\n",anynumber);
        break;
  case 1:
        printf("%d is 1 more than a multiple of 3\n",anynumber);
        break;
  case 2:
        printf("%d is 1 less than a multiple of 3\n",anynumber);
}
```

PROGRAM TRACE   Let's trace some examples.

◆ If **anynumber** has the value 11, **remainder** is 2, and we print a message that 11 is 1 less than a multiple of 3.

◆ If **anynumber** is 7, **remainder** is 1, and we print a message that 7 is 1 more than a multiple of 3.

◆ If **anynumber** is 24, **remainder** is 0, and we print a message that 24 is a multiple of 3.

In this example, the *switch* statement provides a convenient way of selecting one of three alternatives.

STYLE WORKSHOP We can eliminate the variable *remainder* and use *anynumber % 3* directly, as follows:

```
switch (anynumber % 3)  {
  ...
}
```

THE *break* STATEMENT

Now let's discuss the role of the **break** statement, which is often included in each group of statements except the last one. In general, C uses the **break** statement to terminate a control structure. As we'll soon see, **break** can terminate execution of a loop. In a **switch** statement, **break** comes at the end of a group of statements to terminate the action. Including **break** is not strictly necessary, but if it is omitted, we "fall through" from one group of statements to another.

For instance, in Example 6-9, assume that **anynumber** has the value 24. If we remove the **break** statement in **case 0**, we fall into the next group of statements after printing the message saying **anynumber** is a multiple of 3. As a result, we also print a message saying **anynumber** is 1 more than a multiple of 3, which is not true.

There are some rare cases when we purposely want to go from one group of statements to the next, but almost every **switch** statement has **break** statements to separate groups. The last group does not need a **break** statement (why not?), but some people put one in anyway so that additional conditions can be easily added.

ANOTHER EXAMPLE OF A *switch* STATEMENT: THE *default* CLAUSE

Let's consider another example, which shows that several values of the selector can lead to the same action. It also illustrates a **default** clause.

EXAMPLE 6-10 We read in an integer value from 2 to 9 and classify it into one of four categories: an even prime number (2), an even number which is not prime (4, 6, or 8), an odd prime number (3, 5, or 7), or an odd number which is not prime (9). In this example, we use a **default** clause to catch illegal values (this is called **error trapping**).

Here is a **switch** statement that performs the classification and prints the result:

```
int number;

printf("\ntype in a number from 2 to 9>: ");
scanf("%d",&number);
switch (number)  {
  case 2:
      printf("\n%d is an even prime\n",number);
      break;
  case 4:
  case 6:
```

```
        case 8:
            printf("\n%d is an even nonprime\n",number);
            break;
        case 3:
        case 5:
        case 7:
            printf("\n%d is an odd prime\n",number);
            break;
        case 9:
            printf("\n%d is an odd nonprime\n",number);
            break;
        default:
            printf("\n%d is not in the range from 2 to 9\n",number);
    }
```

Note that it is possible to have more than one value in a particular alternative. For example, 4 and 6 are both classified as even nonprime numbers. Each of the values from 2 to 9 should be mentioned explicitly as a possible value for the selector.

Now let's discuss the *default* clause. We have provided for possible values of *number* from 2 to 9, but it can hold many other possibilities. If, through some error in typing in data, some other value is stored in *number*, a *switch* statement without a *default* clause does nothing. It is better to catch this mistake and print an error message. The remaining alternatives can be grouped together in a *default* clause; the action of this group is to print an error message.

For example, if *number* holds 3, a message saying 3 is an odd prime number is printed; if *number* holds 8, a message saying 8 is an even nonprime number is printed. However, if *number* holds an inappropriate value (for example, 15, which is a value of type *int* but not something we are trying to classify), an error message is printed by the *default* clause.

STYLE WORKSHOP Without a *switch* statement, how could we solve the problem of classifying the numbers? One possibility is a long series of *if* statements, one for each possible value of *number*; another is a single nested *if*. By comparison, the *switch* statement is much simpler to write and easier to follow. Notice how close the C statements are to the English-language description of the process. The natural correspondence is not nearly as clear if we use some other method. In general, anything that can be done with a *switch* statement can also be done with a series of *if* statements or a nested *if* construction (see Exercise 24). However, if the problem can be solved with a *switch* statement, that is usually preferable to some type of *if*.

RESTRICTIONS ON THE USE OF A *switch* STATEMENT

Unfortunately, there are some limitations on the *switch* statement.

◆ The most important one is that the selector must be an expression whose underlying data type is an integer: *int* or *char*. For example, an expression of type *double* or *float* cannot be used. In this case, a programmer has the inconvenience of translating a noninteger type into an appropriate form.

◆ Second, each possible value for the selector must be a constant, not a variable or an expression.

◆ A third major restriction is the need for a **break** statement if we do not want to drop from one group of statements to the next. (Curiously, Example 6-10 can be reorganized to give an equivalent result without a **break** on each path. See Exercise 23.)

C LOOP CONTROL FEATURES: *break* AND *continue* STATEMENTS

C has two statements which are useful for loop control: **break** and **continue**. These statements can be used in all three types of loops (**for** loops, **while** loops, and **do-while** loops).

In a typical situation, the body of a **for** loop is executed a fixed number of times, depending upon the starting value of the **for** loop index and the test condition. In the simplest case, on each iteration through the body of the loop, the control variable increases by 1. For example, consider this **for** loop header:

```
for (i = 4; i <= 6; i++)
```

We expect the body of this loop to be executed exactly three times, with *i* having the values 4, 5, and 6. However, there may be situations when the programmer wants to skip a particular iteration of the body of the loop or terminate the execution of the entire loop before all values of the **for** loop index have been used. The **continue** statement can be used in the first case and the **break** statement in the second.

Let's first consider a situation in which, for certain values of the **for** loop index, we want to skip execution of some or all of the code within the body. To do this, we can use the **continue** statement.

EXAMPLE 6-11   Assume that we have this loop, which is designed to skip part of the processing if *i* has the value 5 but do all of it if *i* has the value 4 or 6. In general, the code for *first part of the process* and *second part of the process* can be any combination of C statements; in this particular example, each part consists of a single **printf**.

```
for (i = 4; i <= 6; i++)  {
    /* first part of the process */
    printf("first part with i = %d\n",i);
    if (i == 5)
        continue;
    /* second part of the process */
    printf("second part with i = %d\n",i);
}
```

PROGRAM TRACE   As usual, the body of this **for** loop is executed for each value of *i* from 4 to 6.

◆ When *i* has the value 4, the program does both parts of the processing, and two lines of output are printed.

◆ When *i* is 5, the first part of the processing is done, but the **continue** statement causes the second part to be skipped. Only a single line of output is printed.

◆ The program continues with the next iteration through the body of the loop with *i* = 6. On this pass, both lines of output are printed.

Therefore, execution of the *for* loop generates the following output:

```
first part with i = 4
second part with i = 4
first part with i = 5
first part with i = 6
second part with i = 6
```

Now let's discuss a situation where we want to terminate the entire execution of the *for* loop. To do this, we can use the *break* statement.

EXAMPLE 6-12 Consider the following version of Example 6-11, in which the *continue* statement is replaced by a *break* statement. This loop terminates when *i* has the value 5.

```
for (i = 4; i <= 6; i++)  {
    /* first part of the process */
    printf("first part with i = %d\n",i);
    if (i == 5)
        break;
    /* second part of the process */
    printf("second part with i = %d\n",i);
}
```

PROGRAM TRACE

◆ When *i* has the value 4, the program does both parts of the processing, and two lines of output are printed.

◆ When *i* is 5, the first part of the processing is done, but the *break* statement terminates the entire loop. Only a single line of output is printed. Note that *i* never has the value 6.

Execution of this loop produces the following output:

```
first part with i = 4
second part with i = 4
first part with i = 5
```

After a loop terminates because of a *break* statement, the program resumes execution with the statement after the loop. In a sense, we "break out" of the loop. In contrast, a *continue* statement does not terminate the entire loop; instead the loop "continues."

USING *break* AND *continue* WITH A *while* OR *do-while* LOOP

As we noted, *break* and *continue* statements can be used with *while* or *do-while* loops as well.

EXAMPLE 6-13 Assume that we want to use a loop to read in a series of data values and process them. If a data value is positive, we want to do both steps of the processing. If the data value is negative, we want to perform step 1 but skip step 2. In either case, we want the loop to keep executing. However, if the data value is 0, we want the loop to terminate after processing steps 1 and 2 with the 0 value.

Here is a piece of code which implements these ideas using a *do-while* loop (for simplicity, we have used pseudocode for the two processing steps):

```
int datavalue;

do  {
        printf("\ntype in a data value; use 0 to terminate:> ");
        scanf("%d",&datavalue);
        step 1 of the processing
        if (datavalue < 0)
            continue;
        step 2 of the processing
}  while (datavalue != 0);
```

Do you see how this works? Can you predict what will happen for the values 15, –3, and 0?

Now let's consider a version of the problem from Example 6-13 in which the value 0 is a termination signal (and everything else stays the same), but the 0 should not be processed at all. In this case, we can use a *while* loop with a peculiar header condition: *while (1 == 1).*[4] Normally, this condition causes an infinite loop (why?). However, because we have added a *break* statement, the loop can terminate when the value of *datavalue* is 0.

EXAMPLE 6-14 Here is a *while* loop containing both *break* and *continue* statements which implements these ideas:

```
int datavalue;

while (1 == 1)  {
        printf("type in a data value; use 0 to terminate:> ");
        scanf("%d",&datavalue);
        if (datavalue == 0)
            break;
        step 1 of the processing
        if (datavalue < 0)
            continue;
        step 2 of the processing
}
```

What happens if a positive value is read in? What if a negative value is read in? What if *datavalue* is 0?

---

[4]In fact, we can use the header *while (1)*; see Exercise 32.

THE *exit* FUNCTION

C has other ways to control program execution; the most important is the *exit* **function**. If either a function or a main program is executing, a call to the function *exit* immediately terminates the entire program, returning control to the operating system. By convention, if the termination is normal, the call to the function looks like this, with 0 sent as a parameter to *exit*:

```
exit(0);
```

If the termination is considered abnormal, a value other than 0 is sent to the *exit* function. For example, a call to the function can look like this:

```
exit(1);
```

EXAMPLE 6-15   In the function *classify*, if the value for *month* (or *day*) is not valid, *classify* can stop the program and signal that it has detected bad data by using the following:

```
if (month < 1 || month > 12)  {
    printf("\n%d is not a valid value for the month\n",month);
    printf("program will terminate prematurely\n");
    exit(1);
}
else  ...
```

This call to *exit* terminates the entire program. (Exercises 28 to 33 contain more material on the features we've discussed.)

STYLE WORKSHOP Different codes can signal various error conditions. The return value can be checked by other programs which may use this program's results or by the operating system (this is most common in Unix). Many programmers consider it good style to terminate every main program with *exit(0)* for normal completion.

THE *goto* STATEMENT

C has an additional control structure, called a *goto* **statement**, that also controls execution of a loop. In general, the *goto* statement allows a program to transfer control from one point to any other point. (In fact, calls to *break* and *continue* can be thought of as special cases of the *goto* statement.) Unfortunately, unrestricted use of the *goto* leads to programs that are very hard to debug or modify. For this reason, structured programming (see Chapter 4, Section 5) strongly discourages its use. Given all the control structures available in C, programmers should never have to use a *goto*. Therefore, we do not use it.

SELF-CHECK 6-8

1.   Can a *switch* statement replace a nested *if* in all cases?

2.   In Example 6-10, what happens if the *break* statements are removed from each group? For example, what is printed for 2? For 6? For 5? Are any of the answers still correct?

3. If a main program calls function *func1*, and function *func1* calls function *func2*, what happens if *func2* executes the statement *exit(1)*?

SECTION 8 **LOGICAL AND RELATIONAL OPERATORS, SHORT-CIRCUIT EVALUATION**

Program 6 introduced several new operations that are useful with complex questions. Our last topic in this chapter is to study these operations, which are performed by logical and relational operators. We also talk briefly about short-circuit evaluation of expressions.

THE RELATIONAL OPERATORS

The six basic **relational operators** were introduced in Chapter 2, Section 4. They are: <, <=, >, >=, ==, and !=. Each relational operator takes as operands two expressions and produces an answer which is either true or false. More precisely, false corresponds to the integer value 0, and true corresponds to any other integer value, but we think of it as associated with 1.

THE LOGICAL OPERATORS

There are three **logical operators**: && (conjunction—read as *and*), || (disjunction—read as *or*), and ! (negation—read as *not*). The logical operators act on one expression (for !) or two expressions (for && and ||) and produce a result which is either true or false.

Often the result of a relational operator is sent as an operand to a logical operator. For example, we could have the expression *! (x > 2)*. Because of the parentheses, we first apply the relational operator (>) to obtain a true or false value for *x > 2*; this value is then negated. The result from one logical operator can also be sent as an operand to another. For example, consider the expression *! (x > 2) && (y = 3)*. In order to evaluate it, we have to discuss the precedence rules for logical and relational operators.

PRECEDENCE RULES FOR LOGICAL AND RELATIONAL OPERATORS

Here are the precedence rules for logical and relational operators (see Table 6.2):

◆ Negation (!) has the same precedence as the other unary operators, including unary minus and the increment and decrement operators; their precedence is higher than any of the other arithmetic operators (see Chapter 2, Section 4).

◆ The relational operators have lower precedence than any of the arithmetic operators, except for the assignment operators (for example, = or +=).

◆ The logical operator && has lower precedence than the relational operators.

◆ The logical operator || has lower precedence than &&.

◆ Both && and || have higher precedence than the assignment operators, which have the lowest precedence.

◆ In a given expression, two or more logical operators with the same precedence are grouped from left to right (except for ! which is grouped from right to left).

◆ Parentheses can override these rules. Anything inside a pair of parentheses is done first; within the parentheses, operations are performed in order of precedence.

STYLE WORKSHOP It is a good idea to include parentheses in certain situations where they are not strictly necessary. Almost everyone knows the C precedence rules for arithmetic operations (e.g., multiplication before addition), but many inexperienced programmers are not positive about the ones for the logical and relational operators. (This problem is aggravated by the fact that the rules in C are different from those in other computer languages, say Pascal.) Therefore, extra parentheses are sometimes added for clarity.

Table 6.2 summarizes the precedence rules for all of the operators we have used so far, including logical and relational operators.

TRUTH TABLES FOR THE LOGICAL OPERATORS

In order to evaluate an example involving logical operators, we need a set of standard tables describing how they work. These tables, often called **truth tables**, are given in Table 6.3. In the tables, a and b are any two boolean expressions. A **boolean expression** is one that evaluates to a boolean value— either true or false. A logical operator is sometimes called a boolean operator since its result is a boolean value. In Table 6.3, we represent true by T and false by F.[5]

These tables are read in the following way: If a is T, then ! a is F. If a is T and b is T, a && b is T ($a \parallel b$ is also T in this case), and so on. Note that $a \parallel b$ is false only when both a and b are false; a && b is true only when a and b are both true. These tables are "known" by the C compiler, and a programmer should know them as well.

TABLE 6.2 Precedence of Arithmetic, Assignment, Logical, and Relational Operators

Precedence	Operation	Associativity
highest precedence	! – (unary) + (unary) ++ ––	right to left
(done first)	* / %	left to right
	+ –	left to right
	< <= > >=	left to right
	== !=	left to right
	&&	left to right
	||	left to right
lowest precedence	= += –= *= /= %=	right to left
(done last)		

---

[5]Recall that C considers 0 to be false and any other value to be true.

TABLE 6.3   Truth Tables for the Logical Operators

Table for !			Tables for &&, ‖			
if *a* is	then ! *a* is		if *a* is	and if *b* is	then *a* && *b* is	then *a* ‖ *b* is
T	F		T	T	T	T
F	T		T	F	F	T
			F	T	F	T
			F	F	F	F

The meaning of && in C is identical to and in English. Similarly, ‖ in C works just like or in English. Actually, we use two different kinds of or in English: **inclusive or** (one or the other, or both) and **exclusive or** (one or the other, but not both). The operator ‖ corresponds to the use of inclusive or. (Exercise 26 discusses modeling the exclusive or operation.)

EVALUATING EXPRESSIONS USING LOGICAL AND RELATIONAL OPERATORS

Now that we know how logical operators work, let's look at a few examples of evaluating boolean expressions.

EXAMPLE 6-16   The first example has two boolean operators: && and ‖.

```
int x = 4, y = 0, z = 1;

if (x < y || z >= x && x != 0)
    printf("it is true\n");
else
    printf("it is false\n");
```

Before we go step-by-step through the evaluation, let's note the following: Since && has higher precedence, it is done before ‖. The two boolean expressions that && works on are *z >= x* and *x != 0*. The two boolean expressions that ‖ works on are *x < y* and the result of the &&.

PROGRAM TRACE   Now we can trace the example in detail:

◆   First, we substitute numerical values:

$(4 < 0 ‖ 1 >= 4 \&\& 4 != 0)$

◆   Next we evaluate the relational operators: $4 < 0$ is *F*, $1 >= 4$ is *F*, and $4 != 0$ is *T*.

◆   We now have the following:

$(F ‖ F \&\& T)$

◆ Now && has precedence over ||. We evaluate F && T which yields F. Then we have the following:

$(F \, || \, F)$

◆ Since $F \, || \, F$ is F, the entire expression is false.

◆ We execute the ***else*** statement. This prints the following line of output:

```
it is false
```

Now let's trace a more complete example, including parentheses and arithmetic operators.

EXAMPLE 6-17   Assume that we have this ***if-else*** statement, where *st-1* and *st-2* are any C statements:

```
if (a * 2 > b || ! (c == 6) && d - 1 <= e)
        st-1;
else
        st-2;
```

PROGRAM TRACE   Assume that ***a*** is 2, ***b*** is 4, ***c*** is 7, ***d*** is 4, and ***e*** is 3.

◆ As before, we start by substituting numerical values:

$(2 * 2 > 4 \, || \, ! \, (7 == 6) \, \&\& \, 4 - 1 <= 3)$

◆ Then we perform operations which are inside the innermost parentheses. In this case, the condition $7 == 6$ is false so we have the following:

$(2 * 2 > 4 \, || \, ! \, F \, \&\& \, 4 - 1 <= 3)$

◆ Negation (!) has highest precedence so we do ! F, which is T. This gives

$(2 * 2 > 4 \, || \, T \, \&\& \, 4 - 1 <= 3)$

◆ Now the multiplication $(2 * 2)$ has highest precedence, so we have

$(4 > 4 \, || \, T \, \&\& \, 4 - 1 <= 3)$

◆ The subtraction now has highest precedence, so we have

$(4 > 4 \, || \, T \, \&\& \, 3 <= 3)$

◆ Next we do the relational operators. Technically, they are done one at a time, from left to right, but we can show both at once since they don't interact with each other: $4 > 4$ is false, but $3 <= 3$ is true. So we have

$F \, || \, T \, \&\& \, T$

◆ Now && has precedence over ||; T && T is T.

$F \, || \, T$

◆ Finally, $F \, || \, T$ is T.

◆ The entire ***if*** condition is true, so we execute *st-1*.

SHORT-CIRCUIT EVALUATION OF BOOLEAN OPERATORS

The rules in C to evaluate boolean operators are slightly different from what we have implied. In giving the rules for evaluating the && of two expressions, we have suggested that C evaluates each of them, then sees whether their && is true. Actually, C uses a shortcut method, called **short-circuit evaluation**.

HIGHLIGHTS

The && of two expressions is true only if both the expressions are true. If, for example, the first expression is false, it is impossible for the entire && expression to be true. In such a case, C does not bother to evaluate the second expression. It short-circuits the evaluation process and concludes that the boolean expression using && must be false.

EXAMPLE 6-18

Let's assume that we want to divide one variable y by another variable x, then see whether or not this result is greater than z. We can use y/x for the division, comparing the result to z, but there is a problem if x has the value 0. In languages that do not have short-circuit evaluation, we must use an extra *if* statement to avoid this problem (see Exercise 27). But in C, we can do something like this:

```
if (x != 0 && y / x > z)
    st-1;
else
    st-2;
```

PROGRAM TRACE Let's trace what happens in this example, assuming first that x has the value 4, y has the value 20, and z has the value 3.

◆ First, we substitute numerical values: 4 != 0 && 20 / 4 > 3.

◆ The first expression, 4 != 0, is true so the evaluation continues.

◆ The second expression, 20 / 4 > 3, which becomes 5 > 3, is true, so the entire && is true.

◆ We execute *st-1*.

Now let's assume that y and z have the same values, but x has the value 0. We substitute values to get 0 != 0 && 20 / 0 > 3.

◆ The first expression, 0 != 0, is false. Therefore, the entire && must be false, and C does not evaluate the second expression. Since the entire && is false, we execute *st-2*.

This is exactly the desired result in this case, because if 20 / 0 is evaluated, it causes a division-by-zero error.

Short-circuit evaluation of an || condition can also occur. If the first expression in an || is true, the entire || expression must be true, and C short-circuits the evaluation of the second expression.

SELF-CHECK 6-9

1. If the && of two expressions is false, what can you say about the two expressions? What if the && is true?

2. If the || of two expressions is false, what can you say about the two expressions? What if the || is true?

SUMMARY

ONE FUNCTION CALLING ANOTHER

1. One C function can call another, which makes it possible for a main program to call a function. The function that issues the call is the calling function; the function named in the call is the called function. Each returns to the function that called it.

do-while LOOPS

2. A *do-while* loop is an alternative to a *while* loop. The general form of a *do-while* loop is shown here. Because a set of braces has been used, the body of the loop can consist of any number of C statements; *cond* is a condition that evaluates to true or false.

```
do  {
       body of the loop
}  while (cond);
```

3. The *do-while* loop is executed as follows: Initially, the body of the loop is executed. When the *while* clause is reached, *cond* is evaluated. If the condition is true, the body of the loop is repeated, and *cond* is evaluated again. If the condition is false, the body of the loop is not repeated, the loop is terminated, and the program continues with the statement after the *while* clause. In general, the body of the loop is repeated as long as the condition evaluates to true.

4. The only major difference between a *while* loop and a *do-while* loop is that the *while* loop tests the condition before entering the body of the loop, whereas the *do-while* loop tests it after executing the body. Therefore, the body of a *do-while* loop is always executed at least once.

if STATEMENT

5. A single *if-else* statement can be used to select one of two alternatives. A C program can choose one of three (or more) alternatives by using a series of *if* statements.

NESTED *if* STATEMENT

6. A nested *if* construction, in which the first or second clause is another *if-else* statement, can be used to select one of three or more paths.

7. The simplest form of a nested *if* is shown here (*cond-1* and *cond-2* are conditions that evaluate to true or false; *st-1*, *st-2*, etc. are C statements):

```
if (cond-1)
     st-1;
else if (cond-2)
          st-2;
else
     st-3;
st-4;
```

8. This nested *if* is executed in the following way: If *cond-1* is true, *st-1* is executed; if *cond-1* is false and *cond-2* is true, *st-2* is executed; if *cond-1* is false and *cond-2* is false, *st-3* is executed. The statement following the entire nested *if*, *st-4*, is always executed.

9. Any statement in a nested *if* can be replaced by a compound statement; a pair of braces is used to execute more than one statement. Here is an example of a compound statement used with each *else*:

```
if (cond-1)
     st-1;
else  {
     st-2;
     if (cond-2)
          st-3;
```

(continued)

(*continued*)

```
     else   {
            st-4;
            st-5;
        }
    }
    st-6;
```

In case *cond-1* is false, *st-2* is executed, and *cond-2* is tested. If this condition is true, then *st-3* is executed, but if it is false, *st-4* and *st-5* are both executed. In every case, the program continues with *st-6*.

switch STATEMENT

10. The *switch* statement provides another convenient way to select one from a series of alternatives. Here is the general form of a *switch* statement:

```
switch (selector)   {
    case value-1:
          group-1 of statements;
    case value-2:
          group-2 of statements;
    ...
    case value-n:
          group-n of statements;
}
```

11. In this form, *selector* must be an expression of some integer-valued type (*int* or *char;* it cannot be *float* or *double)*; each *value-i* is a constant representing a possible value for *selector;* each *group-i* is any number of C statements. It is possible to have more than one constant value in a particular alternative; the keyword *case* is followed by a constant value and a colon for each value covered by that alternative.

12. The *switch* statement is executed as follows: The value of *selector* is computed and compared to *value-1*. If they are equal, *group-1 of statements* is selected to be executed. If the values are not equal, the process is repeated for each possible value until a match is found. If a selected group ends in a *break* statement, the rest of the alternatives are skipped; however, if *break* is not present, execution of one group of statements goes on to the next.

13. A *default* clause, which covers all other possible values, can be used as the last choice. This clause is selected if no match is found. In the event that there is no *default* clause, the *switch* statement does nothing.

break AND *continue* STATEMENTS; *exit* FUNCTION

14. The statements *break* and *continue* control execution of a loop, whether it is a *for* loop, a *while* loop, or a *do-while* loop. If the *break* statement is executed inside the body of a loop, the entire loop terminates. If the *continue* statement is executed inside the body, the particular iteration terminates, but the loop continues.

15. For example, consider this *for* loop. The *continue* statement terminates the iteration when *i* has the value 3, and the *for* loop continues with *i* as 4, then 5, etc. If the variable *x* has a value greater than 15, the *break* statement terminates the entire loop.

```
for (i = 1; i <= 10; i++)   {
    ...
    if (i == 3)
        continue;
    ...
    if (x > 15)
        break;
    ...
}
```

16. The **exit** function also regulates the flow of control by terminating execution of an entire program, whether it is called from a main program or a function. If termination is normal, **exit** is usually sent 0 as a parameter, as in **exit(0)**. If termination is abnormal, **exit** is usually sent another value, as in **exit(1)**.

LOGICAL AND RELATIONAL OPERATORS

17. The logical or boolean operators (&&, ||, and !) can be used to formulate complex conditions. For example, using && (and) makes it possible to test if two conditions are both true; using || (or) makes it possible to test if either (or both) of two conditions is true. The operator ! (not) negates a condition.

18. The logical operators receive either one (for !) or two (for && and ||) true-false values and produce an answer that is either true or false. The logical operator ! has the highest precedence (the same as unary minus). The logical operator && has lower precedence than ! but higher precedence than the logical operator ||. Two or more operators in a row with the same precedence are evaluated from left to right.

19. The logical operator ! has higher precedence than any of the relational operators ($<$, $<=$, $>$, $>=$, $==$, and $!=$). The relational operators have higher precedence than logical operators && and ||. Parentheses override the precedence rules for logical and relational operators.

20. The truth tables for logical operators provide a convenient summary of the rules for evaluating them. In these tables, true and false are represented by T and F. For example, T && F is F; F || T is T; $!F$ is T.

21. With boolean expressions, C uses short-circuit evaluation. In evaluating the && of two expressions, if the first one is false, the overall expression must be false, and C does not evaluate the second. Similarly, in evaluating the || of two expressions, if the first is true, the overall expression must be true, and C does not evaluate the second.

EXERCISES

TRACING EXERCISES:

1. Use the following declaration for this problem:

```
int i,j,k,x;
```

For the three sets of values (1) to (3), show what is stored in the variable *x* by each of the following program segments. If *x* is not assigned a value by the code segment, indicate one by ?.

(1) *i* = 1; *j* = 2; *k* = 3;
(2) *i* = 7; *j* = 10; *k* = 4;
(3) *i* = 5; *j* = 4; *k* = 3;

```
a.  if (j > k)            b.  if (i > j)            c.  if (i > j)
        x = 2;                    x = 1;                    x = 5;
    if (i > k)            else                      else if (j > k)
        x = 3;               if (j > k)                    x = 1;
                                 x = 2;               else if (i > k)
                             else                         x = 3;
                                 x = 3;
```

2. Show what is printed by the following C statements when the variables *a, b, c, d,* and *e* have
    the values shown in parts (1) to (4) below. In addition, show the intermediate result of each
    logical and relational operator.

    (1) *a* = 2;   *b* = 1;   *c* = 3;   *d* = 0;   *e* = 1;
    (2) *a* = 3;   *b* = 3;   *c* = 3;   *d* = 3;   *e* = 3;
    (3) *a* = 5;   *b* = 0;   *c* = 0;   *d* = 3;   *e* = 2;
    (4) *a* = 3;   *b* = 5;   *c* = 7;   *d* = 4;   *e* = 2;

```
int a,b,c,d,e;

if (a < b || d > e)
    if (b > c && c > d)
        printf("win\n");
    else if (d < e)
            printf("place\n");
        else
            printf("show\n");
else
    printf("FInish\n");
```

3. For each set of initial values for the variables, evaluate the following series of statements ac-
    cording to C precedence rules and show what is printed.

    (1) *a* = 6;   *b* = 7;   *c* = 3;   *d* = 2;   *e* = 16;
    (2) *a* = 1;   *b* = 18;   *c* = 6;   *d* = 42;   *e* = 8;

```
int  a,b,c,d,e;
  ...
if ( ! (a = b && c * c <= 100 || d <> e % 8) )
    printf("valid\n");
else
    printf("invalid\n");
if (1000 > a + b * b * 9 || !(e * d == a / d))
    a += b;
else
    a -= b;
printf("%d\n",a);
```

4. For each set of values for the variables (1) to (3), show what is printed by code segments (a),
    (b), and (c). Assume that *p, q,* and *r* are all expressions whose values are equal to one of the
    constants defined here:

```
#define TRUE 1
#define FALSE 0
```

    (1) p = TRUE;   q = TRUE;   r = FALSE;
    (2) p = TRUE;   q = FALSE;   r = TRUE;
    (3) p = FALSE;   q = FALSE;   r = FALSE;

a.
```
if (p && q || r)
    printf("true");
else
    printf("false");
```

b.
```
if (p || !(q && r))
    printf("true");
else
    printf("false");
```

c. if (!p || (q || r) && !q)
```
        printf("true");
    else
        printf("false");
```

5. For these two programs, substitute each of the following specific conditions one at a time for *condition* in the loop control, then trace the loop. Show what is printed in each case. Will any of these cause an infinite loop or some other error? Here are the five conditions:

(1) (sum <= 12)
(2) (num > 4 && sum == num)
(3) (sum < 12 || num < 16)
(4) (num <= 32)
(5) (sum >= 0)

a.
```c
#include <stdio.h>
main()
{
    int num = 2,sum = 0;

    while (condition) {
        num *= 2;
        sum += num;
        printf("%d %d\n",num,sum);
    }
    printf("%d %d\n",num,sum);
}
```

b.
```c
#include <stdio.h>
main()
{
    int num = 2, sum = 0;

    do {
        num *=2;
        sum += num;
        printf("%d %d\n",num,sum);
    } while (condition);
    printf("%d %d\n",num,sum);
}
```

6. Show what is printed by each of these program segments:

a.
```c
int a = 2,z = 16;

do {
    z -= a;
    a += z /2;
    printf("%d %d\n",a,z);
} while (z >= a);
```

b.
```c
int i = 4,j = 9;

do {
    i += j;
    j--;
    printf("%d %d\n",i,j);
} while (i < j);
```

7. a. Construct a table to verify that the nested *if* statement in Example 6-3 correctly translates Figure 6-3.
   b. Do the same for the nested *if* in Example 6-4 that translates Figure 6-4.

8. For each of the sets of values below, determine which statement (*st-1* or *st-2*) is executed by the following *if-else* statement. In addition, show the intermediate result of each logical and relational operator.

   (1) *x* = 7; *y* = 3; *z* = 1; *r* = 3;
   (2) *x* = –1; *y* = –2; *z* = –7; *r* = 5;
   (3) *x* = 8; *y* = 2; *z* = 1; *r* = –10;

   ```
   if (x > 2 * y && y - z % 2 < r + 2 * 6 || x == -1)
       st-1;
   else
       st-2;
   ```

9. Translate the following *while* loops into *do-while* loops that do the same thing.

   a.
   ```
   int a = 19,b = 7;

   while (b <= a)
       b += 3;
   b += 2;
   ```

   b.
   ```
   int a = 10,b = -6;

   while (a != b || a > 0)
       a += b;
   ```

10. Show what is printed by each of the following segments. Are (a) and (b) equivalent? What about (c) and (d)?

    a.
    ```
    int a = 1,b = 1,c = 10;

    do {
        printf("%d\n",a);
        a += b;
        c++;
    } while (a <= c);
    printf("%d %d %d\n",a,b,c);
    ```

    b.
    ```
    int a = 1,b = 1,c = 10;

    while (a <= c) {
        printf("%d\n",a);
        a += b;
        c++;
    }
    printf("%d %d %d\n",a,b,c);
    ```

    c.
    ```
    int a = 1,b = 1,c = 10;

    do {
        printf("%d\n",a);
        a += b;
        b++;
        printf("%d\n",a);
    } while (a <= c);
    printf("%d %d %d\n",a,b,c);
    ```

    d.
    ```
    int a = 1,b = 1,c = 10;

    while (a <= c) {
        printf("%d\n",a);
        a += b;
        b++;
    }
    printf("%d %d %d\n",a,b,c);
    ```

11. Show what is printed by the following program. Assume that the set of data consists of these numbers, typed in one at a time in response to the prompt: 12 9 8 6 14 13 10 2.

    ```
    #include <stdio.h>
    main()
    {
        int i,size;
    ```

```
        for (i = 1; i <= 8; i++)  {
            printf("please enter the size> ");
            scanf("%d,&size);
            switch (size)  {
              case 9:  case 11:  case 13:  case 15:
                  break;  /* do nothing for larger odd sizes */
              case 2:  case 4:  case 6:  case 8:
                  printf("the dress size is %d",size);
                  printf(" it is small\n");
                  break;
              case 10:  case 12:
                  printf("the dress size is %d",size);
                  printf(" it is medium\n");
                  break;
              default:
                  printf("the dress size is %d",size);
                  printf(" it is large\n");
            }
        }
    }
```

12. Answer questions (a) to (c) for the following program.

```
#include <stdio.h>
main()
{
    int s1,s2,s3;
    int code = 0;

    do  {
        printf("please enter the 3 sides of a triangle, one at a time\n");
        scanf("%d",&s1);
        scanf("%d",&s2);
        scanf("%d",&s3);
        if ( (s1 == s2 || s1 == s3 || s2 == s3)  &&
             (s1 != s2 || s1 != s3 || s2 !=  s3) )  {
            printf("isosceles triangle: %d %d %d\n",s1,s2,s3);
            code = 1;
        }
    }  while (code != 1 && s1 != 0);
}
```

   a. Show what is printed by the program above. Use this set of data: 6 3 1   1 6 4   1 3 3   0 1 6 (assume that each group of three numbers is typed in response to the prompt).
   b. What happens if we add 3 9 12 to the end of the set of data? What about 3 9 9? Or 3 3 3? What if these values are added to the beginning of the set of data?
   c. What is the purpose of testing whether *s1* is equal to 0?

13. In the following program segment, the function *sums* calls the function *product*. For each call to a function, identify the calling function and the called function. Indicate where control returns after the call. Show what is printed, assuming that the data values are 5 and 8.

```
#include <stdio.h>
int product(int, int);
int sums(int, int);
main()
{
    int x,y,ans;

    printf("enter values one at a time for x and y\n");
    scanf("%d",&x);
    scanf("%d",&y);
    ans = sums(x,y);
    printf ("x = %d    y = %d    ans = %d\n",x,y,ans);
}

int product(int g,int h)
{
    if (g * h >= 40)
        return 3;
    else
        return g - h;
}

int sums(int i,int j)
{
    int a,b;

    a = product(i,j);
    b = product(a,j);
    return a + b;
}
```

14. a. Here is a main program, together with two functions. Assume that the set of data consists of the integers from 1 to 5 in order. Show what is printed as this program is executed. Note that function **sub2** calls function **sub1**.

```
#include <stdio.h>
int sub1(int, int);
int sub2(int, int);
main()
{
    int d,e,f,g,h,i,j,k;

    scanf("%d %d %d %d %d",&g,&h,&i,&j,&k);
    f = sub1(g,h);
    printf("first call: %d %d %d\n",g,h,f);
    e = sub2(i,j);
    printf("second call: %d %d %d\n",i,j,e);
    d = sub1(g,k);
    printf("third call: %d %d %d\n",g,k,d);
}
```

```
int sub1(int x,int y)
{
    if (x + y == 3)
        return 3;
    else return y - x;
}

int sub2(int p,int q)
{
    int r,s;

    r = sub1(p,q);
    s = sub1(q,p);
    return r + s;
}
```

b. Make up a different set of data and repeat the exercise.

15. Assume that *cond-1* and *cond-2* are conditions or questions which evaluate to either true or false. For parts (a) to (d) below, identify what statement(s) is executed in each situation:

(1) *cond-1* evaluates to true and *cond-2* to false
(2) *cond-1* evaluates to false and *cond-2* to true
(3) both conditions evaluate to true
(4) both conditions evaluate to false

a.
```
if (cond-1)
    st-1;
if (cond-2)
    st-2;
```

b.
```
if (cond-2)
    st-2;
if (cond-1)
    st-1;
```

c.
```
if (cond-1)
    st-1;
else
    if (cond-2)
        st-2;
```

d.
```
if (cond-2)
    st-2;
else
    if (cond-1)
        st-1;
```

ANALYSIS EXERCISES

16. In Exercise 10, parts (a) and (b), how does changing the limiting value inside the **while** or **do-while** loop affect the execution? In parts (c) and (d), how does a change in the increment affect things?

17. Show that anything which can be done with a **do-while** loop can be rewritten for a **while** loop and vice versa. Remember that the key difference between the two is that the body of a **do-while** loop always executes at least once (see Figure 6-1).

18. Rewrite the following segment using a **switch** statement instead of the nested **if**. Then rewrite it using a cascading nested **if** with full indentation. Finally, rewrite it using a series of **if** statements instead of a nested **if**. Which version is most efficient? Which is easiest to follow? In the nested **if** versions, why can we use simplified **if** conditions? For example, we can use **if (exam >= 80)** instead of **if (exam >= 80 && exam < 90)**.

```
int exam;

if (exam >= 90)
    printf("grade = A");
else if (exam >= 80)
    printf("grade = B");
else if (exam >= 70)
    printf("grade = C");
else if (exam >= 60)
    printf("grade = D");
else
    printf("grade = F");
```

19. Assume that we have the following problem: The variable x holds some initial value. If the value of x is greater than 99, subtract 25 from it; if the original value is in the range from 80 to 99, add 10 to it; otherwise add 1 to x. For example, if x starts at 120, it ends up as 120 − 25 = 95; if x is 98, it becomes 98 + 10 = 108; if x is 37, it is set to 37 + 1 = 38.

    a. What is wrong with using this series of C statements to solve the problem?

    ```
    int x;
    . . .
    if (x > 100)
        x -= 25;
    if (x >= 80 && x <= 99)
        x += 10;
    if (x < 80)
        x++;
    ```

    b. Modify the series of *if* statements in part (a) so that it does solve the problem.
    c. Use a nested *if* to solve this problem.
    d. Is it possible to use a *switch* statement to solve this problem? Explain.

20. Assume that we want to process a set of data, with 0 as the trailer value at the end (the 0 value is not processed). At first glance, these two segments seem to be equivalent. However, only the one on the right processes the data correctly. Assume that the set of data consists of 2 31 14 0, typed in one at a time.

    (1) `int num;`   (2) `int num;`

    ```
    num = 1;                                    scanf("%d",&num);
    while (num != 0)  {                         while (num != 0)  {
        scanf("%d",&num);                           process num
        process num                                 scanf("%d",&num);
    }                                           }
    ```

    a. Show which values are processed by each segment.
    b. What is the purpose of setting *num* to 1 in segment (1)? What is wrong with that segment?
    c. What is the purpose of each *scanf* in segment (2)?
    d. Show how to accomplish the same thing as segment (2) with a *do-while* loop.

21. In a nested *if* which contains a large number of conditions to be tested, it is often more efficient to rearrange the order of the questions, especially if the nested *if* has to be executed many times. For example, consider the nested *if* statement in Exercise 18.

    a.   In its current form, which condition is tested in every case (for every possible letter grade)? Which condition is tested in only one case?

    b.   Assume that this nested *if* statement appears in a loop, where it is executed once for each of 5000 students in a college. Most of the students received a grade of 90 or above on the exam. Is the current form a reasonable way to arrange the nested *if* statement? (*Hint*: If you change the order of the questions, how many conditions have to be tested to assign a grade to the majority of the students?)

    c.   Assume that most of the students received a grade of 50 or below on the exam. Is the current form reasonable? What is a more efficient way to rearrange the questions in the nested *if*?

    d.   What if most of the students received a grade in the range from 60 to 69. Is there a more efficient way to rearrange the nested *if* in this case?

22. a.   What happens in a *switch* statement if a particular constant value for the selector appears two or more times in the list of alternatives? First, try to predict what happens; then write a program to determine what C does in this situation.

    b.   What happens in a *switch* statement if the value for the selector does not appear in the list of alternatives (and there is no *default* clause)? First, try to predict what happens; then write a program to determine what C does in this situation.

    c.   If you have access to another C compiler, try running the programs on it as well.

23. Consider the following version of a *switch* statement, in which most of the *break* statements have been eliminated.

```
int number;

printf("type in a number from 2 to 9>: ");
scanf("%d",&number);
switch (number)   {
  case 2:
      printf("\n%d is a prime number",number);
  case 4:
  case 6:
  case 8:
      printf("\n%d is an even number\n",number);
      break;
  case 3:
  case 5:
  case 7:
      printf("\n%d is a prime number",number);
  case 9:
      printf("\n%d is an odd number\n");
  }
```

    a.   What is printed if the user types in the following values: 4 7 9 2? Are these correct answers?

b. If the **break** statements are put back in on each path, what does this version print? Are these correct answers?

24. Show that anything that can be done with a **switch** statement can also be done with a nested **if** construction. (*Suggestion*: Take the general form of a **switch** statement from Section 7 and show how it can be replaced by a nested **if**.)

25. Are there any differences among the code segments in each group below? Explain.

    a. (1) `if (!(x == 0)) ...`   (2) `if (x != 0) ...`
        (3) `if ( (x == 0) == 0) ...` (4) `if ( x == 0 == 0) ...`
    b. (1) `if ( !(p || q)) ...`   (2) `if ( !p && !q) ...`
    c. (1) `if ( !(p && q)) ...`   (2) `if ( !p || !q) ...`

The equivalences in parts (b) and (c) are called **deMorgan's Laws**.

26. Although C does not, some other computer languages (e.g., Turbo Pascal) have an exclusive-or operator, which we will denote by *xor*. If *p* and *q* are each either true or false, the expression *p xor q* is true if *p* is true or *q* is true, but false if they are both true or both false.

    a. Construct a truth table for the *xor* operator.
    b. Show how to simulate *xor* in C using the other three boolean operators. (*Suggestion*: There are several ways.)

27. In Section 8, Example 6-18 shows how short-circuit evaluation of boolean operators in C can eliminate a possible divide-by-zero error. Show how to solve the problem discussed there without taking advantage of short-circuit evaluation. (*Hint*: Consider the following two nested **if** statements.)

```
if (cond-1)            compared to        if (cond-1 && cond-2)
    if (cond-2)                               ...
        ...
```

28. a. What is printed by the following program?

```
#include <stdio.h>
main()
{
    int i,sum = 0;

    for (i = 1; i <= 5; i++) {
        if (i == 2)
            continue;
        sum += i;
        printf("the sum is %d and i is %d\n",sum,i);
    }
    printf("after the loop, the total sum is %d\n",sum);
}
```

    b. In the program above, replace the **continue** statement by a **break** statement and show what is printed by the new program.
    c. In the program above, replace the **continue** statement by a call to **exit** and show what is printed by the new program.

29. a. In the program in Exercise 28, replace the entire *if* statement by the following:

```
if (i % 2 == 0)
     continue;
```

Show what is printed by the new program. Is the output the same as from part (a) of Exercise 28? Explain.

    b. Repeat parts (b) and (c) of Exercise 28 using the *if* statement from part (a) of this exercise. Is the output from each of the new programs the same as from the corresponding original program? Explain.

30. a. Show what is printed by the following program, assuming that the data values 4 9 23 0 are entered, one at a time, in response to the prompts.

```
#include <stdio.h>
main()
{
    int numb;

    printf("type in a number; use 0 to stop. ");
    scanf("%d",&numb);
    while (numb != 0)  {
        if (numb == 6)
            continue;
        printf("%d is being processed",numb);
        statements to process numb
        printf("type in a number; use 0 to stop.> ");
        scanf("%d",&numb);
    }
}
```

    b. Repeat the exercise, assuming that the user intends to type in the numbers from 1 to 10, followed by 0. Explain what goes wrong. (*Hint*: What happens when the user types in the value 6?)

31. a. In Example 6-11, a *for* loop contains a **continue** statement. Show how to rewrite the loop without using one. (*Suggestion*: Consider using an *if-else* statement so the program can skip part of the body of the loop.)

    b. Repeat part (a) for Example 6-12, in which a *for* loop contains a **break** statement. (*Suggestion*: You may find it helpful first to rewrite the *for* loop with a more complicated condition controlling the loop, then modify the new loop to allow early termination.)

    c. Repeat part (a) for the *while* and *do-while* loops which contain **break** and/or **continue** statements (examples 6-13 and 6-14).

    d. Can you replace calls to *exit* by using other features of C? Explain.

32. a. Are there any differences between the *while* loop headers in (1) and (2) below? Explain.

```
(1)  while (1 == 1)
(2)  while (1)
```

    b. Normally, a *while* loop with a header like this leads to an infinite loop. Why?

c. Below is an example (in pseudocode) of a *while* loop with such a header:

```
while (1)  {
        read in a value for x
        if x is negative, terminate the loop
        print x
}
```

(1) Without changing the header of the loop, but using the new C statements in this chapter (*break*, *continue*, etc.), show how to translate this into C code. Explain how the *while* loop you use terminates.

(2) By changing the header of the loop and using other features of C introduced earlier in the text (but not in this chapter), show how to translate this into C code.

33. In Exercise 32, we discussed *while* loops that seem to lead to infinite loops but actually terminate under certain conditions. Show how to do similar things with *do-while* loops.

MODIFYING PROGRAM 6

34. The original version of Program 6 assumes that winter consists of the entire months of December, January, and February (and makes similar assumptions for the other seasons). Rewrite Program 6 so that winter covers the period from December 21 to March 20, and so on for the other seasons.

35. The original version of Program 6 assumes that all months have precisely 31 days. Rewrite Program 6 so that April, June, September, and November have 30 days, February has 28 (we will ignore leap year), and the rest of the months have 31. (*Suggestion*: The only time this modification changes the answer computed in the function *whichweek* is when the month is one of the five listed here and the week is number 5.)

36. a. In Program 6, the allowed values for *day* are in the range from 1 to 31. Assume that we remove checking for bad data from *classify*. What happens if the user types in an illegal value, say 37, for *day*?

    b. Under the same assumption, what happens if the user types in an illegal value for *month*?

    c. Modify the main program so that if the user types in an illegal value for *day*, the main program immediately requests another in the correct range. Do the same for an illegal value for *month*. Compare this method of error checking to the one in Program 6.

37. In Program 3, we introduced a trailer value to end a set of data. Compare the use of a trailer value to the new method in Program 6, where the user has the opportunity to continue or stop after each element is processed. Which method gives the user greater flexibility? Which method limits the values usable as data? Which requires the user to enter more responses?

38. a. In our first attempt to write the function *whichseason*, we included the following line:

```
if (month == 12 || 1 || 2 ) ...
```

According to the C precedence rules in Section 8, in what order are the operations performed? Does this cause an error? (Run a test program to check your answer.) How can we modify this statement to correct the order of operations?

b. Show how to rewrite **whichseason** with a nested **if** statement rather than a series of **if** statements. Can you use a **switch** statement? Explain why or why not.

39. In the function **whichweek**, we used a series of **if** statements to determine in which week a given date belongs. This exercise offers a number of other ways to accomplish this.

    a. Rewrite **whichweek** using a separate **if** statement for each possible value of **day**. (How many **if** statements do you need?)
    b. Rewrite **whichweek** using a nested **if**.
    c. Rewrite **whichweek** using a **switch** statement.
    d. Rewrite **whichweek** using integer division to determine the week number.

40. a. Write a nested **if** version of **translate**.
    b. In this version of **translate**, in what order should the months be listed if you know that most people are born in the summer?
    c. What if the fewest people are born in the summer?
    d. Would this special information about the months make any difference in the original version of **translate**?

41. In Program 6, the user is asked to enter either *y* or *n* to indicate whether the loop in the main program should continue.

    a. What happens if the user enters a value that is not one of these two responses? For example, what does the program do if the user enters some nonsensical thing like *H* or *5*? Is what the program does a reasonable way to handle typing in a response of this kind?
    b. What happens if the user enters the value *N*? Although this response correctly answers the question, will it be handled in a reasonable way?
    c. One possible solution to the problem in part (b) is to test for either '*n*' or '*N*'. Show how to modify the program to do this.
    d. C has a function **toupper** which can convert a lowercase letter into its uppercase equivalent. For example, **toupper('a')** returns '*A*'. Show how to use this function to solve the problem of alternate responses.
    e. The revision from part (d) does not handle all possible correct responses. What happens if the user enters the value *f* (for false)? Is this a "reasonable" response? Will it be handled correctly? Is there any method to handle all possible user responses?
    f. What if the user enters a response that is more than one character (for example, if the user enters *Y, e, s* and then a carriage return)?

PROGRAMMING PROJECTS

42. Assume that you are working on a linguistics research project. You want to classify the letters of the alphabet: The letters '*b*' and '*d*' are type 1; the letters '*c*', '*j*', and '*q*' are type 2; '*a*' is type 3; '*h*' and '*r*' through '*z*' are type 4; the rest of the letters are type 5. You want to read in a character (stored in **letter**) and determine its type (which is stored in **lettertype**). For this problem, assume that the person typing in data definitely enters one of the 26 lowercase letters.

    a. Write a program which performs this classification. Use a series of **if** statements. (*Suggestion*: You can handle each value of **letter** separately or use the logical and relational operators to combine cases like this):

    ```
    if (letter >= 'r' && letter <= 'z') ...
    ```

    b.   Use a nested *if* instead of a series of *if* statements.

    c.   Use a *switch* statement to classify the letters. Note that a variable of type *char* can be the selector in a *switch* statement.

43. In Exercise 42, we assume that the user enters one of the 26 lowercase letters. But in fact there are actually 256 possible values of type *char* that can be typed in. Show how to use each of the following methods to prohibit the selector's value from falling outside the indicated range.

    a.   Prompt the user to type in only a lowercase letter and assume he or she follows directions (this is the method used in Exercise 42).

    b.   Before the *if* or *switch* statement, check that the value typed in is within the allowed range from '*a*' to '*z*'.

    c.   As part of the *if* or *switch* statement, list each of the 256 values of type *char* with an appropriate action for each.

    d.   Can you think of any other ways to limit the legal values which can be entered?

    e.   Which method is the most reliable? Which method did you refuse to do? Which method depends upon the user's following directions? Which method is the best solution to the problem?

44. Assume that the set of values to be typed in as data for a program consists of a series of positive integers, then a single negative integer, then a second series of positive integers (terminated by 0). For example, the set of data may be 13 2 15 –8 9 87 1 2 1 1 21 0. Write a program that reads in the data, then prints two counts at the end: how many positive integers appear before the negative number and how many appear after. (The set of data shown earlier has three positive integers in the first set and seven in the second.) You can use either *while* or *do-while* loops (or one of each).

45. Write a program that does the following: Read a number *change* from a set of data. The value of *change* should be in the range from 0 to 99, representing a number of pennies. Your program finds the most economical way (using as few coins as possible) to represent the value *change*, using quarters, dimes, nickels, and pennies. Assume that this is the most economical way (is it the best?): Always give as many quarters as possible; for whatever amount is left, always give as many dimes as possible, and so on. For example, if *change* is 87, give three quarters, one dime, no nickels, and two pennies. (*Suggestion*: You can use either a *while* loop, a *do-while* loop, or some other method using integer division to determine how many quarters, dimes, and so on should be given.)

46. Write a complete C program to do the following: The main program reads in (and prints) a set of three student exam grades, then calls a function to check whether they are valid. If the function says they are, the main program calls a series of other functions to classify the grades. At the end of the data set, the main program print three counters. Here are the details:

    a.   The main program reads in three values.

    b.   The main program calls a function *validgroup* to determine if this set of three values forms a valid group. The function *validgroup* receives three parameters. For the group to be valid, each number must be in the range from 0 to 100. If the group is valid, the function prints a message. If one or more of the numbers is negative or greater than 100, the function prints an overall message saying the group is invalid. In addition, for each invalid value, the function prints the invalid grade and a message (for example, if all three are negative, it prints three values and messages).

If the function says the group is not valid, the main program skips the processing and goes on to the next group of three values.

c. If the function says the group is valid, the main program calls a function **trends** to determine what trend the grades follow. The function **trends** receives three parameters: call them **n1**, **n2**, and **n3**. The function classifies these three values in one of four ways: **n1 <= n2 <= n3**; **n1 >= n2 >= n3**; **n1 >= n2** and then **n2 < n3**; or **n1 <= n2** and then **n2 > n3**. The function prints an appropriate message—for example, the numbers increase, the numbers increase and then decrease, etc.

d. Then the main program calls a function **comparegrades**, sending it the three grades as parameters. The function **comparegrades** determines which of the following cases holds true: all three values are the same; two are the same and the third is larger; two are the same and the third is smaller; all three are different. Either the function or the main program prints an appropriate message.

e. Finally, the main program goes on to the next group of three values. When the main program runs out of groups (you must decide when), it prints the final values of three counters it has been keeping track of: the total number of groups processed, the number of valid groups, and the number of invalid groups.

Be sure to include a complete set of test data, covering all the possible cases. Here are some examples:

If the original group of data values is –2 173 280, the output is

```
-2 173 280 is an invalid set
-2 is negative    173 is too big    280 is too big
```

If the original group is 79 84 84, the output is

```
79 84 84 is a valid set
the grades go up
two are the same and the third is smaller
```

47. Write a C program to do the following: The main program reads in three integers, representing the degree measurement of three angles of a triangle, and sends them to a function. If the function says that the three integers form a valid triangle, the main program calls another function to classify the triangle. After repeating this process for the entire set of data, the main program prints how many groups formed valid triangles and how many formed invalid ones.

The first function, which checks for validity, uses the following rule: The three angles form a valid triangle if they add up to 180 and each one is greater than 0. For example, 40 60 80 is a valid set, but –10 40 150 is invalid (the numbers add up to 180, but one is negative), as is 20 40 100.

The classification function calls two additional functions. One of them determines if the triangle is equiangular (all three angles equal), isosceles (exactly two angles equal), or scalene (all three angles different). The other function determines if the triangle is right (has one angle with 90 degrees), obtuse (one angle above 90), or acute (all three below 90). Each function prints an answer giving its part of the classification process.

Include at least 15 groups with at least 5 of them invalid. Be sure to cover all the possible combinations (isosceles right, scalene acute, etc.).

Here are some sample sets of output:

```
20 60 100 is a valid group
the triangle is scalene
the triangle is obtuse

40 50 60 is an invalid group

-10 40 150 is an invalid group
```

48. Repeat Exercise 47 using the sides of a triangle rather than the angles. Three numbers are valid as the sides of a triangle if each one is positive, and the sum of every two numbers is greater than the third. For example, 4 6 7 is valid; 4 –1 3 is not valid; and 4 5 10 is also invalid.

   The sides can be classified in two ways: First, determine if the triangle is equilateral (all three sides equal), isosceles (exactly two sides equal), or scalene (all three sides different). Second, determine whether or not the triangle is a right triangle (the sum of the squares of two sides is equal to the square of the third side). For example, 6 10 8 is a right triangle, but 5 6 7 is not.

49. Write a program which allows the user to perform simple tasks on a calculator. A series of functions allows the user to select an operation to perform and then enter operands.

   The first function displays a menu, giving the user the choice of typing in any one of the following:

+, –, *, /, or %	representing the usual arithmetic operators
A	representing the average of two numbers
X	representing the maximum of two numbers
M	representing the minimum of two numbers
S	representing the square of a number
Q	indicating the user wants to quit the program

   The program reads the user's response into a variable of type *char*. Using a *switch* statement or a series of *if* statements, the program determines what function to call to process the user's request. For example, if the user enters +, another function asks for two integers. Then it finds the sum of the two integers. If the user enters *X*, a function asks for two integers and finds the larger of the two. If the user enters *S*, a function asks for one value and finds the square of that value. If the user enters *Q*, the program stops.

   For each calculation, the program prints the user's original input and the result.

ARRAYS

SYNTAX CONCEPTS: arrays, subscript notation, array of *char*, arrays as parameters, casting, two-dimensional arrays

PROGRAMMING CONCEPTS: parameter (or header) value, storing data in an array, using an array in a function, finding the maximum of a list of numbers

CONTROL STRUCTURES: *for* loop to process an array; the parameter method and the *EOF* method of detecting the end of a set of data

PROBLEM-SOLVING TECHNIQUES: modular programming, error checking

HOW TO READ CHAPTER 7

It is possible to cover Section 3 without first doing Section 2. However, sections 2 and 3 should be completed before continuing with sections 4, 5, and 6.

OUTLINE:

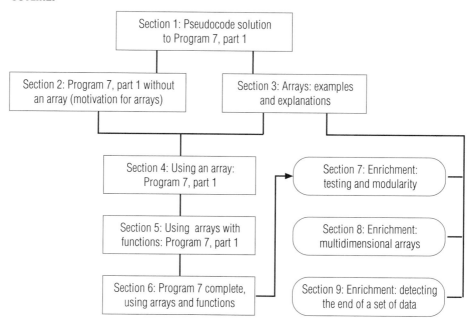

INTRODUCTION

This chapter starts with a problem that comes up often in programming applications: finding the average (sometimes called the mean) of a list of numbers. Even more important is the introduction of a new way to store information, called an array. After discussing arrays, we use one to solve the rest of Problem 7. One new part of the problem involves comparing all of the values in the array to the average. Arrays, and other data structures based on them, are of central importance to computer science. We will solve the averaging part of the problem without arrays, then with them, so that the advantages are apparent. Since all of our programs from this point on use the ideas developed here, make sure that you understand this chapter. Problem 7 also introduces a parameter value (sometimes called a header value).

STATEMENT OF THE PROBLEM

PROBLEM 7

An instructor has given an exam in class and wants to find the average mark and the highest mark. Write a complete C program to do the following: Read in and print the data, find the average mark in the class and the highest mark, then find how many grades are above, how many are below, and how many are equal to the average. At the end, print the results.

There are no more than 40 students in the class. The data format is as follows: a number n, called the parameter value, saying how many marks there are for the class, followed by that many marks. For example, the complete set of data might be this:

    3   91   94   65

The 3 is the parameter, promising three marks for the class. They are 91 94 65. Naturally, a real example would be much larger, but the format of the data remains the same.

In this case, the average of the marks for the class is $(91 + 94 + 65)/3 = 83.33$. The highest mark is 94. The number of grades greater than the average is 2, the number less than the average is 1, and the number equal to the average is 0.

SECTION 1   **HEADER (OR PARAMETER) VALUES; PSEUDOCODE FOR PROBLEM 7**

This section introduces a header value and uses it in developing and refining pseudocode for the first part of Problem 7—finding the average of a set of numbers. Of the two remaining parts of Problem 7, finding the highest mark can be solved with what you already know. However, finding the number of marks greater than, less than, and equal to the average cannot, and that part must wait until after Section 3. We will delay finding the highest mark until then as well.

A HEADER OR PARAMETER VALUE

In one sentence, the first part of Problem 7 can be described as reading in and finding the average of a series of numbers. But there is an important point to be resolved. How will the program know when it has read the last number?

We already have two methods to determine this. One is to use a trailer or sentinel to indicate the end of data. As a second method, the program in Chapter 6 asked the user about being finished, but this makes sense only for a program that uses interactive data entry. Rather than use either method, we would like to introduce a third.

The new method is called the **header value method**. A **parameter** or **header value** is a number which tells us how many actual pieces of data there are. A program which uses a header value first reads it in, then uses that value to determine how many more data values to read in. For example, in the list 5 12 24 56 34 84, the 5 is the header value, telling the program that there are five data values to be read in. The data values are 12 24 56 34 and 84.

Of course, this method also has its flaws and is not always the best choice, but it gives us a third alternative. In a given situation, we can use whichever method seems best. Section 9 introduces a fourth method and compares all four, as does Exercise 9.

CAUTION Notice that the word *parameter* is used in a new way here, different from the meaning it had when we were referring to a value passed to a function. Unfortunately, it is traditional to use the same word for both situations. Try to keep the two meanings separate. It should be clear from the context what the word means.

PSEUDOCODE VERSION OF PROBLEM 7

We will write several versions of Program 7, each time adding new features and taking care of more parts of the original problem. To start, let's just read in the data and find the average for the class. As usual, we begin with a rough pseudocode solution to the problem, then refine it until we reach a level close to C.

The first thing we must do is read in the marks. Each mark should be printed as well so that we can check our computed averages.

> *read and print the data,*
> *including the parameter* n

STYLE WORKSHOP Printing the data values as they are read in is more important when they are coming from a file than when they are entered interactively. We have written Program 7 as though the data values are being entered interactively. However, by this time, your instructor may have introduced redirection, so the input may be coming from a data file.

Finding the average for the class is quite easy. We add up the marks (in a variable we'll call *sum*) and divide by the total number of marks (*n*, in our case) to find the average. We store the average in *avgmark* and print it. The rest of the pseudocode is as follows:

> *set* sum *to the sum of the marks*
> *set* avgmark *to* sum *divided by* n
> *print* avgmark

REFINING THE PSEUDOCODE: USING THE HEADER VALUE

The next steps to refine are *read and print the data* and *set **sum** to ....* Let's first look at reading in the data. Note that the first number of the set (the 3 in the set 3 91 94 65) has to be treated in a different way from the rest since it is not one of the marks to be averaged. Our program must indicate that the first number determines how many other numbers will be read in. To make this clear to the computer, we'll read **n** in separately:

> *read* n
> *print* n

After **n** is read in, we want to read in **n** marks and add them up; to do this, we set up a loop to execute **n** times. In the loop, we read (one at a time) a series of values into the variable **mark** and print each **mark** value. Here is the outline of the loop:

> *for each of* n *marks* {
>   *read* mark
>   *print* mark
>   ...
> }

To determine how many numbers have been read, we use a counter, **count**; it starts at 0, as usual, and increments to **n–1**. The next version of the pseudocode includes the counting, which occurs in the header of a **for** loop:

> for (count = 0; count < n; count++) {
>   *read* mark
>   *print* mark
>   ...
> }

Now let's concentrate on translating *set **sum** to the sum of the marks*. Computing the sum should be standard by now, with an initialization of **sum** to 0 and a step that adds a new term to **sum**. Each value read into **mark** is added to **sum**. Finally, when we have added all of the marks, we divide by **n** to compute the average. Here is the final version of the pseudocode:

> *read* n
> *print* n
> sum = 0;
> for (count = 0; count < n; count++) {
>   *read* mark
>   *print* mark
>   *add* mark *to* sum
> }
> *set* avgmark *to* sum *divided by* n
> *print* avgmark

Notice that we start counting from 0 in the header of the *for* loop because that is traditional in C. As you will see in Section 3, however, starting from 0 is necessary in the second version of the program. Meanwhile, there is an added benefit of starting at 0: Each time we reach the top of the loop, the variable *count* holds the number of marks that have already been processed. (See Exercise 10 and Chapter 3, Exercise 45.)

SELF-CHECK 7-1

1. In the following list, which number is the parameter value? What information does it provide?

    4 27 59 87 98

2. As we read in a series of *n* numbers, should we count the value we read in for *n* as one of them?

3. If we start counting from 1, how does the condition in the loop header of the pseudocode have to be changed?

SECTION 2 PROGRAM 7, PART 1

This section translates the pseudocode from Section 1 into C, producing a program that reads in values and finds the average for the class. For reasons which will become clear shortly, we will write the first version of the program without functions and revise it later.

HEADER AND DECLARATIONS

Before we translate the pseudocode, let's write the main program header and declarations. Note that *avgmark* is declared to have data type *double* because an average usually is not an integer.

```
/*
 * Program prog7a.c:
 * finds the average of the grades for one class,
 * reading in data using a parameter value
 */
#include <stdio.h>
main()
{
    int     count,n,sum=0;
    int     mark;
    double avgmark;
```

READING IN THE PARAMETER VALUE

Now we must decide how we intend to read in the data: interactively or by redirecting input from a file (see Appendixes V and VI). We will put in prompts and read in the data interactively. However, since this program can handle a large number of students per class, or, with modifications, a large number of classes, some users may want to redirect *stdin* to come from a file.

The pseudocode says to read the parameter value into *n* and print out its value:

```
printf("Enter the number of marks> ");
scanf("%d",&n);
printf("There are %d marks\n",n);
```

ERROR CHECKING: DOES *n* HAVE A REASONABLE VALUE?

Actually, we are not ready to write the *for* loop header; the program should not continue without doing some error checking on the value entered for *n*. Certain values of *n*—for example, 0 or −1—will cause the rest of the program to make no sense and can result in an execution error. If *n* is 0 or negative, the program will not read in any data values (which by itself is not a problem), but it will try to compute the average of the data values. This *is* a problem, especially if *n* is 0. If *n* is negative, the average will be incorrect, but if *n* is 0, finding the average will crash the program.

A programmer can handle a bad parameter value several ways. One option is to terminate the program; another is to continue to ask the user to enter a parameter value until it is in the proper range. In this case, we will terminate the program; we leave the other option for Exercise 11. We can revise the section of code to check the value of *n* and terminate if it is invalid:

```
if (n > 0)
    printf("There are %d marks\n",n);
else {
    printf("invalid number of marks\n");
    exit(1);
}
```

Remember from Chapter 6, Section 7 that a call to *exit* terminates the program; sending *exit* a value other than 0 means an error.

THE LOOP CONDITION

Now we can write the loop to read in the rest of the data. The pseudocode has already translated the header of the *for* loop into C. Let's check the loop condition. The value of *count* starts at 0 and increments each time through the loop until the condition *count < n* is false. What is the final value of *count*? If you are counting five things starting at 1, you go from 1 to 5. However, if you count starting from 0, you go from 0 to 4, one less than the total. We are counting **n** things starting from 0, so we go to **n−1**. When **count** gets the value **n**, we fall out of the loop. We have the following **for** loop header:

```
for (count = 0; count < n; count++)
```

READING IN THE DATA AND FINDING THE AVERAGE

Within the loop, we read in a mark, print it, and add it to **sum**, which was initialized in the declaration. As we translate the loop into C, we include a comment describing the action of the loop.

```
/*
 * find average of n marks by adding
 * them to sum and dividing by n
 */
for (count = 0; count < n; count++) {
    printf("Enter a mark> ");
    scanf("%d",&mark);
    printf("%d\n",mark);
    sum += mark;
}
```

Since we have added all the marks, we can divide **sum** by **n** to obtain the average. We then print the average.

```
avgmark = sum / n;                                    /* incorrect */
printf("The average is %6.2f\n",avgmark);
```

NUMBER CONVERSIONS

Before we put the program together, there is a problem to fix. The program tries to find the average as follows:

```
avgmark = sum / n;
```

The program will run, and you will get a value for **avgmark**, but it isn't the one you expect. If **sum** has the value 180 and **n** has the value 3, **avgmark** has the expected value of 60. However, if **sum** has the value 182 and **n** has the value 3, **avgmark** still has the value 60, not 60.666. In C, dividing an integer by an integer produces an integer. When we divide **sum** by **n**, C saves only the integer portion of the quotient; assigning the result to a variable with type **double** is irrelevant because the fractional part of the answer has already been discarded.

There are two ways to solve this problem. One is to assign one of the integer values to a variable of type **double** before dividing:

```
double dsum;

dsum = sum;
avgmark = dsum / n;
```

Because one of the operands (*dsum*) has type *double*, this forces C to do real division, producing a real result. The fractional portion is not lost, and *avgmark* has the correct value (in this case, 60.67, if shown with two decimal places).

CASTING

The other solution is to use a more general technique called **casting** or **type casting**. Casting is a method for explicitly requesting type conversion. It allows the program to specify the type of result from an operation.

Casting is carried out by placing the desired type in parentheses in front of an operand:

```
avgmark = (double) sum / n;
```

Casting *sum* as type *double* has the same result as using the variable *dsum*. It makes a temporary copy of *sum* with type *double* and uses that value in the division. By casting *sum*, we guarantee that the C compiler performs real division, saves the fractional part of the result, and makes it available when the result is assigned to *avgmark*. We can obtain the same result by casting *n* as *double*:

```
avgmark = sum / (double) n;
```

CAUTION It is important to note that the following cast does not work:

```
avgmark = (double)(sum / n);
```

This cast is done too late to accomplish what we want. The division is done first, producing an integer; the result is cast as *double*, but the fractional part has already been lost.

FINDING THE AVERAGE (FIRST VERSION)

Let's put the program together so we can trace it.

 PROGRAM LISTING

```
/*
 * Program prog7a.c:
 * finds the average of the grades for the class,
 * reading in data using a parameter value
 */
#include <stdio.h>
main()
{
    int    count,n,sum=0;
    int    mark;
    double avgmark;

    printf("Enter the number of marks> ");
    scanf("%d",&n);
```

```
    if (n > 0)
        printf("There are %d marks\n",n);
    else {
        printf("Invalid number of marks\n");
        exit(1);
    }
    /*
     * find average of n marks by adding
     * them to sum and dividing by n
     */
    for (count = 0; count < n; count++) {
        printf("Enter a mark> ");
        scanf("%d",&mark);
        printf("%d\n",mark);
        sum += mark;
    }
    avgmark = (double) sum / n;
    printf("The average is %6.2f\n",avgmark);
}
```

PROGRAM TRACE Let's trace the program (ignoring printing) with this set of data: 3 91 94 65. Note that *n* never changes, *mark* holds the successive numbers to be averaged, *count* counts the number of *mark* values read in, and *sum* holds the sum of the *mark* values.

◆ Initially, *sum* is 0 and *count* is 0, indicating that we have not yet read in any *mark* values.

◆ We first read 3 into *n*, which tells the program that there are three marks in the set of data; the *for* loop will go from 0 to 2.

◆ Inside the body of the loop, when *count* is 0, we read 91 into *mark* and add it to *sum*, which becomes 91.

◆ At the top of the loop, *count* becomes 1, indicating that we have read in one mark.

◆ Inside the body of the loop, we read 94 into *mark* and add it to *sum*, which becomes 91 + 94 or 185.

◆ At the top of the loop, *count* becomes 2.

◆ Inside the body of the loop, we read 65 into *mark* and add *mark* to *sum*, which becomes 185 + 65 or 250.

◆ Then *count* becomes 3, which is too large. We fall out of the *for* loop with the final values for *count*, *mark*, and *sum*.

3	3	65	250
count	*n*	*mark*	*sum*

◆ Outside the loop, we cast *sum* to type *double*, which makes it 250.00; then we divide this value by *n*, which is 3, to give *avgmark* the value 83.33, which is printed.

This completes the first version of Program 7, which finds the average of the marks. This first version simply serves as a base for what we want to do. Before we rewrite the program, we will introduce the new concept that is the focus of this chapter.

SELF-CHECK 7-2

1. Why will entering 0 as the value for *n* cause the program to crash?
2. What is the final value of *count*?
3. What is the relationship between *count* and the number of values read in?

SECTION 3 ARRAYS

This section introduces an array, the first data structure in this book. A **data structure** is a method of grouping and organizing information in a way that reflects the relationships among data values.

PROBLEMS WITH THE FIRST VERSION

The program presented in Section 2 works as promised. However, we often find an average as part of a larger problem, as in complete Program 7, and for that reason, the program can be improved. Imagine that we have just completed calculating the average. Can we answer these questions?

1. What was the first grade averaged?
2. The second?
3. The last?
4. Which grade is closest to the average?
5. How many grades are above or below the average?

We can't tell what the first (or second) number was because each was read into *mark*, then replaced by the next. Questions 4 and 5 are also impossible to answer (and question 5 is part of Problem 7). We can answer only question 3 since the last number read in is still in *mark*.

Here is a grotesque way to solve some of these problems:

◆ Read the first number into a variable called ***mark1***.

◆ Read the second into a new variable, ***mark2***.

◆ Read the third into ***mark3*** (and so on).

Since each number is in a distinct variable, if we are asked about one specifically, we know where to look.

This may be a good idea, but it entails much extra work. Each variable, ***mark1***, ***mark2***, ***mark3***, ..., must be declared. Even worse, we can no longer use a loop to read in the numbers. Each number has to be read, printed, and added to ***sum*** separately because each has its own name. Thus, to add 10 numbers and find their average is burdensome. To add 25 or 30 requires a large (and repetitious) program. It is clear that this is not a clever way to solve the problem.

There is another problem with using many different variables. Suppose we want to read in values in the main program or a function and then call another function to compute the average. How many arguments do we send to the function? The number depends on the value of ***n***, which is not known until the program is running, when we read in a value for ***n***. Even in ***prog7a.c***, where we store the data values sequentially in ***mark***, it is impossible to send all of them to a function at one time. This is why we have written the first version of Program 7 without a function.

THE CONCEPT OF AN ARRAY

Fortunately, C (as well as almost every programming language) has a way of assigning unique names to the variables so that one value does not have to be written on top of another, but without the tremendous effort involved in separate variable names. An **array** allows us to use a single variable to store a number of values with the same data type. Each element of the array has its own storage location, which can be referenced like any other variable. The elements of an array are stored in consecutive storage locations in memory and identified by the name of the array followed by a number in brackets; these numbers start at 0. Thus, in an array of numbers called ***num***, we can refer to the first ***num*** value, the second ***num*** value, and so on. In mathematics, we would identify these values as num_0, num_1, etc. In C, the components of a five-element array ***num*** are ***num[0]***, ***num[1]***, ***num[2]***, ***num[3]***, and ***num[4]*** (see Figure 7-1). An array gives us a way to store all the marks for a class and then refer to a specific student's mark.

HIGHLIGHTS

◆ Each number 0, 1, 2, 3, 4 is called a **subscript** or an **index**; individual elements of the array are called **subscripted variables**.

◆ Square brackets distinguish array subscripts from other types of parenthesized expressions.

◆ The subscripts of all arrays in C are numbered starting with 0 and increase each time by 1.

FIGURE 7-1 Array *num*

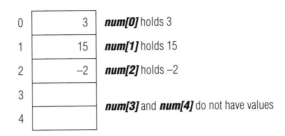

NAMING THE ELEMENTS OF AN ARRAY

This simple analogy explains the relationship of the individual elements to the entire array. Within the Smith family, the individual members can be referred to by their first names—Joan or Bob or Carol. All of them share a common last name. When we want to distinguish one family from another, we use the last name—the Smith or the Taylor family. When we want to choose a single individual, we use both names—Joan and Smith.

An array is similar. All elements of the *val* array share the common name *val*. They are distinguished from each other by their individual subscripts. To refer to an element in the *val* array, we give the array name and the subscript or location within it—*val* and 3 designate *val[3]*. Just as there can be a Joan Smith and a Joan Jacobs, there can be a third element in the *val* array (called *val[2]*) and one in the *num* array (called *num[2]*). (You'll get used to counting from 0 in time.)

SELF-CHECK 7-3

1. What is the purpose of an array?

2. Which of the following games use an array in their scoring mechanisms? For each one, identify what a single element of the array represents.

    a. tennis   b. bowling   c. darts   d. baseball

3. How large an array do you need to represent each of the following collections of information?

    a. the days in the week   b. the months in the year

USING ARRAYS

The elements of the array can be treated like simple variables. Each element can be assigned a value, tested, printed, or used in an expression.

EXAMPLE 7-1

Here are some examples using elements of array **num** instead of simple variables:

```
num[3] = 5;   or   printf("%d",num[4]);   or   result = 2 * num[0];
```

A more interesting and powerful feature lets the subscript itself be a variable.

EXAMPLE 7-2

Let's use *i* as the subscript of array **num**:

```
i = 4;
num[i] = 7;
```

The variable *i* is set to 4 by the first line. The reference in the second line to the subscripted variable *y[i]* really means *y[4]*, and that storage location is set to 7.

Finally, let's look at the almost perfect marriage between arrays and *for* loops. The array subscript can be changed in the *for* loop header, allowing us to fill consecutive elements efficiently.

EXAMPLE 7-3

What does this loop do?

```
for (i = 0; i < 5; i++)
    num[i] = i * 3;
```

It assigns each element of array **num** a value which is three times its subscript; that is, **num[0]** gets the value 0, **num[1]** gets 3, **num[2]** gets 6, **num[3]** gets 9, and **num[4]** gets 12.

 CAUTION Make sure that you know the difference between the value stored in an array element (9 in **num[3]**) and a subscript like 3.

DECLARING AN ARRAY

To use an array, we must declare it. For example, an array called **nums** that can hold ten integers is declared as follows:

```
int nums[10];
```

- ◆ The 10 specifies the number of elements in the array (usually referred to as the **size** or **dimension**). Array **nums** has ten elements, numbered from 0 to 9.
- ◆ 0 is the **lower bound** or smallest subscript in every array.
- ◆ 9 is the **upper bound** or largest subscript.
- ◆ In the program, a subscript which refers to **nums** should be in the range from 0 to 9.
- ◆ The type in the array declaration tells what data type applies to each element, from the lower to the upper bound; in the array **nums**, the data type for each element is *int*.

Keep in mind that the declaration sets aside ten storage locations for the **nums** array, but the program does not have to use them all.

🖐 **CAUTION** Even though there are ten elements in the array, the highest subscript is 9. An attempt to use subscript 10 references a storage location outside the array, which is usually the location of another variable. If you assign or read a value into that location, you will destroy the value of the other variable. C does not send an error message since it does not check for invalid subscripts.

It is possible to initialize some or all of the elements in an array in the declaration, although that usually makes sense only for small arrays. The following declaration initializes all ten elements in the *nums* array:

```
int nums[10] = {5,11,-1,17,30,6,47,48,21,-32};
```

ARRAYS OF OTHER DATA TYPES

Although the examples so far have all been arrays of type *int*, we can have arrays of other data types, such as *float*, *double*, or *char*.

EXAMPLE 7-4 We want an array *sales* to hold a company's sales data for three years, 1994 to 1996. The sales data will be values of type *double*. The declaration and initialization for the array *sales* can be the following:

```
double sales[3] = {123.45, 23456.78};
```

The lower bound for the array is 0; the upper bound is 2, giving a total of three storage locations. Each location can hold a number of type *double*. Note that we have initialized only the first two elements in the array; *sales[0]* is initialized to hold the sales for 1994, and *sales[1]* holds the sales for 1995. The third element, *sales[2]*, will hold the sales for 1996 when that value is entered. Figure 7-2 diagrams what the array *sales* looks like after it has been initialized.

INTERPRETATION OF SUBSCRIPTS

Since C requires that subscripts begin at 0, we can't use ones that might otherwise seem logical. For example, the year can't be the subscript in the *sales* array. Instead, we must interpret the subscripts in the program code, as shown in Example 7-5.

FIGURE 7-2 Array *sales*

```
double sales[3] = {123.45, 23456.78};
```

	sales
0	123.45
1	23456.78
2	

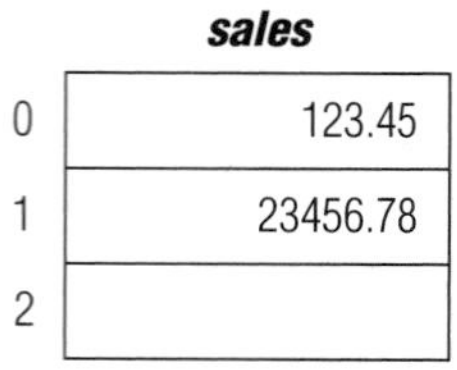

EXAMPLE 7-5

Suppose we want to read in amounts to update the array **sales** from Example 7-4. Each transaction consists of two pieces of data: first, the year which is being updated, and then the new amount to add to the total. There may be several transactions for each array element, and the transactions are not necessarily in any order. This means we cannot use the index of the loop to select array elements. The following code updates the appropriate element and then prints the entire array.

```
double sales[3] = {0,0,0};
double amount;
int    year,count,numtrans;

printf("Enter the number of transactions> ");
scanf("%d\n",&numtrans);
for (count = 0; count < numtrans; count++) {
    scanf("%d",&year);
    scanf("%lf",&amount);
    switch (year) {
      case 1994:
            sales[0] += amount;
            break;
      case 1995:
            sales[1] += amount;
            break;
      case 1996:
            sales[2] += amount;
            break;
      default;
    }
}
printf("sales for 1994 are %8.2f\n",sales[0]);
printf("sales for 1995 are %8.2f\n",sales[1]);
printf("sales for 1996 are %8.2f\n",sales[2]);
```

There is a relationship between the years (1994, 1995, and 1996) and the subscripts (0, 1, and 2). We can use this mathematical relationship to replace the **switch** statement with the following simple statement:

```
sales[year - 1994] += amount;
```

Using the same principle, the three calls to **printf** can be replaced by the following loop:

```
for (i = 0; i < 3; i++)
    printf("sales for %d are %8.2f\n",i+1994,sales[i]);
```

ARRAY OF *char*

Let's take a more careful look at an array of **char**, since that is special in C. An array of **char** is declared like others.

EXAMPLE 7-6

The following declaration sets up an array **message** that can hold 20 characters:

```
char message[20];
```

We can assign values to each array element, either in the declaration or through assignment statements. Each element can hold a single value of type *char*, including special values like the newline character '*\n*', the tab character '*\t*', or the null character '*\0*'.

The **null character**, like the newline character, requires two symbols to represent it but is treated as one character in C. This character is extremely important in processing strings in C because it is the string terminator.[1]

An array of *char* can be initialized element by element in the declaration or assignment statements, as shown in Example 7-7.

EXAMPLE 7-7   Here we initialize the first five elements in the declaration and assign values to the next seven; the other elements remain uninitialized:

```
char message[20] = {'w','e','i','r','d'};

message[5] = ' ';          /* this assigns a blank to message[5] */
message[6] = 's';
message[7] = 't';
message[8] = 'u';
message[9] = 'f';
message[10] = 'f';
message[11] = '\0';        /* this assigns the null character to message[11] */
```

What is special about an array of *char* is the way it can be used. In addition to working with the individual elements, we can treat it as a unit. Examples 7-8 and 7-9 illustrate this flexibility with two different ways to print the array *message*.

EXAMPLE 7-8   The array *message* can be printed character by character. Assume that *message* has been initialized as shown in Example 7-7. In the code below, we look for the '*\0*' as a signal to stop printing (in this case, we stop at the end of the filled elements in the array).

```
int  i=0;
char message[20];

/* message initialized as in Example 7-7 */

while (message[i] != '\0') {
    printf("%c",message[i]);
    i++;
}
```

The same thing can be done with a *for* loop:

```
for (i = 0; message[i] != '\0'; i++)
    printf("%c",message[i]);
```

---

[1]We learn more about the null character in Chapter 9.

Either loop prints the individual elements of **message** one at a time, next to each other, so that the resulting output looks like a string:

> `weird stuff`

 CAUTION The next technique *requires* the null character to be assigned to the array element that follows the last character to be printed.

Example 7-9 shows how an array of **char** can be printed as one entity.

EXAMPLE 7-9 Assume that **message** has been initialized as shown in Example 7-7. The null character signals to the computer that it has reached the end of the filled elements in the array.

```
printf("%s\n",message);
```

This call to **printf** prints **message** all at once, stopping at the null character:

> `weird stuff`

Note the new conversion character in the control string of the call to **printf**. The conversion specification **%s** means that the value is a string.[2]

SELF-CHECK 7-4

1. What is the appropriate declaration for each of the following?
   a. an array of 50 numbers with decimal places
   b. an array of 26 characters

2. Answer the following questions about this declaration:

   `int amount[25];`

   a. How many elements are in the array?
   b. What are the upper and lower bounds of the array?

3. What is special about an array of **char**?

EXPRESSIONS AS SUBSCRIPTS

Actually, we have been more restrictive than is necessary. All the subscripts in our examples have been integer constants or variables, but this is not required. A subscript can be an expression as long as it evaluates to an integer.

---

[2]In Chapter 9, we discuss working with strings.

EXAMPLE 7-10   Here is the declaration for an array *item* and a variable *i*. Below the declaration is an assignment using a valid subscript reference.

```
int i=4;
int item[20];

item[2*i + 3] = 76;
```

To which element does the subscript refer? First, the subscript $2*i + 3$ is evaluated to an integer value; call it *val*. In this case, the subscript *val* evaluates to $2*4 + 3 = 8 + 3 = 11$, so the value 76 is assigned to *item[11]*.

Although a subscript can be any integer expression, by far the most common choice is an integer variable such as *i* or a minor modification like $i + 1$. Let's illustrate this with a simple example.

EXAMPLE 7-11   Assume we have read a series of letters into the eight-element array *letters*. For example, the array might contain 'Y', 'A', 'M', 'L', 'N', 'M', 'M', and 'J'. Figure 7-3 shows the array with these values (the subscripts are along the bottom):

We want to check if any two consecutive entries are equal. Here is a portion of a program to print a message every time there is a match:

```
char letters[8];
int  i;

for (i = 0; i < 7; i++)
    if (letters[i] == letters[i + 1])
        printf("%c is repeated\n",letters[i]);
```

We have declared *letters* as an array of *char*. Inside the *for* loop, the subscript *i* refers to an element of the array. The subscript $i + 1$ refers to the next element of the array.

You may wonder why the *for* loop index goes from 0 to 6 ($i < 7$) even though there are eight elements in the array. Remember that the highest subscript in the array is 7; when *i* is 6, $i + 1$ is 7, so we will be comparing the next-to-last element (*letters[6]*) with the last (*letters[7]*). (If we allowed *i* to go from 0 to 7, the last comparison would use *letters[8]*, which is out of bounds.)

An alternate way to process the array is to have the subscript *i* refer to an element and use $i - 1$ as the subscript of the previous element.

FIGURE 7-3   *letters* array

'Y'	'A'	'M'	'L'	'N'	'M'	'M'	'J'
0	1	2	3	4	5	6	7

PARALLEL ARRAYS

The same subscript can be used for more than one array at the same time. Two arrays which use the same variable as a subscript in a loop are called **parallel arrays**. Consider a situation where we have two arrays, one to store students' ID numbers and another to store the same students' averages. Let's call the two arrays *idnum* and *average*. A logical way to store the information is to keep each student's ID number in the same position of the *idnum* array as that student's average occupies in the *average* array. Thus, *average[0]* belongs to *idnum[0]*, *average[1]* to *idnum[1]*, and so on (see Figure 7-4).

To print out each student's ID number, followed by that student's average, we can use the same subscript. Example 7-12 shows how to do this.

EXAMPLE 7-12

```
int     i;
int     idnum[20];
double  average[20];

for (i = 0; i < 20; i++)
     printf("student %d has an average of %6.2f\n",idnum[i],average[i]);
```

As *i* varies from 0 to 19, it allows us to access a new element from both arrays. The element accessed from the *idnum* array will always have the same subscript as the one from the *average* array.

SENDING A SINGLE ELEMENT OF AN ARRAY AS A PARAMETER

A single element of an array is treated like any simple variable of its type. We can send it as a parameter to an array, as we did in Example 7-12, where *idnum[i]* and *average[i]* are parameters for *printf*. Example 7-13 shows how to send an element of an *int* array to a function.

FIGURE 7-4   Parallel arrays, *idnum* and *average*

	idnum			average	
0	123		0	65.45	
1	234		1	95.67	
2	345		2	86.56	
	.			.	
	.			.	
	.			.	
19	890		19	77.47	

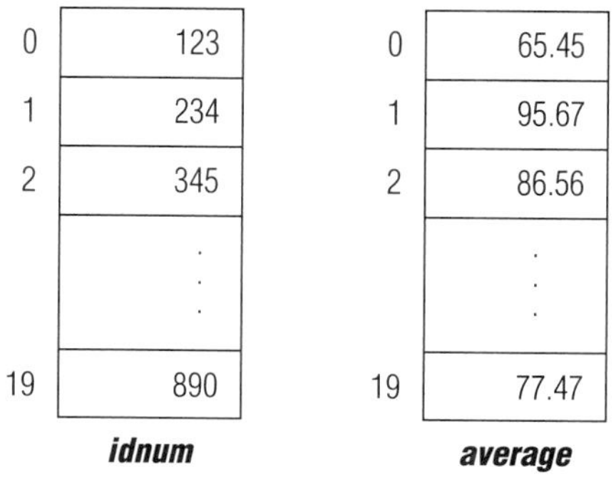

EXAMPLE 7-13   The function **add** adds two numbers together and returns the result. Here are its prototype and header:

prototype   **header**

```
int add(int,int);
```
```
int add(int first,int second)
```

The calling function can send any integer variable to match parameters **first** and **second**. The call below sends the first two elements of the **nums** array:

```
int result,nums[10];
...
result = add(nums[0],nums[1]);
```

Passing an entire array as a parameter is more complex and is discussed in Section 5.

SELECTING BOUNDS FOR AN ARRAY

Let's look at some other features of arrays. Suppose an array **test** is declared to have 40 storage locations. It is certainly legal to fill only 3 of them since we can leave storage locations unused. However, suppose we provide only 2 locations by using this declaration:

```
int test[2];
```

Whether this is a problem depends on the size of the set of numbers. The program must provide enough space to hold all the data. If there are only one or two numbers, this array can store all the values. But if the set of data has three numbers, we have a problem: the third value goes into **test[2]**, which is outside the array. Declaring **test** to have 3 locations solves the problem for this set of data, but if the data set has four values, the problem arises again.

It is foolish to write a program that is so sensitive to the slightest change in the size of the data set. We should not have to revise the declaration and recompile the program every time the size changes. Declaring arrays with very large bounds is one way to make sure that we won't be caught short, but it is wasteful and inefficient. As a rule, it is best to choose array bounds that are large enough to hold most sets of data comfortably but are not unwieldy. We usually declare our arrays to hold several more items than we expect. If we expect 120 numbers, we declare 150 locations:

```
int test[150];
```

NOTE   The space is reserved regardless of whether it is filled.

CAUTION A programmer must be careful to reserve enough memory locations for an array and keep all subscripts within the established bounds. Since C does not check to see whether a subscript is out of bounds, using one greater than the upper bound does not generate a warning or error message. C uses the subscript to calculate a memory location and utilizes that location even if it is allocated to another variable.

USING A CONSTANT AS THE ARRAY SIZE

It would be convenient to use the variable *num* in the declaration, as follows:

```
int num = 150;
int test[num];                              /* illegal */
```

It would seem that, once *num* gets a value, we can use it to declare an array of exactly the right size. However, this form is illegal since the compiler must know how much space to assign to the array before the program starts to run (before *num* receives a value).

We can, however, use a constant as the size of the array; to modify the size, we simply change the constant definition.

```
#define NUM 150
int test[NUM];
```

The value 150 is substituted for *NUM* prior to setting up storage for the array, making this a legal declaration.

SELF-CHECK 7-5

1. Given this declaration, answer the following questions.

    ```
    int item[25], amount[25],i;
    ```

    a. If *i* = 8, what array element is referred to by *item[i–3]*?
    b. If *i* is 24, what element is *amount[i+1]*?

2. Show how to fill all the elements in the *item* array in question 1 with sequential values, starting from 1.

3. In Example 7-12, why can't the information for arrays *idnum* and *average* be stored in one array?

SECTION 4 USING AN ARRAY—PROGRAM 7, PART 1

This section illustrates how to use an array by rewriting the part of Program 7 we have done so far.

THE *mark* ARRAY

Instead of a single variable called *mark*, we can use an array called *mark*.

◆ The first number to be averaged goes into *mark[0]*.

◆ The second number to be averaged goes into *mark[1]*.

◆ The last number to be averaged goes into *mark[n–1]*.

This method of naming the elements is close to what we proposed in Section 3 (*mark1*, *mark2*, *mark3* ...). Now, because the named elements are part of an array, the notation will help rather than hinder us. When we print and add to *sum*, we use a particular element of the *mark* array. Thus, at the end of the averaging process, we still have all the values stored in the *mark* array.

To instruct the computer to use *mark[0]* first, then *mark[1]*, we need a variable for the subscript that can increase from 0 to *n–1*. Luckily, there already is such a variable, *count*, the index of the *for* loop, which can be the array subscript. Before the first mark is read in, *count* has the value 0. Then *count* is 1 after the first mark has been processed. The index *count* continues to increase by 1 as each new *mark* value is used.

If we designate *mark[count]* as the variable to hold the numbers, the values to be averaged are put successively into *mark[0]*, *mark[1]*, ..., *mark[num–1]*. The only changes we have to make to use an array in Program 7 are to replace *mark* by *mark[count]* and revise the declaration.

PROGRAM 7: SECOND VERSION, USING AN ARRAY

Now let's rewrite the program. We said that the professor never has more than 40 students in a class. Therefore, we set up the following array declaration (note that we allow for a few extra elements as a precaution):

```
#define SIZE 50
int mark[SIZE];
```

Now that we are using an array, we must add an additional check to parameter value *n*. It is no longer sufficient to check whether *n* is greater than 0; *n* must be appropriate for the bounds of the array: in this case, *n* must be less than *SIZE*. A program which reads data into an array should always make sure not to exceed the bounds. Here is the complete new version of the program, using an array to hold the marks:

PROGRAM LISTING

```
/*
 * Program prog7b.c:
 * finds the average of the grades for the class
 * using a parameter value and an array
 */
#include <stdio.h>
#define SIZE 50
main()
{
    int     count,n,sum;
    int     mark[SIZE];
    double  avgmark;

    printf("Enter the number of marks> ");
    scanf("%d",&n);
```

```
        if (n > 0 && n <= SIZE)
            printf("There are %d marks\n",n);
        else {
            printf("Invalid number of marks\n");
            exit(1);
        }
        /*
         * find average of n marks by adding
         * them to sum and dividing by n
         */
        sum = 0;
        for (count = 0; count < n; count++) {
            printf("Enter a mark> ");
            scanf("%d",&mark[count]);
            printf("%d\n",mark[count]);
            sum += mark[count];
        }
        avgmark = (double) sum / n;
        printf("The average is %6.2f\n",avgmark);
}
```

The array version is almost identical to the original. To verify this, you should trace it with the same set of values that we used for the first version. Now, however, each value is stored in its own array location; even after the average has been computed, all of the values in **mark** are still available for other computations.

A MODULAR VERSION OF PROGRAM 7

To illustrate the importance of having all the values available throughout the program, we will rewrite it using two loops rather than one. Each loop performs a separate task. The first loop reads in and prints the data, and the second finds the average, using the values which are still in the array. Each loop is thus a self-contained unit, or module, which we can use here or somewhere else. Notice that each module performs a separate task, as a function would. This will help us in the next version of this program.

PROGRAM 7: THIRD VERSION, USING AN ARRAY AND TWO LOOPS

Here is the new version of the program so far:

🖥 PROGRAM LISTING

```
/*
 * Program prog7c.c:
 * finds the average of the grades for the class
 * using a parameter value, an array, and two loops
 */
```

(continued)

(*continued*)

```c
#include <stdio.h>
#define SIZE 50
main()
{
     int    count,n,sum;
     int    mark[SIZE];
     double avgmark;

     printf("Enter the number of marks> "):
     scanf("%d",&n);
     if (n > 0 && n <= SIZE)
         printf("There are %d marks\n",n);
     else {
         printf("Invalid number of marks\n");
         exit(1);
     }
     /*
      * read n marks into the mark array
      * and print each mark as it is read in
      */
     for (count = 0; count < n; count++) {
         printf("Enter a mark> ");
         scanf("%d",&mark[count]);
         printf("%d\n",mark[count]);
     }
     /*
      * find average of n marks by adding
      * them to sum and dividing by n
      */
     sum = 0;
     for (count = 0; count < n; count++)
         sum += mark[count];
     avgmark = (double) sum / n;
     printf("The average is %6.2f\n",avgmark);
}
```

SELF-CHECK 7-6

1. a. What is the advantage of the array version of the program?
    b. What changes are necessary to use an array in Program 7?

2. Can we have separate modules to read and print?

3. If we omit *[SIZE]* from the declaration of **mark**, what type of variable does the compiler think **mark** is?

USING ARRAYS WITH FUNCTIONS—PROGRAM 7, PART 1

Now that we have seen how to work with arrays, we must learn how to use an array in a function. To illustrate this, let's rewrite Program 7, part 1.

RECEIVING AN ARRAY AS A PARAMETER: PROTOTYPE AND FUNCTION HEADER FOR *sumarray*

We want to write a function called **sumarray** that finds the sum of the elements in the **mark** array. Of course, we won't sum all the elements in the array, just those filled with useful values. The easiest way to specify this is to use another parameter, say **n**, to hold the number of values we want to sum (as opposed to the size in the declaration). Inside the function, we call the array **num**. We want the function to add the array elements from **num[0]** to **num[n–1]** and return this value. We call the formal parameter **num** instead of **mark** for two reasons: one is so we can distinguish between the formal and actual parameter if necessary; the second is so we can reuse this function for any array of integers and still have a meaningful name.

First, let's look at the prototype of the function **sumarray**, where the array is the first parameter, and **n** is the second:

```
int sumarray(int [], int);     or     int sumarray(int num[], int n);
```

In the left version of the prototype, we do not give names to the formal parameters, while in the version on the right, we do give them names. Some people prefer a name when the parameter is an array, even if they just write **int array[]**, using **array** as the name of the parameter.

The header of the function follows logically from the prototype, although, of course, a name must be given to the formal parameter. Once again, we use *[]*, with no size, to indicate the array parameter:

```
int sumarray(int num[], int n)          /* function header */
```

CAUTION In a function prototype or header, insert brackets following the data type (or name, if supplied) of the parameter, to indicate that it is an array.

◆ Do not omit the array brackets. If you do, the compiler will expect the parameter to be a simple integer variable rather than an array.

◆ It is not necessary to put a size into the array brackets. If you supply one, it will be ignored.

In a function that receives an array as a parameter, the formal parameter can be matched up with an array of any size. However, the actual and formal parameters must have the same underlying type (array of **int** or array of **double**). This means that we can use **sumarray** to sum integer arrays of different sizes.

THE FUNCTION *sumarray*

The rest of the function is very straightforward. Assume that a separate function, **readdata** (to appear shortly), has already read values into the array before this function is called. All *sumarray* has to do is add up the elements in the array (which is what we did earlier in the main program) and return the result. Here is the entire function:

```
/*
 * Function sumarray:
 * Input:
 *    num: an array of integers
 *    n: the number of elements in the array
 * Process:
 *    finds the sum of the first n elements
 *    in the num array
 * Output:
 *    returns the sum to the calling function
 */
int sumarray(int num[], int n)
{
    int sum,count;

    sum = 0;
    for (count = 0; count < n; count++)
        sum += num[count];
    return sum;
}
```

THE FUNCTION *avgarray*

Now that we have a simple example of an array as a parameter to a function, we are ready to write the function for Program 7. To do this, we need a function to find an average, not a sum. We can call the function *avgarray*. Let's again call the parameters to this function *num* and *n*; in fact, we can use *num* and *n* in all the functions. Note the type of answer the function returns.

```
double avgarray(int num[], int n)                    /* function header */
```

To find an average, we add up a series of numbers (in this case, *n* of them) and divide by the total number of values (again *n*). One way to do this is to write a *for* loop to sum the *num* array, then have a last step which divides this sum by *n*. This isn't hard to do, but we want to limit the burdensome work we must do as programmers by having the computer do it for us. There is an easy way to sum the *num* array by using the function *sumarray*. In other words, the function *avgarray* calls the function *sumarray*. The answer from *sumarray* is put into the local variable *total*.

```
total = sumarray(num,n);
```

The answer stored in *total* is cast as *double*, divided by *n*, and then returned:

```
return (double) total / n;
```

Actually, the local variable ***total*** can be eliminated. In the version of ***avgarray*** below, we get rid of ***total***. Here is the entire function:

```
/*
 * Function avgarray:
 * Input:
 *    num: an array of integers
 *    n: the number of elements in the array
 * Process:
 *    calls sumarray to find the sum of the first n elements
 *    in the num array; divides the returned value by n to obtain the average
 * Output:
 *    returns the average to the calling function
 */
double avgarray(int num[], int n)
{
    return (double) sumarray(num,n) / n;
}
```

In this version, the value returned from the function ***sumarray*** is used directly in the computation; this value is cast as ***double*** and then divided by ***n*** without first being stored in ***total***.

THE FUNCTION *readdata*

In order to write a complete version of Program 7, we also need a function ***readdata*** to read in and print the data. The ***readdata*** function performs the same task as the first loop of the modular version of the program. It does not, however, print a heading on the output since the main program does that. The function ***readdata*** reads in the values from the set of data; first it reads in ***n***, and then it reads ***n*** values into an array ***num***, which holds the numbers we have read in.

Clearly, ***readdata*** should receive as a parameter the array which we want to fill. However, you may recall from Chapter 5 that functions in C don't change the value of their parameters because C passes parameters by value. That is, any change to the variable inside the function is not reflected when we return to the calling function. Fortunately, the value that is passed for an array parameter allows changing the array's values within the function.[3]

CHANGING AN ARRAY IN A FUNCTION

When we send an array as a parameter, the value we send to the function is the actual *location* of the variable in storage. This means that the values in an array can be changed within a function and will retain their new values upon return to the calling function.

---

[3]Changing values in a function is discussed in more detail in Chapter 8; in particular, that discussion clarifies how an array is passed as a parameter.

We send the *mark* array to *readdata*, and it receives values within the function. The variable *n* must also have a value read into it, but we have not yet introduced a way to allow a value read into *n* in the function *readdata* to remain when we return to the calling function. Therefore, *readdata* reads the size of the array into a local variable and returns that value to the main program to be used in later functions. Let's look at the prototype and header of the function:

prototype

```
int readdata(int []);
```

header

```
int readdata(int num[])
```

You may ask why *readdata* can't return the array. Remember that a function can only return a single value. Which value of the array would it return? The first? The last? None of these makes sense. The array cannot be returned but must have its values changed instead.

Here is the complete function *readdata*:

```
/*
 * Function readdata:
 * Input:
 *    num: the array to fill
 *    parameter is uninitialized upon entry
 * Process:
 *    reads n and reads n values
 *    into the num array; prints n and num
 * Output:
 *    fills array num
 *    prints num array
 *    returns n
 */
int readdata(int num[])
{
    int count,n;

    printf("Enter the number of marks> ");
    scanf("%d",&n);
    if (n > 0 && n <= SIZE)
        printf("There are %d marks\n",n);
    else {
        printf("Invalid number of marks\n");
        exit(1);
    }
    for (count = 0; count < n; count++) {
        printf("Enter a mark> ");
        scanf("%d",&num[count];
        printf("%d",num[count]);
    }
    return n;
}
```

When we send the *mark* array to *readdata*, it contains no values; it receives its values in *readdata*. After the function returns to the main program, the array *mark* that was

FIGURE 7-5 Sample values of **num** and **n** as changed by **readdata**

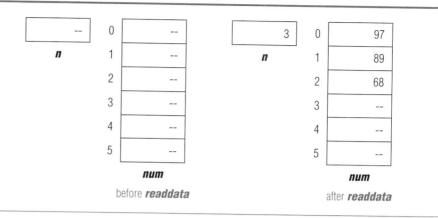

matched with the formal parameter **num** holds the information read in by the function **readdata** (see Figure 7-5). Of course, if the value entered for **n** is invalid, the program terminates, and the function does not return to the main program. (In Section 9 and Exercise 11, we explore other ways of handling invalid data.)

REVISING THE MAIN PROGRAM: SENDING AN ARRAY AS A PARAMETER

We have written the functions; now we must write the main program. The main program has to establish the prototypes, call the functions, and print out the results.

To send an array as a parameter to a function, we include its name in the parameter list of the function call, just as we would any other variable name. Here are the two function calls:

```
n = readdata(mark);
avgmark = avgarray(mark,n);
```

Here is the complete main program, including the calls:

```
/*
 * Program prog7d.c:
 * finds the average of the grades for the class using
 * functions readdata, sumarray, and avgarray
 */
#include <stdio.h>
#define SIZE 50
int readdata(int []);
int sumarray(int [], int);
double avgarray(int [], int);
main()
{
    int     n;
    int     mark[SIZE];
    double  avgmark;
```

(continued)

(continued)

```
        /* call functions to read and process the marks */
        n = readdata(mark);
        avgmark = avgarray(mark,n);
        printf("The average is %6.2f\n",avgmark);
    }
```

FOURTH VERSION OF PROGRAM 7

Now we are ready to combine the functions with the (revised) main program.

PROGRAM LISTING

```
/*
 * Program prog7d.c:
 */
#include <stdio.h>
#define SIZE 50
int readdata(int []);
int sumarray(int [], int);
double avgarray(int [], int);

main()
{
    int    n;
    int    mark[SIZE];
    double avgmark;

    /* call functions to read and process the marks */
    n = readdata(mark);
    avgmark = avgarray(mark,n);
    printf("The average is %6.2f\n",avgmark);
}

/* ... */
int readdata(int num[])
{
    int count,n;

    printf("Enter the number of marks> ");
    scanf("%d",&n);
    if (n > 0 && n <= SIZE)
        printf("There are %d marks\n",n);
    else {
        printf("Invalid number of marks\n");
        exit(1);
    }
    for (count = 0; count < n; count++) {
        printf("Enter a mark> ");
```

```
            scanf("%d",&num[count];
            printf("%d",num[count]);
        }
        return n;
}

/* ... */
int sumarray(int num[], int n)
{
        int sum,count;

        sum = 0;
        for (count = 0; count < n; count++)
            sum += num[count];
        return sum;
}

/* ... */
double avgarray(int num[], int n)
{
        return (double) sumarray(num,n) / n;
}
```

SELF-CHECK 7-7

1. a. Why is it necessary for **avgarray** to have a return value of type **double**?
   b. Why doesn't the main program have to call **sumarray**?
2. How is a parameter identified as an array in the prototype?
3. What is the reason for omitting the size of an array in the prototype and function header?
4. Upon its return from **readdata**, the **mark** array has values in it. How?

SECTION 6 **THE REST OF PROGRAM 7**

This section gives an algorithm for finding the maximum of a list of numbers, which we incorporate into Program 7. We write a function for Program 7 to find the number of marks less than, greater than, and equal to the average. Then we complete Program 7.

FINDING THE MAXIMUM

We have two more sections of Program 7 to write. First, the professor wants to know the highest grade in the class. We already have the grades stored in an array where we can look at each one. To find which grade is the highest, we could say, "Look through the grades for a 100—if it is there, it must be the highest; if not, look for a 99, and so on." However, this method is incredibly inefficient, especially if the highest grade is something like 73 or, even worse, 54. We need to devise an algorithm for finding the largest number.

AN ALGORITHM FOR FINDING THE LARGEST ELEMENT IN AN ARRAY

Let's take a look at a possible algorithm for finding the largest element in an array.

Algorithm for Finding the Largest Element in an Array

◆ *Initially, pick the first number in the array to be the largest so far.*

◆ *Compare this number to the next one in the array. If the next is larger, then it is the largest so far; otherwise do nothing.*

◆ *Repeat this process until every number in the array has been compared to the largest so far.*

◆ *Whichever number is the larger after the last comparison (the largest so far at the end) is the largest in the entire array.*

Before we refine this, let's make sure that the algorithm is correct. It's impossible that an earlier losing number can be larger than the value of the largest so far at the end; therefore, this algorithm works. Now we can use it to find the largest value in an array.

Here is a pseudocode version of this algorithm, applied to the first n elements of the *num* array:

> *largest so far = first number in the* num *array*
> *for each of the remaining* n-1 *numbers in the array*
>   *compare largest so far with this number*
>   *if this number > largest so far*
>   *largest so far = this number*

This is easy to translate into C. Let's use *largestsofar* for the variable that holds the largest number seen so far in the array. We can initialize *largestsofar* to an actual candidate for the largest number, *num[0]*:

```
largestsofar = num[0];
for (count = 1; count < n; count++)
    if (largestsofar < num[count])
        largestsofar = num[count];
```

PROGRAM TRACE Let's trace this code before writing the function, using the set of data shown earlier (grades 91, 94, 65 in the *num* array, and *n* equal to 3).

◆ We initialize *largestsofar* to the value of *num[0]*, which is 91.

◆ Then we enter the loop, where we compare *largestsofar* with *num[1]*, which is 94.

◆ Since *largestsofar* is smaller, we assign the new value of 94 to *largestsofar*.

◆ The second time through the loop, we compare *largestsofar* with *num[2]*, which is 65. Since *largestsofar* is larger, we do nothing.

◆ When we fall out of the loop, *largestsofar* has the value of the highest grade in the array, which is 94.

CAUTION Some programmers initialize *largestsofar* to a small number like 0, rather than the first element in the array; however, there are a few cases where this does not work. For example, suppose that all the elements in the array are negative. Then no element will be greater than *largestsofar*, and the program will not find the largest value in the array.

THE FUNCTION *findmax*

Now we modify the C code to fit our particular situation. Let's call our function *findmax*. It has to return one value, the highest grade. The parameters this function needs are the array and the number of array elements that have to be searched for the highest grade. Here is the prototype:

```
int findmax(int [], int);
```

In the main program, the parameters are called *mark* and *n*; in the function, they are called *num* and *n*. Here is the call from the main program:

```
higrade = findmax(mark,n);
```

The array *mark* is matched with *num* in *findmax*, and *n* is matched with *n*. The body of *findmax* is what we just traced. Here is the entire function:

```
/*
 * Function findmax:
 * Input:
 *   num: an array of integers
 *   n: the number of elements in the array
 * Process:
 *   finds the highest value in the first
 *   n elements of the num array
 * Output:
 *   returns the maximum of the elements
 */
int findmax(int num[], int n)
{
    int largestsofar,count;

    largestsofar = num[0];
    for (count = 1; count < n; count++)
        if (largestsofar < num[count])
            largestsofar = num[count];
    return largestsofar;
}
```

STYLE WORKSHOP It is not necessary to use an array to find the largest of a list of numbers. The same algorithm can be applied to numbers as they are being read in and processed. Similarly, in Section 2 of this chapter, we found the average without using an array by processing numbers as they were read in. To find the largest without using an array, set *largestsofar* to the first number read in and, as each subsequent number is read in, compare it with *largestsofar*. We have used an array because this way we can perform this task as an independent module through a function.

FINDING THE NUMBER OF MARKS ABOVE, BELOW, AND EQUAL TO THE AVERAGE

Now let's turn to the last task of Program 7: finding and printing the number of grades above, below, and equal to the average. This the only part which really requires an array because the comparison with *avgmark* cannot be performed until *avgmark* has been computed. Without an array, the individual marks won't be available once *avgmark* has been computed.

PSEUDOCODE

As usual, we start by writing pseudocode. This is at heart a comparison and counting problem. We must compare each mark with the average; if the mark is less, we increment one counter; if it is greater, we increment a different counter; if it is equal, we increment a third counter. Here is the pseudocode (assuming that *avgnum* holds the average):

> *for each mark*
> > *compare it with* avgnum
> > *if the mark is less than* avgnum, *increment* numless
> > *if the mark is greater than* avgnum, *increment* numgreater
> > *if the mark is equal to* avgnum, *increment* numequal
> *print* numless, numgreater, *and* numequal

THE FUNCTION *countmarks*

The function—we'll call it *countmarks*—is simple to write from the pseudocode. We send the function three parameters: the array of marks; *n*, the number of elements in the array; and *avgnum*, the average of the marks in the array. Since there are three values computed in *countmarks*, but a function can return only a single value, *countmarks* is a void function which prints its results. Here is the prototype:

```
void countmarks(int [], int, double);
```

Here is the complete function *countmarks*:

```
/*
 * Function countmarks:
 * Input:
 *    num: an array of integers
 *    n: the number of elements in the array
 *    avgnum: the average of the elements in the array
 * Process:
 *    find how many grades in the array num are greater than avgnum
```

```
 *     find how many grades in the array num are less than avgnum
 *     find how many grades in the array num are equal to avgnum
 * Output:
 *    print numless, numgreater, and numequal
 */
void countmarks(int num[], int n, double avgnum)
{
    int count,numless=0,numgreater=0,numequal=0;

    for (count = 0; count < n; count++)
        if (num[count] < avgnum)
            numless++;
        else if (num[count] > avgnum)
            numgreater++;
        else
            numequal++;
    printf("the number of marks less than the average is %d\n",numless);
    printf("the number of marks greater than the average is %d\n",numgreater);
    printf("the number of marks equal to the average is %d\n",numequal);
    return;
}
```

That's all there is to this function; we can put it into the final version of Program 7. The only remaining question is when the main program calls *countmarks*. It must call *countmarks* sometime after it calls *avgarray*.

FIFTH VERSION OF PROGRAM 7: MAIN PROGRAM, *findmax*, AND *countmarks*

Here is the the main program for the complete version of Program 7, including the functions for finding the maximum mark and the number of marks above, below, and equal to the average, with simplified comments:

🖥 PROGRAM LISTING

```
/*
 *   Program prog7e.c
 */
#include <stdio.h>
#define SIZE 50
int readdata(int []);
int sumarray(int [], int);
double avgarray(int [], int);
int findmax(int [], int);
void countmarks(int [], int, double);

main()
{
    int    n;
    int    mark[SIZE];
```

(continued)

(continued)

```
        double avgmark;
        int    higrade;

        /* call functions to read and process the marks */
        n = readdata(mark);
        avgmark = avgarray(mark,n);
        printf("The average is %6.2f\n",avgmark);
        higrade = findmax(mark,n);
        printf("The highest mark is %d\n",higrade);
        countmarks(mark,n,avgmark);
}

/* other functions go here */

/* ... */
int findmax(int num[], int n)
{
    int largestsofar,count;

    largestsofar = num[0];
    for (count = 1; count < n; count++)
        if (largestsofar < num[count])
            largestsofar = num[count];
    return largestsofar;
}

/* ... */
void countmarks(int num[], int n, double avgnum)
{
    int count,numless=0,numgreater=0,numequal=0;

    for (count = 0; count < n; count++)
        if (num[count] < avgnum)
            numless++;
        else if (num[count] > avgnum)
            numgreater++;
        else
            numequal++;
    printf("the number of marks less than the average is %d\n",numless);
    printf("the number of marks greater than the average is %d\n",numgreater);
    printf("the number of marks equal to the average is %d\n",numequal);
    return;
}
```

In this version, the main program calls **readdata** to read in and print the data. The function **readdata** gets the value for **n**, fills the array with values, and returns **n** and the filled array to the main program. Then the main program calls **avgarray** to compute the average for the class. The function **avgarray** calls the function **sumarray** to find the sum of the marks in the class and return the sum to ***avgarray***. Then ***avgarray*** divides the sum by the number of students to get the average, which it returns to the main program. Next, the main program calls ***findmax*** to find the highest grade in the class. Finally, the main program calls ***countmarks***, which finds and prints the number of marks above, below, and equal to the average.

STYLE WORKSHOP In writing Program 7, we have made extensive use of stepwise refinement. We started with a simple version of the program and gradually refined it to handle more and more details of the task. This is an important skill to master.

SELF-CHECK 7-8

1. What is the difference between the way a person finds the maximum of a list of numbers and the way a computer does it?

2. What happens if we pick −1 as ***largestsofar*** and the elements in the array are −100, −34, −76, −92, and −3?

3. What is an algorithm for finding the smallest element in a list of numbers? The second largest? What if there are ties?

SECTION 7   ENRICHMENT: ANALYSIS OF PROGRAM 7: TESTING AND MODULARITY

This section discusses testing and error checking in Program 7. In addition, it analyzes the contribution of arrays to programming modularity.

TESTING PROGRAM 7

Now that we have written the entire program, we must test it. Of course, we could have tested each function as we incorporated it into the program. For example, we could have tested ***sumarray*** before writing ***avgarray***. In this particular case, we can trust ***sumarray*** because it basically repeats a module which we know works from a previous program.

You may think that we don't need to test ***readdata*** since it prints the data that it reads in; you are wrong. For the first time, we have written a function which changes one of its parameters. You must make sure that it does what it should. The simplest way to test ***readdata*** is to print out the ***mark*** array after returning to the main program. Since ***readdata*** already prints, you will have two lists of values to compare. If there is any discrepancy, something is wrong. To test the error checking, try entering different parameter values, including a positive number, a negative number, and 0.

To test ***avgarray*** and ***sumarray***, we can send as parameters arrays containing varying numbers of elements; within each array, the elements should have simple values whose average we can easily compute by hand. Within ***sumarray***, we can print the sum of the array and ***n***. Upon our return to ***avgarray***, we can again print the sum and ***n***, as well as the computed average. Finally, upon our return to the main program, we can print the returned average as a comparison. If any computed values do not match, or if the results do not jibe with computations done by hand, we have an error.

For *findmax* and *countmarks*, we can send in a few arrays, one at a time. For *findmax*, if we already know the largest value in each array, we can compare our hand-computed results with the value returned. For *countmarks*, if we already know the average of the array, we can count by hand the number of values greater than, less than, and equal to the average and compare the results with those printed.

SELECTING TEST DATA

In testing *findmax*, we should be careful to use all possible sets of values. We should test a case where the highest grade is in the first position of the array, one where it is in the middle, and one where it is last. In addition, we should add a set of test data where the highest grade occurs twice or three times, or all the grades are the same. Frequently, a program is written so that it works for the expected set of data but not for unexpected combinations; often, first and last elements in an array or list are treated differently, and a good set of test data uncovers any errors in processing these anomalous cases.

In our test data for the calls to *readdata* and *avgarray*, we should also use a range of possible cases; in particular, we should include a set of data where *n* is 0, one where *n* is negative, and one where *n* does not actually match the number of grades. If we include test data of this sort, we have a better chance of discovering flaws in our program.

Program 7 should work for all sets of data. (See Section 9 for further discussion of error checking and Exercise 13 for one remaining problem.) Actually, thinking through the possible values that may occur in a set of data is a good way to discover errors like dividing by 0 if there are no students in the class.

ADVANTAGES AND DISADVANTAGES OF ARRAYS

This is a good point to evaluate the use of an array in solving Problem 7. The first version of the program could average a set of marks of any size, but the array versions must have some prior knowledge of the amount of data. In that sense, the first version is superior; there are problems which are solvable only without an array. (For example, suppose you are asked to average a list of numbers, but you do not know how many numbers are in the list; no matter how many numbers there are, the problem can be solved without an array. However, an array solution needs an upper bound.)

On the other hand, there are some clear advantages to the array versions. An important one has already been mentioned. After computing the average, every piece of data is still available for further processing. For example, we were able to find the average and the maximum, and also the number of elements above, below, and equal to the average. We could also have found the grade closest to the average. In order to find the average and maximum grades, we need to go through the array entries only once; however, if we want to find the grade closest to the average, we must go through the values more than once. This can be done only if we have saved all the array entries. Later programs exploit the flexibility of being able to use the same data for different calculations.

MODULAR VERSION OF PROGRAM 7

There is another important advantage to the array method. In the first version of the program, we read in a **mark** value, printed it and added it to **sum**, then read in another **mark**, and so on. In other words, we processed each **mark** value completely before going on to the next. With arrays, we were able to use a more modular method in the third version of the program: First, read in all the data; then print all the data (we decided to combine the reading and printing); finally, add all the data together. This method of solving the problem is possible only with arrays because all the values of **mark** must be saved.

A diagram illustrating this idea is shown in Figure 7-6. Such a diagram is called a **functional flowchart** since it illustrates the functions or jobs to be performed and the flow of control through them.

In a further step toward modularity, arrays allow us to write Program 7 using functions. We can write a function to add up the marks for each class because we do not have to know in advance how many marks there are. Without arrays, we would need a function with

FIGURE 7-6 Functional flowchart for Problem 7

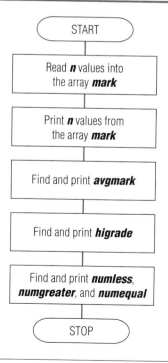

three parameters for this class, perhaps another one with eight parameters for a different class, and maybe another one with four parameters for a third class (and each class would have to be exactly this size). However, we can write one function that accepts an array (of any size) as its principal parameter. This array can contain a variable number of marks, thus increasing the flexibility of the function.

Using an array is helpful for the following reasons:

HIGHLIGHTS

◆ It gives us the ability to store and retrieve large amounts of data without declaring many separate variable names.

◆ It allows us to break a program down into modules or functions which can then be programmed one at a time in a straightforward way.

Modules provide reusable code to perform tasks that we do frequently. They can be used as building blocks in later, more complex programs.

SELF-CHECK 7-9

1. What happens in Program 7 if the parameter value *n* is given the value 0?

2. Why is it important to select test data carefully?

3. What are some advantages of modular programming?

SECTION 8 ENRICHMENT: TWO-DIMENSIONAL ARRAYS

This section introduces two-dimensional arrays. We also briefly mention arrays with more than two dimensions.

STORING FOUR GRADES FOR EACH STUDENT IN A CLASS

Let's imagine a slight modification of Problem 7. Assume that each student in the class has four grades, rather than one, representing marks on four exams. The instructor still wants to do things like find the average mark or the highest or lowest mark in the entire class. In addition, the instructor wants to be able to find each student's average and the class average on each of the four exams.

This is a large amount of information. There are potentially 50 students in the class, and each student has four marks. It is necessary to deal with each mark several times—for example, we need to use the same mark to find a student's average and the class average on a particular exam. Therefore, after we process a mark once, we still need to have it available.

The need to keep many values available suggests an array. However, some major questions have to be resolved about how to organize the data.

How can we store the grades using arrays? Each student has four grades, and there are up to 50 students. One possibility is to have a separate array for each student, with four entries. If this is our choice, finding a particular student's average is easy: just add up the elements of that student's array and divide by 4. But the class average on the first exam is much harder to compute. We have to jump from array to array, adding all the first elements. Also each of these 50 arrays has to be given a distinct name and declared.

This method obviously has problems so let's try to think of another way to store the data. Another possibility is to set up one array for each exam. In this case, we have to declare each of the four arrays. To find the class average on an exam, we can sum the appropriate array and divide by the number of students. But using this method to find individual student averages is more complicated. Overall, this method is much better than the first but still not very good.

TWO-DIMENSIONAL ARRAYS

A better way to store the data is to use a new data structure called a **two-dimensional array**. (We can call the arrays so far one-dimensional.) A two-dimensional array is useful when we need to keep track of two coordinates of data—for example, a company may have sales data for three stores for the 12 months of the year. A scientist may have data from ten experiments performed on five subjects. A two-dimensional array can be visualized as a rectangle, as shown in Figure 7-7.

To locate a particular point in the array, we must specify two positions or subscripts: one to describe how far down the point is, one to say how far across. The subscript governing how far down we go is called the **row subscript**; the one determining how far across is the **column subscript**. To describe any entry in the array accurately, we need the row and column subscripts.

EXAMPLE 7-14

In Figure 7-7, the rows are numbered from 0 to 2; the columns are numbered from 0 to 5. The number 10 is in the first row, third column. The number 98 is in the third row, fifth column.

In our program, we want a two-dimensional array with 50 rows, one for each student, and 4 columns, one for each exam. To locate a particular mark, we specify which student got it (the row) and on which exam (the column). Figure 7-8 provides an illustration of such an array with some entries filled in.

FIGURE 7-7   A two-dimensional array with 3 rows and 6 columns

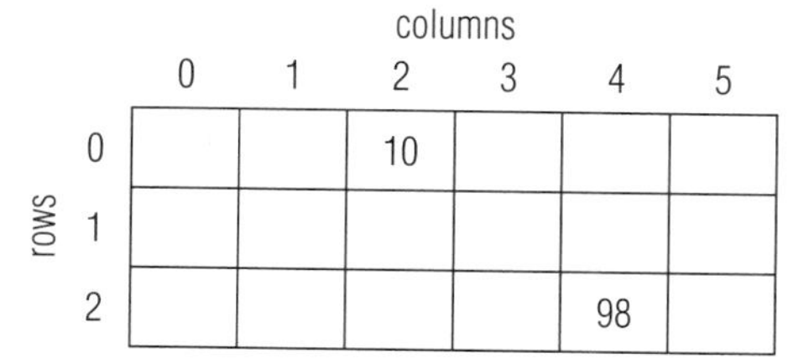

FIGURE 7-8 A two-dimensional array with 50 rows and 4 columns

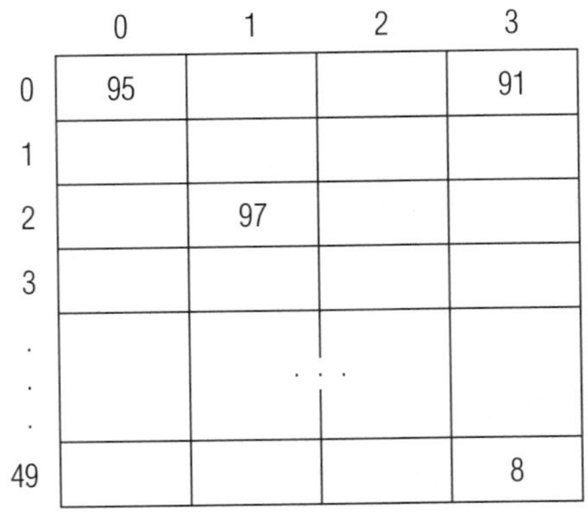

We can call this array **grade**. Each element in **grade** is selected by specifying first a row and then a column.

EXAMPLE 7-15 In Figure 7-8, **grade[0][0]** holds 95. The 91 is in **grade[0][3]**, the first row and the fourth column; **grade[49][3]** is 8; 97 is in **grade[2][1]**. In all, the **grade** array has room for $50 \times 4 = 200$ marks.

ANALYSIS OF THE DATA STRUCTURE

Let's see how a two-dimensional array helps solve this problem. To find a student's average, we average a row of the two-dimensional array; for example, we use row 2 for the third student's average. To find the class average on an exam, we average a column of the two-dimensional array; for example, we use column 0 for the class average on the first exam. The other parts of the problem are also easy because of the way we have decided to store the marks.

STYLE WORKSHOP Note that we decided which major data structure to use even before we started to talk about writing the program in C. A programmer must often think as much about how to store data as process it. A clever choice of how to organize data—a useful data structure—makes the rest of the program much easier, while a poor choice leads to all sorts of programming problems.

DECLARING A TWO-DIMENSIONAL ARRAY

Of course, we must declare the two-dimensional array **grade** before we can use it in the program. The declaration is similar to the one for a one-dimensional array; we must provide the number of rows, followed by the number of columns. Here is a possible declaration:

```
int grade[50][4];
```

This says that **grade** has 50 rows, numbered from 0 to 49; each row has 4 column entries, numbered 0 to 3.

Assuming that we have defined the constant **MAXSIZE**, we can use the following declaration for the array:

```
#define MAXSIZE 50

int grade[MAXSIZE][4];
```

Similarly, we can use a constant to define the number of columns. For clarity in the first part of this section, however, we will use a constant for the number of rows but 4 for the number of columns.

SELF-CHECK 7-10

1. In the declaration for this array, how many rows are there? How many columns?

    ```
    int grade[25][5];
    ```

2. Give the declaration for a two-dimensional array **labdata** which can hold data collected from ten experiments performed on five subjects. Assume that each piece of lab data is a value of type **double**.

3. Show how to locate the items in the **labdata** array from question 2 which represent the data collected from the first experiment on the second subject and the fourth experiment on the third subject.

PROCESSING A TWO-DIMENSIONAL ARRAY IN A MAIN PROGRAM

Let's see how to use a two-dimensional array to extend Program 7. We can process a two-dimensional array directly in a main program or pass it as a parameter to a function. To illustrate both methods, we read values into the array in a main program, then show how to find each student's average in a function.

Assume that the variable *class_size* holds the number of students in the class. The maximum value for *class_size* is 50, but it may very well be less. A moment's thought suggests that we employ a *for* loop to read in the grades. We will call the control variable for this *for* loop *stnum* (short for student number) since it runs through all the students. Here is a main program that reads in a value for *class_size*, then uses that value to control a loop which reads in four grades for each student:

```
/*
 * program to read data into
 * a two-dimensional array
 */
#include <stdio.h>
#define MAXSIZE 50
main()
{
    int grade[MAXSIZE][4];
    int class_size;
    int stnum;
```

(continued)

(*continued*)

```
        printf("how many students in the class?> ");
        scanf("%d",&class_size);
        for (stnum = 0; stnum < class_size; stnum++)  {
            printf("type in four grades for the next student> ");
            scanf("%d",&grade[stnum][0]);
            scanf("%d",&grade[stnum][1]);
            scanf("%d",&grade[stnum][2]);
            scanf("%d",&grade[stnum][3]);
            printf("the grades were: %d %d %d %d\n",grade[stnum][0],
                    grade[stnum][1],grade[stnum][2],grade[stnum][3]);
        }
    }
```

PROGRAM TRACE Let's see how this works on a simple set of data.

◆ The program starts by asking how many students are in the class. If the user types in 3, the *stnum* loop will run from 0 to 2.

◆ In the body of the loop, the user is asked to type in four values. The first time through the loop, these four values are read into columns 0 to 3 in the first row of *grade*. For example, the user could type 5, 6, 7, and 98. Then 5 goes into *grade[0][0]*, 6 into *grade[0][1]*, 7 into *grade[0][2]*, and 98 into *grade[0][3]*.

◆ Then the user types four more grades into the second row of *grade*, and so on for the third row.

Figure 7-9 shows the *grade* array after reading in values for three students.

PASSING A TWO-DIMENSIONAL ARRAY AS A PARAMETER TO A FUNCTION

To illustrate how to pass a two-dimensional array as a parameter, we can write a function, *findstudentavg*, to find and print the average for each student in the class. Let's begin by writing the prototype. Since the function prints every student's average without returning

FIGURE 7-9 *grade* array after reading in the data for three students

	0	1	2	3
0	5	6	7	98
1	93	71	53	38
2	95	97	93	96
3				
.			. . .	
.				
.				
49				

any value to the main program, it is a void function. The array **grade** must be a parameter to the function and looks like this in the prototype:

```
void findstudentavg(int grade[][4], ...
```

The parameter includes the data type for the elements of the array (optionally followed by the name of the array), followed by two sets of brackets, one for each subscript. The second set of brackets must contain the number of columns (in this case, four). The set of brackets for the rows can be empty (any value placed here is ignored). This allows the function to receive as a parameter an array with any number of rows but four entries in each row.

Now suppose we define a constant for the number of exams:

```
#define MAXSIZE 50
#define NUMEXAMS 4
    ...
int grade[MAXSIZE][NUMEXAMS];
```

In that case, the constant **NUMEXAMS** should be used to specify the parameter:

```
void findstudentavg(int grade[][NUMEXAMS], ...
```

Since the function needs to know the number of students in the class, **class_size** is also a parameter to the function. Here are three equivalent function prototypes:

```
void findstudentavg(int grade[][NUMEXAMS], int);

void findstudentavg(int grade[MAXSIZE][NUMEXAMS], int); /* MAXSIZE is ignored */

void findstudentavg(int [][NUMEXAMS], int);              /* omits the array name */
```

The main program reads in the data, then calls the function. Here is the call to the function:

```
findstudentavg(grade,class_size);
```

THE FUNCTION *findstudentavg*

Finally, we can write the function. Let's use the same names, **grade** and **class_size**, for the formal parameters in the function. Here are the comment and function header:

```
/*
 * Function findstudentavg:
 * Input:
 *    two-dimensional array grade holds
 *    NUMEXAMS grades for each of class_size students
 * Process:
 *    finds each student's average
 * Output:
 *    prints each student's average
 */
void findstudentavg(int grade[][NUMEXAMS], int class_size)
```

Note once again that, in the function header, we must specify the number of columns (*[NUMEXAMS]*), but the number of rows is indicated by an empty set of brackets (*[]*). A two-dimensional array is stored as a collection of rows; the number of columns tells how many elements are in each row. The function is sent the name of the array (*grade*) plus the number of columns (*NUMEXAMS*). In this way, the function knows when one row ends and the next one begins.

Inside the function, we must find each student's average. Here is a pseudocode version of the body of the function:

```
for (stnum = 0; stnum < class_size; stnum++)  {
      find the average for student number stnum
      print the average
}
```

To find the average for each student, average that student's row. Finding the average for student number *stnum* is similar to what we did in Program 7. First, initialize *sum* to 0; then add to *sum* each grade in the row for student number *stnum*; at the end, divide by *NUMEXAMS*. To add the grades, we need not mention each column explicitly since the number of exams is now defined as a constant.

Instead, there is a better method to add up the marks in row number *stnum*. We can use a second *for* loop; the first loop is for the rows, and the second for the columns. We put one *for* loop inside another, forming a nested *for* loop (see Chapter 4, Section 4). Here is the code for the function (including the declaration of local variables):

```
/* ... */
void findstudentavg(int grade[][NUMEXAMS], int class_size)
{
      int     stnum,exam,sum;
      double avg;

      for (stnum = 0; stnum < class_size; stnum++)  {
          sum = 0;
          for (exam = 0; exam < NUMEXAMS; exam++)
              sum += grade[stnum][exam];
          avg = (double) sum / NUMEXAMS;
          printf("student number %d had an average of %6.2f\n",stnum,avg);
      }
}
```

We have used *stnum* as the control variable for the rows and *exam* as the control variable for the columns, running from 0 to *NUMEXAMS – 1*, or 3. Inside both *for* loops, *grade[stnum][exam]* refers to the particular mark we are interested in.

PROGRAM TRACE We trace this function on the data shown in Figure 7-9. Assume that we are working with a class of three students.

◆   The outer *for* loop processes each of the students; the inner loop processes each grade of each student.

◆ The outer loop starts with **stnum** equal to 0. In the inner loop, row 0 of **grade**, from **grade[0][0]** to **grade[0][3]**, is summed to obtain 116. After the inner loop ends, the average is computed to be 29.00, and this is printed as the average of student number 0.

◆ Then **stnum** is incremented to 1, and **sum** is reset to 0 for the second student (otherwise **sum** for this student would start with 116). Row 1 of **grade**, from **grade[1][0]** to **grade[1][3]**, is summed to obtain 255, so the average is 255/4, which is 63.75. This is printed as the average of the second student.

◆ Then **stnum** is increased again to 2, and we set **sum** back to 0 and sum the third row, which totals 381; the average here is 381/4 = 95.25, and this is printed.

Finally, we exit from the outer loop. The entire output from this function looks like this:

```
student number 0 had an average of  29.00
student number 1 had an average of  63.75
student number 2 had an average of  95.25
```

PROCESSING DOWN A COLUMN OF A TWO-DIMENSIONAL ARRAY

Once the data values have been stored, we can use a nested loop to process a two-dimensional array in other ways. In general, one *for* loop controls the row subscript, and the other controls the column subscript. For example, by interchanging the row and column loops, we can process down a column.

EXAMPLE 7-16   We can write a function *findexamavg* to find the class's average on each exam. The function has to find the average value in each column:

```
/* ... */
void findexamavg(int grade[][NUMEXAMS], int class_size)
{
    int    stnum,exam,sum;
    double avg;

    for (exam = 0; exam < NUMEXAMS; exam++)  {
        sum = 0;
        for (stnum = 0; stnum < class_size; stnum++)
            sum += grade[stnum][exam];
        avg = (double) sum / class_size;
        printf("exam number %d had an average of %6.2f\n",exam,avg);
    }
}
```

Here are the function prototype and the call to the function:

```
void findexamavg(int grade[][NUMEXAMS], int);

findexamavg(grade,class_size);
```

We leave it to the reader to trace this function for the grades shown earlier.

Finally, a single row of a two-dimensional array can be sent as a parameter to a function. In this case, we specify only the row subscript. For example, we can use the function *sumarray* from Section 5 to sum the elements in row 1 of the two-dimensional array. Here is the call to *sumarray*:

```
sum = sumarray(grade[1],NUMEXAMS);
```

MULTIDIMENSIONAL ARRAYS

It is also possible to have an array with more than two dimensions. As an example, we might want to extend the two-dimensional array *grade* to include information about five classes. To do this, we could form a new array by adding a third dimension.

EXAMPLE 7-17   Consider a three-dimensional array called *marks*; three subscripts are required to locate a particular entry.

◆   the first subscript of *marks* selects one of five classes;

◆   the second subscript picks one of 50 students;

◆   the third subscript chooses one of four exams.

For example, the assignment statement *marks[3][1][2] = 5* means that in the fourth class, for the second student, the third mark is set to 5. Similarly, *marks[1][6][0]* is a reference to the second class, seventh student, first mark.

The declaration for *marks* must specify bounds for all three dimensions. We can use something like this:

```
int marks[5][50][4];
```

Actually, almost all C compilers allow more than three dimensions in an array. You can use four, five, six, or more subscripts. In general, any array with more than one dimension is called a **multidimensional array**. However, past the second or third dimension, it becomes harder and harder for most people to visualize a multidimensional array. The basic data structure in such a program is probably too complex and should be simplified. In addition, the amount of space occupied by, for example, a five-dimensional array can become astronomical. Let's assume that each of the five dimensions has bounds 0 to 9, which is not that large. Then the total number of storage locations is 10^5 or 100,000. Quite possibly, this number exceeds the space allocated to your program, causing an error. Therefore, except in rare circumstances, three-dimensional arrays are the largest used.

STYLE WORKSHOP   In most cases, a one-dimensional array is sufficient to represent the information in a program. In a few situations, a two-dimensional array is more useful. It is very rare that a program needs more than two dimensions.

SELF-CHECK 7-11

1.   When passing a two-dimensional array to a function, which dimension must be stated explicitly in the function header and prototype?

2. Give a declaration for a three-dimensional array *sales* which holds sales data for five stores, for 12 months, for three years.

SECTION 9   ENRICHMENT: DETECTING THE END OF A DATA SET: *EOF* METHOD; RETURN VALUE FROM *scanf*

This section discusses various ways of detecting the end of a set of data, in the process introducing the *EOF* method. It also shows how to test the return value from *scanf*.

THE *EOF* METHOD COMPARED TO OTHER METHODS OF DETECTING THE END OF A SET OF DATA

When reading in values, it is often necessary to determine when the set of data has ended, whether the set of data is entered interactively or from a file. (A **file** is a collection of data values on a disk—see appendices V and VI.) So far, we have discussed three methods, which we summarize below; then we introduce a fourth method, called the *EOF* method (*EOF* stands for end of file). Each method has advantages and disadvantages, and sometimes a program uses more than one (see Exercise 9).

The **trailer** or **sentinel method** requires that the program specify a single value as a signal that the set of data is complete. The last item should be this value. (We used this method in Program 3 with the phony value –1111.) Each data value that is read in is compared to the trailer value to determine if it is a real piece of data. There are two basic advantages to this method: It is not necessary to know in advance how many items are in a set of data (compare with the parameter or header method), and it is possible to have separate groups of data, each with its own trailer value (compare with the *EOF* method).

The **user-response method** asks the user to answer a question. Usually it is something like "Do you want to continue (y/n)?" This method works best with interactive programming. The user enters the character *y* to continue and *n* to stop. (We used this method in Program 6.) One disadvantage of this method is that it requires a response from the user each time, which is time consuming and can be annoying.

The **parameter** or **header method** uses a signal at the beginning of each group of data. The first item read in is a number indicating how many pieces of data follow. (We used this method in Program 7.) The major disadvantage of this method is the need to know this number in advance, since an incorrect value often leads to an execution error. The advantages of the parameter method are that it does not require the use of a phony value, and it allows more than one group of data, each with its own parameter value. It can be used with interactive data entry as well as data from a file. Almost all of our later programs use the parameter method to detect the end of a set of data, sometimes together with the *EOF* method.

There are problems with all these methods of indicating the end of a set of data. The trailer or sentinel method requires that you devise a phony value which cannot exist in the set of data, but sometimes it is impossible to find a phony value. The user-response method requires that the program be run interactively so that the user can answer (unless you put responses in the data file, which is a distortion); in addition, the user must be asked an additional question each time a data value is entered. The parameter method requires that you know in advance how many values are in the data set.

The fourth method, called the **EOF method**, is simpler. It has the computer test for the actual end of the set of data. One advantage of the **EOF** method is that the computer, rather than the programmer, handles the details of detecting the end of the set of data. No phony values are needed, and the person entering the data does not have to know how many values there are. The method can be used whether the program is run interactively or not. When the program tries to read past the last element in the file, the end-of-file condition is true. When using interactive data entry, the **EOF** method requires entering a special character, called the **end-of-file character**, to indicate the end of the set of data.

The end-of-file character is entered by pressing (CTRL)-(Z) in DOS or (CTRL)-(D) in Unix. If data values are coming from the keyboard, the user can enter the end-of-file character when the program requests a new value. When an input function like *scanf* reads this character, it stops looking for data values.

One disadvantage is that this method cannot be used in every situation. As an example, some programs read several sets of data in separate loops. If data values are entered interactively, each group can be terminated with the end-of-file character. However, if the data values come from a file on disk, **EOF** is returned only when the physical end of the file is reached. The idea of reading several sets of data into a program is explored further in Exercise 16.

THE CONSTANT *EOF*

C has a predeclared constant **EOF** which indicates that the end of a file has been reached. The definition of this constant is contained in the header file *stdio.h*; it usually has a negative value.

As we discussed in Chapter 5, Section 7, *scanf* returns an integer which normally represents the number of values it successfully reads in and converts. If no data value can be converted successfully, *scanf* returns 0. However, if there are no characters in the input stream, or if the user explicitly enters the end-of-file character, *scanf* returns **EOF**. Chapter 5, Section 7 contains examples illustrating this feature.

CHECKING THE RETURN VALUE FROM *scanf* IN PROGRAM 7

In *readdata*, the input function for Program 7, we checked the value of the header *n* to make sure it was positive and less than *SIZE*. However, we did not do all the checking we could have. By testing the return value of *scanf*, we can catch other errors, such as having a noninteger typed in as the value of *n*, or having no value read in at all. If we don't check, and the value read into *n* is invalid, the program behaves in an unexpected manner (it may loop forever or do nothing). Example 7-18 rewrites the function *readdata* from Program 7 to check each data value as it is entered.

EXAMPLE 7-18   If a piece of data is missing or if there is an error in reading the data, this program prints a message and terminates, using the *exit* function (see Chapter 6, Section 7). The program checks whether *scanf(...) != 1*; this is equivalent to *if (scanf(...) == EOF || scanf(...) == 0)*.

```
/*
 * Function readdata:
 */
int readdata(int num[])
{
    int count,n;

    printf("Enter the number of marks> ");
    if (scanf("%d",&n) != 1) {
        printf("Missing or bad header value\n");
        exit(1);
    }
    if (n > 0 && n <= SIZE)
        printf("There are %d marks\n",n);
    else {
        printf("Invalid number of marks\n");
        exit(1);
    }
    for (count = 0; count < n; count++) {
        printf("Enter a mark> ");
        if (scanf("%d",&num[count]) != 1) {
            printf("Missing or bad mark value\n");
            exit(1);
        }
        printf("%d\n",num[count]);
    }
    return n;
}
```

STYLE WORKSHOP It is good C style to make sure that each data value has been successfully read in. When data is entered interactively, it is unlikely that the user will skip entering a value; however, when data values are typed into a file for a program to read, some may be omitted. Bad data, on the other hand, is possible with any form of entry.

When C is used in a commercial environment, where it is crucial that data values have a particular format, it is common to test every call to *scanf* to make sure that successful conversions have taken place. In a student environment, it is not so critical to verify this fact. To keep our programs uncluttered, we have usually not tested the value returned by *scanf*; however, you can incorporate this feature into your own programs.

SELF-CHECK 7-12

1. What kind of value is returned by *scanf*?

2. How does an interactive user signal the end of the set of data using the *EOF* method?

3. What are four methods of testing for the end of a set of data?

SUMMARY

PARAMETER (OR HEADER) VALUES

1. A parameter or header value is a number entered prior to a set of data values which tells how many data values are in the set. Using a header value has several advantages, including the ability to read several different sets of data, one after another.

2. A program can read the parameter value *n*, then read *n* groups of values from the set of data. The value read for the parameter must be treated differently from the rest of the data.

COMPUTING THE AVERAGE OF A LIST OF NUMBERS

3. The average or mean of a list of numbers can be computed in the following way: Initialize a sum to 0. Each time through a loop, add another number to the sum. After adding the entire list, divide by the number of values to obtain the average.

CASTING

4. Casting converts the type of a variable or an expression where it is not automatically changed by C.

5. When dividing integer operands, casting is necessary to obtain a result of type *float* or *double*. To cast a variable as another type, place the desired type in parentheses in front of the variable:

```
double ans;
int    num,n;

ans = (double) num / n;
```

Without casting, the result of the division (*num / n*) is an integer, which is stored in a variable of type *double*.

ARRAYS

6. If a program reads a series of numbers into a variable called *x*, at the end of the process, only the last value of *x* is available for further use. All previous values stored in *x* are lost since a storage location can hold just one value at a time.

7. However, using an array for *x* solves this problem. The array provides a separate storage location for each value. Each location within the array is referenced by giving the name of the array and the subscript or position (*i*), where *i* may be a constant or a variable. The subscripted variable *x[i]* can be treated like any variable, appearing on either side of an assignment statement or in a call to *printf* or *scanf*, for example.

8. In addition to the usual data type such as *int* or *double*, the declaration must also specify the size of an array. For example, we can use this declaration:

```
int x[25];
```

This says that *x* is an array of integers which can hold 25 values; it has a lower bound of 0 and an upper bound of 24. All subscripts referring to elements of the array must be between 0 and 24.

9. A *for* loop is useful to access the elements of an array. In most common situations, the *for* loop index acts as the array subscript. As the index ranges from the lower to the upper bound, the array elements can be processed one by one.

10. One major advantage of an array is the ability to divide a large program into smaller, relatively self-contained units called modules. These modules

can transform a large, unwieldy program into a series of easy-to-follow functions.

11. One disadvantage of an array is the need to specify a size, which limits a program. This size can be adjusted by modifying the declaration for the array, although the adjustment requires the program to be recompiled. In most programs, the benefits of using arrays far outweigh the disadvantages.

ARRAY OF *char*

12. An array of *char* is in most ways like any other array. It has the special feature that it can be treated as a unit. When the null character, '\0', is placed in one of the array positions, all characters prior to it can be printed together, as in the following example:

```
char list[5] = {'w','a','i','t','\0'};

printf("%s",list);
```
This prints the word "wait".

ARRAYS AS PARAMETERS

13. To send an array as a parameter to a function, the formal parameter in the prototype and the function header must be declared as an array.

14. To send array *x* from paragraph 8 to function *func*, we can use the following prototype:

```
int func(int []);
```
or
```
int func(int array[]);
```
In the second prototype, *array* is a dummy name, used so the brackets aren't standing alone.

15. To send array *x* to function *func*, we can use the following function header:

```
int func(int x[])
```

16. The declaration in a function prototype or header omits the size of the array. This allows the function to receive an array of any size. Of course, the data type of each array sent as an actual parameter must match that of the formal parameter.

17. An array cannot be the return value of a function. It also cannot be treated as a single unit, so it is not possible to read an entire array at once, print it, or copy it to another array in a single assignment statement.

FINDING THE LARGEST NUMBER IN A LIST

18. Here is an algorithm for finding the largest in a list of numbers: Pick the first number as the largest seen so far. Compare this to each number in turn. If the new number is larger, make it the largest value seen so far. At the end of the process, the largest value seen so far is the largest in the entire group.

TWO-DIMENSIONAL ARRAYS

19. A data structure is a framework for organizing and storing information. A one-dimensional array is a simple data structure. A two-dimensional array is a generalization of a one-dimensional array.

20. Every element or storage location in a two-dimensional array is specified by two subscripts. If you picture the array as a grid, the row subscript indicates how far down the element is, and the column

subscript indicates how far across. Each element is uniquely determined by the combination of row and column. The declaration for the two-dimensional array gives the number of rows, followed by the number of columns. For example, the following declaration specifies that *sales* is a two-dimensional array of real numbers, with rows numbered from 0 to 5, and columns from 0 to 9.

```
double sales[6][10];
```

21. A *for* loop can appear within the body of another *for* loop, producing a nested *for* loop construction which is extremely useful with a two-dimensional array. Typically, one *for* loop controls the row subscript, and the other controls the column subscript. By changing the relative positions of the row and column loops and/or using a specific value for one subscript, a programmer can process the entire two-dimensional array, process across a row, or process down a column.

22. Here is a *for* loop that processes across the rows of a two-dimensional array. It prints the entire two-dimensional array, with the entries for each row on a new line (the format specification *%6d* aligns the values in a given column):

```
int num[10][5];
int i,j;
...
for (i = 0; i < 10; i++)  {
    for (j = 0; j < 5; j++)
        printf("%6d",num[i][j]);
    printf("\n");
}
```

23. Here is a *for* loop that processes down the columns of the two-dimensional array declared in paragraph 22. It finds the sum of the entries in each column.

```
for (j = 0; j < 5; j++)  {
    sum = 0;
    for (i = 0; i < 10; i++)
        sum += num[i][j];
    printf("%d is the sum",sum);
    printf("for column %d\n",j);
}
```

24. Here is a loop that prints every element in a particular row (in this case, the third row) of the same two-dimensional array:

```
for (j = 0; j < 5; j++)
    printf("%6d",num[2][j]);
printf("\n");
```

25. Arrays can be generalized to three or even more dimensions. For example, in a three-dimensional array, three subscripts are necessary to reference a particular location. However, very few problems require the use of an array with more than two or at most three dimensions. In fact, one-dimensional arrays are by far the most common.

THE *EOF* METHOD AND *scanf*

26. The constant *EOF*, defined in *stdio.h*, indicates the end of a set of data.

27. A call to the function *scanf* returns *EOF* if there are no more characters in the input stream. This is used by the *EOF* method of detecting the end of a set of data. The following loop reads in and prints a series of numbers, terminating when there are no more values.

```
int num;

while (scanf("%d",&num) != EOF)
    printf("%d\n",num);
```

28. A user can signal the end of a set of data by pressing CTRL-Z in DOS or CTRL-D in Unix.

29. When reading values, it is useful to check for bad data as well as *EOF*. The following loop stops if there are no more data values or if an error occurs entering a data value:

```
int num;

while (scanf("%d",&num) == 1)
    printf("%d\n",num);
```

EXERCISES

TRACING EXERCISES

1. For each part of this exercise, assume that the array **a** starts with the values in Figure 7-10. For each of the program segments, show what values are stored in **a** after executing the segment. Use this declaration for each part:

```
int a[6];
int i,j,q;
```

a.
```
a[4] = a[2] + a[2 + 1];
a[0] = a[6 - 1] + a[6 - 2];
```

c.
```
i = 1;
j = i + 2;
a[i] = a[j] + a[j + 1];
```

b.
```
j = 4;
a[3] = a[j] + a[j - 1];
a[2] = a[j + 1];
```

d.
```
for (i = 0; i < 5; i++)
    a[i] = a[i + 1];
```

2. Show what values are stored in the **x** array after executing this program segment. Also show what is printed.

```
int x[5] = {2,2,1,3,1};
int y;

y = x[1] + 1;
printf("%d\n",y);
x[4] = 1;
printf("%d\n",x[x[4]]);    /* be careful of the subscript here */
y--;
printf("%d %d\n",y,x[y]);
```

FIGURE 7-10   Array **a** for Exercise 1

	a
0	7
1	−1
2	0
3	4
4	15
5	3

3.   Show what is stored in the *x* and *y* arrays after the following program segment is executed. Also show what is printed. Assume that the arrays have the initial values in Figure 7-11.

```
int  x[6],y[6];
int  i;
...
x[3] = x[3] + x[5];
y[1] = y[2] + y[3];
x[5] = x[0] + x[2];
x[1] = x[4] + x[x[1]];
for (i = 0; i <= 5; i++) {
    if (x[i] > 10)
        printf("%d\n",x[i]);
    if (x[i] < 50)
        printf("%d\n",y[i]);
}
```

4.   Show what is printed by each of these programs. If the program reads in data, the values are shown after it:

a.
```
#include <stdio.h>
main()
{
    int i,k,m;
    int a[9];

    for (i = 0; i <= 8; i++)
        a[i] = 0;
    m = 1;
    k = 5;
    for (i = -2; i <= 2; i++) {
        a[i + k] = 20 * i;
        m = -m;
        k += m;
        printf("k = %d   m = %d\n",k,m);
    }
}
```

FIGURE 7-11   Arrays *x* and *y* for Exercise 3

x		y	
0	−5	0	75
1	3	1	−1
2	40	2	−4
3	19	3	50
4	3	4	10
5	10	5	15

```
                    printf("i = %d   k = %d   m = %d\n",i,k,m);
                    for (i = 0; i <= 8; i++)
                        printf("%d        %d\n",i,a[i]);
             }
```

b.
```
     #include <stdio.h>
     main()
     {
         double a[20],b[20],large[20];
         int    num,i;

         scanf ("%d",&num);
         for (i = 0; i < num; i++)  {
             scanf ("%lf",&a[i]);
             scanf ("%lf",&b[i]);
             if (a[i] > b[i])
                 large[i] = a[i];
             else
                 large[i] = b[i];
         }
         for (i = 0; i < num; i++)
             printf("large[%d]= %f\n",i,large[i]);
     }
```

Here are the input data values:

6
−4.2 1.56   0 8   1.0 6.75   20.3 −1   −54.2 −33.7   −41.3 −41.3

c.
```
     #include <stdio.h>
     main()
     {
         int f[21], x

         for (x = 8; x <= 14; x++)
             f[x] = 3 * x - 5;
         printf("for the function f(x) = 3x - 5\n");
         for (x = 8; x <= 14; x++)
             printf("f(%d)= %d  \n",x,f[x]);
     }
```

d.
```
     #include <stdio.h>
     void calc_tax(double [], double []);
     main()
     {
         double sales[4], tax[4];
         int    season;

         for (season = 0; season < 4; season++)
             scanf("%lf",&sales[season]);
         calc_tax(sales,tax);

         printf("\tsales\ttax\n");
         for (season = 0; season < 4; season++)
             printf("%10.2f\t%10.2f\n",sales[season],tax[season]);
     }
```
(continued)

(continued)

```
void calc_tax(double sales[], double tax[])
{
    int season;

    for (season = 0; season < 4; season++)
        tax[season] = sales[season] * 0.20;
    return;
}
```

Here are the input data values:

12000   24000   21000   46000

5. a.   Draw a picture of the **a** and **b** arrays after executing this program segment. Assume that the set of data consists of 23 100 231 245 9.

```
#include <stdio.h>
main()
{
    int a[5],b[5];
    int i,j=0;

    for (i = 0; i <= 4; i++)  {
        scanf("%d",&a[i]);
        if (a[i] > 100)  {
            b[j] = a[i];
            j++;
        }
    }
}
```

   b.   Describe what happens if the initialization *j = 0* is removed from this program. Is there any set of data for which this does not lead to an error?

6.   In Exercise 5(a), assume that the following call to *printf* is added after the *for* loop:

```
printf("%d is the second value greater than 100\n",b[1]);
```

   a.   What does this new call to *printf* do? Will it work correctly on this set of data?
   b.   Is there any case where it will not work correctly? Explain.
   c.   Give a method that works in all cases. Your method should print the second value greater than 100, if there is such a value, and an appropriate message if there isn't.

7.   Assume that we want a set of data to contain a parameter value of 5 and then five numeric values. Which of the following show the correct form for the data? Which work but do not read in all the data shown? Which run out of data? Which return *EOF*?

   a.   6 12 3 4 5 19   d.   5 12 3 4 5 19 87
   b.   5 5 5 5 5   e.   5 3 5 4 3 t
   c.   5 12 3 4 5 19

8.   What is the result of each of the following, using the declarations shown after them?

```
int    first=26,second=4;
double ans,dval=4.52;
```

a.   `ans = first / second;`
b.   `ans = (double) (first / second);`
c.   `ans = (double) first / second;`
d.   `ans = first / (double) second;`

e.   `ans = first;`
f.   `first = dval;`
g.   `ans = dval / second;`
h.   `first = dval / second;`

ANALYSIS EXERCISES

9. This exercise compares the various methods for detecting the end of a set of data.

   a. You want to find the average of a series of real numbers (allowing all possible values, positive, negative, or 0). Can you use a trailer value? If you do not know in advance how many values there are, is it possible to use a parameter value? Explain. What method works best?

   b. You want to find the average of a series of numbers with this extra information: No two consecutive values can be the same. Describe a way to use the trailer method to detect the end of the set of data. What if two, but never three, consecutive values can be equal?

   c. You want to find the averages of two series of numbers from two different groups of data, one following the other. What method(s) can you use?

MODIFICATIONS OF PROGRAM 7

10. Program 7 finds *avgmark* by dividing *sum* by *n*. We use *n* as the divisor because it represents the number of marks entered.

    a. At this point in the program, does *count* also represent the number of marks entered?
    b. Can the code be changed to calculate *avgmark* by dividing *sum* by *count*?
    c. Can we say *avgmark* = *(double) sum / count* if we start *count* at 1? Why or why not? (*Hint*: This is a tricky problem when using a *for* loop and deserves careful consideration—try it on some sample data.)
    d. Can we say *avgmark* = *(double) sum / count* if we use a *while* loop with *count* < *n* as the condition? Does it depend on whether *count* starts at 0 or 1?
    e. Suppose an error occurs during data entry so that not all the values are entered. Does either *n* or *count* reflect the number of data values added to *sum*? Does it depend on factors in parts (c) and (d)?

11. a. Rewrite *prog7a.c* so that it reports an error in reading in the value for *n* and gives the user a chance to correct the error before continuing.
    b. Why do we use *exit(1)* if *n* <= *0*? What happens as a result of calling *exit*? How is a normal exit indicated? In this case, what happens to the rest of the program?
    c. If you type in a bad response when you are using the cash machine at your bank, does the program terminate? What happens?
    d. While the way errors are handled in *prog7a.c* may be adequate in a student program, would it work in a commercial environment?

12. In Program 7, we wrote functions *sumarray* and *avgarray* to do much of the processing as modules in a large program.

    a. Write a driver program that tests these two functions separately. Which one should be tested first?

b. Instead of having *avgarray* call *sumarray*, it is possible to have *avgarray* compute the array average directly. Show how to do this. What are the advantages and disadvantages of this approach?

13. In Program 7, we checked for the possibility that *n* was less than 1. Can we catch the error where *n* is less than the number of values in the data? For example, what happens if the parameter *n* is 2, but there are three grades?

14. Before deciding to allow function *readdata* to return the value for *n*, we suggested that there are other methods of handing this problem. One method is to let the main program read a value into *n* before calling *readdata*. (*Note*: This method isn't true to the idea that all the data in this program is read into the function *readdata*.) Rewrite Program 7 using this method of getting a value into *n*.

15. In the functions for Program 7, instead of calling the array *mark* or *grade*, we used the generic name *num*. We did this so that we could reuse the functions in other programs without having to rename the arrays. However, several functions, primarily *readdata* and *countmarks*, have features which make them inappropriate in a different program. What are they? Fix these features so that these functions are reusable.

16. a. Rewrite Program 7 so that it performs the same tasks for three classes rather than just one. This requires the program to read in three sets of data. Consider carefully which method of detecting the end of the set of data works in this case. If you use the header method, how many header values do you need? If you use the *EOF* method, how many times do you need to indicate *EOF*? If you redirect the data to come from a file, can you use the *EOF* method?

b. Rewrite Program 7 so that it performs the same tasks for three classes, rather than just one. This version requires at least three arrays (one for each class). In addition, have the program calculate the overall average for the three classes, the highest and lowest marks overall, and the total number of marks above, below, and equal to the overall average. (*Hint:* The simplest method of doing this part of the problem is to combine the grades from all three classes into one large array.)

TWO-DIMENSIONAL ARRAY EXERCISES

17. a. Give the declaration for a two-dimensional array *sales* which can hold sales data for three stores for each of 12 months. Assume that each piece of sales data is a value of type *double*.

b. Show how to locate the items in the *sales* array which represent the sales of the first store in May, the second store in June, and the third store in January.

18. Assume that a two-dimensional array of integers, called *y*, initially has the values in Figure 7-12. Show what values are stored in the array after executing each of these program segments. Each part uses this declaration and starts from these values:

```
int y[3][4];
int i,j;
```

a.
```
y[1][2] = y[0][3] + y[1][1];
y[0][3] = y[2][0] + y[2][1];
y[1][3] = y[0][1] + y[1][3];
```

b.
```
i = 0;
y[i+1][0] = y[i+1][i+3];
i = 1;
y[0][3] = y[2][i-1];
```

FIGURE 7-12   Array **y** for Exercise 18

	0	1	2	3
0	5	11	6	0
1	91	3	−12	2
2	14	1	219	7

c.
```
i = 1;    j = 2;
y[2][1] = y[2][0] + y[1][2];
y[i][j] = i + j + y[2][3];
```

19. a.   Draw a picture showing the values stored in **array2** after executing this program segment. Assume that the user types in the integers from 1 to 24 in order.

```
int array2[6][4];
int i,j,num;

for (i = 5; i >= 0; i--)
    for (j = 0; j < 4; j++)  {
        scanf("%d",&num);
        if (j > i)
            num++;
        array2[i][j] = num;
    }
```

b.   Rewrite the program using a third (outermost) loop. This loop supplies the values (integers from 1 to 24) to use for **num**.

20. For each of the following program segments, show exactly what is printed. Also draw a picture showing the final values stored in the array **arr**. If a storage location does not have a value, indicate its value with ?. Use this declaration for each part:

```
int arr[5][6];
int i,j;
```

a.
```
for (i = 0; i < 5; i++)
    for (j = 0; j < 6; j++)  {
        arr[i][j] = 10 * i + j;
        printf("i = %d, j = %d, the array %d\n",
            i,j,arr[i][j]);
    }
```

b.
```
for (i = 5; i < 10; i++)
    for (j = 6; j > 2; j--)
        if (i > j)
            arr[i-5][j-1] = i + j;
        else
            arr[j-i+1][j-1] = 19;
```

(continued)

(continued)

```
for (i = 0; i < 5; i++)
    for (j = 0; j < 6; j++)
        printf("i = %d, j = %d, the array %d\n",
               i,j,arr[i][j]);
```

PROGRAMMING PROJECTS

21. Write a program to do the following: Read a series of numbers into an array *numb* (there are never more than 50 numbers). Then multiply each number by 3, storing the new values in an array *prod*. Write the program using a parameter value to govern the amount of data read in.

22. Write a program that reads a series of numbers into an array *numb* (there are no more than 100 numbers). Go through the elements of the *numb* array one by one, moving the positive (or 0) elements to an array *pos* and the negative elements to an array *neg*. For example, if *numb* holds 5 −9 2 −7 −4 0 2, then array *pos* gets 5 2 0 2, and array *neg* has −9 −7 −4. Print the three arrays.

23. a. Write a program that reads in a number *ans* of type *double* and a parameter value *n*, then reads *n* numbers of type *double* into an array *results* (assume there are no more than 500 numbers). Determine which of these numbers is closest in absolute value to *ans*. Find the average of the *results* values and the number closest to it.

    b. Can this exercise be solved without using an array? Explain. Do you need an array if the set of data contains the value for *ans* after the values for *results*?

24. Write a program that reads in a parameter value *n*, then reads *n* numbers into the *x* array. It then reads in another parameter value *m*, and reads *m* values into the *y* array. It finds the average of the *n* values in the *x* array and the *m* values in the *y* array. Then it copies both arrays into a single large array, *z* (which consists of the elements of *x* followed by those from *y*). Finally, it finds the average of the *n* + *m* values in the *z* array.

25. Write a program that reads a series of integer values into an array, then finds the mode of the array, which is the number that occurs most often. (*Suggestion*: One possible method is to count how many times each value occurs, then find which of these counts is the largest.)

26. A company manufactures two items, each with a price that can vary. The company receives orders which contain two numbers for each item; the first represents the number of units ordered, and the second number represents the price of that item. A program has been written to find the total cost of the order by reading the amounts ordered, then multiplying the price of the first item (stored in *price1*) by the amount ordered (read into *amt1*) and adding this to the total cost for item two, which is computed in the same way.

    The company expands its product line to include ten items instead of two. One way to handle this is to introduce variables for each of the new prices and amounts, then multiply the appropriate values and add the total costs for the ten items. Another method is to store the ten prices in an array, read the ten amounts ordered into another array, then multiply the corresponding elements of the two arrays. Write a program that uses the first method, then another program that uses the second method. Compare the two programs.

27. Write a program that counts the number of votes received by each of 20 candidates in an election. Each piece of data is a number from 0 to 19, with 0 representing a vote for candidate 0,

1 for candidate 1, and so on. The program reads in an arbitrary number of votes. At the end of the set of data, it prints the number of votes received by each candidate. Determine which candidate receives the most votes. (*Suggestion*: Store the vote totals in an array, using the piece of data as the subscript.)

28. The well-known Fibonacci series consists of the numbers 1, 1, 2, 3, 5, 8, 13, ... The first two terms are both 1; thereafter, each term is the sum of the two previous terms (e.g., $8 = 3 + 5$, $13 = 5 + 8$).

    a. Write a program (without an array) to read in a value *n*, then compute and print the values of the first *n* terms of the Fibonacci series. (*Suggestion*: You have to keep track of the last term and the next-to-last term and update them at the appropriate time.)

    b. Solve the same problem using an array to hold the terms of the series. (This is significantly easier than part (a) but is limited by the bounds of the array.)

29. a. Write a function *smallarr* that returns the smallest element in an array. The function receives two parameters: an array *x* of numbers of type *double* and an integer *n*, representing the number of values in the array *x*.

    b. Write a main program that tests the *smallarr* function. The main program calls the function with several different arrays, containing varying numbers of elements.

    c. Write a function *avg_large_and_small* that returns the average of the largest and smallest elements in an array. (*Suggestion*: The function can use *smallarr* and a version of *findmax* from Program 7, revised to operate on numbers of type *double*.)

30. Write a program that calls a function *poslarg* that returns the position of the largest element in an array. The function receives as parameters an array of integers *val* and an integer *n*, representing the number of elements in the array. (*Note*: This function finds the subscript or position of the largest value, not the value itself.) For example, if the array holds 5 7 3 2 6, then the function returns 1 since the largest element (7) is in position 1. If the largest value occurs several times, return the first occurrence.

31. a. Write a function *zerotest* that searches for an array element with a value of 0. The function receives as parameters an array of integers *s* and an integer *r*, representing the number of values to be tested in the array. The function returns 1 (true) if 0 occurs one or more times in the first *r* positions of *s*; it returns 0 (false) if no 0 is present. Here is the function prototype:

```
int zerotest(int [],int);
```

    b. Write a driver program that tests the function *zerotest*. The driver program should use several arrays and sizes. For example, if the *x* array holds 7 4 3 2 0 –1 0 5, *zerotest* can be called with the first four elements of *x*, the first six, and so on.

32. a. Write a function *zeroposit* which modifies the function *zerotest* from Exercise 31. Instead of returning true or false, *zeroposit* returns the position of 0 within the first *r* elements of the *s* array. If 0 occurs several times, the function returns the position of the first 0; if it does not occur at all, the function returns –1, indicating failure.

    b. Write a driver program to test *zeroposit*. On the array *x* in Exercise 31(b), *zeroposit*(*x*,6) is 4; *zeroposit*(*x*,8) is also 4; *zeroposit*(*x*,3) is –1.

33. Write a function *search* to generalize the function *zeroposit* from Exercise 32. Instead of always searching for the position of 0, *search* receives the number to be located as one of its

parameters. The function receives an array of integers **numb**, a size **m**, and a particular integer **p**. It returns the position of the first value of **p** within the first **m** elements of the **numb** array; it returns –1 if **p** does not occur. (The problem of searching for a particular value is extremely common in business and commercial situations. It is discussed in Chapter 10.)

34. You have been hired as a programmer by a major bank. Your first project is a small banking transaction system. Each account consists of a number and a balance. The user of the program (the teller) can create a new account, as well as perform deposits, withdrawals, and balance inquiries.

    Initially, the account information of existing customers is to be read into a pair of parallel arrays—one for account numbers, the other for balances. Use the following function to read in the data values:

    ```
    int read_accts(int acctnum_array, double balance_array, int max_elems);
    ```

    This function fills up the account number and balance arrays (up to **max_elems**) and returns the actual number of accounts read in (later referred to as **num_elems**).

    The program then allows the user to select from the following menu of transactions:

    Select one of the following:
       W – Withdrawal
       D – Deposit
       N – New account
       B – Balance
       Q – Quit

    Use the following function to produce the menu:

    ```
    char menu(void);
    ```

    This function displays the menu and reads in the user's choice. You should verify that the user has typed in a valid selection (otherwise print out an error message and repeat the prompt). The user's selection is returned by the function.

    Once the user has entered a selection, one of the following functions should be called to perform the specific transaction. At the end, before the user quits, the program prints the contents of the account arrays.

    ```
    int findacct(int acctnum_array, int num_elems, int account);
    ```

    This function returns the index of **account** in **account_array** if the account exists, and –1 if it doesn't. It is called by all the remaining functions.

    ```
    void withdrawal(int acctnum_array, double balance_array, int num_elems);
    ```

    This function prompts the user for the account number. If the account does not exist, it prints an error message. Otherwise, it asks the user for the amount of the withdrawal. If the account does not contain sufficient funds, it prints an error message and does not perform the transaction.

    ```
    void deposit(int acctnum_array, double balance_array, int num_elems);
    ```

    This function prompts the user for the account number. If the account does not exist, it prints an error message. Otherwise, it asks the user for the amount of the deposit.

```
int new_acct(int acctnum_array, double balance_array, int num_elems);
```

This function prompts the user for a new account number. If the account already exists, it prints an error message. Otherwise, it adds the account to the account array with an initial balance of 0. It returns the new number of accounts.

```
void balance(int acctnum_array, double balance_array, int num_elems);
```

This function prompts the user for an account number. If the account does not exist, it prints an error message. Otherwise, it prints the account balance.

```
void print_accts(int acctnum_array, double balance_array, int num_elems);
```

This function prints all customer information—account number and balance.

PROGRAMMING PROJECTS FOR TWO-DIMENSIONAL ARRAYS

35. The arrays x and y both have five rows and three columns. Write two functions, one to do each of the following:

    a. Determine if every storage location in x holds the same value as the corresponding location in y.

    b. Determine if any storage location in y holds the same value as the corresponding location in x.

    Print an appropriate message for each case. Write a main program that tests these functions. Test your program with various sets of data.

36. Assume that values have been read into the array a, which has four rows and nine columns.

    a. Write a function that adds 10 to each negative value stored in the array (if $a[2][3] =$ −19, it should be changed to −9).

    b. Modify your function from part (a) so that, instead of adding 10 just once, it adds 10 repeatedly until the value is no longer negative (−19 becomes −9 and then +1; −7 becomes +3; −30 becomes 0).

37. A square two-dimensional array has equal numbers of rows and columns (e.g., five of each). Given such an array called x, the locations with equal row and column subscripts ($x[1][1], x[2][2]$, etc.) form the main diagonal of the array. These entries go from upper left to lower right. The antidiagonal consists of the entries from lower left to upper right.

    Write a function to sum the entries on the main diagonal of an array. Write a function to sum the entries on the main diagonal and the antidiagonal. Write a main program that tests these functions.

38. Write a complete program to do the following: A function interactively reads in nine values, each of which is the character X or O, corresponding to moves on a tic-tac-toe board. (Assume that the first row is read in, then the second row, then the third row.) Another function prints the board in the form of a three-by-three array, with an X or an O in the appropriate location. Another function determines the winner of the game (whichever player has three marks in a row: horizontally, vertically, or on either diagonal). The function determines if X won, if O won, if the game is a draw, or if the result is impossible. (Many results are impossible—for example, if there are two winners. What are some other impossible results?)

39. Write a program that plays tic-tac-toe. Instead of simply reading in the moves, it decides which move to make in a given situation, based on rules that you provide. For example, if the opponent has two marks in the same column, the machine should select the third position in that same column. Write two versions of the program: one in which the machine plays interactively with a human opponent and one in which the machine makes the moves for both sides.

40. a. Assume that a two-dimensional array *letter* with four rows and four columns holds a single character in each storage location (*letter[2][1]* might hold 'y'). Write a function that determines whether any row or column or either diagonal of the array consists of the characters 'h', 'e', 'l', 'p', either forward or backward.

    b. Modify your function from part (a) so that the array *letter* has six rows and six columns. See if any four consecutive row (or column or diagonal) entries contain the sequence of characters 'h', 'e', 'l', 'p', either forward or backward.

41. Write a program that does grade analysis using the two-dimensional *grade* array from Section 8. Each row contains the grades for one student; each column reflects the grades on a given exam. There should be four exams. The set of data starts with a parameter value indicating the number of students. Then the program reads in and prints four grades for each student. The program does the following tasks, each in its own function.

    a. Finds and prints the class average on each exam.
    b. Finds and prints the highest mark on each exam.
    c. For each exam, finds and prints how many grades are above, below, and equal to the average.
    d. Finds and prints each student's average. Use the *grade* array subscript to identify each student.
    e. Finds the overall class average. There are three ways to do this: averaging the individual student averages, averaging the four class exams, and averaging all the separate grades.

        (1) Try to estimate the number of arithmetic operations needed for each method.
        (2) Which method requires the fewest arithmetic operations?
        (3) Of the three methods, which is the most reliable? That is, which does not depend upon previous calculations?

42. Expand the program from Exercise 41 by adding functions for each of the following parts:

    a. Determine each student's high and low grades, the exam on which they were obtained, and the difference between the high and low grades.
    b. In the entire class (and for each student separately), find the number of grades that are 90 or more, 80 to 89, and so on.
    c. Print the number of every student who receives at least one grade of 90 or more. If a student has two or more grades in this range, print the number only once. Use the *grade* array subscript to identify each student.
    d. Go through the array and make sure that every mark is valid (in the range from 0 to 100). If any mark is invalid, print an error message and the position of the invalid mark.
    e. Convert invalid grades to valid ones in the following way: If the grade is negative, make it positive (if necessary, apply the next step as well). If the grade is over 100, keep only the last two digits of the number. For example, 687 becomes 87; 135 becomes 35; –200 becomes 200 and then 0.

f.	Before computing each student's average, drop the lowest grade. For example, if a student's grades are 90 45 89 91, drop the 45, and the other three grades average to 90.00.

g.	Assume that the last test is optional. If student number *i* took the test, then (in row *i*) the fourth column of the **grade** array holds the grade, but if the student didn't, the fourth column of **grade** holds –1. Modify the function which computes student averages to handle this feature. (Do any other functions have to be modified to make this change?)

h.	In the original version of the program, each exam had equal weight. Assume that the weight of each exam is not the same. Instead, each exam has associated with it an integer (you determine how these integers receive values) such that the sum of the four is 100. Each integer is the relative weight of that exam. For example, to give the exams equal weight, each integer would be 25. But if the weights are 20 20 20 40, then the last exam counts twice as heavily as the others. Modify the function which computes student averages to handle this feature. (Do any other functions have to be modified to make this change?)

43.	A company has records for the hours worked by each employee per week. Each employee's record consists of the hourly rate of pay and seven numbers, representing the hours worked by the employee on the seven days of the week. For example, a typical entry could be the following:

```
13.25  1.3  7  8  0  4.7  0  0
```

The first piece of data entered (not shown) is a parameter value, specifying the number of employees (there are no more than 20).

Write a program that reads in the specified data and then does the following:

a.	For each employee, finds the total number of hours worked for the week.

b.	For each employee, finds the weekly pay by multiplying the hours worked by the rate per hour.

c.	Finds the number of employees absent on each day of the week. An employee is considered absent on a given day if the hours worked are less than 1.

d.	Finds which day has the most absentees.

44.	The game of Life was developed by a mathematician named John Conway. It is intended to provide a model of life, death, and survival among simple organisms that inhabit an *n* by *m* board. The current population of the board comprises one generation. A cell's neighbors are the eight cells surrounding it, as shown in Figure 7-13. There are only four rules that govern the birth or death of cells from one generation to the next:

(1)	Every empty cell with three living neighbors comes to life in the next generation.

(2)	Any cell with one or no neighbors dies of loneliness.

(3)	Any cell with four or more neighbors dies from overcrowding.

(4)	Any cell with two or three neighbors lives into the next generation.

All births and deaths occur simultaneously.

Why is Life a game? It turns out that some starting populations die out quickly, while others form interesting patterns that repeat, grow, or move across the board as they go from generation to generation.

FIGURE 7-13   Cell **x** and its eight neighboring cells

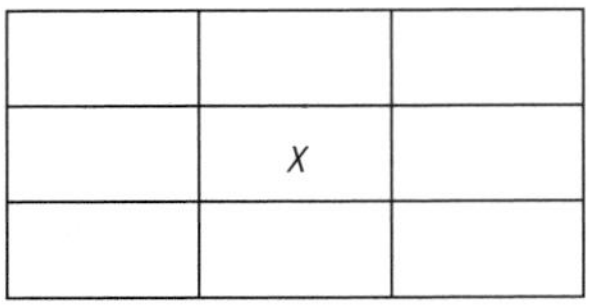

a.   Write a program that plays Life on the screen. Let the program user specify the locations of the starting population as well as the number of generations that should be
shown as output. Use a two-dimensional array to represent the board. In order for the
board to fill the screen, use an array with rows from 0 to 24 and columns from 0 to 79.
Use a letter, like x, to represent each living cell.

b.   Write a function that pauses between generations so that the screen image can be
printed.

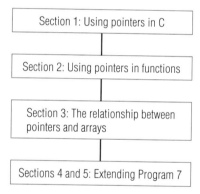

POINTERS

8

SYNTAX CONCEPTS: pointers, pointer notation, ∗ and & operators, *sizeof* operator, pointer arithmetic

PROGRAMMING CONCEPTS: use of pointers, dereferencing, indirect addressing, parameters which are pointers, input and output parameters

HOW TO READ CHAPTER 8

It is possible to cover sections 1 through 3 without having done Program 7.

OUTLINE:

Section 1: Using pointers in C

Section 2: Using pointers in functions

Section 3: The relationship between pointers and arrays

Sections 4 and 5: Extending Program 7

INTRODUCTION AND STATEMENT OF THE PROBLEM

This chapter introduces pointers. Pointers play a crucial role in C, second only to functions, and give the language much of its distinctive flavor. Rather than introducing a completely new problem in this chapter, we will simply modify our solution to Problem 7 by adding a few new pieces. The study of pointers is a rich topic, and there is plenty to discuss without a new problem.

SECTION 1   POINTERS

BITS AND BYTES

The memory of a computer is divided into small units called **bytes**. Each byte is further divided into eight **bits**, short for **binary digits**. A bit can hold one of two simple values, 1 or 0. Bits are combined into bytes just as letters form words.

A single byte can have 256 (2^8 = 256) different values, ranging from 00000000 to 11111111; each value can be interpreted as a character, a number, even a color. Part of the power of computers comes from the ability to assign many different interpretations to byte values in memory.

For some values, a byte is not large enough. To represent a wider range of values, we combine bytes into larger units. Their size, names, and uses depend on the type of computer.

◆ PCs and compatibles use a two-byte unit (16 bits) to represent the *int* data type.

◆ Sun workstations use a four-byte unit (32 bits) to represent the *int* data type.

◆ Most other machines use one of these two standard units.

The size of the unit determines the number of values which can be represented. In each system, one bit is used for the sign (positive or negative) and the remaining bits for the value. The largest *int* value on a PC is 32,767 ($2^{15} - 1$), while on a workstation, it is over two billion ($2^{31} - 1$).

A simple way to determine the size in bytes of an integer on your system is through the *sizeof* operator (see Exercise 13 for other uses of *sizeof*). Try running the following line of code on your system:

```
printf("the number of bytes used for an integer is %d",sizeof(int));
```

ADDRESS OF A STORAGE LOCATION

Every byte or storage location in the memory of the computer has a number which identifies it uniquely, just as a house or an apartment does. This identifying number (or letter) is called its **address**. Addresses start at 0 and go up; the upper limit is determined by the amount of memory in the machine (see Figure 8-1). Individual bits do not have addresses, just as your kitchen or living room does not have one.

Every variable in a C program is assigned a spot in memory and thus an address. When we declare a variable, we tell the computer two things:

◆ the type of variable we want, and

◆ the name of the variable.

A declaration is a way of telling the computer to set aside a specific chunk of memory and assign it a name. The type of the variable tells the computer, among other things, how large a storage location is needed. For example, a variable of type *double* occupies more space than one of type *char* or *int*.

FIGURE 8-1   Addresses in memory

FIGURE 8-2 Address (name) versus value of storage location *num*. *A*, on a PC; *B*, on a workstation.

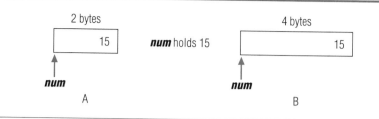

Let's take apart the following declaration as an example:

```
int num;
```

The compiler, seeing this declaration, sets aside the appropriate-size storage location for type **int** and assigns it the name **num**. This name is associated with the address of the first byte in that storage location (see Figure 8-2).[1] Whenever we refer to **num** in our program, the computer goes to the address in memory which it has associated with **num**. This technique allows us to use names for variables.

 CAUTION Note that the *address* of a variable is not the same as its *value*, just as your address is not the same as your house. The value of a variable can change during a program, but the address cannot.

POINTERS AND THE USE OF THE ADDRESS OPERATOR &

Sometimes, however, it is handy to be able to refer to a variable's address. For this, we use pointers. A **pointer** is a variable that can hold an address as its value. One way to access the address of a variable is by placing the **address operator**, an ampersand (&), in front of its name.

EXAMPLE 8-1

Here are declarations and address references for variables of three different data types:

declaration	address
`int    num;`	`&num`
`double sales;`	`&sales`
`char   initials;`	`&initials`

Some possible values for the addresses and values of these variables are shown in Figure 8-3.[2]

---

[1]In this and the other figures, numerical values appear in decimal notation, although they are really stored in binary.

[2]In this and succeeding figures, the address numbers are not meant to be accurate. They are chosen solely for purposes of illustration.

FIGURE 8-3 Contrasting addresses and values

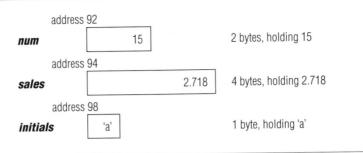

CAUTION Only an object stored in memory has an address. We cannot refer to the address of an expression or a constant. The following are illegal references:

◆ *&(7)*—an illegal reference to the address of the constant 7

◆ *&(x + 2)*—an illegal reference to the address of the expression *x + 2*

The notation *&num* is read as "address of *num*." A call to the *scanf* function also uses this notation. It is helpful to make this connection more explicit. The *scanf* function receives two (or more) parameters. For example, to read a value into the variable *num*, we use the following call to *scanf*:

```
scanf("%d",&num);
```

In general, the first parameter to *scanf* is a string containing one or more conversion specifications, and each of the other parameters is the address of a storage location which receives a value in the function. In this call, because we have specified *&num* instead of *num* as the second parameter, the value sent to *scanf* is the address of *num*. Figure 8-4 shows the difference between the type of parameter sent to *scanf* and the type sent to *printf*.[3]

DECLARING A POINTER VARIABLE

We can declare a pointer variable—that is, we can say a certain variable points to, or holds the address of, an object of a certain type. To do this, we use this notation:

```
int *p;
```

This is read as "*p* is a pointer to an integer" or "*int* star *p*." A variable of type *int* * can hold the address of a variable of type *int*.

Similarly, we can declare a variable to be a pointer to a character or a double, using the following declarations:

```
char   *cp;
double *dp;
```

---

[3]It may have occurred to you that the *scanf* function is odd because it changes the value of its parameters. In Section 2, we fully explain the operation of the *scanf* function.

FIGURE 8-4 Parameter transmission in a call to **_scanf_** versus a call to **_printf_**. A, a call to **_scanf_**; B, a call to **_printf_**.

The first declaration says **_cp_** is a pointer to a character value and can hold the address of a variable of type **_char_**. We read the declaration as follows: "**_cp_** has type **_char_** star" or "**_char_** star **_cp_**." The second says **_dp_** is a pointer to a value of type **_double_**, so it can hold the address of a variable of type **_double_**. We say "**_dp_** has type **_double_** star."

CAUTION Each pointer variable points to an object of a specific type. For example, **_dp_** points to a value of type **_double_**, not type **_int_**.

The address of a storage location can be assigned to a pointer variable. For example, the address of integer variable **_a_** can be assigned to pointer variable **_p_** by using the statement in Figure 8-5.

THE DEREFERENCING OPERATOR *

As part of the declaration of a pointer variable, we use the symbol *. This symbol can also be used as an operator, called the **dereferencing** or **indirection operator**. The notation *_p_ means the object that **_p_** points to or the location whose address is stored in **_p_**. This operator allows us to access and change the value stored at that location. This is called **indirect addressing**.

USING POINTERS WITH * AND &

Using the two operators, * and &, we can work with storage locations, pointers to these locations, and their values in a variety of ways. Let's look at some examples.

FIGURE 8-5 Storing an address in a pointer variable

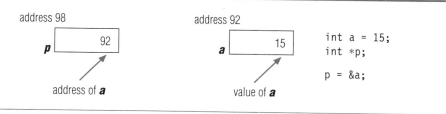

FIGURE 8-6   Accessing a value using a pointer (Example 8-2). *A*, after the declaration; *B*, after **p = &a**.

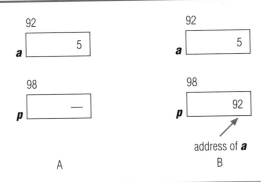

EXAMPLE 8-2

```
int a=5;
int *p;

p = &a;
printf("a holds: %d",a);
printf(" and the thing p points to holds: %d\n",*p);
```

Consider the declarations. First, *a* is a standard integer variable, but the data type for *p* is *int **. Therefore, *p* is a pointer to an integer, which means *p* can hold the address of an integer. Initially, *p* points to nothing; then *p* is assigned the address of *a*. This is the printout:

> a holds 5 and the thing p points to holds 5

PROGRAM TRACE   Let's go through this more carefully:

◆   The variable *a* is assigned the value 5. At this point, *p* has not yet been assigned a value (see Figure 8-6A).

◆   Then *p* is assigned the value of the address of *a*. Since *p* is a variable of type *int **, it can hold the address of a variable of type *int* (see Figure 8-6B).

◆   The first call to *printf* prints the value stored in *a*, which is 5.

◆   The second call to *printf* prints 5, the value at the location that *p* points to. Since *p* holds the address of *a*, *p* points to *a*, which holds the value 5.

SELF-CHECK 8-1

1.   How many different values can a bit have? How many different values can a byte have? On your system, how many bytes are used to store a value of type *int*?

2.   Can the addresses of two distinct variables, *x* and *y*, ever be the same? Can the values stored at these addresses ever be the same?

3.   Which of the following assignment statements are incorrect? Explain your answers.

```
int    *p;
int    a;
double d;

p = d;
p = a;
p = &d;
p = &a;
```

CHANGING THE VALUE OF A POINTER VARIABLE

The value of a pointer can change, as shown in Example 8-3.

EXAMPLE 8-3

```
int *p;
int a=5,b=3;

p = &a;
printf("a holds: %d, b holds: %d\n",a,b);
printf("and the thing p points to holds: %d\n",*p);
p = &b;
printf("a holds: %d, b holds: %d\n",a,b);
printf("and the thing p points to holds: %d\n",*p);
```

Here is the printout from this code:

```
a holds: 5,  b holds: 3
and the thing p points to holds: 5
a holds: 5,  b holds: 3
and the thing p points to holds: 3
```

At first, *p* holds the address of *a* (see Figure 8-7A), but later it holds the address of *b* (see Figure 8-7B). However, *&a* and *&b* do not change, nor do the values stored in *a* and *b*.

USING THE DEREFERENCING OPERATOR TO CHANGE A STORAGE LOCATION'S VALUE

The dereferencing operator ∗ can be used to change the value of a storage location. In fact, the declaration for a pointer variable suggests this. Consider the following declaration:

```
int *p;
```

Technically, the declaration says that *p* has type *int* ∗, but there is another way to interpret it. Break it apart so that we have *int* and then *∗p*. You can think of this as saying that *∗p* can hold an integer value. If *p* is a pointer to an integer variable, then *∗p* refers to or dereferences

FIGURE 8-7 Changing the value of a pointer (Example 8-3). *A*, after *p = &a*; *B*, after *p = &b*.

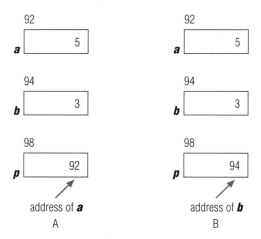

the value of that variable. The dereference can occur in an expression or on the left-hand side of an assignment statement.

EXAMPLE 8-4

We can use a pointer *p* to change the value stored in *a* as follows:

```
int *p;
int a=5;

p = &a;
*p = 10;
*p = *p + 1;
```

The first assignment statement stores the address of *a* in *p*. The second one changes the value at the address *p* points to. Since *p* holds the address of *a*, this changes the value stored in *a* to 10. The third assignment statement adds 1 to that value (see Figure 8-8).

FIGURE 8-8 Changing a value using a pointer (Example 8-4). *A*, the value of *a* after **p = 10*; *B*, the value of *a* after **p = *p + 1*.

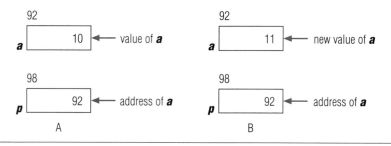

r-value VERSUS *l-value*

Note that *p* has different meanings on the two sides of the assignment statement *p* = *p* + *1*, just as *x* does on the two sides of the assignment statement *x* = *x* + *1*. When *p* (or *x*) appears on the right-hand side, the machine uses the value of the expression *p* (or *x*). This is called an **r-value**. When *p* (or *x*) appears on the left-hand side, the computer goes to a storage location, *p* (or *x*), and changes its value. This is called an **l-value**. In general, *p* on the right-hand side of an assignment statement means to access the value at a storage location; *p* on the left-hand side means to change the value at the location whose address is stored in *p*.

PRECEDENCE OF THE ∗ OPERATOR

There is another way to write the last assignment statement in Example 8-4, using the increment operator:

```
(*p)++;
```

This increments the value of the variable whose address is stored in *p*. Note the parentheses around *p*. The increment operator has higher precedence than the ∗ operator. If we omit the parentheses, the statement will not do what we want:

```
*p++;
```

This increments the pointer *p* itself so that it points to a different memory location. In order to accomplish what we want, we must put parentheses around *p*. (Appendix III contains a complete list of the operators in C, showing the relative precedence of ∗ and &.)

PRINTING A POINTER OR AN ADDRESS

Although it is not normally useful, we can print the value of a pointer variable *p*; we can also directly print the address of a storage location. Here are some examples.

EXAMPLE 8-5

```
int a=5;
int *p;

p = &a;
printf("the address of a is: %u\n",&a);
printf("the value of p is: %u\n",p);
```

This section of code prints the following when run in Turbo C:

```
the address of a is: 65524
the value of p is: 65524
```

When the code is run using ANSI C on a Sun, the printout looks like this:

```
the address of a is: 4160748316
the value of p is: 4160748316
```

STYLE WORKSHOP The conversion specification we use to print both the address of *a* and the value of *p* is *%u*, used for unsigned decimal values. In general, the *%p* conversion specification is the usual way to print pointers and addresses. However, for our purposes, it is simpler to use *%u*, which prints the value of a pointer in decimal notation.

EXAMPLE 8-6 It is interesting to print the address of two consecutive storage locations in an array. For example, consider this code:

```
int a[5] = { 10, 20, 30, 40, 50 };
int *p,*q;

p = &a[0];
q = &a[1];
printf("the address of a[0] is: %u\n",&a[0]);
printf("the address of a[1] is: %u\n",&a[1]);
printf("the value of p is: %u\n",p);
printf("the value of q is: %u\n",q);
printf("the value of a[0] is: %d\n",a[0]);
printf("the value of a[1] is: %d\n",a[1]);
```

When this runs under Turbo C on a PC and ANSI C on a Sun, the output is the following:

Turbo C

```
the address of a[0] is: 65516
the address of a[1] is: 65518
the value of p is: 65516
the value of q is: 65518
the value of a[0] is: 10
the value of a[1] is: 20
```

ANSI C

```
the address of a[0] is: 4026530892
the address of a[1] is: 4026530896
the value of p is: 4026530892
the value of q is: 4026530896
the value of a[0] is: 10
the value of a[1] is: 20
```

Note that storage locations *a[0]* and *a[1]*, whether viewed as addresses or as values of pointer variables, are exactly two bytes apart in Turbo C (and four bytes apart in ANSI C). This is because each integer in the array occupies two bytes on a PC and four bytes on a Sun workstation.

CAUTION Because the particular value of an address varies from system to system (and depends on the order of the program's declaration), it is dangerous for a program to attempt to use it. For instance, in Example 8-6, the fact that *q* holds an address is important; the fact that it holds precisely 65518 (or 4026530896) is meaningless.

USING * AND & IN ONE EXPRESSION

We can also combine the operators * and & in one expression. For example, we can take the * of the address of a variable. If we take an address and dereference it using *, we end up with the original value of the variable.

EXAMPLE 8-7

Here is an example showing the combination of & and *:

```
int a=5;
int *p;

p = &a;
printf("the answer is: %d\n",*&a);
printf("this way it is: %u\n",&*p);
```

As we know, the value of the address of **p** changes from system to system. If this program is run, the following output is printed:

Turbo C

```
the answer is: 5
this way it is: 65524
```

ANSI C

```
the answer is: 5
this way it is: 4026530908
```

PROGRAM TRACE

◆ The first call to ***printf*** prints *&a*, which is the value stored at the address of **a**. Obviously, this is the value of **a**, which is 5.

◆ The second call to ***printf*** prints &*p, which is the address of the integer value that **p** points to. Therefore, this prints the value of **p**, which is the address of **a** (note the conversion specification **%u**).

In these examples, we see that printing an address or the value of a pointer variable is not very meaningful. On the other hand, printing the value stored at an address or pointed to by a pointer, is meaningful.

INITIALIZATION OF A POINTER VARIABLE

It is possible to initialize a pointer variable in a declaration. However, we must be careful about the order of the declarations. Let's look first at the right way to do things, then the wrong way.

EXAMPLE 8-8

```
int a=5;
int *p=&a;

printf("a holds: %d",a);
printf(" and the thing p points to holds: %d\n",*p);
```

This is equivalent to Example 8-2, and the output is identical. In the declaration, **a** is given type ***int*** and is initialized to the value 5; then **p** is given type ***int*** * and is initialized to the address of **a**.

TABLE 8.1   Expressions Involving * and &

Expression	Value
p	the address of the location *p* points to
*p	the value at the location *p* points to
a	the integer value stored at location *a*
&*a*	the address of *a*
*&*a*	the integer value stored at location *a*
&*p*	the address of the location *p* points to

CAUTION Normally, a declaration with an initialization can be rewritten as first a simple declaration and then an assignment statement by cutting the original apart and repeating the variable name in each new statement. For example, *int a = 5* can be separated into *int a* and *a = 5*. However, for a pointer variable, we must be more careful. The declaration for *p* is not equivalent to *int *p* and then *p = &a*. That would initialize *p* to the address of *a*. Instead, the declaration can be separated into the following:

```
int *p=&a;    is equivalent to    int *p;
                                   p = &a;
```

The variable is *p*, not *p*; the data type for *p* is *int *, not *int*.

Now let's consider what happens if we interchange the order of the two declarations from Example 8-8:

<table>
<tr><td>EXAMPLE 8-9</td><td>

```
int *p=&a;                      /* incorrect order of declarations */
int a=5;
```

</td></tr>
</table>

Why is this order incorrect? The top line initializes *p* to the address of *a*, but *a* has not yet been declared. Therefore, the compiler cannot find *a* and gives an error message.

Table 8.1 illustrates many things we have discussed in this section. Assume the following declarations:

```
int *p;
int a;
```

SELF-CHECK 8-2

For this self-check, assume the following two declarations:

```
int a;
int *p;
```

1. What conversion specification is used to print each of the following?

    a.   the value stored at location *a*

    b.   the value stored at location *p*

    c.   the value at the location *p* points to

2. Does the following statement assign to **p** the address of **a** or the value of **a**?

```
p = &a;
```

3. Does the following statement store the value of **a** or the address of **a**? Where does it store this?

```
*p = a;
```

SECTION 2 USING PARAMETERS WHICH ARE POINTERS (A SECOND LOOK)

What we have said about pointers so far is really an introduction to their use in functions and arrays. In this section, we discuss how a programmer can use pointers in a function, expanding the ideas in Chapter 5, Section 8. (It is not necessary to read that section before this one.)

FUNCTIONS THAT CHANGE THEIR PARAMETERS

Functions in C can do more complicated things than we have shown so far. In fact, with the exception of the ones in Chapter 5, Section 8, all our examples of programmer-defined functions have ignored a powerful feature. A function can change the value of one or more of its formal parameters; by doing this, in certain cases, a function can change the value pointed to by one or more of its actual arguments.

A FUNCTION THAT TRIES TO ADD 1 TO ITS PARAMETER: *trytoadd1*

As our first example, let's write a function that increments or adds 1 to the value of its parameter. The function does not return the new value; instead, it tries to modify the value of the parameter. Although this is not the easiest way to solve this problem, it illustrates the difficulty of changing the value of a parameter in C.

We can call this function ***trytoadd1*** (because our first version doesn't work). It receives one parameter, an integer called **x**, and does not return an answer. In the body of the function, we simply use **x++** to increment **x**. To make sure everything works, we add extra print statements, one before and one after incrementing.

EXAMPLE 8-10
(not correct)

Here is the entire function ***trytoadd1***:

```
/* function that tries to add 1 to its parameter x */
void trytoadd1(int x)
{
    printf("in the function, before adding: %d\n",x);
    x++;
    printf("in the function, after adding: %d\n",x);
    return;
}
```

Let's write the call to this function from a main program. The main program will initialize a variable, print its value, call the function, then print again. As usual, we include a function prototype. Here is the entire driver program to test **trytoadd1**:

```
/* driver program to test trytoadd1 */
#include <stdio.h>
void trytoadd1(int);
main()
{
    int k=5;

    printf("in the main program, before the call: %d\n",k);
    trytoadd1(k);
    printf("in the main program, after the call: %d\n",k);
}
```

Although we expect this program to correctly add 1 to the parameter, it does not work. If we actually run the program, we get the following output:

```
in the main program, before the call: 5
in the function, before adding: 5
in the function, after adding: 6
in the main program, after the call: 5
```

WHAT WENT WRONG?

Everything is perfect until we get back to the main program after the call. At that point, the main program prints the original value for **k**, not the incremented value printed in the function. To see exactly what went wrong, let's go through the function more carefully.

The formal parameter **x** in the function is given the *value* of the actual parameter **k** in the main program. As we saw in Chapter 5, Section 2, the formal parameter can be viewed as a local variable inside the function. It starts out with the value of the actual argument (see Figure 8-9A). But if the parameter **x** changes in the function, as it does here, the main program's **k** does not change (see Figure 8-9B). The main program does not know about any local variables in a function. The communication between actual and formal parameters is one-way: from the main program to the function.

CAUTION If the value of a formal parameter in a function changes, the value of the actual parameter in the calling function does not change.

THE USE OF POINTERS AS PARAMETERS: *add1* AS THE CORRECT VERSION OF *trytoadd1*

There is a way to write a function to add 1 to its parameter: using pointers. To make **trytoadd1** work correctly, we have to change both the function and the way the main program calls it.

FIGURE 8-9   *A*, the value of **k** is transmitted to **x**; *B*, the value of **x** is not transmitted back to **k**.

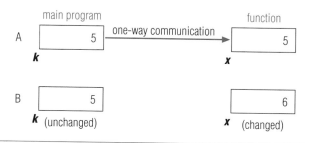

First, the function header has to change. (We will also change the function's name to **add1** since this version works.) The new header looks like this:

```
void add1(int *x)                                    /* this header is complete */
```

The difference is in the data type for **x**. Originally, it was **int**; now it is **int ***, pointer to integer. In other words, **x** is going to hold the *address* rather than the *value* of the integer. A parameter of this type is called a **pointer parameter** or a **parameter which is a pointer**.

The body of the function must also change. In the original version, we simply added 1 to the value of **x**, but now it is not **x** that we want to increment. Instead, we want to increment the *value* at the location that **x** points to. To do this, we must use the dereferencing operator:

```
(*x)++;
```

Recall that if **p** is an address, then **p* is the thing that **p** points to. In **add1**, **x* is the integer whose value we want to print and increment. So in every place that we used **x** in the original version, we substitute **x*.

THE COMPLETE FUNCTION *add1* AND THE CALL FROM THE MAIN PROGRAM

The entire function **add1** is shown in Example 8-11.

EXAMPLE 8-11

```
/* ... */
void add1(int *x)
{
    printf("in the function, before adding: %d\n",*x);
    (*x)++;
    printf("in the function, after adding: %d\n",*x);
    return;
}
```

In the main program, the call to the function also has to change. The new version of the function expects to get the address of an integer variable. Therefore, the main program must send the address, rather than the value of **k**. To do this, we use **&k** for the actual parameter in the function call. Although the function replaced every use of **x** by **x*, the main program replaces **k** by **&k** just once: in the call to the function. (The prototype for **add1** must also change to match the new function header.)

EXAMPLE 8-11
(continued)

Here is a driver program to test the function **add1**:

```
/* driver program to test add1 */
#include <stdio.h>
void add1(int *);
main()
{
    int k=5;

    printf("in the main program, before the call: %d\n",k);
    add1(&k);
    printf("in the main program, after the call: %d\n",k);
}
```

PROGRAM TRACE Let's trace this new driver program.

◆   The main program prints an initial message with **k** having the value 5.

◆   We call the function, sending the address of **k**. In this case, we are sending the address of a storage location which holds the value 5 (see Figure 8-10A).

◆   This address is matched to the formal parameter **x**, which is also a pointer to, or the address of, an integer. So **x** points to a location that has the value 5—that is, *x* has the value 5.

◆   In the function, *x* increments to 6, meaning the value at the storage location that **x** points to changes to 6 (see Figure 8-10B). This new value prints inside the function.

◆   The storage location which **x** points to is the variable **k**. Back in the main program, the value stored in **k** changes to 6, and this value prints.

If we run this program, we get the following output:

```
in the main program, before the call: 5
in the function, before adding: 5
in the function, after adding: 6
in the main program, after the call: 6
```

FIGURE 8-10 Using a pointer as a parameter (the function **add1**). A, the address of **k** is transmitted to **x**; B, the value in the location **x** points to is changed.

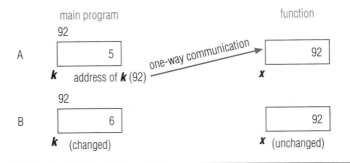

To sum up, the call to the function has the overall effect of changing the value pointed to by the actual parameter.

SELF-CHECK 8-3

1. In the function ***trytoadd1***, what is the value of the formal parameter? Inside the body of the function, does the value of the formal parameter change? What is the value of the actual parameter after returning from the function?

2. In the function ***add1***, what is the value of the formal parameter? (*Hint*: This is not the same as question 1.) Inside the body of the function, does the value of the formal parameter change? What changes in the main program after the call to the function?

3. What is wrong with each of the following calls from a driver program to the function ***add1***?

    ```
    int k=5;

    add1(k);
    add1(*k);
    ```

RETURNING MORE THAN ONE VALUE FROM A FUNCTION

Obviously, we could have written ***add1*** so that it returns the new value of ***k***, which avoids the entire issue of changing the value of a parameter. However, there are cases where we can't solve the problem by returning a single value. In Chapter 5, Section 8, we looked at a function that changes two values. Now that we understand the use of parameters which are pointers, let's look at that function again.

EXAMPLE 8-12

Here is a function ***findmaxmin*** which finds and returns to the calling function both the larger and smaller of its first two parameters. It returns these values by using the third and fourth parameters. In the function, new values are assigned to ****max*** and ****min***, which has the effect of changing two variables in the calling function.

```
/*
 * Function findmaxmin:
 * Input:
 *    x and y have values to compare
 *    max and min point to locations that
 *    will be assigned values in the function
 * Process:
 *    the function stores the larger of x and y
 *    in *max; it also stores the smaller in *min
 * Output:
 *    the locations max and min point to get values
 */
```

(continued)

(continued)

```
void findmaxmin(int x, int y, int *max, int *min)
{
    if (x > y)  {
        *max = x;
        *min = y;
    }
    else  {
        *max = y;
        *min = x;
    }
    return;
}
```

CALLS TO THE FUNCTION *findmaxmin*

We can use the following driver program to test *findmaxmin*:

```
/* driver program to test findmaxmin */
#include <stdio.h>
void findmaxmin(int, int, int *, int *);
main()
{
    int a=1,b=2,larger,smaller;

    findmaxmin(a,b,&larger,&smaller);
    printf("the larger is %d    and the smaller is %d\n",larger,smaller);
}
```

Note that the data type for *max* is *int* *. The address of *larger* is stored in *max*. Similarly, the address of *smaller* is stored in *min*. As the function executes, both *larger* and *smaller* are given values. Figure 8-11 illustrates the matchup of actual and formal parameters.

INPUT AND OUTPUT PARAMETERS

A parameter such as *max* or *min* in Example 8-12, whose initial value is not used but which holds a value assigned in the function, is called an **output parameter**. This term signifies that the value it carries on input to the function is not important; the value it holds on output is.

In the same way, an **input parameter** provides some type of input to the function, but it is not used to communicate the results of the function to the outside world. Almost all of the parameters we have used so far have been input parameters.

FIGURE 8-11   Matchup of actual and formal parameters in a call to ***findmaxmin***

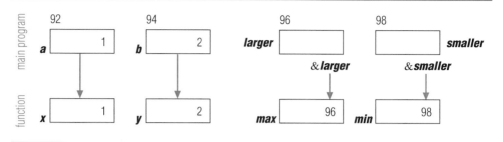

Finally, a parameter whose value is both used by the function and changed by the function is called an **input-output parameter**. In the function ***add1*** from Example 8-11, the value of the location pointed to by the parameter is incremented by the function. Since we use the value on input and modify it on output, it is an input-output parameter.

PARAMETER TRANSMISSION: PASSING BY VALUE

C has just one way of sending parameters to a function. This method is called passing a parameter by value or **call by value**. Before the function starts, the value of the argument or actual parameter is copied into the corresponding formal parameter (see Figure 8-12). That has the same effect as this assignment statement:

```
formalparameter = actualparameter;
```

The value of the formal parameter may or may not be changed in the function. However, when we return to the calling function, any change is not reflected in the corresponding argument (analogously, even if ***formalparameter*** changes, ***actualparameter*** does not). Thus, when the function is complete, the matching argument in the calling function has the same value that it had originally.

FIGURE 8-12   Passing a parameter by value

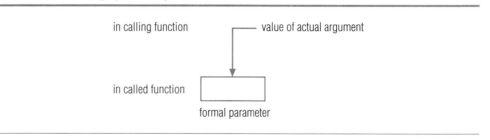

PARAMETER TRANSMISSION USING POINTERS AS PARAMETERS

However, a parameter can be a pointer, as we have just seen. In this case, the value sent to the function is the address of a variable. The address allows the function to access the value of the variable. The specific value sent as the argument, which is an address, does not change in the function. However, the value stored at that address can be changed.

Let's diagram what happens in the function header for *findmaxmin*:

$$\text{values} \qquad\qquad \text{pointers}$$
$$\downarrow \qquad \downarrow \qquad\quad \downarrow \qquad\qquad \downarrow$$
```
void findmaxmin(int x, int y, int *max, int *min)
```

This is paralleled by what happens in the call to the function:

$$\text{matched to values}$$
$$\downarrow \;\; \downarrow$$
```
findmaxmin(a+b,9,&c,&d);
```
$$\qquad\qquad\quad \uparrow \;\; \uparrow$$
$$\text{matched to pointers}$$

Since only the values of the first two actual arguments are needed in the function, they are not preceded by ampersands in the call. However, the third and fourth arguments, which are matched to the pointer parameters in the function, are preceded by ampersands so that their addresses (rather than their values) are sent to the function.

A FUNCTION TO INTERCHANGE THE VALUE OF ITS PARAMETERS

Assume we have two variables—call them *a* and *b*—and we want the value currently in *a* to be placed in *b*, while the value in *b* is moved to *a*. We want to do this swap in a function called *swap*, which interchanges the values of its two parameters.

This function is the classic example of why pointers as parameters are needed. If functions could not change parameters, such a swap function would be impossible. Since a function is restricted to returning a single value (or no value in a void function), we would have to choose between returning *a* or *b*. And even if we could somehow return both *a* and *b*, we could never actually interchange their values. Clearly, we need a new mechanism. However, before we can talk about the function, we have to discuss the simpler question of how to interchange the value of two variables.

INTERCHANGING TWO VALUES

The first idea that occurs to most people is simply to move *a* into *b* and *b* into *a*. That is, we can try something like this:

```
a = b;                                          /* incorrect */
b = a;
```

This seems easy enough, but it doesn't work.

Let's say, for example, *a* is 5 and *b* is 3 to start (see Figure 8-13A). We want *a* to become 3, and *b* to become 5. But this is not what occurs. The top line sets *a* to 3, which is fine (see Figure 8-13B); the bottom line sets *b* to the current value of *a*, which is 3, not the old value, which was 5 (see Figure 8-13C). Both *a* and *b* are now 3, which isn't what we want.

Changing the order of assignments doesn't help since both locations then end up holding the value 5:

```
b = a;                                              /* also incorrect */
a = b;
```

The problem is that we want *a* and *b* to change values simultaneously. But in a program, things aren't done simultaneously; one must come first. It seems that whichever statement comes first destroys the other value. How, then, can we swap two numbers?

Here is an analogy: If you have two boxes, one to your left and one to your right, how do you switch their positions? You pick both boxes up at the same time, then move your left hand to the right, and your right hand to the left.

But suppose you can use only one hand to switch the boxes.

◆ You move one box, say the left, temporarily to the middle (see Figure 8-14A).

◆ Then you move the box on the right to the vacant left position (see Figure 8-14B).

◆ Finally, you move the box in the middle to the right (see Figure 8-14C).

It takes three steps and requires an extra place to store the first box temporarily, but the exchange is possible.

FIGURE 8-13 Incorrect way to swap the values of *a* and *b*. A, the initial values; B, the values after *a = b*; C, the values after *b = a*.

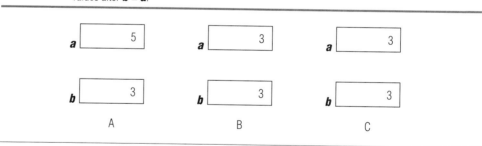

FIGURE 8-14 Correct way to interchange the positions of two boxes. A, step 1; B, step 2; C, step 3.

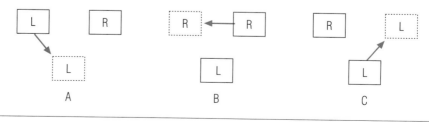

The same principle can be used to swap **a** and **b**. Here is an algorithm to perform this task:

Algorithm to Interchange the Values of *a* and *b*

- ◆ *Temporarily move **a** to some new location; call it **temp**. This saves the old value.*
- ◆ *Move **b** into **a**, destroying whatever was there.*
- ◆ *Finally, move **temp** into **b**, which has the effect of moving the original value of **a** into **b**.*

EXAMPLE 8-13   In C, the following three assignment statements swap the values of **a** and **b**:

```
temp = a;
a = b;                          /* swapping the values of */
b = temp;                       /* the variables a and b  */
```

There is only one way to modify the order of the steps. If we start with **temp = b**, then the continuation must be **b = a**, then **a = temp**.

There is a simple way to remember the correct order of statements. Each of the three variables (**a**, **b**, and **temp**) should appear on the left-hand side of one assignment statement and the right-hand side of another; the two uses of **a** and **b** can be connected by upward arrows as shown below:

```
temp = a;                                temp = b;

a = b;              or                   b = a;

b = temp;                                a = temp;
```

THE FUNCTION *swap*

Now let's see how to do the same thing in a function called **swap**. Our job is to write a function that receives two parameters. The function swaps or interchanges the values of two storage locations in the calling program. In order to change the values, the function has to receive pointers, rather than values. If **a** and **b** are pointers to integers, then **a* and **b* are the underlying values we want the function to swap.

EXAMPLE 8-14   Here is the complete function to swap the values of two variables:

```
/*
 * Function swap:
 * Input:
 *    a and b: pointers to two integer values
 * Process:
 *    interchange the values pointed to by a and b
 * Output:
 *    values have been interchanged
 */
```

```
void swap(int *a, int *b)
{
    int temp;

    temp = *a;
    *a = *b;
    *b = temp;
    return;
}
```

This is almost identical to the direct swap of two values in Example 8-13. The only difference is that *a and *b have replaced a and b.

CALLING *swap* FROM A MAIN PROGRAM

Now let's see how a main program (or any other function) uses the **swap** function.

EXAMPLE 8-14
(continued)

Here is a driver program to test **swap**:

```
/* driver program to test the function swap */
#include <stdio.h>
void swap (int *,int *);
main()
{
    int x,y;

    x = 5;
    y = 3;
    printf("before the call:\n");
    printf("x is: %d, and y is: %d\n",x,y);
    swap(&x,&y);
    printf("after the call:\n");
    printf("x is now: %d, and y is now: %d\n",x,y);
}
```

Note that the name of each variable to be interchanged must be preceded by an & so that an address is sent to the **swap** function. The address of x is matched to a, and that of y is matched to b. Inside the function, the values pointed to by a and b are exchanged, which means the values at the addresses &x and &y are interchanged. The overall effect of the function call is to swap the values of x and y.

If the driver program is run, the following prints:

```
before the call:
x is: 5, and y is: 3
after the call:
x is now: 3, and y is now: 5
```

THE FUNCTION *scanf*

Now that we have seen how to use pointers as parameters, we can explain how the function *scanf* works. Let's look back at the situation we have been discussing:

```
int num=5;

scanf("%d",&num);
```

$\rightarrow$ (at the site of the first arrow)

$\rightarrow$ (at the site of the second arrow)

At the site of the first arrow, before the call to the *scanf* function, *num* has the value 5 from the initialization in the declaration. At the site of the second arrow, after the call to the *scanf* function, *num* has whatever value has been read in by the function. The value of the storage location passed to the function changes as a result of the function call.

Now that we understand pointers as parameters, it is easy to explain exactly how the *scanf* function works. The header for the function[4] indicates that the second parameter is a pointer so that it can be matched to an address (in this case, the address of *num*). This parameter is an output parameter for *scanf* since only its value at the end of the function is important. Inside the function, the value referenced by that parameter is changed; the variable *num*, which is the corresponding object in the calling program, picks up the change; as a result of the function call, the value of *num* is modified.

SELF-CHECK 8-4

1. Show how to interchange the values of two variables *d1* and *d2* of type *double*.

2. If we are swapping the values of *a* and *b*, and the first step is *temp = b*, why is there only one possible continuation?

3. What happens if we forget to include an ampersand before the name of a variable in a call to *scanf*? What happens if we use the following call?

```
int num;

scanf("%d",num);
```

SECTION 3 **POINTERS AND ARRAYS**

In this section, we discuss the intimate relationship between pointers and arrays.

WHY ARRAYS ARE DIFFERENT

Now that you have seen what it takes for a function to change the value of one of its parameters, you may be wondering about an exception to this rule that we used in Program 7. We

---

[4]We have not shown the actual function header for *scanf* because additional features make it quite complicated.

wrote a function ***readdata*** which read values into the ***mark*** array without using pointer notation for the formal parameter and seemingly without sending an address as a parameter. Here are the function header and the call from the main program:

```
int readdata(int num[])                      /* function header */

n = readdata(mark);                          /* call to the function */
```

The function header declares ***num*** to be an array, but it does not have ∗ in front of the name; the call to the function uses the name of the array ***mark***, but it does not have & in front of the name. How can the function modify the array without these additional operators?

The answer to this question relates to the value C assigns to the name of an array. Suppose we have an array ***mark***, declared as follows:

```
int mark[5];
```

You know from Chapter 7 that the ***mark*** array has five elements, numbered from 0 to 4, and that it makes sense to refer to ***mark[0]*** or ***mark[3]***. In C, a reference to the name of an array, without a subscript, means the address of the array (see Figure 8-15). More precisely, the name of the array refers to the address of the element in position 0. Similarly, the notation we use in a function prototype or header to indicate that a parameter is an array (***int[]*** or ***int array[]***) also means that the parameter is an address.

When a main program sends an array as a parameter to a function, the array is assigned storage only in the main program. The function is told where this storage is located. When a main program (or any calling function) sends an array to a function, it sends the address of the array, not all the individual elements. The address allows the function to use the storage already allocated for the array without having to assign new space. Because the array name is itself an address, we do not preface it by an ampersand (&). In a function header that uses brackets to indicate an array, it is not necessary to use ∗ to make the formal parameter a pointer because the name of the array is already a pointer. Thus, a function can always change the values in an array.

THE USE OF ∗ IN THE FUNCTION HEADER FOR AN ARRAY PARAMETER

In fact, we can make the use of pointers explicit in the function header. If the formal parameter is, for example, an array of integers, we can use ***int ∗*** as its type instead of ***int []***. In this case, the function ***readdata*** can use the header below, which is equivalent to the original one above:

```
int readdata(int *num)                       /* an equivalent function header */
```

FIGURE 8-15   The name of an array

mark[0] mark[1] mark[2] mark[3] mark[4]

mark

This header says the formal parameter **num** is a pointer to an integer (the address of an integer), which is exactly the type of actual argument it is matched to as part of the function call.

STYLE WORKSHOP The * notation (as in **int** *) is often used in the header of a function that has an array as a parameter (especially an array of characters, as we will see in Chapter 9). The new header for **readdata** is completely equivalent to the function header which uses subscript notation (**int []**).

 CAUTION Despite the equivalence of **int []** and **int** * in a function header, the following declarations are *not* equivalent in a main program:

```
int num[100];        not equivalent to        int *num;
```

The declaration on the left sets aside space in memory for 100 consecutive storage locations, each of which holds an integer. The identifier **num** is the address of the first of these, position 0 in the group of storage locations (see Figure 8-16A).

The declaration on the right sets aside space in memory for one pointer variable, which points to the location of an integer. The identifier **num** holds the address of this location (see Figure 8-16B). There is not room to store 100 integers.

We discuss a further difference between these two declarations in the next example.

THE VALUE OF A POINTER VARIABLE VERSUS THE ADDRESS OF AN ARRAY

A pointer variable holds a value (an address); because it is a variable, its value can change. On the other hand, an array name is a constant, and it cannot change. For example, if **num** is an array, the name **num** holds a constant address—the address of the first location in the array. It is illegal to change this value.

EXAMPLE 8-15 Here is an example to clarify these points. First, let's look at some legal changes in the value of a pointer variable:

```
int a,b;
int *p;
int num[100];

p = &a;                                    /* these are all legal */
p = &b;
p = num;
```

PROGRAM TRACE The first few assignments give various values to the pointer variable *p*.

◆ First, *p* is assigned the address of *a* (see Figure 8-17A).

◆ Next, *p* is assigned the address of *b* (see Figure 8-17B). This changes the value of *p*.

◆ Finally, *p* is set to **num**, which means *p* holds the address of the first integer stored in the array (see Figure 8-17C). In each of these cases, the pointer variable is assigned the address of an integer, which is legal.

FIGURE 8-16 *A*, declaring an array versus *B*, declaring a pointer

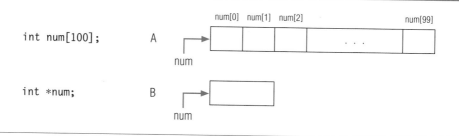

FIGURE 8-17 Changing the value of a pointer. *A*, after ***p = &a***; *B*, after ***p = &b***; *C*, after ***p = num***.

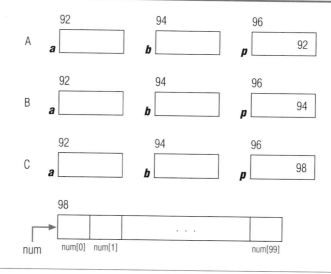

Example 8-16 shows that new values cannot be assigned to the name of an array, even though that name is a pointer.

EXAMPLE 8-16

```
int num[100];
int a;
int *p;

num = &a;                              /* these are illegal */
num = p;
```

Either assignment to ***num*** is illegal since ***num*** is a constant (holding the address of the first location in the array; see Figure 8-17C).

USING & TO SEND AN ADDRESS TO AN ARRAY PARAMETER

In the call to a function, we can explicitly send the address of a particular position in the array as a parameter. For example, we can call the function **readdata** with this statement:

```
n = readdata(&mark[0]);                    /* an equivalent function call */
```

In this call, the actual parameter to the function is the address of position 0 in the **mark** array. This address can be matched to either form of the formal parameter, *int ** or *int []*.

STYLE WORKSHOP Although sending the address of position 0 is equivalent to sending the name of the array as a parameter, this notation is not frequently used. It is much more common to specify the array name.

It is possible to use address notation to send the address of the third or fifth element in the array rather than the first. We exploit this idea in Chapter 9 when we work with arrays of characters. For now, here is a simple example that shows how to use address notation to sum a range of values in an array.

EXAMPLE 8-17   Let's start by recalling the function **sumarray** from Chapter 7:

```
/* ... */
int sumarray(int num[], int n)
{
    int sum,count;

    sum = 0;
    for (count = 0; count < n; count++)
        sum += num[count];
    return sum;
}
```

In Chapter 7, we used this function call to sum the first **n** elements in the **mark** array (positions 0 to **n – 1**):

```
sum = sumarray(mark,n);
```

To sum the array elements from **mark[5]** to **mark[11]**, we can use this call:

```
sum = sumarray(&mark[5],7);
```

By sending the address of a later position in the array, such as **&mark[5]**, we can sum values from that position. The address is matched to the corresponding formal parameter inside the function. We also have to adjust the second parameter, which says how many positions to sum. For example, to sum positions 5 to 11, we use 7, which is the number of elements (11 – 5 + 1).

In this call, **&mark[5]** is matched to **num** inside the function; **7** is matched to **n**. From the function's point of view, we are summing an array that starts at position 0 and goes on for seven locations (see Figure 8-18A). However, from the calling program's point of view, we are summing the **mark** array, starting at position 5 and going on for seven locations (see Figure 8-18B).

FIGURE 8-18 Using address notation to sum part of an array. *A*, the function's point of view; *B*, the calling program's point of view.

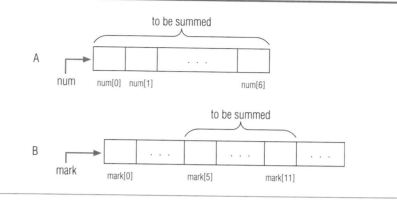

POINTER ARITHMETIC

C provides a method, called **pointer arithmetic**, for moving from one storage location to another. Through pointer arithmetic, it is possible to address the elements in an array without subscripts. Instead, we use direct address manipulation to move from one array element to the next. The technique uses **displacement** or **offset**, which is a measure of how far an element is from the beginning of the array.

In C, offset is measured in array positions or elements. Figure 8-19 shows array *num*, with the offset of each element from position 0. Note that the offset is measured in positions, not bytes; adjacent elements are exactly one position apart. This offset is independent of the size of the array elements.

If the array *num* has five elements, the first is at an offset of 0, since it is at the beginning of the array. The third element is at an offset or displacement of two positions from the beginning (one position from the second element). In either an array of *char* or one of type *double*, the fifth element is offset four positions from the first. However, each element in the array of *char* is much smaller than one in the array of type *double*.

FIGURE 8-19 Array *num*, declared by *int num[5];*

subscript	0	1	2	3	4
	10	25	45	50	68
offset	+0	+1	+2	+3	+4

REFERENCING ARRAY ELEMENTS USING POINTER NOTATION

We can reference array elements using pointer notation and move from one element to the next with pointer arithmetic. The following assignment statements give new values to the first and second elements of array **num**.

```
*(num+0) = 17;
*(num+1) = 54;
```

Note that adding 1 to **num** really means adding the number of bytes in an integer (either two or four) to its address.

The offset can be a variable, as shown in Example 8-18.

EXAMPLE 8-18   The following code shows how we can fill all the elements of array **num** with consecutive integers 15 through 19:

```
int i,count=15;
int num[5];

for (i = 0; i < 4; i++)  {
    *(num+i) = count;
    count++;
}
```

Subscript and pointer notation provide two equivalent ways to reference array elements. If **num** is an array, the following notations are completely equivalent, either in a main program or a function:

HIGHLIGHTS   num[i]   *is equivalent to*   *(num + i)

In the header for a function, these notations are also completely equivalent:

int num[]   *is equivalent to*   int *num

USING A POINTER VARIABLE TO PROCESS AN ARRAY

We can take advantage of pointer arithmetic to process an array using a pointer variable. This is illustrated in Example 8-19.

EXAMPLE 8-19   Consider the following *for* loop to sum the values in an array:

```
int i,sum=0;
int num[100];

for (i = 0; i < 100; i++)
    sum += num[i];
```

Using pointer notation, the **for** loop can be written as follows:

```
for (i = 0; i < 100; i++)
    sum += *(num + i);
```

We can also use a pointer variable to traverse an array without even mentioning the array in the body of the loop. Example 8-20 shows how to do this.

EXAMPLE 8-20

```
int *p;
int i,sum=0;
int num[100];

p = num;
for (i = 0; i < 100; i++)  {
    sum += *p;
    p++;
}
```

Before we trace this piece of code, note that the **for** loop header is the same as the one in Example 8-19. However, the body of the loop does not mention **i** (or the array **num**). This time, the sole purpose of the variable **i** is to count from 0 to 99 so that we go through the body of the loop 100 times. Traversing the array is accomplished by manipulating the pointer **p** (see Exercise 15).

PROGRAM TRACE   Let's go step by step through the processing of the array in Example 8-20.

♦   The assignment **p = num** assigns the address of the array to the pointer variable. After this assignment, **p** holds the address of the first element.

♦   Inside the body of the loop, because ***p** is **num[0]**, we add **num[0]** to **sum**.

♦   The next statement to be executed is **p++**, which increments the address stored in **p**. Therefore, **p** points to the next element in the array, which is **num[1]**.

♦   We add **num[1]** to **sum** and increment the address stored in **p**.

♦   Each time through the body of the loop, we add to **sum** the element pointed to by **p** and increment **p** so that it points to the next element in the array.

 CAUTION   It is tempting to use a statement like this to advance the pointer:

```
num++;                        /* illegal */
```

However, as we noted above, this is illegal because **num** is a constant.

SENDING THE ADDRESS OF A LOCATION IN AN ARRAY TO A FUNCTION

We can use pointer notation to send a function the address of a location in an array. Consider the function call from Example 8-17:

```
sum = sumarray(&mark[5],7);
```

This call, using an ampersand to supply the address of **mark[5]**, is equivalent to the following one, which uses an offset of 5 to select the address:

```
sum = sumarray(mark+5,7);
```

In this version of the call, the first parameter to the function is the address **mark+5**. Recall that this notation means five elements past the address of the beginning of the array. Therefore, it refers to the address of **mark[5]**, or **&mark[5]**, which is exactly what we used earlier. In fact, the form using an offset is probably more common than the one using the address operator.

SELF-CHECK 8-5

1. Use * notation to give the header for a void function called **arraywork** that receives one parameter, a pointer to an array called **values** of type **double**.

2. Use * notation to give the header for a void function **twochars** that receives two parameters, **s1** and **s2**, each of which is an array of characters.

3. Show how to call the function **sumarray** so that it finds the sum of the elements in positions 6 to 15 in an integer array called **x**.

SECTION 4 MODIFYING SOME FUNCTIONS FROM PROGRAM 7

In this section, we use the ideas introduced in this chapter to modify and expand the tasks of two of the functions from Program 7.

MODIFYING THE *readdata* FUNCTION

We will start by modifying the **readdata** function. Recall that this function received as a parameter an array called **num**. The function read in an integer **n**; then it read **n** data values into the **num** array. Finally, it returned the value of **n** to the main program. Thus the function communicated with the main program in two ways: by modifying an array and returning a value. It is usually considered better style to have a function communicate in just one way. Now that we know how to use pointers as parameters, we can modify **readdata** so that it changes two parameters, the array and the size. In that case, the function does not have to return an explicit value.

Let's first look at the original version of the function from Chapter 7, Section 5:

```
/* ... */
int readdata(int num[])
{
    int count,n;

    scanf("%d",&n);
    for (count = 0; count < n; count++)  {
```

```
            printf("Enter a mark> ");
            scanf("%d",&num[count]);
            printf("%d",num[count]);
        }
        return n;
    }
```

To modify the function, we alter the header by changing the return type from *int* to *void* and adding a new pointer parameter; we change the body of the function so that it uses the pointer parameter instead of the local variable *n*; and we do not return the value of *n* (instead, we modify the pointer parameter). The next example rewrites *readdata* so that it uses a parameter which is a pointer to return the number of elements in the array.

EXAMPLE 8-21   Here is the revised function *readdata*:

```
/*
 * Function readdata:
 * Input:
 *    n: the size of the array (pointer parameter)
 *          ...
 * Output:
 *          ...
 *    returns the size of the array as a pointer parameter
 */
void readdata(int num[], int *n)
{
    int count;

    scanf("%d",n);
    for (count = 0; count < *n; count++) {
        printf("Enter a mark> ");
        scanf("%d",&num[count]);
        printf("%d",num[count]);
    }
    return;
}
```

Note the following changes in the body of the function: First, since *n* is now a parameter, we no longer declare it to be a local variable. In addition, the *for* loop header is now this:

```
    for (count = 0; count < *n; count++)
```

In this case, we simply replace *n* by *∗n* since *n* is a pointer. The *return* statement is also modified so that it no longer returns an explicit value.

Finally, there is a strange modification in the call to *scanf*. We now use the following:

```
    scanf("%d",n);      instead of      scanf("%d",&n);
```

Since *n* is now a parameter which is a pointer, *∗n* refers to the value in its storage location; the call to *scanf* would say *& ∗n*. However, as we pointed out in Section 2, this is equivalent to just *n*.

MODIFYING THE MAIN PROGRAM TO CALL THE NEW VERSION OF *readdata*

In the next section, we rewrite Program 7 using pointers and include a main program to call the revised function *readdata*. In the meantime, here are the new function prototype, with one array and one pointer parameter, and the new call to the function, sending two parameters, the array *mark* and the address of *n*.

```
void readdata(int [], int *);        /* function prototype */

readdata(mark,&n);                   /* call to the function */
```

MODIFYING THE FUNCTION *findmax* TO A NEW FUNCTION *findlimits*

We also expand the function *findmax* from Program 7, giving it an additional task. In Chapter 7, Section 6, the original function found the largest value in the array and returned it to the main program. The new function, *findlimits*, finds both the largest and smallest values in the array, returning both (via parameters which are pointers) to the main program. This function illustrates how parameters which are pointers permit a function to send back more than one value.[5]

Unlike *findmax*, the new function does not return an explicit answer; instead, it communicates with the main program by modifying two parameters which are pointers, *largest* and *smallest*. Inside the body of the function, *largest* is set to the largest value stored in the array, and *smallest* to the smallest.

EXAMPLE 8-22   Here is the entire new function *findlimits*, showing all changes:

```
/*
 * Function findlimits:
 * Input:
   ...
 *   largest, smallest: pointer parameters which
 *   will be set to the largest and smallest values
 * Process:
 *   finds the largest and smallest values in the
 *   first n elements of the num array
 * Output:
 *   modifies two pointer parameters largest and
 *   smallest to hold these values
 */
void findlimits(int num[], int n, int *largest, int *smallest)
{
    int largestsofar,smallestsofar,count;
```

---

[5]The function *findlimits* is similar to *findmaxmin* in Section 2, so we only sketch its development. The new function finds the largest and smallest values in an array, whereas *findmaxmin* found the larger and smaller of just two values.

```
        largestsofar = num[0];
        smallestsofar = num[0];
        for (count = 1; count < n; count++)  {
            if (largestsofar < num[count])
                largestsofar = num[count];
            if (smallestsofar > num[count])
                smallestsofar = num[count];
        }
        *largest = largestsofar;
        *smallest = smallestsofar;
        return;
    }
```

Note that we compute both the largest value in the array and the smallest in a single loop; this can also be done in two separate loops. Also note that we use local variables *largestsofar* and *smallestsofar*. We could instead use **largest* and **smallest*. The next section shows how to call this function from the main program.

MODIFYING THE FUNCTION *countmarks*

Finally, we modify the function *countmarks*. The original function received three parameters: the array *num*, the number of elements *n*, and the average *avgnum*. The function used local variables *numless*, *numgreater*, and *numequal* to determine how many values were above, below, and equal to the average, and it printed these three counters. The new version uses the three counters as pointer parameters to carry values back to the main program. The new function header looks like this:

```
void countmarks(int num[], int n, double avgnum, int *numless,
                int *numgreater, int *numequal)
```

The function now uses **numless*, **numgreater*, and **numequal* to refer to the three counters.

EXAMPLE 8-23   Below is the complete new function *countmarks*. Note that printing has shifted to the main program.

```
/*
 * Function countmarks:
 * Input:
 *   ...
 *   numless, numgreater, numequal: pointers to three counters
 *   ...
 *   modifies the pointer parameters to hold the counts
 */
void countmarks(int num[], int n, double avgnum, int *numless,
                int *numgreater, int *numequal)
{
    int count;
```

(continued)

(continued)

```
        *numless = 0;
        *numgreater = 0;
        *numequal = 0;

        for (count = 0; count < n; count++)
            if (num[count] < avgnum)
                (*numless)++;
            else if (num[count] > avgnum)
                (*numgreater)++;
            else
                (*numequal)++;
        return;
    }
```

The next section shows how to call the new version of ***countmarks*** from the main program.

SELF-CHECK 8-6

1. In the new version of the function ***readdata*** (Example 8-21), why must the first call to ***scanf*** (which reads the number of elements in the array) be the following?

   `scanf("%d",n);`   *instead of*   `scanf("%d",&n);`

2. What are the differences between finding the largest value in an array and finding the smallest?

3. Show how to rewrite ***findlimits*** using *largest* and *smallest* for the comparisons, instead of the local variables ***largestsofar*** and ***smallestsofar***.

SECTION 5   ## PROGRAM 8: USING POINTER NOTATION FOR THE ARRAYS IN PROGRAM 7

In this section, we rewrite Program 7 and combine it with the new versions of the functions from the last section, this time using pointer notation for the arrays.

RULES FOR USING POINTER NOTATION IN A FUNCTION

Recall from Section 3 the following rules for pointer notation for array elements:

◆ If ***num*** is an array, these forms of notation are completely equivalent, either in a main program or a function:

   `num[i]`   *is equivalent to*   `*(num + i)`

◆ In the header or prototype for a function (but only there), these forms of notation are completely equivalent:

   `int num[]`   *is equivalent to*   `int *num`

We use these two rules to rewrite the various functions from Program 7.

REWRITING THE FUNCTION *readdata* USING POINTER NOTATION

Let's start by rewriting the **readdata** function. We use the version from Section 4, which has two parameters, and modify the function header and body according to our two rules. Here is the entire new version of the function **readdata**:

```
/* ... */
void readdata(int *num, int *n)
{
    int count;

    scanf("%d",n);
    for (count = 0; count < *n; count++) {
        printf("Enter a mark>");
        scanf("%d",num + count);
        printf("%d",*(num + count));
    }
    return;
}
```

Note that the second call to **scanf** replaces **&*(num + count)** with **num + count**, which is equivalent.

REWRITING THE FUNCTION *findlimits*

Now let's rewrite the function **findlimits** from Section 4. Once again, the two rules make the process straightforward.

```
/* ... */
void findlimits(int *num, int n, int *largest, int *smallest)
{
    int largestsofar,smallestsofar,count;

    largestsofar = *num;
    smallestsofar = *num;
    for (count = 0; count < n; count++)  {
        if (largestsofar < *(num + count))
            largestsofar = *(num + count);
        if (smallestsofar > *(num + count))
            smallestsofar = *(num + count);
    }
    *largest = largestsofar;
    *smallest = smallestsofar;
    return;
}
```

Note the initializations for **largestsofar** and **smallestsofar**. The notation ***num** means the value stored at the address of the first element in the array, exactly what we want as the initial value.

The other functions, **sumarray** and **avgarray**, are even easier to rewrite with pointer notation and are shown with the entire rewritten program below.

USING POINTER NOTATION IN THE MAIN PROGRAM

As we discussed in Section 3, the main program must still use subscript notation to declare the **mark** array. In the calls to the functions **readdata** and **findlimits**, the main program uses an ampersand each time it needs to send an address which is not an array. However, the calls to the remaining functions are unchanged. Finally, the function prototypes can use either subscript or pointer notation to indicate array parameters.

PROGRAM 8 (PROGRAM 7 MODIFIED AND REWRITTEN USING POINTER NOTATION)

Here is entire Program 8, using pointer notation in the function prototypes. In most cases, the comments have been abbreviated.

🖥 PROGRAM LISTING

```
/*
 *  Program prog8.c:
 *  rewrite Program 7 using pointer notation
 *  and modify a few of the old functions
 */
#include <stdio.h>
#define SIZE 50
void readdata(int *, int *);
int sumarray(int *, int);
double avgarray(int *, int);
void findlimits(int *, int, int *, int *);
void countmarks(int *, int, double, int *, int *, int *);
main()
{
    int     n;
    int     mark[SIZE];
    double  avgmark;
    int     higrade;
    int     lograde;
    int     less,greater,equal;

    /* call the functions to read and process the marks */
    printf("The grades for the class:\n");
```

```
        readdata(mark,&n);
        avgmark = avgarray(mark,n);
        printf("The average grade in the class is %6.2f\n",avgmark);
        findlimits(mark,n,&higrade,&lograde);
        printf("The highest grade in the class is %d\n",higrade);
        printf("The lowest grade in the class is %d\n",lograde);

        countmarks(mark,n,avgmark,&less,&greater,&equal);
        printf("The number of marks less than the average is %d\n",less);
        printf("The number of marks greater than the average is %d\n",greater);
        printf("The number of marks equal to the average is %d\n",equal);
}

/* ... */
void readdata(int *num, int *n)
{
    int count;

    scanf("%d",n);
    for (count = 0; count < *n; count++) {
        printf("Enter a mark>");
        scanf("%d",num + count);
        printf("%d",*(num + count));
    }
    return;
}

/* ... */
int sumarray(int *num, int n)
{
    int sum,count;

    sum = 0;
    for (count = 0; count < n; count++)
        sum += *(num + count);
    return sum;
}

/* ... */
double avgarray(int *num, int n)
{
    return (double) sumarray(num,n) / n;
}

/* ... */
void findlimits(int *num, int n, int *largest, int *smallest)
{
```

(continued)

(*continued*)

```
    int largestsofar,smallestsofar,count;

    largestsofar = *num;
    smallestsofar = *num;
    for (count = 0; count < n; count++)  {
        if (largestsofar < *(num + count))
            largestsofar = *(num + count);
        if (smallestsofar > *(num + count))
            smallestsofar = *(num + count);
    }
    *largest = largestsofar;
    *smallest = smallestsofar;
    return;
}

/* ... */
void countmarks(int *num, int n, double avgnum, int *numless,
                int *numgreater, int *numequal)
{
    int count;

    *numless = 0;
    *numgreater = 0;
    *numequal = 0;

    for (count = 0; count < n; count++)
        if (*(num + count) < avgnum)
            (*numless)++;
        else if (*(num + count) > avgnum)
            (*numgreater)++;
        else
            (*numequal)++;

    return;
}
```

SELF-CHECK 8-7

1. In the function **readdata**, when we refer to elements of the array **num**, the call to **printf** uses a *, but the call to **scanf** does not. Why?

2. In the header for the function **findlimits**, **int** * is used as the data type for three of the parameters. Explain what it means in each case.

3. Rewrite the function prototypes for Program 8 using subscript notation for each array.

SUMMARY

ADDRESSES AND THE ADDRESS OPERATOR &

1. The memory of a computer is divided into small units called bytes. Each byte has a number associated with it, called its address. A byte is further subdivided into eight smaller components called bits; each bit can hold a single 1 or 0. However, individual bits do not have addresses.

2. Each variable in memory holds a value; in addition, each variable has an address, which identifies its position in memory. (If the variable occupies more than one byte, the address is that of the first.) If *num* is a variable in memory, *&num* is the address of the variable. For example, the statement below reads an integer value into the storage location which is the address of the variable *num*.

```
scanf("%d",&num);
```

3. The address operator & can take the address of any variable but not that of an expression. The variable *x* has an address, denoted by *&x*. However, an expression like *x+1* has no address.

POINTERS AND ADDRESSES

4. A pointer variable can point to or hold the address of another variable. A pointer variable is also called a pointer.

5. Here are the declarations for two pointer variables, *iptr* and *dptr*, and a way to assign each one the address of a storage location in memory:

```
int     num,val;
double  avg;
int     *iptr;
double *dptr;
```

```
iptr = &num;
dptr = &avg;
```

The third line of the declaration says that *iptr* is a variable of type pointer to *int*, which means *iptr* can hold the address of an integer. The first assignment statement gives *iptr* the value of the address of *num*. Similarly, *dptr* is declared to be a pointer to *double*, and the second assignment statement gives it the value of the address of *avg*, a variable of type *double*.

THE DEREFERENCING OPERATOR *

6. The * or dereferencing operator can be used to reference the value stored at a particular address stored in a pointer. When part of an expression, **iptr* refers to the value stored at the location *iptr* points to. This is called indirect addressing. Here is an example, using the variables already declared:

```
iptr = &num;
val = *iptr + 1;
```

The first assignment sets *iptr* to the address of *num*; the second changes *val* so that it holds one more than the value stored in *num*.

7. By using **iptr* on the left-hand side of an assignment statement, a program can change the value stored at a particular address. Here is an example, using the same variables:

```
iptr = &num;
*iptr = *iptr + 1;
```

The first statement sets *iptr* to the address of *num*. In the second statement, **iptr* on the right-hand side refers to the value of *num*; **iptr* on the left-hand side refers to the address of the variable *num*. The value in the location that *iptr* points to (the value of *num*) is incremented by 1.

8. Using *p* on the right-hand side of an assignment statement accesses the value at a storage location; this is called an r-value. Using *p* on the left-hand side of an assignment statement changes the value at the location whose address is stored in *p*; this is called an l-value.

9. The increment operator can also be used with a pointer as shown below. In this form, the parentheses are necessary because the precedence of ++ is higher than that of the * operator.

```
(*iptr)++;
```

This statement is equivalent to the following:

```
*iptr = *iptr + 1;
```

USING POINTERS IN FUNCTIONS

10. Because a pointer can be used to change the value stored at a particular address, a function can employ pointers to achieve the indirect effect of modifying one or more arguments in the calling function. Here is an example of a function that adds 7 to the values pointed to by both formal parameters:

```
void add7(int *p, int *q)
{
    *p += 7;
    *q += 7;
    return;
}
```

Each formal parameter has type *int* *, which means that each holds an address. The body of the function adds 7 to the values stored at those addresses. Since it is a void function, **add7** does not directly return these new values. However, the calling function can access them.

11. Here is a main program that uses the function **add7**:

```
#include <stdio.h>
void add7(int *,int *);
main()
{
    int a=5,b=3;

    printf("the original values are: ");
    printf("%d and %d\n",a,b);
    add7(&a,&b);
    printf("the new values are: ");
    printf("%d and %d\n",a,b);
}
```

The main program sends the addresses (**&a** and **&b**) of two variables (**a** and **b**) as parameters to the function. The function has the effect of adding 7 to the values stored at these addresses. The main program prints the following:

```
the original values are: 5 and 3
the new values are: 12 and 10
```

INTERCHANGING THE VALUES OF TWO VARIABLES

12. Parameters which hold addresses are called pointer parameters or parameters which are pointers. One important use of parameters which are pointers is in a function to interchange or swap two values. In the function **swap** below, three statements, plus an additional variable, are needed to interchange the values.

```
void swap(int *a, int *b)
{
    int temp;

    temp = *a;
    *a = *b;
    *b = temp;
    return;
}
```

13. A calling function can use the following call to *swap* to interchange the values of two variables *day1* and *day2*:

```
swap(&day1,&day2);
```

The arguments sent to the function are the addresses of the two variables. After the call to the function, the values of these variables are interchanged.

14. If a formal parameter is used only to carry a value into a function, it is called an input parameter to the function. A formal parameter which is used only to send an answer back to the calling function is called an output parameter. If the formal parameter's original value is used, and the same parameter is also used to return a value, it is called an input-output parameter. Most of the formal parameters so far have been input parameters. The parameters *p* and *q* from paragraph 10 are input-output parameters.

CALL BY VALUE AND THE USE OF PARAMETERS WHICH ARE POINTERS

15. C has only one way of transmitting a parameter to a function. The method is called passing a parameter by value or call by value. At the time the function is called, the actual argument is evaluated, and its value is assigned to the corresponding formal parameter. A change in the value of the formal parameter does not change the corresponding actual parameter.

16. By using parameters which are pointers, it is possible for a function to modify variables in the calling function. If the formal parameter is a pointer, the called function receives the address or storage location of the corresponding argument. Using the dereferencing operator, the called function can access and/or modify the value stored at this address.

17. An array name is the address of the first element in the array. When an array is sent as an actual parameter to a function, the corresponding formal parameter is a pointer to the first element in the array. This means that, if the array is modified in the function, the calling function recognizes the change in the corresponding actual argument.

POINTER ARITHMETIC

18. If *p* is a pointer, then *p + 2* refers to an element which is two storage locations past the address that *p* is pointing to. This notation, called pointer arithmetic, can be used instead of subscript notation to refer to elements of an array. If the array *num* is declared as shown, then the expressions on the left and right are completely equivalent ways to refer to the array and its elements:

```
int num[10];
```

num	*is equivalent to*	&num
num[0]	*is equivalent to*	*(num + 0)
	or just	*num
num[5]	*is equivalent to*	*(num + 5)
num[i]	*is equivalent to*	*(num + i)

19. In the header for a function (or in a function prototype), the following are equivalent ways to refer to an array of integers:

```
void func(int *num)
```

is equivalent to

```
void func(int num[])
```

In either case, the formal parameter *num* is a pointer to *int* because the array name *num* is simply the address of the first element. Only the address of the first element of an array is sent to a function, not the entire set of storage locations in the array.

EXERCISES

TRACING EXERCISES

1. What is printed by the following program?

```c
#include <stdio.h>
void whatisit(int *, int *);
main()
{
    int m=5,n=13,p=7;

    printf("m is: %d, n is: %d, p is: %d\n",m,n,p);
    whatisit(&m,&n);
    printf("m is: %d, n is: %d, p is: %d\n",m,n,p);
    whatisit(&p,&n);
    printf("m is: %d, n is: %d, p is: %d\n",m,n,p);
    whatisit(&p,&m);
    printf("m is: %d, n is: %d, p is: %d\n",m,n,p);
}

void whatisit(int *a, int *b)
{
    int temp;

    if (*a < *b)  {
        temp = *a;
        *a = *b;
        *b = temp;
    }
    return;
}
```

2. Here are a main program and two functions. Show what is printed as this program is executed.

```c
#include <stdio.h>
int findval(int,int);
void compute(int,int,int,int *);
main()
{
    int w,x,y,z;

    for (x = 5; x >=1; x--)  {
        y = 3;
        z = findval(x,y);
        compute(x,y,z,&w);
        printf("%d %d %d %d\n",x,y,z,w);
    }
}
```

```
void compute(int a, int b, int c, int *d)
{
    if (a > b)
        *d = a + c;
    else
        *d = a + b;
    return;
}

int findval(int a, int b)
{
    int c;

    c = a + b;
    if (c > 4)
        return a;
    return c + a;
}
```

3. a. Show what is printed by the following program.

```
#include <stdio.h>
void changer(int, int *);
main()
{
    int a = 4, b = 6, c = 2;

    changer(b,&a);
    printf("MAIN %d %d %d\n",a,b,c);
    a = 15;      b = 25;      c = 20;
    changer(a,&c);
    printf("MAIN %d %d %d\n",a,b,c);
}

void changer(int first, int *second)
{
    int c;

    printf("TOP %d %d\n",first,*second);
    if (first < *second)
        c = -1;
    else c = 10;
    first += c;
    *second = *second * c;
    printf("BOTTOM %d %d %d\n",first,*second);
    return;
}
```

b. Consider the following calls to the function *changer* (they use the variables declared in the main program). Mark each one as valid or invalid. If you mark a call as invalid, explain why.

(1) b = changer(a,&b)   (2) changer(a+1,&b)   (3) changer(a, &b+1)

4. The person using the program below is ready to type in the integers 1 to 10 in order. However, the program may stop before the user can type in all these values. Show exactly what is printed by the program before it stops.

```c
#include <stdio.h>
void add(int *);
void subtract(int *);
main()
{
    int x = 22, y = 1;

    while (y != 5)  {
        scanf("%d",&y);
        printf("%d and %d\n",x,y);
        if (y == 1)
            add(&x);
        if (y == 2)
            subtract(&x);
        if (y == 3)
            x *= 2;
        if (y == 4)
            printf("illegal input\n");
        if (y == 5)
            printf("no action\n");
    }
    printf("\nat the end: %d and %d\n",x,y);
}

void add(int *w)
{
    *w += 5;
    printf("in add: %d\n",*w);
    return;
}

void subtract(int *z)
{
    *z -= 10;
    printf("in subtract: %d\n",*z);
    return;
}
```

5. a. Show what is printed by the following program.
   b. Modify the program so that it no longer returns a value; instead, (1) the function becomes a void function; and (2) the second parameter to the function is a pointer, and the function uses it to return an answer.
   c. Show what the new program prints.

```c
#include <stdio.h>
int add(int, int);
main()
{
    int a,sum,ans;
```

```
            ans = 0;
            for (a = 1; a <= 5; a++)  {
                ans += add(a,sum);
                printf("in main: %d %d\n",a,ans);
            }
        }

        int add(int a, int sum)
        {
            if (a != 3)
                sum += 10 * a;
            else
                sum = 100;
            printf("in add: %d %d\n",a,sum);
            return sum;
        }
```

6. Show what is printed by the following program.

```
#include <stdio.h>
void flipit(int *, int *,int);
main( )
{
    int a = 2, b = 5, c = 10, *f;

    f = &a;
    printf("first: %d %d %d %d\n",a,b,c,*f);
    flipit(&b,f,c);
    printf("now: %d %d %d %d \n",a,b,c,*f);
}

void flipit(int *p, int *q, int r)
{
    (*p)++;
    (*q)++;
    r = (*p) * (*q);
    printf("in flipit: %d %d %d\n",*p,*q,r);
    return;
}
```

7. Show what is printed by the following program.

```
#include <stdio.h>
int notachanger(int, int);
main( )
{
    int e=15,f=6,g=3;

    e = notachanger(f,g);
    printf("in the main pgm: %d %d %d\n",e,f,g);
}
```

(continued)

(*continued*)
```
int notachanger(int a,int b)
{
     int c = 5;

     a++;
     c = b + a;
     b = b % 2;
     printf("in notachanger: %d %d %d\n",a,b,c);
     return c;
}
```

8. Show what is printed by the following program.

```
#include <stdio.h>
int flipagain(int, int *, int *);
main( )
{
     int a = 2, b = 5, c = 7, f[3];

     f[0] = 10;
     f[1] = 100;
     f[2] = -10;
     printf("first: %d %d %d %d %d %d\n",a,b,c,f[0],f[1],f[2]);

     c = flipagain(a,&b,f);
     printf("now: %d %d %d %d %d %d\n",a,b,c,f[0],f[1],f[2]);
}

int flipagain(int q, int *p, int *r)
{
     int s;

     q++;
     *(r+1) += 5;
     *(r+2) -= 3;
     s = (*p) * (*r);
     printf("in flipagain: %d %d %d\n",*r, *(r+1), *(r+2));
     printf("still here: %d %d %d\n",q, *p, s);
     return s;
}
```

9. Show what is printed by the following program.

```
#include <stdio.h>
void adder(int, int *);
main( )
{
     int x,z = 7;

     x = 5;
     printf("first: %d %d\n",x,z);
     adder(x,&z);
```

```
          printf("second: %d %d\n",x,z);
    }

    void adder(int a, int *b)
    {
        a++;
        (*b)++;
        printf("third: %d %d\n",a,*b);
        return;
    }
```

10. Show what is printed by the following program.

```
    #include <stdio.h>
    void somechanges(int *, int *, int);
    int answer(int,int);
    main()
    {
        int a=20, b=7, c=5;
        int result;

        result = answer(a,b);
        printf("%d %d %d %d\n",result,a,b,c);

        somechanges(&a,&b,c);
        printf("%d %d %d\n",a,b,c);

        a = 1;
        b = 8;
        c = 6;
        somechanges(&a,&b,c);
        printf("%d %d %d\n",a,b,c);
    }

    void somechanges(int *a, int *b, int c)
    {
        *a += 4;
        c--;
        if (*a > *b)
            if (*b < c)
                    *a = 15;
            else
                    *b = 100;
        else
            c += 1000;
        printf("in change %d %d %d\n",*a,*b,c);
        return;
    }

    int answer(int x,int y)
    {
        int c,d;
```

(continued)

(*continued*)

```
        c = x / y + 3;
        d = x % (y + 3);
        printf("c is %d, d is %d\n",c,d);
        if (c > d)
            return c;
        else
            return d;
}
```

11. Show what is printed by the following program.

```
#include <stdio.h>
void modify(int, int *);
main( )
{
        int x,z = 7;
        int *y = &z;

        x = 5;
        printf("first: %d %d %d \n",x,z,*y);
        printf("second: %d \n",*&x);

        modify(x,y);
        printf("third: %d %d %d \n",x,z,*y);
}

void modify(int a, int *b)
{
        a++;
        (*b)++;
        printf("%d %d\n",a,*b);
        return;
}
```

ANALYSIS EXERCISES

12. Show the result when the conversion specification **%p** is used to print the value of a pointer. To do this, take each of the examples in Section 1 that print a pointer using **%u** and replace **%u** by **%p**. What can you conclude about the use of **%u** versus **%p**?

13. a. Show how to use the **sizeof** operator to determine the number of bytes your compiler allocates to a variable of type **double**.

    b. Do the same for a variable of type **char** (do you think this changes from one compiler to another?).

    c. Do the same for some other types—e.g., **float**, **long**, and **short**.

14. Assume we are processing an array of integers **num** which has been sent as a parameter to a function. In addition to the array, the function gets another parameter **n**, which is the number of elements to be processed.

a. In the function, there are two basic ways to represent the array: using subscripts or pointer notation. For each way, give the function header, the *for* loop header, and the details of how the body of the loop references the elements of the array.

b. In the main program, there is only one way to declare this array. What is it?

c. Why is the main program only allowed to use one way? What is wrong with the other method?

15. This exercise refers to Example 8-20.

    a. Can the body of the loop be replaced by either of the statements shown below?

       (1) `sum += *(p++);`   (2) `sum += (*p)++;`

       If the parentheses are removed from either one, are the operations still done in the same order?

    b. Can the header of the loop (and the assignment statement above it) be replaced by the following?

       `for (p = num; p < num + 100; p++);`

       If yes, explain how this works. If no, explain why it does not work.

PROGRAMMING PROJECTS

16. a. Write a function *findaverage* which finds the average of the values in an array. The function uses pointer notation to process the array. The parameters to the function are a pointer to an array of type *double* and an integer representing the size of the array.

    b. Show how to call the function *findaverage* from a main program and print the average. The main program sends *findaverage* an array *numbers*, consisting of ten elements. The answer returned is stored in a variable the main program calls *the_avg*.

    c. In the main program, give the function prototype and the declaration for each variable mentioned in the call to the function.

17. Write a function *makefirstmax* which receives the addresses of two integer parameters, *a* and *b*. The function stores the larger of the two values at the address of *a* and stores the smaller at the address of *b*.

18. a. Write a void function, *changetoavg*, which has three parameters:

       numbs—an array of values of type *double*

       n—an integer from 1 to 100, representing the number of values in the *numbs* array

       avg—a pointer to a value of type *double*

    The function determines the average of the first *n* elements in the *numbs* array. It prints this average and stores the result in **avg*. Then the function sets each of the first *n* elements in the array to the value computed for the average.

    For example, assume that *n* is 4 and the array holds 5.0 –7.0 3.0 6.0. The function prints a message saying the average is 1.75, stores the average, and changes each of the first four elements of the array to this value. The new array holds these values: 1.75 1.75 1.75 1.75.

b. Write a main program that uses the function ***changetoavg*** to modify the first 20 elements in an array called ***xyz***, storing the average in a variable called ***xyzavg***. When the function returns, the main program prints the average and the new values in the array. Assume that the array ***xyz*** holds no more than 100 values of type ***double***.

19. Rewrite Program 6 so that the main program calls a function to read in the two data values (a month and day). The function sends this information back to the main program using pointer parameters. Why isn't this method used in the original version of Program 6?

20. Rewrite Program 3 so that it uses a function to read in the payroll data for each employee (the ID number, hours worked, and rate of pay). What other changes will you have to make to the program? (*Hint*: The original program reads in the data in various places.)

21. In paragraph 10 of the chapter summary, there is a (void) function called ***add7*** that adds 7 to the location pointed to by each of its parameters. Assume that a program wants to add some value other than 7 to a group of variables.

   a. Is it possible to use ***add7***?
   b. Show how to modify ***add7*** to a new function, ***addk***, that does the following: The function ***addk*** receives three parameters. The first two (***p*** and ***q***) are the same as the two parameters to ***add7***; the third, ***k***, specifies the value to add to ***p*** and ***q***.
   c. Show how to call ***addk*** from a main program so that it does each of the following jobs: adds 10 to ***x*** and ***z***; adds –3 to ***bob*** and ***jennifer***; adds 7 to ***time*** and ***rate***; adds ***bonus*** (a variable) to ***pay1*** and ***pay2***.

22. Write a function, ***countem***, which does the following. Given an array of ***n*** integers, the function counts how many of the array elements are positive, how many are negative, and how many are 0. Using parameters which are pointers, the function returns these three counters.

23. Write a complete program containing a main program and a function to do the following: The main program calls a function to read in an arbitrary number of integer values. (You decide how to detect the end of the set of data—see Chapter 7, Section 9). The function counts how many values are positive, how many are negative, and how many are 0. The function uses pointer parameters to return these counters to the main program where they are printed. (*Note*: The individual values read in do not have to be stored anywhere.)

24. Rewrite the function from Exercise 23 so that it stores the counts in an array of counters, rather than three separate pointer variables. Modify the main program so that it uses the new version of the function.

25. Write a complete program to do the following:

   a. Write a function called ***readdata*** which receives two parameters, an integer ***n*** and an array of integers called ***vals***. The function is sent a value for ***n***. It reads in ***n*** integers, storing the data values in the array ***vals***. Print the data values as they are read in. In this and the other functions, use pointer notation to represent the array.
   b. Write a function called ***countzeros*** which receives two parameters, an integer ***n*** and an array ***vals***. The function counts how many of the first ***n*** elements of the ***vals*** array are 0. Print the number of 0 values (in either the main program or the function). For example, if the array holds 66 0 –4 0 4 31 with ***n*** = 6, it has two 0 values.
   c. Write a function called ***add4toall*** which adds 4 to each element stored in the array (it receives the same two parameters as ***countzeros***). Assume the array initially holds 66 0 –4 0 4 31 with ***n*** = 6; after the function call, the array holds 70 4 0 4 8 35.

d.   Write a main program which calls these functions. First the main program reads in an integer which it calls **size**. Then the main program calls **readdata** to read a set of data containing **size** elements into an array called **numbers**, which contains no more than 100 integers. Then the main program calls the function **countzeros** to find how many of the **size** array elements are 0. Next, the main program calls **add4toall** to modify the **numbers** array. The new values in the array are printed (in either the main program or the function). Finally, the main program calls the function **countzeros** again to determine how many elements in the new array are 0.

26. Write a complete program to do the following: The main program calls a function **readdata** to read in a set of integers representing IQ scores. Then the main program calls another function **aboveandbelow**, which determines how many of the scores are above 100 and how many are 100 or below. The function sends these two counters back to the main program where they are printed.

Write the functions two ways, once using subscript notation and once using pointer notation for the arrays. (In **aboveandbelow**, you need to use pointer notation for the counters regardless of what notation is used for the array.)

27. The Euclidean Algorithm is a convenient way to compute the greatest common divisor (*gcd*) of two numbers without doing any division. The *gcd* of two positive integers, x and y, is the largest integer, k, that evenly divides both x and y. For example, the *gcd* of 8 and 4 is 4; the *gcd* of 18 and 14 is 2; the *gcd* of 6 and 5 is 1.

The Euclidean Algorithm works as follows (assume that $x >= y$): subtract y from x, getting a result of z. Then subtract the smaller of y and z from the larger. Repeat this process until 0 is reached for the result of a subtraction. The last non-zero value is the *gcd* of x and y. Here are some examples:

$18 - 14 = 4, 14 - 4 = 10, 10 - 4 = 6, 6 - 4 = 2, 4 - 2 = 2, 2 - 2 = 0.$

Therefore, 2 (the last non-zero value) is the *gcd* of 18 and 14.

$6 - 5 = 1, 5 - 1 = 4, 4 - 1 = 3, 3 - 1 = 2, 2 - 1 = 1, 1 - 1 = 0.$

Therefore, 1 is the *gcd* of 6 and 5.

Write a program which uses the Euclidean Algorithm to compute the *gcd*. The program should have at least three functions. One function reads in two data values. The other two divide up the algorithm: one subtracts the smaller value from the larger, and the other subtracts the most recent subtraction result from the previous smaller value (or vice versa).

CHARACTER STRINGS

SYNTAX CONCEPTS: array of **char**, **char** ∗ data type, null character, functions from **string.h**, functions from **ctype.h**, input/output functions for characters and strings, **NULL** constant, strings as parameters, arrays of strings

PROGRAMMING CONCEPTS: replacing one string by another, editing a text

CONTROL STRUCTURES: pointer notation, using a flag

HOW TO READ CHAPTER 9

Section 1 is required for all but Section 6. Section 2 is not required for Section 3. Section 5, however, depends on sections 1 through 4. Section 6 is independent of the rest of the chapter and can be covered at any time after functions. Section 7 requires only sections 1 and 2, but Section 4 is helpful.

OUTLINE:

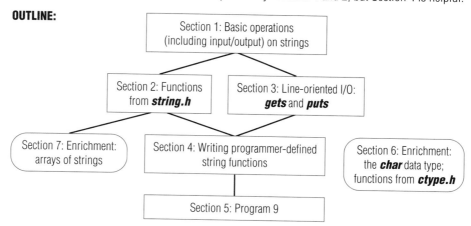

Section 1: Basic operations (including input/output) on strings

Section 2: Functions from **string.h**

Section 3: Line-oriented I/O: **gets** and **puts**

Section 7: Enrichment: arrays of strings

Section 4: Writing programmer-defined string functions

Section 6: Enrichment: the **char** data type; functions from **ctype.h**

Section 5: Program 9

INTRODUCTION AND STATEMENT OF THE PROBLEM

C has no string data type. Despite this fact, there are obviously strings in C: we have printed strings like "Admit" or "The table is finished". In fact, C has numerous library functions for string input/output and manipulation. This chapter discusses how strings are handled in C.

In this chapter, you will learn how to assign a value to an array of **char**, how to handle strings with array and pointer notation, how to read and print a string, and how to compare two strings. Here's a preview of some of the other things you will learn:

◆ To add an *s* to the end of a word;

◆ To count the number of times the letter *e* occurs in a string;

◆ To change the third letter of a string to some new value; and

◆ To replace all occurrences of "his" by "her."

Notice that each example accesses some part of a string, rather than the whole.

A direct-mail advertising agency has decided to personalize its sweepstakes offers. It has prepared a basic letter with a particular customer's name, address, spouse's name, and other personal information. The company would like a computer program to make the appropriate changes to address each customer individually. As a first test, the company would like the program to make one set of changes: to replace all occurrences of

PROBLEM 9

1.	Smith	by	Johnson
2.	Mr.	by	Ms.
3.	421 Main St.	by	18 Windy Lane
4.	wife	by	husband
5.	Susan	by	Robert
6.	her	by	his

Here is the basic letter:

Congratulations, Mr. Smith! The Smith family of 421 Main St. may already have won a new one-million-dollar house!! Your neighbors at 421 Main St. will be so surprised when you, Mr. Smith, move into your new house with your wife, Susan! And her eyes will light up with joy at her fabulous new home! Enter the sweepstakes now, and you and the Smith family may win it all!

Write a C program that reads in the text line by line, displays each line as it is read in, makes the designated changes, and displays the revised text.

DECLARING, INITIALIZING, PRINTING, AND READING STRINGS

This section introduces the string data structure and elementary operations that can be performed on strings. It also introduces or reviews string declaration, character-by-character assignment, printing strings, and reading strings using *scanf*. These are all the things that can be done without using the string functions from the standard library.

WHAT IS A STRING?

So far, we have done very little with strings, largely because C doesn't have a string data type. In C, a string is a data structure (a more complex object built out of simpler pieces) based on an array of *char*. In Chapter 7, we learned how to declare an array of *char*. In Chapter 8, we learned how to use pointers. Now we are ready to discuss how to work with strings.

A string, called a **character string** or a **string of characters,** is a sequence of elements of the *char* data type. Therefore, each position in a string can hold any character you can type on the keyboard; in addition, a string can contain special characters, like the newline or tab characters, which are typed as two symbols but stored as a single character in memory.

A **string literal** is a sequence of characters enclosed by double quotation marks like "this is a string." (In contrast, individual values of type *char* are enclosed by single quotation marks, like *'a'*.) A string literal is a constant; its value cannot be changed.

HOW IS A STRING STORED?

A string, even a literal one, is very similar to an array of characters. In fact, the only difference between an array of *char* and a string is that a string must end in a special character called the null character or **null byte**—a single character (with ASCII code 0) created by typing two symbols (**\0**). Each two-symbol character starts with \ and is stored as a single character in memory.

If you use a literal string in a program (e.g., in a *printf* function call), it is stored in consecutive bytes in memory, and the compiler places the null character at the end. Figure 9-1 shows the storage for the literal string "Figure 9-1".

DECLARING STRING VARIABLES

A string is declared like an array of characters. We can declare a variable which can hold a name of up to 20 characters as follows:

```
char name[21];
```

As with any array, the number in brackets is the size, or maximum length, of the variable. For example, giving *name* a size of 21 means that it can store up to 20 characters plus the null character. More precisely, the entire storage location *name* is divided into 21 boxes, called bytes, each of which holds one character. Each character is an element of data type *char*—a letter, number, blank, punctuation mark, and so on.

THE NULL CHARACTER

The null character marks the end of a string. In some cases, you must explicitly insert a null character to terminate a string. In other cases—for example, in a literal string—the null

FIGURE 9-1 Storage for a literal string

F	i	g	u	r	e		9	-	1	\0
0	1	2	3	4	5	6	7	8	9	10

character is inserted automatically. The null character occupies a space in a string, as shown in Figure 9-1. An extra position must be provided in each string declaration to include room for it. A string of 20 bytes has room for only 19 characters. For a string to hold 20 characters, it must have 21 bytes.

CAUTION An array of *char* does not need a null character, but, without one, it cannot be treated as a string without courting disaster. For example, trying to print a string which lacks a null character can cause long stretches of irrelevant characters until the next null character is found in memory.

STRING SIZE AND LENGTH

In the declaration, an array of *char* is allocated a specific number of bytes; this is called its **size**. For example, *name* has size 21.

A string also has a **length**, which is different from its declared size. The length is the number of characters stored in the string up to, but not including, the null character. (In Section 2, we learn to use a function to determine the length of a string.)

Figure 9-2 shows a string *first*, which fills only the first four of ten declared positions. The size of *first* is 10, and its length is 3.

As with other arrays, the individual positions in a string are numbered, starting from 0, and can be accessed individually. Thus in Figure 9-2, *first[1]* has the value *'e'*, while *first[3]* has the value *'\0'*, the null character. Actually, positions *first[4]* through *first[9]* have values as well, but they are of no interest to us right now and may be characterized as "garbage."

INITIALIZING IN THE DECLARATION

As with any array, it is possible to initialize an array of *char* in the declaration. Example 9-1 shows two equivalent ways of initializing an array of *char* with array notation.

EXAMPLE 9-1

```
char first[10] = {'t','a','b','l','e','\0'};
char second[10] = "table";
```

The method used to initialize *first* treats the string as an array of *char* and assigns values to the individual positions. In this case, it is necessary to assign the null character. The method used for *second* initializes the string as a unit, and the null character is supplied automatically by the compiler, as it is for literal strings. The values stored for these two strings are identical.

FIGURE 9-2 String *first*

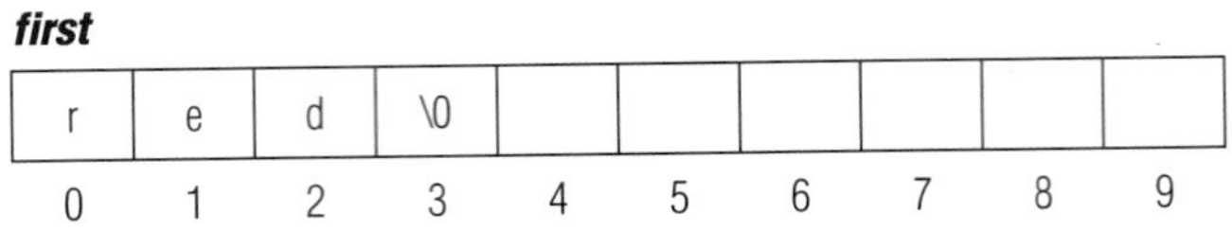

first

r	e	d	\0						
0	1	2	3	4	5	6	7	8	9

STYLE WORKSHOP Because the method used to initialize the variable **second** in Example 9-1 is much easier to type, we will use it in the text.

A POINTER TO A STRING OF CHARACTERS

The name of a string can be viewed as a constant pointer to a string, even when we are not using pointer notation. However, it is possible to declare a pointer to a string explicitly, as follows:

```
char *sptr;
```

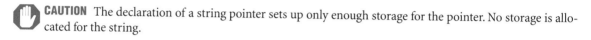 **CAUTION** The declaration of a string pointer sets up only enough storage for the pointer. No storage is allocated for the string.

Since the declaration does not allocate storage for the string, a string pointer should only point to strings for which storage has already been set up. One common use of string pointers is in the declaration of a formal parameter in a function.[1]

LEGAL CHARACTERS

A string literal is delimited or marked off by double quotation marks, while a character is delimited by single quotation marks (apostrophes). Both double quotation marks (") and the apostrophe (') are legal characters in a string. Nothing special needs to be done to include an apostrophe in a string. However, each occurrence of double quotation marks has to be preceded by the escape character (\) to tell the compiler that this is a character, not a delimiter (see Table 2.4, page 86). The same thing has to be done to include the backslash itself in a string. Example 9-2 illustrates this point.

EXAMPLE 9-2
```
char apos[10] = "won't fit";
char quotes[20] = "the \"king\" of rock";
char filename[20] = "c:\\hwork\\prob9.c";
```

From this declaration, **apos** gets the value "won't fit", **quotes** gets the value "the "king" of rock", and **filename** gets the value "c:\hwork\prob9.c". Each character preceded by the escape character is stored as a single character, as you can see in Figure 9-3.

INITIALIZING A STRING IN THE CODE

To initialize a string in the body of the code, we can explicitly assign a value to each character and insert the null character after the last one. Let's look at an example.

---

[1]In Chapter 12, Section 3, we discuss dynamic storage allocation, another way to provide storage for a string.

FIGURE 9-3   *A,* string ***apos***; *B,* string ***quotes***; *C,* string ***filename***.

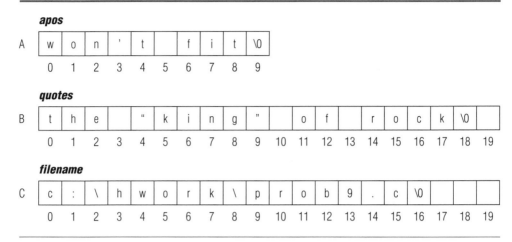

FIGURE 9-4   String ***city*** initialized to "L.A."

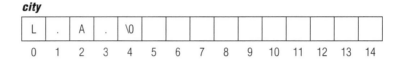

EXAMPLE 9-3

```
char city[15];

city[0] = 'L';
city[1] = '.';
city[2] = 'A';
city[3] = '.';
city[4] = '\0';
```

The array now holds the string "L.A.", which has a length of 4; the string is terminated by the null character in position 4, as shown in Figure 9-4.

IN DEPTH

Character by character assignment, as shown in Example 9-3, is the only technique for giving a string a value *in the body of the code* without using the functions from Section 2. In fact, this is one of the techniques used in those functions.

SELF-CHECK 9-1

1. a.   What is the size of a string?
    b.   What is the length of a string?
    c.   Why is the size always different from the length?

2. What is the purpose of the null character?

3. Give a declaration for a string called **student**, which holds up to 50 characters. Show two ways to initialize the string in the declaration.

A STRING AS AN ARRAY OF *char*

Since a string is an array of **char**, it is possible to work with the individual string positions as with array elements. Example 9-4 shows how to copy a single character from a string to a variable of type **char**.

EXAMPLE 9-4

An individual component of a string is a character and can be assigned to a **char** variable.

```
char c,d;
char str[5] = "wing";

c = str[3];
d = str[0];
```

As a result of these assignments, **c** has the value '*g*', and **d** has the value '*w*'.

It is also possible to change the value of a string variable by changing one or more of its positions. Example 9-5 shows how to do this.

EXAMPLE 9-5

We have the variable **item**, shown below:

```
char item[10] = "compater";
```

Suppose we want to change the value of **item** to "computer". Figure 9-5A shows the variable with the original value. In order to change the value of the string, all we need to do is change the value of the character in **item[4]** from '*a*' to '*u*'. We can do that this way:

```
item[4] = 'u';
```

After this change, the variable **item** looks like Figure 9-5B.

FIGURE 9-5 *A*, string **item** with incorrect value "compater"; *B*, string **item** with changed value "computer".

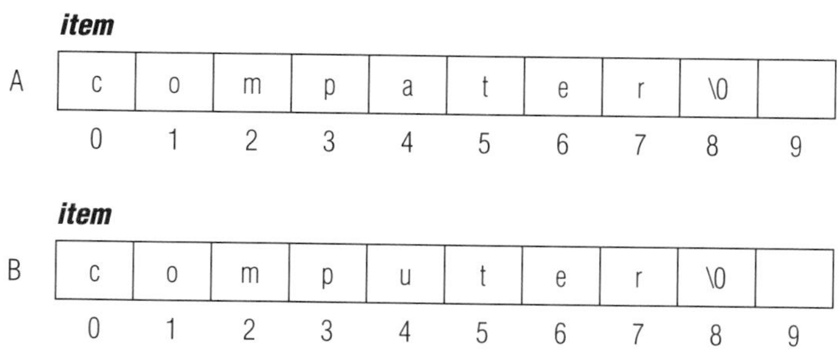

item

A	c	o	m	p	a	t	e	r	\0	
	0	1	2	3	4	5	6	7	8	9

item

B	c	o	m	p	u	t	e	r	\0	
	0	1	2	3	4	5	6	7	8	9

CAUTION Don't replace the null byte by any other character unless you insert a new null byte in a different position in the string. A string must end with a null character.

A STRING VERSUS AN ARRAY OF *char*

Even though a string is an array of *char*, it can be treated as a unit because, unlike a regular array of *char*, it is terminated by the null character. It is also possible to copy, compare, or move a block of characters from a string. And, as with any array, it is possible to manipulate the individual elements.

You may recall that we discussed arrays of *char* in Chapter 7; Example 7-7 initialized a *char* array (as we did in Example 9-3) and explicitly inserted the null character at the end; then it printed the array as a unit. That example treated the array of *char* as a string. Let's take a closer look at that technique.

PRINTING A STRING

It is possible to print a string using *printf*. As long as the string is terminated by a null character, the *printf* function prints all the characters up to, but not including, the null character.

Example 9-6 illustrates printing a string literal and a string variable declared as an array of *char*. Remember that the *printf* conversion specification for a string variable is *%s*. Notice that a conversion specification is necessary to print the value of a variable, not a literal. In Section 2, we learn how to use another function dedicated to printing strings.

EXAMPLE 9-6

```
char first[11] = "Andy";

printf("The name is %s\n",first);
printf("What a nice guy!\n");
```

This prints the following:

```
The name is Andy
What a nice guy!
```

The first call to *printf* prints the literal string "The name is", followed by the value of *first*, declared as an array of *char* and initialized in the declaration. Then the second call to *printf* prints another literal string on a new line; since no variables have to be inserted into the second string during printing, no conversion specifications are required.

LIMITATIONS ON AN ARRAY OF *char*

It is not possible to assign a value to an array of *char* as if it were a simple variable, except in a declaration. The following assignment is illegal:

```
city = "L.A.";                                              /* illegal */
```

It is also impossible to compare an array of **char** with a string value: The following comparison is legal but doesn't compare the value in **city** with the string literal:

```
if (city == "L.A.")                              /* legal, but misleading */
    ...
```

Instead, it compares the address of **city** with the address where the literal string "L.A." is stored. These addresses are not equal, regardless of the value stored in **city**.

In order to do significant work with strings in C, we must employ additional tools, either our own or those supplied with most C compilers. Typically, we use the library functions contained in **string.h**. With these functions, we can assign values to an array of **char**, compare two strings, extract part of a string, and combine strings in different ways. Without these functions, we must do all of these operations character by character. Sections 2 and 3 discuss the most common string library functions.

READING STRINGS USING *scanf*

It is possible to read a string using **scanf**, although many C programmers feel that it is dangerous and should be avoided. However, the technique is simple to use in a beginning programming course. The conversion specification for reading a string using **scanf** is **%s**, just as in **printf**. Example 9-7 shows a section of code which reads in a string.

 CAUTION The & symbol is not used with the name of a string variable getting a value from **scanf** because a string variable is an array. Since the name of an array is an address, the symbol & is not needed.

EXAMPLE 9-7

```
char name[16];

printf("Enter a name of up to 15 characters> ");
scanf("%s",name);
```

Whatever the user types in (as long as it has no blanks) is stored in **name** and is automatically followed by the null character. For example, if the user types in the value "Eleanor", the variable **name** has that value, as shown in Figure 9-6, and has a length of 7.

FIGURE 9-6 String **name** after reading in "Eleanor"

name															
E	l	e	a	n	o	r	\0								
0	1	2	3	4	5	6	7	8	9	10	11	12	13	14	15

When typing in string data, be sure not to type the quotation marks. A string literal must appear within quotation marks in the program but not in the set of data. Also be sure to press (ENTER) after typing the data value.

PROBLEMS WITH USING *scanf*

There are a few problems with reading strings using *scanf*. The first is based on *scanf*'s treatment of whitespace characters.

 CAUTION The *scanf* function stops reading at the first whitespace character—you may remember from Chapter 3 that whitespace characters are spaces, tabs, and newline characters.

One solution to this problem, shown in Example 9-8, is to read in each part of the string as a separate unit.

EXAMPLE 9-8 Suppose we want to read in the name "Anna Ruiz". We can do it as follows:

```
char first[16];
char last[16];

printf("Enter a first name of up to 15 characters> ");
scanf("%s",first);
printf("Enter a last name of up to 15 characters> ");
scanf("%s",last);
```

If the user types in the name, "Anna" is stored in *first* and "Ruiz" is stored in *last*. If we wish, we can use one of the techniques described later to combine these two into a single string.

STYLE WORKSHOP If you use *scanf* with strings, we recommend that you always read in each value in a separate call to *scanf*. Many people consider it bad style to do either of the following:

◆ read more than one value in a single *scanf* function call:

```
scanf("%s %s",first,last);                    /* bad style */
```

◆ read in a string value in the same *scanf* function call as a value of another type:

```
scanf("%s %d",first,number);                  /* bad style */
scanf("%d %s",number,first);                  /* bad style */
```

In fact, many C programmers will not read in more than one item (of any type) with a single *scanf*. When reading strings, this is even more critical because of the way whitespace characters are treated. Furthermore, many C programmers will not read a string with any function except *fgets* (see Appendix VII).

The most serious problem with reading in a string using *scanf* is that there is no way to set a limit on the size of the value read in. The *scanf* function reads until it finds a whitespace character; if it reads more characters than the variable can hold, those characters are stored in the adjacent memory locations, even if they overwrite existing values of other variables. If the string typed in for the *scanf* in Example 9-7 happened to be 20 characters long, 5 of them would overwrite memory locations assigned to another variable.

CAUTION When typing in string data, never enter a value which is longer than the number of characters in the variable's declaration minus 1. If you do, there is no place to store the null character within the variable, and the results are unpredictable.

The *gets* function (Section 3) and the *fgets* function (Appendix VII) are better ways to read in strings because they allow for whitespace characters. In addition, *fgets* lets the programmer limit the number of characters read in, thus avoiding the problem of overwriting other variables.

SELF-CHECK 9-2

1.   Why is it wrong to use the & symbol when reading in a string with *scanf*?

2.   Show three different ways to give the value "animal" to the string variable *str*, declared as follows:

```
char str[10];
```

3.   a.   What is stored in *str* if each of the following values, separately, is read in using a single call to *scanf*?

    (1) cityscape   (3) thingamajig

    (2) New York   (4)   (one or more blanks)

    b.   Which of the input values in part (a) causes unpredictable results?

SECTION 2   STRING MANIPULATION FUNCTIONS FROM THE STANDARD LIBRARY

To do more than simple printing of strings in C, we must either write functions or use those from the standard library. This section discusses string manipulation functions from the standard library *string.h*. In later sections, we use these functions and the string input/output (I/O) functions from *stdio.h* to write Program 9.

FUNCTIONS FROM THE STANDARD LIBRARY

The standard library *string.h* contains many functions for string manipulation. Among them are the following:

◆   *strcpy*, which allows us to give a string an initial value as a unit, rather than character by character;

◆   *strlen*, which allows us to determine the length of a string;

◆   *strcmp*, which allows us to compare one string with another;

◆ *strcat*, which allows us to combine two strings;

◆ *strncpy*, which allows us to copy a block of *n* characters from one string to another; and

◆ *strncmp*, which allows us to compare a block of *n* characters from one string with those in another.

In addition, the operator *sizeof*, which is not limited to strings, is especially handy in string processing.

USING *string.h*

To use these library functions, we must include the *string.h* header file in our program. The *#include* directive for this header file, shown below, is placed with *#include <stdio.h>* and the *#include* directives for any other header files. These headers can appear in any order.

```
#include <string.h>
```

The file *string.h* includes the prototypes for the string manipulation functions, just as *math.h* contains the ones for mathematical functions and *stdio.h* contains those for I/O functions.

A POINTER TO A STRING

Each function from *string.h* accepts pointers to one or more strings as parameters. Although pointers were discussed in detail in Chapter 8, we need to look at them in the context of strings.

◆ Since a string is an array of *char*, the name of the string is the address of the array or a pointer to the string; *str* is a pointer to the *str* array.

◆ To refer to a position past the beginning of a string, use the & operator to specify the address of that position, rather than its value: *&str[3]* is a pointer to the fourth position in the *str* array, while *str[3]* means the value at that address.

◆ As an alternative, the pointer notation *str+3* means the same thing as *&str[3]*. The notation *str+3* means the position three elements past the beginning of the *str* array or the address of the fourth position (since the first position is at *str+0*). In pointer notation, *(str+3)* means the value at the address *str+3*.

ASSIGNING A VALUE TO A STRING VARIABLE: *strcpy*

It is possible to give a string a value as a unit; however, as we said earlier, since a string has its home in an array, it can't be given a value by an assignment statement. The name of a string, like the name of any array, is a constant; it cannot be used on the left-hand side of an assignment statement.

In place of assignment, we use the *strcpy* function to assign a value to a string. The *strcpy* function lets us copy a string from one location to another. The string to be copied can be a literal string or a string already stored in an array of *char*. The *strcpy* function will copy the entire string, including the terminating null character, to the new location.

General Form of a Call to *strcpy*

```
strcpy(dest,source);
```

The ***strcpy*** function has two parameters; both are pointers to strings: The first is the **destination**—a string variable whose value is going to be changed; the second is the **source**—the string literal or variable which is going to be copied to the destination. Figure 9-7 shows the flow of information in the ***strcpy*** function.

The ***strcpy*** function copies characters from the source to the destination until it finds and copies a null character. (Remember that a literal is automatically terminated by a null character.) Once a string variable has been given a value, by whatever means, ***strcpy*** can copy that value to another string variable. Example 9-9 shows how to use the ***strcpy*** function.

EXAMPLE 9-9

```
char first[21];
char last[21];

strcpy(first,"Wayne Smith");
strcpy(last,first);
```

After the two calls to ***strcpy***, ***first*** and ***last*** each have the value "Wayne Smith\0".

HIGHLIGHTS

When copying from a string literal, the ***strcpy*** function automatically copies the null character. Remember from Chapter 7 that an array can be changed in a function, even though the name of the actual array parameter is not preceded by & in the call to the function. In Example 9-9, the arrays ***first*** and ***last*** are changed in the function ***strcpy***.

SPECIFYING AN ADDRESS PAST THE BEGINNING OF A STRING

A call to ***strcpy*** can be used to copy just part of a string. Either or both of the parameters can refer to addresses past the beginning of their strings. The ***strcpy*** function copies characters from the designated starting position through the first null character.

The name of a string is an address and can be sent as a parameter to a function without the & operator. However, to specify the address of a position past the beginning of a string, we must use either the & operator or pointer notation. Example 9-10 illustrates both methods.

FIGURE 9-7 Direction of the copy operation in ***strcpy***

EXAMPLE 9-10

```
char name[20] = "Alice Larrenson";
char newname[10] = "Lee Davis";

strcpy(&name[6],&newname[4]);        or        strcpy(name+6,newname+4);
```

This call to **strcpy** copies "Davis" from **newname** to replace "Larrenson". The source is specified as **&newname[4]** or **newname+4**, which is the position of the character **'D'**. The function copies characters beginning at that location up to the null character. The characters are copied to the position **&name[6]** (or **name+6**), which is the position of the **'L'**.

Figure 9-8 shows the result of this function call. Notice that some characters of "Larrenson" are not replaced by this call to **strcpy**; however, because the null character copied with the string "Davis" terminates the string in position 11, the characters "son" are not accessed.

CAUTION The **strcpy** function continues to copy characters up to and including the first null character. If the source string does not contain a null character, **strcpy** copies until it finds one in memory, which can be many bytes past the end of the string.

In addition, the **strcpy** function does *not* check to see whether there is room for the resulting string at the specified location. If there is no room, it copies characters on top of whatever variables follow in memory. This may destroy the contents of other variables.

Therefore, the programmer is responsible for making the destination large enough that the copy does not overlay (and thus wipe out) the values of adjacent variables. An especially common error is failing to leave room for the null character. If you work with the resulting string, you may have strange results; the new string may appear to have the entire long value that you gave it, while other variables before or after it may be changed. The copy may have overwritten important program information so you may get messages like "Abnormal program termination" (in DOS) or "Memory fault, core dumped" (in Unix).

FIGURE 9-8 *A,* **name** *and* **newname** *initially; B,* **name** *after* **strcpy(&name[6],&newname[4])**

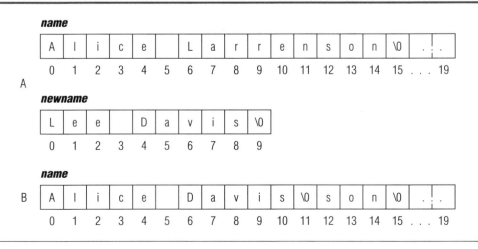

DETERMINING THE LENGTH AND SIZE OF A STRING: *strlen* AND *sizeof*

Since C doesn't protect you from making mistakes when copying string values (or using them with other string functions), it is important to determine the length of the string you are copying. The **strlen** function can be used to find the length of the string in bytes. The **sizeof** operator can be used to determine the declared size of a string. It accepts one operand, a variable or a type, and returns the number of bytes allocated to it.

General Form of a Call to *strlen*

The general form of a call to **strlen** is the following:

```
length = strlen(str);
```

The parameter to **strlen**, **str**, is a string; the return value, **length**, is an integer representing the current length of **str** in bytes, excluding the null character. For example, if **str** has the value "howdy\0", **strlen** returns 5. If **str** has the value "\0", **strlen** returns 0. Note that the length does not depend upon the number of characters specified in the declaration for **str**.

General Form of *sizeof*

The general form of **sizeof** is the following:

```
size = sizeof item;     or     size = sizeof(typename);
```

The **sizeof** operator takes a single operand, which can be a type or a variable. If the operand is the name of a type, like **typename**, parentheses are required; if it is a variable, like **item**, parentheses are optional, but many programmers use parentheses in all cases. The result, in this case assigned to **size**, is an integer representing the size of the operand in bytes.

If **item** is the name of a variable, including an array, **sizeof** returns its size in bytes; for example, if **item** has been declared **char item[30]**, **sizeof** returns 30. If the operand is the name of a type, **sizeof** returns the number of bytes allocated to that type in the system (see Chapter 8 for more on **sizeof**).

CAUTION In a function where **str** is sent as a parameter, **sizeof str** returns the size of the pointer **str** rather than the declared string. The only way to know the declared size of a string parameter in a function is to pass the size as a parameter.

USING *strlen* AND *sizeof*

Example 9-11 shows how to use **strlen** and **sizeof** to avoid a problem when copying a string.

EXAMPLE 9-11

```
int  length,size;
char dest[25];
char source[30];

scanf("%s",source);
length = strlen(source);
size = sizeof dest;
if (length < size)
     strcpy(dest,source);
else
     printf("won't fit\n");
```

Using **strlen** allows checking the length of **source** before copying it to **dest**. If the source string is too long, the copy operation is not performed. Another function, **strncpy**, can be used to copy only part of a string.

STYLE WORKSHOP The following condition eliminates the variables **length** and **size** and uses the values returned by the function calls directly:

```
if (strlen(source) < sizeof dest)
     strcpy(dest,source);
```

COMPARING STRINGS: *strcmp*

String comparison is simply an extension of character comparison. In Chapter 2, Section 5, we saw that each element of data type **char** has a numeric equivalent, called its **ASCII code**. Because values of type **char** are assigned numbers in consecutive order, characters can be put in order or alphabetized. The number for a is less than the one for b which is less than the one for c, etc. The capital letters are assigned a sequence of numbers in a different range, smaller than all the lowercase letters. Thus $A < Z < a < z$. A blank has a numeric value lower than all printable characters, and the null byte has the lowest value of all. Some sample characters and their ASCII codes are shown in Table 9.1. A complete list is in Appendix II.

The computer compares pairs of characters, one from each string, until it finds a pair that are not the same. If the first characters are alike, it looks at the next character in each string, until it gets to the end of one of the strings or finds a pair of characters that are not alike. Thus when comparing "car" with "cat", it finds the first two characters are alike; then it determines that "car" is less than "cat" because '*r*' is less than '*t*' (see Figure 9-9). Similarly, both "car" and "cat" are less than "cloth" (because '*a*' is less than '*l*').

Normally, the length of the strings is not a factor because the character-by-character comparison starts at the left end. However, there is a special case where two strings have

TABLE 9.1 Selected Characters and Their Numeric Equivalents

Character	'\0'	' '	'A'	'B'	'Z'	'a'	'b'	'c'	'z'
ASCII code	0	32	65	66	90	97	98	99	122

FIGURE 9-9 *Comparison of two strings*

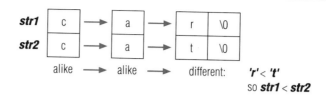

different lengths and are identical in all positions up to the end of the shorter one. In this case, the shorter string is called a **prefix** of the other. The prefix is considered less because the null byte has the lowest numeric value of all characters. '\0' is less than 'a': thus "cat" is less than "catalog".

Notice, too, that "cat" and "Cat" are different strings since uppercase and lowercase letters have different numeric values. "Cat" is less than "cat" because uppercase letters have smaller numeric values.

A function to compare two strings is included in the standard library of functions. It is called **strcmp**. The **strcmp** function takes pointers to two strings as parameters and returns an integer value based on the relationship between the two strings.

General Form of a Call to *strcmp*

The general form of the call to **strcmp** is the following, where either parameter may be a string literal or variable:

```
result = strcmp(first,second);
```

The function **strcmp** returns an integer determined by the relationship between the strings pointed to by the two parameters. While the result is an integer, we usually don't care about its exact value, just whether it is positive, negative, or 0:

result > 0 if **first** > **second**   (the strings, not the pointers)
result = 0 if **first** == **second**
result < 0 if **first** < **second**

Example 9-12 shows the results of comparing some literal strings.

EXAMPLE 9-12

```
int result;

result = strcmp("cat","car");          /* result > 0 */
result = strcmp("big","little");       /* result < 0 */
result = strcmp("ABC","abc");          /* result < 0 */
result = strcmp(" ab","ab");           /* result < 0 */
result = strcmp("pre","prefix");       /* result < 0 */
```

(continued)

(*continued*)
```
result = strcmp("potato","pot");         /* result > 0 */
result = strcmp("cat","cat");            /* result == 0 */
```

Each call to **strcmp** produces the same result if the parameters are names of variables. Example 9-13 gives two illustrations.

EXAMPLE 9-13
```
int  result;
char first[15]="cat",second[15]="car";

result = strcmp(first,second);           /* result > 0 */
result = strcmp(first,"catalog");        /* result < 0 */
```

STYLE WORKSHOP It is common to use the **strcmp** function in a condition without assigning its return value to a variable, as shown in Example 9-14.

EXAMPLE 9-14
```
char first[20],second[20];

scanf("%s",first);
scanf("%s",second);
if (strcmp(first,second) == 0)
    printf("they are equal\n");
```

This prints a message if the two values read in are the same. If **first** is less than **second**, or **second** less than **first**, we do not print the message; we don't care which integer is returned from **strcmp** as long as it is not 0.

It is also possible to begin a comparison from a position other than the beginning of a string. To do this, the parameter to **strcmp** must be an address, specified by the & operator (illustrated in Example 9-10) or pointer notation.

SELF-CHECK 9-3

1. Assuming the following declarations, show how to use **strcpy** to do the following:
```
char str[10];
char input[80];
```
   a. copy "toad" to **str**
   b. copy **str** to **input**

2. Show the result of using **sizeof** and a call to **strlen** on each of the following strings.
   a. `char s[5] = "bird";`
   b. `char buffer[80] = "oops";`

3. Show the value returned by *strcmp* in each of the following comparisons:

    a.   `strcmp("apple","orange")`

    b.
```
char tree[10] = "oak";
char bush[8] = "privet";

strcmp(bush,tree);
strcmp(tree,bush);
```

    c.   `strcmp("Apple","apple");`

CONCATENATION: JOINING TWO STRINGS TOGETHER

Often it is useful to **concatenate**, or join together, two strings. The *strcat* function can do this. The resulting string has only one null character, at the end.

General Form of a Call to *strcat*

The general form of the call to the *strcat* function is the following, where both *first* and *second* are pointers to strings:

```
strcat(first,second);
```

After the call, *first* contains all the characters from *first*, followed by the ones from *second* up to and including the first null character in *second*.

CAUTION The *strcat* function stops copying when it finds a null character. If the second string does not contain a null character, *strcat* continues copying bytes from memory until it finds a null character, no matter how far away.

In addition, like *strcpy*, the *strcat* function does *not* check to see whether there is room for the resulting string at the specified location. Therefore, the programmer must check to make sure that the resulting string fits in the variable.

Figure 9-10 and Example 9-15 illustrate concatenation using *strcat*.

EXAMPLE 9-15

```
char bigstr[1024];
char dest[30]   = "computer";
char second[15] = " programming";

strcat(dest,second);
strcpy(bigstr,dest);
strcat(bigstr," is fun and also very demanding");
```

The first call to *strcat* gives *dest* the value "computer programming"; this easily fits in the 29 available bytes. However, a cautious programmer is much more careful. The resulting string could easily be more than 29 characters, depending on the original value of *dest*. The second

FIGURE 9-10 Action of *strcat(first,second)*. A, *first* and *second* before the call; B, *first* after the call.

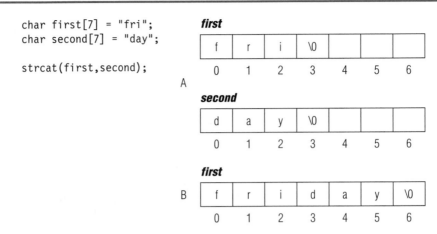

```
char first[7] = "fri";
char second[7] = "day";

strcat(first,second);
```

method, which copies the first string to a much larger "work area" variable (*bigstr*) before performing the concatenation, is a much safer procedure. In this example, first *dest* is copied to *bigstr*, which is very large; then *bigstr* is concatenated with the literal string to create the string "computer programming is fun and also very demanding".

Example 9-16 shows how to use *strlen* and *sizeof* to perform concatenation safely without using a large work area:

EXAMPLE 9-16

```
char dest[30] = "computer";
char second[15] = " programming";

if (strlen(dest) + strlen(second) < sizeof dest)
    strcat(dest,second);
else
    printf("error: can't concatenate-destination is too small");
```

Notice that *strlen* returns the length of the current value of the string sent as its parameter. We are comparing the combined lengths of *dest* and *second* with the declared length of *dest*, which is calculated by *sizeof*.

SUBSTRING FUNCTIONS: *strncmp* AND *strncpy*

All of the functions we have explored so far work on an entire string (or from the specified starting position to the end of the string). Many times, however, we want to extract a portion of a string and copy it to a new location or want to see whether a string matches part of another string. In these cases, we need functions which look at a part of a string, or a **substring**. Let's first look at the **strncmp** function.

THE *strncmp* FUNCTION

Suppose that we want to discover whether the first four characters of two strings are the same or whether the section of a string starting at the third character has the value "ron". We could do a character-by-character comparison, but it is easier to use the **strncmp** function.

General Form of a Call to *strncmp*

The general form of a call to the **strncmp** function is the following, where **firstaddress** and **secondaddress** are pointers to strings, and **numchars** is an integer:

```
result = strncmp(firstaddress,secondaddress,numchars);
```

The **strncmp** function compares up to **numchars** characters from the two strings, starting at the addresses specified (**firstaddress** and **secondaddress**). Like **strcmp**, the function returns an integer representing the relationship between the compared string sections.

Like **strcmp**, the **strncmp** function stops at a null character. It compares character by character until it finds a null character or characters that are different or until it has compared **numchars** characters.

Example 9-17 demonstrates using **strncmp** to determine whether the first four characters of two strings are identical.

EXAMPLE 9-17

```
char first[30] = "strong";
char second[10] = "stopper";
int  numchars;

if (strncmp(first,second,4) == 0)
    printf("first four characters are alike\n");
else if (strncmp(first,second,4) < 0)
    printf("first four characters of first string are less\n");
else
    printf("first four characters of first string are greater\n");
```

In this example, **strncmp** compares up to four characters from the strings **first** and **second**. If the first four match, **strncmp** returns 0, the condition is true, and the message "first four characters are alike" is printed. If the first four don't match, **strncmp** returns a negative or positive value; depending on this value, the appropriate message is printed.

Example 9-18 demonstrates how to find a string of characters in the middle of another string.

EXAMPLE 9-18 Suppose we want to find whether the string "ron" occurs in position 2 of the string *first*.

```
char first[30] = "strong";
int  numchars;

if (strncmp(&first[2],"ron",3) == 0)
    printf("ron is found in position 2\n");
else
    printf("ron is not found\n");
```

In this example, *strncmp* compares three characters from the address *&first[2]* with three from the string "ron". Since they match, *strncmp* returns 0, the condition is true, and the first message is printed. If they did not match, the second message would be printed.

THE *strncpy* FUNCTION

The *strncpy* function allows copying just a section of a string. It allows us to extract a substring from one string and copy it to another location.

General Form of a Call to *strncpy*

The general form of a call to the *strncpy* function is the following:

strncpy(dest,source,numchars);

The *strncpy* function takes three parameters: *dest* is a pointer to the destination; *source* is a pointer to the source; and *numchars* is an integer that specifies how many characters to copy. This call to *strncpy* copies up to *numchars* characters from *source* to *dest*.

 CAUTION Unlike *strcpy*, *strncpy* does not automatically append a null character. If the extracted string does not end with a null character, the programmer has to supply one.

Extracting a substring and copying it to a new location is such a common task that many computer languages build in this function. Example 9-19 shows using *strncpy* to extract a substring from a string.

EXAMPLE 9-19 This section of code extracts a three-character substring from string *source*, copies it to *dest*, and then prints it.

```
char source[20] = "computers are fun";
char dest[10];

strncpy(dest,source+3,3);          /* same as strncpy(dest,&source[3],3); */
dest[3] = '\0';
printf("%s\n",dest);
```

As illustrated in Figure 9-11, the ***strncpy*** instruction copies the three characters "put," from ***source+3*** to ***dest***. Then the null character is copied after the '**t**'. The call to ***printf*** prints the following:

```
put
```

It is also possible to copy to a destination other than the beginning of the string. Example 9-20 shows how to perform an insert operation without overwriting existing characters.

EXAMPLE 9-20 This example inserts "big " into the string ***result*** to create the new string, "I have a big cat". In order to insert the new word without losing any characters from the original string, we must first make room in string ***result***.

```
char result[18] = "I have a cat";
char insert[10] = "big ";

len = strlen(insert);
strcpy(result+9+len,result+9);
strncpy(result+9,insert,len);
```

The length of string ***insert*** determines how much room is needed in ***result***; in this case, four characters must be moved. The call to ***strcpy*** copies four characters starting at ***result+9*** ("cat\0"). They are copied ***len*** positions toward the end of the string, leaving four positions that can be overwritten.

The call to ***strncpy*** copies the four characters "big " (including the space) to ***result+9***, producing the string "I have a big cat". In this case, ***strncpy*** must be used because ***strcpy*** would copy the null character, cutting off the end of the new string. (Exercise 17 asks you to trace this example.)

Although there are other string-processing functions, the ones here are among the most useful.

FIGURE 9-11 *A,* ***source****; B,* ***dest*** after the call to ***strncpy****; C,* ***dest*** at the end of this section of code.

A ***source***

c	o	m	p	u	t	e	r	s		a	r	e		f	u	n	\0		
0	1	2	3	4	5	6	7	8	9	10	11	12	13	14	15	16	17	18	19

B ***dest***

p	u	t							
0	1	2	3	4	5	6	7	8	9

C ***dest***

p	u	t	\0						
0	1	2	3	4	5	6	7	8	9

SELF-CHECK 9-4

1. What is the result of the following operations? Does each work? Do any destroy other variables? Start in each case from the original values.

```
char big[50] = "a sunny day";
char little[5] = "was";
char middle[15] = "in the park";
```

   a. strcat(big,little);   c. strcat(big,middle);
   b. strcat(little,middle);

2. What is the result of these operations?

```
char big[50] = "sun in the daytime";
char little[10] = "sunshine";
char middle[15] = "a sunny day";
```

   a. strncmp(middle+2,little,4);   b. strncmp(middle+8,big+11,5);

3. Using the values in the variables from question 2, write a section of code to put each of these values into a variable, **dest**.

   a. "day"   b. "sun"

SECTION 3   **STRING INPUT/OUTPUT FUNCTIONS:** *gets, puts*

In this section, we will learn how to use the input/output (I/O) functions **gets** and **puts**, which are designed for doing I/O on string values. The prototypes for these functions are in **stdio.h**. The corresponding file functions **fgets** and **fputs**, which are generally preferred, are introduced in Appendix VII.

LINE-ORIENTED VERSUS TOKEN-ORIENTED INPUT/OUTPUT

So far, we have seen only the kind of input/output performed by **scanf** and **printf**. This kind of I/O processes individual units—characters, integers, strings—separated by whitespace characters. The individual units are called **tokens**, and this kind of I/O is called **token-oriented I/O**. The second kind of I/O, introduced here, is carried out by the functions **gets** and **puts**. This type processes entire lines and is called **line-oriented I/O**.

PRINTING A STRING: *puts*

Although we can print a string with the **printf** function, it is better to use the **puts** function, which is dedicated to printing strings. Here is the format of a call to the **puts** function:

General Form of a Call to the *puts* Function

```
puts(str);
```

The ***puts*** function takes a pointer to a string ***str*** as a parameter and sends ***str*** to ***stdout***, the standard output stream (see Appendix V). After printing the string, ***puts*** prints the newline character, which has the effect of printing an entire line. Although ***puts*** returns a value (on success, a nonnegative value; on error, ***EOF***), it is usually called as a void function.

Example 9-21 shows how the ***puts*** function works.

EXAMPLE 9-21

```
char str[25] = "This is a string to display";

puts(str);
```

This call to ***puts*** prints the string below and then goes to a new line:

```
This is a string to display
```

READING A VALUE INTO A CHARACTER ARRAY: USING *gets*

Although we can read in a string value using the ***scanf*** function, normally ***scanf*** stops when it reads a whitespace character. This makes ***scanf*** inappropriate for performing a task like reading in an entire line of input (possibly containing whitespace characters). An alternative is the string input function ***gets***.

The ***gets*** function allows reading in an entire line of input, including whitespace characters. It reads everything up to a newline character (created by pressing the (ENTER) key).

Here is the standard format for a call to the ***gets*** function:

General Form of a Call to the *gets* Function

```
result = gets(instring);      or      gets(instring);
```

The parameter ***instring*** is a pointer to a character array; ***gets*** returns a value of type ***char*** ∗ (or ***NULL***—see below—if it fails to read a string).

The ***gets*** function fills the array ***instring*** with a line of input from ***stdin***, the standard input stream (see Appendix V), replacing the terminating newline character with a null character. In addition, ***gets*** returns a pointer to the array it has filled. The call on the left assigns that pointer to a ***char*** ∗ variable (***result***). After the call on the left, the programmer can work with the string using pointer notation. The sample call on the right invokes ***gets*** like a void function. After either call, the programmer can work directly with the array using the name ***instring***.

Example 9-22 illustrates reading a line with ***gets*** and printing it with ***puts***.

EXAMPLE 9-22

```
char str[128];

gets(str);
puts(str);
```

The function **gets** is called to read a value into **str**. If the call to **gets** is successful, **str** has a value. Suppose the user types in "Oh boy!", followed by pressing ENTER. In that case, **str** has the value shown in Figure 9-12. The call to **puts** prints "Oh boy!" and goes to a new line.

STYLE WORKSHOP For protection, we usually declare character arrays used as input areas (called **input buffers** or just **buffers**) quite a bit longer than we need. Since C doesn't check the length of the value assigned or read into a string variable with **gets**, you can get into trouble if the value read in is longer than the size specified in the declaration. To avoid this problem, use the **fgets** function, introduced in Appendix VII.

Example 9-23 repeats Example 9-22 using the pointer returned by the **gets** function; the pointer is assigned to the **char ∗** variable **instring**.

EXAMPLE 9-23

```
char str[128];
char *instring;

instring = gets(str);
puts(instring);
```

Remember that **str** is allocated 128 bytes of storage, but **instring** has space only for a pointer. If the **gets** function is successful, **str** has a value, and **instring** points to that value. If the user types in "here we are", **str** gets the value shown in Figure 9-13. The string read in is printed by **puts**.

FIGURE 9-12 **str** after the call to **gets**

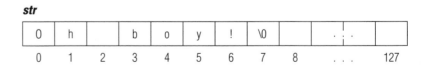

FIGURE 9-13 **str**, pointed to by **instring** and filled by **gets**

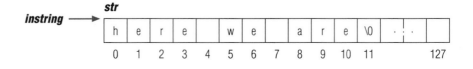

THE *NULL* POINTER AND ERROR CHECKING

When working with pointers, there is a special value which means that the pointer currently isn't pointing to anything. In C, this value is called *NULL*. It is not necessary to declare *NULL* in your program since it is a constant defined in *stdio.h*.

If the **gets** function fails to read in a value, it returns *NULL*. *NULL* is returned automatically if there are no more strings to be read in from an input stream; when entering data interactively, the user can signal *NULL* by pressing CTRL-Z ENTER (in DOS) or CTRL-D in Unix (the same signal as for *EOF*). A programmer should check for this value to make sure that the function has successfully read in the input. This is very similar to the error checking used with calls to **scanf**. Examples 9-24 and 9-25 show calls to **gets**, comparable to those in Examples 9-22 and 9-23. In each example, the call to **gets** is in a loop, and the return value from the function acts as the loop control.

EXAMPLE 9-24A

This example, like Example 9-22, reads a string into a character array and prints the array. The example assigns the return value from **gets** to a *char* * variable *result*, but *result* is used only to check the result of the **gets** function. When the value of *result* is *NULL*, there is no more input.

```
char str[128];
char *result;

result = gets(str);
while (result != NULL) {
    puts(str);
    result = gets(str);
}
```

Notice that, as usual in a structured read loop, we have one call to **gets** outside the loop to "prime the pump."

Example 9-24B performs the same task as Example 9-24A, but calls the function and tests the return value in the loop condition. (For further explanation on how examples 9-24B and 9-25B work, see Chapter 12, Section 4.)

EXAMPLE 9-24B

```
char str[128];
char *result;

while ((result = gets(str)) != NULL)
    puts(str);
```

In this example, the two calls to **gets** have been collapsed into one, which is in the **while** condition. The call to **gets** is done first, followed by the test of its return value. The parentheses around *result = gets(str)* are necessary to override the fact that != has higher precedence than =.

Example 9-25A rewrites Example 9-23. It processes the string using the pointer returned by **gets** and puts the call to **gets** into a loop controlled by the return value.

EXAMPLE 9-25A

```
char str[128];
char *instring;

instring = gets(str);
while (instring != NULL) {
     puts(instring);
     instring = gets(str);
}
```

The loop condition looks odd, because it appears that we are comparing a string without using *strcmp*. In fact, we are comparing one pointer (***instring***, which points to the string stored in ***str***) with another (***NULL***). This is not a string comparison.

 CAUTION We cannot use the following as the loop condition because ***str*** is the address of a string in memory, and it will never have the value ***NULL***:

```
while(str != NULL)                      /* invalid comparison */
```

Example 9-25B rewrites Example 9-25A, putting the call to ***gets*** inside the loop condition, as in Example 9-24B.

EXAMPLE 9-25B

```
char str[128];
char *instring;

while ((instring = gets(str)) != NULL)
     puts(instring);
```

Here again, we take advantage of the compact code which C permits.

PROBLEMS WITH *gets*

While ***gets*** is designed to be used with strings, it has a great potential for disaster. The function doesn't check to see whether there is room for the string which is being read in. Unfortunately, this means that even though a call to ***gets*** may be successful, the value read in may overwrite (and destroy) other variables in your program. Example 9-26 shows how this can happen.

EXAMPLE 9-26

Here is an accident waiting to happen:

```
int  value=3;
char inarea[25];
int  num=5;

gets(inarea);
puts(inarea);
printf("value is %d and num is %d\n",value,num);
```

Suppose the user types in a line of input more than 24 characters long. Depending on the operating system, DOS or Unix, either ***value*** or ***num*** will be overwritten by the extra characters. The output from the call to **puts** will not show the error because the entire input value will print, even though it exceeds the bounds of **inarea**. The result of **printf**, however, will be odd indeed because the value of one of the variables (**value** or **num**) will have been destroyed. (Exercise 18 asks you to run this section of code to see what happens.)

 CAUTION When reading in data using **gets**, make sure that the values entered are shorter than the variable into which they are being read.

Because **gets** can cause such problems, professional programmers prefer not to use it. Instead, they use **fgets**, the corresponding file input/output function, which allows the programmer to specify the length of the input string. We discuss **fgets** in Appendix VII.

SELF-CHECK 9-5

1. How is reading a string with **gets** different from reading with **scanf**?

2. Which of these statements are legal? If a statement is illegal, explain why.

```
char text[80];
int  num=5;
```

a. gets(text);
b. puts(num,text);
c. gets(num);

d. puts(text);
e. puts(num," values were entered");
f. gets("%s",text);

SECTION 4   WRITING SOME USEFUL STRING FUNCTIONS OF OUR OWN

Now that we have seen the string functions available in C, it is time to write our own functions to work with strings. This section explains programmer-defined functions using strings.

SENDING A STRING AS A PARAMETER

Let's start with a simple function called **length**. Like **strlen**, it receives one string as a parameter and returns its length.

EXAMPLE 9-27 The function **length** is sent one parameter, the string whose length is to be determined. It returns an integer representing that length. Thus the function prototype can be either of the following:

```
int length(char []);      or      int length(char *);
```

The main program calls **length** as follows:

```
int  len;
char str[80];

gets(str);
len = length(str);
```

Now let's write the **length** function. In its body, we must look character by character until we find the end of the string (the null character), counting each character as we examine it. Since *i*, the index variable of the loop, starts at 0 and increments as we go through the string, it serves as both the index and the counter. Here is the function:

```
/* returns an integer representing the length of parameter str */
int length(char *str)
{
    int i=0;

    while (str[i] != '\0')                 /* or while (*str+i) != '\0') */
        i++;
    return i;
}
```

If *str* has the value "winter", **length** returns 6. If *str* is the null string "\0", **length** returns 0. In the pointer notation in the comment, the * operator extracts the character at position *str+i* for comparison with '\0'.

CAUTION If we wrote **while(str+i != '\0')**, we would be comparing the *address* of each position in the string with the *value* '\0', and these would never be equal.

COUNTING HOW OFTEN A CHARACTER APPEARS IN A STRING: THE FUNCTION *countchar*

Now let's write one of the functions we promised earlier, a function to count the number of times a character appears in a string.

EXAMPLE 9-28 This function is not much different from the one in Example 9-27, except that we check each value passed on the way to the end of the string. The function, which we call **countchar**, receives two parameters: the first is the string to examine, and the second is the character we want to count.

```
/* returns an integer representing the # of occurrences of let in str */
int countchar(char str[],char let)
{
    int i=0,count=0;

    while (str[i] != '\0') {
        if (str[i] == let)
            count++;
        i++;
    }
    return count;
}
```

As in the function **length**, *i* moves us through the string. We compare each character with **let**; if **str[i]** is equal to **let**, we increment **count**. If, at the end, **count** is still 0, **let** did not appear in **str**.

For example, if we count the number of times the character *e* appears in the string "the elephant is early", *countchar* returns 4. If we count the number of times the character *s* appears in the string "hallelujah", *countchar* returns 0.

DETERMINING THE POSITION OF A CHARACTER IN A STRING: THE FUNCTION *findchar*

Now let's write a more complex function. The *findchar* function accepts two parameters, a string and a character. It determines whether the character is found in the string; it returns the position where the character is found or –1 if it isn't found.

Here is the prototype:

```
int findchar(char *,char);        or        int findchar(char[],char);
```

Here is a sample call to the function:

```
int  position;
char str[50] = "hand";
char let = 'a';

position = findchar(str,let);
```

EXAMPLE 9-29   Within the function *findchar*, we don't know whether the character we are searching for will be found. Therefore, we must continue searching until one of two things occurs: we find the character, or we reach the end of the string. The loop structure is identical to the one in the function *length*. What is different is determining whether the character has been found. We return *i* immediately if we find the character *let* in *str*. If we fall out of the loop, then *let* has not been found in *str*, and we return –1.

```
/*
 *    returns an integer representing the position of let within str
 *    if not found, returns -1
 */
int findchar(char *str,char let)
{
    int i=0;

    while (str[i] != '\0') {
        if (str[i] == let)
            return i;
        i++;
    }
    return -1;
}
```

The call to *findchar* above Example 9-29 finds 'a' in position 1 of "hand" and returns 1. If *str* is "hand" and *let* is 'k', the function processes the entire string without finding *let*. After falling out of the loop, the function returns –1 to indicate that 'k' has not been found.

STYLE WORKSHOP Some programmers dislike the style in Example 9-29 because the function has two *return* statements. The next subsection provides an alternative.

SETTING A FLAG OR SENTINEL

There is a way to write *findchar* to return the correct value of *i* without multiple **return** statements. The new method uses a flag. A **flag** or **sentinel** is a variable which is set when a particular event happens. The flag is tested in the condition of the loop to determine whether to terminate. Example 9-30 rewrites *findchar* using a flag and pointer notation.

EXAMPLE 9-30
The variable *found* acts as a flag or sentinel to indicate whether or not the character *let* has been found. Initially, *found* is 0; if *let* is found in *str*, *found* is set to 1. The additional test in the loop header is *!found*, so that we enter the loop when *found* is 0, but we fall out when *found* is 1.

```
/* finds position of let in str using a sentinel */
int findchar(char *str,char let)
{
    int i=0,found=0;

    while (*(str+i) != '\0' && !found)
        if (*(str+i) == let)
            found = 1;
        else
            i++;
    if (!found)
        i = -1;
    return i;
}
```

Notice that we must test the value of *found* after falling out of the loop to determine which condition in the loop header failed.

Setting a flag is an alternative to the **break** statement and can often be used when a **break** statement cannot. (Exercise 23 asks you to rewrite the *findchar* function using **break**.)

ADDING AN *s* TO THE END OF A WORD

Let's solve another of the problems mentioned earlier. This time we will write a section of code to add an *s* to the end of a word.

Actually, adding an *s* is not as simple as it may sound. First, we have to decide what we mean by the end of a word. To simplify the task, assume that it means after the last character currently in the string. Second, we must make sure there is room for the letter we are adding. For example, if the '\0' is in the last position, there is no room for the *s*.

EXAMPLE 9-31
This section of code tests the current length of *str* and adds an *s* if there is room. To perform this task in a function, we would have to pass the declared size of *str* as a parameter.

```
char str[10] = "animal";
int  len;

len = strlen(str);
```

```
    if (sizeof str > len+1) {
        str[len+1] = '\0';
        str[len] = 's';
    }
```

The first line finds the current length of the string and puts it in **len**. This means that **str[len]** contains the last character in the string (which must be '**\0'**). The next line checks to see whether the declared size of the string is at least one byte greater than the current length; if it is, there is room to add the character s. We first move the '**\0'** one position toward the end of the string by copying it to **str[len+1]**. The last assignment moves s to **str[len]**. (See Figure 9-14.)

A FUNCTION WHICH RETURNS A VALUE OF TYPE *char* *: THE FUNCTION *classify*

The functions **length** and **findchar** receive strings as parameters, but each one simply computes and returns an integer value. A more complex function can return a pointer to **char**; a function can also change its string parameters. Note that a function can return a pointer to **char**, since a pointer is a variable; however, a function cannot return a string.

Our first example is a function which returns a value of type **char** *. We will write a function **classify** which is a variant on Problem 6, classifying a month into one of the four seasons. This time, the main program reads in the name of a month, rather than a number, and sends the string to **classify** to be categorized into one of four seasons. The **classify** function returns a pointer to a string. Example 9-32 shows the main program and the function **classify**.

FIGURE 9-14   **str** before and after adding the character s

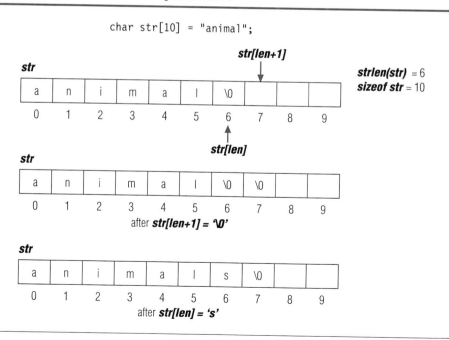

EXAMPLE 9-32 Let's begin with the main program. This version of the main program calls **classify**, sending the string **month** as a parameter. The function **classify** returns a pointer, indicated by a return type of **char** * in the function prototype.

```
/*
 * reads in a month name
 * calls classify to classify it into one of four seasons
 */
#include <stdio.h>
#include <string.h>
char *classify(char *);
main()
{
    char month[10],*season;

    printf("Enter month> ");
    scanf("%s",month);
    season = classify(month);
    if (strcmp(season,"error") != 0)
        printf("%s is in %s\n",month,season);
    else
        printf("%s is not a valid month\n",month);
}
```

Since the pointer **season** points to the value returned by **classify**, it doesn't have storage allocated in the main program. The main program checks the return value to see if the month is valid and prints the result.

Now we write the function **classify**, which receives a string **monthname** as a parameter. Its task is to classify **monthname** into one of four seasons. To do so, it makes up to 12 calls to **strcmp**, each time sending **monthname** and one of the 12 months of the year as parameters. When **strcmp** finds a match for **monthname**, **classify** returns a pointer to the appropriate season; otherwise it returns an error message.[2] (See Section 7 for another version of **classify**.)

```
/*  classifies monthname into one of four seasons */
char *classify(char *monthname)
{
    if (strcmp(monthname,"December") == 0)
        return "winter";
    if (strcmp(monthname,"January") == 0)
        return "winter";
    if (strcmp(monthname,"February") == 0)
        return "winter";
    if (strcmp(monthname,"March") == 0)
        return "spring";
    if (strcmp(monthname,"April") == 0)
        return "spring";
```

[2]Some people consider it bad style for a function to have multiple returns. To avoid the issue, this function can be written to change the parameter **season**; a solution using a local variable requires the variable to be **static** (see Chapter 12, Section 2).

```
    if (strcmp(monthname,"May") == 0)
        return "spring";
    if (strcmp(monthname,"June") == 0)
        return "summer";
    if (strcmp(monthname,"July") == 0)
        return "summer";
    if (strcmp(monthname,"August") == 0)
        return "summer";
    if (strcmp(monthname,"September") == 0)
        return "autumn";
    if (strcmp(monthname,"October") == 0)
        return "autumn";
    if (strcmp(monthname,"November") == 0)
        return "autumn";
    return "error";
}
```

In *classify*, the value typed in (now called *monthname*) is compared with each month of the year until a match is found. If *monthname* is equal to the current value, *strcmp* returns 0, and the name of the appropriate season is assigned to *season* and returned to the main program.

A FUNCTION WHICH CHANGES ITS STRING PARAMETERS

Finally, let's write a function which changes its string parameters. Because a string is an array, we don't use the & operator. (See Chapter 8, Section 3, on changing array parameters in functions.)

We write a function *split*, which accepts a string *stringtosplit* as an input parameter and breaks the string into two parts at the first blank. For example, if the parameter has the value "New York", the function splits it into two units: "New" and "York". The function assigns the two parts to output parameters *first* and *second*. If there is no blank in the string, the function returns –1, and the values of *first* and *second* are unchanged.

The function prototype is either of the following:

```
int split(char [], char[], char[]);   or   int split(char *, char *, char *);
```

The main program sends the string *stringtosplit* to the function *split*; if the string has been successfully split, the main program prints the two halves in reverse order (*second* and then *first*). Here are the declarations and the call:

```
char *stringtosplit;
char buffer[50];
char first[50], second[50];
int  result;

stringtosplit = gets(buffer);
result = split(stringtosplit,first,second);
if (result >= 0)
    printf("%s %s\n",second,first);
else
    printf("no blank in string\n");
```

THE FUNCTION *split*

Now let's write the function **split**. For simplicity, we'll use the same names in the calling program. Within the function, we want to look at each character of the string **stringtosplit** to find the first one which is a blank. Since there is no guarantee that a blank occurs, we must continue looking until we find a blank or reach the end of the string.

Does this sound familiar? Finding a blank is a special case of finding any character in the string. In fact, we have already written a function **findchar** which finds a specified character in a string. Modular programming suggests that we use it for our current task. That means we must include the prototype for **findchar**:

```
int findchar(char *,char);
```

EXAMPLE 9-33 The function **split** calls **findchar** to find the first blank in the string **stringtosplit**. If **findchar** returns –1, there is no blank in the string and **split** returns –1. If **findchar** returns anything else, we split the string at that position, using **strcpy** and **strncpy**; then we return the position of the blank. Here is the complete function **split** (**findchar** is shown in Example 9-30).

```
/*
 *  calls findchar to find first occurrence of blank in stringtosplit
 *  if findchar returns -1, first and second are unchanged
 *  otherwise, returns position of blank; first and second have new values
 */
int split(char *stringtosplit, char *first, char *second)
{
    int pos;

    pos = findchar(stringtosplit,' ');
    if (pos >= 0) {
        strncpy(first,stringtosplit,pos);
        *(first+pos) = '\0';
        strcpy(second,stringtosplit+pos+1);
    }
    return pos;
}
```

If **findchar** finds a blank in **stringtosplit**, it returns its position. Then **split** calls **strncpy**, telling it that **first** should get the value of the characters in the string up to the blank. We must insert a null character to terminate the new value in **first** since **strncpy** does not append a null character. Then we call **strcpy** to copy the remainder of the string (from position **pos+1** to the end) to **second**.

PROGRAM TRACE Let's trace this function on the string "North Dakota", sent in as the value of **stringtosplit**. Figure 9-15 shows the strings involved.

◆ The function **split** calls **findchar**, which returns position 5 to be stored in **pos**.

◆ Then **split** calls **strncpy**, telling it to copy five characters, or "North", from **stringtosplit** to **first**.

◆ Then **split** inserts a null byte at position 5 of **first**.

FIGURE 9-15 Action of function **split** on string "North Dakota"

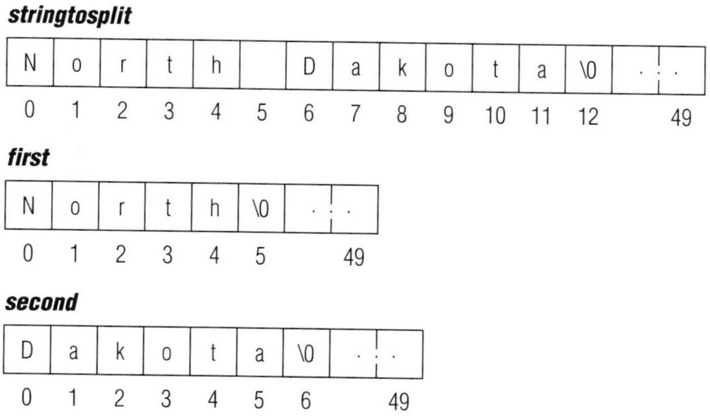

stringtosplit

N	o	r	t	h		D	a	k	o	t	a	\0	.	.	.
0	1	2	3	4	5	6	7	8	9	10	11	12		49	

first

N	o	r	t	h	\0	.	.	.
0	1	2	3	4	5		49	

second

D	a	k	o	t	a	\0	.	.	.
0	1	2	3	4	5	6		49	

◆ Then **split** calls **strcpy**, telling it to copy to **second** the rest of the string starting at **stringtosplit+pos+1**, which is **stringtosplit+6**. Copying begins at the **'D'** and continues until the null character.

◆ Then **split** returns 5, which is the position of the blank.

◆ Since **result** is 5, which is >0, **split** prints the two strings.

If we send in the string "San Jose State", essentially the same thing happens, with **pos** equal to 3. The string is split at the first blank into "San" and "Jose State". The second blank is treated like any other character.

Finally, if we send in the string "Indiana", which has no blanks in it, **findchar** returns –1, and **split** simply returns –1 without splitting the string.

SELF-CHECK 9-6

1. Write the prototype for a function **twostr** which accepts pointers to two strings as parameters and returns a pointer to a string.

2. How does a string function typically find the end of a string?

3. Rewrite the **return** statement from **findchar** (Example 9-30) so that it uses the conditional operator to return **i** or –1.

SECTION 5   PROGRAM 9

In this section, we write Program 9. We use the string functions from previous sections and write some new ones specifically designed for the program. We write Program 9 with array notation. (Exercise 26 asks you to rewrite it using pointer notation.)

PSEUDOCODE FOR THE MAIN PROGRAM

As usual, we begin Program 9 with pseudocode.

>*while there is a line of the letter to read*
>>*read in a line of the original letter*
>>*print the original line*
>>*replace the old strings in the line by the new ones*
>>*print the new line*

ARRAY OR NOT ARRAY?

We can get started from this pseudocode quickly. Let's begin with the first two lines. We can choose to process the letter in one of two ways: read in a single line of the letter, print it, and process it before reading in the next line; or read the entire letter into an array, then process the array a line at a time. We will do the first.

STYLE WORKSHOP While it is possible to use an array of strings in C, it is not customary. In general, C programmers avoid two-dimensional arrays, such as an array of strings. However, Section 7 does show how to use one.

FUNCTIONS FOR PROGRAM 9

We need a function to read in a line of the letter, another to print out the line, and a third to replace one string by another.

Let's focus on the I/O. Since the input is lines of text containing whitespace characters, we can't use **scanf** to read it in; instead we must use a line-oriented I/O function. The function **gets** reads in a line of input, strips off the newline character, and returns a pointer to the string. To match the line-oriented input, we use **puts** to do line-oriented output.

The **replace** function is the only one we have to write from scratch. The function **replace** accepts as a parameter the line of the letter to change. For each line, the **replace** function reads in a series of old and new string pairs and replaces each old string with the new. Before we write pseudocode for **replace**, let's look at the main program.

THE MAIN PROGRAM

The program reads in the original letter one line at a time, calls **replace** to make all changes on that one line, and then repeats the process. It uses the **EOF** method to detect the end of the letter (see Chapter 7, Section 9); however, since we are using **gets**, the signal is **NULL**. The variable **text** holds each line of data as it is read in; we declare **text** as an array of 120 characters, large enough to hold either the original or the changed string. (We also define **REPSIZE**, used later as the size of the old and new strings.)

The outline of the main program looks like this:

```
/*
 * Program prob9.c:
 * reads in a form letter and replaces all
 * occurrences of old strings by new strings
 */
```

```
#include <stdio.h>
#include <string.h>
#define LINESIZE 120
#define REPSIZE 15
/* function prototypes go here */
main()
{
    char text[LINESIZE];

    while (gets(text) != NULL) {
        puts(text);
        replace(text);
        puts(text);
    }
}
```

If the lines of data are input from the keyboard, the first call to **puts** seems redundant, repeating what is already on the screen. However, it does check that the value has been read in correctly. If, on the other hand, **stdin** is redirected to come from an external file, this line is our only view of the data prior to the changes. Later on, one (or both) of the calls to **puts** can send output to the printer or a file.

In keeping with top-down programming, we leave the main program and discuss the functions.

PSEUDOCODE FOR *replace*

Let's start by developing pseudocode for **replace**. The first thing **replace** has to do is read in data values. The string **text** is sent to **replace** as a parameter. In order to make the replacements, the function **replace** has to read in each set of **oldstr** and **newstr** values once for each line of text. This suggests a loop that reads in sets of data values until there are no more.

> *while there are data values*
> *read in a set of replacements (*oldstr *and* newstr*)*

After reading in the value for string **oldstr**, **replace** tries to find **oldstr** in **text**. If it finds **oldstr**, **replace** replaces it by **newstr**. Here is the complete pseudocode:

> *while there are data values*
> *read in a set of replacements (*oldstr *and* newstr*)*
> *while* oldstr *occurs in text*
> *search for next occurrence of* oldstr *in text*
> *replace* oldstr *by* newstr

BREAKING THIS TASK INTO FUNCTIONS

Let's consider how to make the changes called for in the **replace** function. To make things concrete, concentrate on replacing **oldstr**, which has the value "Smith", by **newstr**, which has the value "Johnson", in **text**. Assume that **text** has this value:

```
Congratulations, Mr. Smith! The Smith family of 421 Main St. may already
```

To replace "Smith" by "Johnson", first we see if "Smith" occurs in **text**. If it does, we replace it; if it does not, we continue with the next part of the processing.

To determine whether **oldstr** occurs within **text**, we write another function called **pos**. We also need one or more functions to actually replace *oldstr* by **newstr**. We look at **pos** first.

A FUNCTION TO FIND ONE STRING IN ANOTHER STRING: THE FUNCTION *pos*

Let's write pseudocode for the **pos** function, which is essentially a pattern-matching function. The function receives two parameters, **text** and **oldstr**. The **pos** function searches **text** for the first occurrence of **oldstr** and returns the position in the array where it is found. If it doesn't find **oldstr**, the function returns –1. In either case, the return value is an integer.[3] Here is the pseudocode for **pos**:

search for oldstr *in* text
if oldstr *is found in* text
    return position of oldstr *in* text
else
    return –1

The first line of pseudocode needs to be refined further. Searching for a string within another string is more complicated than what we did in the function *findchar* in Example 9-29, although there are some similarities. To find character **let** within string **str**, *findchar* had to compare **let** with each character in **str**. Finding a string **oldstr** within a string **text** is an extension of this.

Each character in **text** is a potential starting position for string **oldstr**. Suppose **text** has the value "neither", and **oldstr** has the value "the". We must look at each consecutive three-letter unit within **text** to see if it matches **oldstr**. First we have to look at "nei", then at "eit", then at "ith", then at "the", where we find a match (see Figure 9-16).

Clearly, we must use a loop to make a series of comparisons, each starting with the next position in string **text**. Here is the complete pseudocode for the **pos** function:

while (characters remain in text*)*
    compare oldstr *with characters from* text
    if oldstr *is found in* text
        return position of oldstr *in* text
return –1

WRITING THE FUNCTION *pos*

Let's start developing the loop in this pseudocode. To look at each of the characters in string **text**, we start comparing **oldstr** with the string starting at **text[0]**, then **text[1]**, and so on. We use a variable **i** to hold the starting position of each comparison in the array. When the

---

[3] C has a library function, **strstr**, which does essentially the same thing, but it returns a pointer to the position at which the substring is found. Exercise 33 asks you to use this function.

FIGURE 9-16 Strings **text** and **oldstr**, showing sequential comparisons

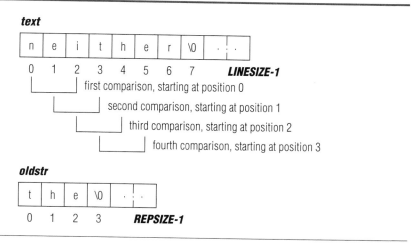

character at **text[i]** is the null character, we are finished. (We can actually stop several positions before that. See Exercise 32.) Here is an outline of the loop so far:

```
int i=0;

while (text[i] != '\0') {
        compare oldstr with characters from text
        if oldstr is found in text
                return position of oldstr in text
        i++;
}
```

The next line of pseudocode says to compare **oldstr** with a limited number of characters from **text**—for example, five, if **oldstr** has the value "Smith". Since **strcmp** does not stop until it finds a null character in one string, we must use **strncmp**, which allows us to specify how many characters to compare.

As parameters to **strncmp**, we send the string **text** from position **i** on; this is the string to search. The string to search for is **oldstr**. Finally, we send the number of characters to compare: the length of **oldstr**. Let's add all this to the function:

```
int lenold,result,i=0;

lenold = strlen(oldstr);
while (text[i] != '\0') {
        result = strncmp(&text[i],oldstr,lenold);
        if oldstr is found in text
                return position of oldstr in text
        i++;
}
```

The call to **strncmp** now says to compare **lenold** (in this case, five) characters from the address **&text[i]** with **lenold** characters from **oldstr**.

If **oldstr** is found in **text**, the call to **strncmp** returns 0. At that point, **pos** returns **i**, which holds the position of **oldstr** within **text**. If **oldstr** is not found in **text** on a given call to **strncmp**, **pos** increments **i**. The loop can be revised as follows:

```
int lenold,result,i=0;

lenold = strlen(oldstr);
while (text[i] != '\0') {
    result = strncmp(&text[i],oldstr,lenold);
    if (result == 0)
        return i;
    i++;
}
```

If we get to the end of the string without finding a match, **oldstr** is not contained within **text**, and **pos** returns −1. This is shown in the final version below.

THE FUNCTION *pos*

Here is the complete function **pos**; its prototype will be shown with the main program.

```
/*
 * Function pos:
 * Input:
 *    oldstr: string to search for
 *    text: string in which to find oldstr
 * Process:
 *    finds position of first occurrence of oldstr in text
 * Output:
 *    if found, returns position; if not found, returns -1
 */
int pos(char text[], char oldstr[])
{
    int lenold,result,i=0;

    lenold = strlen(oldstr);
    while (text[i] != '\0') {
        result = strncmp(&text[i],oldstr,lenold);
        if (result == 0)
            return i;
        i++;
    }
    return -1;
}
```

IMPLEMENTING *replace*

There are several ways to implement the **replace** function. Our method is to split the string **text** into two components and then reassemble them, with **newstr**, to form a new string. For the first task, we write a function **splitup**, similar to the **split** function from Example 9-33, but more general. (Exercise 24 asks you to compare **split** and **splitup**.) Several other ways to develop the **replace** function are explored in Exercises 29 to 31.

SPLITTING THE STRING

The **splitup** function breaks the string **text** into two components: the part preceding the string **oldstr**, and the part following it. The function receives five parameters: the first is **text**, the input parameter containing the text to split. Surprisingly, **oldstr**—the string to remove—does not have to be one of the parameters. All **splitup** needs to know is the position of **oldstr**, sent as **p**, and its length, sent as **lenold**. Finally, we send output parameters **part1** and **part2** to hold the two parts of the split text.

Figure 9-17 illustrates the action of **splitup**. If **text** has the value "Mr. Smith! The ...", and **replace** intends to replace "Smith", then **part1** gets the string "Mr. ", while **part2** gets the string "! The ...". "Smith" is not copied.

If the string **oldstr** is found in position 4, the string that is copied to **part1** goes from position 0 to position 3, the first four characters. More generally, if the string **oldstr** is found in position **p**, the string that is copied to **part1** goes from position 0 to position $p-1$, the first **p** characters. The value of **p** is returned by **pos**.

Here are the statements to copy the first part of **text** to **part1**. Although we can do the copying character by character, we use **strncpy** to copy **p** characters. Notice that we must explicitly move a null character to position **p** after using **strncpy**.

```
strncpy(part1,text,p);
part1[p] = '\0';
```

The function **splitup** copies to **part2** everything past the substring "Smith". If the 'S' of "Smith" is in position **p**, then the position following the 'h' is $p+5$. More generally, the position

FIGURE 9-17 Action of function **splitup** on string **text**

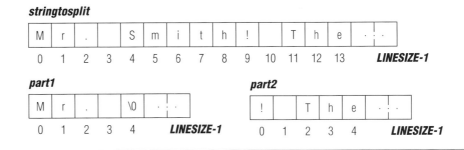

following the characters that match **oldstr** is **p+strlen(oldstr)** or **p+lenold**. To copy everything from **text[p+lenold]** to the end of **text**, we use **strcpy**. The following call copies the remaining part of the string to **part2**:

```
strcpy(part2,&text[p+lenold]);
```

THE FUNCTION *splitup*

Let's put the parts of the **splitup** function together. Notice that the function doesn't return a
value but simply changes its parameters.

```
/*
 * Function splitup:
 * Input:
 *    text: string to split; lenold: length of oldstr
 *    p: position of oldstr within text; part1, part2: strings to fill
 * Process:
 *    splits text at positions p and p+lenold;
 *    part1 gets text prior to oldstr; part2 gets text following oldstr
 * Output:
 *    part1 and part2 have new values
 */
void splitup(char text[], int lenold, char part1[], char part2[], int p)
{
    strncpy(part1,text,p);
    part1[p] = '\0';
    strcpy(part2,&text[p+lenold]);
    return;
}
```

PUTTING THE STRING BACK TOGETHER

The second function called by **replace** constructs the new string **text** by concatenating
part1, the replacement string **newstr**, and **part2**. We call this function **reassemble**. It should
receive four strings as parameters: **text** is an output parameter, while **newstr**, **part1**, and
part2 are input parameters.

Since the new string is assembled in the variable **text**, the first task of **reassemble** is to
copy **part1** to **text**, using **strcpy**. Then it calls **strcat** twice, once to concatenate **newstr** to
text, and again to concatenate **part2** to **text**.

THE FUNCTION *reassemble*

Here is the complete function **reassemble**:

```
/*
 * Function reassemble:
 * Input:
 *    newstr: the replacement word or phrase
 *    part1, part2: first and last parts of the original string text
```

```
 *  Process:
 *      using concatenation, reassembles text from part1, newstr, and part2
 *  Output:
 *      text has new value--part1+newstr+part2
 */
void reassemble(char text[], char newstr[], char part1[], char part2[])
{
        strcpy(text,part1);
        strcat(text,newstr);
        strcat(text,part2);
        return;
}
```

Let's look at what happens in *reassemble*. Figure 9-18A shows the values of the parameters. Since only *text* changes in *reassemble*, we do not show *part1*, *newstr*, and *part2* again. First, *reassemble* calls *strcpy* to copy *part1* to *text*, which changes the value of *text* as

FIGURE 9-18   *A,* parameters to function **reassemble**; *B,* **text** as changed by **strcpy**; *C,* **text** as changed by **strcpy** and the first call to **strcat**; *D,* **text** as changed by **strcpy** and both calls to **strcat**.

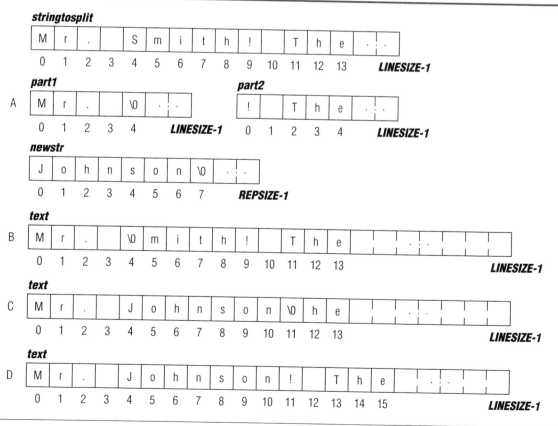

shown in Figure 9-18B. The part of **text** following the null character is still there, but we ignore it. Next, **reassemble** calls **strcat** to concatenate **newstr** to **text**, which changes **text** as shown in Figure 9-18C. Finally, **reassemble** calls **strcat** to concatenate **part2** to **text**, which changes **text** as shown in Figure 9-18D.

WRITING THE *replace* FUNCTION

Now let's return to function **replace**. It receives **text** (a single line of the original letter) as a parameter, reads in data values for **oldstr** and **newstr**, calls **pos** to find the position of **oldstr** within **text**, and calls **splitup** and **reassemble** to make the replacements. Here is a revision of the earlier pseudocode:

while there are data values
    *read in a set of replacements (*oldstr *and* newstr*)*
    while oldstr *occurs in* text
        call pos *to search for next occurrence of* oldstr *in* text
        call splitup *to break up* text
        call reassemble *to reconstruct* text

Each time it is called, **replace** executes a nested loop to make all replacements in **text**. The outer loop reads in each of the several sets of values for **oldstr** and **newstr**: "Smith" and "Johnson", "Mr." and "Mrs.", etc. This loop continues to execute as long as sets of **oldstr** and **newstr** values are entered. (The **while** condition tests only **oldstr** since we assume the replacements come in pairs.) The inner loop replaces every occurrence of **oldstr** in **text** by **newstr**. Here are the header, declaration, and outline of the function so far:

```
/*
 * Function replace:
 * Input:
 *    text, a string in which to make replacements
 * Process:
 *    reads in strings oldstr and newstr
 *    calls pos to find position of oldstr in text
 *    calls splitup to remove oldstr and give values to part1 and part2
 *    calls reassemble to create new text by concatenating part1+newstr+part2
 * Output:
 *    text has a new value with all replacements made
 */
void replace(char text[])
{
    int  p,lenold;
    char part1[LINESIZE],part2[LINESIZE];
    char *oldstr, *newstr;
    char oldin[REPSIZE], newin[REPSIZE];

    while ((oldstr = gets(oldin)) != NULL) {
        newstr = gets(newin);
            ...
    }
```

Once it has values for *oldstr* and *newstr*, *replace* calls the functions which replace *oldstr* by *newstr*. First, it calls *pos* to find the location of *oldstr* in *text*. If it finds *oldstr* in *text*, *replace* calls *splitup* to separate *text* into two components and *reassemble* to create a new *text*, with *newstr* in place of *oldstr*.

After making a replacement, *replace* should continue to search for *oldstr* in each line, stopping only when *pos* returns –1. Then we are ready to read in a new set of values for *oldstr* and *newstr*. To continue the search, *replace* must call *pos* again inside the loop to find the next occurrence of *oldstr* within the revised *text*. If *replace* doesn't call *pos* in the loop, the value of *p* remains unchanged from the first call, and the loop makes incorrect replacements. Here is the final version of *replace*:

```c
/* Function replace */
void replace(char text[])
{
    int   p,lenold;
    char  part1[LINESIZE],part2[LINESIZE];
    char  *oldstr, *newstr;
    char  oldin[REPSIZE], newin[REPSIZE];

    while ((oldstr = gets(oldin)) != NULL) {
        newstr = gets(newin);
        p = pos(text,oldstr);
        lenold = strlen(oldstr);
        while (p != -1) {
            splitup(text,lenold,part1,part2,p);
            reassemble(text,newstr,part1,part2);
            p = pos(text,oldstr);
        }
    }
    return;
}
```

Actually, the way that the function *pos* is called from *replace* is not as efficient as it might be. Each time *pos* is called, it must search the entire string from the beginning rather than starting where it left off. Improving the efficiency of calls to *pos* is the subject of Exercise 32.

ACTION OF THE *replace* FUNCTION

Let's verify that the complete *replace* function works.

PROGRAM TRACE Assume the string *text* has the value shown in Figure 9-19A.

◆ First, we send *text* to *pos*, together with *oldstr*, which has the value "Smith"; *pos* returns 21, which is the position of "Smith" within *text*.

◆ Because *p* is not equal to –1, *replace* calls *splitup* to break *text* into two parts: *part1* is "Congratulations, Mr. " and *part2* is "! The Smith family of 421 Main St. may already".

◆ Then *reassemble* concatenates *part1*, *newstr*, and *part2* to produce the string in Figure 9-19B.

◆ After "Smith" is replaced by "Johnson", *pos* is called again. This time *pos* finds "Smith" in position 34 of *text*.

FIGURE 9-19   *A*, string ***text*** before any changes; *B*, string ***text*** after first change; *C*, string ***text*** after second change.

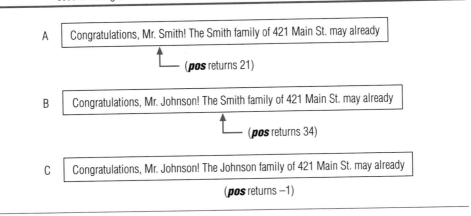

- Again, ***splitup*** and ***reassemble*** are called to replace "Smith" by "Johnson".
- After this replacement, ***pos*** is called once more. This time ***text*** looks like Figure 9-19C; ***pos*** does not find "Smith" in ***text*** and returns –1.

PROGRAM 9 COMPLETE

Here is the complete Program 9:

💻 PROGRAM LISTING

```
/*
 * Program prob9.c:
 * replaces all occurrences of old strings by new strings in a text
 * reads in a line of text, uses splitup and reassemble functions
 * to do the actual replacement of oldstr by newstr
 * and then writes out the line of text
 */
#include <stdio.h>
#include <string.h>
#define LINESIZE 120
#define REPSIZE 15
void replace(char text[]);
int pos(char text[], char oldstr[]);
void splitup(char text[], int lenold, char part1[], char part2[], int p);
void reassemble(char text[], char newstr[], char part1[], char part2[]);
main()
{
    char text[LINESIZE];
```

```
        while (gets(text) != NULL)  {
            puts(text);
            replace(text);
            puts(text);
        }
}

/* Function replace */
void replace(char text[])
{
    int   p,lenold;
    char part1[LINESIZE], part2[LINESIZE];
    char *oldstr, *newstr;
    char oldin[REPSIZE], newin[REPSIZE];

    while ((oldstr = gets(oldin)) != NULL) {
        newstr = gets(newin);
        p = pos(text,oldstr);
        lenold = strlen(oldstr);
        while (p != -1) {
            splitup(text,lenold,part1,part2,p);
            reassemble(text,newstr,part1,part2);
            p = pos(text,oldstr);
        }
    }
    return;
}

/* Function pos */
int pos(char text[], char oldstr[])
{
    int lenold,result,i=0;

    lenold = strlen(oldstr);
    while (text[i] != '\0') {
        result = strncmp(&text[i],oldstr,lenold);
        if (result == 0)
            return i;
        i++;
    }
    return -1;
}

/* Function splitup */
void splitup(char text[], int lenold, char part1[], char part2[], int p)
{
    strncpy(part1,text,p);
    part1[p] = '\0';
    strcpy(part2,&text[p+lenold]);
    return;
}
```

(continued)

(continued)

```
/* Function reassemble */
void reassemble(char text[], char newstr[], char part1[], char part2[])
{
    strcpy(text,part1);
    strcat(text,newstr);
    strcat(text,part2);
    return;
}
```

If you run this program, you will notice that the data entry is very laborious. You must enter every line of the original letter. In addition, you must enter every set of replacements once for each line. Appendix VII introduces functions which allow you to eliminate most of this work by using files.

You may find a few kinds of replacements for which this program does not work (Exercise 27 explores some of the problems).

SELF-CHECK 9-7

1. Why doesn't the function **pos** return 0 if it doesn't find the character it is looking for?

2. What happens if the original string does not contain the value to be replaced even once?

3. Can the function **reassemble** join **newstr** and **part2** and then copy this new string to the end of **part1**?

SECTION 6 ENRICHMENT: USING DATA TYPE *char*: *getchar*, *putchar*; FUNCTIONS FROM *ctype.h*

In this section, we discuss using data type **char**. We introduce character I/O functions **getchar** and **putchar**, whose headers are in **stdio.h**. In addition, we explain functions which allow us to check and change the values of variables of type **char** (or individual characters in a string). The headers for these functions are located in the file **ctype.h**.

CHARACTER-ORIENTED I/O

So far, we have discussed token-oriented I/O, performed by the functions **scanf** and **printf**, and line-oriented I/O, performed by **gets** and **puts**. C has a third kind, **character-oriented I/O**, which reads in or prints out one character at a time. Character-oriented I/O is performed by the functions **getchar** and **putchar**.

THE *getchar* FUNCTION

The library function specifically designed for input of character values is **getchar**. It reads a single character (including a whitespace character) from the keyboard and returns it. Typically, the value returned is assigned to a variable.

General Form of a Call to *getchar*

```
c = getchar();
```

The function *getchar* doesn't receive parameters. It returns a single value, which is the character just read in from *stdin*, or else is *EOF* (see Example 9-35). Because it can be assigned the value *EOF*, the variable *c* should have type *int* rather than *char*.

MORE ON DATA TYPE *char*

It may be surprising that *getchar* returns a value of type *int* since its job is to read in a character. As noted in Chapter 2, data type *char* is a subset of data type *int*; each value of type *char* has a numeric value (called its ASCII code) within the range of type *int*. The character 'a', for example, has ASCII code 97. Escape sequences like '\n' and '\t' are considered single characters with distinct ASCII codes. There are 256 values of type *char* with numeric values from 0 to 255. A value of type *char* can be interpreted as a character or an integer, and an integer in the range of type *char* can be interpreted as a character, as shown in Table 9.2.

Example 9-34A shows a simple way to use the *getchar* function.

EXAMPLE 9-34A

Suppose we want to continue processing in a program if the user enters *y*, but terminate if the user enters *n*. (This is an example of the user-response method introduced in Chapter 6.) The code below reads in a single character, assigns it to the variable *answer*, and continues processing if *answer* equals 'y':

```
int answer;                                          /* incorrect */

do {
    action of the loop goes here
    printf("Do you want to continue? y/n");
    answer = getchar();
} while (answer == 'y');
```

TABLE 9.2 Results of Printing *char* Values

Declarations: `int stuff=98;`
`int ch='a';`

Statement	Result	Comment
printf("%c",ch);	a	%c prints a *char* value as a character
printf("%d",ch);	97	%d converts *ch* to the equivalent number
putchar(ch);	a	a *char* variable
putchar('V');	V	a *char* constant
putchar('\n');	newline	a character in single quotation marks
printf("\n");	newline	a two-byte string: "\n\0" (because of double quotation marks)
putchar(stuff);	b	*putchar* converts type *int* to type *char*
stuff += 4;		
printf("%c\n",stuff);	f	%c converts type *int* to type *char*

- ◆ If the person using the program types in *y* (and then ⌷ENTER⌷), ***answer*** gets the value '*y*'. The ***while*** condition is true, and the loop repeats.

- ◆ If the person using the program types in the letter *n* (and then ⌷ENTER⌷), ***answer*** gets the value '*n*'. The ***while*** condition is false, and the loop terminates.

- ◆ If the user enters a response like *M* or *?* or even *Y*, the loop also terminates.

Unfortunately, this loop does not work correctly. The next subsection explains the problem.

BUFFERING OF INPUT

The function ***getchar*** may appear not to work properly in some circumstances, as in Example 9-34A. When the user types *y* ⌷ENTER⌷ in response to the prompt, the loop continues one more time and then stops without offering a chance to enter another value.

This happens because pressing ⌷ENTER⌷ causes the entire line to be stored in an input area called a **buffer**. An input function like ***getchar*** retrieves data values from the input buffer. In this case, the buffer contains two characters: '*y*' and '\n'. The '*y*' is read first by ***getchar***, causing the loop to repeat. However, the next call to ***getchar*** doesn't wait for the user to enter a new value; instead, it reads '\n' from the input buffer and takes it as a signal to stop.

You may think that changing the loop condition will make the loop wait for an '*n*' to stop:

```
while (answer != 'n');
```

However, this also won't work. Each user response of '*y*' causes the loop to execute twice, once for '*y*' and once for the newline character. Example 9-34B shows a simple solution to this problem.

EXAMPLE 9-34B

To eliminate the newline character, place an extra ***getchar*** in the loop (to read the newline character) and throw away the value that it reads:

```
int answer,trash;

do {
    action of the loop goes here
    printf("Do you want to continue? (y/n)> ");
    answer = getchar();
    trash = getchar();
}  while (answer == 'y');
```

The response is read into ***answer***, and the newline character is read into ***trash***, which is ignored. The line ***trash = getchar()*** can be simplified to ***getchar()***.

THE CONSTANT *EOF*

The ***getchar*** function is often used to read in a number of character values sequentially. In such a case, it is necessary to determine when the sequence ends. The predeclared constant ***EOF*** is used for this purpose. If the user enters the end-of-file character, the ***getchar*** function returns the constant ***EOF***. Remember that the end-of-file character is entered by pressing ⌷CTRL⌷-⌷Z⌷ in DOS, or ⌷CTRL⌷-⌷D⌷ in Unix.

So that it can be distinguished from a normal character value, the constant **EOF** does not have a value within the range of type **char**; instead, it has a value outside the range of **char**. This is why the variable into which the characters are read must have type **int**. Example 9-35 illustrates this.

EXAMPLE 9-35

Suppose we want to determine the total number of characters in the input data, including all whitespace characters. We can read in the characters and count them one by one, stopping when we reach end-of-file. The following loop accomplishes this.

```
int c,count=0;

c = getchar();
while (c != EOF)  {
     count++;
     c = getchar();
}
printf("there are %d characters in the input\n",count);
```

If the user enters the string "what a day this has been", followed by ENTER and the end-of-file character, this loop counts 25 characters in the input. If the user enters c ENTER TAB a ENTER t ENTER and the end-of-file character, this counts 7 characters in the input.

THE *putchar* FUNCTION

Hand in hand with reading in characters goes printing. The function **putchar** has the task of printing **char** values.

General Form of a Call to *putchar*

```
putchar(ch);
```

The **putchar** function takes one parameter—the **char** value to print (in this example, **ch**)—and sends it to **stdout**. It returns a value of type **int** which is usually ignored.

Example 9-36 modifies Example 9-35 to display each character as it is read in.

EXAMPLE 9-36

The following loop reads, displays, and counts the characters read in, including whitespace characters, stopping when it reaches end-of-file.

```
int c,count=0;

c = getchar();
while (c != EOF)  {
     putchar(c);
     count++;
     c = getchar();
}
printf("\nthere are %d characters in the input\n",count);
```

Table 9.2 shows the result of printing **char** and **int** values with the **putchar** and **printf** functions.

SELF-CHECK 9-8

1. What is the purpose of the **getchar** function?

2. Why is it usually necessary to declare a variable **int** if the variable is to hold values read in by the **getchar** function?

3. Suppose a program contains the following lines of code:

```
int let;

let = getchar();
putchar(let);
```

If the call to **getchar** reads in '\n', what is the effect of the subsequent call to **putchar**?

TESTING THE TYPE OF A *char* VALUE

Often it is useful to know what kind of value is stored in a variable of type **char** (or an element of an array of **char**). For example, you may want to know whether the character is a letter, a digit, a space, or a piece of punctuation, or whether an alphabetic character is uppercase or lowercase (so that you can change its case).

It is possible to test the value of a specific character by comparing it with others in a specific range. For example, we can write a function to detect a lowercase alphabetic character, as shown in Example 9-37.

EXAMPLE 9-37

Here is a possible definition for the function **islower**, which receives a character **ch** as a parameter and returns 1 (for true) if **ch** is a lowercase alphabetic character; otherwise the function returns 0 (for false):

```
/* returns 1 if ch is lowercase letter, 0 if anything else */
int islower(char ch)
{
    if (ch >= 'a' && ch <= 'z')
        return 1;
    return 0;
}
```

We can write similar functions for the other tasks described above, but some of them are rather complicated (the **char** values representing punctuation, for example, have ASCII codes which are not adjacent). To make the task simpler, C has functions to perform these checks. Some are **isalpha**, **isdigit**, **isalnum**, **isspace**, **ispunct**, **islower**, and **isupper**. Each function takes a single character as its sole parameter and returns 1 (for true) or 0 (for false). The prototypes for these functions are in **ctype.h**, and a program which uses them should insert the following line with the other **#include** directives:

```
#include <ctype.h>
```

Table 9.3 shows the task of each of the functions.

TABLE 9.3 Selected Functions from *ctype.h*

Function	Checks
isalpha	is the parameter alphabetic (*A..Z* or *a..z*)?
isdigit	is the parameter a digit (*0..9*)?
isalnum	is the parameter alphabetic or a digit?
isspace	is the parameter a space (' ')?
ispunct	is the parameter a piece of punctuation?
islower	is the parameter a lowercase alphabetic character (*a..z*)?
isupper	is the parameter an uppercase alphabetic character (*A..Z*)?

Example 9-38 shows how to use these functions to count the number of each type of character received as input.

EXAMPLE 9-38   The following section of code uses four function calls to determine the type of each character read in and count how many there are of each type.

```
int ch;
int alpha=0,digit=0,space=0,punct=0;

ch = getchar();
while (ch != EOF) {
    getchar();
    if (isalpha(ch))
        alpha++;
    else if (isdigit(ch))
        digit++;
    else if (isspace(ch))
        space++;
    else if (ispunct(ch))
        punct++;
    ch = getchar();
}
printf("The number of alphabetic characters is %d\n",alpha);
printf("The number of digits 0-9 is %d\n",digit);
printf("The number of spaces entered is %d\n",space);
printf("The number of pieces of punctuation is %d\n",punct);
```

An alternative way of reading the data in this example is to use the following header:

```
while ((ch = getchar()) != EOF)
```

The line *ch = getchar()* at the end of the loop is then omitted. Chapter 12, Section 4 (on side effects) explains how this works.

UPPERCASE AND LOWERCASE: THE *toupper* AND *tolower* FUNCTIONS

Often it is useful to change the case of a character, if only for testing purposes. For example, we can ask a user to enter a response (*y* for yes or *n* for no). The user may assume that *Y* and

N are equally good responses, and our program must be prepared. We can use the ***toupper*** or the ***tolower*** function in a case like this.

◆ The ***toupper*** function takes a character as a parameter and returns the corresponding uppercase character.

◆ The ***tolower*** function takes a character as a parameter and returns the corresponding lowercase character.

If sent anything else as a parameter, either function returns the value unchanged. Example 9-39 gives an example of a user-response loop, first without ***toupper*** and then with it.

EXAMPLE 9-39A

Without using ***toupper*** (or ***tolower***), here is what we have to do to allow the user to enter either *n* or *N* to stop executing the loop:

```
int ch;

do {
    ...
    printf("Do you want to continue? (y/n)");
    ch = getchar();
    getchar();
} while (ch == 'y' || ch == 'Y');
```

Actually, if the user enters any character but *y* or *Y,* the loop will terminate. This is also true in Example 9-39B.

EXAMPLE 9-39B

With ***toupper,*** the same test is much simpler:

```
int ch;

do {
    ...
    printf("Do you want to continue? (y/n)");
    ch = getchar();
    getchar();
} while (toupper(ch) == 'Y');
```

In this case, if the user enters *y,* '*y*' is sent to ***toupper,*** which returns '*Y*' for the == test. If the user enters *Y* (or any nonlowercase character), the character that was entered is returned.

The call to ***toupper*** in Example 9-39B doesn't change the value of ***ch***. If you want to change the value of the character sent to ***toupper*** or ***tolower***, you must assign the return value to a variable (this can be the same variable as the parameter). Example 9-40 shows how to use ***tolower*** this way.

EXAMPLE 9-40

```
char str[15];
int  i=0;

strcpy(str,"alPHABetic");
```

```
while (str[i] != '\0') {
    str[i] = tolower(str[i]);
    i++;
}
```

Each call to **tolower** sends one character from string **str** as a parameter. It also assigns the return value (the corresponding lowercase character, if there is one) to the same position in the array. Let's look at one particular call:

```
str[2]  = tolower(str[2]);
```

The '*P*' from **str[2]** is sent to the function **tolower**, which returns '*p*'; this value is then assigned to **str[2]**, replacing '*P*'.

SELF-CHECK 9-9

1. What value is returned by each of the following calls?

    a. isdigit('a');   e. toupper('P');
    b. ispunct('?');   f. toupper('j');
    c. isupper('t');   g. tolower('M');
    d. islower('k');   h. isalpha('c');

2. What happens if we use the function **islower** from Example 9-37 in a program and then want to use the function **islower** from **ctype.h**?

SECTION 7   ENRICHMENT: ARRAYS OF STRINGS

This section shows how to declare and use arrays of strings, including reading and printing, sending elements as parameters, and referencing individual characters.

DECLARING AN ARRAY OF STRINGS

The declaration for an array of strings looks odd. Once we get past that, using the array is quite simple. What is odd about the declaration is that each string in the array is itself an array of **char**. Thus an array of strings is an array of arrays, or a two-dimensional array (see Chapter 7, Section 8). To declare an array of strings, we must specify two subscripts: the number of strings in the array and the number of characters in each string.

EXAMPLE 9-41   Suppose we want to declare an array to hold the names of the 12 months of the year. We can call the array **months**. There should be 12 elements in array **months**, and each element should be ten characters long, since the longest month name, September, contains nine characters. Here is a declaration for **months**:

```
char months[12][10];
```

Figure 9-20 shows what this array looks like when filled.

FIGURE 9-20 The ***months*** array

months[0]	J	a	n	u	a	r	y	\0		
months[1]	F	e	b	r	u	a	r	y	\0	
. . .	. . .									
months[11]	D	e	c	e	m	b	e	r	\0	
	0	1	2	3	4	5	6	7	8	9

IN DEPTH

If you are familiar with two-dimensional arrays, the order of the subscripts in the declaration of ***months*** makes sense. The first subscript corresponds to the number of rows in a two-dimensional array, and the second subscript to the number of columns.

Even though an array of strings is technically a two-dimensional array, it is possible to use elements of the array by specifying only one subscript, as with one-dimensional arrays. That is because an array of ***char*** is treated as a unit, a string. As shown in Figure 9-20, each array element is identified by a single subscript like ***months[4]***. We need two subscripts only to refer to a particular character in a string in the array. In pointer notation, we can refer to ***months[4]*** as ***months+4***.

READING AND PRINTING AN ARRAY OF STRINGS

Examples 9-42 and 9-43 do input/output on arrays of strings using ***printf*** and ***scanf***.

EXAMPLE 9-42

The following section of code initializes and then prints the elements of the ***months*** array:

```
char months[12][10] = {"January","February","March","April","May","June",
                "July","August","September","October","November","December"};
int  i;

for (i = 0; i <= 11; i++)
     printf("%s\n",months[i]);
```

Now let's look at a loop that reads values into an array of strings. Example 9-43 uses the ***EOF*** method of reading in data.

EXAMPLE 9-43

```
char str[10][20];
int  i=0;

while (scanf("%s",str[i]) != EOF) {
     printf("%s\n",str[i]);
     i++;
}
```

This loop reads data into the **str** array, which can hold up to ten strings, each up to 20 characters in length. Each call to **scanf** reads a string into an element of the **str** array. Then the call to **printf** prints the string just stored. Since the call to **scanf** is in the header of the loop, we don't need another. Whenever **scanf** determines that there are no more data values, the loop terminates.

IN DEPTH

In past uses of **scanf**, we have checked its return value in the following way to see whether we have successfully read in a data value:

```
while (scanf("%s",str[i]) == 1)
```

When reading numeric values, this check serves two purposes: it checks for **EOF** and also for bad data—for example, entering a character where a numeric value is required. When reading string values, however, there is no such thing as bad data—numeric values are read in as characters. Thus checking for **EOF** is sufficient.

USING ELEMENTS OF A STRING ARRAY IN STRING FUNCTIONS

Let's look at how we send an element of an array as a parameter to a string function from the standard library. Example 9-44 sends elements of a string array to the functions **strcpy** and **strcmp**.

EXAMPLE 9-44

```
char animal[3][12];
int  i,result;

strcpy(animal[0],"giraffe");
strcpy(animal[1],"tiger");
strcpy(animal[2],"rhinoceros");
for (i = 0; i <= 2; i++) {
    result = strcmp(animal[i],"tiger");
    if (result == 0) {
        printf("tiger was found in position %d\n",i);
        break;
    }
}
```

In this example, we first assign values to the **animal** array of strings. Then we compare each element in the array with "tiger" to see if there is a match. If there is, we print a message and break out of the loop. In this case, we print the following:

```
tiger was found in position 1
```

A FUNCTION THAT USES AN ARRAY OF STRINGS: THE FUNCTION *classify*

Let's write a function **classify** which is a variant on Problem 6, classifying a month into one of four seasons. We wrote a version of this function as Example 9-32 in Section 4. This time, the function uses an array of strings for comparison.

Example 9-45 shows the function *classify*.

EXAMPLE 9-45

The function *classify* receives a string *monthname* as a parameter and classifies *monthname* into one of four seasons. To do so, it uses an array of strings, *months*. It sends *monthname* and one of the elements of the array *months* to the function *strcmp* for comparison. If *strcmp* finds a match for *monthname*, *classify* returns a pointer to the appropriate season; otherwise it returns an error message.

```
/*
 * Function classify:
 *    finds monthname in array months and
 *    classifies its position into one of four seasons
 */
char *classify(char *monthname)
{
    char months[12][10] ={"January","February","March","April","May",
        "June","July","August","September","October","November","December"};
    int  i,found=0;

    for (i = 0; i <= 11 && !found; i++)
        if (strcmp(monthname,months[i]) == 0)
            found = 1;
    if (!found)
        return "error";
    switch (i-1) {
        case 11: case 0: case 1:  return "winter";
        case 2:  case 3: case 4:  return "spring";
        case 5:  case 6: case 7:  return "summer";
        case 8:  case 9: case 10: return "autumn";
    }
}
```

In *classify*, the value which is typed in (now called *monthname*) is compared with each element in the *months* array. If it is equal to the current value, *strcmp* returns 0; otherwise *strcmp* returns a positive or negative value. For comparison purposes, positive or negative values are interpreted as non-zero. The rest of the function uses *i*, which represents the position of *monthname* within the array *months*, to determine *monthname*'s season.

REFERENCING A CHARACTER IN AN ELEMENT OF A STRING ARRAY

To refer to a single character in a string which is an element of a string array requires two subscripts:

```
months[3][1]
```

This refers to position 1 in the string *months[3]*. If the *months* array is initialized as shown in Figure 9-20, *months[3]* has the value "April", and position 1 of that string is the character *'p'*. Example 9-46 illustrates how to change and print a single character of a string from the *months* array.

EXAMPLE 9-46

```
months[3][1] = 'v';
printf("%c\n",months[0][0]);
```

The first line changes "April" to "Avril". The second line prints the character *'J'* from "January".

SELF-CHECK 9-10

1. Give a declaration for each of the following:

    a. ***courses***: an array of 20 strings, each of which can hold up to 30 characters
    b. ***lines***: an array of 50 strings, each of which can hold up to 80 characters

2. What is wrong with the following declaration?

```
char strarr[10][3] = {"hopes","happiness","success");
```

3. What is wrong with the following attempt to print an array ***stuff***, which has already been initialized?

```
char stuff[10][15];
int  i;
...
for (i = 0; i < 15; i++)
     printf("%s\n",stuff[i]);
```

SUMMARY

STRING BASICS

1. Although it has no string data type, C has numerous library functions for performing I/O on strings and manipulating them.

2. A string in C is actually an array of characters which is treated in a special way. The null character ("\0") is placed at the end as the string terminator.

3. The declaration specifies the maximum number of characters that can be stored in the array:

```
char str[8];
```

When the array of characters is treated as a string, one position in the array must be reserved for the null character. Thus this declaration can hold a string of up to seven characters plus the null character.

4. The maximum number of characters (in this example, eight), is known as the size of the string.

5. The actual number of characters stored in a string, not including the null character, is called its length.

6. A string of length 0 is called an empty or null string and is represented by two quotation marks placed side by side ("") or surrounding the null character ("\0").

7. A string can be initialized in the declaration or character by character, as shown below:

```
char str[20] = "handy";
char letters[10];

letters[0] = 'a';
letters[1] = 'p';
letters[2] = 'e';
letters[3] = '\0';
```

8. Since a string is an array, its name is an address. Individual positions in a string can be accessed using either subscript or pointer notation. Either notation can also be used to specify an address in the middle of a string.

STRING FUNCTIONS

9. All other operations on strings are performed through functions. The library functions designed for strings have their headers in *string.h*.

10. The *strcpy* function is used to copy a value to a string variable; this action cannot be performed by a simple assignment statement. Its first parameter is the string to be changed; the second is the value to be copied. The *strcpy* function stops after copying a null character.

11. The *strcmp* function is used to compare two strings. It receives two strings as parameters and returns an integer representing their relationship; it returns 0 if the strings are equal, a positive value if the first string is greater, or a negative value if the first string is less than the second. The *strcmp* function stops comparing when it reaches a null character in one of the strings.

12. The *strlen* function is used to determine the current length of a string. It takes one parameter, the address of a string, and returns an integer representing the string's length.

13. The *sizeof* operator is used to determine the size of a variable or a type in bytes. For a string, the value returned is an integer representing the declared size; for other types, the value returned is the size of that type in bytes.

14. The *strlen* and *sizeof* functions are especially useful because the *strcpy* and *strcat* functions do not check to see whether the destination string is large enough to hold all the characters copied or concatenated from the source string.

15. The *strcat* function is used to concatenate one string to the end of another to produce a longer string. It takes two parameters, both of which are addresses of strings, and it concatenates the second string to the end of the first. The first parameter must be the address of a variable. The *strcat* function does not check to see whether there is room for the concatenated string and can easily overlay the values of other variables.

16. The *strncpy* function copies up to *n* characters from the second parameter to the first. The third parameter specifies how many characters are to be copied.

17. The *strncmp* function compares up to *n* characters in two strings sent as parameters. The third parameter specifies how many characters are to be compared. The function returns values that match those of *strcmp*.

LINE-ORIENTED INPUT/OUTPUT

18. The I/O functions used until now—*printf* and *scanf*—perform token-oriented I/O; they read (or print) one item at a time. This item is called a token. A call to *scanf*, which performs token-oriented I/O, reads until it finds a whitespace character, and then stops. The functions *gets* and *puts* use another method, line-oriented I/O, which allows a program to read or print an entire line as a unit.

19. The *gets* function is used to read in a line of input from *stdin*, which is usually the keyboard. It takes one parameter, the address of an array of *char*, and returns a pointer to that string. If nothing is read in, *gets* returns *NULL*—the null pointer.

20. The *puts* function is used to send a line of output to *stdout*, which is usually the screen. It takes one parameter, a pointer to an array of *char*.

USING STRINGS WITH FUNCTIONS

21. A string can be sent as a parameter to a function. As with any array, the name of the string is a pointer, making the & symbol unnecessary. The string can be matched with a formal parameter of type *char* * or *char[]*. A function can also return a value of type *char* *.

THE *char* DATA TYPE AND ITS FUNCTIONS

22. The *char* data type has 256 characters, including all the letters, digits, and symbols on the keyboard. Each character of a string is a member of the *char* data type. The *char* data type is a subset of type *int*, and each character has a numerical equivalent—called its ASCII code—in the range from 0 to 255. Simple conversions are permitted.

23. Along with token-oriented and line-oriented I/O, C also has character-oriented I/O, which allows input or output to be done one character at a time. Among the functions for character-oriented I/O are *putchar* and *getchar*.

24. The *putchar* function displays a character to *stdout*.

25. The *getchar* function reads in one character at a time from *stdin*. A call to *getchar* returns the next character in the input stream, or *EOF* if there is none. A call to *getchar* looks like this:

```
int ch;

ch = getchar();
```

The return value of *getchar* is usually assigned to a variable of type *int*.

26. The constant *EOF*, standing for end-of-file, has a numerical value outside the range of type *char*. Since it differs from all other characters, it indicates the end of a set of data. However, because the value of *EOF* is outside the range of type *char*, a variable which may get this value through a call to *getchar* must have type *int*.

27. The *getchar* function reads in whitespace characters like the newline character. If the user types the letter *y* followed by (ENTER), two characters are stored in the input buffer. If the newline character is not discarded, it becomes the data value for the next call to *getchar*. To discard the extra character, insert an extra call to *getchar* to read the newline character and simply ignore the value it reads in.

28. The header file *ctype.h* contains the prototypes for a number of functions dedicated to testing and manipulating characters.

29. Among the functions in *ctype.h* are *ispunct*, *isdigit*, *isalpha*, *islower*, *isupper*, *isspace*, and *isalnum*. These functions accept a character as a parameter and classify the character as, respectively, punctuation, a digit, an alphabetic character, lowercase, uppercase, a space, or an alphanumeric character (a letter or a digit). Each function returns a value other than 0 to indicate success.

30. Two other useful functions from *ctype.h* are *toupper* and *tolower*. These allow conversion of a letter from lowercase to uppercase and vice versa. Conversions of this sort allow the programmer to simplify conditions which test a user's response.

31. It is possible, though not common, to use an array of strings in a C program. An array of strings is a two-dimensional array (better implemented as an array of pointers). Here is a sample declaration:

```
char names[10][20];
```

This declaration sets up an array of ten names, each of which can hold up to 20 characters. To access any single string in an array of strings requires one subscript; to access a character in that string requires two subscripts.

TRACING EXERCISES

1. Suppose you have the following declaration.

```
char str[5];
```

Which of the following values can be given to the variable **str**? If any value can't, explain why not.

a. "dog"   b. "rope"   c. "table"

2. What declaration is necessary for a variable **item** if the largest value it can hold is as long as "cantaloupe"? What if the largest value is as long as "antidisestablishmentarianism"?

3. Show how to represent each of the following in both array notation and pointer notation:

a. the character in position 5 of **arr**   c. the character in position 3 of **str**
b. the character in position 4 of **hold**   d. the character in position 1 of **line**

4. Show the result of a call to **sizeof** and one to **strlen** on each of the following strings, declared and initialized as shown.

a. `char str[25]="Happy birthday to you!";`   b. `char name[10] = "Winnie";`

5. For (a) and (b), show what each variable contains after the series of statements is executed. Use these declarations for each part:

```
char str[80];
char str1[10];
char str2[3];
char str3[25];
int  i,j;
```

a. `strcpy(str1,"fantastic");`   b. `strcpy(str3,"waterfall");`
   `strcpy(str3," weekend");`   `j = strlen(str3);`
   `strcpy(str,str1);`   `i = sizeof str3;`
   `strcat(str,str2);`

6. Show the value returned by **strcmp** in each of the following comparisons:

a. `char flower[10] = "tulips";`   b. `char wood[10] = "live oak";`
   `char plant[6] = "tulip";`   `char table[10] = "oak";`

   `strcmp(flower,plant);`   `strcmp(&wood[5],table);`
   `strcmp(plant,flower);`   `strcmp(table,wood+5);`

7. What is the result of each of the following calls to **strcmp**? Use these declarations for each part:

```
char str[10]  = "water";
char str2[20] = "waterfall";
char str3[15] = "what";
```

a. `strcmp(str,"water");`   c. `strcmp(str,str3);`   e. `strcmp(str2,str);`
b. `strcmp(str3,str);`   d. `strcmp(str,str2);`   f. `strcmp(str3,"where");`

8. What is the result of each of the following operations? Does each work? Do any of them destroy other variables? (Start in each case from the original values.)

```
char big[50]   = "a sunny day";
char little[10] = "was";
char middle[15] = "in the park";
```

a. `strcat(middle,little);`   c. `strcat(big,middle+6);`
b. `strcat(middle,big);`

9. For each of the following, show what values are assigned to the variables. Start from the following declaration and initial values for each part:

```
char str[80] = "good morn";
char str1[10] = "good";
char str2[5] = "bad";
```

a. `strncpy(str1,&str[2],2);`   c. `strncpy(str1,str+5,4);`
b. `strncpy(str,str2,3);`   d. `strncpy(str2+1,str+6,3);`

10. What is the result of each of the following operations?

```
char big[50] = "sun in the daytime";
char little[10] = "sunshine";
char middle[15] = "a sunny day";
```

a. `strncmp(&middle[2],big,3);`   b. `strncmp(little+5,big+4,3);`

11. Assuming the following declarations, show how to use **strcpy** to assign values to these strings as indicated in (a) through (c).

```
char str[10];
char input[80];
```

a. copy "catalogs" to **input**
b. copy **input** to **str**
c. copy "logs" from **input** to **str**

12. Using only the values in the variables **big**, **little**, and **middle**, write code to put each of the following values into the variable **dest**. (*Hint:* There may be more than one way to do some of these.)

```
char big[50] = "sun in the daytime";
char little[10] = "sunshine";
char middle[15] = "a sunny day";
char dest[7];
```

a. "in"   b. "me"   c. "time"   d. "shine"

13. Show what is printed by the following programs:

a.
```
#include <stdio.h>
#include <string.h>
main()
{
    char str1[6];
    char str2[20];
    char str3[25];
    int  i;

    strcpy(str1,"first");
    strcpy(str2,"alexander");
    strcpy(str3,str2);
    i = strlen(str3);
    strcat(str3,str1);
    printf("%s %s %s %d\n",
        str1, str2, str3, i);
}
```

b.
```
#include <stdio.h>
#include <string.h>
main()
{
    char str[25];
    char str1[25];
    int  k, m, n;

    strcpy(str,"jacksonville fl");
    m = strlen(str);
    strcpy(str1,"here is ");
    strcat(str1,str);
    k = sizeof str1;
    n = strlen(str1);
    printf("%s %s\n",str, str1);
    printf("%d %d %d\n", k, m, n);
}
```

14. Show what is printed by the following program:

```c
#include <stdio.h>
#include <string.h>
main()
{
    char str[25],temp[25];
    int  i,k;

    strcpy(str,"large array of char");
    k = strlen(str);
    for (i = 0; i <= k; i += 5) {
        strcpy(temp,str+i);
        printf("%s %s\n",temp,str);

    }
}
```

15. What is the output from the following program?

```c
#include <stdio.h>
#include <string.h>
main()
{
    char str[10] = "artist";
    char arraystr[7] = "xyzabc";
    int  i;
    char str1[7];
    char str2[13];

    for (i = 0; i < 6; i++)
        printf("Element number %d is %c\n",i, arraystr[i]);
    strcpy(str1,"hunger");
    strcpy(arraystr,str);
    printf("\n");
    for (i = 0; i < 6; i++)
        printf("%s",arraystr);
    printf("\n");
    strcpy(str2,str1);
    strcat(str2,arraystr);
    printf("The new string is %s\n",str2);
    strcpy(arraystr,"widget");
    printf("arraystr is now %s\n", arraystr);
}
```

16. What is the output from this program?

```c
#include <stdio.h>
#include <string.h>
main()
{
    char str[5]="sale";
    char strarray[5];
    char bigstr[12];
    int  i;
```

```
            strcpy(strarray,str);
            for (i = 0; i < 4; i++)
                printf("%c",strarray[i]);
            printf("\n");
            strarray[0] = 'b';
            strarray[3] = 'k';
            for (i = 0; i < 4; i++)
                printf("%c",strarray[i]);
            printf("\n");
            strarray[3] = 'l';
            for (i = 0; i < 4; i++)
                printf("%c",strarray[i]);
            strarray[0] = 'l';
            strcpy(bigstr,strarray);
            strcat(bigstr,"me!!");
            printf("\n\n");
            printf("%s",bigstr);
        }
```

17. Trace Example 9-20. Show step by step what is in each variable after executing each line of the code.

MODIFICATIONS TO PROGRAM 9 AND EXAMPLES

18. Incorporate the code from Example 9-26 into a complete program and run it to see what happens.

19. a. Rewrite function *length* from Example 9-27 using a *for* loop.
    b. What happens if we write the loop header as *while(str+i != '\0')*?

20. a. Rewrite function *countchar* from Example 9-28 using a *for* loop.
    b. Rewrite Example 9-28 using pointer notation.

21. Write a function *adds* which adds an *s* to the end of a string sent as a parameter (see Example 9-31).

22. Why doesn't the function *classify* from Example 9-45 require a *break* after each *case*?

23. a. Rewrite function *findchar* from Example 9-30 so that it uses *break*.
    b. Rewrite the *return* statement from *findchar* so that it uses the conditional operator.
    c. Try to rewrite *findchar* so that it does the same thing without using a flag.

24. Compare the function *split* from Example 9-33 with the function *splitup* in Program 9. Are they performing the same task? Is it possible to revise function *split* so that it can be used in Program 9 in place of *splitup*? If so, write the function; if not, explain why not.

25. a. Rewrite Example 9-44 so that it prints a message if "tiger" is not found in the array.
    b. Revise the code so that it finds all the occurrences of "tiger" in the *animal* array.

26. a. Rewrite function *pos* using pointer notation.
    b. Rewrite function *splitup* using pointer notation.
    c. Rewrite function *reassemble* using pointer notation.
    d. Rewrite the complete Program 9 using pointer notation.
    e. Rewrite function *pos* using a *for* instead of a *while* loop.

27. There are several problems that can arise with the version of ***replace*** given in Section 5.

    a. If the string to be replaced begins with a capital letter (e.g., at the start of a sentence), then it will not be replaced. For example, replacing "her" by "his" will not work for "Her eyes will light up...". Suggest a way to solve this problem.

    b. Another problem occurs if the string to be replaced is found in an inappropriate place. For example, if we replace "her" by "him" in "here is my mother.", then the new string is "hime is my mothim." Suggest several ways to solve this problem.

    c. A more serious problem arises in a situation like this: Replace "he" by "she" or "Mr." by "Mrs.". In this case, the replacement string contains another occurrence of the old string to be replaced. Why does this cause a problem? How can it be solved? (*Hint*: Instead of looking for the old string ***old*** anywhere in ***str***, start searching for it past the last occurrence.)

    d. Can you think of any other problems?

28. Rewrite the ***replace*** function from Section 5 so that it calls the ***pos*** function only once, in the header of the ***while*** loop.

29. There are several ways of carrying out the ***replace*** function other than splitting the string into three components and reassembling them. You can implement ***replace*** by calling functions ***delete*** and ***insert***, described below.

    a. Write a function ***delete*** which finds a string within a longer one and deletes it from the string, closing up the string afterward. The function receives two parameters: ***oldstr***, the string to search for, and ***text***, the string in which to search. It should change the value of the second string parameter.

        For example, ***delete*** ("rain","drainboard") causes "drainboard" to change to "dboard" because all the characters after "rain" are moved toward the beginning of the string. The function ***delete*** can use character-by-character movement or call ***strcpy***.

    b. Write a function ***insert*** which inserts a string into another, changing the second string. The function receives three parameters: ***new***, the string to insert; ***text***, the string in which to place it; and ***p***, the desired position within that string. It should change the value of the second parameter. (*Hint*: See Example 9-20.)

        For example, ***insert***("isk","dboard",1) says to insert "isk" into "dboard" at position 1, changing it to "diskboard". Since "isk" is three characters long, all characters from position 1 to the end of the string must be moved three positions toward the end of the string; then "isk" can be inserted at position 1. Be sure to have the function check that it does not exceed the length of the string ***text***.

30. The method explained in Exercise 29 requires a lot of character movement. Another way of carrying out the ***replace*** function is by writing a single function that inserts the replacement string into ***text*** right after moving characters toward the end of the string, without moving any characters back. This function, called ***outandin***, accepts four parameters: ***text***, the string to change; ***oldstr***, the old string to be replaced; ***newstr***, the string to insert; and ***p***, the position of the replacement. By using concatenation, create a new string from the part prior to ***p***, ***newstr***, and the part following ***oldstr***. Copy the result back to ***text***.

31. Which of these methods to write ***replace*** (the original, and the methods from exercises 29 and 30) is most modular? Which provides functions which are likely to be reusable? Which involves the most character movement? Which involves the least character movement?

32. The *pos* function as written in Section 5 is not as efficient as it might be.

    a. First, the function starts to search *text* for *oldstr*, starting at position *text[0]* each time. Where can *pos* begin its search that takes advantage of what it already has calculated? (*Hint:* This requires a third parameter.)

    b. Write a new version of the *pos* function that starts its search in a new position each time; send the starting position as a parameter. Be careful how you select the starting position: If you search for "dog" in *text*, which is "dogsdoggy", and replace each occurrence by "orange", where should you begin your next search after the first replacement, "orangesdoggy"?

    c. Second, the function continues to search even though there are not enough positions past the starting position to hold *oldstr*. For example, in the string "carts", where should the function stop searching for the string "cat"? Each time through the loop, *pos* examines three positions. The first time, *pos* looks at positions 0-1-2; the second time, at 1-2-3; the third time, at 2-3-4; should it continue? Why or why not?

    d. Write a new version of the *pos* function that stops when the characters remaining are fewer than the number of characters in *oldstr*.

33. Rewrite Program 9 so that it calls the library function *strstr* instead of *pos*. The function *strstr* receives two strings as parameters and returns a pointer to the location of the second string within the first, or *NULL* if the string is not found. Here is an example:

```
char *pos1,*pos2;
char first[20]="alfalfa";

pos1 = strstr(first,"fa");
pos2 = strstr(first,"ba");
```

The first call to the function assigns *pos1* a pointer to the location of the first occurrence of "fa" within *first*, or *first+2*. The second call assigns *pos2* the value *NULL*.

34. a. Rewrite the main part of Program 9 so that it reads in all data from a file (using redirection—Appendix V—or *fscanf*—Appendix VI). If you are using *fscanf*, try it two ways: (1) hard-code the name of the file, and (2) ask the user to input the name of the file.

    b. Rewrite the main program so that it writes all output to a file (using redirection or *fprintf*—Appendix VI). If you are using *fprintf*, try the same methods as part (a).

PROGRAMMING PROJECTS

35. a. Write a function, like the one in Example 9-37, that performs the same task as *isdigit*.

    b. Do the same for *isupper, isalpha, isalnum*, and *isspace*.

36. a. Write a function *removeblanks* to delete blanks from a string. The function receives a string variable as a parameter and returns the string with all blanks removed. For example, if the value sent to *removeblanks* is " I am sad " the function returns "Iamsad".

    b. Modify the function so that only trailing blanks are deleted. Call the new function *trailing*. It receives a variable *str*, an array of *char*, as a parameter and returns the string with all trailing blanks removed. For example, if the value sent to *trailing* is "I me you ", the function returns "I me you".

    c. Write parts (a) and (b) using a void function. Each function modifies a string sent as a pointer parameter.

37. Write a function *rev_position* that receives two string parameters, *str1* and *str2*. It returns the position where *str2* in reverse order starts in *str1*. For example, if *str1* is "melon" and *str2* is "nol", then *rev_position* returns 2 (since the reverse of *str2* is "lon" and "lon" starts in position 2). If *str1* is "melon" and *str2* is "lon", the function returns –1.

38. Write a function *right_position* that receives two string parameters, *str1* and *str2*. It returns the start of the last occurrence of *str2* in *str1*. For example, if *str1* is "messes" and *str2* is "es", the function returns 4. If the string is not found, it returns –1.

39. a. Write a function *reverse* that receives a string *str* as a parameter and returns the characters in *str* in reverse order. For example, if the value sent to *reverse* is "I me ", the function returns " em I".

    b. Write a void function version of *reverse* that receives two parameters. One parameter holds the original string. The second is an output parameter to hold the reversed string produced by the function.

40. a. Write a function *countblanks* that receives a string *str* as a parameter and returns the number of blanks in *str*. For example, if the value sent to *countblanks* is " help me ", the function returns 4. The function should not change the value of the parameter.

    b. If you use the function *removeblanks* from Exercise 36, there is a very simple version of *countblanks*. What is it?

    c. Write a function *count* that receives a string *str* and a character *ch* as parameters. It returns the number of times that *ch* occurs in *str1*. Do not change either parameter.

    d. Modify *count* from part (c) so that it takes two strings, *str1* and *str2*, as parameters and counts the number of times that *str2* occurs in *str1*. However, each character in *str1* can be counted only once. For example, "eve" occurs just once in "eveve".

41. a. Write a function *non_alpha* that receives a string *str* as parameter and returns the position of the first nonalphabetic character in *str*. For example, if *str* has the value "stev7n", the function returns 4. If none is found, the function returns –1.

    b. Write a function *alpha* that receives a string *str* and returns the position of the first alphabetic character in *str*. For example, if *str* has the value "3315 Main St.", the function returns 5. If none is found, the function returns –1.

    c. Write a function *after* that receives a string *str* and returns the position of the first alphabetic character that occurs after a nonalphabetic character. For example, if *str* has the value "stev9n", the function returns 5; if *str* has the value "stev9 n", the function returns 6. If none is found, the function returns –1.

42. Assume you have two strings, *s1* and *s2*, and you want to determine if the characters in one are a rearrangement of the ones in the other. Write a function *order* to solve this problem.

43. a. Write a function *common* that receives two parameters, strings *s1* and *s2*. The function returns a string consisting of the characters which appear at least once in both strings. For example, if *s1* has the value "johnson" and *s2* has the value "honor", then the function returns "hon" (or these characters in some other order).

    b. Write a program that reads in a series of names (first name, last name). It calls the function *split* from Example 9-33 to break each name up into its two components. Next, it calls *common* to determine if there are any letters in common in the first and the last name. It returns a string containing the common letters. You can make the letters all capitals, all lowercase, or ignore case. For example, if the name is "JOHN JONES", then the two parts are "JOHN" and "JONES". The letters in common are "JON".

c. Write a version of **common** that does the same thing as (b) but leaves no repeated letters in the output string. For example, if the name is "BOB BOKO", the returned string is "BO".

Test the functions with the following strings:

JOHN JONES	madonna	WILSON ACTS
april fresh	SANDY E. LANDY	anna anna

For exercises 44 and 45, assume that all words are composed of only lowercase letters.

44. Write a function **code** that receives two parameters, a string **words** and an integer **m**. The function encodes each letter in **words** into a new letter **m** positions down in the alphabet. For example, if **m** is 3, then '*a*' is encoded as '*d*', '*k*' as '*n*', '*y*' as '*b*', and so on. (Assume that the alphabet is circular, so that *z* is followed by *a*.) All nonalphabetic symbols in **words** are unchanged. Write a driver program to test **code**.

45. Write a complete program that calls the functions described below, first to encode and then to decode a series of strings. The main program tests **encode** and **decode**. It reads a 26-letter alphabet string indicating what code is to be used. Then it reads a series of strings. Each string is encoded by **encode**. The new string is then decoded by **decode**. (What happens if we call them in reverse order?)

a. Write a function **encode** that receives two string parameters, **str** and **alpha**. The first parameter is a word to be encoded; the second is a permutation of the 26 letters of the alphabet. Each letter in **str** is encoded according to this scheme: If a letter in **str** is the **k**th letter of the alphabet in the usual order, then its encoding is the letter in **alpha** that is in position **k**. For example, if **alpha** starts with "eps...", then each '*a*' in **str** becomes '*e*', each '*b*' becomes '*p*', and so on.

b. Write a function **decode** that receives the same parameters as **encode**. This function decodes **str** letter by letter. If a particular letter of **str** occurs in position **k** of **alpha**, it is decoded into the letter at position **k** in the alphabet. For example, if **alpha** starts with "txe...", each '*t*' in **str** becomes '*a*', each '*x*' becomes '*b*', and so on.

c. Modify the main program to do error checking. For example, the alphabet string must contain each letter exactly once. Are there any restrictions on the individual strings?

46. a. Write a program that reads in a series of strings, then determines whether or not each string is a valid "mini-C" identifier. Here is a brief summary of the rules: The name may be up to 30 characters long; the first character must be a letter; every remaining character must be a letter, a digit (0 to 9), or an underbar symbol.

In your program, use the following functions:

size: to determine if the size of the identifier name is within the allowed range;
first: to determine if the name starts with an allowed symbol; and
others: to determine if all other characters are allowed symbols.

You should decide exactly what parameter(s) are required by these functions and whether they should be void functions.

If an identifier name is valid, print "ok". If it is invalid, print at least one thing that is wrong with it (e.g., "it does not begin with a letter").

b. Modify the program to reject keywords as well. Use a function ***iskey*** to determine if the string is a keyword. Assume that there are only five keywords: ***if, for, while, do,*** and ***else.***

c. Modify the program to reject an identifier name that has appeared previously. Use a function ***repeated*** to determine if the string repeats an earlier valid name. (*Hint:* Use an array to hold the valid names.)

d. Modify the program to convert an invalid identifier name to a valid one. If the first character is not a letter, add '***x***' at the front of the string. If there are illegal symbols in the string, delete them.

47. Write a complete program that calls ***convert***, described below, to convert dates from one format to another. Test the program with the following dates, among others:

    11/17/29   01/01/00   12/31/99

    a. Write a function ***convert*** that receives as a parameter a string ***date*** of the form "mm/dd/yy". For example, ***date*** can be "11/17/29". The function converts this value to the form "month day, year". For example, "11/17/29" becomes "November 17, 1929" (all years are in the twentieth century).

    b. Modify the function to allow one or two digits for the month and/or day. For example, "5/17/29" becomes "May 17, 1929".

    c. Modify the function to reject an invalid string. What constitutes one?

48. Write a function to break a sentence into individual words and produce a new sentence made up of the words in reverse order. Thus, if the original is "I am eating eggs", the result is "eggs eating am I".

49. Write a program to read in a word and send it to a function ***find2*** to determine whether it contains any double letters, and if so, how many sets. Test ***find2*** on the following words, among others: "spelling" (double *l*), "bookkeeper" (three sets of double letters), "helper" (no double letters, even though the *e* is repeated).

50. Write a program to read in a string and send it to a function ***IsPal*** to determine whether it is a palindrome. A string is a palindrome if it reads the same backward and forward, like "Madam, I'm Adam". You can make the letters all capitals, all lowercase, or ignore case. You should ignore punctuation in the string.

51. Write a program to read in a string that is a sentence and send it to a function ***lettercount***. The function counts how many times each letter in the sentence occurs. The program produces a printed list of each letter and the number of times the letter appears. Write the program in two different forms:

    a. Produce a list containing counts for only those letters which actually occur in the string.

    b. Produce a list containing counts for all the letters in the alphabet. If a letter does not occur in the string, it appears on the list with a count of 0.

    Do these alternatives suggest two very different ways of counting the letters? Before you start, think carefully about the various ways you can count.

52. Write a program that reads in and prints a text, line by line, and calls a series of functions. The main program calls a function ***diffwords*** to count the number of different words in the entire text (ignoring case). It also calls a function ***wordcount*** to count the number of times

each word appears in the text. Then it calls a function ***printcount*** to print a list of all the words in the text, together with the count of the number of times they appear. For example, if a word occurs twice in the text, it appears only once on the list, with a count of 2. Print the list of words in alphabetical order. Use other functions wherever appropriate.

For example, suppose the text is this:

The elephant ate the banana and the giraffe ate the banana.

The function ***diffwords*** produces a count of 6 ("the", "elephant", "ate", "banana", and "giraffe"); ***wordcount*** produces this list:

and	1	banana	2	giraffe	1
ate	2	elephant	1	the	4

53. Write a program that reads in a string and calls a function ***uplow*** to convert each letter to the opposite case: if the letter is lowercase, ***uplow*** converts it to a capital; if it's a capital, it becomes lowercase. If a character in the string is not a letter, ***uplow*** leaves it the same. The program prints the original string and the converted string. For example, if the string is "IBM is in New York, USA", ***uplow*** produces the string "ibm IS IN nEW yORK, usa".

54. Write a program that reads in a string and translates it into Pig Latin. Pig Latin is a secret language that converts words in the following way:

    a. If the word starts with a consonant, the consonant moves to the end of the string and is followed by an "ay": the words "pig latin" become "igpay atinlay".

    b. If the word begins with a vowel, the letters "ay" are added to the end of the word: the words "is any" become "isay anyay".

    Write a function to split the string into words. Write another function to convert each word to Pig Latin. Print the original string and the converted string.

55. Write a program that reads in a string and translates it into Algebra. Algebra is a secret language that converts words in the following way:

    a. If the word starts with a consonant or a group of consonants, the letters "iaz" are added after the consonant or group of consonants: the words "crazy cat" become "criazazy ciazat".

    b. If the word begins with a vowel, the letters "iaz" are added to the beginning of the word: the words "is any" become "iazis iazany".

    Write a function to split the string into words. Write another function to convert each word to Algebra. Print the original string and the converted string.

56. Write a program that reads in a series of strings, stopping when there are no more strings. For each string, it should call each of the following functions and print the results:

    cat: Takes two strings, ***s1*** and ***s2***, as parameters. Concatenates ***s2*** to the end of ***s1***, changing ***s1***. (This function may not call ***strcat***.)

    remove: Takes a string, ***s***, and a character, ***c***, as its parameters. Removes all occurrences of ***c*** from ***s***, changing ***s***.

57. Write a program that plays a simplified form of Hangman. Your program prints out the length of a word (using underscores), and the player tries to guess what the word is by filling in letters. Each time the player guesses a letter, the program checks to see if the word

contains that letter. If it does, the program fills in the letter wherever it occurs and prints again. If it does not, the program adds the letter to a list of unsuccessful letters. A player wins by replacing all the underscores with letters in seven or fewer guesses (seven guesses correspond to drawing the head, neck, two arms, body, and two legs in Hangman).

After the game is over, the user should be given the option of playing again. Your program should have an array of words, so that the player is given a different word each time. Include both long and short words, easy ones and hard ones. Include some words that have a lot of repeated letters and some that have none.

SORTING
AND SEARCHING

PROGRAMMING CONCEPTS: sorting, linear sort, bubble sort, interchanging two values, searching, linear search, binary search

PROBLEM-SOLVING TECHNIQUES: analysis of algorithms, bottom-up approach

HOW TO READ CHAPTER 10

It is possible to cover sections 4 and 9 before sorting. Program 10 can use the bubble sort from Section 3 instead of the linear sort from sections 1 and 2.

OUTLINE:

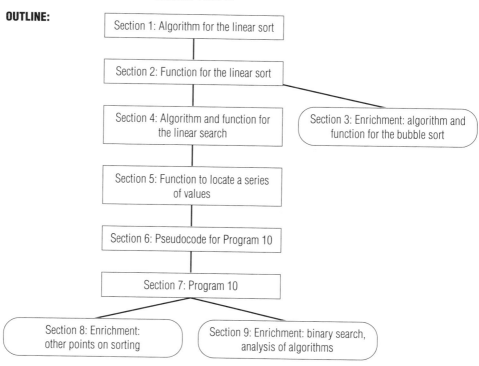

Section 1: Algorithm for the linear sort

Section 2: Function for the linear sort

Section 4: Algorithm and function for the linear search

Section 3: Enrichment: algorithm and function for the bubble sort

Section 5: Function to locate a series of values

Section 6: Pseudocode for Program 10

Section 7: Program 10

Section 8: Enrichment: other points on sorting

Section 9: Enrichment: binary search, analysis of algorithms

INTRODUCTION AND STATEMENT OF THE PROBLEM

INTRODUCTION

This chapter starts by introducing **sorting**—one of the most common applications of computers today. For example, a bank's files of its customers and their transactions, a college registrar's student records, and the names in a telephone book are all sorted to make access easier. Simply stated, sorting means to put objects into order (numerical for numbers or alphabetical for characters), either ascending or descending.

We discuss two sorting methods: a linear or selection sort and a bubble sort. Neither is particularly efficient or used very often in the business or scientific world. We study them because for most small cases (fewer than 100 numbers), they are adequate. A more practical reason is that these two methods are closest to the way a person sorts. Thus they are probably easiest to describe in an algorithm and use in a program. The sorting methods used for actual commercial or scientific applications (e.g., to sort 100,000 numbers) are much too complicated for our current programming ability. Any further discussion has to be postponed until a higher-level course in data structures. [For examples, see *Data Structures in C and C++* by Y. Langsam, M. Augenstein, and A. Tenenbaum (Englewood Cliffs, N.J.: Prentice-Hall, Inc., 1996).]

In addition to sorting, the chapter introduces **searching**—another widely used computer function. Searching means finding a value in a list. We discuss several types of searches; the decision of which to use is largely based on whether the list has been sorted.

Let's start with the statement of the problem:

PROBLEM 10

Read a parameter value, which we will call *n*, then read a set of *n* numbers. Print the numbers in their original order. Sort the numbers into ascending order. Print the numbers in sorted order. Then read in a second set of data, consisting of numbers which may or may not occur in the original list. For each such number, print its position in the list or print a message saying that it doesn't occur.

We use a bottom-up approach to solve the problem. We start by writing a function to sort an array. (In fact, we will write two functions which sort in different ways.) Next we add the searching component. Then we combine these pieces with other functions to read in and print a set of data. Finally, we tie everything together with a main program that calls the functions.

We write this program in a modular way. We present two sorting methods, either of which can be used to sort the list of numbers. We also present two searching methods. Once again, either can be used to search the sorted list. The decision on which sort or search to use is somewhat arbitrary, although the chapter does analyze and compare the various sorting and searching methods. These functions are like tools or books in a library. A programmer can decide which one to use in a given situation.

SECTION 1 ◆ USING A LINEAR OR SELECTION SORT

Much of Problem 10 consists of things that we have done before (reading in and printing a set of numbers) so we concentrate first on the new portions: sort the numbers into ascending order and then search through the list. The next few sections are devoted to sorting. After that, we discuss searching.

In this section, we develop an algorithm for sorting, using what is called a linear or selection sort. We trace the algorithm on a few examples and then translate it into pseudocode.

SORTING INTO ASCENDING ORDER

It seems clear that the numbers to be sorted should be stored in an array. Therefore, we need an algorithm describing how to sort an array into ascending order. Ascending order means that the numbers are increasing. For the moment, we assume that no two numbers are equal so that we do not have any repeated elements.

Let's store the numbers to be sorted in an array called **numb**. Rather than specifying a particular size (e.g., 50 or 100) for the array, assume that it has **n** values to be sorted; these values are stored in positions 0 to **n - 1** within the array. The problem boils down to this: Given the **numb** array, rearrange the first **n** elements so that they are in increasing order. Figure 10-1 provides an example of the **numb** array before and after sorting (with **n** equal to 5).

AN INFORMAL ALGORITHM FOR SORTING

Now we must construct an algorithm for sorting the **numb** array. We can't be vague and say "put the numbers in order." We need a step-by-step process that can be written as a program.

Here is a possible way to approach the problem:

◆ Start by finding the smallest number in the array and putting it in the first position since in the final sorted array, the smallest element comes first.

◆ Look through the rest of the numbers for the smallest one left, which goes into the next position of the array.

◆ Do the same to find the next smallest and so on until all the positions have been filled.

CAUTION Once we have determined the proper item for a position, we cannot consider that item in determining the proper item for other positions because we already know it is smaller than the remaining values.

FIGURE 10-1 **numb** array before and after sorting

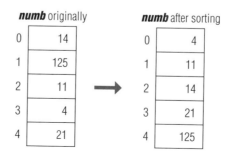

This is not quite precise enough to be an algorithm, but we can continue to improve this method until it becomes an algorithm. The first step is to find the smallest number in the array and put it in the first position. We did something similar when we found the largest of a set of marks in Program 7. Finding the smallest is exactly the same idea.

ALGORITHM TO FIND THE SMALLEST ELEMENT IN AN ARRAY

◆ *Pick one of the numbers (usually, the first element) in the array as the smallest so far.*

◆ *Compare it to each of the other numbers.*

◆ *If one of them is smaller, this new value becomes the smallest so far.*

◆ *Continue to compare the smallest so far to the rest until all the numbers have been compared.*

The method for finding the smallest can be combined with the informal sorting algorithm to create a more precise one. This sorting algorithm is called a **linear** or **selection sort** since we compare the elements in linear order (first, second, third, etc.) as we select the correct one for each position in the array.

A FORMAL ALGORITHM FOR SORTING

Now we modify this algorithm so that it can be used to sort the elements of the *numb* array. We pick *numb[0]* to be the initial value for smallest so far since that is where we want the smallest value to end up. To find the smallest, compare each element in the array with *numb[0]*. If the new value is less than *numb[0]*, we swap their positions within the array (this allows us to save the old value of *numb[0]*); if the new value is greater than or equal to *numb[0]*, we do nothing. (This also takes care of the question of repeated elements—do you see how?) Then we do the same thing for the other positions in the array.

Here is a complete algorithm for sorting the first *n* elements of the *numb* array:

ALGORITHM FOR THE LINEAR OR SELECTION SORT

◆ *Find the smallest element in the array and put it in **numb[0]**. Compare each array element to **numb[0]**. If it is smaller, swap it with **numb[0]** (if not, do nothing).*

◆ *Ignore the element in position 0 and repeat the process for the rest of the elements to find which one belongs in position 1—**numb[1]**.*

◆ *Repeat the process for the other positions in the array down to the next to last.*

We stop at the next-to-last position because filling it leaves only one number, which automatically goes in the last position.

PSEUDOCODE TRANSLATION OF THE ALGORITHM

Now let's translate the algorithm into pseudocode in preparation for writing a function to sort. Looking at the algorithm, we see a nested loop structure. One loop handles successive positions within the array, and the other determines which of the candidates for a particular position should go there. Here is the algorithm rewritten in pseudocode:

PSEUDOCODE FOR THE LINEAR SORT

for each position in the array (except the last)
  for each candidate for that position
    compare the candidate to the element currently in that position
    if the candidate is smaller
      swap them

What do we mean by the phrase *for each candidate for that position*? At any point in the process, the only candidates for a given position are those elements whose subscript is greater than that of the given position. For example, the candidates for position 3 have subscripts of 4 or higher.

TRACING THE PSEUDOCODE FOR THE LINEAR SORT ALGORITHM

Let's trace an example to verify that our pseudocode translation of the linear sort algorithm works.

EXAMPLE 10-1

Assume that the *numb* array holds 14 125 11 4 21 (with $n = 5$). We simplify our trace by showing only the numbers, not the subscripts from the *numb* array. We also use) to stand for a comparison between any two elements. If the two are swapped, then we rewrite the entire revised array immediately to the right.

PROGRAM TRACE Figure 10-2 shows a trace of the first pass through the algorithm to find the smallest number and put it into *numb[0]*. First 14 is compared to 125. Since it is less, we do nothing. Then 14 and 11 are compared, and these two items must be swapped. We move to the second column in the figure. Now 11 (the smallest so far) and 4 are compared; once again, these two items must be swapped. We move to the third column in the figure. Finally, 4 is compared to 21, and there is no change. Note that 4, the smallest number, is now correctly placed in *numb[0]*.

Once the first pass is complete, we start a second pass to fill the second position. (In Figure 10-3, we use a vertical line to separate passes from each other.) For the second pass, we ignore *numb[0]*. We want to determine the second smallest in the entire array, the smallest in the remaining group. We start by comparing 125 to 14, and

FIGURE 10-2 Trace of the first pass of the pseudocode for the linear sort algorithm: Example 10-1 ($n = 5$)

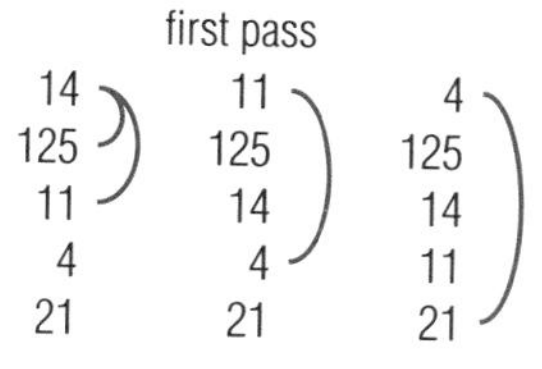

first pass

14	11	4
125	125	125
11	14	14
4	4	11
21	21	21

these two values swap places. Then we compare 14 and 11, resulting in another swap. Finally, 11 and 21 are compared, but they do not swap.

The second pass is followed by a third pass to determine the third smallest, and a fourth one to determine the fourth (and also fifth) position. On the third pass, 125 and 14 swap, but 14 and 21 do not. On the fourth pass, 125 and 21 swap. The complete trace of the pseudocode for the algorithm is shown in Figure 10-3.

SELF-CHECK 10-1

1. In the linear sort algorithm, why is the element chosen for a position not considered for any other position?

2. If we sort 5 elements, how many passes are needed? If we sort 56, how many are needed? If we sort *n* elements, how many do we need? On each pass, how many items are put in their correct position?

3. If we want to sort a group of two or three numbers, is it necessary to store them in an array? What if we have four or five numbers? What if we have an arbitrary number (that is, *n* values)?

SECTION 2   FUNCTION FOR THE LINEAR SORT

In this section, we translate the pseudocode into a function to perform a linear sort. This function is then used in Program 10. (Concentrating on the functions before the main program is called a bottom-up approach to solving a problem; see Section 6.)

A FUNCTION TO SORT

We've traced a few examples to prove that the algorithm and pseudocode are correct; now it is time to write a function. Since there is no single answer to return, we use a void function. Instead of returning an answer, the function changes the values stored in the entire array.

We write a function called ***linearsort*** to sort or rearrange the ***numb*** array, assuming that values have already been stored in positions 0 to *n* − *1*. Later we show how to call this function from a main program.

FIGURE 10-3   Complete trace of the pseudocode for the linear sort algorithm: Example 10-1 (*n* = 5)

first pass			second pass			third pass		fourth pass	
14	11	4	4	4	4	4	4	4	4
125	125	125	125	14	11	11	11	11	11
11	14	14	14	125	125	125	14	14	14
4	4	11	11	11	14	14	125	125	21
21	21	21	21	21	21	21	21	21	125

Here is the comment, followed by the function header:

```
/*
 * Function linearsort:
 * Input:
 *    numb: the array to sort
 *    n: the number of elements to sort in the array
 * Process:
 *    linear sorts into ascending order
 *    the first n values of the numb array
 * Output:
 *    function modifies array numb
 */
void linearsort(int numb[], int n)
```

Notice once again that **numb** is changed in the function. This is crucial because we must have the changed order of the array available in the main program once we return from the function.

Let's look at the pseudocode again:

for each position in the array (except the last)
*   for each candidate for that position*
*   compare the candidate to the element currently in that position*
*   if the candidate is smaller*
*   swap them*

The outer loop takes care of positions in the array. When $n = 5$, it takes 4 passes through the body of the outer loop to sort the array; when $n = 6$, there are 5; if $n = 100$, there will be 99 passes. In general, it takes $n - 1$ passes to sort n values since each pass except the last fills one position, and the last pass fills two. Following normal C practice, we start counting at 0 so we number these passes $0, 1, 2, ..., n - 2$. For example, if n is 5, the passes are 0, 1, 2, 3.

On each pass, we want to do the same job—find the smallest value of the elements of the array still left and put it into the correct position in **numb**. Thus we can use a **for** loop, with index **pass**, to take care of the $n - 1$ passes. Notice that we've modified the pseudocode now that the identifier **pass** is a reference.

```
int pass;

for (pass = 0; pass < n - 1; pass++)
```
    `for` *each candidate for position* `pass`
       compare the candidate to the element in position `pass`
           `if` *the candidate is smaller*
               swap it with the element in position `pass`

Inside the **pass** loop, we want to compare each of the remaining numbers to the value that is in position **pass** of **numb**. However, as we noted earlier, we don't want to consider any number that has already been chosen. Using our example, note that once 4 is chosen to go in *numb[0]*, it is not a candidate for *numb[1]*; once 11 is fixed in *numb[1]*, neither 4 nor 11 should go in *numb[2]*, and so on.

Let's use *cand* as the control variable of the *for* loop to run through the candidates. The candidates for position *pass* are the values in *numb[pass + 1]*, *numb[pass + 2]*, . . ., *numb[n – 1]*. Each candidate should be compared to *numb[pass]*. If it is smaller, it is swapped with *numb[pass]*. Therefore, we have this nested *for* loop construction (and an additional declaration for *cand*):

```
int pass,cand;

for (pass = 0; pass < n - 1; pass++)
    for (cand = pass + 1; cand < n; cand++)
        if (numb[pass] > numb[cand])
            swap them
```

Note that the outer or *pass* loop only goes up to *n – 2* because the last pass determines the position of two elements. The inner or *cand* loop goes up to *n – 1* because each element in the array must be considered. In the last comparison of the entire nested loop, *pass* equals *n – 2* and *cand* equals *n – 1*, so *numb[n – 2]* is compared to *numb[n – 1]*. For example, if *n* is 5, the last comparison is *numb[3]* to *numb[4]*.

DISSECTING THE LINEAR SORT FUNCTION

Before going on, let's check that this portion of the pseudocode has been translated correctly.

PROGRAM TRACE We return to our example: *n* = 5, *numb* holding 14 125 11 4 21. Let's analyze the overall setup. Note that *n – 1* is 4, and *n – 2* is 3.

◆ The outer loop has *pass* going from 0 to 3 since we want to fix the values for *numb[0]* to *numb[3]* (*numb[4]* is the value which is left).

◆ The inner loop has *cand* going from *pass + 1* to 4.

◆ For position 0, the candidates are *numb[1]* to *numb[4]*, competing with *numb[0]*.

◆ For position 1, the candidates are *numb[2]* through *numb[4]*, competing with *numb[1]*.

◆ For position 2, they are *numb[3]* and *numb[4]*, competing with *numb[2]*.

◆ For position 3, just *numb[4]* and *numb[3]* compete.

◆ Finally, *numb[4]* must be the largest.

Note once again that *numb[4]* can be a candidate for the other passes, but no separate pass determines position 4.

The trace matches the step-by-step analysis of the algorithm and pseudocode in Figure 10-3. We urge you to do a detailed trace on an example with five or six elements to prove the code works.

INTERCHANGING TWO VALUES

We must still interchange the two values, *numb[pass]* and *numb[cand]*, in case there is a swap. Recall from Chapter 8, Section 2 the method to interchange two values. (In Section 8 of this chapter, we show how to use the function **swap** from Chapter 8, Section 2.) The following three statements interchange the two array elements:

```
temp = numb[pass];                    /* swapping the values of    */
numb[pass] = numb[cand];              /* numb[pass] and numb[cand] */
numb[cand] = temp;
```

In the sorting function, we want to interchange the two values only if they are out of order—if **numb[pass]** is greater than **numb[cand]**. Therefore, we use the following **if** statement:

```
if (numb[pass] > numb[cand])  {
    temp = numb[pass];                /* swapping the values of    */
    numb[pass] = numb[cand];          /* numb[pass] and numb[cand] */
    numb[cand] = temp;
}
```

THE *linearsort* FUNCTION

Here is the entire **linearsort** function:

```
/* ... */
void linearsort(int numb[], int n)
{
    int pass,cand;
    int temp;

    for (pass = 0; pass < n - 1; pass++)
        for (cand = pass + 1; cand < n; cand++)
            if (numb[pass] > numb[cand])  {
                temp = numb[pass];
                numb[pass] = numb[cand];
                numb[cand] = temp;
            }
    return;
}
```

PROGRAM TRACE To make sure the function works, let's trace a simple example with four elements: 8 23 6 5 ($n = 4$).

♦ The outer **for** loop sets **pass** to 0, which is less than or equal to **n – 2** (4 – 2 is 2).

♦ The inner **for** loop sets **cand** to **pass + 1**, which is 0 + 1 or 1. This value is less than or equal to **n – 1**.

♦ The first comparison is **numb[0]**, which is 8, to **numb[1]**, which is 23. They are in order so we do nothing.

♦ Then **cand** increments to 2, and we compare position 0 (which holds 8) and position 2 (which holds 6). Since 8 > 6 is true, we interchange these two values.

♦ Next **cand** increments to 3 (which is still less than or equal to **n – 1**). We compare position 0 (which now holds 6) and position 3 (which holds 5), and these values are swapped.

♦ Then **cand** increments to 4, which terminates the inner loop. The first pass is complete, and the smallest value (5) is now in position 0. The array holds the following values: 5 23 8 6.

♦ Next *pass* increments to 1. A new *cand* loop starts with *cand* initialized to 1 + 1, which is 2.

♦ We compare position 1 (which holds 23) and position 2 (which holds 8). They swap places.

♦ Then *cand* increments to 3, and we compare position 1 (which now holds 8) with position 3 (which holds 6). They swap places.

♦ Then *cand* increments to 4, which terminates the inner loop. The second pass is complete, and the second smallest value (6) is now in position 1. The array holds the following values: 5 6 23 8.

♦ Next *pass* increments to 2. A new *cand* loop starts with *cand* initialized to 2 + 1 = 3.

♦ We compare position 2 (which holds 23) with position 3 (which holds 8). They swap places.

♦ Then *cand* increments to 4, which terminates the inner loop. The third pass is complete, and the third smallest value (8) is now in position 2; in addition, the largest value (23) is in the last position. The array holds the following values: 5 6 8 23.

THE *linearsort* FUNCTION REWRITTEN USING POINTER NOTATION

NOTE   This subsection assumes that you have already covered Chapter 8. If necessary, review the discussion there on pointers and arrays.

As the last part of this section, let's rewrite the entire function using pointer rather than subscript notation for the array. The only changes necessary are the declaration of the array in the header and the reference to the array elements.

The new function header looks like this:

```
void linearsort(int *numb, int n)
```

Recall that this declares *numb* to be a pointer to an integer, which is exactly what the name of an array is.

Inside the body of the function, references to the array look like this:

```
if (*(numb+pass) > *(numb+cand))
```

Recall that this notation (*numb+pass* or *numb+cand*) says each element in the array is offset by *pass* or *cand* positions from the position of the first element.

Here is the entire function rewritten with pointer notation:

```
/* ... */
void linearsort(int *numb, int n)
{
    int pass,cand;
    int temp;

    for (pass = 0; pass < n - 1; pass++)
        for (cand = pass + 1; cand < n; cand++)
            if (*(numb+pass) > *(numb+cand))  {
                temp = *(numb+pass);
                *(numb+pass) = *(numb+cand);
                *(numb+cand) = temp;
            }
    return;
}
```

SELF-CHECK 10-2

1. Trace the *linearsort* function on this set of numbers: 20 100 –12 5 (*n* = 4)

2. In the *linearsort* function, what is the purpose of the *pass* loop? What is the purpose of the *cand* loop?

3. Is tracing the pointer version of *linearsort* any different from tracing the original version?

SECTION 3   **ENRICHMENT: USING A BUBBLE SORT**

This section shows a second way to sort an array, called a bubble sort, and briefly compares the two methods.

PROBLEMS WITH THE LINEAR SORT

Why do we need another sorting method? Imagine the following situation: The *numb* array holds the numbers from 1 to 78, followed by 80 and then 79, so it is in ascending order except for the last two items, which are swapped.

A person would quickly notice that the numbers from 1 to 78 are in order, then swap 80 and 79, but it takes the linear sort function a long time to sort this array. The program does not (why not?) notice that the items are almost all in their correct positions. Instead, it first determines the smallest number and puts it in *numb[0]*. This takes 79 comparisons. Then it ignores that number and determines the second smallest by comparing the second number to each of the others. This process goes on for a total of 79 passes and slightly over 3000 comparisons. (See Exercise 9 for a way to calculate the precise number.)

This is not even the worst possible case. What if the entire array is in order to begin with? The same number of passes and comparisons are used. Thus we have an incredible situation where it takes more than 3000 comparisons to "sort" a sorted array. No matter what the original order, the linear sort algorithm uses the same comparisons to sort an array with 80 elements (see Exercise 7). Of course, in an array that is almost sorted, there are relatively few swaps, and this saves time.

A NEW APPROACH USING ADJACENT POSITIONS

The problem is that the linear sort does not take advantage of any information that it has already obtained about the array. A "smarter" sorting algorithm could use the results of earlier comparisons to decide what to do next. For example, if *numb[3]* < *numb[4]* and *numb[4]* < *numb[5]*, it is stupid to compare *numb[3]* and *numb[5]*. Shortcuts like this are used by a person to speed up the sorting process. Let's build a smarter algorithm that uses some of these shortcuts.

Assume that we find the following:

◆   *numb[0]* < *numb[1]*

◆   *numb[1]* < *numb[2]*

◆ *numb[2] < numb[3]*

...

◆ *numb[n – 2] < numb[n – 1]*

The *numb* array must be in order. If each number is in the correct position relative to the one after it (and, therefore, the one before it), the array is sorted.

This means that we can use only neighboring positions in our comparisons. Instead of comparing *numb[0]* to *numb[1]*, *numb[2]*, ..., *numb[n – 1]*, we need only compare *numb[0]* to *numb[1]*. If it is less than (or equal to—do you see why?) *numb[1]*, we compare *numb[1]* to *numb[2]*. If a number is larger than the one after it, we swap the two of them and continue. But we must be a little more careful. If, for example, *numb[1]* and *numb[2]* are swapped, perhaps the old value of *numb[2]*, now in *numb[1]*, is also smaller than *numb[0]*. For example, if *numb* holds 14 125 11 4 21, 125 and 11 should swap, but 11 is also less than 14. If we stop after one pass, the array holds 14 11 4 21 125, which is not in sorted order (although 125, the largest element, is in the correct position).

Therefore, when we finish going through the array, we must go back to the beginning and start over. The numbers are gradually put into their correct positions starting from the end of the list. If we ever have one pass through the entire array without a swap, we are done. In that case, *numb[0] < numb[1]*, *numb[1] < numb[2]*, ..., *numb[n – 2] < numb[n – 1]*. We know this means the array is sorted.

ALGORITHM AND PSEUDOCODE FOR THE BUBBLE SORT

This new method is called a **bubble sort** for reasons that become clear when we trace a few examples. Here is the bubble sort algorithm to sort the first *n* elements of the *numb* array:

ALGORITHM FOR THE BUBBLE SORT

Repeat the following process until an entire pass has no swaps:

◆ *Compare adjacent elements of the array (**numb[0]** with **numb[1]**, **numb[1]** with **numb[2]**, ..., **numb[n – 2]** with **numb[n – 1]**).*

◆ *If they are out of order, swap them.*

Here is a pseudocode version of this algorithm:

PSEUDOCODE FOR THE BUBBLE SORT

    do the following as long as there has been a swap on the last pass
      for each element of the array
        compare the element to its neighbor
        if they are out of order
          swap them

TRACING THE BUBBLE SORT ALGORITHM

Let's trace an example before going on.

EXAMPLE 10-2   Assume that **numb** holds 14 125 11 4 21 ($n = 5$). We use the earlier conventions in the trace, which is illustrated in Figure 10-4.

PROGRAM TRACE

◆   In the first pass, we compare 14 and 125, and they are in correct order.

◆   In the linear sort, we would compare 14 and 11, but, in the bubble sort, we compare 125 and 11. They swap positions.

◆   Then we compare 125 and 4, which also get swapped, as do 125 and 21. This ends the first pass.

◆   Because there has been at least one swap in the first pass, we must have a second.

◆   In the second pass, 14 and 11 (and then 14 and 4) swap places so we need a third pass.

◆   The third pass swaps 11 and 4, requiring a fourth. There are no swaps; we are done.

There are several ways to speed up the bubble sort algorithm; a few are explored in exercises 12 through 14.

EXAMPLE 10-3   Let's try another example: **numb** = 4 7 11 15 20 13 ($n = 6$). On this example, which is almost in order to start, the bubble sort is significantly better than the linear sort (see Figure 10-5).

FIGURE 10-4   Trace of the pseudocode for the bubble sort algorithm: Example 10-2 ($n = 5$)

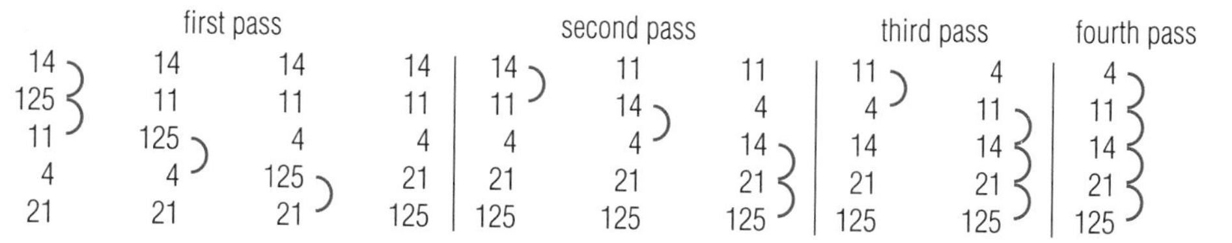

FIGURE 10-5   Trace of the pseudocode for the bubble sort algorithm: Example 10-3 ($n = 6$)

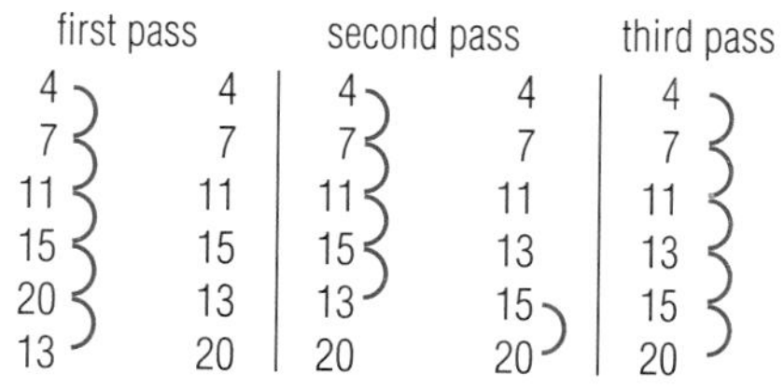

CAUTION While a bubble sort is usually better than a linear sort, there are cases where it is worse, for example, on an array that starts in reverse order.

EXAMPLE 10-4

As an example where the bubble sort does very poorly, let **numb** = 7 6 5 4 (**n** = 4). Trace this one on your own.

In general, the bubble sort works best if the original array is almost sorted. For a random array, this is quite rare, but it is fairly common in practice. For example, if you have a sorted array and want to add two new elements, you can place them in the front (why is this better than the rear?) and do a relatively fast bubble sort.

A trace of the bubble sort shows elements moving to their correct locations like bubbles in water. In Figure 10-4, watch a large number like 125 descending and a small number like 4 rising. Figure 10-5 shows 13 rising while 15 and 20 descend.

COMPARISON OF THE TWO ALGORITHMS

In many cases, the bubble sort is not much better than the linear sort. However, if the array is fairly close to sorted order, the bubble sort is a significant improvement. Thus, for relatively small applications (**n** < 100), where an extremely efficient sort is not necessary, the bubble sort is preferred. Another advantage of the bubble sort is that the numbers to be compared are always adjacent in the array, whereas the linear sort often compares numbers that are widely spread. In certain circumstances, this takes longer.

One curious feature about the bubble sort algorithm is that there is no way to predict exactly how many passes are necessary to sort **n** numbers. The number of passes ranges from a low of one (if the array is in order) to a high of **n** (if the array is completely reversed). The linear sort always takes **n – 1** passes. (See Exercise 9 for an analysis of the sorting algorithms.)

Neither sort is useful in real business or scientific applications where the amount of data is in the thousands or larger.

FUNCTION FOR THE BUBBLE SORT

Now let's translate the pseudocode for the algorithm into a function. The bubble sort algorithm says to repeat something as long as an event, *a swap on the last pass*, occurs. In addition, we must go through the process at least once. As we saw in Chapter 6, the best way to implement such a structure is with a *do-while* loop.

We want to repeat the body of the loop as long as a swap occurs on each pass. In fact, we use that as our condition controlling the *do-while* loop:

```
do  {
     . . .
}  while (there has been a swap on the last pass);
```

Inside the *do-while* loop, we want to have a complete pass through the array, comparing each position to the one after it; for this, we use a *for* loop. If we use *pos* as the *for* loop index, the two items to be compared are **numb[pos]** and **numb[pos + 1]**. The **for** loop index **pos** goes from 0 to **n – 2** (we use **n – 2** so that we don't compare the last item in the array to the one after it). Here is the first version of the function for the bubble sort:

```
/*
 * Function bubblesort:
 * Input:
 *    numb: the array to sort
 *    n: the number of elements to sort in the array
 * Process:
 *    bubble sorts into ascending order
 *    the first n values of the numb array
 * Output:
 *    function modifies array numb
 */
void bubblesort(int numb[], int n)
{
    int pos;

    do  {
        for (pos = 0; pos < n - 1; pos++)
            if (numb[pos] > numb[pos + 1])
                swap them
    }  while (there has been a swap on the last pass)
    return;
}
```

Let's check this. The body of the **do-while** loop continues to be executed as long as a swap was made on the last pass. This means that at least one more pass is needed to check for further swaps. If we ever escape from the loop, it is because an entire pass of the **for** loop did not cause a swap. This means that **numb[0]** and **numb[1]**, **numb[1]** and **numb[2]**, ... , **numb[n – 2]** and **numb[n – 1]** are all correctly positioned relative to each other so the entire array is sorted.

 CAUTION A common mistake is to use the following **if** condition:

```
if (numb[pos] > numb[pos] + 1) ...
```

This is wrong because the + 1 has been moved outside the array brackets. Inside the brackets, + 1 means add 1 to the subscript; outside the brackets, it means add 1 to the value of **numb[pos]**. We are asking if the value of **numb[pos]** is greater than itself plus one, and this can never be true.

DETERMINING WHETHER A SWAP HAS BEEN MADE

We still have to define the **while** condition of the loop. To tell if a swap was made on the last pass, we can use a signal or flag. A value of 0 indicates that no swap was made, while 1 means a swap was made. (The declaration for this variable, which we call **swapped**, is shown in the complete function later in this section.) The condition to be tested is this: **while (swapped == 1)**. This can be abbreviated to **while (swapped)** since **swapped** is true as long as **swapped** is not 0. This leads to the following format for the outer loop structure:

```
do  {
    ...
}  while (swapped);
```

There are still a few loose ends. One fundamental problem is where to give **swapped** a value to indicate whether a swap has been made. Since **swapped** equal to 1 indicates a swap, the natural time to set **swapped** to 1 is when we interchange the two values. This means we should insert the statement **swapped = 1** inside the compound statement that swaps **numb[pos]** and **numb[pos + 1]**. This time, we also include the actual statements to do the swap:

```
do  {
    for (pos = 0; pos < n - 1; pos++)
        if (numb[pos] > numb[pos + 1])  {
            /* swap the values */
            temp = numb[pos];
            numb[pos] = numb[pos + 1];
            numb[pos + 1] = temp;
            swapped = 1;
        }
}  while (swapped);                                      /* incomplete */
```

Unfortunately, this leads to the following situation: we have set **swapped** to 1 at one point, and we have checked to see if **swapped** is not 0, but we have never given **swapped** the value 0. If the array is initially unsorted, the **do-while** loop will continue forever because the condition **while(swapped)** is always true.

CAUTION An infinite loop, caused by forgetting to initialize (or reinitialize) a variable, is a common error with a **do-while** loop.

The problem can be solved by giving **swapped** an initial value of 0 somewhere. One possibility is to set it to 0 in an **else** statement:

```
if (numb[pos] > numb[pos + 1])  {
    /* swap the values */
    temp = numb[pos];
    numb[pos] = numb[pos + 1];
    numb[pos + 1] = temp;
    swapped = 1;
}
else
    swapped = 0;                                         /* incorrect */
```

However, this is not the correct spot. For example, if **numb[1]** and **numb[2]** swap, but **numb[2]** and **numb[3]** don't, **swapped** should remain at 1 to indicate the swap on this pass.

We want *swapped* to be 0 only if an entire pass through the inner loop does not produce a swap. This suggests setting *swapped* to 0 between the two loops.

THE *bubblesort* FUNCTION

Here is the complete version of the bubble sort function:

```
/* ... */
void bubblesort(int numb[], int n)
{
      int pos,swapped;
      int temp;

      do  {
          swapped = 0;
          for (pos = 0; pos < n - 1; pos++)
              if (numb[pos] > numb[pos + 1])  {
                  /* swap the values */
                  temp = numb[pos];
                  numb[pos] = numb[pos + 1];
                  numb[pos + 1] = temp;
                  swapped = 1;
              }
      }  while (swapped);
      return;
}
```

PROGRAM TRACE Let's trace the function on the set of values we used in Example 10-3: *numb* = 4 7 11 15 20 13 (*n* = 6).

◆   The *do-while* loop starts, and *swapped* is set to 0.

◆   The *for* loop starts, and *pos* is initialized to 0, which is less than the limiting value of *n – 1*.

◆   The first comparison is *numb[0]* to *numb[1]*. Since 4 > 7 is false, we do nothing.

◆   Then *pos* increments to 1, and we compare position 1 (which holds 7) to position 2 (which holds 11). Once again they are already in order.

◆   We compare positions 2 and 3, and then positions 3 and 4, without change.

◆   Then *pos* increments to 4, and we compare position 4 (which holds 20) and position 5 (which holds 13). They swap places, and we also set *swapped* to 1, indicating a swap was made.

◆   Next *pos* increments to 5, but now the condition (*pos < n – 1*) is false, and we fall out of the *for* loop.

◆   Then we test the *while* condition. Since *swapped* is 1, the condition is true, and the body of the *do-while* loop is executed again. The array now holds the following values: 4 7 11 15 13 20.

◆   On the second pass, *swapped* is set to 0, and the *for* loop starts again with *pos* set to 0.

◆   We compare positions 0 and 1, 1 and 2, 2 and 3, all without a swap taking place.

◆ We compare position 3 (which holds 15) to position 4 (which holds 13). They swap places, and ***swapped*** is set to 1.

◆ Then we compare position 4 (which holds 15) to position 5 (which holds 20). They do not swap.

◆ Next ***pos*** increments to 5, and we fall out of the ***for*** loop.

◆ When we test the condition at the bottom of the ***do-while*** loop, it is true since there was a swap on the last pass. The array now holds the following values: 4 7 11 13 15 20. This happens to be in sorted order, but we must have another pass through the ***do-while*** loop to verify that.

◆ In the new pass, ***swapped*** is set to 0, and the ***for*** loop starts with ***pos*** set to 0.

◆ We compare positions 0 and 1, 1 and 2, 2 and 3, 3 and 4, 4 and 5 without any swaps taking place. Eventually, ***pos*** increments to 5, and we fall out of the ***for*** loop.

◆ The condition at the bottom of the ***do-while*** loop is now false since ***swapped*** is still 0. Therefore, the ***do-while*** loop ends, and the sort is complete.

CAUTION In both the linear and the bubble sort, we do not swap two elements if they are equal, but only if the first is greater than the second. In the linear sort, this is done for efficiency. However, in the bubble sort, it is crucial not to swap adjacent elements that are equal. (See Exercise 8 for details.)

DISSECTING THE BUBBLE SORT FUNCTION

This function contains two loops, which serve very different purposes. The outer or ***do-while*** loop forces us to repeat the ***for*** loop as long as swaps of adjacent elements are made. The inner or ***for*** loop lets us compare all pairs of adjacent elements in the ***numb*** array. The body of the ***for*** loop is done exactly $n - 1$ times for each execution of the outer loop. The outer loop is repeated an unknown number of times [see Exercise 9(b)] until ***swapped*** is 0. When this occurs, it means that an entire pass through the array has not found two adjacent elements out of order and the array has been sorted.

THE *bubblesort* FUNCTION REWRITTEN USING POINTER NOTATION

Once again, it is possible to rewrite the entire function with pointer rather than subscript notation for the array. The changes are similar to the ones we made for the pointer version of the ***linearsort*** function.

SELF-CHECK 10-3

1. Trace the pseudocode for the bubble sort algorithm on the following set of numbers: 20 0 –2 15 ($n = 4$).

2. Is it possible to initialize ***swapped*** to 0 as part of the ***for*** loop header? If yes, show how to do it. If no, explain why it is not possible.

3. Why must the ***while*** condition controlling the outer loop eventually become false? That is, why must there be a pass where no swap takes place?

SECTION 4 SEARCH TECHNIQUES: LINEAR SEARCH

One of the most common ways to take advantage of the speed and power of a computer is to search through a list. This section examines the most basic technique to do this, called a linear or sequential search.

A SIMPLE SEARCHING PROBLEM

Assume we are given an initial list of *n* numbers. Then we receive a series of new numbers, which are read in one at a time. We want to see if each number in the new series occurs in the original list. If it does, we want to print its position. If it doesn't, we want to print a message saying it was not found. For example, assume that the original list contains five numbers: 4 99 2 90 16. The first new number is 90, and the second is 7. The number 90 is found in position 3 of the original list; the number 7 is not found.

The first simplification we will make is to concentrate on searching for a single item at a time instead of worrying about the entire set of new values. We will write a function to search a list of numbers and determine the location of a single new value. (Later we will use this function as part of Program 10.)

We start by talking about a searching method that does not require a sorted list. In Section 9, we present an algorithm which takes advantage of searching a list that is already sorted. However, it is not always more efficient to sort the list before starting to search. For example, if we are searching for only one or two items, it is not worthwhile to sort the list.

On the other hand, if we are searching hundreds, thousands, or even millions of times, it is more efficient if the list is sorted before the search. Consider how often people look up numbers in the phone book.

ALGORITHM FOR THE LINEAR OR SEQUENTIAL SEARCH

Our first searching technique uses an algorithm called the **linear** or **sequential search**. We start with an array of numbers called **numb**, a new integer to locate in the array, called **newnumber**, and the number of elements to search in the array, called **n**. The algorithm determines the position of **newnumber** within the array **numb**.

The algorithm simply compares **newnumber** to each element of the array. If they are equal, it returns the position of the element. If it does not find **newnumber**, it signals that fact.

Here is a more formal version of the algorithm with these variable names:

ALGORITHM FOR THE LINEAR SEARCH

◆ *Compare* newnumber *to each element in the* numb *array.*

◆ *If a particular element is equal to* newnumber, *return the position of that element.*

◆ *If a particular element is not equal to* newnumber, *try the next element.*

◆ *If no element is equal to* newnumber, *return a failure signal.*

As usual, we translate the algorithm into pseudocode before writing a function to do the search. Looking at the algorithm, we see an obvious loop to go through all positions in the array. In this loop, we compare **newnumber** to the element in the array at that position. Here is the algorithm rewritten in pseudocode:

PSEUDOCODE FOR THE LINEAR SEARCH

> *for each position in the* numb *array*
>> *compare the element in that position to* newnumber
>> *if they are equal*
>>> *return the position in the array*
> *if no element is equal to* newnumber,
>> *return a failure signal*

THE FUNCTION *linearsearch*

Now we are ready to write a function, called **linearsearch**, which translates the algorithm into C. The function receives the following parameters: **numb**, **n**, and **newnumber**. There is an obvious answer to return—the position of **newnumber** in the array—so we write **linearsearch** as a function that returns an integer value. Consider the five numbers at the start of this section: 4 99 2 90 16. If **linearsearch** is asked to locate 90, it returns 3. If it is asked to locate 7, it returns a signal that 7 does not occur. Any number which can't be an array position is a good signal; we can use –1.

Here are the function comment and header:

```
/*
 * Function linearsearch:
 * Input:
 *   numb: the array to search
 *   n: the number of elements to search in the array
 *   newnumber: the value to search for
 * Process:
 *   using a linear search, determines the position of
 *   newnumber within the first n elements of numb
 * Output:
 *   returns the position of newnumber in the array;
 *   returns -1 if newnumber is not found
 */
int linearsearch(int numb[], int n, int newnumber)
```

The pseudocode translates naturally into a *for* loop, with each position from 0 to *n – 1* being tested for **newnumber**. If the value in the array at a particular position matches **newnumber**, we return that position, terminating the *for* loop and the function. If the *for* loop does not terminate prematurely, the new value has not been found, and the function returns –1 to signal failure. Because the entries are checked one after another, this method is called a linear or sequential search.

Assume that **newnumber** is somewhere in the array. Regardless of whether it is found in the first or last position, or somewhere in between, the ***return position*** statement terminates the function, sending back the position of **newnumber**. However, if **newnumber** is not found in the array, then **return –1** terminates the function. Here is the body of the function:

```
{
        int position;

        for (position = 0; position < n; position++)
            if (numb[position] == newnumber)
                return position;
        return -1;
}
```

We are assuming that each value occurs just once in the array **numb** (or if it occurs several times, we are interested only in the first one). This means that once a match has been found, it is not necessary to search any further. It is possible to modify the search so that it finds all occurrences.

PROGRAM TRACE Let's trace the two examples from earlier in this section. Here are the parameters to the function: the array **numb** holds 4 99 2 90 16, **n** is 5, and we are searching for 90 as **newnumber**.

◆   Inside the function, the **for** loop compares 90 to each element in the array, for **position** equal to 0, 1, ...

◆   A match is found at the fourth element in the array with **position** equal to 3.

◆   This value is returned to the calling program, and the function terminates.

Assume now that **newnumber** is 7.

◆   In the function, the entire **for** loop, from 0 to **n – 1**, is processed without finding a match.

◆   After the loop ends, the function returns –1 to the calling program. If the loop ends without executing the **return position** statement, it must be because **newnumber** has not been found.

STYLE WORKSHOP Note that the **return** statement in the middle of the loop terminates both the loop and the function. As an alternative, we can use a **break** statement (see Chapter 6, Section 7) to get out of the loop, then modify the single **return** statement at the end of the loop to return the appropriate value (see Exercise 40).

ANALYZING THE LINEAR SEARCH ALGORITHM

The algorithm for the linear search seems efficient since each entry in the array of numbers is checked at most one time per new number. If nothing is known about the original array (the array is not sorted, and all elements are equally likely to be selected), this search method is as good as any other. However, in many situations, we know that the array is in sorted order. In that case, the linear search is extremely inefficient. To determine why, we must analyze the behavior of the linear search algorithm.

AVERAGE BEHAVIOR OF THE LINEAR SEARCH ALGORITHM

Assume we have 100 elements in an array of integers and all elements are equally likely to be selected.

◆ On the average, it takes approximately 50 comparisons to find the position of a new number if it is already in the array. It actually takes anywhere from 1 to 100 comparisons, depending on the position of the number.

◆ If the new number is not in the array, we have to search all 100 elements to find out.

Now assume we have 1000 entries in the array (of course, the constant definition has to change to accommodate an array this size).

◆ An average of 500 comparisons is required to find an entry if it is present.

◆ A thousand comparisons are necessary to verify that an entry is not present.

Finally, assume we have an array of **n** numbers.

On the average, to find the position of a given number takes **n** / 2 comparisons.

◆ **n** comparisons are needed to show that a number is not there.

These results are tabulated in Table 10.1.

The key observation about the linear search is that the average number of comparisons required remains the same, regardless of how the values are ordered in the array.

ACCELERATED REJECTION IN A SORTED LIST

As we have already noted, it is usually not more efficient to sort a list before a search; but, if the list has already been sorted, this extra information can increase the efficiency of the search. If the array is sorted, one improvement is to accelerate the rejection process. As soon as the number being checked is larger than the new number, we can exit the search loop and return a signal that the new number is not in the list without checking the rest of the array. (A more detailed discussion of this method, called the **accelerated rejection method**, is found in exercises 26 and 33.)

POINTER NOTATION VERSION OF *linearsearch*

This subsection assumes you have already covered Chapter 8. If necessary, review the discussion there on pointers and arrays.

TABLE 10.1 Analysis of the Linear Search Algorithm

	Average number of tries using linear search to	
n	Locate	Reject
7	4	7
100	50	100
1,000	500	1,000
1,000,000	500,000	1,000,000

We now rewrite the entire function with pointer notation. There is just one line in the body of the function, plus the header, that must be changed.

```
/* ... */
int linearsearch(int *numb, int n, int newnumber)
{
    int position;

    for (position = 0; position < n; position++)
        if (*(numb + position) == newnumber)
            return position;
    return -1;
}
```

SELF-CHECK 10-4

1. Why doesn't the *linearsearch* function return 0 if an item is not found in the array?
2. Why must the *linearsearch* function return an integer if an item is not found, rather than some other type of answer?
3. Trace the linear search algorithm and function on the following lists and new values to be located:

   a. list: 7 2 4 –2 0 8 15 34 6   new values: 4 and then 1
   b. list: 10 20 30 ... 100   new values: 5 and then 20

SECTION 5   A FUNCTION TO LOCATE A SERIES OF VALUES

LOCATING A SERIES OF NEW VALUES

In the original statement of Problem 10, we specified a series of items whose location in the array should be determined. However, to simplify our discussion in Section 4, we wrote a function, *linearsearch*, to find the position of a single item in the array. Now we show how to use that function together with a new function to locate the position in an array of each item in a series.

CAUTION In Program 10, the array is sorted by the time we start to locate new values. However, we do not take advantage of that fact in writing this new function.

The new function, which we call *locatevalues*, is given two parameters, the array *numb* and *n*, the size of the array. It asks the user to type in a new number whose position in the array is to be found. Then it calls *linearsearch*, sending it the three required parameters: the array, its size, and the new number to be located. When *linearsearch* returns with an answer, the *locatevalues* function prints an appropriate message. Then it asks the user whether to continue.

In Chapter 6, we had a similar situation when we classified month/day combinations. In that chapter, we decided to use a loop with a question at the bottom asking the user whether to continue. We use a similar structure in the *locatevalues* function. Here is a pseudocode version of the function:

> *repeat the following as long as the user wants to continue:*
> *ask the user to type in a value for* newnumber
> *call* linearsearch *to find the position of* newnumber *in the array*
> *print the position*
> *ask whether the user wants to continue*

Recall that we translated this structure into a **do-while** loop. Here is the next version of the pseudocode, showing this loop structure and making the input more specific:

```
do {
      printf("Please enter a number to locate within the array\n");
      scanf("%d",&newnumber);
      call linearsearch to locate newnumber in the numb array
      print the answer returned by linearsearch
      printf("do you want to continue (y/n)? \n");
      scanf(" %c\n",&answer);
} while (answer != 'n');
```

Note the blank space before **%c** in the *scanf* for **answer**. When the user-response method was introduced in Chapter 6, we noted that the space matches the newline character typed in after the value for **newnumber**.

Although this is not quite C code, it is close. At this point, we can write the function.

THE FUNCTION *locatevalues*

First, we give the function header and comment for *locatevalues*. Unlike *linearsearch*, this function does not return a value.

```
/*
 * Function locatevalues:
 * Input:
 *    two input parameters
 *       numb: an array of integers
 *       n: the size of the array
 *    also reads in a series of new values one by one
 * Process:
 *    for each new value, calls the function linearsearch
 *    to find the location of each new value in the numb array
 * Output:
 *    prints a message giving the location of each new value
 */
void locatevalues(int numb[], int n)
```

Now we translate the remaining pseudocode into C. The function *linearsearch* returns an integer value, which we store in a local variable called *location*. Therefore, the call from *locatevalues* to the function *linearsearch* looks like this:

```
location = linearsearch(numb,n,newnumber);
```

We shouldn't simply print the value stored in *location*. If the *linearsearch* function does not find *newnumber*, it returns –1. What happens if we use the following statements?

```
location = linearsearch(numb,n,newnumber);
printf("%d is located in position %d\n",newnumber,location);
```

If we print the value returned directly and *newnumber* is not found, it will certainly look awkward to have a message saying *newnumber* is located in position –1. To fix this problem, we ask a question to determine the correct way to phrase the message describing the position of *newnumber*. This question appears in the final version.

In addition, to make the program easier to use, we allow the user to type either *N* or *n* in response to the prompt at the end of the loop. This is taken care of by the call to the function *toupper* (see Chapter 9, Section 6). Once the *do-while* loop ends, nothing else is necessary, and the function also ends. Here is the entire *locatevalues* function:

```
/* ... */
void locatevalues(int numb[], int n)
{
    int  newnumber,location;
    char answer;

    do  {
        printf("Please enter a number to locate within the array\n");
        scanf("%d",&newnumber);
        location = linearsearch(numb,n,newnumber);
        if (location >= 0)
            printf("%d occurs at position %d\n",newnumber,location);
        else
            printf("%d does not occur\n",newnumber);
        printf("do you want to continue (y/n)? \n");
        scanf(" %c\n",&answer);
    }  while (toupper(answer) != 'N');
    return;
}
```

Since we have already traced the *linearsearch* function, it is easy to trace *locatevalues*. Let's assume that the array holds the same values (4 99 2 90 16), and the series of values to be located consists of 90 and 7.

PROGRAM TRACE

◆   The *locatevalues* function asks the user to type in a value for *newnumber*. The user enters 90.

◆   This value is sent to *linearsearch*, together with the array *numb* and the value of *n*.

◆ In this case, *linearsearch* returns the value 3 to the function *locatevalues*, and this is stored in *location*.

◆ The *if* statement determines that this is an actual position, and the following message is printed:

> 90 occurs at position 3

◆ The user is asked whether to continue, and the user types in y (or Y). The *while* condition is true, and the *do-while* loop repeats the series of instructions.

◆ The user is asked for a new value to locate, and the user types in 7 as the value for *newnumber*.

◆ This value is sent to *linearsearch* (together with the same values for *numb* and *n*).

◆ The *linearsearch* function sends back –1 to indicate that 7 does not occur in the array.

◆ The *if* statement determines that this is not an actual position so the following message is printed:

> 7 does not occur

◆ The user is asked whether to continue and types in n (or N). The *do-while* loop terminates since the *while* condition is false.

◆ The *locatevalues* function returns to the program which called it.

SELF-CHECK 10-5

1. What is the smallest number of new values that can be searched for in Program 10? What is the largest number?

2. Trace the *locatevalues* function on the following lists and new values to be located:

    a. list: 7 2 4 –2 0 8 15 34 6   new values: 4 1 7 15 6 7 5
    b. list: 10 20 30 ... 100   new values: 5 20 0 60 –11

3. Write a pointer version of *locatevalues*.

SECTION 6   PSEUDOCODE FOR PROBLEM 10: BOTTOM-UP APPROACH

In this brief section, we give a pseudocode solution to Problem 10, using a bottom-up approach. In the next section, we translate this pseudocode into a complete program.

PSEUDOCODE FOR THE MAIN PROGRAM

From the statement of the problem, it is easy to give a first version of the pseudocode for Program 10. As usual, we write the program so that each task is handled by a function: one to read in the data, one to print the data, one to sort, etc. The main program continues to use the variable names *n* and *numb*.

Here is the pseudocode:

call a function readarray *to read* n, *then read* n *numbers into an array* numb
call a function printarray *to print the array in the original order*
call a function linearsort *to sort the array into ascending order*

call a function `printarray` *to print the array in sorted order*
call a function `locatevalues` *to locate the position of a series of new values in the array* numb

The first two tasks of the main program are handled by functions which read in the set of data and print an array. Then we call the *linearsort* function from Section 2 to sort the array. This is followed by another call to *printarray* to print the newly sorted array. Finally, we call the function *locatevalues* from Section 5 (which calls *linearsearch* from Section 4). In the pseudocode, the *linearsort* function is called to perform the sort. We could instead use the *bubblesort* function from Section 3.

Notice that the same function, *printarray*, prints both the original and the sorted array. The main program differentiates between these two by printing a message before it calls the function to print the numbers stored in the array. Also notice that the function *readarray* performs a task identical to the one in programs 7 and 8. Therefore, we can reuse this function when we put everything together for Program 10.

DIVISION INTO MODULES; BOTTOM-UP APPROACH

Problem 10 divides up easily into a series of steps. However, the approach we use in attacking this problem differs from the top-down design. We consider each of the steps to be a separate subproblem for which we create a function. After writing the functions, we devise a main program to call them. This method of attacking a problem is called a **bottom-up approach**.

COMPARISON TO TOP-DOWN DESIGN

This approach is not the same as the top-down method we introduced in Chapter 4 and have used since then. With the top-down approach, we started by planning the main program. As we developed the main program, we recognized distinct tasks to be performed by functions. Once the plan for the main program was complete, we wrote the individual modules to perform these tasks. The bottom-up method starts with the modules (functions), then writes a main program to put the pieces together. Usually, this approach is followed when it is clear in advance that the overall task divides up into a series of well-defined subtasks which can become functions. However, the top-down approach is more flexible and minimizes the possibility of confusion in communication between the main program and the functions (e.g., in parameter transmission).

Most programmers use a combination of the two techniques. For example, a programmer may start by dividing the job into a series of tasks, then work on some simple modules, then link them together. In any case, the bottom-up method offers another way of attacking a problem.

SELF-CHECK 10-6

1. Is it possible to use two separate print functions, one to print the original and one to print the sorted array? Does it make sense to do this?

2. Why doesn't the main program call *linearsearch*?

3. In a bottom-up design, what is the last step worked on? In a top-down approach, what is the last step?

SECTION 7   PROGRAM 10

In this section, we combine the pseudocode from Section 6 with the individual functions from earlier sections to write a complete C program to solve Problem 10.

THE MAIN PROGRAM

Let's start with the initial portion of the main program, up to the declaration of variables.

```
/*
 * Program prog10.c:
 * sorting using the linear sort algorithm
 * searching using the linear search algorithm
 */
#include <stdio.h>
#define SIZE 50
main()
{
    int numb[SIZE];
    int n;
```

In the first sections of this chapter, we examined the sorting phase of Problem 10. In the last two sections, we handled the searching phase. As a last step, we write the easy parts of the program: the calls to the functions which read in the original data, sort and search the array, and print both the original and the sorted array.

The function *linearsort* was given in Section 2, the function *locatevalues* appeared in Section 6, and *linearsearch* was in Section 5. Another function we need is *readarray*, to read a set of data into an array and return its size. This function was used in chapters 7 and 8, and we will adapt it for Program 10. (The original version printed the data read in; the new version will not since we now have a separate function to print.) The call from the main program to *readarray* is similar to the one used earlier. It looks like this:

```
n = readdata(numb);
```

Then we need a function *printarray* to print a set of data stored in an array. The call to *printarray* is preceded by a message printed by the main program. This message displays a heading above the printed array. By varying the message, we can print appropriate headings for both the original data and the sorted array. Here is the first call to *printarray*, which prints the original set of data:

```
printf("original data\n\n");
printarray(numb,n);
```

For the call to *linearsort*, we use the following:

```
linearsort(numb,n);
```

The second call to *printarray*, after the array has been sorted, looks like this:

```
printf("\n\nsorted array\n\n");
printarray(numb,n);
```

Then the main program calls *locatevalues* to read in the new set of values to locate within the array.

```
locatevalues(numb,n);
```

This completes the body of the main program. The only things left to include are the prototypes and definitions for all the functions. These are given below with the entire program.

COMPLETE PROGRAM 10

🖳 PROGRAM LISTING

```
/*
 * Program prog10.c:
 * sorting using the linear sort algorithm
 * searching using the linear search algorithm
 */
#include <stdio.h>
#define SIZE 50

void linearsort(int [], int);
int readdata(int []);
void printarray(int [], int);
int linearsearch(int [], int, int);
void locatevalues(int [], int);

main()
{
    int numb[SIZE];
    int n;

    n = readdata(numb);                        /* call readdata to read in the data */

    printf("original data\n\n");
    printarray(numb,n);                     /* call printarray to print the original array */

    linearsort(numb,n);                        /* call linearsort to sort the array */

    printf("\n\nsorted array\n\n");
    printarray(numb,n);                      /* call printarray to print the sorted array */

    locatevalues(numb,n);
}
```

(continued)

(*continued*)

```c
/* Function readdata */
int readdata(int numb[])
{
    int i,n;

    printf("enter the number of elements in the array\n");
    scanf("%d",&n);
    for (i = 0; i < n; i++)  {
        printf("enter a number to be put into the array\n");
        scanf("%d",&numb[i]);
    }
    return n;
}

/* Function printarray */
void printarray(int numb[], int n)
{
    int i;

    for (i = 0; i < n; i++)
        printf("%d\n",numb[i]);
    return;
}

/* Function linearsort */
void linearsort(int numb[], int n)
{
    int pass,cand;
    int temp;

    for (pass = 0; pass < n - 1; pass++)
        for (cand = pass + 1; cand < n; cand++)
            if (numb[pass] > numb[cand])  {
                temp = numb[pass];
                numb[pass] = numb[cand];
                numb[cand] = temp;
            }
    return;
}

/* Function locatevalues */
void locatevalues(int numb[], int n)
{
    int  newnumber,location;
    char answer;

    do  {
        printf("Please enter a number to locate within the array\n");
        scanf("%d",&newnumber);
        location = linearsearch(numb,n,newnumber);
```

```
            if (location >= 0)
                printf("%d occurs at position %d\n",newnumber,location);
            else
                printf("%d does not occur\n",newnumber);
            printf("do you want to continue (y/n)? \n");
            scanf(" %c\n",&answer);
    } while (toupper(answer) != 'N');
    return;
}

/* Function linearsearch */
int linearsearch(int numb[], int n, int newnumber)
{
    int position;

    for (position = 0; position < n; position++)
        if (numb[position] == newnumber)
            return position;
    return -1;
}
```

This completes Program 10. We have written Program 10 to read in the original set of data interactively and send output to the screen. You can easily revise the program to read some of the data from an external file (see Appendix VI) or through redirection (see Appendix V), and send the output to the screen, the printer, or an external file (see Exercise 24).

PROGRAM 10 USING POINTER NOTATION

In Section 2, we gave a version of *linearsort* which used pointer rather than subscript notation to represent elements of the array, and we did the same thing for *linearsearch* in Section 4. We can also change the functions *locatevalues*, *readdata*, and *printarray* to use pointer notation. (These ideas are explored in the exercises.)

SELF-CHECK 10-7

1. Make up a set of data with five values (*n* is 5), plus some new values to be located, and trace Program 10.

2. Write function prototypes for *linearsort* and *linearsearch* that use pointer notation for the array. From the compiler's point of view, is there any difference between these function prototypes and the original ones?

3. Show how to use the function *bubblesort* in Program 10.

SECTION 8 ENRICHMENT: OTHER POINTS ON SORTING

In this section, we discuss more on sorting, including a function to interchange two array elements.

SORTING INTO DESCENDING ORDER; ALLOWING REPEATED ELEMENTS

First, let's learn how to sort numbers into descending instead of ascending order. We simply replace the condition on the left (or the corresponding line in a bubble sort) by the opposite condition on the right:

```
if (numb[pass] > numb[cand])      by      if (numb[pass] < numb[cand])
    ...                                        ...
```

That's it! Try an example to see that this works.

We have mentioned that two equal numbers in a list do not cause a problem; for example, the values 14 125 11 4 14 21 are sorted into 4 11 14 14 21 125. This is true because when the repeated elements are compared, they do not swap places, but they eventually end up in adjacent positions.

SORTING NONINTEGER VALUES; ASCII CODES

Both sorting programs assume that the *numb* array holds integers. To sort real numbers, the only change is a trivial one. The declarations for *numb* and *temp* (why is *temp* important?) have to be modified, but nothing else in the body of the function is altered.

For example, in the *bubblesort* function, to sort values of type *double*, we use the following header and declaration of local variables (the array is still called *numb*):

```
void bubblesort(double numb[], int n)
{
    int    pos,swapped;
    double temp;
```

In the rest of the program, only the function prototype and the main program's declaration of the array change. Here is the new function prototype:

```
void bubblesort(double [], int n);
```

Finally, here is the new declaration for the array in the main program:

```
double numb[SIZE];
```

Of course, the other functions, including *readdata*, *printarray*, etc., also have to be modified.

What about sorting variables of type *char*—for example, putting letters into alphabetical order? Even this is quite simple. As we noted in Chapter 9, Section 2, each individual character (including digits, letters, punctuation, etc.) is represented in a computer by a number, called its ASCII code (see Appendix II). The numbers are selected so that the one for *a* is less than the one for *b*, and so on. (This should be clear if you understand how types *char* and *int* are related; see Chapter 2, Section 5.) If *c1* and *c2* are two characters, when we ask, "Is *c1* > *c2*?", the computer interprets this as "Is the number for *c1* greater than the one for *c2*?" It is not necessary to explain that *a* < *b* because this is automatically built into the system. Therefore, our two sorting methods work on any type of data.

SORTING STRINGS

What about sorting strings—for example, putting names into alphabetical order? To mention just one problem: In numerical order, any three-digit number (112) is larger than a two-digit one (98), but in alphabetical order, some three-letter words come before two-letter ones (*and,* for example, comes before *me*). Fortunately, we don't have to explain this to the computer. Modifying our original function to sort strings consists of changing the declarations, plus one other change. However, changing the declarations for strings is a little complicated.

To clarify things, let's change the name of the array we are sorting from **numb** to **name**. So **name** is an array of strings—that is, an array of pointers to **char**. In a function header, the parameter for this array is represented by the following:

```
char *name[]                            /* name is an array of strings */
```

This says that **name** is an array whose underlying elements are **char** ∗. The size of each string is determined by the program that calls the sorting function.

Recall the local variable **temp**, used to hold a value as we swap two array elements. Because it is a local variable and not a parameter, its data type cannot be **char** ∗. Instead, we need to allocate an explicit amount of space for this string. Let's assume that 25 characters are sufficient. (The size should match the strings in the original array.)

Once we have changed the declarations, we can give the function header and declaration of local variables for a function to sort strings. (We use the **linearsort** function, rather than the **bubblesort** function, but this is not crucial.)

```
void linearsort(char *name[], int n)
{
    int  pass,cand;
    char temp[25];
```

THE FUNCTIONS *strcmp* AND *strcpy*

There are other changes that must be made when sorting strings because of the way we compare and switch them.

◆   Recall from Chapter 9 that we must use **strcmp** (whose function prototype is in the file **string.h**) to compare two strings. If the first parameter is larger than the second, **strcmp** returns an answer which is positive.

◆   In addition, we must use **strcpy** (its prototype is also in **string.h**) to move the value of one string into another.

Here is code for the function **linearsort** to sort strings:

```
if (strcmp(name[pass],name[cand]) > 0)  {
    /* statements to interchange the two strings */
    strcpy(temp,name[pass]);
    strcpy(name[pass],name[cand]);
    strcpy(name[cand],temp);
}
```

Now we rewrite the entire function to sort strings using a linear sort.

```
/* ... */
void linearsort(char *name[], int n)
{
      int  pass,cand;
      char temp[25];

      for (pass = 0; pass < n - 1; pass++)
          for (cand = pass + 1; cand < n; cand++)
              if (strcmp(name[pass],name[cand]) > 0)  {
                  /* statements to interchange the two strings */
                  strcpy(temp,name[pass]);
                  strcpy(name[pass],name[cand]);
                  strcpy(name[cand],temp);
              }
      return;
}
```

ALPHABETIZING STRINGS

The problem mentioned earlier about the size of strings is a phony one. When two strings are compared by *strcmp*, they are matched character by character, starting at the left. For example, the string "and" starts with the character *a*, and "me" starts with *m*. Since *a* is numerically less than *m*, "and" is alphabetized before "me".

Here are some things to remember about alphabetizing strings:

◆   Under usual ASCII ordering, the values for capitals are less than those for lowercase letters.

◆   A blank is assigned a value which is less than any printable character.

◆   If all characters match, but one string has trailing blanks, the longer string is considered greater.

EXAMPLE 10-5   Here are some examples of *strcmp*:

Case	Reason
strcmp("a","b") < 0	'a' < 'b'
strcmp("Z","a") < 0	'Z' < 'a'
strcmp("bob","Bob") > 0	'b' > 'B'
strcmp("ccc","cc") > 0	"ccc" is longer than "cc"
strcmp("an ","an") > 0	"an " is longer than "an"
strcmp("an"," Bob") > 0	'a' > ' '
strcmp("an","an") == 0	the strings are identical

A FUNCTION TO INTERCHANGE TWO ARRAY ELEMENTS

In Section 2, when we wrote the *linearsort* function, we interchanged the values of two array elements by writing three assignment statements. This section shows how to use the *swap* function from Chapter 8 (shown below) to perform the interchange in Program 10.

```
void swap(int *a, int *b)
{
    int temp;

    temp = *a;
    *a = *b;
    *b = temp;
    return;
}
```

USING *swap* IN *linearsort*

Instead of three assignment statements to interchange the values of the two array elements, the *linearsort* function can use the following call to *swap*:

```
swap(&numb[pass],&numb[cand]);
```

Let's rewrite the *linearsort* function, showing the call to *swap* in context:

```
/* ... */
void linearsort(int numb[], int n)
{
    int pass,cand;

    for (pass = 0; pass < n - 1; pass++)
        for (cand = pass + 1; cand < n; cand++)
            if (numb[pass] > numb[cand])
                swap(&numb[pass],&numb[cand]);
    return;
}
```

Note that we can drop the declaration of the local variable *temp*, and we no longer need a compound statement after the *if* condition. The *swap* function also works with the *bubblesort* function.

CAUTION This version of *swap* works only if we want to exchange integers, not values of a different type. A separate version of *swap* is needed to exchange characters or reals or strings.

In Chapter 11, we discuss a structure to store related items which do not have the same data type—for example, the name, age, and occupation of a person. To sort an array of these structures based on the name, it is necessary to exchange the additional information on age and occupation. Exercises 45 and 46 discuss this idea, together with a suggestion on using a version of *swap* to interchange the names.

SELF-CHECK 10-8

1. Trace the linear sort (either algorithm or function) on the following set of data: 50.1 6.3 4.4 50.1 6.3 4.4 ($n = 6$).

2. In the version of **linearsort** which uses the function **swap**, why isn't it necessary to declare a local variable **temp**?

3. Show how the **bubblesort** function can use **swap**. (Don't forget the variable **swapped**.)

SECTION 9 ENRICHMENT: BINARY SEARCH

In this section, we provide a searching algorithm which is much better than the sequential search. However, it can be used only if the array is already sorted. The new algorithm is called a binary search.

THE BINARY SEARCH METHOD

The original linear search algorithm and its accelerated rejection version from Section 4 are hopelessly inefficient for searching a long list. For example, if you used either method to look up a name in the telephone directory of a large city with perhaps one million names, it would take an incredibly long time. Without even realizing it, most people probably use a variant of the **binary search** method. The basic idea is not to do an element-by-element linear search but make better and better "guesses" as to where the new element must be.

Assume that we have a sorted array called **numb**; the variable **n** holds the number of elements in the array; we are looking for the position of **newnumber**. At the beginning, the entire array from the lowest position (0) to the highest ($n - 1$) must be searched. We start by "guessing" that **newnumber** occurs halfway between the low and high elements; we test whether **newnumber** is equal to the array element at this position. For example, in Figure 10-6, we first guess that **newnumber** occurs at position 3, which is halfway between 0 and 6 (assume that **newnumber** is 50).

Note the following facts for developing the binary search algorithm:

♦ If the array element in the tested position is equal to **newnumber**, the search is over since **newnumber** has been found.

♦ If the array element in the tested position is larger than **newnumber**, all elements after it must also be larger and can be ignored. Thus, if **newnumber** is in the array, it must lie in the portion between the first element and the tested one, and this is the section we should search further.

♦ Similarly, if the array element in the tested position is smaller than **newnumber**, all elements before it can be ignored; the array should be searched from the element after the tested position to the end.

The binary search then repeats the same process: Make guesses and test the value at the position halfway between the low and high elements until **newnumber** is located. This idea of halving explains the name of the method: binary search.

FIGURE 10-6   First step of the binary search algorithm to locate a new value

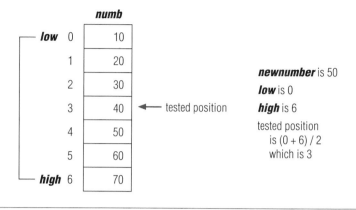

ALGORITHM FOR THE BINARY SEARCH

Let's formalize the binary search algorithm. Assume again that we have a sorted array called **numb** which has **n** elements; we are looking for the position of **newnumber**. Initially, the entire array, from **low** = 0 to **high** = **n – 1**, is to be searched. Here is the algorithm:

ALGORITHM FOR THE BINARY SEARCH

♦   *Initialize* low *to 0 and* high *to* n - 1.

♦   *Continue the following process as long as* newnumber *has not been found and* low *is less than or equal to* high.

♦   *Test whether the array element halfway between positions* low *and* high *is equal to* newnumber.

♦   *If the element is equal to* newnumber, *the search is successful.*

♦   *If the array element at the position tested is too large, change the value of* high *to one less than the tested position.*

♦   *If the array element at the position tested is too small, change the value of* low *to one more than the tested position.*

Now we translate the algorithm into pseudocode and write a function to do the binary search. The algorithm says to continue as long as **low** is less than or equal to **high**. For the pseudocode, we translate this into a loop. In this loop, we determine our next guess as to where **newnumber** occurs, then compare **newnumber** to the element in the array at that position. Depending upon the outcome, we either stop searching because we have found **newnumber** or adjust our search range by changing **low** or **high**. Here is the algorithm re-written in pseudocode:

PSEUDOCODE FOR THE BINARY SEARCH

```
low = 0;
high = n - 1;
while (low <= high)
```
look at the element halfway between positions low *and* high
if (*the element in the tested position is equal to* newnumber)
return the position of newnumber
else if (*the element is larger than newnumber*)
high = *the tested position – 1*
else
low = *the tested position + 1*

Before we write this as a function, let's look at some examples.

EXAMPLE 10-6   Consider the array in Figure 10-7. Assume that the new number we are seeking is 50.

Figure 10-7A shows that initially the entire array, from a low of 0 to a high of 6, must be searched.

◆   The first position tested is 3. The element in position 3 is smaller than **newnumber** so the next pass of the algorithm is restricted to positions 4 to 6 of the array.

FIGURE 10-7   Using the binary search algorithm to locate a new value

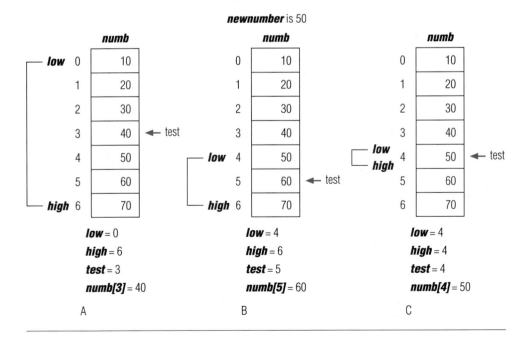

A   B   C

♦ The next test is position 5 (see Figure 10-7B). The number in position 5 is too large so the next pass is restricted to the range 4 to 4, which is just position 4.

♦ The third test is position 4 (see Figure 10-7C), and the item is found there.

Of course, it is possible that **newnumber** is not in the original array. The algorithm determines this when the range that must still be searched is empty. This occurs if we just had a pass where the high and low values to be searched are equal and **newnumber** is not there. In that case, **low** becomes greater than **high**, and we fall out of the loop.

EXAMPLE 10-7 Consider the same array as Example 10-6, but assume that 15 is the value of **newnumber**.
Figure 10-8A shows that initially the entire array, from a low of 0 to a high of 6, must be searched.

♦ The first position tested is 3. The element in position 3 is larger than **newnumber** so the next pass of the algorithm is restricted to positions 0 to 2 of the array.

♦ The next test is position 1 (see Figure 10-8B). The number in position 1 is too large, so the next pass is restricted to the range 0 to 0, which is just position 0.

♦ The third test is position 0 (see Figure 10-8C), which has a value that is too small. Now the low value of the range shifts to 1, while the high value remains at 0.

♦ The low value is larger than the high value, which means that the range to be searched is empty, and 15 has not been located (see Figure 10-8D).

FIGURE 10-8 Using the binary search algorithm to determine that a new value is not in the array

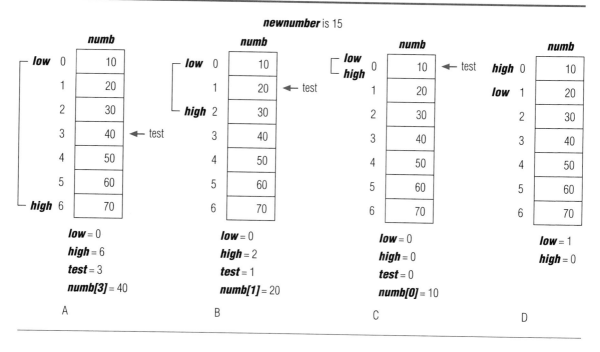

FUNCTION FOR THE BINARY SEARCH

The function for the binary search method is a straightforward translation of the pseudo-code. We continue to call the formal parameters **numb**, **newnumber**, and **n** to correspond with the names in **linearsearch**.

```
/*
 * Function binarysearch:
 * Input:
 *   numb: the array to search--the array must be sorted
 *   n: the number of elements to search in the array
 *   newnumber: the value to search for
 * Process:
 *   using a binary search, determines the position of
 *   newnumber within the first n elements of numb
 * Output:
 *   returns the position (test) of newnumber in the array numb;
 *   returns -1 if newnumber is not found
 */
int binarysearch(int numb[], int n, int newnumber)
```

The function needs local variables to hold the low and high points for the searching range, and these are initialized to 0 and **n − 1**. In addition, the function needs another local variable to hold the guess as to where to look next for **newnumber**. We call this variable **test**. The declaration for these variables looks like this:

```
{
    int low,high,test;
```

This is followed by a loop. In this case, a **while** loop seems most appropriate. The **while** loop is controlled by the relative values of **high** and **low**. Here is the loop header:

```
low = 0;
high = n - 1;
while (low <= high)
```

Inside the body of the **while** loop, **test** holds the current guess as to where to look within the array. Initially, it is the midpoint of the entire array, but later **test** is the midpoint of the section of the array which must still be searched. To assign **test** a value that is midway between **high** and **low**, use integer division on the sum of **high** and **low**:

```
while (low <= high)  {
    test = (low + high) / 2;
```

This gives **test** an integer value, appropriate for a subscript of the **numb** array. Once we have calculated the midpoint of the section of the array being searched, a nested **if** statement compares the value in position **test** with **newnumber**.

```
while (low <= high)  {
    test = (low + high) / 2;
    if (numb[test] == newnumber)
```

```
            return test;                        /* newnumber found at test */
        else if (numb[test] > newnumber)
            high = test - 1;                            /* adjust range */
        else
            low = test + 1;
    }
```

When we terminate the **while** loop, we return –1 (a failure signal), then end the function.

```
        return -1;                              /* newnumber not found */
    }
```

THE FUNCTION *binarysearch*

Let's put the whole thing together:

```
/* ... */
int binarysearch(int numb[], int n, int newnumber)
{
    int low,high,test;

    low = 0;
    high = n - 1;
    while (low <= high)  {
        test = (low + high) / 2;
        if (numb[test] == newnumber)
            return test;                        /* newnumber found at test */
        else if (numb[test] > newnumber)
            high = test - 1;                            /* adjust range */
        else
            low = test + 1;
    }
    return -1;                                   /* newnumber not found */
}
```

USING A BINARY SEARCH IN PROGRAM 10

Once we have the **binarysearch** function, we can use it in Program 10 since the array is sorted by the time we search. Here is the relevant portion of the function **locatevalues** (note that the search function is called by **locatevalues** rather than the main program):

```
location = binarysearch(numb,n,newnumber);
if (location >= 0)
    printf("%d occurs at position %d\n",newnumber,location);
else
    printf("%d does not occur\n",newnumber);
```

EXAMPLE 10-8   Let's trace the *binarysearch* and *locatevalues* functions on the two earlier examples, one where *newnumber* is present and another where it isn't. Assume that the set of data stored in the array contains the values 10 20 30 40 50 60 70 (*n* is 7). Note that these values are in sorted order, which is crucial to the operation of the binary search algorithm.

PROGRAM TRACE Let's assume that, inside the function *locatevalues*, the user asks to find the position of 50 in the array, so *newnumber* is 50.

♦   The function *locatevalues* calls *binarysearch*, sending it the relevant parameters (see Figure 10-7).

♦   Inside the *binarysearch* function, *low* is set to 0 and *high* to 6. In the body of the *while* loop, *test* is set to (0 + 6) / 2, which is 3; *numb[3]* contains 40. Since *numb[3]* is not equal to or greater than *newnumber*, *low* is set to 3 + 1, which is 4.

♦   We reenter the body of the loop, and *test* is set to 5. Since *numb[5]* contains 60, which is greater than *newnumber*, *high* is set to 5 – 1, which is 4.

♦   We reenter the body of the loop, where *test* is set to 4. Now *numb[4]* contains 50, which is equal to *newnumber*. The value of *test*, which is 4 in this case, is returned to the *locatevalues* function.

♦   The *locatevalues* function tests the answer returned, then prints the following output:

> `50 occurs at position 4`

Now the user asks to locate 15 (*newnumber*). The function *locatevalues* calls *binarysearch* (see Figure 10-8).

♦   The first few steps inside the *binarysearch* function are exactly the same: *low* is set to 0 and *high* to 6, the *while* loop condition is true, and *test* is set to 3.

♦   Since *numb[3]* contains 40, *high* is set to 2.

♦   We reenter the body of the loop; *test* is set to 1; since *numb[1]* contains 20, *high* is set to 0.

♦   This time through the body of the *while* loop, *test* is set to 0. Now *numb[0]* contains 10, and *low* is set to 1. Note that *low* is now greater than *high*.

♦   Since the *while* condition (1 <= 0) is false, we continue after the end of the loop. The function returns –1 because *newnumber* does not occur in the array.

♦   The *locatevalues* function tests the answer returned, then prints the following:

> `15 does not occur`

CAUTION It is imperative that the original array be in order. In practice, this is often true, but in some situations, it may not be. In that case, the binary search method cannot be applied.

ANALYSIS OF THE BINARY SEARCH ALGORITHM

Here is a brief analysis of the efficiency of the binary search algorithm. In our two examples of the binary search, *n* was equal to 7. It took three guesses to locate 50 and three to determine that 15 was not in the array.

Three guesses were needed because the number 8 (which is one more than the number of elements in the array) must be divided in half three times before 1 is reached. In general,

TABLE 10.2 Analysis of the Linear Search and the Binary Search

	Average number of tries using linear search to		Maximum number of tries using binary search to	
n	Locate	Reject	Locate	Reject
7	4	7	3	3
100	50	100	7	7
1,000	500	1,000	10	10
1,000,000	500,000	1,000,000	20	20

if the number of array elements plus 1 ($n + 1$) must be divided in half k times before 1 is reached, no more than k guesses are needed to find an element in the array (or reject it).

How does the binary search algorithm do on larger values of n? Table 10.2 compares the efficiency of the linear and binary searches for various values of n. The accelerated version of the linear search discussed in exercises 26 and 33 is not much better than the original. It is clear that the binary search is significantly more efficient than the linear search, both in locating and rejecting, for values of n as small as 100. The advantage becomes even greater as the value of n increases.

SELF-CHECK 10-9

1. Exactly why is it crucial for the array to be in order before a binary search is performed?

2. Trace the binary search algorithm and the *locatevalues* function on the following lists and new values to be located:

    a. list: –2 0 2 4 6 7 8 15 34   new values: 4 1 7 25
    b. list: 10 20 30 ... 100   new values: 20 5 –11

3. If a sorted list of items contains four million values, how many guesses does it take the binary search algorithm to locate the position of an item?

SUMMARY

BOTTOM-UP VERSUS TOP-DOWN DESIGN

1. A large program often divides into a series of relatively simple parts. Each part can be solved in an individual module; the modules are combined to form a program. A top-down approach starts with a main program, refines it into modules, and then works on each module. A bottom-up design starts with the individual modules, then works on the main program which calls them. Many programmers use a combination of the two techniques.

SORTING

2. Sorting, which means putting a list of objects into order (either ascending or descending), is an extremely common and important application of computers.

3. There are many possible sorting methods. Unfortunately, the most efficient ones are rather difficult to program. The two discussed in this chapter are easy to program but not very efficient. However, for small cases (under 100 items), they are adequate. Understanding these simple methods is useful before learning more complex techniques.

LINEAR SORT

4. An algorithm for the linear sort of an array into ascending order consists of these steps:

    Find the smallest element in the array and place it in the first position. Do this by comparing each element of the array to the one in the first position. If the new element is smaller, swap it with the element in the first position. Repeat this process for the other positions in the array, at each stage ignoring all elements whose positions have already been filled.

5. The function for the linear sort implements this algorithm by using a nested *for* loop construction. The outer loop corresponds to the various positions to be filled; the inner loop considers all possible candidates for that position. A total of *n – 1* passes through the outer loop is needed to sort *n* elements. Each pass determines one position, except for the last, which determines two.

BUBBLE SORT

6. The bubble sort improves on the linear sort algorithm by comparing only adjacent elements of the array. The key to the bubble sort is this observation: If each element is in order relative to its two neighbors, the entire array is in sorted order. Here is the bubble sort algorithm:

    Repeat the following process as long as each entire pass through the array has a swap: Compare each element of the array to the one after it; if they are out of order, swap them; continue processing until the end of the array.

7. The module for the bubble sort implements this algorithm using a *do-while* loop that contains a *for* loop. The outer loop repeats the inner loop as long as an entire pass has at least one swap of adjacent elements. The inner loop compares each element to the one after it, swapping them if they are out of order and noting that a swap has been made.

ANALYSIS OF THE TWO SORTING ALGORITHMS

8. Although the linear sort is easy to program, it is incredibly inefficient since it makes the same number of comparisons in every case. One of the exercises shows that a total of $n^2 / 2$ comparisons are needed to sort *n* elements, regardless of what order they are in. This includes an array that is already in order. A "smarter" algorithm takes advantage of previous information to decrease the number of comparisons.

9. In the worst case, the bubble sort is about as poor as the linear sort is in every case. But if the elements are almost in sorted order, the bubble sort is significantly faster. Although this is unlikely to happen randomly, in practice it is fairly common to have an array where most of the elements are in order except for a few misplaced values. Nevertheless, neither sort is useful in real-world applications.

SORTING VARIATIONS

10. Sorting into descending order is a trivial modification of sorting into ascending order: Replace the test for "greater than" by "less than." The sorting algorithms work for integers or real numbers as well as other data types, simply by changing the declarations. Characters can be sorted into alphabetical order by the same method since each character has a numerical value, called its ASCII code, which is used in the comparisons. Sorting strings can also be done with only a few changes.

SEARCHING

11. There are also several searching techniques discussed in the chapter, all having the following goal: Given a list of items, determine if a new item is an element of the list. If it is, return the position of the new item; if it is not, return some indication of failure (typically –1). If an item occurs several times, report only the first occurrence.

LINEAR OR SEQUENTIAL SEARCH

12. The linear search (also called a sequential search) algorithm is the simplest searching method. Each element in the array is compared sequentially to the new item. If the two match, the subscript of the array element is the position of the new item. After searching the entire array, if a match has not been found, the item is not in the array.

BINARY SEARCH

13. If the array is in sorted order, another searching method, called the binary search, can be used. Instead of searching the array sequentially, the binary search method guesses that the new item is the middle element among the remaining elements. At each step of the algorithm, the number of elements to be searched is cut in half, from n to $n/2$ to $n/4$, ... Either the new item is found on one of these guesses, or eventually there are no more items to be searched, which means that the new item is not in the array.

14. Here is an outline of the binary search algorithm:

    Initially, set low = 0 *and* high = n - 1. *Set position* test *halfway between* low *and* high. *If the new item equals the element at position* test, *the search is successful. If the element in position* test *is too large, set* high *to one less than* test. *If the element in position* test *is too small, set* low *to one more than* test. *Repeat this process until either the new item is found (success), or* low *is greater than* high *(failure).*

ANALYSIS OF THE SEARCHING ALGORITHMS

15. If no special information is known about the elements in the array, the linear search method is as good as any other. However, if the array is in sorted order, the linear search algorithm is extremely inefficient. Given an array with n elements, on the average it takes $n/2$ comparisons to locate the position of a new item, but it always takes n comparisons to determine that a new item is not present. These values are independent of the order of the elements in the array. As a minor improvement, in a sorted array, the average number of comparisons needed to determine that an item is not in the array can be reduced to $n/2$ by using an accelerated rejection process.

16. The maximum number of tests required by the binary search algorithm to locate or reject an item is $\log_2 (n + 1)$, where $\log_2 (n + 1)$ is the smallest integer k such that 2^k is at least $n + 1$. For example, if n is 100, no more than seven tests are needed (since $2^7 = 128$); if $n = 1000$, no more than ten tests are required ($2^{10} = 1024$). On the average, if the number of elements to be searched is doubled, only one more test is needed.

EXERCISES

Note: The exercises for sorting and searching are grouped separately. In addition, the programming exercises which assume a knowledge of strings are grouped together at the end.

TRACING EXERCISES

1. Trace the linear sort algorithm on each of the following lists of items. Then do the same for the bubble sort algorithm.

    a. $n = 6$ 45 32 17 6 1 0
    b. $n = 5$ 3 –8 129 2 3
    c. $n = 7$ –1 –76 508 –87 –34 124 –54
    d. $n = 4$ 2 1 18 5
    e. $n = 8$'s' 'x' 'q' 'u' 'b' 'a' 'V' 'T'
    f. $n = 5$ 12.3 154.56 97.5 3.37 –5.32
    g. $n = 6$ 9 9 6 1 –3 2
    h. $n = 13$ "WenEng" "Ayshea" "Hong" "Alex" "Dmitry" "Ari" "Yukie" "Malky" "Henry" "Vitaly" "Ezhar" "Boris" "Yuriy"

2. Given the following set of strings, sort them in ascending alphabetical order. Does it matter whether we use a linear or a bubble sort?

    "a"   "b"   "an"   "a "   "a "   " a"
    " an"   "and"   "Bob"   "bob"   " Bob"   "an "

3. a. Modify the function for the linear sort so that it can be used to sort the types of values in Exercise 1(e). Then trace the function on the values shown. Do the same for the bubble sort function.
    b. Repeat part (a) for the data in Exercise 1, parts (f) and (h).
    c. Make up your own set of data with $n = 8$. Trace the linear sort and the bubble sort on it.

4. In translating the linear sort algorithm into pseudocode, is it possible to eliminate either loop from the nested loop structure?

5. In the **linearsort** function, the inner **for** loop header looks like this:

    ```
    for (cand = pass + 1; cand < n; cand++)
    ```

    What happens if this is changed to each of the following?

    a. `for (cand = pass + 1; cand <= n; cand++)`
    b. `for (cand = pass; cand < n; cand++)`
    c. `for (cand = pass + 1; cand < n - 1; cand++)`
    d. `for (pass = pass + 1; pass < n; pass++)`

    If you are unsure of an answer, try running a program using each header on a set of data.

6. a. Assume that you want to sort the values stored in the three variables, *n1*, *n2*, and *n3*, into order so that *n1* holds the smallest and *n3* holds the largest value. Show how to do this using a nested *if* or a series of *if* statements.
   b. Repeat part (a) for four variables, *n1* to *n4*. [*Hint*: This is much harder than part (a).] If you are successful, try the same thing for five variables.
   c. Assume that you have values in six variables, *n1* to *n6*, and you want to sort them. Show how to use an array to accomplish this task.
   d. In order to sort a group of numbers, is it necessary to store them in an array? Is it helpful?

ANALYSIS OF THE SORTING ALGORITHMS

7. Show that the linear sort algorithm uses precisely the same set of comparisons to sort an array of *n* elements regardless of the order of the values. (*Suggestion*: You can list the exact set of comparisons that the algorithm uses.)

8. In both the linear and the bubble sort, we do not swap two elements if they are equal but only if the first is greater than the second.
   a. In the linear sort function, what happens if we replace the test

   `if (numb[pass] > numb[cand])` *by* `if (numb[pass] >= numb[cand])` ?

   b. In the bubble sort function, what happens if we replace the test

   `if (numb[pos] > numb[pos + 1])` *by* `if (numb[pos] >= numb[pos + 1])` ?

   Run a program for each part on a simple example with a repeated value (e.g., 5 7 3 5). The results may surprise you.

9. a. Given an array with *n* elements, how many passes does the linear sort algorithm require to sort it? On each pass, how many comparisons are necessary? What is the total number of comparisons required to sort *n* elements using the linear sort algorithm? (*Hint*: The sum of the first *n* numbers is roughly $n^2 / 2$. See Chapter 4, Exercise 19.)
   b. Given an array with *n* elements, what is the maximum number of passes required by the bubble sort algorithm to sort it? (This is called the **worst case behavior** of the algorithm.) What is the minimum number? (This is called the **best case behavior**.)
   c. On each pass, how many comparisons are necessary? In the worst case, what is the total number of comparisons required to sort *n* elements using the bubble sort algorithm?

10. a. Evaluate your answers from Exercise 9 assuming that *n* = 10, *n* = 100, *n* = 1000.
    b. In the worst case, the best sorting algorithms require about 1.5 *n* log$_2$ *n* comparisons. Using this fact, verify the following: For the values of *n* from part (a), the worst case behavior of the best sorting algorithms requires roughly 50, 1000, and 15,000 comparisons, respectively.
    c. What can you conclude about using the linear or the bubble sort for large (*n* > 500) examples?

MODIFICATIONS TO THE SORTING ALGORITHMS

11. The linear sort algorithm in the text can be improved so that it does not make as many switches of array elements. (However, it still makes the same number of array comparisons.) It is not necessary to interchange two array elements every time the first one is not

smaller. Instead, on each pass through the array, the program can keep track of the position of the smallest element seen on that pass. At the end of each pass, the smallest element can be interchanged with the one currently in that array position.

Show how to use this idea in the linear sort function. Trace a few examples to compare this new version to the original function. Compare the number of comparisons and the number of switches.

12. The bubble sort algorithm in the text can be improved in several ways. The next few exercises discuss a few improvements.

The maximum number of passes through the outer or *do-while* loop can be predicted in advance. Since each pass determines the position of at least one element, the maximum number of passes is *n − 1*, where *n* is the number of values to be sorted. One simple way to take advantage of this is to count, within the outer loop, the number of passes that have been made. Then change the condition tested in the *while* clause so that it also checks the count of the number of passes. The loop continues as long as both of the following are true: *count* is less than *n − 1* (fewer than *n − 1* passes have been completed) and *swapped == 1* (each pass has had a swap).

Show how to use this idea in the bubble sort function. Trace a few examples to compare this new version to the original function.

13. Once the suggestion from Exercise 12 has been followed, there is another improvement that can also be made. The first pass through the outer loop determines the largest element; the next pass determines the second largest, and so on. We can use a variable *count* to count how many positions have already been determined. The inner *for* loop [*for (pos = 0; ...)*] need not go from position 0 to position *n − 2* each time. For example, on pass 2 (when *count* = 1), *pos* need only go from 1 to *n − 3*; on pass 3 (when *count* = 2), *pos* need only go from 1 to *n − 4*, and so on. To convince yourself, review the traces from Section 3.

Show how to use this idea in the bubble sort function by modifying the *for* loop header. Trace a few examples to compare this latest version to the function from Exercise 12 and the original bubble sort function.

14. Here is another possible improvement to the bubble sort algorithm: If two adjacent array elements (say *numb[4]* and *numb[5]*) are out of order, swap them. However, instead of comparing the new *numb[5]* to *numb[6]*, determine the correct location of *numb[4]* by allowing it to "bubble up" in the array. For example, compare the new *numb[4]* to *numb[3]*. If *numb[3]* is greater, swap them and compare *numb[3]* to *numb[2]* until an equal or smaller value is encountered or you reach *numb[1]*. In this way, the value originally in *numb[5]* moves into *numb[4]*, *numb[3]*, ..., as it seeks its ultimate location.

Show how to use this idea in the bubble sort function [what other change(s) should be made?]. Trace a few examples.

PROGRAMMING PROJECTS INVOLVING SORTING

15. In order to interchange the values of two variables, *a* and *b*, it is necessary to use three statements and one temporary storage location.

a. Show how to interchange the values of three variables, *a*, *b*, and *c* (*a* to *b*, *b* to *c*, *c* to *a*). How many statements must be used? How many temporary locations?

b. Show how to interchange the values of four variables, *a*, *b*, *c*, and *d* (*a* to *b*, *b* to *c*, *c* to *d*, and *d* to *a*).

c. Show how to interchange the values of *n* variables stored in array *x* (*x[0]* to *x[1]*, ..., *x[n – 1]* to *x[0]*).

16. Assume that the first *n* elements of the *numb* array have been sorted into ascending order.
  a. Show how to print the values in descending order.
  b. Show how to sort the array into descending order.

17. Give an algorithm for the following: Given an array with *n* elements, sort the elements into ascending order and discard all duplicates; if necessary, modify *n*. For example, if the original array holds 3 7 2 3 7 3 (*n* = 6), the final array is 2 3 7 (*n* = 3).

18. a. Write a function *findsecond* that finds the second-smallest element in an array. The function receives the array *x* and the number of elements as parameters. The function can use the function *bubblesort*; however, the program that calls *findsecond* does not expect the array to be sorted. Therefore, *findsecond* should make a copy of the array parameter and ask *bubblesort* to sort the copy.
  b. Write a function *median* that finds the median of an array. The median is the array element such that half the elements are greater and half are less (if *n* is even, it is the average of the middle two elements). The function receives the array *x* and the number of elements as parameters. As in part (a), ask *bubblesort* to sort a copy of the array.
  c. Write a function *sortmedian* that does two things: sort an array that is sent as a parameter, and find the median of the array. Should *sortmedian* be written as a void function or as one that returns a value?
  d. Write a function *mode* that finds the mode of an array. The mode is the value that occurs most frequently. The function receives the same parameters as *median* in part (b). It also has the same restriction on sorting the original array.
  e. Write a function *sortmode* to sort an array and find the mode.
  f. Is it possible to solve parts (a), (b), or (d) without first sorting the array?

19. Give an algorithm for the following: Insert a new number *x* into its proper location within a sorted array (assume that there is room in the array to add another element). For example, if *numb* holds 2 7 11 12 13, and *x* is 10, then *x* is inserted into position 2, and the values after it are shifted.

    Is it better to start *x* at the front of the list or the back? Is it easier if the list is in ascending or descending order? Explain.

20. a. Write a function *elimdups* that eliminates the duplicate elements in an array. The function receives as parameters an array of integers *numb* and an integer *n* representing the number of elements in *numb* that are to be processed. The function removes duplicate elements from the array, shifting the other elements down and modifying *n* if necessary. For example, if *n* = 5 and an array holds 3 7 3 7 2, then after the call to *elimdups*, the array holds 3 7 2 and *n* is 3. Write *elimdups* without sorting the *numb* array since the remaining elements should be in their original order.
  b. Assume that you can use the function *bubblesort* and that *elimdups* can change the order of the elements in the *numb* array. Use *bubblesort* to simplify *elimdups*.

21. Write a function *sortpart* that sorts part of an array. The function receives as parameters the name of the array to be sorted (*y*), and the first (*first*) and last position (*last*) to be sorted. The function sorts the elements of the *y* array from positions *first* to *last* inclusive. For example, if *y* holds 14 7 5 6 2, *first* = 1, and *last* = 3, the *y* array holds 14 5 6 7 2 after the partial sort is complete.

22. Write a function ***sorteither*** that receives an extra parameter called ***order***. This parameter indicates whether the array is to be sorted into ascending (+1) or descending (−1) order. Try to do this without two separate sets of sorting instructions. (*Hint*: If ***a*** > ***b***, then −1 ∗ ***a*** < −1 ∗ ***b***.)

23. a. Write a function ***sorthigh*** (with two parameters ***numb*** and ***n***) that does two things: sorts the first ***n*** elements of the ***numb*** array and returns the largest element in the array. For example, if an array with four elements holds 5 3 7 6, the function changes the array to hold 3 5 6 7 and also returns 7.

    b. Rewrite ***sorthigh*** as a void function (with the obvious modifications).

    c. Is it better to write ***sorthigh*** as a void function or one that returns a value?

24. a. Rewrite Problem 10 so that it uses redirection to read the original data from a file rather than interactively from the keyboard.

    b. Which version (interactive or reading from a file) is more useful for a set of 10 numbers? 1,000 numbers? 10,000 numbers? Which sort would you use in each case?

    c. Rewrite Problem 10 so that it uses redirection to send the output to a file rather than the screen. Then rewrite it again so that it sends the output to the printer.

    d. Which version (printer, screen, or file) would be more useful for a set of 10 numbers? 1,000 numbers? 10,000 numbers?

25. Write a complete program to do the following:

    The main program calls three functions. One reads in a set of ID numbers and donations to a charity. The second sorts the ID numbers into numerical order, being sure to carry along the corresponding donations. (See Exercise 45.) The third function prints the sorted lists, giving both ID numbers and donations. The same function sorts the donation amounts into ascending order, carrying along the corresponding ID numbers.

    Here are the details:

    a. The main program calls a function to read in the data. The data set consists of a parameter value which the main program calls ***n*** and ***n*** groups of data, each of which contains a person's three-digit ID number and an integer (e.g., 456 20000 or 123 30234).

       The main program calls these arrays ***idnumbers*** and ***donations***. A separate printing function prints the original set of data in the form of a neat table. When the arrays print, there should be an overall heading, plus headings for the columns of ID numbers and donations.

    b. Then the main program sends the array of ID numbers, the array of donations, and the size ***n*** to a sorting function. This function sorts the ID numbers into numerical order. Be sure to maintain the matchup of ID numbers and donations. For example, 456 should always be associated with 20000, no matter where 456 moves in numerical order; similarly, 123 should stay with 30234.

       When the sorting function finishes and returns control to the main program, main calls the printing function to print the two arrays.

    c. Next the main program calls the sorting function again, sending it the same three parameters. This time the function sorts the donations into numerical order, being sure to maintain the linkup of ID numbers and donations.

       When the sorting function finishes and returns control to the main program, main calls the printing function to print the two arrays with appropriate headings.

Your arrays should have room for up to 50 entries. To test the program, have a set of data with at least 15 to 20 values in each array. Make sure that your original order is not close to numerical order for either array and that the two numerical orders are not close to each other.

ANALYSIS OF THE SEARCHING ALGORITHMS

26. This exercise discusses the accelerated rejection searching algorithm from Section 4. Here is a more precise version:

   Assume that **numb** is an array of **n** integers in ascending order; **newnumber** is the integer whose position in **numb** is to be determined. The algorithm works as follows:

   Compare newnumber *to the elements of* numb *in order. If the current element is less than* newnumber, *compare* newnumber *to the next element. If* newnumber *is equal to the current element, the search is over (success). If* newnumber *is less than the current element, the search has failed since every later element in* numb *must also be greater than* newnumber.

   a. Write pseudocode for the accelerated rejection version of the linear search.
   b. Write a function **fastreject** that receives as parameters **numb**, an array of integers in ascending order; an integer **n**, the size of the array; and an integer **newnumber**. Use the accelerated rejection algorithm to return the location of **newnumber** within the first **n** elements of **numb** (return –1 if it is not found).

27. Assume that an array **vals** of integers holds the following numbers: 3 7 12 14 16 35 123. Here is the list of values whose positions (if any) in **vals** are to be located: 8 16 12 26 112 35 6 7 14 13.

   a. Trace the linear search algorithm in processing this set of data. Find the average number of comparisons required to locate an integer in the array and the number needed to show that a new value is not present.
   b. Repeat part (a) using the binary search algorithm.
   c. Compare your answers from parts (a) and (b). Is this a good test of the two algorithms? Explain.

28. Select a page at random from a telephone directory. Make up 15 to 20 names that are in the range covered by this page, including some that are in the directory and some that are not. Then repeat Exercise 27 using the page of the directory as the array **vals** and the names you made up as the items to be located.

29. Repeat Exercise 28 using 20 pages from the directory. What trend do you see as the size of the original list increases?

30. In order to use the binary search algorithm to look up a name in the telephone directory, we must assume that the list is in alphabetical order. Since the directory has an immense number of names (100,000 or more), it is quite time consuming to arrange the list in alphabetical order. Explain why this is not as great a problem as it seems. You may want to consider the following in your answer: the use of clever sorting methods that are much faster than the linear or the bubble sort; the number of times the directory is used compared to the number of times the entries must be sorted; the ease of updating (inserting or deleting names from) an already sorted list (see exercises 43 and 44).

31. The binary search algorithm assumes that the original array is in increasing (or alphabetical) order. Show how to modify it to work on an array that is in decreasing order.

32. This exercise analyzes the linear search algorithm from Section 4.

    Assume that **numb** is an array of **n** integers in ascending order; **newnumber** is the integer whose position in **numb** is to be determined. If **newnumber** is in **numb**, it requires a minimum of one and a maximum of **n** steps to determine this fact, where each step consists of a comparison of **newnumber** to an element in the array.

    a. Give an example that requires one step and an example that requires **n** steps.
    b. On the average, how many steps are required?
    c. In every case, it requires **n** steps to show that **newnumber** is not in **numb**. Why?
    d. Show that these results are true regardless of the order of the elements in **numb**.

33. This exercise analyzes the accelerated rejection method from Section 4 and Exercise 26.

    a. If **newnumber** is in **numb**, the accelerated rejection algorithm still requires an average of **n**/2 steps to locate its position. Explain why.
    b. If **newnumber** is not in **numb**, it takes a minimum of one and a maximum of **n** steps to determine this fact. Give an example that requires one step and an example that requires **n** steps.
    c. On the average, how many steps are required to reject a new value?
    d. Compare these results to the linear search algorithm. If you expect to find almost every new value somewhere in the original array, is the accelerated rejection process worthwhile? What if most new values are not found?

34. a. Actually, the accelerated rejection algorithm is worse than we have implied since two comparisons are required for each step, as opposed to one for the linear search algorithm. Explain why this is true.
    b. In addition, in order to use the accelerated rejection algorithm, the array **numb** must be in sorted order. Explain why this is true.

    Therefore, the accelerated rejection algorithm is very rarely used.

35. This exercise analyzes the binary search algorithm from Section 9.

    a. The minimum number of steps needed to locate a new value is one and the maximum is $\log_2 (n + 1)$. Give examples for both.
    b. The number of steps required to show that a new value is not in the **numb** array is always $\log_2 (n + 1)$. Justify this statement.
    c. Explain why it is relatively unimportant if each step consists of one or two comparisons.

36. Assume that the number of elements in the original array is doubled (for example, **n** is increased from 100 to 200). Analyze the effect this has on the performance of the linear search, accelerated rejection, and binary search algorithms. (*Hint*: One of them requires just a single extra step. Which one?)

37. Assume that the array **numb** contains a particular number twice. Assume that this value is equal to the new number we are seeking.

    a. In the linear search algorithm, which of the two occurrences of the number is selected? Explain.
    b. In the binary search algorithm, which of the two occurrences of this value is selected? Explain. Does this cause any problems?

MODIFICATIONS TO THE SEARCHING ALGORITHMS

38. Modify the functions *linearsearch* and *binarysearch* so that they work on an array of real numbers (or an array of characters) rather than integers. Are any changes needed in the basic algorithms?

39. a. Modify the function *linearsearch* so that, rather than returning the position where it finds the new number, it simply indicates whether the search has been successful. (Depending on the application, you may want *linearsearch* to do this or to indicate the position in the array where the element is found.)

    b. How does the main program's call to *linearsearch* have to be modified to accommodate this change?

    c. How does the main program's processing after the return from *linearsearch* have to be changed?

40. In the function *linearsearch*, we used two *return* statements: one in the middle of the loop and one after the end of the loop. Rewrite the function so that it uses a single *return* statement at the end of the loop. To do this, use a *break* statement to exit the loop in case *newnumber* has been found. In addition, modify the *return* statement at the end of the loop so that it returns the appropriate value (either the position of *newnumber* or –1). (*Hint*: At the end of the loop, how can you tell which value should be returned?)

PROGRAMMING PROJECTS INVOLVING SEARCHING

41. a. Write a function *shift* that receives as parameters an array of integers *arr*; an integer *n*, representing the number of elements in the array; and two integers, *first* and *last*, representing the first and last positions in the array to be moved. The function shifts each element in the array from position *first* to *last* forward one place, and adds 1 to *n*. Thus, *arr[first]* ends up in *arr[first + 1]*, *arr[first + 1]* in *arr[first + 2]*, ..., *arr[last]* in *arr[last + 1]*. (Assume that the array has a position *last + 1*.) Can you move the elements in this order?

    b. Write a function *shiftsome* that receives one extra parameter, a positive integer *k* representing the number of positions to be shifted. (Assume that there is room in the array to shift as far as *k* positions.) For example, if *k* is 3, *shiftsome* shifts each element three positions. Do not use *shift* in writing *shiftsome*.

    c. Rewrite *shiftsome* by calling *shift* a total of *k* times. Compare the efficiency of the two versions.

42. Write a function *shiftback* with the same parameters as *shift* that shifts backward each array element from position *last* to position *first*. Thus *arr[last]* ends up in *arr[last – 1]*, ..., *arr[first]* in *arr[first – 1]*. Assume that *first* is not 0. Why must we make this assumption?

43. a. Write a function *insert* that receives as parameters *numbers*, a sorted array of integers, an integer *n* representing the size of the array, and an integer *newnumber*. The function inserts *newnumber* into its correct position in ascending order within the array. (*Note*: In addition to changing certain positions in *numbers*, the function must modify *n* as well. Why?)

    b. Rewrite the function *insert* using the function *shift* from Exercise 41.

  c. Rewrite the function **insert** to handle the case where the array is full, and it is impossible to insert a new element. What should the function do?

44. Write a function **delete** that receives the same parameters as the function **insert** (see Exercise 43). It deletes **newnumber** from the array **numbers**. This involves shifting certain elements of the array and modifying **n**. Assume that **newnumber** does occur in the **numbers** array. You can use a function from an earlier exercise (which one?) if it is helpful.

EXERCISES INVOLVING STRINGS

45. In most applications of sorting, there is usually other information associated with each element of the array. For example, consider the following problem: Read in a parameter value **n**, then read in **n** groups of data, each consisting of a name and a number. Typical groups might be: "Rocky" 5, "Space" 1999, or "Indy" 500. Sort the numbers into alphabetical order. Print the values after sorting.

  If a programmer solves this problem in a naive way, the final printout may be some mishmash like this:

```
Indy        5
Rocky    1999
Space     500
```

When sorting, we must maintain the association of name and number. Every time two names swap places, the corresponding numbers must also swap.

  Write a program that solves this problem by carrying along extra information. You may want to use a version of the **swap** function from Section 8 to interchange the names while maintaining the association with numbers.

46. (*Note:* If you have already covered Chapter 11, store the data for this exercise in an array of structures. If you have not yet covered Chapter 11, use a series of arrays. In either case, try to use a version of the **swap** function.)

  A set of data consists of groups of information, consisting of people's names, ages, and social security numbers. Sort the list of ages into ascending order, being sure to carry along the names and social security numbers. Then sort the names into alphabetical order, carrying along the other data. Finally, sort the social security numbers. Print each sorted list, together with the associated information, with appropriate headings.

  (*Warning:* A social security number, with nine digits, may be larger than the largest integer value in your system, and thus it cannot be represented using data type **int**. Think of another representation. *Suggestion:* A social security number is never used in mathematical computations but is simply a string of digits.)

47. A set of data consists of a series of names and numbers. Sort the numbers into ascending order. If two or more numbers are equal, sort their corresponding names into alphabetical order. For example, 5 "Pieces" comes before 5 "Rocky".

48. A set of data consists of a series of names and numbers. Sort the names into alphabetical order. If a name occurs more than once, remove the extra name(s) but modify the number to the sum of the numbers for the separate occurrences. For example, if you find "Rocky" 5 and "Rocky" 11, the final list shows only "Rocky" 16.

49. In a commercial or scientific application, the amount of information carried along as an array is sorted may be very large (e.g., 70 to 80 pieces of data per person). Therefore, it is helpful to minimize the number of times this extra information must be swapped. Devise an algorithm that does not require every piece of extra information to be swapped each time the actual values are. [*Suggestion*: Swap only the values but keep track of their original positions within the array. Once a given value is permanently placed, move its extra information. (Is it even necessary to swap the actual values?)]

50. Suppose that you have two arrays, *name* and *grade*. The *name* array contains students' names, and *grade* contains their grades on a test. Write a program that finds all the students who have a grade of 90 to 100 and prints their names and their grades in numerical order.

STRUCTURES

11

SYNTAX CONCEPTS: data type *struct*, accessing members of a structure, dot operator, -> operator, nested structures, *typedef*, data type *union*

PROGRAMMING CONCEPTS: setting up a menu

PROBLEM-SOLVING TECHNIQUES: creating and accessing a database

HOW TO READ CHAPTER 11

Section 2, which introduces basic concepts about structures, is the most important part of the chapter and can be covered before Section 1. Section 3 requires both earlier sections. Sections 4 and 5 introduce *typedef* and data type *union*, which are related to structures but not required for Program 11.

OUTLINE: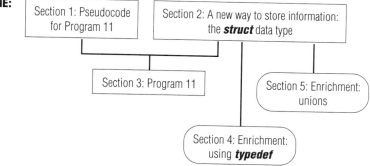

Section 1: Pseudocode for Program 11

Section 2: A new way to store information: the *struct* data type

Section 3: Program 11

Section 5: Enrichment: unions

Section 4: Enrichment: using *typedef*

INTRODUCTION AND STATEMENT OF THE PROBLEM

In this chapter, we introduce an important C data type called a structure. This data type provides the focus for the entire chapter and Problem 11. In Program 11, we read in data about a series of contestants for a quiz show, followed by some questions about the data. Using fancier terminology, we can say that Program 11 creates a database and responds to a series of questions or queries about it. A **database** is a collection of related information organized in a way that permits easy access. In C, it can be implemented by using a structure or an array of structures, or some other storage mechanism. Before we write code for Program 11, we have to discuss structures.

PROBLEM 11

A television quiz show has information about a number of people who want to become contestants. The name of each potential contestant and some personal characteristics are on file. The quiz show producer wants to get an answer to a question such as "Which contestants have blonde hair?" or "Which contestants are 21 years old?"

Write a complete C program to do the following: Read in information for a group of contestants; count the number of contestants read in. The information about each contestant consists of

name (last name, then first name)
sex (F or M)
hair color (red, black, brown, blond, gray, or bald)
age
title of job
annual salary (with two decimal places)

Here is a typical entry for a contestant:

Smith   Mary F brown   27   lawyer   85456.78

Mary Smith is a female with brown hair, 27 years old, a lawyer, and earns $85,456.78 per year.

Once the information on the entire group of contestants has been read in, print it in tabular form under a set of column headings (e.g., Name, Sex, etc.). The contestant's name should appear in normal order (first name, last name) with a single space between the two parts. The salary should be printed with a dollar sign and decimal point. For example, the line in the table for Mary Smith should look like this:

Mary Smith F brown   27   lawyer $85456.78

Then print a menu on the screen, allowing the user to select a particular trait which is desired in a contestant. The menu contains the names of all possible traits: age, hair color, salary, sex, and title. In addition, the menu offers the option of quitting the program.

After identifying the trait that is desired, prompt the user to enter a value that corresponds to that trait (e.g., 17 for age, or M representing male, or 50000 for salary). The program prints a list of all contestants who have the selected value for the chosen trait (for salary, we want all contestants whose salary is greater than or equal to the number requested). The program prints their names as they appear in the table. There should also be a heading indicating what question is being answered. For example,

Contestants whose age is 27

Mary Smith
Paul Cooper

Then the program presents the menu again to allow the user to make another selection. The program continues to process requests until the user selects *quit* from the menu.

SECTION 1   PSEUDOCODE FOR PROGRAM 11

This section develops pseudocode for Program 11 in top-down fashion, beginning with the main program. Before actually solving the problem in Section 3, we introduce structures in Section 2.

PSEUDOCODE FOR THE MAIN PROGRAM

Let's begin our top-down analysis of Program 11 by deciding upon the overall organization. Suppose we divide up the work as follows: The main program calls a function—***readdata***—to read in from a data file information about the contestants. This information is stored to form a database. Then the main program calls a function, ***prettyprint***, to print the entire collection of data in a nice format with column headings.

Here's the pseudocode for the first section of the main program:

> *call* readdata *to read in data about the contestants*
> *and store the data values in a database*
> *call* prettyprint *to print the contestant database*

This section of the program needs to be executed only once. After the data values have been read in and stored, they can be used many times until the program terminates.

Next, the main program calls a function, ***printmenu***, to produce a menu of choices on the screen for the user. The user's choices are *sex, age, hair color, title,* and *salary.* Another function, ***selecttrait***, reads in the user's choice and asks for the specific value desired.

For example, the user may select *age* from the menu, and then enter 27, meaning, "List all contestants whose age is 27." Another possible selection could be *salary* and 50000, meaning, "List all contestants whose salary is greater than or equal to $50,000." The ***selecttrait*** function calls other functions to do the processing necessary to produce the list of contestants meeting the criteria.

Before we write the rest of the pseudocode, one question remains. Should we write the program so that the user can process only one request? It seems more efficient to let the program continue until the user is finished asking questions. In fact, we will make *quit* one of the options in the menu. If the user selects *quit*, the program terminates. Here is the pseudocode for the second part of the main program:

> *while user wishes to continue {*
>   *call* printmenu *to print a menu of traits on the screen*
>   *call* selecttrait *to respond to a particular query*
> *}*

This is all the pseudocode necessary for the entire main program. As usual, there are many other ways to organize the program, some of which are discussed in the exercises. Now, let's write pseudocode for each function.

PSEUDOCODE FOR THE FUNCTION *readdata*

The function **readdata** sets up the database. The function reads in a series of sets of data values until there are no more values; it counts the number of contestants and returns that value as a parameter value (we'll call it **num**). Here is the pseudocode for **readdata**:

```
/* readdata */
num = 0;
```
while there are data values
> *read in data for each contestant*
> *add 1 to* num

PSEUDOCODE FOR THE FUNCTION *prettyprint*

The function **prettyprint** accomplishes a simple task: printing the database in a nice format. Since we are still writing pseudocode, we won't worry about the details. Here is the pseudocode for **prettyprint**:

```
/* prettyprint */
```
print headings
for each of the num *contestants*
> *print database information in a neat format*

SETTING UP A MENU—PSEUDOCODE FOR THE FUNCTION *printmenu*

To set up a menu, all the program has to do is print the words that we want on the screen. The **printmenu** function simply prints messages on the screen in an attractive format; the **selecttrait** function does the rest of the work by reading in the user's selection. Here is pseudocode for **printmenu**:

```
/* printmenu */
```
print instructions to the user
print a heading
print choices for the user
ask the user to make a selection

PSEUDOCODE FOR THE FUNCTION *selecttrait*

The **selecttrait** function is actually the heart of Program 11. Once **printmenu** has presented the user's list of choices and asked for a selection, **selecttrait** takes over. The **selecttrait** function determines the user's choice; if the user chooses to quit, the function returns a value signaling the main program to terminate; otherwise, **selecttrait** calls another function appropriate to the choice. For example, if the user selects *age*, **selecttrait** calls a function **findage**; if the user selects *hair color*, **selecttrait** calls a function **findhair**, and so on. Here is the pseudocode for **selecttrait**:

```
/* selecttrait */
```
read in the user's choice

> *if user selects* `"quit"`
> *terminate*
> *else*
> *call the appropriate function to search the database*

Of course, we can not complete the pseudocode for ***selecttrait*** until we see what goes on in each of the functions it calls. Since each function does essentially the same thing, we can use ***findage*** as an example.

THE *findage* FUNCTION

The function that is selected asks the user for a value for the trait and then searches the database for all contestants satisfying the request. The function ***findage*** asks the user for an age; if the user enters 27, ***findage*** creates a list of all those contestants whose age is 27. Similarly, the ***findhair*** function asks the user for a hair color; if the user chooses *red*, ***findhair*** creates a list of all contestants whose hair is red.

The function prints the query and a list of all contestants satisfying it. If there are no contestants who do, it prints a message to that effect. Here is the pseudocode for ***findage***:

> `/* findage */`
> *ask user for the desired age value*
> *search the database for contestants matching the requested age value*
> *print a list of contestants with the requested age*
> *if there are none, print a message*

Each function discussed here performs a task which is quite straightforward. The only remaining problem is how to store the data. Section 2 introduces a new data structure suitable for this task, and we use it in Section 3 to write Program 11.

SELF-CHECK 11-1

1. Can you think of a way to store the data for Program 11? What is the problem with using an array? How about a collection of parallel arrays?

2. Suggest some other ways to organize the solution to Problem 11 by dividing the tasks into different modules.

SECTION 2   **A NEW WAY TO STORE INFORMATION: THE *struct* DATA TYPE**

This section introduces the declaration and use of structures.

ORGANIZING THE DATA FOR THIS PROGRAM

You already know enough to write Program 11. The data can be stored in a collection of arrays, one for the first name of each contestant, one for the last, one for the sex, and so on. Although you may consider using a two-dimensional array, with all of the data about one contestant constituting a row, this is not permitted because all elements of an array, regardless of the number of dimensions, must be of the same type.

Using separate arrays to store the data is possible but awkward. It forces us to jump back and forth from array to array as we process each contestant. This method also scatters information about one contestant in many different places instead of concentrating it in a single location. Because the pieces of data are clearly related to each other, there should be a way of storing them that indicates this connection. In fact, we will solve Program 11 by using a new data type, called a structure, rather than using arrays.

HIGHLIGHTS

A programmer must often think as much about how to store as how to process the data. A clever principle of organization—that is, a useful data structure—often makes the rest of the program much easier, while a poor choice can lead to all sorts of problems.

TWO RESTRICTIONS ON ARRAYS

Before discussing structures, let's point out two restrictions imposed by arrays. One has already been noted: All elements of an array must have the same data type—for example, *int* or *double* or *char[25]*. In other words, an array must consist of homogeneous data.

The second restriction is more subtle: All elements of the array must be at the same level of organization; there is no hierarchy among elements. For example, in an array called *x*, *x[0]* is not more basic, more complex, or in any way more important than *x[1]*, *x[2]*, or any other array element. This may not seem like much of a restriction, but when we present the alternative, you will see that it is.

AN EXAMPLE OF A STRUCTURE

There is an alternative to an array. A **structure**, declared using the *struct* data type, allows grouping of data values which are heterogeneous; it also imposes on the various parts of the data a hierarchy which reflects the relationships among them. The best way to convey the idea of a structure is with a picture. Figure 11-1 is a picture of a structure called *address*, which consists of a house number and a street name. In a moment, we will show how to declare *address* so that it has this organization.

DEFINING A STRUCTURE

There are several ways to define a structure. The simplest is by using the data type *struct*. A structure is a composite data type which contains declarations for several items called

FIGURE 11-1   The structure *address*

members. The members of a structure can have any data type allowable in C, including data type **struct**.

A structure declaration does not set up any storage; it defines a template, or pattern, for variables. In a sense, a structure declaration defines a type. (In Section 4, we show how to make this explicit by using **typedef**.) Example 11-1 first shows how to define a structure type and then how to use it to declare variables; it also shows how to combine the two ideas.

EXAMPLE 11-1A

Assume that we want to define the structure **address**, illustrated in Figure 11-1. The structure consists of a house number (an integer) and a street name (a string). We can define this structure as follows:

```
struct address {
    int  housenumb;
    char streetname[20];
};
```

In this case, the new type is **struct address**. Once the structure has been defined, we can declare variables using the new type:

```
struct address home_address, work_address;
```

Defining the structure and using it to declare a variable can be combined, as shown in Example 11-1B.

EXAMPLE 11-1B

The variables **home_address** and **work_address** declared in this example are identical in organization to those in the two-part form of Example 11-1A. Each has two components: an integer **housenumb** and a string **streetname**.

```
struct address {
    int  housenumb;
    char streetname[20];
} home_address, work_address;
```

General Form of a *struct* Definition

```
struct struct_tag {
    type_1 var_1;
    type_2 var_2;
    ...
    type_n var_n;
} structvar1, structvar2;
```

◆   The word **struct** is a keyword in C.

◆   The item identified as **struct_tag** is called a **tag** and identifies the structure later in the program. While the tag can be omitted, doing so makes it impossible to define other structures with this format later.

◆   Each *type_1 ... type_n* can be any data type in C, including another structure.

- ◆ The items *var_1*, *var_2*, ... *var_n* are the members of the structure.

- ◆ The items **structvar1** and **structvar2** are variables which have the format of the structure **struct_tag**.

ACCESSING MEMBERS OF A STRUCTURE: THE DOT (.) OPERATOR

In Example 11-1, we declared two structures, **home_address** and **work_address**, each of which has the same two members: **streetname** and **housenumb**.

A member of a structure is identified and accessed using the **dot operator** (.). The dot operator connects the member name to the name of its containing structure:

```
structurename.membername
```

EXAMPLE 11-2   The members of the structures **home_address** and **work_address** are identified and distinguished from each other by using the dot operator. The four members are accessed this way:

```
home_address.housenumb          work_address.housenumb
home_address.streetname         work_address.streetname
```

It is legal (though perhaps not the best style) to have a simple variable with the same name as a member of a structure since the way structure members must be addressed guarantees that there is no ambiguity. The compiler will always be able to distinguish between a variable called **housenumb** and **home_address.housenumb** or **work_address.housenumb**.

Example 11-3 shows how to give values to the members of structures **home_address** and **work_address**.

EXAMPLE 11-3   Using the structure variables **home_address** and **work_address**, we can give values to the members in any of the usual ways:

```
home_address.housenumb = 123;
strcpy(home_address.streetname,"Main");
scanf("%s",work_address.streetname);
scanf("%d",&work_address.housenumb);
```

STRUCTURE ASSIGNMENT

It is legal to copy one entire structure to another with the same **struct** type by using a simple assignment statement, as shown in Example 11-4:

EXAMPLE 11-4   Once **new_address** has values, they can be copied or assigned to the corresponding members in **home_address** in one assignment statement:

```
struct address {
    int  housenumb;
    char streetname[20];
} home_address, new_address;

...
home_address = new_address;
```

MORE EXAMPLES OF STRUCTURES

Let's look at a few more simple examples of structures. Figure 11-2 shows a structure tagged *student*. As you can see, the structure *student* has three component parts: *name*, *average*, and *lettergrade*. In Example 11-5, we define a structure, *student*, and then declare two variables with type *struct student*, each matching Figure 11-2.

EXAMPLE 11-5

```
struct student {
    char    name[40];
    double average;
    char    lettergrade;
} freshman;
struct student beststudent;
```

Notice that we have declared the two variables in different ways. The variable *freshman* is declared with the structure definition; the variable *beststudent* is declared in a separate statement. Nonetheless, the two structures have the same type—*struct student*.

Example 11-6 shows sample statements using the members of the structures *freshman* and *beststudent*.

EXAMPLE 11-6

Assume that the members of the structures *freshman* and *beststudent* have been given values. We can use a member of either structure like any simple variable. Here are some examples:

```
if (freshman.average > 3.5)
    freshman.lettergrade = 'A';

if (freshman.average > beststudent.average) {
    strcpy(beststudent.name,freshman.name);
    beststudent.average = freshman.average;
    beststudent.lettergrade = freshman.lettergrade;
}
```

Because a structure can be copied as a unit, the last *if* statement can be written more easily:

```
if (freshman.average > beststudent.average)
    beststudent = freshman;
```

As another example, suppose a used car dealer needs to store information about each vehicle in the showroom. The dealer may use the structure with the tag *vehicles*, which is shown in Figure 11-3.

Example 11-7 shows a possible definition for the structure tagged *vehicles* and a declaration of variables *v1* and *v2* using that structure.

FIGURE 11-2 *struct student*

FIGURE 11-3 *struct vehicles*

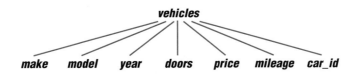

EXAMPLE 11-7   Here is a possible definition for *struct vehicles*, based on Figure 11-3:

```
struct vehicles {
    char    make[10];
    char    model[10];
    char    year[5];
    int     doors;
    double  price;
    int     mileage;
    char    car_id[25];
};
struct vehicles v1,v2;
```

The dealer can use a statement like this to compare the cars and their mileage:

```
if (v2.year < v1.year && v2.mileage < v1.mileage)
    printf("This %s %s %s is a great buy!",v2.year,v2.make,v2.model);
```

INITIALIZING A STRUCTURE

It is possible to initialize a structure (or part of one) in the declaration. The technique is similar to initializing an array except that the members of a structure may have different data types. Example 11-8 shows how.

EXAMPLE 11-8
```
struct student {
    char    name[40];
    double  average;
    char    lettergrade;
} freshman = {"Sam Starter", 2.0, 'C'};
struct student sophomore = {"Lyn Later",3.45};
```

The first initialization gives *freshman.name* the value "Sam Starter", *freshman.average* the value 2.0, and *freshman.lettergrade* the value 'C'. Omitting values in the list of initial values leaves the corresponding member uninitialized. The member *sophomore.name* is given the value "Lyn Later", *sophomore.average* is initialized to 3.45, but *sophomore.lettergrade* is uninitialized. It is not possible to omit a value in the middle of a list.

CAUTION An initialization in a declaration does not give values to the template for the structure; it affects only the specific structure being initialized. For example, the initialization of the structure *freshman* in Example 11-8 does not initialize the template *student*. Any other structure that is defined as having type *struct student* is not given these values.

SELF-CHECK 11-2

1.   What are the advantages of a structure over an array?

2.   Write a definition for a structure **bus**, which contains all the information about a specific bus route, including the name of the route (a code like *B* or 4 or 63), the number of times that buses run that route each day, the starting and ending points for the route (street names), and the cost of the fare (1.50 or .75).

3.   Show two ways of declaring variables using the structure type defined in question 2.

A STRUCTURE VERSUS AN ARRAY

Because structure members have names, a structure is often better even in a situation where an array could be used. Example 11-9A shows the structure *mortgage*.

EXAMPLE 11-9A

```
struct loan {
      double years;
      double rate;
      double apr;
      double amount;
      double month_interest;
      double month_principal;
      double month_payment;
} mortgage;
```

alternative declaration, showing factoring:

```
struct loan {
      double years, rate, apr, amount, month_interest;
      double month_principal, month_payment;
} mortgage;
```

Because the members of this structure all have the same type, an array of **double** could be used to store the same information. However, a structure allows the programmer to use names rather than subscripts; this makes the program easier to write and debug.

Example 11-9B shows the difference between using an array and a structure containing the same information.

EXAMPLE 11-9B

With the structure definition of *mortgage* from Example 11-9A, the following statements will calculate interest and monthly payments:

```
mortgage.years = 30;
mortgage.rate = 8.5;
mortgage.apr = mortgage.rate / 100;
mortgage.amount = 150000;
mortgage.month_interest = mortgage.amount * mortgage.apr / 12;
```

In contrast, suppose we declare *mortgage* as an array:

```
double mortgage[7];
```

```
mortgage[0] = 30;                                          /* years */
mortgage[1] = 8.5;                                 /* interest rate */
mortgage[2] = mortgage[1] / 100;          /* annual percentage rate */
mortgage[3] = 150000;                           /* amount borrowed */
mortgage[4] = mortgage[3] * mortgage[2] / 12;
                                       /* interest = amount * apr / 12 */
```

Notice that the code needs numerous comments to clarify how the variables are used, while this clarity is built into the structure solution.

Another reason for using a structure rather than an array is that items in an array usually have more in common than their data type. For example, you may have an array of test scores, but the test average is usually not stored in one element of the array; instead, it is stored in a separate variable.

MORE COMPLICATED STRUCTURES

The members of a structure may be arrays, pointers, or even other structures. Let's first look at some structures that have an array as a component. (We have already used an array of *char* in several structures.) The structure *triangle*, shown in Figure 11-4 and defined in Example 11-10A, contains two arrays.

EXAMPLE 11-10A   Here is the declaration of *struct triangle* from Figure 11-4.

```
struct triangle {
    char type[12];
    int  angle[3];
} t1;
```

Type *struct triangle* includes an integer array, *angle*, to hold the angles, and a *char* array, *type*, to hold the type of the triangle: equilateral, isosceles, or scalene.

FIGURE 11-4 *struct triangle*

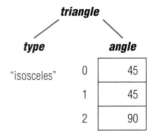

Since **angle** is an array, its elements are identified by subscripts. The first element of the **angle** array is identified as follows:

```
t1.angle[0]
```

EXAMPLE 11-10B   The following classifies triangle **t1** as equilateral, scalene or isosceles.

```
if (t1.angle[0] == t1.angle[1] && t1.angle[1] == t1.angle[2])
    strcpy(t1.type,"equilateral");
else if (t1.angle[0] == t1.angle[1] || t1.angle[1] == t1.angle[2]
        || t1.angle[0] == t1.angle[2])
    strcpy(t1.type,"isosceles");
else
    strcpy(t1.type,"scalene");
```

NESTED STRUCTURES

A structure can be a member of another structure. This is called a **nested structure**.

Suppose a library wants to store information for each of its books: the author's name (first and last), the title, the publication details (publisher name, city, and state), and the year the book was published, as well as information such as the call number and the number of copies. Figure 11-5 shows one possible hierarchy for this structure.

EXAMPLE 11-11   Here is a definition for the structure from Figure 11-5:

```
struct books {
    char lastname[20];
    char firstname[20];
    char title[30];
    char pubname[25];
    char pubcity[20];
    char pubstate[3];
    int  yearpub;
    char call_number[15];
    int  numcopies;
};
```

The problem with this structure is that it is too flat; that is, the structure's hierarchy has only one level. That's like having a company where all the employees report to the same

FIGURE 11-5   struct books

person. The hierarchy doesn't reflect the actual relationships among the data values represented in the structure.

Suppose we create some smaller structures to represent some of the lower-level components of the ***books*** structure, such as the author's name, as shown in Figure 11-6.

EXAMPLE 11-12A   The structure in Figure 11-6 can be represented by this definition:

```
struct name {
    char last[20];
    char first[20];
};
```

Similarly, several items are all related to the publisher of the book: the publisher name, city, and state. Figure 11-7 shows the relationship of this information.

EXAMPLE 11-12B   The structure in Figure 11-7 can be represented by this definition.

```
struct pub_info {
    char name[25];
    char city[20];
    char state[3];
};
```

FIGURE 11-6   ***struct name***

FIGURE 11-7   ***struct pub_info***

FIGURE 11-8   ***struct books***

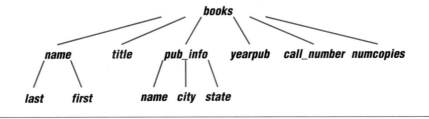

Once the structure types **name** and **pub_info** have been defined, we can use them in the **books** structure, as shown in Example 11-12C.

EXAMPLE 11-12C   This structure definition uses the structure types **name** and **pub_info** from Examples 11-12A and 11-12B to revise the **books** structure defined in Example 11-11.

```
struct books {
    struct name author;
    char    title[30];
    struct pub_info publisher;
    int     yearpub;
    char    call_number[15];
    int     numcopies;
} book;
```

When we nest one structure within another, we are declaring a variable of the structure type. The structure **books** contains a variable, **author**, which has type **struct name**. The structure **books** also contains a variable, **publisher**, which has type **struct pub_info**.

The structure with tag **books** from Example 11-12C now more accurately reflects the relationship between its members, apparent from Figure 11-8.

ACCESSING MEMBERS OF A NESTED STRUCTURE

Using a nested structure is only slightly more complex than using a single-level structure. A member must be identified by its full name, which uses the dot operator to connect all its levels. Thus, in the variable **book**, which has type **struct books**, the publisher's name can be accessed as follows:

```
book.publisher.name
```

The author's last name can be accessed like this:

```
book.author.last
```

Notice that the names in the full identification of a member are always the variable names, not the tags associated with the structure types. We use the variable **author**, not the tag **name**, and the variable **publisher**, not the tag **pub_info**.

REUSABILITY OF STRUCTURE DEFINITIONS

One advantage of defining small structures which can be nested in others is that the definitions are reusable. For example, we can modify the structure **student** from Example 11-5 to separate the name into two parts for easy alphabetization; in addition, separating the name from the grade reflects the hierarchy more accurately. Here is the original definition:

original:

```
struct student {
    char    name[40];
    double  average;
    char    lettergrade;
} freshman;
```

Example 11-13A shows the revised definition (which we call **student2** for clarity).

EXAMPLE 11-13A To define **student2**, we use the structure **name** from Example 11-12A (originally defined for the **books** structure), as well as a new structure, **classmark**.

```
struct name {
    char last[20];
    char first[20];
};
struct classmark {
    double average;
    char    lettergrade;
};
struct student2 {
    struct name sname;
    struct classmark grade;
} freshman;
```

Figure 11-9 shows a picture of the revised **student2** structure. Example 11-13B shows how to access the members of nested structure **freshman**.

EXAMPLE 11-13B To access a structure member, use the name of the variable, not the structure tag, at each level:

```
freshman.sname.last                 freshman.grade.lettergrade
freshman.sname.first                freshman.grade.average
```

STYLE WORKSHOP C is designed around the principle of building larger constructs from smaller ones. Defining small structures which can be combined to form larger ones is basic to this principle.

ANOTHER EXAMPLE OF A NESTED STRUCTURE

Let's look at another example of a nested structure. Suppose that we want to store information about employees of a company: the name, social security number, and address.

Figure 11-10 presents a picture of a structure tagged **employee**. It holds varied pieces of information about the employee: the name (first and last); the social security number; the address, made up of street address (which in turn consists of house number and street), city, state, and zip code.

FIGURE 11-9 *struct student2*

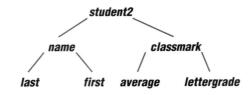

FIGURE 11-10   *struct employee*

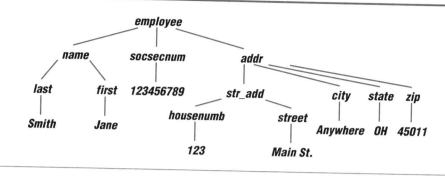

STYLE WORKSHOP   Although social security numbers and zip codes are composed of integers, both are normally treated as strings (see Exercise 13).

Example 11-14 shows how to break this structure up into several smaller ones. Then it combines the smaller structure definitions into a nested definition for *struct employee*.

EXAMPLE 11-14   Since it is clear from the figure that *name* and *addr* are further subdivided, each can be defined as a separate structure. We've already defined *name* in Example 11-12A, and we can reuse it.

Defining *addr* is more complex, because it contains *str_add*, which itself is further divided. The simplest way is to work from the lowest level up. We define a structure type named *str_add*, which is close to the definition of the structure *address* from the beginning of this section:

```
struct str_add {
    int  housenumb;
    char street[20];
};
```

Once *str_add* has been defined, we can use it to declare a structure variable, *street_address*, within the structure type *addr*:

```
struct addr {
    struct str_add street_address;
    char    city[30];
    char    state[3];
    char    zip[6];
};
```

Finally, once we have defined *addr*, we can define the entire structure *employee*, as well as a variable *emp*, which has type *struct employee*:

```
struct employee {
    struct name empname;
    char    socsecnum[10];
    struct addr address;
} emp;
```

CAUTION When smaller structures are incorporated into larger ones, the order of their definitions matters. A structure type must be defined before it is used.

Example 11-15 illustrates reading in values for the structure *emp*, defined in Example 11-14. Notice that the type of the member determines whether the & operator must be used. All the structure members except ***emp.address.street_address.housenumb*** are strings (arrays of ***char***) and thus do not need the & operator.

EXAMPLE 11-15

```
scanf("%s",emp.empname.last);
scanf("%s",emp.empname.first);
scanf("%s",emp.socsecnum);
scanf("%d",&emp.address.street_address.housenumb);
scanf("%s",emp.address.street_address.street);
scanf("%s",emp.address.city);
scanf("%s",emp.address.state);
scanf("%s",emp.address.zip);
```

Notice that we entered the data in the order of the declaration. This is, of course, not the only possible order to enter data.

 CAUTION A structure may not contain another structure of its own type (although it may contain a pointer to a structure of its own type). We discuss structures containing pointers more fully in Chapter 12, Section 3.

SELF-CHECK 11-3

1. In Program 11, why use a structure rather than an array?
2. Write statements to initialize all the members of the structure *class* in code, rather than in the declaration.

```
struct courseinfo {
    int    coursenumber;
    double num_credits;
    int    class_size;
};
struct classinfo {
    char    department[20];
    struct courseinfo course;
} class;
```

3. What is the purpose of a nested structure?

AN ARRAY OF STRUCTURES

As you may imagine, we can declare an array of structures. Example 11-16 shows a declaration for an array *emp*, with room for 100 employees.

EXAMPLE 11-16

```
struct employee {
    struct name empname;
    char    socsecnum[10];
```

```
                                struct addr address;
                            } emp[100];
```

Each element of an array of structures is referenced using normal subscript notation, with the subscript right after the name of the array variable. To print the zip code of *emp[0]*, we write the following:

```
        printf("%s\n",emp[0].address.zip);
```

Example 11-17 illustrates how to access the elements of an array of structures in a *for* loop.

EXAMPLE 11-17

Let's print the first ten names (in the order of first name, then last name) from the *emp* array.

```
        for (i = 0; i < 10; i++)
            printf("%s %s\n",emp[i].empname.first,emp[i].empname.last);
```

As another example, suppose we want to print a list of the names of all the employees who live in New Jersey (represented by "NJ"). Example 11-18 shows how to do this.

EXAMPLE 11-18

```
        printf("All employees who live in New Jersey:\n");
        for (i = 0; i < 100; i++)
            if (strcmp(emp[i].address.state,"NJ") == 0)
                printf("%s,%s\n",emp[i].empname.last,
                                emp[i].empname.first);
```

USING AN ARRAY AT A MIDDLE LEVEL

So far, we have seen an example where a structure contains an array as a member—that is, at the lowest level (the structure *triangle* from Example 11-10A). We also have seen an example of an array of structures—that is, an array at the highest level (the array of structures *emp[100]* from Example 11-16). It is possible to have an array of structures at a middle level and to have arrays at more than one level. In every case, the appropriate subscript is always used after the name of the array variable. To illustrate this concept, suppose we modify the *student2* structure from Example 11-13A:

◆ It should hold the student's overall average and information about the student's grades for up to five classes.

◆ For each class, it should contain the average and letter grade, plus an array of the student's test grades which were used to compute the average.

EXAMPLE 11-19

Here is the structure *student3*, which modifies the structure *student2* from Example 11-13A:

```
        struct name {
            char last[20];
            char first[20];
        };                                        /* this part remains the same */
        struct classmark {
            int    test[5];                       /* array of tests for each class */
                                                          (continued)
```

(*continued*)
```
    double average;
    char    lettergrade;
};
struct student3 {
    struct name sname;
    int    numclasses;          /* number of classes in array class */
    struct classmark class[5];    /* new array, one for each class */
    double overallavg;            /* new average for all classes */
} stu;
```

Figure 11-11 illustrates the structure for the variable **stu**, showing only **class[0]**. Since the structure **student3** reserves space for five classes, the **class** structure is repeated five times. (When we need to show an array, we will use variable names, rather than tags, as in this figure.)

When accessing an element from a structure which contains an array at a middle level, the subscript is attached to the level to which it refers. Example 11-20 shows how to do this using structure **stu**.

EXAMPLE 11-20 To refer to student **stu**'s grade on test 2 in class 3, we write the following:
```
stu.class[3].test[2]
```
The student's average in class 4 is the following:
```
stu.class[4].average
```

Example 11-21 uses **struct student3** to show how to access an array of elements in a structure.

EXAMPLE 11-21 Let's find student **stu**'s average and print the name and average using a nested loop structure.
```
int    i,j,k,sum;
double sum_classavg=0;
```

FIGURE 11-11   Structure **stu** showing **class[0]**

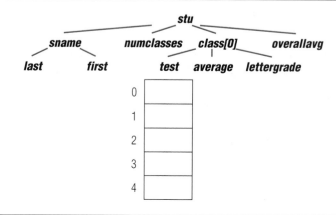

```
for (i = 0; i < stu.numclasses; i++) {
    sum = 0;
    for (j = 0; j < 5; j++)
        sum += stu.class[i].test[j];
    stu.class[i].average = (double)sum / 5;
    sum_classavg += stu.class[i].average;
}
stu.overallavg = sum_classavg / stu.numclasses;
printf("%s, %s %8.2f\n",stu.sname.last,stu.sname.first,stu.overallavg);
```

A POINTER TO A STRUCTURE

Pointers can be used also with structures. We can create a pointer to a structure the same way we create a pointer to any other type. Example 11-22 shows how.

EXAMPLE 11-22   To create a pointer to type **struct student3**, we can write the following:

```
struct student3 {
    struct name sname;
    int    numclasses;
    struct classmark class[5];
    double overallavg;
};
struct student3 *studptr;
```

CAUTION   The declaration for a pointer to a structure (**studptr** in Example 11-22) does not allocate storage for a structure, but only for a pointer. Typically, pointer notation is used in a function which receives a pointer to a structure as a parameter. To use the pointer **studptr** and pointer notation in a main program, storage must be allocated for a structure by using the function **malloc** (see Chapter 12, Section 3), or by adding this declaration and assignment:

```
struct student3 stud;
```

```
studptr = &stud;
```

Examples 11-23 and 11-24 assume that storage has been allocated in some manner.

Accessing members of a structure with a pointer can be done with the * operator. However, because the dot operator has precedence over the * operator (see Appendix III), we use parentheses to override the precedence rules, as shown in Example 11-23.

EXAMPLE 11-23   We can assign a value to **overallavg**, pointed to by **studptr**, as follows:

```
(*studptr).overallavg = 3.15;
```

To print **numclasses** and **last**, we can use the following:

```
printf("%d\n",(*studptr).numclasses);
printf("%s\n",(*studptr).sname.last);
```

To give a value to a member of a structure which is a string, we use the same notation. Here is a call to **strcpy** to provide a value for the member **first**:

```
strcpy((*studptr).sname.first,"Kate");
```

When reading in values using **scanf**, the notation parallels that for simple variables; the & (address) operator is required for all variables except strings, whose names are already addresses. Here are statements to read values into members **numclasses** and **first**:

```
scanf("%d",&(*studptr).numclasses);
scanf("%s",(*studptr).sname.first);
```

CAUTION Even though the & and * operators are adjacent, because of the parentheses, they do not cancel one another out.

THE —> OPERATOR

There is another notation which means the same thing as (***ptr**) and looks simpler. It uses the –> operator (a minus sign followed immediately by the greater than symbol). Spaces before and after –> are optional. Example 11-24 uses the –> operator.

EXAMPLE 11-24   To assign a value to members **numclasses** and **overallavg** of a structure pointed to by **studptr**, we can write the following:

```
studptr -> numclasses = 5;     is equivalent to     (*studptr).numclasses = 5;
studptr -> overallavg = 3.15;
```

To print the value of members **numclasses** and **last** pointed to by **studptr**, we can write the following:

```
printf("%d\n",studptr -> numclasses);
printf("%s\n",studptr -> sname.last);
```

To use **strcpy** to give a value to a structure member which is a string, we use the same notation as for **printf**. Here is a call to **strcpy** to provide a value for the member **first**:

```
strcpy(studptr -> sname.first,"Kate");
```

To read a value pointed to by **studptr**, the notation parallels what is used for simple variables. We can read in a value for member **last** using the same notation as for **printf**:

```
scanf("%s",studptr -> sname.last);
```

However, to read in an integer, we must use the & operator.

```
scanf("%d",&studptr -> numclasses);
```

Table 11.1 summarizes the notation used with pointers to members of structures. The form for integer variables applies to all nonstring variables.

TABLE 11.1 Notation for Pointers to Structures

	Forms Used with (*ptr) Notation		Forms Used with ptr-> Notation	
	assignment, strcpy or printf	scanf	assignment, strcpy or printf	scanf
integer	(*ptr).intval	&(*ptr).intval	ptr -> intval	&ptr -> intval
string	(*ptr).str	(*ptr).str	ptr -> str	ptr -> str

SELF-CHECK 11-4

1. Use this declaration to answer the questions below:

```
struct petinfo {
    char species[10];
    char sex;
    int  age;
    char name[15];
};
struct petinfo pet[6];
```

Write statements to assign values to **pet[0]**. Assume the pet is a cat, female, two years old, named Diva.

2. Show the declaration for a pointer **petptr** which points to a structure of type **struct petinfo**.

3. Show two ways to refer to the members **age** and **name** of the structure pointed to by **petptr**.

USING A STRUCTURE IN A FUNCTION

A structure can be sent as a parameter to a function, it can be the value returned by a function, and it can be changed in a function. To send a structure as a parameter (or to return a structure), we use the **struct** type as the type of the formal parameter (or the return value) in the function header. Unlike an array, a structure is sent to a function as a value parameter.

CAUTION The position of declarations is important when you use a structure in both the main program and the function. You must place the structure definition where it can be seen by both of them. The structure type cannot be defined inside the main program. Instead, it must be defined above the main program so that the function can find it. (Any structure variables should be declared within the individual functions.) This is the same rule that we have already followed for **#define** and **#include** directives and for function prototypes.

ANSI C under Unix is even more exacting: it requires that the structure definition come before any prototypes that use it. Although Turbo C does not require this order, we will use it so that our programs work on both systems.

Let's first look at an example which sends a single structure to a function to be printed. We'll outline a program that calls a function to print the values in a structure **worker** which has type **struct employee**.

EXAMPLE 11-25   This program defines *struct employee* before all functions, so that *employee* can be accessed by the main function as well as *printemp*. The main function declares the structure *worker*, reads values into it, and then sends the structure to *printemp* to be printed.

```c
/* prints components from the worker structure */
#include <stdio.h>
struct name {
     char last[20];
     char first[20];
};
struct str_addr {
     int  housenumb;
     char street[20];
};
struct addr {
     struct str_addr street_address;
     char   city[30];
     char   state[3];
     char   zip[6];
};
struct employee {
     struct name empname;
     char   socsecnum[10];
     struct addr address;
};

void printemp(struct employee);

main()
{
    struct employee worker;

    /* read in data */
    ...
    printemp(worker);
}

/* Function printemp */
void printemp(struct employee worker)
{
     printf("%s %s\n",worker.empname.last,worker.empname.first);
     printf("%s\n",worker.socsecnum);
     printf("%d %s\n",worker.address.street_address.housenumb,
             worker.address.street_address.street);
     printf("%s %s %s\n", worker.address.city, worker.address.state,
             worker.address.zip);
     return;
}
```

HIGHLIGHTS

Example 11-25 illustrates one of the most important features of structures: they group logically related data values. Without a structure, we would have to send eight parameters to *printemp*; with a structure, we send only one.

CHANGING A STRUCTURE IN A FUNCTION

Changing a structure in a function is more complex. Remember that a structure is passed as a value parameter, like an ordinary variable; it is *not* passed like an array. In order for a function to change values in a structure, it must receive a pointer to the structure as a parameter.

Let's review the notation to send a pointer to a structure as a parameter to a function. To illustrate, we'll give the call, prototype, and header for a function *reademp*, which receives a structure of type *struct employee* as a parameter; the function reads values into that structure.

To change a variable in a function, we send the address of that variable as the parameter by putting the & operator in front of the variable's name. For the function *reademp* to read values into the *worker* structure, we use the following call:

```
reademp(&worker);                                              /* call */
```

If the actual parameter is an address, the prototype and header must use * to indicate that the formal parameter is also an address. For this call to *reademp*, the prototype and header are the following:

```
void reademp(struct employee *);                           /* prototype */

void reademp(struct employee *worker)              /* function header */
```

If a pointer to a structure is passed as a parameter, then, inside the function, *worker* is a pointer. You can use either pointer notation from Table 11.1. However, from here on, we use only the –> operator for pointers.

Example 11-26 shows a main program that calls a function *reademp* to read values into a single structure. This example completes Example 11-25.

EXAMPLE 11-26

```
/*
 * calls reademp to fill worker structure
 * calls printemp to print worker structure
 */
#include <stdio.h>
struct employee {
    ...
};
void reademp(struct employee *);
void printemp(struct employee);

main()
{
    struct employee worker;
```

(continued)

(*continued*)

```
        reademp(&worker);
        printemp(worker);
}

/* Function printemp */
    ...

/*
 * Function reademp:
 * reads values into the structure pointed to by worker
 */
void reademp(struct employee *worker)
{
    scanf("%s",worker -> empname.last);
    scanf("%s",worker -> empname.first);
    scanf("%s",worker -> socsecnum);
    scanf("%d",&worker -> address.street_address.housenumb);
    scanf("%s",worker -> address.street_address.street);
    scanf("%s",worker -> address.city);
    scanf("%s",worker -> address.state);
    scanf("%s",worker -> address.zip);
    return;
}
```

SENDING AN ARRAY OF STRUCTURES AS A PARAMETER

To send an array of structures as a parameter to a function requires no special operators since the name of an array of structures is an address. Example 11-27 shows a main program that calls a function ***readvotes*** to read in and print out an array of structures of type ***struct votes***.

EXAMPLE 11-27 This program sets up an array of structures of type ***struct votes***. The components are the names of candidates and the number of votes each candidate received. The main program declares an array of up to 100 candidates, and the function ***readvotes*** fills as many elements of the array as there are candidates.

```
/*
 * establishes a database of candidates and their votes
 */
#include <stdio.h>
struct votes {
    char name[20];
    int  numvotes;
};

void readvotes(struct votes *, int *);

main()
{
```

```
        struct votes cands[100];
        int    numcands;

        readvotes(cands,&numcands);
}

/*
 * Function readvotes:
 * reads in and prints the cand array of structures
 */
void readvotes(struct votes *cand, int *numcands)
{
    int i;

    scanf("%d",numcands);
    for (i = 0; i < *numcands; i++) {
        scanf("%s",cand[i].name);
        scanf("%d",&cand[i].numvotes);
        printf("%s\n",cand[i].name);
        printf("%d\n",cand[i].numvotes);
    }
    return;
}
```

When using pointer notation together with a subscript, parentheses must be used for precedence:

```
scanf("%s",(cand+i) -> name);
scanf("%d",&(cand+i) -> numvotes);
```

When an array of structures is sent to a function, the notation in the header (and similarly in the prototype) can be either of the following:

```
void readvotes(struct votes *cand, ...)
```

or

```
void readvotes(struct votes cand[], ...)
```

A FUNCTION WHICH RETURNS A STRUCTURE

A function can also return a structure by using the structure type as the return value. Example 11-28 illustrates returning a structure from a function.

EXAMPLE 11-28   This program calls a function **whowon**, sending it as a parameter an array of structures of type **struct votes**. Assume that this structure has been declared and filled by function **readvotes** from Example 11-27. The function **whowon** determines which candidate has the highest number of votes and returns a structure containing that candidate's name and number of votes. (It does not allow for ties.) Notice the use of structure assignment.

```
/*
 * calls whowon to determine who has highest number of votes
 * whowon returns a structure
 */
#include <stdio.h>
#include <string.h>
struct votes {
    char name[20];
    int  numvotes;
};
struct votes whowon(struct votes *,int);
void readvotes(struct votes *,int *);

main()
{
    struct votes cands[100],winner;
    int    numcands;

    readvotes(cands,&numcands);                    /* from Example 11-27 */

    winner = whowon(cands,numcands);
    printf("%s won with %d votes\n",winner.name,winner.numvotes);
}

/*
 * Function whowon:
 * returns a structure which contains name and number of votes of
 * candidate with highest number of votes
 */
struct votes whowon(struct votes *v,int numcands)
{
    int    i;
    struct votes highest;

    strcpy(highest.name,v[0].name);
    highest.numvotes = v[0].numvotes;
    for (i = 1; i < numcands; i++)
        if (v[i].numvotes > highest.numvotes)
            highest = v[i];
    return highest;
}
```

When a function returns a structure, the return type is sometimes placed on a separate line from the rest of the function header (or prototype) for readability. This is illustrated by the header for the function **whowon**:

```
struct votes
whowon(struct votes *v,int numcands)
```

STYLE WORKSHOP The task from Example 11-28 can be handled in many other ways: by returning the subscript *i*, by returning a pointer to an element of the array of structures, or by sending a pointer to a structure as a third parameter to **whowon**. These techniques are explored in Exercise 26.

HIGHLIGHTS

There are three things to understand to work with structures comfortably. One is the picture of the structure in our minds or on paper; this picture has a tree structure and shows the hierarchy and relationships among the elements.

The second is the way to declare a structure. Start by defining any structures used as components. Once a structure type is defined, it can be used to declare a variable—either a simple one or a component of another structure.

The third is the way elements of a structure are accessed, using the . operator. To identify a member, specify each level in the structure; use the names of the variables, not the tag names of the structure types. If any level is an array, place the subscript next to the array name.

SELF-CHECK 11-5

1. Write the header for a void function ***fillstudent*** which should be able to modify a structure of type ***struct student***.

2. Write the header for a function ***findtop*** which receives as parameters an array of structures of type ***struct class*** and an integer ***numclasses***. The function returns a pointer to ***struct class***.

SECTION 3   PROGRAM 11

This section solves Problem 11 using the pseudocode from Section 1; the program uses an array of structures to store the data.

PSEUDOCODE FOR THE MAIN PROGRAM

Let's take another look at the pseudocode for the main program before we translate it into C:

> *call* readdata *to read in data about the contestants*
>   *and store the data values in a database*
> *call* prettyprint *to print the contestant database*
> *while user wishes to continue*
>   *call* printmenu *to print a menu of traits on the screen*
>   *call* selecttrait *to respond to a particular query*

STORING THE DATA IN AN ARRAY OF STRUCTURES

The first line of the pseudocode says *call **readdata** to read in data ... and store the data values in a database*. Before we can read in the data, we must decide how to store the values—that is, the internal form of the database. After Section 2, you should realize that an array of structures is the most logical data structure to use. We call this array of structures ***contestant***.

Before we give the declaration for ***contestant***, let's look at a typical element of the array, say ***contestant[5]***. An obvious way to divide ***contestant*** is into ***name***, which consists of ***last*** and *first*; and *personal*, which holds the personal traits—*sex*, *age*, *job*, and so on. One of these, *job*, is itself divided into *title* and *salary*. A single array cannot hold this information (unless we consider each piece of information to be a string—see Exercise 16). Supplying data for the sixth contestant, we can draw a picture that looks like Figure 11-12.

THE DECLARATION FOR *contestant*

Once the picture is clear, the declaration for *contestant* is straightforward. We define several smaller structures, then combine them into a structure type *con*. We use that type to declare an array in the main program, assuming a maximum of 50 contestants, with the actual number specified by *num*. Here is the definition for the structure:

```
#define NUMCONS 50
struct conname {
     char last[20];
     char first[20];
};
struct jobinfo {
     char   title[15];
     double salary;
};
struct persinfo {
     char   sex[2];
     char   haircolor[7];
     int    age;
     struct jobinfo job;
};
struct con {
     struct conname name;
     struct persinfo personal;
};
```

FIGURE 11-12   Structure *contestant[5]*, showing values stored in the members

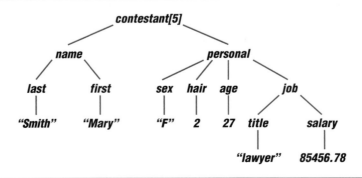

Because reading in data of type *char* together with values of other types can be a problem, we declare *sex* as a string, even though it holds a single letter. In the main program, we include this declaration to establish the *contestant* array of structures:

```
struct con contestant[NUMCONS];
int     num;
```

We use the names *contestant* and *num* in each function in Program 11.

THE MAIN PROGRAM

Now that we have decided on the structure of the database, we can continue to translate the pseudocode. The main program is divided into two parts: Part I consists of reading in the original database and printing it in a nice format, and Part II processes the queries about the database.

To start Part I, the main program calls a function *readdata*, which reads in information for all contestants, returning the number of contestants in *num*. Since the function changes the entire array of structures and also *num*, it receives pointers to both parameters. Then the main program calls the function *prettyprint* to print the entire database in a nice format. The *prettyprint* function needs the same parameters as *readdata* (but this time, they do not need to be pointers). Here are the calls from Part I of the main program:

```
/*
 * Program prob11.c:
 * Part I: calls readdata to read the original database
 * then calls prettyprint to print it
 */
readdata(contestant,&num);
prettyprint(contestant,num);
```

Next the main program calls functions to handle Part II—answering queries about the database. The pseudocode says that the main program calls a function *printmenu* to display a menu of the possible traits. This function does not need any parameters since it only prints some information on the screen. After *printmenu* sets up the menu, the main program calls the function *selecttrait* to allow the user to choose from the menu. Like *prettyprint*, *selecttrait* needs *contestant* and *num* as parameters.

As the pseudocode shows, the calls to *printmenu* and *selecttrait* are repeated until the user is finished. Since the user selects *quit* from the menu and this selection is handled within *selecttrait*, the *while* loop can continue until *selecttrait* returns a value meaning quit. We put the call to *selecttrait* in the loop condition; when the return value is 0, the loop terminates.

```
/* Part II--calls functions to read and process the requests */
do {
    printmenu();
} while (selecttrait(contestant,num) != 0);
```

Let's add the *#include* directives and the function prototypes before writing the functions. An outline of the whole program so far is on the following page.

🖳 PROGRAM LISTING

```
/*
 * Program prog11.c:
 * creates a database about quiz show contestants,
 * then answers questions about the database
 */
#include <stdio.h>
#include <stdlib.h>
#include <string.h>
#define NUMCONS 50

/* structure definitions go here */

void readdata(struct con *,int *);
void prettyprint(struct con *,int);
void printmenu(void);
int selecttrait(struct con *,int);

main()
{
    struct con contestant[NUMCONS];
    int    num;

    /* Part I: calls readdata to read the original database
     * then calls prettyprint to print it
     */
    readdata(contestant,&num);
    prettyprint(contestant,num);

    /* Part II: calls functions to read and process the requests */

    do {
        printmenu();
    } while (selecttrait(contestant,num) != 0);
}
```

THE FUNCTIONS FOR PART I: CREATING AND PRINTING THE DATABASE

Part I of the program sets up the database by calling the function *readdata*; then the main program calls *prettyprint* to print the data. Let's write the functions one at a time from the pseudocode.

THE FUNCTION *readdata*

The function *readdata* sets up the database. Here is its pseudocode:

> num = 0;
> *while there are data values*
>   *read in data for each contestant*
>   *add 1 to* num

The function reads in data from a file, which we have called "p11.dat".[1] From the file, *readdata* reads sets of data into the ***contestant*** array of structures; each time it reads a set of data, it increments a counter.

CAUTION For DOS and Windows users: To use a file in a subdirectory, prefix the path separator (\) with the escape character (also \) so that C will correctly identify the path character; for example, "c:\\homework\\p11.dat". In Unix, which uses the / character for directory paths, this is not a problem.

Here are the data values for one contestant:

```
Smith  Mary  F  brown  27 lawyer  85456.78
```

The data file contains seven items of data for each contestant. The items must be separated by whitespace characters: tabs, spaces, or newline characters. A sample data file (with two contestants) might look like this:

```
White    William
M red   52 analyst 100635.12
Smith
Mary
F brown
27 lawyer 85456.78
```

We can expand the pseudocode for ***readdata*** into the following:

num = 0;
while there are data values
    read data into the contestant *array:*
        read name (last, first)
        read personal data (sex, haircolor, age, title, salary)
        add 1 to num

Now let's write the ***readdata*** function from the pseudocode. The function opens and closes the data file. Since it makes no sense to continue the program if the file is not opened correctly, the function terminates the entire program if there is an error. Notice that ***readdata*** uses a local variable ***count*** to count contestants, changing ***num*** at the end; this makes the code clearer than using ***num*** directly:

```
/*
 * Function readdata:
 * Input:
 *    values are read from the file cfile
 *    contestant: the array to fill
 *    num: the actual number of contestants
 *    both parameters are uninitialized upon entry
 * Process:
 *    reads in data values from file cfile
```

(continued)

---

[1]Appendix VI covers explicitly reading data from a file. If you have not covered this material, mentally convert each *fscanf(filename,...)* to *scanf(...)* and each *fprintf(filename,...)* to *printf(...)* as you read through the examples.

```
(continued)
 *    into the contestant array of structures
 *    counts the number of contestants
 * Output:
 *    gives values to parameters contestant and num
 * Called by: main        Calls: none
 */
void readdata(struct con *contestant, int *num)
{
     FILE *cfile;
     int  count;

     cfile = fopen("p11.dat","r");
     if (cfile == NULL) {
         fprintf(stderr,"Error opening input file\n");
         exit(1);
     }
     count = 0;
     while (fscanf(cfile,"%s",contestant[count].name.last) != EOF) {
         fscanf(cfile,"%s",contestant[count].name.first);
         fscanf(cfile,"%s",contestant[count].personal.sex);
         fscanf(cfile,"%s",contestant[count].personal.haircolor);
         fscanf(cfile,"%d",&contestant[count].personal.age);
         fscanf(cfile,"%s",contestant[count].personal.job.title);
         fscanf(cfile,"%lf",&contestant[count].personal.job.salary);
         count++;
     }
     *num = count;
     fclose(cfile);
     return;
}
```

NEW FEATURE OF COMMENTS: FUNCTION DEPENDENCIES

There is one unusual feature in this function. We have added a line to the comment. In this program, the last line of each function's comment indicates what function(s) that function is called by and what functions (other than standard library functions) it calls. In a large program, this information is very useful in debugging.

STYLE WORKSHOP You may wish to print the data in rough format in **readdata** as a check against the neatly printed output from the **prettyprint** function. After using this kind of "debug printout," programmers comment out the extra print statements once the program works correctly. (If you are using an interactive debugger, you may not need debug printout.)

CAUTION The Turbo C++ and Borland C++ compilers have an anomaly. If it is not obvious from the function header or declarations that **scanf** is used to read in a floating point variable (**salary**, in this case), these compilers do not link in the floating point formats for **scanf**; the program compiles, but it will not run. This version of *readdata* does not work with these compilers, because we sent ***readdata*** a pointer to the structure that contains ***salary***. A simple solution is to read ***salary*** into a local variable with type ***double***. The program on the disk included with your text contains a fix for this error, but it is not shown in the program listing in the text. If you are using some other C compiler, you should not have a problem running this program.

THE FUNCTION *prettyprint*

To complete Part I, we write the function ***prettyprint***. It accomplishes a simple task, printing the database in a nice format. Here is the pseudocode for ***prettyprint***:

> *print headings*
> *for each of the* num *contestants*
> > *print database information in a neat format*

DESTINATION OF THE OUTPUT

Let's consider where ***prettyprint*** should direct its output. Certainly, ***prettyprint*** could send the nicely formatted database to the screen, but the output may be too long to fit; besides, we need a permanent copy of the formatted database. Since we want ***prettyprint*** to produce a printed listing of the database, the function should direct its output to a file, which we can later print. The ***prettyprint*** function opens and closes the file; if there is an error, ***prettyprint*** terminates the program after printing a message.

PLANNING THE APPEARANCE OF THE OUTPUT

It is helpful to decide what we would like the report to look like. Then we can figure out how to format it. Since we have to print seven different values for any number of contestants, it makes sense to print the output in columns with headings. Figure 11-13 shows the output as we intend to print it using ***prettyprint*** (this is only one possible format):

We use tabs to space the output and align the data under headings, as we did in Chapter 2. You may find that you need to adjust the number of tabs based on the size of your data values.

FIGURE 11-13   Output from ***prettyprint***

```
                    Contestants in the Database

    Name                Sex     Hair     Age     Title    Salary

    William White       M       red      52      analyst  $100635.12
    Mary  Smith         F       brown    27      lawyer   $ 85456.78
    John  Smith         M       gray     67      retired  $     0.00
```

CAUTION It is difficult to produce neatly formatted output in C. Tabs do not always produce neat columns; we were careful to select data values that do not cause a problem. Since tab positions are eight characters apart, the effect of a tab depends on the length of the preceding value. A name or title which goes past the next tab position destroys the appearance of the table.

```
/*
 * Function prettyprint:
 * Input:
 *   contestant: the array to print
 *   num: the number of contestants
 * Process:
 *   sends the database in a nice format to the file dbfile
 * Output:
 *   nicely displayed listing of array of structures in file dbfile
 * Called by: main      Calls: none
 */
void prettyprint(struct con *contestant, int num)
{
    int  count;
    FILE *dbfile;

    dbfile = fopen("p11.out","w");
    if (dbfile == NULL) {
        fprintf(stderr,"error opening output file\n");
        exit(1);
    }
    fprintf(dbfile,"\t\tContestants in the Database\n\n");
    fprintf(dbfile,"Name \t\tSex \tHair \tAge \tTitle \tSalary\n\n");
    for (count = 0; count < num; count++) {
        fprintf(dbfile,"%s ",contestant[count].name.first);
        fprintf(dbfile,"%s\t",contestant[count].name.last);
        fprintf(dbfile,"%s\t",contestant[count].personal.sex);
        fprintf(dbfile,"%s\t",contestant[count].personal.haircolor);
        fprintf(dbfile,"%d\t",contestant[count].personal.age);
        fprintf(dbfile,"%s\t",contestant[count].personal.job.title);
        fprintf(dbfile,"$%8.2f\n",contestant[count].personal.job.salary);
    }
    fclose(dbfile);
    return;
}
```

THE FUNCTIONS FOR PART II: INTERROGATING THE DATABASE

We now write the functions for Part II of the program—answering queries about the database. The function ***printmenu*** sets up a menu from which the user can select a trait or choose to quit; then ***selecttrait*** reads in the user's request and either terminates the program (if the user asks to quit) or calls the appropriate function to process the query. The functions ***printmenu*** and ***selecttrait*** are called over and over until the user asks to quit. Let's take another quick look at Part II of the main program:

```
/* Part II: calls functions to read and process the requests */
do {
    printmenu();
} while (selecttrait(contestant,num) != 0);
```

SETTING UP A MENU: THE FUNCTION *printmenu*

To set up a menu, we have to print a series of choices on the screen, along with an indication of how the user can select them. Here is the pseudocode for ***printmenu***:

> *print instructions to the user*
> *print a heading*
> *print choices for the user*
> *ask the user to make a selection*

This part of the program is interactive, letting the user enter requests from the keyboard and receive responses on the screen. Here is the entire function:

```
/*
 * Function printmenu:
 * Input:
 *   none
 * Process:
 *   sets up a menu of from which the user
 *   may choose a trait or choose to quit
 * Output:
 *   displays a menu on the screen
 * Called by: main    Calls: none
 */
void printmenu(void)
{
    fprintf(stdout,"\n\n\n\n\n\n");
    fprintf(stdout,"To obtain a list of contestants with a given trait,\n");
    fprintf(stdout,"select a trait from the list and type in the number\n");
    fprintf(stdout,"corresponding to that trait.\n\n");
    fprintf(stdout,"To quit, select 0.\n\n");
    fprintf(stdout,"\t*****************************\n");
    fprintf(stdout,"\t        List of Choices        \n");
    fprintf(stdout,"\t*****************************\n");
    fprintf(stdout,"\t   0 -- quit\n");
    fprintf(stdout,"\t   1 -- age\n");
    fprintf(stdout,"\t   2 -- sex\n");
    fprintf(stdout,"\t   3 -- hair color\n");
    fprintf(stdout,"\t   4 -- title\n");
    fprintf(stdout,"\t   5 -- salary\n");
    fprintf(stdout,"\n\n\tEnter your selection, 0 through 5 > ");
    return;
}
```

STYLE WORKSHOP The ***printmenu*** function uses ***fprintf*** instead of ***printf***. Since other parts of the program send output to a file, we use ***fprintf*** for all output. However, it is possible to use ***printf***.

You should make sure that the number of lines in a menu does not exceed the number of lines on the screen (25 for most monitors); this ensures that the entire menu is displayed on the screen.

Notice that we have printed some blank lines to clear part of the screen before producing the menu. If your compiler has a function to clear the screen (Turbo C has one called **clrscr**, whose prototype is in **conio.h**), you may want to call it from **printmenu**.

THE FUNCTION *selecttrait*

Once **printmenu** has presented the user's list of choices, the main program calls **selecttrait**. This function reads in the user's choice and then either terminates the program or calls the appropriate function to search the database. Here is the pseudocode for **selecttrait**:

> *read in the user's choice*
> *if user selects* "quit"
>   *terminate*
> *else*
>   *call the appropriate function to search the database*

Since the main program expects a return value of 0 from **selecttrait** if the user wants to quit, **selecttrait** returns an integer. The header and comment for **selecttrait** are the following:

```
/*
 * Function selecttrait:
 * Input:
 *   reads a value typed from the keyboard
 * Process:
 *   based on the value typed in, either terminates
 *   the program or calls a function to search the database
 * Output:
 *   returns user's choice to main
 */
int selecttrait(struct con *contestant, int num)
```

Since **printmenu** has already asked the user to enter the selection, **selecttrait** simply reads in the choice and calls the appropriate function to continue the search. For example, if the user enters 2, **selecttrait** calls **findsex**, which prompts the user to enter the value *M* or *F* and then finds all the contestants who meet the criterion (all the males, or all the females).

The setup here is perfect for a **switch** statement. Using **choice** as a selector, the **switch** statement calls **findage**, **findsex**, **findhair**, **findtitle**, or **findsalary**. Each of the five search functions is sent two parameters: **contestant** and **num**. A curious point: Notice that **selecttrait** doesn't use **contestant** or **num**, but it has to receive both parameters so that it can send them on to the functions it calls.

If the user chooses to quit, **selecttrait** returns 0; a simple way to handle this is to let **selecttrait** return the user's choice. Here is the heart of the **selecttrait** function:

```
     fscanf(stdin,"%d",&choice);
     switch(choice) {
       case 0: break;
       case 1: findage(contestant,num);
               break;
       case 2: findsex(contestant,num);
               break;
       case 3: findhair(contestant,num);
               break;
       case 4: findtitle(contestant,num);
               break;
       case 5: findsalary(contestant,num);
               break;
       default: fprintf(stdout,"Incorrect value; try again\n");
                fprintf(stdout,"\n\tEnter your selection, 0 through 5 > ");
     }

     ...
     return choice;
```

STYLE WORKSHOP The function uses *fscanf* instead of *scanf*; this gives us the flexibility to switch the source of the data quickly from *stdin* to a file.

One issue remains for *selecttrait*. Since the program is run interactively, what should *selecttrait* do if the user enters an incorrect choice, for example, 6 or 9? The best thing is to give the user another chance to enter a correct value; therefore, we incorporate the *switch* statement into a loop that continues as long as the user enters an incorrect value. On error, the *default* clause prints a message and prompts the user to enter another choice.

THE ENTIRE FUNCTION *selecttrait*

Here is the complete function *selecttrait*:

```
/* Function selecttrait */
int selecttrait (struct con *contestant, int num)
{
    int choice;

    do {
        fscanf(stdin,"%d",&choice);
        switch(choice) {
          case 0: break;
          case 1: findage(contestant,num);
                  break;
          case 2: findsex(contestant,num);
                  break;
          case 3: findhair(contestant,num);
                  break;
```

(continued)

(*continued*)

```
            case 4: findtitle(contestant,num);
                    break;
            case 5: findsalary(contestant,num);
                    break;
            default: fprintf(stdout,"Incorrect value; try again\n\n");
                     fprintf(stdout,"\tEnter your selection, 0 through 5 > ");
        }
    }  while (choice < 0 || choice > 5);
    return choice;
}
```

The function *selecttrait* calls one of the five functions to answer a particular question. The function that is called asks for the desired trait and prints the list of matching contestants.

STYLE WORKSHOP The functions *printmenu* and *selecttrait* are called from inside a loop in the main program. If the *default* clause and the loop in *selecttrait* are omitted, the program works much the same way: the menu is presented, and the user is asked to make a selection. The difference is that there is no error message printed, and the user has no way of knowing why the last request remains unfulfilled. Printing the error message and giving the user a second chance to respond is part of making a program user friendly.

ACCESSING THE DATABASE: THE SEARCH FUNCTIONS

Now we are ready for the most interesting part: finding all contestants who have the requested trait. We have to write five functions to process the queries. Each function should ask the user for a value and then print the query as a heading. The query may be something like "Contestants whose age is 27", "Contestants whose hair is red", or "Contestants whose salary is over $25,000". The function then searches the database for all contestants satisfying the criterion. Below the heading, the function prints the first and last names of the contestants who have that trait; if no contestants do, the function prints "No matching contestants".

THE *findage* FUNCTION

We will write the function *findage*, which is typical. It asks the user for an age value; if the user enters 27, it creates a list of all contestants who are 27.

Here is the pseudocode for *findage*:

ask user for the desired age value
search the database for contestants matching the requested age value
print a list of contestants with the requested age
if there are none, print a message

In *findage*, we call the value we are looking for *agewanted*; the function continues to use *contestant* and *num* for the array and the number of contestants. Here are the comment and header for the function:

```
/*
 * Function findage:
 * Input:
 *    reads requested value from the keyboard into agewanted
 *    contestant: array of structures
 *    num: number of elements in the contestant array
 * Process:
 *    finds all contestants in array contestant
 *    with age equal to agewanted
 * Output:
 *    prints the first and last name of all contestants
 *       with age equal to agewanted
 *    otherwise prints a message that none were found
 * Called by: selecttrait     Calls: pause
 */
void findage(struct con *contestant, int num)
```

The first thing the function does is ask the user for the desired age and print the query:

```
fprintf(stdout,"\n\nEnter the age that you want > ");
fscanf(stdin,"%d",&agewanted);
fprintf(stdout,"\n\nContestants whose age is %d\n\n",agewanted);
```

Then the function must find all contestants with that age. As we saw in Chapter 10, Section 4, if the set of data is not sorted, the simplest way of finding all contestants with a given value is a sequential search. That is, the function goes through the entire list of contestants one by one, comparing each one's age to what we want. Each time it finds a contestant of the right age, it prints the name:

```
for (count = 0; count < num; count++)
    if (contestant[count].personal.age == agewanted)
        fprintf(stdout,"%s %s\n",contestant[count].name.first,
                contestant[count].name.last);
```

However, what if no contestant is that age? If we leave the page blank or print a heading with no names under it, the output looks incomplete. To avoid this problem, it is customary to print a message when there is no list—in this case, saying that no contestants are that age.

To know when to print this message, we can use a variable, *found*, to indicate whether the search was successful. This variable keeps track of how many matching contestants have been found. Initializing *found* to 0 at the beginning of the function indicates that initially we have found no contestants of the right age. Each time we find such a contestant, we increment *found*. After the *for* loop ends, if *found* still has the value 0, there are no contestants of the appropriate age, and we print a message saying this; otherwise, we print the number of matching contestants. Here is the body of *findage* revised to print a message if no contestants match the query:

```
int count,agewanted,found=0;

for (count = 0; count < num; count++)
    if (contestant[count].personal.age == agewanted) {
```

(continued)

(continued)

```
        fprintf(stdout,"%s %s\n",contestant[count].name.first,
            contestant[count].name.last);
        found++;
    }
  if (!found)
      fprintf(stdout,"No contestants of this age\n\n");
  else
      fprintf(stdout,"%d contestants found\n",found);
```

PAUSING A PROGRAM

The *findage* function (and each of the other search functions) has one more task to perform that is not obvious until you actually run the complete program. At that point, the output printed by the *findage* function disappears off the screen, pushed off by the action of the *printmenu* function, which is called from *main* as soon as *findage* completes its task.

An interactive program needs to display its output on the screen until the user has a chance to look at it. We can write a function that stops the program until the user presses a key. The function, *pause*, is called at the end of *findage* and all the other search functions.

THE FUNCTION *pause*

The function *pause* is simple. It prints a message on the screen: "Press <Enter> to continue". Then it uses *getchar* to read the key pressed. Because the sole purpose of *pause* is to wait until the user presses ENTER, the actual value of the key pressed is discarded. The function begins by using a call to *getchar* to clear the buffer (see Chapter 9, Section 6). Here is the complete function *pause*:

```
/*
 * Function pause:
 * Input:
 *    key pressed from stdin
 * Process:
 *    delays program by waiting for key to be pressed
 * Output:
 *    displays "Press <Enter> to continue" on stdout
 * Called by: findage,findhair,findsex,findtitle,findsalary   Calls: none
 */
void pause(void)
{
    getchar();
    fprintf(stdout,"\n\nPress <Enter> to continue");
    getchar();
    return;
}
```

The *pause* function is called at the very end of *findage*, after *findage* has displayed all its output, but before it returns:

```
if (!found)
    fprintf(stdout,"No contestants of this age\n\n");
else
    fprintf(stdout,"%d contestants found\n",found);
pause();
return;
```

The complete version of *findage* appears at the end of this section.

THE OTHER FOUR FUNCTIONS

The other four functions are similar to *findage*, requiring only trivial modifications. In *findsalary*, our comparison is somewhat different since we want to find all contestants with a salary greater than or equal to the value specified. Other functions need to use *strcmp* to make the comparison. (Writing the rest of the four functions is left as an exercise.)

COMPLETE PROGRAM 11

We are finally finished with Program 11. Here is the final version, showing the entire main program plus all the functions and prototypes (except the four left as an exercise):

PROGRAM LISTING

```
/*
 * Program prog11.c
 * creates a database about quiz game contestants,
 *  then answers questions about the database
 */
#include <stdio.h>
#include <stdlib.h>
#include <string.h>
#define NUMCONS 50

struct conname {
    char last[20];
    char first[20];
};
struct jobinfo {
    char    title[15];
    double salary;
};
struct persinfo {
    char    sex[2];
    char    haircolor[7];
```

(continued)

(continued)

```
        int    age;
        struct jobinfo job;
};
struct con {
        struct conname name;
        struct persinfo personal;
};
void readdata(struct con *, int *);
void prettyprint(struct con *, int);
void printmenu(void);
int selecttrait(struct con *, int);
void findage(struct con *, int);
void findsex(struct con *, int);
void findhair(struct con *, int);
void findtitle(struct con *, int);
void findsalary(struct con *, int);
void pause(void);

main()
{
        struct con contestant[NUMCONS];
        int    num;

        readdata(contestant,&num);
        prettyprint(contestant,num);

        do {
                printmenu();
        } while (selecttrait(contestant,num) != 0);
}

/* ... */
void readdata(struct con *contestant, int *num)
{
        FILE *cfile;
        int  count;

        cfile = fopen("p11.dat","r");
        if (cfile == NULL) {
                fprintf(stderr,"Error opening input file\n");
                exit(1);
        }
        count = 0;
        while (fscanf(cfile,"%s",contestant[count].name.last) != EOF) {
                fscanf(cfile,"%s",contestant[count].name.first);
                fscanf(cfile,"%s",contestant[count].personal.sex);
                fscanf(cfile,"%s",contestant[count].personal.haircolor);
                fscanf(cfile,"%d",&contestant[count].personal.age);
                fscanf(cfile,"%s",contestant[count].personal.job.title);
```

```
                    fscanf(cfile,"%lf",&contestant[count].personal.job.salary);
                    count++;
            }
        *num = count;
        fclose(cfile);
        return;
    }

    /* ... */
    void prettyprint(struct con *contestant, int num)
    {
        int   count;
        FILE *dbfile;

        dbfile = fopen("p11.out","w");
        if (dbfile == NULL) {
            fprintf(stderr,"error opening output file\n");
            exit(1);
        }
        fprintf(dbfile,"\t\tContestants in the Database\n\n");
        fprintf(dbfile,"Name \t\tSex \tHair \tAge \tTitle \tSalary\n\n");
        for (count = 0; count < num; count++) {
            fprintf(dbfile,"%s ",contestant[count].name.first);
            fprintf(dbfile,"%s\t",contestant[count].name.last);
            fprintf(dbfile,"%s\t",contestant[count].personal.sex);
            fprintf(dbfile,"%s\t",contestant[count].personal.haircolor);
            fprintf(dbfile,"%d\t",contestant[count].personal.age);
            fprintf(dbfile,"%s\t",contestant[count].personal.job.title);
            fprintf(dbfile,"$%8.2f\n",contestant[count].personal.job.salary);
        }
        fclose(dbfile);
        return;
    }

    /* ... */
    void printmenu(void)
    {
        fprintf(stdout,"\n\n\n\n\n\n");
        fprintf(stdout,"To obtain a list of contestants with a given trait,\n");
        fprintf(stdout,"select a trait from the list and type in the number\n");
        fprintf(stdout,"corresponding to that trait.\n\n");
        fprintf(stdout,"To quit, select 0.\n\n");
        fprintf(stdout,"\t******************************\n");
        fprintf(stdout,"\t        List of Choices        \n");
        fprintf(stdout,"\t******************************\n");
        fprintf(stdout,"\t    0 -- quit\n");
        fprintf(stdout,"\t    1 -- age\n");
        fprintf(stdout,"\t    2 -- sex\n");
        fprintf(stdout,"\t    3 -- haircolor\n");
        fprintf(stdout,"\t    4 -- title\n");
        fprintf(stdout,"\t    5 -- salary\n");
        fprintf(stdout,"\n\n\tEnter your selection, 0 through 5 > ");
      return;
    }
```

(*continued*)

(continued)

```c
/* ... */
int selecttrait(struct con *contestant, int num)
{
    int choice;

    do {
        fscanf(stdin,"%d",&choice);
        switch(choice) {
          case 0: break;
          case 1: findage(contestant,num);
                  break;
          case 2: findsex(contestant,num);
                  break;
          case 3: findhair(contestant,num);
                  break;
          case 4: findtitle(contestant,num);
                  break;
          case 5: findsalary(contestant,num);
                  break;
          default: fprintf(stdout,"Incorrect value; try again\n\n");
                   fprintf(stdout,"\tEnter your selection, 0 through 5 > ");
        }
    } while (choice < 0 || choice > 5);
    return choice;
}

/* ... */
void findage(struct con *contestant, int num)
{
    int agewanted,count,found=0;

    fprintf(stdout,"\n\nEnter the age that you want > ");
    fscanf(stdin,"%d",&agewanted);
    fprintf(stdout,"\n\nContestants whose age is %d\n\n",agewanted);
    for (count = 0; count < num; count++)
        if (contestant[count].personal.age == agewanted) {
            fprintf(stdout,"%s %s\n",contestant[count].name.first,
                    contestant[count].name.last);
            found++;
        }
    if (!found)
        fprintf(stdout,"No contestants of this age\n\n");
    else
        fprintf(stdout,"%d contestants found\n",found);
    pause();
    return;
}

/* other functions--findsex, findhair, findtitle, findsalary--go here */
```

```
/* ... */
void pause(void)
{
    getchar();
    fprintf(stdout,"\n\nPress <Enter> to continue");
    getchar();
    return;
}
```

SELF-CHECK 11-6

1. If we use arrays instead of a structure in Program 11, how many arrays are needed?

2. If we use arrays instead of a structure in Program 11, how many arrays have to be sent to each function?

SECTION 4 **ENRICHMENT: USING** *typedef*

This section introduces *typedef*, a mechanism for defining new types.

USING *typedef*

In keeping with its focus on building larger structures from smaller ones, C allows programmers to define their own types from simpler ones. We have seen how a programmer can define a *struct* type by using a tag. By using *typedef*, a programmer can explicitly create a new type which can be used later in the program to declare variables.

General Form of a *typedef* **Definition**

> typedef *definition* newtype;

The word *typedef* is a keyword; *definition* represents the actual items that make up the new type, and *newtype* is its name.

USING *typedef* TO DEFINE NEW TYPES

A common use of *typedef* is to define types more complicated than the basic ones available in C. Each definition establishes a new type which can then be used just like a predefined type such as *int*, *char*, or *double*.

Using a type definition gives the programmer the same advantage that the *#define* directive does: a type can be used throughout the program but defined in one location. The programmer can associate a specific type with a specific task and more easily ensure that declarations are compatible. Furthermore, any changes can be made in a single location, minimizing the possibility of missing some of the references.

Example 11-29 shows some simple examples of types defined using *typedef*.

EXAMPLE 11-29

```
typedef int bigarray[1000];
bigarray nums;                  is equivalent to         int nums[1000];
```

Type **bigarray** represents an array of 1000 integers.

```
typedef char string[80];
string buffer;                  is equivalent to         char buffer[80];
```

Type **string** represents an array of 80 characters.

```
typedef int *intptr;
intptr p;                       is equivalent to         int *p;
```

Type **intptr** represents a pointer to an integer.

The first two **typedef** statements define types based on arrays, while the third defines one based on a pointer to an integer. Each type, once defined, is used to declare a variable.

USING *typedef* TO DEFINE *struct* TYPES

A more common use of **typedef** is to define structure types. The general form of **typedef** for this purpose is shown below:

General Form of a *typedef* Definition for a Structure

```
typedef struct tag {
    type_1  id_1;
    type_2  id_2;
    ...
    type_n  id_n;
} typename;
```

Here, **typename** is the name of the new **struct** type, and each *type...id* pair represents a member of the structure. The item **tag** is optional; if a name is used here, the phrase **struct tag** is equivalent to **typename**.

Example 11-30 uses **typedef** to define a structure type and then uses that new type to declare several variables.

EXAMPLE 11-30

```
typedef struct addr {
    int  housenumb;
    char streetname[10];
} address;
address home_address,work_address;
struct addr new_address;
```

The definition establishes a new type, **address**, which is a structure type. Because **address** has been defined using **typedef**, it is used to declare variables without repeating the word **struct**. Since a tag—**addr**—is supplied, we can declare variables either using type **address** or type **struct addr**.

LOCATION OF *typedef* DEFINITIONS

A type must be defined before it is used. Typically, *typedef* definitions are placed at the very beginning of the program prior to other declarations. If a type defined using *typedef* is used in a main program and functions, the definition should be placed outside the main program, prior to the prototypes for any functions that use it.

STYLE WORKSHOP Some programmers, especially those who have previously used Pascal, prefer to use *typedef* whenever they are defining a structure type.

It is also common to use *typedef* in a user-defined header file to define variables that will be shared among programmers working on a project.

SELF-CHECK 11-7

1. If you have a *typedef* definition in a program, where should it be defined?

2. Suppose you have the following definition:

```
typedef struct part {
    char part_num;
    int  quantity;
} part_type;
```

Show two ways to declare a variable *inventory*, which is an array of 100 elements of type *part_type*.

SECTION 5 ENRICHMENT: UNIONS

Another data type is *union*, which looks like a structure but has a different purpose. A **union** allows a single storage location to be associated with several different variables. At any given time, however, only one of these variables can actually use the space. A union can be used by itself or as part of a *struct* definition.

GENERAL FORM OF A UNION

A union definition looks like a *struct* definition.

General Form of a Union Definition

```
union union_tag {
    type_1  var_1;
    type_2  var_2;
    ...
    type_n  var_n;
} uvar;
```

FIGURE 11-14 Space allocation in the union *occupation* (assumes *double* is eight bytes)

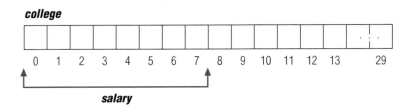

◆ The tag **union_tag** is used to identify the union later in the program.

◆ Each *type_1 ... type_n* can be any data type in C, including an array, a structure, or another union (except one of the type being defined).

◆ The items *var_1, var_2, ... var_n* are the members of the union.

◆ The item **uvar** is a variable which has the format of the union **union_tag**.

HIGHLIGHTS

The critical difference between a structure and a union is that only one of the *type_1 ... var_1* pairs exists at any given time. Space is reserved for the largest of the alternative members; whichever one is active occupies as much of that space as it requires.

EXAMPLE 11-31

A high school might use the following union to keep track of its graduates in the years immediately after graduation. If the graduate is in college, the college's name is stored; if the graduate has a job, the salary is stored.

```
union occupation {
    char    college[30];
    double salary;
} current;
```

This union can be included in the structure stored for each student. Figure 11-14 illustrates how this union is stored, with *college* and *salary* occupying some of the same memory locations.

ACCESSING A MEMBER OF A UNION

Once a union has been defined, its members are accessed like those of a structure, using the dot operator or the -> operator (with pointers). Example 11-32 shows how to access a member of a union.

EXAMPLE 11-32

```
union occupation {
    char    college[30];
    double salary;
} current,past;                    /* declares two variables */
union occupation *old;             /* pointer to union occupation */

...
printf("%s\n",current.college);
```

```
old = &past;
old -> salary = 12345.67;
```

The first part declares two variables of type **union occupation**. The union **current** is accessed directly using the dot operator; the pointer **old** is used to access the union **past**.

DETERMINING WHICH MEMBER EXISTS

Since only one member of a union can exist at a time, the programmer is responsible for determining which one is active so that the program can refer to it properly. (Accessing the wrong one is legal but may produce odd results, such as printing a string as a number.) Another variable or a constant can be used to determine which member is currently active, as shown in Example 11-33.

EXAMPLE 11-33

```
union occupation {
     char   college[30];
     double salary;
} current;
int incollege;

scanf("%d",&incollege);
if (incollege)
     strcpy(current.college,"University of Wherever");
else
     current.salary = 12345.75;
```

If **incollege** is true (nonzero), member **college** is active; otherwise member **salary** is active.

USING A UNION IN A STRUCTURE

A union can be part of another union or a structure. Example 11-34 shows the union from Example 11-33 as part of a larger structure.

EXAMPLE 11-34

```
struct alumni {
     char name[30];
     char address[40];
     char citystate[30];
     int  incollege;
     union occupation {
          char   college[30];
          double salary;
     } current;
} grad[100];

...
if (grad[0].incollege == 1)
     printf("%s\n",grad[0].current.college);
else
     printf("%9.2f\n",grad[0].current.salary);
```

A UNION THAT CONTAINS A STRUCTURE

A union can contain a structure (or another union) as one of its members. All of the members of the contained structure or union are active or inactive at the same time.

As an example, let's look at the structure used in Program 11. Each contestant has the same structure, divided into **name** and **personal**, with the same members in each. However, by using unions, we can form a different structure for each contestant.

Suppose that we want to keep information about three types of contestants: prospective contestants, scheduled contestants, and contestants who have already appeared on the show. For each type, we have different information.

◆   For a contestant who has already appeared on the show, we want to keep track of the date, the amount won (if any), and the social security number, so that we can report to the Internal Revenue Service the amount of winnings.

◆   For each prospective contestant, we want to keep track of the date when the person is available.

◆   For a scheduled contestant, we want to keep track of the date when the person will appear.

Although we could provide a field in every structure for each piece of information, a union is logically more compelling and also saves space. Figure 11-15 shows a picture of the data that must be stored, and Example 11-35 shows a union to represent this information.

EXAMPLE 11-35   Here are two ways to define the union **showinfo**; in each case, a variable **state** is declared:

nesting a structure definition in the union

```
union showinfo {
    char date_avail[9];
    char date_sched[9];
    struct past_con {
        char    date_appeared[9];
        double amount_won;
        char    socsecnum[10];
    } onshow;
} state;
```

FIGURE 11-15   The components of the union **showinfo**

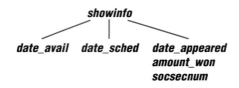

FIGURE 11-16   Use of memory by the union *state*

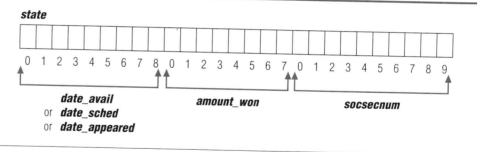

defining the structure separately from the union

```
struct past_con {
    char    date_appeared[9];
    double  amount_won;
    char    socsecnum[10];
} onshow;

union showinfo {
    char    date_avail[9];
    char    date_sched[9];
    struct past_con onshow;
} state;
```

With either definition, references to the members of *state* can be made as follows:

```
state.date_avail   or   state.date_sched   or   state.onshow.date_appeared
                                                 state.onshow.amount_won
                                                 state.onshow.socsecnum
```

Figure 11-16 shows how union *state* occupies memory.

USING A UNION IN PROGRAM 11

In order to use the union from Example 11-35 in a program, we must add some way to determine which alternative of the union is active. Example 11-36 shows how to do this.

EXAMPLE 11-36   The declaration on the next page modifies the array of structures from *prog11.c* to incorporate the union *state* from Example 11-35. The member *status* is used to determine which alternative is active. The possible values of *contestant.status* are defined as constants: *PROSPECTIVE*, *SCHEDULED*, and *PAST*.

```
#define PROSPECTIVE  1
#define SCHEDULED    2
#define PAST    3
...
```

(continued)

(*continued*)

```
struct con { .
    struct conname name;
    struct persinfo personal;
    int     status;
    union   showinfo state;
};
struct con contestant[NUMCONS];
```

The following section of code tests the value of ***contestant[0].status*** to see which alternative of ***state*** is active; it prints the values for that alternative.

```
if (contestant[0].status == PAST)
    printf("%s %f %s\n",contestant[0].state.onshow.date_appeared,
            contestant[0].state.onshow.amount_won,
            contestant[0].state.onshow.socsecnum);
else if (contestant[0].status == PROSPECTIVE)
    printf("%s\n",contestant[0].state.date_avail);
else if (contestant[0].status == SCHEDULED)
    printf("%s\n",contestant[0].state.date_sched);
```

CAUTION The programmer must be careful not to attempt to access a member that is not in the currently active alternative. The compiler stores a union by reserving enough space in each structure for the longest possible variant (but not the sum of all possible variants). In the case of union ***state***, the members ***date_avail***, ***date_sched***, and ***date_appeared*** are the same size and thus occupy exactly the same storage location. Giving a value to one wipes out any value previously given to another. However, no other variables share the space with ***amount_won*** and ***socsecnum***, and their old values remain even if the value of ***status*** changes. In Example 11-36, it is possible to print ***contestant[0].state.onshow.amount_won*** once it has been assigned a value, even if ***status*** is currently ***SCHEDULED*** or ***PROSPECTIVE***.

STYLE WORKSHOP We often store dates as ***char date[9]***, assuming that the dates are in the format yy/mm/dd. For example, December 1, 1996, would be stored as "96/12/01". This format is convenient for comparisons and sorting.

SELF-CHECK 11-8

1. What is the difference between a union and a structure?

2. How do we control which alternative of a union is currently active?

3. In general, how much memory is allocated for a union?

SUMMARY

STRUCTURES VERSUS ARRAYS

1. There are two major restrictions imposed by arrays. First, all elements must be homogeneous; that is, they must share a single data type. The second restriction is that all elements of the array must be at the same level of organization; no hierarchy is possible.

2. C provides another method of storing information, called a structure, that eliminates these two restrictions. The data in a structure need not be homogeneous, and the structure establishes a hierarchy or relationship between the parts.

ORGANIZATION AND DECLARATION OF STRUCTURES

3. A structure can be viewed as an inverted tree, with one element at the top, and branches or subdivisions leading to further elements. The subdivisions impose a hierarchical structure on the data. Figure 11-17 shows an example.

4. The general form of a definition for a structure is as follows:

    ```
    struct struct_tag {
        type_1 var_1;
        type_2 var_2;
        ...
        type_n var_n;
    } structvar1, structvar2;
    ```

    Following the keyword **struct** is **struct_tag**, the name of the structure type being defined. Each

    type_1 ... var_1 pair is a member of the structure, representing a data item. Only the members of a structure hold data values. The items **structvar1** and **structvar2** are variables declared to have type **struct struct_tag**.

5. Here is a declaration for the structure in Figure 11-17. First, we define the structure **struct bookinfo**. Then we use the defined structure to declare variables in two ways:

    ```
    struct bookinfo {
        char callnumber[20];
        char author[30];
        char title[40];
    } book;
    struct bookinfo novel;
    ```

IDENTIFYING STRUCTURE MEMBERS

6. A member of a structure is referenced by specifying all the parts on a path from the top down to the member, with dots separating the names of the parts. For example, **novel.author** is the **author** part of the structure **novel**. The dot operator joins the parts of the name.

7. One advantage of using a structure is that it allows grouping related data while giving each item a label. This makes a structure useful even if the grouped items all have the same data type and could be stored in an array.

MORE COMPLEX STRUCTURES

8. A structure can contain an array or another structure. A structure that contains another is called a nested structure. It is also possible to declare an array of structures.

9. On the following page is a declaration for a nested structure. In this example, we define smaller

    structures for the component parts of **struct students**; then we use these structure definitions to build the large one. The structure **students** contains an integer **id**, an array **grade**, as well as structures **name** and **class**. The structure **class** contains array **tests** as one of its members.

FIGURE 11-17 *struct booksinfo*

```
struct sname {
    char first[10];
    char last[10];
};
struct oneclass {
    char    name[15];
    int     tests[4];
    double  average;
};
struct students {
    struct sname name;
    int     id;
    struct oneclass class;
    char    grade[5];
};
struct students freshman;
```

10. To refer to a member of a nested structure, we must include all names on the path from the top of the tree to the member. When an array element which is part of a structure is referenced, the array subscript must appear next to the level to which it applies. Some of the members from the structure *freshman* are *freshman.name. first* and *freshman.grade[4]*.

11. In a structure definition, an array can appear at any level—including the top—so that there is an array of structures.

12. Because a member of a structure is always identified by its complete name, including all levels, names can be reused without ambiguity. A name can be used in different places in a nested structure, in different structures, or in a structure and as a single variable.

USING MEMBERS OF A STRUCTURE

13. In a program, a structure member can be used wherever a single variable can be used—for example, on either side of an assignment statement or in a function call. When a member of a structure is sent as a parameter as a function, the corresponding formal parameter is a simple variable.

USING COMPLETE STRUCTURES

14. All values in a structure can be copied to another structure with the same **struct** type by using a single assignment statement; this is called structure assignment. If **first** and **second** are structures with the same type, it is possible to write the following line:

```
first = second;
```

15. It is possible to initialize an entire structure, or part of one, in the declaration.

USING STRUCTURES WITH FUNCTIONS

16. An entire structure can be sent as a parameter to a function. The data type of the formal parameter must be the structure type declared for the actual parameter.

17. An advantage of using a structure is that a single parameter, rather than many, can be passed to a function.

18. If a structure definition is used both in the main program and in a function, it must be placed in a position where it is accessible by all functions that use it. This can be accomplished by placing the definition outside the main program, above the function prototypes.

19. Unlike an array, a single structure is sent as a value parameter. An array of structures can also be sent to a function. Since an array of structures is an array, its name is already a pointer, which means that the & operator is not needed on the actual parameter.

20. To change a single structure in a function, the program must send a pointer to that structure as a parameter. A structure can also be returned from a function.

USING POINTER NOTATION WITH STRUCTURES

21. It is possible to use pointer notation with structures. The following two forms of notation are equivalent as a means of addressing a member of an array of structures:

    ```
    part[i].quantity
    ```

    is equivalent to

    ```
    (*part+i).quantity
    ```

    The order of the * and the parentheses is required because the . operator has precedence over the * operator.

22. If a pointer to a structure which is not an array is sent to a function, the members of the structure can be referred to using pointer notation as follows:

    ```
    part.quantity
    ```

    is equivalent to

    ```
    (*part).quantity
    ```

23. To change a value of a structure member in a function using pointer notation, we must add the & operator unless the member is a string.

24. The notation in paragraphs 22 and 23 can be replaced by the arrow operator, ->. In each case, the notation on the left is equivalent to that on the right:

    ```
    part -> quantity      (*part).quantity
    &part -> quantity     &(*part).quantity
    ```

MISCELLANEOUS TOPICS

25. A database is a collection of related groups of information organized in a way which permits easy access. In C, the most natural way to implement a database is through an array of structures.

26. A program can receive input from and send output to several different places. For example, Program 11 receives input both from an external file and the keyboard; it sends output both to the screen and the printer.

27. A menu is presented to a user by using *printf* to print each of the desired messages. The user can be offered a selection of items and asked to choose one.

28. In interactive programming where output is sent to the screen, it is sometimes necessary to pause the program so that the output can be read. A function to do this is shown in the text.

USING *typedef*

29. A new type can be defined using *typedef*. Once defined, this new type, which can be a *struct* type, can be used to declare variables. Here is an example which defines a pointer type:

    ```
    typedef intptr *int;

    intptr p;
    ```

30. Here is a *typedef* which defines a *struct* type *sname* and uses it to declare a variable *name*:

```
typedef struct {
    char first[10];
    char last[10];
} sname;
sname   name;
```

USING UNIONS

31. A union allows a programmer to assign different variables to the same storage location. Which variable is active is dependent on another variable in the program.

32. A union definition resembles a *struct* definition. Here is an example:

```
union union_tag {
    type_1 alternative_1;
    type_2 alternative_2;
```

```
    ...
    type_n alternative_n;
} uvar;
```

Only one of the *type...alternative* pairs is active at a time.

33. Each alternative in a union can be a single variable, a structure, another union, or an array.

EXERCISES

DECLARATION AND TRACING EXERCISES

1. Each of the pictures in Figure 11-18 describes a structure. Assume that all variables have type *int*.
   a. Give a declaration for each structure.
   b. Describe each picture in English (e.g., *a* is divided into ...).
   c. How many data items can be stored in each structure?

2. Given the tree structure in Figure 11-19, write a definition for *struct orderinfo* as requested:
   a. Write a definition for *struct orderinfo* without using individual *struct* definitions for any of the nested structures. Write a declaration for a structure *order* using this type definition.

FIGURE 11-18 Structures for Exercise 1

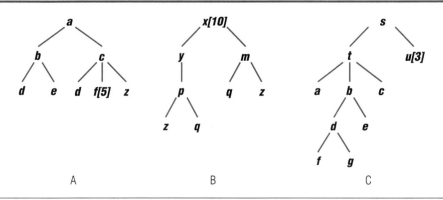

FIGURE 11-19 Tree structure of *orderinfo*

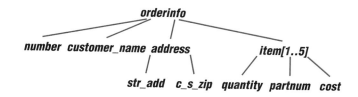

b. Write an individual *struct* definition for *addressinfo* and one for *iteminfo*, and use them in the definition of *orderinfo*. Write a declaration for *order* using these *struct* definitions.

c. Write definitions for new types *addressinfo* and *iteminfo* using *typedef*. Write a declaration for a structure *order* using these type definitions.

d. Write a declaration for an array *orders*, which consists of 300 elements of type *struct orderinfo*.

3. For each of the following descriptions, draw a picture of a structure. Then give a declaration for the structure. How many data items can be stored in each structure?

a. A small library has fiction and nonfiction books with up to ten copies of each. Each book has a title, an author, a classification number (e.g., QA237), a publication date (e.g., 1992), and the number of pages.

b. A club has 30 members. Each member has a name (divided into first and last), a member number (e.g., 27) and up to five interests. Each interest consists of a name (e.g., chess or video games) and an integer from 1 to 10 representing the level of interest.

4. a. Here is a declaration for a structure *subscriber*. Draw a picture for this structure. Describe it in English as well.

```
struct nameinfo {
    char title[5];
    char firstinit[3];
    char last[20];
};
struct addressinfo {
    char first_line[30];
    char second_line[40];
};
struct subinfo {
    struct nameinfo mailing_name;
    struct addressinfo address;
    char    date_end[9];
} subscriber;
```

b. Assume that a set of data contains the following:

Mrs. R. Kuhn 1900 CherryBlossom St. Cincinnati OH 45231 05/02/98

Write one or more C statements to read these pieces of data into the structure declared in part (a).

c. Modify the structure so that its parts are defined using *typedef*. Does the way you read in the data change?

d. Modify the structure (either change the structure itself or add more declarations) to allow up to 50 subscribers.

e. Note that the subscriber's address consists of two strings rather than a house number, street, city, and zip code in separate variables. Compare the two methods of storing the addresses. For example, how easy is it to read the data in the two formats? How easy is it to access the zip code?

5. Show what is printed by the following program segment. Assume that the set of data consists of the following:

```
25   Sue   Juan   35
```

```c
#include <stdio.h>
main()
{
     struct stuff {
          int  id;
          char name[10];
     } person;

     scanf("%d",&person.id);
     scanf("%s",person.name);
     printf("%d %s\n",person.id,person.name);
     scanf("%s",person.name);
     scanf("%d",person.id);
     printf("%d %s\n",person.id,person.name);
}
```

6. Show what is printed by the following program. (The set of data appears after it.)

```c
#include <stdio.h>
struct studtype {
     char   name[15];
     int    grade[2];
     double avg;
};
void mark(struct studtype *);
main()
{
     struct studtype student;
     int    i,j,num;

     scanf("%d",&num);
     for (j = 0; j < num; j++) {
          scanf("%s",student.name);
          for (i = 0; i < 2; i++)
               scanf("%d",&student.grade[i]);
          mark(&student);
          printf("%s %d %d %5.2f\n",student.name, student.grade[0],
               student.grade[1], student.avg);
     }
}
```

```
void mark(struct studtype *stuptr)
{
    stuptr->avg = (double)(stuptr->grade[0] + stuptr->grade[1]) / 2;
    return;
}
```

Use the following data:

3   Smart 96 94   Stupid 48 54   SoSo 71 68

7. Show what is printed by the following program.

```
#include <stdio.h>
#include <string.h>
struct studtype {
    char    name[20];
    double index;
    char    major[10];
};
void sub1(struct studtype *);
main()
{
    struct studtype student;

    strcpy(student.name,"Joe College");
    student.index = 1.78;
    strcpy(student.major,"football");
    sub1(&student);
    printf("%s %3.2f %s\n",student.name,student.index,student.major);
}

void sub1(struct studtype *studptr)
{
    char temp[20];

    printf("%s %3.2f %s\n",studptr->name,studptr->index,studptr->major);
    studptr->index += 0.25;
    strcpy(temp,"Mr");
    strcat(temp," ");
    strcat(temp,studptr->name);
    strcpy(studptr->name,temp);
    return;
}
```

8. Show what is printed by this program. Assume that the set of data contains the following:

Armstrong machinist 4 7 6.3 8.2 9.4 10.1 0

```
#include <stdio.h>
struct workertype {
    char    name[15];
    char    title[10];
    double hours[7];
};
```

(continued)

(continued)

```
int most(struct workertype, int);
main()
{
     struct workertype worker;
     int   i,j,k;

     scanf("%s",worker.name);
     scanf("%s",worker.title);
     for (i = 0; i < 7; i++)
         scanf("%lf",&worker.hours[i]);
     printf("%s %s\n",worker.name,worker.title);
     for (i = 0; i < 7; i++)
         printf("%f\n",worker.hours[i]);
     k = most(worker,5);
     j = most(worker,7);
     printf("Day %d had the most hrs in the first 5\n",k);
     printf("Day %d had the most hrs in the week\n",j);
}

int most(struct workertype worker, int day)
{
     int top=0,i;

     for (i = 1; i < day; i++)
         if (worker.hours[top] < worker.hours[i])
             top=i;
     return top;
}
```

9. For each of the following situations, would you use an array, a structure, or one or more single variables to hold the information? Give a one or two sentence justification for each answer.

    a. Find the average of an arbitrary (maybe 10, maybe 500, maybe 10,000 or more) number of integers.

    b. In a list of 50 names, see if one occurs twice.

    c. Store payroll data (including name, address, annual salary, dependents, etc.) for an employee of a company.

    d. Store a student's marks on five exams.

    e. Store a student's grade point average.

    f. Store a student's name, marks, and grade point average.

    g. Store 50 students' names, marks, and grade point averages.

10. Answer these questions based on the following structure declarations, used to hold information on two car-rental companies.

```
struct descrip {
     char model[13];
     int  year;
     char color[9];
};
```

```
struct mileinfo {
    long starting;
    long ending;
};
struct carinfo {
    struct descript description;
    struct mileinfo mileage;
} rentacar[10], carforhire[10];
```

Write one or more C statements that will

a. Read data to fill both arrays (*%ld* is the conversion specification for type *long*).
b. Compute the distance traveled (ending minus starting mileage) for each car owned by *rentacar*.
c. Print the model of each car (of either company) whose color is red.
d. Count how many elements of *carforhire* have a value for year in the range between 1994 and 1996 (inclusive).
e. Copy the information for the third *rentacar* to the fifth *carforhire*.

11. Add a union to the *struct* type *carinfo* from Exercise 10. If the car is currently rented, the structure should contain the name and address of the person renting the car, as well as the rental date. If the car is in the shop for repair, the structure should contain the date when the car was taken out of service and the reason for the repair.

12. Here is the declaration for *struct contract*; union *aptinfo* holds information pertinent to renting, leasing, or purchasing an apartment, in that order. The member *how_held*, which can have values *RENT*, *LEASE*, or *PURCHASE*, determines which alternative is active.

```
#define RENT 1
#define LEASE 2
#define PURCHASE 3
struct leaseinfo {
    double monthly_lease;
    int    lease_period;
};
struct contract {
    int how_held;
    union aptinfo {
        double monthly_rent;
        struct leaseinfo lease;
        double price;
    } monetary;
} apartment;
```

a. Draw a diagram of the structure *apartment*, showing the possibilities for union *monetary*.
b. Write statements to give values to the fields appropriate for leasing the apartment referred to by structure *apartment*.
c. Write an *if* statement that prints whichever fields of union *monetary* are active, based on the value of the member *how_held*.

13. When storing elements such as zip codes, house numbers, or social security numbers, it is preferable to use strings, not integers, even though this means they occupy more memory. (A five-digit integer can be stored in two bytes on the PC or four bytes on the Sun, while the corresponding five-digit character string requires six bytes.)

    a. Explain why **char zip[6]** is a better data type for **zip** than **int**. (*Hint:* What happens to a zip code of 97302 stored as an integer?) What other C integer data type allows a zip code of this size? (See Chapter 2, Section 5, for a list of possible data types.) But also consider this: How does a zip code of 07093 print if stored as an integer?

    b. Why is **char socsecnum[10]** better for **socsecnum** than **int**? Again consider size. Is there any C integer data type which could store the largest social security number? Suppose you have used that data type to store **socsecnum**; how does the number print? Give a declaration for **socsecnum** which allows these numbers to be printed with hyphenation (e.g., 123-45-6789).

    c. Some people have a house number which can be stored using type **int**. For each of the following, say whether the house number can be stored as an integer.

       (1) 21½ Merwin Ave.   (3) 1239 Windham Ave.   (5) 432a Catalina Ave.
       (2) 56789 Reading Rd.   (4) 110-34 68th Ave.   (6) 3603 Chestnut St.

MODIFICATIONS TO PROGRAM 11 AND TO THE EXAMPLES

14. Show how to solve Problem 11 without using a structure (more precisely, an array of structures). Compare your program to the one using a structure. What is your conclusion?

15. In Program 11, suppose that the data items in the **contestant** structure have been put into alphabetical order based on the last name. If you know this information, is there any way to speed up the search to answer the requests?

16. The set of data for each contestant in Program 11 consists of strings, integers, and real numbers. Therefore, the data for a single contestant cannot be stored in a single array. However, if each piece of information is considered to be a string, we can store the data for each contestant as an array with seven elements. Thus, the array of structures can be transformed into a two-dimensional array of strings. Show how to interpret the age and salary as strings. Is it necessary to change the format of the data? Do we have to change the **fscanf** statements that read in the data? What other change(s) are necessary? Can numerical data always be interpreted as strings? Explain.

17. Rewrite Program 11 so that the set of data for each contestant is input as a single string. Store the data in an array of strings. How does this change the rest of the program?

18. Discuss other ways to do input and output in Program 11. For example, the queries could be entered from a file. The lists of contestants answering a query could be sent to the printer rather than the screen. The database could be output to a file instead of the printer.

    a. Write functions to do the input/output some of these ways.
    b. Write a function that allows the user to select the methods of input and output.
    c. Rewrite the main program to call these functions at appropriate times.

19. In the text, only the **findage** function from Part II is written out explicitly. To complete Program 11, write the other four query-answering functions: **findsex**, **findhair**, **findtitle**, and **findsalary**.

20. Discuss other ways to structure Program 11. For example, *printmenu* could call *selecttrait*, or *selecttrait* could call *printmenu*, or *printmenu* could contain the loop that controls the number of queries entered. Give a brief outline of three or four alternate ways to allocate the work between the main program and the various functions. Compare the alternatives.

21. Write a function *sortname* that receives two parameters, an array of structures *contestant* and an integer *num*, representing the number of elements in the array. The function *sortname* sorts the elements of the *contestant* array into alphabetical order, based on the values stored in *last*, being sure to carry along the rest of the information stored in the structure (see Chapter 10, exercises 45–50).

22. Modify the function *prettyprint* from Program 11 so that it prints the contestants in the database in alphabetical order by last name. You can use the *sortname* function from Exercise 21.

23. Modify the function *selecttrait* so that it calls functions that set up a menu from which the user can choose a value for a trait. For example, the menu for *sex* asks the user to select *M* for male or *F* for female. Which menus are easy to write? Which cannot list all possible choices? What can you do instead?

24. Modify Program 11 so that it uses the structure containing a union from Example 11-36. Write a function that enters data into the array of structures. Then modify the search functions (*findage*, *findsex*, and so forth) so that they do not list people who have already appeared on the show.

25. Modify the program from Exercise 24 so that it accomplishes the same thing without using a union. This means that all fields of the union (*date_appeared*, *amount_won*, *date_avail*, *date_sched*, etc.) must appear in every structure; some of the fields contain legitimate values, but some do not. For example, if a contestant is scheduled to appear on the show, the field *date_sched* contains legitimate information; however, the fields *date_avail*, *date_appeared*, *amount_won*, and *socsecnum* are not relevant.

   This method requires more space in each structure. How much more? Is it harder to write the functions to accommodate this way of storing data? What happens if you try to sort the scheduled contestants according to *date_sched*? Is it easier with or without the union? What happens if *date_sched* is not initialized to some null value for contestants who are not scheduled? What happens if *date_sched* is initialized to "00/00/00"?

26. Rewrite function *whowon* from Example 11-28 so that it returns its results in three different ways:

   a. Have *whowon* return the subscript *i*.
   b. Have *whowon* return a pointer to an element of the array of structures.
   c. Send a pointer to a structure as a third parameter to *whowon*; let *whowon* modify the location pointed to by this parameter.

27. Look back at several of our earlier programs and exercises. For each, determine if a structure or array of structures is an appropriate way to store the information required.

PROGRAMMING PROJECTS

28. Using the array of structures *subscriber* from Exercise 4(d), write a program that does the following:

   a. Reads and prints a list of subscribers.

b. Determines which subscribers live in zip code 10036. Because of the way the address is stored, it requires string manipulation to find each subscriber's zip code.

c. Determines which subscriptions end in May, 1998.

d. Determines which subscribers use Miss as their title.

e. Determines which subscribers satisfy all these criteria.

29. Write a program to compute the course grades for a group of students. Use a structure to hold the data.

The input for each student consists of the name, three quiz grades, and a final exam grade. For example, a typical set of data values looks like this:

```
John Brown   73 57 94 82
```

The program finds the average of the three quiz grades and stores it in the variable **avg**. Then it finds the average of the final exam grade and **avg**, storing this in **numerical**. Based on the numerical average, it determines the student's letter grade (90 to 100 is an A, in the 80s is a B, etc.). Print the results. Use functions to accomplish each task; all the main program should do is call functions.

30. A college housing office is attempting to match prospective roommates. Each student has listed his or her name, student number (a seven-digit code), major, sports interests, and hobbies. These last three are all three-digit numbers. A typical set of data might be this:

```
Jill James   1234567 327 964 135
```

First, read in a series of ten students, storing the data in the structure declared below. Initialize **roommate** to 0 for all students.

```
struct sname {
     char first[10];
     char last[10]
};
struct interestinfo {
     int major;
     int sports;
     int hobbies;
};
struct studinfo {
     struct sname name;
     char    studentnum[8];
     struct interestinfo interests;
     int     roommate;
} student[10];
```

Starting with the first student, find the best possible roommate by matching as many interests as possible. (If there is a tie, resolve it by selecting the first.) That is, go through the remaining students to find someone whose interests match the first student's as closely as possible. Once a match is found, enter the student number for the original student and the matching person in each other's **roommate** field. Then select the next unmatched student (one whose **roommate** field is still 0) and repeat the process. After matching everyone, print the five pairs of roommates. Use functions in your program for modularity.

31. The method described in Exercise 30 won't necessarily produce the best matchups in all cases. A problem arises if the first person takes as a roommate a mediocre match that would be better for someone else. Try to design a better algorithm.

32. Once parents heard of the scheme used in Exercise 30 to match roommates, they immediately protested since it did not take anyone's sex into account. Modify the program to read in a student's sex (male or female), then try to match as roommates only students of the same sex. At the end, print a list of any unmatched students. Why can there be unmatched students now?

33. The students in turn protested the scheme used in Exercise 30. The final compromise had each student specify his or her sex and the sex desired for a roommate. Modify the program to handle this new situation.

34. Write a program that maintains a database for a car dealership. The information stored for each car includes the make and model (like a Chevrolet Blazer), the year, mileage, color, number of doors, the price, and any other information you think is relevant. Store the information in an array of structures.

    First, your program should read in and print out the information about each car in the database. Then it should present a menu to the user (the prospective car buyer), who queries the database. The user may want to see a listing for all red cars, all cars with mileage under 25,000, all cars with four doors, etc. When the user has selected the feature of interest, your program should search the database and print a listing of all cars that satisfy the user's request. Print all the information in the database for each car that matches. If no car meets the requirements, print a message saying so.

    Write a function to read in the data, one to print the data, one to present a menu, one to read in requests, and functions to search the database.

35. Write a program to read in a series of names. The main program calls a function to read in a set of data. The set of data (which can be read from a file or interactively) consists of a parameter value *n* and then *n* strings. Each string represents a person's name—for example, William Chang or Diana Lewis. Each name has exactly one blank separating the first name and the last name. The program should read the data into a structure, storing the entire name in a single field. As each name is read in, it is printed.

    The main program then calls a function to break the name into two pieces—a first name (everything up to the blank) and a last name (everything after the blank). The function stores these two pieces in the appropriate parts of the structure. As each name is broken up, the function prints the original name and the new first and last names.

    The main program calls a function to find the lengths of the original name, the first name, and the last name. These values are printed and stored in the appropriate parts of the structure.

    The main program calls a function to rearrange the first and last names. For example, if the first name is Diana and the last name is Lewis, then the rearrangement would be Lewis, Diana, including the comma. The rearranged name is printed and stored in the structure.

    The main program calls a function which is sent one element of the array of structures. The function neatly prints, with headings or messages, all of the values stored in the structure. Since this function is sent one structure at a time, it is called for each element of the array.

    The main program then calls a function that determines which entire name in the array is the longest, which first name is the longest, and which last name is the longest. These three things are printed, together with identifying messages. Send this function the entire array of structures as a parameter. If you wish, this function may call others to perform the subtasks.

Note: The array of structures should be able to store everything read in and computed (except for the longest names). In particular, for each person, the structure must be able to hold the original name and its size, the first name and its size, the last name and its size, and the rearranged name. The structure definition must be available to both the main program and the functions.

Have at least ten names in the data set. You can assume some reasonable size for the maximum length of the whole name and the first and last names. Some of the names should be short and others long. Be sure that different people have the longest entire name, the longest first name, and the longest last name.

The following projects assume a knowledge of files, covered in Appendix VI.

36. Write a program which reads in data from files *master* and *trans*. Each related group of data in a file is called a record; a record should be stored in a structure. Each record in *master* consists of two values separated by a blank. The first value in the file is the part number of an item, while the second value is the quantity of that item on hand. Here are two examples:

    12345   4   23456   12

    Each record in *trans* contains three items. The first is a letter, *s* or *p*, indicating whether the transaction is a sale or a purchase. The second is a part number, and the third is a quantity. Here are two examples:

    s   12345   2   p   12345   6

    An *s* means that the company has sold some of the item and the quantity should be subtracted from the inventory. A *p* means that the company has purchased more of the item, and the quantity should be added to the inventory.

    Both files are in order by item number, but there may be more than one transaction record for any record in the master file.

    The program reads in a record from file *master*. Then it reads in records from file *trans* as long as the item number is the same. It performs the appropriate update for each transaction record, and writes a new record out to file *newmastr*. It continues to do this until there are no records in file *master* or file *trans*.

    The program checks for one error condition: the part number in *trans* is not found in *master*. If this error occurs, the program writes an appropriate message to file *errors*, including all the information in the record that is in error.

37. The Big Bank maintains two files on its depositors:

    master is the master file, containing records consisting of a five-digit account number and yesterday's balance (a real number).

    trans is the transaction file, containing records consisting of a five-digit account number and either a deposit (positive) or withdrawal (negative); a deposit or withdrawal is a real number. There may be many transaction records per account number. Each related group of data in a file is called a record; a record should be stored in a structure.

    PART 1: Read each file into an array of structures, printing each record as it is read in. Sort each array in order by increasing account number. Send the sorted version of the master file to a new file called **smaster** and the sorted version of the transaction file to a new file called **strans**, printing each record as it is written out.

PART 2: Read in the two sorted files, **smaster** and **strans** and create two new files, **newbal** and **negbal**. The file **newbal** contains a list of account numbers and new balances at the end of the day, and **negbal** contains a list of all customers whose balance was negative at any time during the day; list both account number and balance. Close **smaster**, **strans**, **newbal**, and **negbal**.

PART 3: Open **newbal** and **negbal**. Read records in from **newbal** and **negbal** and print the records from each file on separate pages with headings. Close **newbal** and **negbal**.

Your program must detect the following error conditions and send a message about each to a file **errors**:

a.   duplicate records in **smaster**
b.   records in **strans** which do not appear in **smaster**
c.   any record with improper format

Your program must also create a file **report**, which consists of the following:

a.   a log listing all rejected transactions, with reasons for rejection
b.   the number of records in the original master file
c.   the number of records in the original transaction file
d.   the number of records in the updated master file
e.   the number of transactions applied
f.   the number of transactions rejected

Print files **errors** and **report**.

38.   The Happily Hardware Company has hired you to program its Accounts Receivable department. (Accounts Receivable are accounts that owe money to the company for purchases from the company.)

INPUT: The program reads from these two files:

master is the master file, in ascending order by customer number, containing a five-digit customer number, a 20-character customer name, and a balance due (a real number). If the balance due is negative, the customer has a credit balance.

trans is the transaction file, containing records of each transaction by each customer. This file is in ascending order by customer number. There may be more than one transaction record per master record. Each related group of data in a file is called a record; a record should be stored in a structure.

Each record starts with a character, O for order or P for payment. Each also contains a five-digit customer number, a five-digit transaction number, plus up to three more values:

◆   If the code is O, the record contains the name of the item ordered (20 characters), the quantity ordered (an integer), plus the cost of the item (a real number).

◆   If the code is P, the record contains the amount of the payment (a real number).

PROCESSING: Read in records one at a time from the two files and use the transaction records to update the master file. Process all transaction records for each master record before going on the next master record. If the transaction record contains an O in column 1, calculate the order amount and add it to the balance due. If the record contains a *P* in column 1, subtract the payment amount from the balance due.

Keep a running total of the accounts receivable balance of Happily Hardware Company (that is, the sum of the balances due for each customer).

Your program must detect the following error conditions:

a.   duplicate records in the master file
b.   records in the transaction file with a customer number which does not appear in the master file
c.   any record with improper format; look for characters in numeric fields, missing field values, extra field values, improper code, etc.

OUTPUT: After you have processed a master record and all its transaction records, prepare and print an invoice for the customer, in the following format:

```
                         Customer name
                         Customer number


                              Previous balance        $XXXXXXXX.XX

 transaction number       item ordered                order amount
 transaction number       item ordered                order amount
 transaction number       payment                     payment amount


                              Balance due             $XXXXXXXX.XX
```

The transactions should appear in the order in which they are processed. In the example above, the words in italics indicate the information that should be listed in each location. The words that are not in italics should be printed as is. Indicate a negative previous balance or a negative balance due by printing CR to the right of the amount. Print all dollar amounts with a decimal point. Put a dollar sign on only the first and last amounts in the column, as shown above.

In addition to printing the invoices, your program must produce three reports on disk:

a.   File *error* is a listing of all rejected master records and rejected transaction records. For each record that is rejected, include all the information in the record, plus a message indicating why the record was rejected.
b.   File *log* keeps track of all records processed. Include the following in this file:

    (1) the total number of records in the master file
    (2) the number of rejected records in the master file
    (3) the number of correct records in the master file
    (4) the total number of records in the transaction file
    (5) the number of rejected transaction records
    (6) the number of correct transaction records

c.   File *receive* lists the accounts receivable. In this file, include the customer name, the customer number, and the balance due for each customer. Use one line per customer. At the bottom of the list, include the total accounts receivable balance.

At the end, print all files. Print a heading at the beginning of the output for each printed file.

RECURSION, GLOBAL VARIABLES, DYNAMIC STORAGE ALLOCATION, AND SIDE EFFECTS—A POTPOURRI

SYNTAX CONCEPTS: recursive functions, *malloc* and *free*

PROGRAMMING CONCEPTS: recursion, global or external variables, dynamic storage allocation, side effects

CONTROL STRUCTURES: recursion, global variables, dynamic storage allocation, side effects

PROBLEM-SOLVING TECHNIQUES: recursion

HOW TO READ CHAPTER 12

OUTLINE:

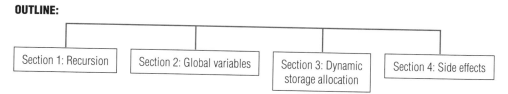

| Section 1: Recursion | Section 2: Global variables | Section 3: Dynamic storage allocation | Section 4: Side effects |

INTRODUCTION

As the name suggests, Chapter 12 is a collection of unrelated sections, which can be covered in any order. Each section introduces a fairly advanced topic. More details can be found in a C language reference manual or a text on data structures in C.

SECTION 1   RECURSION

As you already know, a main program can call a function, and one function can call another. There is an interesting extension of this idea: A function is allowed to call itself. For example, inside the body of function *alpha* there can be an explicit call to function *alpha* itself. A function that calls itself is said to be **recursive**. Also function *alpha* can call function *beta*, which can in turn call function *alpha* again, forming a **recursive chain** (see Exercise 7 for an example).

A recursive definition means that an item is being defined "in terms of itself." Here is an example: We can define a string of digits as either a single digit or a single digit followed by a string of digits (see Figure 12-1). Let's look at a few simple recursive functions.

A FIRST EXAMPLE: THE FACTORIAL FUNCTION

An often-used example is the **factorial function**, usually written as $n!$ in mathematics. The factorial of n (or n factorial) is the product of the integers from 1 to n. More precisely, $n! = 1 \times 2 \times 3 \times ... \times n$. For example, $1! = 1$; $4! = 1 \times 2 \times 3 \times 4 = 24$; $6! = 1 \times 2 \times 3 \times 4 \times 5 \times 6 = 720$.

However, there is another way to look at this definition, as shown in Example 12-1A.

EXAMPLE 12-1A   The product of the numbers from 1 to n, which is $n!$, is equal to n times the product of the numbers from 1 to $n-1$, which is $(n-1)!$. This is true because n is the only term that is present in $n!$ but not in $(n-1)!$.

```
n! = n * (n-1)!        for each        n > 1
```

For example, $6! = 6 \times 5!$. Similarly, $4! = 4 \times 3!$, and $10! = 10 \times 9!$.

Let's look at the recursive definition from Example 12-1A more carefully. The item being defined ($n!$) is described in terms of a similar, but slightly smaller or simpler, one [$(n-1)!$]. In order to find $n!$, we apply the factorial function to $(n-1)$ and then to other smaller values [like $(n-1)-1$]. This repeated use of factorial is what makes the definition recursive. However, there must also be an **escape clause**, also called an **anchor** or **base**, for the recursion. The escape clause gives a fixed value for some particular factorial calculation; this provides a way to stop the recursion. We did not explicitly specify the escape clause for factorial, but it is $1! = 1$. Every recursive definition must contain two elements: an escape clause and a way to express one instance in terms of a simpler one.

EXAMPLE 12-1B   Here is the definition of factorial again, rewritten to emphasize these two elements:

```
1! = 1                                          anchor or escape clause
n! = n * (n-1)!        for each n > 1           recursive reference to a simpler case
```

FIGURE 12-1   Recursive definition of a string of digits

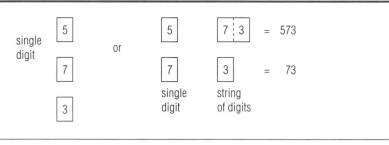

Let's use the definition to write a recursive function ***factorial***, which is defined for any positive integer ***n***. The body of a function to evaluate the factorial of ***n*** looks like this:

```
if (n == 1)
    return 1;                               /* escape clause */
else
    return factorial(n-1) * n;              /* recursive call */
```

Note that the function returns the value 1 in case ***n*** is 1; if ***n*** is greater than 1, the function returns the factorial of ***n–1*** multiplied by ***n***. The two key pieces of the recursion are the escape clause [***if (n == 1)*** ...] and the recursive call, which evaluates the factorial of ***n*** in terms of the factorial of ***n–1***.

The entire ***factorial*** function is shown in Example 12-2A. Note that ***long*** (rather than ***int***) is used for the type of answer returned by the function. To see why this is necessary, compute by hand a factorial like 9! or 10! and see how large the answer is.

EXAMPLE 12-2A   Here is the entire ***factorial*** function:

```
/* recursively compute n! (the product of the numbers from 1 to n) */
long factorial(int n)
{
    if (n == 1)
        return 1;                           /* escape clause */
    else
        return factorial(n-1) * n;          /* recursive call */
}
```

CAUTION   As currently written, the ***factorial*** function works only if ***n*** is greater than or equal to 1. See Exercise 8 for a way to modify the function so that it works for all possible ***n*** values.

TRACING A CALL TO THE FUNCTION *factorial*

Assume that a function ***prob12*** (a main program or some other function) wants to compute the factorial of 4. Inside ***prob12***, we can call ***factorial*** as follows:

```
result = factorial(4);     /* call to the factorial function from outside */
```

Let's see exactly what happens when we reach this statement inside function ***prob12***.

PROGRAM TRACE

◆   Execution of ***prob12*** stops, and control is transferred to ***factorial*** to compute ***factorial(4)***.

◆   In order to do this, we must first find ***factorial(3)*** because the ***else*** statement inside the function says that ***factorial(4)*** is ***factorial(3)*** multiplied by 4. The calculation of ***factorial(4)*** is temporarily suspended until there is a value for ***factorial(3)***.

◆   For the same reason, computing ***factorial(3)*** requires calculating ***factorial(2)***.

◆   Computing ***factorial(2)*** requires ***factorial(1)***.

◆   Computing ***factorial(1)*** is easy. By the escape clause, ***factorial(1)*** is 1.

Here is what we have so far, showing the chain of recursive calls and concluding with the calculation of 1 as *factorial(1)*. The multiplications on the right have not yet been performed. For example, the first multiplication (by 4) is not performed until *factorial(3)* has been evaluated. In fact, since the multiplications are done in reverse order, the first one is the multiplication by 2 on the next to last line.

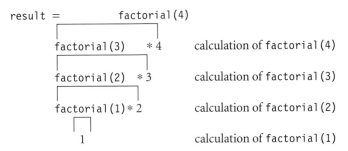

- The value of *factorial(1)*, which is 1, is returned to the calculation of *factorial(2)*, which is waiting for it.
- Now the machine can compute *factorial(2)* as *factorial(1)* * 2 = 2.
- This value of *factorial(2)* is returned to the calculation of *factorial(3)*, which is computed as 2 * 3 = 6.
- This value is returned to the calculation of *factorial(4)*, which is evaluated as 6 * 4 = 24.
- This answer is finally returned to *prob12* and stored in the variable *result*.

Here is a diagram showing the values returned (the last value, 24, is returned to *prob12*):

```
factorial(1) = 1                                    returned to factorial(2)
factorial(2) = factorial(1) * 2 = 1 * 2 = 2         returned to factorial(3)
factorial(3) = factorial(2) * 3 = 2 * 3 = 6         returned to factorial(4)
factorial(4) = factorial(3) * 4 = 6 * 4 = 24        returned to prob12
result = factorial(4) = 6 * 4 = 24                  returned to calling program
```

Notice how much work is involved in tracing the calculation of even a relatively simple value like *factorial(4)*.

STYLE WORKSHOP Recursive definitions are often simple to write but complicated to trace. Usually, a program which uses an iterative process is faster and more efficient than one using a recursive process. Despite this, recursion is an extremely useful programming tool, especially when working with advanced data structures such as binary trees, and you should understand how it works. In addition, there are some cases where a recursive program is just as fast as an iterative one.

USING A LOCAL VARIABLE IN A RECURSIVE FUNCTION

Recursive functions can use local variables to make tracing easier. This is especially helpful to someone who is just learning about recursion. Example 12-2B shows how to use a local variable to store intermediate results.

EXAMPLE 12-2B   This version of the *factorial* function uses a local variable *fact* instead of immediately returning a value:

```
/* ... */
long factorial(int n)
{
```

```
        long fact;

        if (n == 1)
            fact = 1;                              /* escape clause */
        else
            fact = factorial(n-1) * n;             /* recursive call */
        return fact;
    }
```

The trace of this version is quite similar to the original, with one difference. In each case, the value computed for a factorial is stored in *fact* before it is returned to the calling program. For example, if we are computing *factorial(4)*, the value of the recursive call to *factorial(3)* is multiplied by 4 and stored in *fact*, then returned (and similarly on the nested recursive calls).

STYLE WORKSHOP Note that this version has a single *return* statement, which some people prefer.

REVERSING A STRING OF CHARACTERS

Nonnumerical applications provide some of the best and most efficient examples of recursion. We give an example of a function, called *reverse*, which reverses a string of characters. For example, if the original is "help", the reversed string is "pleh". If the original is "not now", the reversed string is "won ton". (See Chapter 9, Exercise 39, for a nonrecursive solution to this problem.)

First, we need a recursive algorithm for reversing a string.

ALGORITHM FOR REVERSING THE CHARACTERS IN A STRING

If *str* is a string of characters, its reverse is defined as follows:

- ◆ *If* str *is the null character or a single character followed by the null character, the reverse is* str *itself.*
- ◆ *If* str *is a single character* ch *followed by one or more characters and then the null character, the reverse is the reverse of the rest of the string, followed by the character* ch, *followed by the null character.*

Note that the position of the null character is unchanged, since it must serve as the string terminator.

The escape clause says that the reverse of any one character is the character itself; the reverse of a string larger than one character is the result of appending the first character to the reverse of the rest of the original string. We trace the algorithm in detail after we translate it into C.

USING RECURSION IN A VOID FUNCTION

The factorial example used a recursive function that returned a value, but void functions can also be recursive. To reverse a string, we use a recursive function with two formal parameters;

one parameter, called **str**, holds the original string to be reversed; a second parameter, called **newstr**, holds the value computed as the reverse of **str**. Here is the function header:

```
void reverse(char *str, char *newstr)
```

THE FUNCTION *reverse*

Once we have decided on the format of the function, the next step is to translate the algorithm into C. Example 12-3 shows the function **reverse**.

EXAMPLE 12-3

```
/* recursively reverse characters in str, storing result in newstr */
void reverse(char *str, char *newstr)
{
    int k;

    k = strlen(str);
    if (k <= 1)
        strcpy(newstr,str);                    /* escape clause */
    else  {
        reverse(str+1,newstr);                 /* recursive call */
        newstr[k-1] = str[0];
        newstr[k] = '\0';
    }
    return;
}
```

PROGRAM TRACE Let's trace the function by reversing "cat\0". (For clarity, we explicitly show the null character.)

◆ For the initial call to the function, the formal parameter **str** is "cat\0". The function starts by testing the length of **str**. Since the length is more than 1, it executes the **else** statement.

◆ The first statement in the **else** is a recursive call to the function (the first call is temporarily suspended). For this second call to **reverse**, the formal parameter **str** has the value "at\0". Since "at\0" has length 2, the **if** condition is again false.

◆ In the **else** statement, **reverse** is called recursively. For the third call, **str** consists of two characters: '*t*' followed by '\0'; this string has length 1. Therefore, at the escape clause, the function copies **str**, which is "t\0", into **newstr**. The function returns to the second call (which is in the middle of computing the reverse of "at\0").

Here is the chain of calls so far, descending to **reverse("t\0",newstr)**:

reverse("cat\0",newstr)	*calls*	reverse("at\0",newstr)
reverse("at\0",newstr)	*calls*	reverse("t\0",newstr)
reverse("t\0",newstr)	*stores*	"t\0" *in* newstr

◆ Control is now back in the second call to **reverse**, right after the recursive call; **newstr** has the value "t\0", and **str** is "at\0". The first character of **str** (the '*a*') is stored in **newstr** on top of the null character to produce "ta". Then a new null character is added to give **newstr** the value "ta\0". The second call is complete and returns to the first call.

◆ Back in the first call, *newstr* has the value "ta\0" and *str* is "cat\0". The first character of *str* (the 'c') replaces the null character in *newstr*; then a new null character is added, producing "tac\0". This value for *newstr* is returned to the program that originally called *reverse*.

Note the following:

1. the call *reverse("t\0",newstr)* stores "t\0" in *newstr*;
2. the call *reverse("at\0",newstr)* stores "ta\0" in *newstr*;
3. the call *reverse("cat\0",newstr)* stores "tac\0" in *newstr*.

A MAIN PROGRAM THAT CALLS *reverse*

The following driver program tests *reverse*. It reads in strings and reverses them, stopping after processing the string "done". For simplicity, we assume the maximum string size is specified by the constant *MAXSIZE*.

```
/* main program to test reverse */
#include <stdio.h>
#include <string.h>
#define MAXSIZE 30
void reverse(char *, char *);
main()
{
        char stringread[MAXSIZE],reversal[MAXSIZE];
        int  k;

        do  {
            printf("type in a string; enter 'done' to stop\n");
            gets(stringread);
            reverse(stringread,reversal);
            printf("%s is the reverse of %s\n\n",reversal,stringread);
            k = strcmp(stringread,"done");
        }  while (k != 0);
}
```

As an example, if we type "help" in response to the prompt, the output looks like this:

```
pleh is the reverse of help
```

If we type in "now is the time", the output is this line:

```
emit eht si won is the reverse of now is the time
```

A MORE COMPLICATED EXAMPLE: THE FIBONACCI NUMBERS

Let's give one last example of a recursive function. In Chapter 4, Exercise 27, and Chapter 7, Exercise 28, we discussed the **Fibonacci numbers**. Briefly, we can define the Fibonacci numbers in the following way: The first two are both 1; each succeeding number is the sum of the two previous numbers in the sequence. The first few Fibonacci numbers are 1, 1, 2, 3, 5, 8, ... In Chapter 7, Exercise 28, you were asked to write a program using an array to compute the first 20 Fibonacci numbers. One solution is given in Example 12-4.

EXAMPLE 12-4

```
/* compute the first 20 Fibonacci numbers */
#include <stdio.h>
main()
{
        int fibonacci[20];
        int term;

        fibonacci[0] = 1;
        fibonacci[1] = 1;
        for (term = 2; term < 20; term++)
                fibonacci[term] = fibonacci[term-1] + fibonacci[term-2];
        ...
}
```

A recursive function *fib* can compute the Fibonacci numbers. Assume that the function is sent one parameter *n* and computes the *n*th Fibonacci number. As usual in a recursion, we need an escape clause. This example has two special cases: $n = 0$ and $n = 1$. The way to go from one case to a simpler one is this: Each Fibonacci number is the sum of the previous two. For example, the fifth number (5) is the sum of the fourth (3) and the third (2). In general, the *n*th Fibonacci number is the sum of the (*n–1*)th and the (*n–2*)th. A recursive function to compute the *n*th Fibonacci number is shown in Example 12-5. It is also possible to write the function with one or more local variables.

EXAMPLE 12-5   Here is the recursive *fib* function:

```
/*  recursively compute term n of the    */
/*  Fibonacci series--1, 1, 2, 3, 5, 8, ... */
int fib(int n)
{
        if (n == 0 || n == 1)
                return 1;
        return fib(n-1) + fib(n-2);
}
```

Tracing this function to evaluate a call to *fib* from some other program may involve a long series of recursive function calls. For example, assume that a calling program wants to find *fib(6)*. The first time through the function *fib* (when *n* is 6) computes the sum of *fib(5)* and *fib(4)*. To evaluate *fib(5)*, we must compute *fib(4)* + *fib(3)*; *fib(4)* is *fib(3)* + *fib(2)*; *fib(3)* is *fib(2)* + *fib(1)*; *fib(2)* is *fib(1)* + *fib(0)*; *fib(0)* and *fib(1)* are both 1 by the escape clause.

Here is a diagram showing the recursive calls used to evaluate *fib(5)*. The number in brackets underneath each function call shows the value computed for that call, either through the escape clause [to evaluate *fib(1)* or *fib(0)*] or through recursive calls.

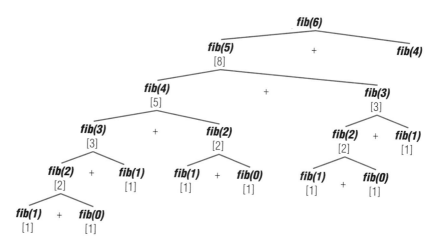

This trace calculates only *fib(5)*, which is the first step in evaluating *fib(6)*; it is also necessary to compute *fib(4)*. Once the calculation of *fib(5)* is complete, the machine starts to compute *fib(4)*. That value is added to the value of *fib(5)* to obtain the original request—the value of *fib(6)*. The final answer returned to the calling program is 13, which is the seventh Fibonacci number. This particular recursive function is incredibly inefficient, but it does illustrate the basic idea.

A programmer who desires to learn more about recursion and its role in computer science is urged to consult a text on data structures.

SELF-CHECK 12-1

1. Why is an escape clause needed in a recursive definition?
2. What makes a function recursive?
3. What is the escape clause for each of the functions in this section?

SECTION 2 GLOBAL (EXTERNAL) VARIABLES

In Chapter 5, we noted that a function can refer to its formal parameters and local variables but not to variables declared in the main program (or in another function). This is true, but it is not the whole truth. In addition to using formal parameters and local variables, a function can also access variables that are declared "globally."

DEFINITION OF A GLOBAL VARIABLE

A **global** or **external variable** is one declared in a file prior to defining the functions contained in that file. Such a variable can potentially be accessed in every function which follows. (Similarly, a function prototype which appears at the top of a file can be accessed by every function in that file.)

✋ **CAUTION** The naive use of global variables can be very dangerous. In general, the use of these variables should be severely restricted, following the guidelines discussed here. A program that does not use global variables is easier to read, debug, and maintain.

AN EXAMPLE THAT USES GLOBAL VARIABLES

A function cannot refer to a variable declared in another function, including the main program. However, a main program or a function can refer to a variable declared outside all of the functions, as illustrated in Example 12-6.

EXAMPLE 12-6   Consider a program where the declarations for three variables, x, y, and z, are outside the main program. The main program and the function *sub* each declare one local variable.

```
#include <stdio.h>
void sub(void);
int x = 1, y = 1, z = 1;
main()
{
    int x = 10;

    printf("in main: %d %d %d\n",x,y,z);
    sub();
    printf("back in main: %d %d %d\n",x,y,z);
}

void sub(void)
{
    double y;

    x = 5;                                          /* global */
    y = 5;                                          /* local */
    z = 5;                                          /* global */
    printf("in sub: %d %f %d\n",x,y,z);
    return;
}
```

In this example, the three variables, x, y, and z, are declared outside any function, making them external. They can be accessed in any function that wants to use them (either intentionally or unintentionally). The main program declares a variable x (of type *int*), and it also refers to two external variables, y and z. In *sub*, the local variable y has data type *double*; the external variables x and z are also referenced. Note that the y from *sub* and the external y are not related. In *sub*, a reference to y means the local variable that has data type *double*. However, when the main program refers to y, it means the external variable.

A function (including the main program) can never access a local variable from another function. Therefore, *sub* is not allowed to use the declaration for x that comes from the main program, and the main program cannot use the declaration for y that comes from *sub*.

PROGRAM TRACE   Now let's see how this program works.

◆   The main program starts by printing the initial values. It prints 10 for the value of the local *x* in the main program; then it prints the initial value 1 for each of the global variables, *y* and *z*:

> in main: 10 1 1

◆   Next the main program calls *sub*, which sets the local *y* and the globals *x* and *z* to 5 and prints them:

> in sub: 5 5.000000 5

◆   After *sub* returns control to the main program, the local *x* is still 10. The global *y* is unchanged at 1 because *sub* modified the local *y*, not the global one. However, the global *z* is changed to 5. The main program prints the following:

> back in main: 10 1 5

Note that the main program and the function *sub* can each change a global variable.

THE NAME SCOPING RULES FOR GLOBAL REFERENCES

C has the following **name scoping rules** for resolving references in a function: If an identifier is declared in a function (including the main program), then it is a local variable, and it is completely distinct from any other variable in the program, even one with the same name. If an identifier is a formal parameter in a function, it is also distinct from any other variable, except it does receive a value from the matching actual argument. However, an identifier used in a function where it is not declared must have an **external declaration** (i.e., one outside any function). A variable used this way is called a global or external variable.

PREVIOUS USE OF GLOBAL REFERENCES

We have taken advantage of these rules for global references before. For example, we have included function prototypes and defined constants and structures. All of these were specified above the main program so that they could be accessed throughout the file. However, in every other case, we have been careful to avoid the use of global references. Something that does not change (e.g., a prototype, constant, or *typedef*) is almost always safe to use as a global reference. Something that can change (notably a variable) is often dangerous to make global, as we will see later.

INTENTIONAL USE OF GLOBAL VARIABLES

In a few cases, using global variables may simplify a program. For example, in Program 11, a main program and a series of functions accessed an array of structures. The definition for the structure preceded the main program, but the main program declared the actual array, and each function received it as a parameter.

As an alternative, we could declare the array of structures externally. In that case, the main program and every function could simply access it without passing it as a parameter (see Example 12-8).

PROBLEMS WITH GLOBAL REFERENCES

Warning one: A global variable must have the same name in the external declaration and every function that uses it. This can severely limit the utility of a function because it can no longer be called several times with different names for the actual arguments each time. Therefore, functions designed to accomplish common tasks (e.g., finding an average, finding the largest element in an array, or sorting) should not use global variables. The functions from Program 11, however, can use global variables because they are special-purpose functions, not intended for use in other programs.

Warning two: An inadvertent use of global references can be very dangerous, as shown in Example 12-7.

EXAMPLE 12-7   Both the main program and the function ***sub*** contain a ***for*** loop whose condition is *i <= n*. The programmer has declared the variables *i* and *n* once, outside the main program. Therefore, the compiler uses the external *i* and *n* in both the main program and ***sub***. This careless use of global variables leads to premature termination of the program. (For convenience, *n* is set to 10, but the exact value is not important.)

```
#include <stdio.h>
void sub(void);
int i,n;
main()
{
    n = 10;
    for (i = 1; i <= n; i++)
        sub();
}

void sub(void)
{
    for (i = 1; i <= n; i++)  {
        ...
    }
    return;
}
```

The unsuspecting programmer predicts that the ***for*** loop in the main program will be executed for *i* = 1, 2, ..., *n*—a total of *n* times. But in fact it is executed just once, as shown in this trace.

PROGRAM TRACE

◆   The main program initializes *i* to 1, enters the body of the loop, and calls the function. All references to *i* and *n*, both in the main program and in ***sub***, are to global variables.

◆ Inside **sub**, the **for** loop executes with $i = 1, 2, ..., n$, finally terminating when i is $n+1$. Then **sub** returns to the main program.

◆ Since i in the main program is the same as i in **sub**, i in the main program's **for** loop is now $n+1$. Therefore, the condition $i <= n$ is already false, even before i is incremented to $n+2$.

◆ After i is incremented, it is compared to n. The condition is false, and the **for** loop in the main program terminates after a single pass.

The foolish use of i and n as global variables causes this error. Almost surely the programmer did not intend for i and n to be shared by the main program and the function.

STYLE WORKSHOP This type of error can be avoided by carefully checking which variables in a function are formal parameters, which are local variables, and which are global. Each variable in a function must fit into one of these three categories. As a general rule, only large data structures (e.g., arrays or structures) should be global variables. If this rule is followed, little variables like i or n that control loops will never be destroyed by accident.

STORAGE CLASSES; AUTOMATIC VARIABLES

In C, each variable has a data type (e.g., **int** or **double**) and a **storage class**, which describes how space for the variable is allocated and where it can be referenced. The most common storage class is **automatic**; other storage classes include **external**, **static**, and **register**. A variable can be given an explicit storage class, or the class can be determined from the context. By default, a local variable in a function (including **main**) has storage class automatic. This means that storage is allocated for the variable when the function is called and freed when it returns; the variable can be referenced as long as the function is active.

A variable declared outside of any function has storage class external. If the external variable is declared at the top of a source file, it can be accessed by any function in the same file.[1] This function (e.g., **main** or **sub** in Example 12-7) can explicitly list each external variable with the keyword **extern**, or the compiler can determine which variables are external from the context. Explicitly listing external variables makes it easier to determine the status of each variable used in a function, as seen in Example 12-8.

EXAMPLE 12-8   In this example, an array of structures is declared before the main program. The main program and **sub** explicitly declare the array to be external.

```
#include <stdio.h>
void sub(int);
#define SIZE 100

struct test {
    char name[20];
    int  grade;
} val[SIZE];
```

(continued)

---

[1]If the program uses separate compilation, a function in another file can make an explicit reference to an external variable.

(continued)

```
main()
{
    extern struct test val[];
    int    i;

    for (i = 0; i < SIZE; i++)
        sub(i);
    process entire val array
}

void sub(int i)
{
    extern struct test val[];

    process val[i]
    return;
}
```

STORAGE CLASSES *static* AND *register*

A local variable with storage class automatic is assigned new space in memory each time the function is called. However, a local variable declared with the keyword *static* retains its storage location and value from one call to the next. Using a static variable gives a function the ability to remember information from one call to the next. As shown in the next example, a function can use a static variable to keep track of how many times it is called.

EXAMPLE 12-9   Here is a function *keeptrack* which calls *exit* with an error signal after it has been called five times:

```
void keeptrack(...)
{
    static int count = 0;

    count++;
    if (count == 5)
        exit(1);
    normal function processing
    return;
}
```

The initialization *count = 0* takes place only on the first call. Each time the function is called, *count* adds 1 to its previous value. For the first four calls, the *if* condition is false, and the function executes the code indicated by *normal function processing*. However, on the fifth call, *count* is incremented to 5, the *if* condition is true, and the function calls *exit* with 1 as an error signal.

An external variable can also be given the keyword *static*. Then it can be referenced only by functions which occur in its own source file after the variable declaration. This provides a way for variables to be shared between certain functions but hidden from others.

Storage class *register* suggests to the compiler variables which, for reasons of efficiency, should be stored in high-speed registers. Typically, this is done for the index of a *for* loop or a subscript in an array. However, the compiler may ignore the suggestion, storing such variables as automatic.

SELF-CHECK 12-2

1. What is a global variable?
2. When can we use a global variable? When shouldn't we use one?
3. What is the default storage class for local variables?

SECTION 3 ▪ DYNAMIC STORAGE ALLOCATION

In Section 2, we learned that local variables with storage class automatic have storage allocated from the beginning of a function until it terminates. In contrast, it is often useful to use dynamic storage allocation to allocate memory as it is needed.

Consider a program which tries to use an array of structures with 150 elements:

```
struct temp {
    char name[50];
    int  num[300];
} big[150];
```

This reserves 150 * 300 or 45,000 storage locations for integers, plus 150 * 50 storage locations for characters. On a PC, it occupies 97,500 bytes or about 97.5K of memory; on a Sun, it uses 187,500 bytes or 187.5K. This array is too large to use in any program running under DOS. Although a program running on a Sun under Unix can accommodate a much larger array, it still has limits: **big[6500]** is acceptable, but **big[7000]** is too large.

Fortunately, most programs don't need such a large array of structures. A programmer may declare a very large array in case the program might use the storage, but the space is often wasted.

DYNAMIC STORAGE ALLOCATION

There is a solution to the size problem: do not set up the array of structures at all. C has a means of getting a new structure whenever we need one. If we need one structure, we can get one; if we need 125, we can get 125. Allocating and freeing storage during execution of the program is called **dynamic storage allocation**.

THE FUNCTION *malloc*

The library function **malloc**, whose prototype is in **stdlib.h** (and also in **malloc.h**), allows allocation of storage as needed. The function accepts one integer parameter, allocates a block of memory of that number of bytes, and returns a pointer to the newly allocated block. The general form of a call to **malloc** is on the following page.

General Form of a Call to *malloc*

```
ptr = (type) malloc(size);
```

The parameter ***size*** is an unsigned integer representing the number of bytes that must be allocated. The parameter can be a constant or the result of using the operator ***sizeof*** (see Chapter 9, Section 2). The return value from ***malloc*** is a pointer of type ***void*** *, called a **generic pointer**. This return value must be cast to the appropriate data type [the casting is indicated by ***(type)***] before assigning it to the pointer ***ptr***.

To use ***malloc***, declare a pointer to a variable of the desired data type (a pointer to a structure is most commonly used) but do not allocate any storage for the variable. Example 12-10 shows how to use ***malloc*** to allocate space for a structure of type ***struct emp***.

EXAMPLE 12-10 Here is the declaration for structure ***struct emp*** and ***worker1***, a pointer to it. We do not need to declare any variables of type ***struct emp***, since we will use ***malloc***.

```
struct emp {
     char    name[20];
     int     empnum;
     double salary;
};
struct emp *worker1;
```

To get a structure of type ***struct emp***, we call the function ***malloc***:

```
worker1 = (struct emp *) malloc(sizeof(struct emp));
```

The operator ***sizeof*** returns the size of ***struct emp*** in bytes; this size is sent as a parameter to ***malloc***. The pointer returned by ***malloc*** is cast to ***struct emp*** * before it is assigned to ***worker1***.

After the call to ***malloc***, the pointer ***worker1*** can refer to the members of the new structure in the usual manner, as shown in Example 12-11.

EXAMPLE 12-11 Here are examples showing how to refer to members of the structure pointed to by ***worker1***:

```
strcpy(worker1 -> name,"John Sullivan");
worker1 -> empnum = 123;
worker1 -> salary = 240.78;
printf("%s\n",worker1 -> name);
worker1 -> salary += 0.25 * worker1 -> salary;
```

FURTHER CALLS TO *malloc*

Each call to ***malloc*** allocates storage for one object. In Example 12-10, we reserved storage for a structure like ***struct emp***, and, in Example 12-11, we initialized some of the structure's members with information about the employee. Now, however, suppose that we hire a second employee. If we call ***malloc*** again, assigning the pointer to ***worker1***, we get a new structure of type ***struct emp***, pointed to by ***worker1***.

Unfortunately, each call to ***malloc*** assigns ***worker1*** a new address, replacing the old one. Assigning a new value to a pointer variable means that it loses the old one; this is not what we want (unless we intend to fire the first employee). Figure 12-2 shows what happens as a result of two consecutive calls to the function ***malloc***.

After the second call, no pointer points to the structure for John Sullivan, the first employee. Without a pointer, there is no way to access, change, or even get rid of this structure. It is simply lost; however, it still occupies all the space allocated for it, wasting that storage. In computer terms, it is "garbage." This space can be recovered only by the operating system.

USING TWO POINTERS

One way to solve the problem is to declare a second pointer of type ***struct emp*** *. When we want another structure of type ***struct emp***, we can call ***malloc*** again, this time assigning the returned address to the second pointer:

```
struct emp *worker1, *worker2;

...
worker2 = (struct emp *) malloc(sizeof(struct emp));
```

After this call, there will be two structures, one pointed to by ***worker1*** and one by ***worker2*** (see Figure 12-3). We can use both structures and their pointers.

CAUTION Be careful when assigning one pointer to another. The assignment ***worker2 = worker1*** does not copy John Sullivan's information to the structure pointed to by ***worker2***. Instead, both pointers point to the structure containing John Sullivan's information, and there is no way to refer to the storage to which ***worker2*** originally pointed (see Figure 12-4). Structure assignment is legal but not with pointers (see Chapter 11, Section 2).

FIGURE 12-2   Two calls to the function ***malloc*** using the same pointer. *A*, after the first call; *B*, after the second call

FIGURE 12-3   Two calls to ***malloc*** using two pointers

FIGURE 12-4   Result of assigning one pointer to another

AN ARRAY OF POINTERS

Although having two pointers is almost as limiting as having one, it leads logically to the next possibility, which is to set up an array of pointers. If we have an array of 100 pointers, each time we need a new employee structure, we can use *malloc* to give a value to the next pointer in the array. Example 12-12 shows how to allocate storage for a new employee.

EXAMPLE 12-12

Here we declare an array of pointers and then allocate storage for element 4 (the fifth worker):

```
struct emp *worker[100];

...
worker[4] = (struct emp *) malloc(sizeof(struct emp));
```

We can refer to this employee's name as *worker[4] –> name*. Other members of the structure are referenced in a similar way.

IN DEPTH

It may seem that an array of pointers uses as much storage as an array of structures, but it doesn't. An array of 100 pointers stores 100 items for a total of 200 or 400 bytes, depending on the system. An array of 100 structures of type *struct emp* stores 300 items (100 names, 100 employee numbers, and 100 salaries). Each structure actually allocated occupies 26 bytes on a PC or 32 bytes on a Sun. With an array of 100 structures, all elements are allocated at the beginning, whether used or not, for a total of 2600 or 3200 bytes. However, with an array of pointers to structures, all the pointers are allocated, but only those structures which are filled use space. If only 10 structures are needed, the total allocation is $200 + (10 \times 26) = 460$ bytes on the PC or $400 + (10 \times 32) = 720$ bytes on the Sun. The larger the structures, the more space is saved by using an array of pointers.

LINKED LISTS

Actually, there is a way to use pointers which allows even more flexibility and saves more storage. A structure definition can include a pointer to another structure of the same type. Example 12-13 shows how to incorporate a pointer into a structure definition.

EXAMPLE 12-13

Here is a structure definition which includes *next*, a pointer to another structure of the same type:

```
struct emp {
    char    name[20];
    int     empnum;
    double  salary;
    struct  emp *next;
};
```

Having a pointer in each structure allows us to set up a chain of structures, each one pointing to the next. This chain is called a **linked list**; each structure in a linked list is called a **node**.

FIGURE 12-5 First node after initialization

NULL AND THE LIST POINTER

A separate pointer points to the beginning of a linked list. This pointer initially points to nothing, which we indicate by giving it the constant value *NULL*:

```
struct emp *list = NULL;
```

If this pointer is not assigned an explicit value, it retains the value *NULL*. This signals that there are no items in the list, and we say that the list is empty.

CREATING A LINKED LIST

Because we put a pointer into the structure definition, we do not have to set up an array of pointers. We assign to *list* the pointer returned by *malloc*:

```
list = (struct emp *) malloc(sizeof(struct emp));
```

Now *list* is no longer *NULL*; it points to the first (and only) node in the list. However, since the pointer in the newly allocated node points to nothing, it must be given the value *NULL*. Example 12-14 shows how to give values to the members of this node.

EXAMPLE 12-14   The following lines give values to the first node in a linked list of workers pointed to by *list*. Figure 12-5 shows the node after initialization.

```
strcpy(list -> name,"John Sullivan");
list -> empnum = 123;
list -> salary = 240.78;
list -> next = NULL;
```

Typically, allocating a node and initializing the pointer to *NULL* is done in a programmer-defined function called something like *getnode* to emphasize its action. Assigning values to the rest of the fields can be done in this function or separately. Example 12-15 shows a possible *getnode* function for *struct emp* and a call to that function.

EXAMPLE 12-15   Here is the function *getnode*:

```
/* allocate a node with struc_size bytes    */
/* and return a pointer of type struct emp * */
struct emp * getnode(int struc_size)
{
    struct emp *p;
```

```
        p = (struct emp *) malloc(struc_size);
        p -> next = NULL;
        return p;
}
```

Here is a call to the function:

```
list = getnode(sizeof(struct emp));
```

The pointer (member **next**) in the newly allocated node can later be assigned a value by **malloc** to get a second node in the list:

```
list -> next = getnode(sizeof(struct emp));
```

This second node also contains a pointer to still another node, and so on. In this manner, each structure points to the next, establishing a linked list, as illustrated in Figure 12-6.

One important feature of a linked list is that it allows a program to allocate exactly the number of structures that are needed; it is not necessary to waste space even for an array of pointers. Every time the program requires a node, it calls **malloc** to provide one; the new structure comes with a pointer to another structure. Each new structure can be linked to the existing list.

TRAVERSING A LIST

We can move one by one through the elements on a list (this is called **traversing the list**) by following the chain of pointers. If we are currently accessing a structure on the list pointed to by **list**, the member **next** in each node points to the next structure.

Since the final pointer has not been used to get a new structure, it still points to **NULL** and signals the end of the list. If there are no items on a list, the list pointer is **NULL** and the list is empty.

To access structures on a list—for example, to print the members of the nodes—we traverse the list by following the chain of pointers. The traversal continues as long as the pointer in the current structure is not **NULL**. Example 12-16 shows how to traverse a list to the end, printing employee names along the way. Figure 12-7 illustrates the process (**info** represents the information stored in each node).

EXAMPLE 12-16   Assume that **list** points to the first item on the list (or **NULL** if the list is empty). The code on the following page prints the names of all the workers in the list.

FIGURE 12-6   A linked list

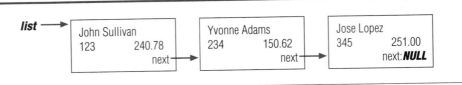

```
struct emp *list, *listptr;

listptr = list;
while (listptr != NULL) {
    printf("%s\n",listptr -> name);
    listptr = listptr -> next;
}
```

In this example, *listptr* is an extra pointer used to traverse the list. It is initially set to the value of *list*. If *listptr* is not equal to *NULL*, there is at least one structure on the list, and we enter the body of the loop. Inside the body of the loop, we print the name in the first structure. Then *listptr = listptr –> next* sets *listptr* to point to the next structure. The traversal continues until the value of *next* in the current structure is *NULL* (which means *listptr* is *NULL*). At that point, we are at the end of the list and fall out of the loop.

ADDING A NODE TO A LINKED LIST

A new node can be added to a linked list in several ways. It is possible to add a node to the beginning or end of a list or somewhere in the middle. Where the node should be added depends on how the list is used. Example 12-17 shows how to add a node to the front (or head) of a linked list. (We leave other insertions for a course in data structures.)

EXAMPLE 12-17   To add a node to the front of the linked list pointed to by *list*, first get a node *p* and fill it (see Figure 12-8A). Then set the *next* member of node *p* to point to the beginning of the list (see Figure 12-8B). Finally, set *list* to point to node *p*, which is the new head of the list (see Figure 12-8C). This works even if the list is originally empty.

```
struct emp *list,*p;

p = getnode(sizeof(struct emp));
fill node p with values
p -> next = list;
list = p;
```

FIGURE 12-7   Traversing a list. *A*, after *listptr = list*; *B*, after first *listptr = listptr –> next*; *C*, after second *listptr = listptr –> next*.

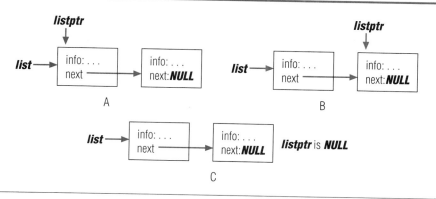

FIGURE 12-8 Adding a node to the front of a linked list. *A*, after ***p = getnode(...)***; *B*, after ***p –> next = list***; *C*, after ***list = p***.

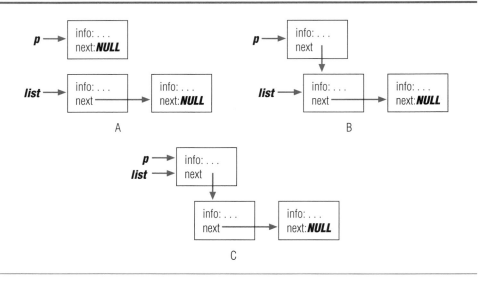

THE FUNCTION *free*

Once we are finished using dynamically allocated storage, we can release it. Suppose we fire an employee. Setting the pointer to the employee's structure to **NULL** does not get rid of the storage for that employee. It prevents our accessing the structure, but the storage is still allocated. Without a way to access the storage, we cannot reuse it.

To solve this problem, C has a library function, *free*, which is the opposite of *malloc*. The prototype for this void function is in *stdlib.h* (and in *malloc.h*). Calling the function *free* with a pointer as a parameter frees the storage pointed to by that pointer. The storage can then be reused later in the program.

General Form of a Call to *free*

> ```
> free(ptr);
> ```

In this case, *ptr* is a pointer to storage which has been allocated by a call to *malloc*.

After the call to *free*, any values stored in the variables are lost unless they have been saved elsewhere. It is not possible to refer to storage which has been freed. Storage may be freed in any order, not just the order in which it was declared.

Example 12-18 shows how to delete a node from the beginning of a linked list and free its storage. (It is possible to delete a node from any position in a linked list, but we leave other deletions for a course in data structures.)

EXAMPLE 12-18   To delete a node from the front of the linked list pointed to by *list*, first set a pointer *p* to point to *list* (see Figure 12-9A). If *p* is *NULL*, the list is empty. Otherwise, set *list* to point to the next node after *p*. This node, which *p –> next* was pointing to, is the new front node (see Figure 12-9B). Then set *p –> next* to *NULL* to detach node *p* from the list (see Figure 12-9C). Finally, free node *p*.

```
struct emp *list,*p;

p = list;
if (p != NULL) {
    list = p -> next;
    p -> next = NULL;
    free(p);
}
```

DANGLING POINTERS

One thing a programmer must be careful to avoid is a **dangling pointer**, one which no longer points to allocated storage. Example 12-19 creates a dangling pointer, *p2*.

EXAMPLE 12-19   In this example, storage for an integer is allocated and assigned to *p1*; *p2* is set to point to the same storage location. When *p1* is freed, *p2* points to nothing.

```
int *p1,*p2;
...

p1 = (int *) malloc(sizeof(int));
*p1 = 15;
p2 = p1;
free(p1);
printf("%d",*p2);                              /* p2 is dangling */
```

FIGURE 12-9   Deleting a node from the front of a linked list. *A*, after *p = list*; *B*, after *list = p –> next*; *C*, after *p –> next = NULL*; *D*, after *free(p)*.

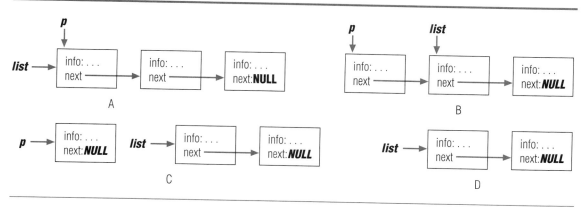

FIGURE 12-10 Creating a dangling pointer. *A,* after call to **malloc**; *B,* after **p2** = **p1**; *C,* after **free(p1)**.

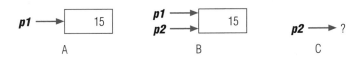

The assignment statement **p2** = **p1** sets the pointer **p2** to point to the same memory location as **p1**. After that, **p1* and **p2* refer to the same value. However, once the space **p1** points to is freed, **p2** is left dangling, pointing to nothing (but it is *not* **NULL.**) The **printf** does not print 15 (see Exercise 20). Figure 12-10 illustrates what happens in this section of code.

A dangling pointer can cause disastrous results in a program. Because a dangling pointer has not been assigned a specific address, it may point to a random location in the memory of the computer, possibly within system memory. It may point to areas which, if accessed, do strange things like causing the computer to reboot or erasing the working copy of the directory of your hard drive. (Fortunately, there is a backup copy of the directory so this is not as disastrous as it sounds!) In Unix on a Sun, a dangling pointer often causes the error message, "Memory fault: Core dumped." Always be careful to free all pointers when your program is finished with them. In Example 12-19, the programmer should write *free(p1)* and *free(p2)* in either order.

Linked lists and other dynamic data structures play a key role in many computer applications. A detailed discussion of the uses of dynamic storage is outside the scope of this textbook. However, pointers and dynamic storage are the basis for many other data structures.

SELF-CHECK 12-3

1. What is the advantage of dynamic storage allocation?
2. What happens as a result of a call to **malloc**? A call to **free**?
3. What is the meaning of a **NULL** pointer in a linked list?

SECTION 4   SIDE EFFECTS OF EXPRESSION EVALUATION

In this section, we introduce side effects. A **side effect** is an instance where a variable is changed as a secondary result of evaluating an expression.

A STATEMENT AS AN EXPRESSION

The right-hand side of an assignment statement is an expression; its value is assigned to a variable on the left-hand side of the assignment operator. In addition, every assignment statement is itself an expression; the value of the expression is the value assigned to the variable. For example, consider this assignment statement:

```
x = 5;
```

This evaluates the right-hand side and assigns the value 5 to **x**; as a side effect, the statement has the value 5.[2] In the simple examples we have used so far, the value of an assignment statement is not used for anything else, so we have avoided discussing side effects, concentrating only on the value assigned. However, C has a number of "idioms" which take advantage of side effects, including the value of an assignment statement.

USING A CALL TO THE *getchar* FUNCTION TO CONTROL A LOOP

As an example of such an idiom, consider this modification of Example 9-35 from Chapter 9.

EXAMPLE 12-20

Suppose we want to determine the total number of characters in the input data, including blanks, tabs, newlines, etc. We use a loop to read in the characters and count them one by one, stopping when we read **EOF**, the end of file. Experienced C programmers write this loop as shown below.

```
int c,count=0;

while ((c = getchar()) != EOF)
    count++;
printf("there are %d characters in the input\n",count);
```

Each time through the **while** loop, the control condition is evaluated. A number of things happen as the condition is evaluated.

◆ First, the assignment statement [**c = getchar()**] nested inside the condition is executed. The function **getchar** reads in a value and assigns it to the variable **c**.

◆ The value read in is also the value of the entire statement **c = getchar()**.

◆ This value is then compared with the constant **EOF**. If the value is equal to **EOF**, we fall out of the loop; otherwise, we enter the loop and count the character.

◆ Then we return to the header and repeat this process as long as the character read in is not **EOF**.

Note that all of this except the counting takes place in the header of the **while** loop. Also note the extra pair of parentheses. Because of the precedence rules, they are needed to make sure the assignment to **c** is done before the comparison with **EOF**.

SIDE EFFECTS OF EVALUATING EXPRESSIONS

There can be many other types of side effects of evaluating arithmetic expressions. In Chapter 1, we introduced the increment and decrement operators and mentioned that there is sometimes a difference between **i++** and **++i**. This difference usually shows up as a side effect of evaluating an expression.

If **i++** and **++i** are stand-alone statements, they have no side effects, and there is no difference between the two expressions, as shown in the example on the next page.

---

[2]Technically the value assigned to **x** is the side effect of the evaluation of the expression.

EXAMPLE 12-21 Both these pieces of code print the value 5.

```
int i = 4;                          int i = 4;

i++;                                ++i;
printf("%d\n",i);                   printf("%d\n",i);
```

However, if an increment operator is part of a larger expression, there can be a difference between i++ and ++i. The expression i++ says to use the value of i and then increment; the expression ++i says to increment and then use the new value.

EXAMPLE 12-22 Here is a slightly modified version of Example 12-21 which illustrates the difference between i++ and ++i:

```
int i = 4;                          int i = 4;

printf("%d ",i++);                  printf("%d ",++i);
printf("%d\n",i);                   printf("%d\n",i);
```

On the left, the value of i is used to print 4; then i is incremented to 5, and the second call to *printf* prints 5 (see Figure 12-11A). Here is the printout from the code:

```
4  5
```

On the right, first i is incremented to 5; then this value is used in each of the calls to *printf* (see Figure 12-11B). Here is the printout from the code:

```
5  5
```

SIDE EFFECTS OF THE INCREMENT OPERATORS

Let's look at some more examples of side effects of the two increment operators. When we introduced the assignment statement in Chapter 1, we said that the variable on the left-hand side gets a new value but variables on the right-hand side are unchanged. Using an increment

FIGURE 12-11 An example of the difference between i++ and ++i; A, i is incremented after printing; B, i is incremented before printing.

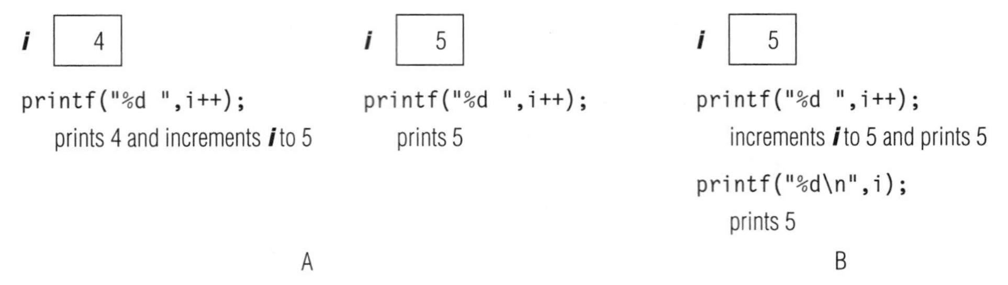

```
i   4              i   5              i   5

printf("%d ",i++);    printf("%d ",i++);    printf("%d ",i++);
  prints 4 and increments i to 5    prints 5    increments i to 5 and prints 5

                                        printf("%d\n",i);
                                          prints 5

        A                                         B
```

operator in the middle of an expression (or as the entire right-hand side) provides an exception to that rule, as shown in Example 12-23.

EXAMPLE 12-23 The following code uses *++c* as the right-hand side of an assignment statement:

```
int num, c = 1;

num = ++c;
```

In this case, as a result of the assignment statement, two variables are changed: ***num*** and ***c***. To see this, we evaluate the assignment statement step by step.

◆ When the expression *++c* is evaluated, *c* is first incremented to 2 (see Figure 12-12A), and this new value is the value of the right-hand side (see Figure 12-12B).

◆ Therefore, ***num*** is given the value 2, and, as a side effect, *c* becomes 2.

EXAMPLE 12-24 Now let's look at the same example with *c++* rather than *++c*.

```
int num, c = 1;

num = c++;
```

This time, *c* is incremented *after* its value is used in the expression to calculate ***num***.

◆ In the expression *c++*, the original value of *c* is used as the value of the expression on the right-hand side (see Figure 12-13A), and then *c* is incremented to 2 (see Figure 12-13B).

◆ Therefore, ***num*** is set to 1, and, as a side effect, *c* becomes 2.

FIGURE 12-12 The use of **++c** on the right-hand side of an assignment statement; A, **c** is incremented; B, **num** gets new value of **c**.

FIGURE 12-13 The use of **c++** on the right-hand side of an assignment statement; A, **num** gets old value of **c**; B, **c** is incremented.

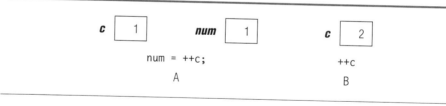

POTENTIAL ERRORS FROM SIDE EFFECTS

Side effects can arise in other situations as well. When they occur unexpectedly, they can cause mistakes that are hard to catch. Let's look at an example illustrating the side effect of an assignment statement and a peculiar feature of an *if* statement. Here a seemingly minor mistake leads to a major misinterpretation.

EXAMPLE 12-25 The code below is designed to read in values for *x* and *y*, then process *y* if the value of *x* is 5.

```
int x,y;

printf("type in values for x and y> ");
scanf("%d",&x);
scanf("%d",&y);
if (x = 5)
        process the value of y
```

Note that the *if* condition is (*x* = 5) rather than (*x* == 5). Although this is probably not what the programmer intended, it is not a compilation error.

◆   Instead, the compiler interprets *x* = 5 as an assignment statement, setting *x* to 5.
◆   As a side effect, the assignment statement has the value 5, which is used as the value of the *if* condition. In an *if* condition, 0 is interpreted as false, and any other value is true. In this case, the value 5 is true.
◆   Regardless of what value has just been read into *x*, the program processes the value of *y*.

In fact, things can be even worse than this. Let's look at a similar example with a *while* loop. In this one, the mistake leads to an infinite loop.

EXAMPLE 12-26 To simplify this example, we show only the *while* loop header:

```
while (x = 5)
    ...
```

Note that the *while* condition is (*x* = 5) rather than (*x* == 5). Therefore, the value 5 is assigned to *x*. This value is the value of the condition used to control the *while* loop. Since 5 is considered to be true, the body of the loop is executed. Then, no matter what happens in the body of the loop, *x* is set to 5 in the header just before the *while* condition is tested again. This produces an infinite loop.

 CAUTION The problem in the last two examples was caused by the careless use of the assignment operator = instead of the comparison operator ==. Be careful whenever you use these operators.

An expression is a complete statement. For example, consider the following:

```
x > y++;
```

The expression *x* > *y*++ is the entire statement. The relational operator > produces a true or false value. The value of the expression is not assigned to any variable, but, as a side effect, the value of *y* is increased by 1.

STYLE WORKSHOP In many cases, the problems associated with side effects can be avoided. For example, if you use the increment operator only in a stand-alone assignment statement, there is no side effect and no difference between *i++* and *++i*. However, side effects do play an important role in the language. As you become more comfortable with C, you should explore certain language idioms, such as the use of *getchar* in the header of the *while* loop in Example 12-20.

SELF-CHECK 12-4

1. Show what is printed by the statements below. Start with the following declaration statements for each part of this question:

```
int  i = 100;
char c = 'M';
```

   a. `printf("%c",c++);`
   b. `printf("%c",++c);`
   c. `printf("%d",i--);`
   d. `printf("%d",--i);`

2. Show what each of these statements does, using the initial values in the declaration.

```
int x = 5, y = 10;
```

   a. `x = (y = 5) + 3;`
   b. `x = (y = 5 + 3);`
   c. `x = y = 5 + 3;`
   d. `x = (y == 5) + 3;`

SUMMARY

RECURSION

1. Every recursive definition must contain two things: (a) an escape clause, which gives a fixed value for one or more simple calculations; and (b) a way of expressing a more complicated calculation in terms of simpler ones. Ultimately, the complicated situation is reduced to the escape clause.

2. As an example, the factorial function, written *n!*, is the product of the numbers from 1 to *n*. For example, $4! = 1 \times 2 \times 3 \times 4 = 24$. This can be defined recursively by noting that $1! = 1$ serves as an escape clause and $n! = (n-1)! \times n$ expresses a more complicated calculation in terms of simpler ones.

3. In a C program, a recursive call is used just like any other function call. For example, in a function called *factorial* which computes *n!*, the key statements look like this:

```
if (n == 1)
    return 1;          /* escape clause */
return factorial(n-1) * n
                       /* recursive call */
```

If *n* is 1, the function returns 1; if *n* is greater than 1, the function returns the product of *n* and the value returned by the recursive call to *factorial(n-1)*.

GLOBAL OR EXTERNAL VARIABLES

4. Each function in a C program can declare local variables. A function can reference its local variables or formal parameters, but it cannot reference variables declared in any other function (including *main*).

5. Constants, function prototypes, and structure definitions can be declared outside of all functions in a file. Then they can be referenced in any function which follows the declaration.

6. A variable declared outside of all the functions in a file is called an external or global variable. It may be referenced in any function (including **main**) which follows the external declaration. If a function has a local variable or a formal parameter with the same name as the global variable, the local reference takes precedence.

7. Each variable has a storage class: automatic, external, static, or register. The default class for a local variable in a function is automatic, which means space is assigned to the variable for the life of the function. If the declaration for a local variable is preceded by the keyword **static**, the variable continues to use the same storage each time the function is called. By default, a global variable has storage class external.

DYNAMIC STORAGE ALLOCATION

8. Dynamic storage allocation allows a program to use exactly the amount of storage that it requires. The program allocates and frees storage during execution. This is important when a program uses a large data structure like an array of structures.

9. Dynamic storage is implemented using pointers. A pointer is declared, but, at that time, no storage is allocated for the variable it points to. During execution, the program explicitly requests a block of storage when needed.

10. The function **malloc** allocates blocks of storage. It accepts as a parameter the size of the desired block and returns a pointer to the newly allocated block. Since the pointer returned by **malloc** has type **void** *, the returned value usually must be cast to the appropriate type before assignment.

11. The number of bytes requested can be specified as an integer or, as is common for structures, a value determined by **sizeof**.

12. Here is an example which uses **malloc** to allocate a structure of type **struct item**:

```
struct item {
    int  num;
    char name[10];
};
struct item *iptr;

iptr = (struct item *) malloc
               (sizeof(struct item));
```

This call to **malloc** allocates a block of storage large enough to hold an integer and a ten-character string; the address of that block is returned, cast to type **struct item** *, and assigned to **iptr**.

13. Once storage has been allocated using **malloc**, it can be accessed using ordinary pointer notation. For example, member **name** can be accessed as **iptr –> name**.

14. Storage which has been allocated using **malloc** can also be freed using the function **free**. It accepts one parameter, which is a pointer to a block of memory. It returns that block of memory to the pool of available storage. Here is an example:

```
free(iptr);
```

15. Several pointers or an array of pointers can be declared; this allows allocation of several structures. A more common technique is defining a structure type which contains a pointer. Structures of this kind can be joined to form a data structure called a linked list. Each structure in a linked list is called a node. A pointer in each node points to the next node.

16. The constant **NULL**, which signifies that a pointer does not point to any storage, indicates the end of a linked list.

SIDE EFFECTS

17. Every assignment statement has two effects: one is to evaluate the expression on the right-hand side and assign this value to the variable on the left-hand side; another is to return this as the value for the entire assignment statement. In the example below, the assignment statement **c = getchar()** is

executed as the *while* loop condition is evaluated. The value read in by *getchar* is stored in *c*, and this value is compared to the constant *EOF*.

```
while ((c = getchar()) != EOF)
    putchar(c);
```

18. Side effects of expression evaluation have an impact in many other places as well—for example, if the increment or decrement operators are used in arithmetic expressions. In the example below, the code on the left assigns the value 4 to both *x* and *y* since the increment is done before the value of *y* is assigned to *x*. The code on the right assigns 3 to *x* and 4 to *y* since the increment is done after the original value of *y* is assigned to *x*.

```
int x, y = 3;            int x, y = 3;

x = ++y;                 x = y++;
```

19. Side effects can cause strange things to occur if the assignment operator (=) and the relational operator (==) are misused. In the code below, the value of *x* + *3* is stored in *y*; then this value is used as the condition of the *if* statement.

```
if (y = x + 3)
    printf("success");
```

The *printf* is executed when the value of the assignment statement is anything but 0.

20. In C, an expression is a complete statement by itself. In the code below, the expression *y* == *x* + *3* is used as a statement, even though no variable is assigned a value. To execute this statement, the value of *x* + *3* is compared to the value of *y*, yielding either 1 (true) or 0 (false). However, this 0 or 1 value is not used for any additional purpose.

```
y == x + 3;
```

EXERCISES

RECURSION

1. Show what is printed by the following program.

```
#include <stdio.h>
int recurs(int);
main()
{
        int x, a, y = 3, z = 5;

        x = recurs(2);
        printf("x is %d\n",x);
        x = recurs(y);
        printf("x is %d\n",x);
        a = recurs(z);
        printf("a is %d\n",a);
}

int recurs(int z)
{
        if (z == 1)
                return 3;
        if (z == 3)
                return 14;
        return 2 * recurs(z-1);
}
```

2.   a.   Rewrite the function *recurs* from Exercise 1 using a single *return* statement.
       b.   Rewrite the function without using recursion.

3.   Rewrite the function *recurs* from Exercise 1 using a void recursive function. To do this, modify the function so that it receives two parameters. The second one should hold the answer that would have been returned.

4.   Here is a recursive function:

```
int testrec(int number)
{
     int temp;

     if (number == 0)
         temp = 0;
     else
         temp = number + testrec(number-1);
     return temp;
}
```

       a.   Evaluate the following calls to the function *testrec*:

           (1) `z = testrec(3);`   (2) `z = testrec(4);`   (3) `z = testrec(6);`

       b.   What mathematical function is computed by this C function?
       c.   Rewrite the function so that it does the same thing without using recursion.

5.   a.   Trace the *factorial* function from Section 1 on some simple values. For example, evaluate step by step the calculation of *factorial(5)* or *factorial(6)*.
       b.   Trace the function *reverse* on some simple strings. For example, give the step-by-step evaluation of *reverse("hi mom")* or *reverse("dad")*.
       c.   Trace the function *fib* on some simple values. For example, trace the complete calculation of *fib(3)* or *fib(4)*. If you have the patience, do the same for *fib(5)* or *fib(6)*.
       d.   Explain why the traces for *fib* are so much more time consuming than those for *factorial* or *reverse*.

6.   What is the difference between a "circular" and a "recursive" definition? What does a recursive definition contain that a circular one does not?

7.   A function *sub* is recursive if the body of the function contains a call to *sub*. However, function *a* can be recursive because it calls function *b*, which calls *a*, forming a recursive chain. Show what is printed by this program which contains a recursive chain.

```
#include <stdio.h>
int first(int);
int second(int);
main()
{
     int i,one,two;

     for (i = 0; i < 5; i++)  {
         one = first(i);
         two = second(i);
         printf("%d %d %d\n",i,one,two);
     }
}
```

```
int second(int n)
{
    if (n == 0)
        return 0;
    return first(n-1) + 1;
}

int first(int n)
{
    if (n == 0)
        return 1;
    return second(n-1);
}
```

8. a. In the **factorial** function as currently written, what happens if *n* is negative or 0?
   b. Show how to modify the function so that it returns an error signal (e.g., –1) if the parameter is negative and the correct answer for all values of *n* which are greater than or equal to 0. (*Note*: In mathematics, 0! is defined to be 1.)
   c. Repeat parts (a) and (b) for the function to compute Fibonacci numbers.

9. Give a recursive definition for addition in terms of adding 1. (*Hint*: If *x* and *y* are nonnegative integers, adding *x* and 0 is *x*; adding *x* and *y* is one more than adding *x* and *y–1*.)

10. Give a recursive definition for multiplication in terms of addition. (*Hint*: The product of *x* and 0 is 0; the product of *x* and *y* is equal to the sum of *x* and the product of *x* and *y–1*.)

11. Give a recursive definition for exponentiation (x^y) in terms of multiplication.

12. a. Give a recursive definition for an arithmetic expression. (*Hint*: You need an escape clause—a specification of the simplest possible arithmetic expression—and a way of expressing a more complicated expression in terms of simpler ones.)
    b. Give a nonrecursive definition for an arithmetic expression.

13. Write a recursive function (with one parameter) to compute and return the reverse of a string. (*Hint*: The space allocated to hold the reverse string cannot be allowed to disappear between calls. Try using a global variable or a local variable which is static.)

GLOBAL VARIABLES

14. If the program from Example 12-7 is run with *n* = 10, exactly which values of *i* are used in the function *sub*? In the main program?

15. Show how to rewrite Program 11 using a global definition for the array of structures. Compare the original program to the new version.

DYNAMIC STORAGE ALLOCATION

16. What is printed by the following program?

```
#include <stdio.h>
#include <stdlib.h>
#include <string.h>
```

(*continued*)

(*continued*)

```
main()
{
    struct rec {
        char name[20];
        int  number;
    };
    struct rec *he,*she;
    int    *iptr1,*iptr2;
    int    x = 51, y = 97;

    scanf("%d %d",&x,&y);
    iptr1 = (int *) malloc(sizeof(int));
    *iptr1 = x;
    printf("x = %d iptr1 = %d\n",x,*iptr1);
    iptr2 = (int *) malloc(sizeof(int));
    *iptr2 = y;
    printf("y = %d iptr2 = %d\n",y,*iptr2);
    he = (struct rec *) malloc(sizeof(struct rec));
    strcpy(he -> name,"Josef Olaf");
    he -> number = 34;
    she = (struct rec *) malloc(sizeof(struct rec));
    strcpy(she -> name,"Wai Ling");
    she -> number = *iptr1;
    printf("he -> name = %s, he -> number = %d\n",
            he -> name,he -> number);
    printf("she -> name = %s,she -> number = %d\n",
            she -> name,she -> number);
    if (he -> number > *iptr1)
        y = he -> number;
    else
        y = *iptr1;
    printf("y = %d\n",y);
}
```

17. What is printed by the program in Exercise 16 if the calls to **malloc** are removed? Try to predict what is printed, then run a program to see if you are correct.

18. A department store normally employs about 300 employees. However, at Christmas and inventory time, the store briefly hires up to an additional 300 people. The structure for each employee looks like the following:

```
struct addrec {
    char str_addr[30];
    char city_state_zip[30];
};
struct emprec {
    char    name[20];
    struct addrec address;
    double rate, hours, pay;
};
```

a. Should the store set up and maintain an array of 600 structures for the entire year? Is there a better way to store the records?

b. Show how to use an array of pointers to set up storage for the store's employees.

c. Show how to use a linked list to maintain storage for the store's employees. Assume that employees are added only to the end of the list.

d. Which method requires the least amount of storage?

19. Show how to use pointers (or an array of pointers) to minimize the number of times information carried along in a sort has to be interchanged (see Chapter 10, Exercise 49).

20. Run the program segment in Example 12-19 and see what is actually printed. If you have access to another C compiler, run the program using that compiler. Are the answers the same?

21. Write a function to insert a node at the end of a linked list. You must determine what parameters to send to the function.

22. Write a function to insert a node into a linked list following node *q*. You must determine what parameters to send to the function.

23. Write a function to delete the node following node *q* from a linked list. You must determine what parameters to send to the function.

24. Write a program that uses a linked list to sort a list of numbers. Read in a sequence of numbers, one at a time. As you read in a number, place it in the linked list in numerical order. (This is called an **insertion sort**.) Use the functions from exercises 21 and 22, together with the functions from Section 3.

SIDE EFFECTS

25. a. Show what is printed by the following program:

```c
#include <stdio.h>
main()
{
    int a = 4, b = 10;

    printf("%d\n",(a++) * (b++));
    printf("%d %d\n",a,b);
}
```

b. What is printed if the first *printf* in the program is replaced by each of the following?

```c
(1) printf("%d\n",(a++) * (++b));
(2) printf("%d\n",(++a) * (b++));
(3) printf("%d\n",(++a) * (++b));
```

26. What does each of the following series of statements do? (For each statement, use the initial values in the declaration.)

```c
int x=5, y=10;
```

a. x = (y == 5 + 3);
b. x = y == 5 + 3;

c. x = x - y++;
d. x = x - ++y;

27. What is wrong with each of the following calls to the **getchar** function?

    a. `getchar(c);`   b.   `c = getchar(c);`

28. Is the following statement legal? If it is, what does it do? If it is not legal, what error message is generated?

    `c = putchar(c);`

29. What storage locations are changed by each of the following statements? Use the following declarations and initial values for each part. Type in and run a simple program to test your answers.

    ```
    int i = 1;
    int a[4] = { 0,10,20,30 };
    ```

    a. `a[i++] = i;`   d.   `a[i] = ++i;`
    b. `a[++i] = i;`   e.   `a[i++] = i++;`
    c. `a[i] = i++;`   f.   `a[++i] = ++i;`

ANSI C KEYWORDS

The following identifiers are keywords in ANSI C. Individual compilers (notably Turbo C++) have added a few others.

auto	extern	sizeof
break	float	static
case	for	struct
char	goto	switch
const	if	typedef
continue	int	union
default	long	unsigned
do	register	void
double	return	volatile
else	short	while
enum	signed	

ASCII CODES

Symbolic characters can be represented by numbers, called ASCII codes; these numbers range from 0 through 255. ASCII codes 32 through 126 have been assigned to the printable character set; 128 through 255 represent the extended character set. Members of the extended character set can be displayed on the screen, but they may not be printable, or they may be interpreted in different ways by different printers. Among these characters are some Greek letters, specialized typographical characters, box drawing characters, and other graphics symbols. The ASCII codes from 0 through 31, together with 127, correspond to control characters (like line feed, carriage return, etc.), and most are interpreted in different ways by different devices.

Here are the printable ASCII characters, together with their codes:

ASCII	char	ASCII	char	ASCII	char	ASCII	char	ASCII	char
32	blank	52	4	72	H	92	\	112	p
33	!	53	5	73	I	93	]	113	q
34	"	54	6	74	J	94	∧	114	r
35	#	55	7	75	K	95	_	115	s
36	$	56	8	76	L	96	`	116	t
37	%	57	9	77	M	97	a	117	u
38	&	58	:	78	N	98	b	118	v
39	'	59	;	79	O	99	c	119	w
40	(	60	<	80	P	100	d	120	x
41	)	61	=	81	Q	101	e	121	y
42	*	62	>	82	R	102	f	122	z
43	+	63	?	83	S	103	g	123	{
44	,	64	@	84	T	104	h	124	|
45	-	65	A	85	U	105	i	125	}
46	.	66	B	86	V	106	j	126	~
47	/	67	C	87	W	107	k		
48	0	68	D	88	X	108	l		
49	1	69	E	89	Y	109	m		
50	2	70	F	90	Z	110	n		
51	3	71	G	91	[	111	o		

C OPERATOR PRECEDENCE TABLE

This table shows the precedence of all operators used in C. Some of these have not been covered in the text.

PRECEDENCE RULES

From Highest Down to Lowest	Associativity
() [] -> .	left to right
! ~ - + ++ -- * & (type) sizeof (all unary)	right to left
* (multiplication) / %	left to right
+ -	left to right
<< >>	left to right
< <= > >=	left to right
== !=	left to right
& (bitwise and)	left to right
^	left to right
|	left to right
&&	left to right
||	left to right
?:	right to left
= += -= *= /= %= &= ^= |= <<= >>=	right to left
,	left to right

SELECTED STANDARD LIBRARY FUNCTIONS

The C standard library consists of more than a hundred functions. The prototype for each library function appears in a header file such as **stdio.h**. This appendix groups some of the most common functions by the header file in which their prototypes are located. For each function discussed in the text, we give a brief description, plus a chapter reference. In a few cases, we've included functions that are not discussed in the text.

NOTE   When the qualifier **const** appears before a parameter (usually a string), it indicates that the function does not change the parameter.

1.   *stdio.h*

Input/output functions

a.   `int fclose(FILE *file);`
closes a file after use; returns **EOF** if an error occurred and 0 otherwise: Appendix VI.

b.   `int fgetc(FILE *file);`
returns a single character read from a file; returns **EOF** if an error occurred or the end of file was reached: Appendix VI.

c.   `char *fgets(char *str, int n, FILE *file);`
reads up to **n-1** characters (stopping at the end of a line) from a file into an array **str** and returns **str**; returns **NULL** if an error occurred or the end of file was reached: Appendix VII.

d.   `FILE *fopen(const char *file, const char *use);`
opens a file for use (**use** is typically "r" for input or "w" for output); if successful, returns a pointer to the file; otherwise returns **NULL**: Appendix VI.

e.   `int fprintf(FILE *file, const char *format, list of expressions to be printed);`
sends output to a file, using the specifications in the format string; returns the number of characters written to the file, or a negative value if an error occurred: Appendix VI.

f.   `int fputc(int c, FILE *file);`
Outputs character **c** to a file; returns the character **c** (as an unsigned **char**) or **EOF** if an error occurred: Appendix VII.

g. `int fputs(const char *str, FILE *file);`
outputs the string **str** to a file; returns **EOF** if an error occurred: Appendix VII.

h. `int fscanf(FILE *file, const char *format,` *list of addresses of variables*`);`
reads input from a file, converting the values read in according to the formats specified and assigning the values to the addresses; returns the number of input items converted and assigned; returns **EOF** if an error occurred before any conversions: Appendix VI.

i. `int getchar(void);`
reads a single character from **stdin** (see **fgetc**): Chapter 9.

j. `char *gets(char *str);`
reads an input line from **stdin** into an array of characters **str** (see **fgets**): Chapter 9.

k. `int printf(const char *format,` *list of expressions to be printed*`);`
sends output to **stdout** (see **fprintf**): Chapter 1.

l. `int putchar(int c);`
outputs character **c** to **stdout** (see **fputc**): Chapter 9.

m. `int puts(const *str);`
outputs the string **str** (and a newline character) to **stdout** (see **fputs**): Chapter 9.

n. `int scanf(const char *format,` *list of addresses of variables*`);`
reads input from **stdin** (see **fscanf**): Chapter 3.

2. ***math.h***

a. `int ceil(double x);`
returns the smallest integer greater than or equal to **x**: Chapter 2.

b. `double cos(double x);`
returns the cosine of angle **x** (measured in radians): Chapter 2.

c. `double exp(double x);`
returns **e** to the **x** power: Chapter 2, Exercises.

d. `double fabs(double x);`
returns the absolute value of **x**: Chapter 2.

e. `int floor(double x);`
returns the largest integer less than or equal to **x**: Chapter 2.

f. `double log(double x);`
returns the natural logarithm of **x**: Chapter 2, Exercises.

g. `double pow(double x, double y);`
returns **x** to the **y** power: Chapter 5, Exercises.

h. `double sin(double x);`
returns the sine of angle **x** (measured in radians): Chapter 2.

i. `double sqrt(double x);`
returns the square root of **x**: Chapter 2.

j. `double tan(double x);`
returns the tangent of angle x (measured in radians): Chapter 2.

3. *ctype.h*

All of these functions are discussed in Chapter 9.

a. `int isalnum(int ch);`—is *ch* alphanumeric?
b. `int isalpha(int ch);`—is *ch* alphabetic?
c. `int isdigit(int ch);`—is *ch* a digit?
d. `int islower(int ch);`—is *ch* a lowercase character?
e. `int ispunct(int ch);`—is *ch* a punctuation symbol?
f. `int isspace(int ch);`—is *ch* a whitespace character?
g. `int isupper(int ch);`—is *ch* an uppercase character?
Each one returns true (1) if *ch* has the specified type; otherwise it returns false (0). For example, if *ch* is an expression of type *char*, then *isupper(ch)* returns 1 if *ch* is an uppercase letter and 0 if it is not.

h. `int tolower(int ch);`
If *ch* is an uppercase letter, returns the corresponding lowercase character; otherwise returns *ch*.

i. `int toupper(int ch);`
If *ch* is a lowercase letter, returns the corresponding uppercase character; otherwise returns *ch*.

4. *string.h*

All of these functions are discussed in Chapter 9 (*strstr* appears in the exercises).

a. `char *strcat(char *str1, const char *str2);`
copies *str2* to the end of *str1*; returns *str1*.

b. `int strcmp(const char *str1, const char *str2);`
compares the strings *str1* and *str2*; returns positive, negative, or 0.

c. `char *strcpy(char *str1, const char *str2);`
copies *str2* to *str1*; returns *str1*.

d. `size_t strlen(const char *str);`
returns the length of *str*.

Note: size_t is predefined as an unsigned integer. This allows the function to work on strings whose length is larger than a usual integer.

e. `char *strncat(char *str1, const char *str2, size_t n);`
copies up to *n* characters from *str2* to the end of *str1*, inserting '\0' at the end; returns *str1*.

f. `int strncmp(const char *str1, const char *str2, size_t n);`
compares up to *n* characters from strings *str1* and *str2*; returns positive, negative, or 0.

g. `char *strncpy(char *str1, const char *str2, size_t n);`
copies up to *n* characters from *str2* to *str1*, padding with additional '*\0*' characters at the end, if necessary; returns *str1*.

h. `char *strstr(const char *str1, const char *str2);`
returns pointer to the first occurence of the string *str2* in the string *str1*; returns *NULL* if it does not occur.

5. *stdlib.h*

a. `int abs(int n);`
returns the absolute value of *n*: Chapter 2.

b. `double atof(const char *str);`
converts *str* to a value of type *double* and returns that value: Appendix VI.

c. `int atoi(const char *str);`
converts *str* to an integer and returns that integer: Appendix VI.

d. `long atol(const char *str);`
converts *str* to a value of type *long* and returns that value: Appendix VI.

e. `void exit(int error_val);`
terminates the program, returning *error_val* to the environment: Chapter 6.

f. `void free(void *p);`
deallocates the space pointed to by *p*: Chapter 12.

g. `void *malloc(size_t size);`
returns a pointer to space for an object of *size* bytes; returns *NULL* if the space cannot be allocated: Chapter 12.

h. `int rand(void);`
returns a random integer in the range from 0 to some maximum value: Chapter 5, Exercises.

i. `void srand(unsigned int seed);`
uses *seed* as the seed to generate a sequence of random numbers: Chapter 5, Exercises.

STANDARD I/O STREAMS, REDIRECTION, AND PIPING; EXECUTING FROM THE DOS COMMAND LINE

STANDARD INPUT/OUTPUT STREAMS

C has three **standard input/output streams**: *stdin*, *stdout*, and *stderr*. A stream is a path by which data can enter or leave a program, as shown in Figure V-1. Each stream is associated with a device but can be connected to a file, another device, or another process. The names *stdin*, *stdout*, and *stderr* are constants, defined in *stdio.h*.

♦ The standard input stream, called *stdin*, is associated by default with the keyboard. Unless you specify otherwise, all input to your program comes from the keyboard. When you use *scanf*, *gets*, or *getchar* to read data which is typed in from the keyboard, you are reading from *stdin*.

♦ Standard output stream *stdout* is associated by default with the monitor. Unless you specify otherwise, all output from your program goes to the monitor. When you use *printf*, *puts*, or *putchar* to display output to the monitor, you are actually sending output to *stdout*.

♦ Standard output stream *stderr* is also associated by default with the monitor. You must explicitly send output to *stderr*; it is not automatic.

Generally, ordinary program output is sent to *stdout* and diagnostics (error messages) are sent to *stderr*. Without I/O redirection, both of these streams go to the monitor, and their output cannot be distinguished.

FILES AND REDIRECTION OF INPUT/OUTPUT

It is possible to redirect I/O. Through output **redirection** in DOS or **piping** in Unix, it is possible to send *stdout* to somewhere other than to the monitor, typically to the printer or to a file on disk.[1] Through input redirection, *stdin* can be assigned to come from somewhere other than the keyboard, typically from a file on disk. A program may even redirect *stderr*, although we do not show how to do so.

---

[1]For more details about using files, see Appendix VI.

FIGURE V-1   Program with standard I/O streams: **stdin**, **stdout**, **stderr**

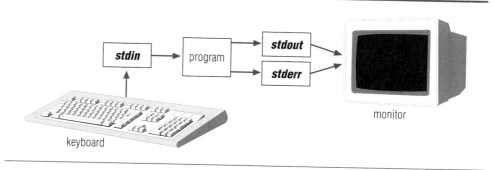

RUNNING FROM THE COMMAND LINE

To use redirection, the programmer must run the program from the **command line** or **command prompt** (e.g., C:> in DOS or > in Unix). A program is executed by typing its name at the command prompt (or by selecting its name or icon from a shell program like Windows). This point is usually quite clear even to beginning programmers who are using Unix (where the executable file **a.out** is executed by typing its name at the command prompt), but it is often unclear to students using DOS. Students using DOS in a university computer center frequently run programs through a menu program. If you are accustomed to selecting *Turbo C++* from a menu and then staying within Turbo C's integrated environment, you have not experienced how programs are actually run. Let's see how to do that.

HOW TO RUN A TURBO C PROGRAM FROM THE COMMAND LINE

In Turbo C, running from the command line means exiting from the integrated environment to run the program from a DOS prompt. To run a program from the command line in Turbo C, do the following:[2]

◆   Press F9 to issue the *Make* command, which compiles and links the program without executing it.

◆   Press ALT-F, D to exit to DOS temporarily. Now you are at the command line.

◆   Type the name of the executable file and press ENTER. If the program is **app5.c**, the executable file is **app5.exe**. To run the program, type the following:

app5

You can run an executable file, without recompilation, by typing its name at the command prompt, just as you can type *tc* to execute the program which brings up the Turbo C++ integrated environment or **win** to run Windows. Even a program compiled and linked

---

[2]More details on this process are provided later in this appendix.

within the integrated environment can be run this way. An executable file can also be run on a computer which lacks a C compiler.

HOW TO RUN A TURBO C++ FOR WINDOWS PROGRAM FROM THE COMMAND LINE

Running from the command line in Windows is done through Program Manager. First, compile and link the program, without running it, by clicking on the icon immediately to the left of the Run icon. In Program Manager, choose File|Run. A Run window will open with an input box labeled *Command Line*. In this box, type the name of the file; if the program is ***app5.c***, the executable file is ***app5.exe***. To run the program, type ***app5*** and then click on OK. Running this way is necessary when using command-line parameters (see Appendix VI).

SENDING *stdout* TO THE PRINTER: REDIRECTION AND PIPING

Sending output to the printer is usually necessary early in a programming course for a number of reasons. Among other things, the output of some programs scrolls off the screen, which makes the output hard to read or print. Output can be sent directly to the printer by using redirection (in DOS) or piping (in Unix).

When ***stdout*** is redirected to the printer, the general diagram shown in Figure V-1 changes to the more specific one shown in Figure V-2.

Sending output from ***stdout*** to the printer is different in DOS than in Unix. In DOS, it can be done through redirection. In Unix, it must be done by **piping**. (In Windows, redirection is not possible; however, the output of a program appears in a separate window which can be viewed or printed in its entirety.) Example V-1 shows how to send ***stdout*** to the printer.

FIGURE V-2 Program with ***stdout*** redirected to the printer

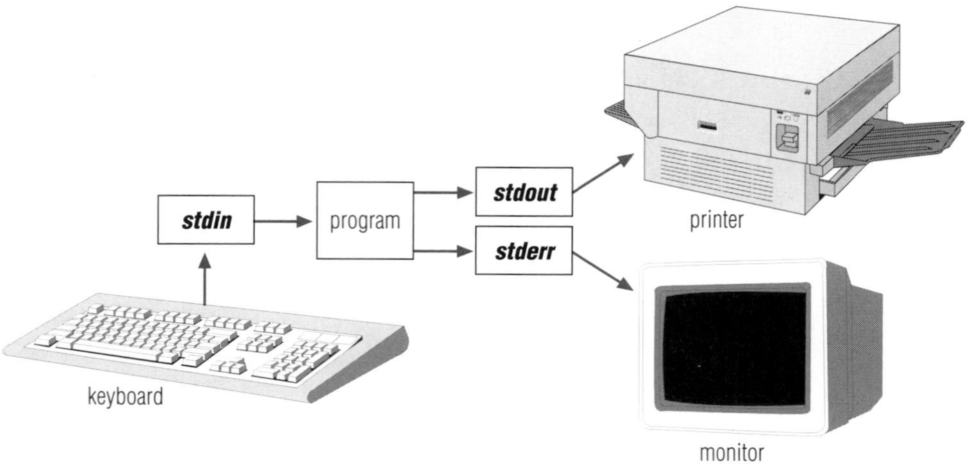

**EXAMPLE V-1A
(DOS)**

Let's assume the output from **prob5** is to go to the printer. In DOS, redirecting **stdout** to the printer requires adding, after the name of the executable file, the output redirection symbol (>) followed by the system's name for the printer. In DOS, the printer is called **prn**.

To redirect **stdout** to the printer in DOS while running **app5**, type the following on the command line:

```
app5 > prn
```

**EXAMPLE V-1B
(Unix)**

In Unix, sending **stdout** to the printer is done by sending it through another program, called **lpr**. The **lpr** program sends lines to the printer. Directing the output of one program through another program is called **piping**, and the symbol for this action is called a **pipe**. To pipe the output through **lpr**, type the name of the program, followed by the pipe symbol (which is |), followed by **lpr**.

To pipe **stdout** to the printer in Unix, type the following on the command line:

```
a.out | lpr
```

It is also possible to redirect output to a file (see Example V-2) and then to print that file.

CAUTION We recommend that you postpone redirecting output until your program is completely debugged. Displaying all output until the program is debugged can save tracing time and paper.

Redirection (or piping) output to the printer might not be recommended in an environment where printers are shared, for example in a computer lab. In that case, your instructor may tell you to send the output to a file and then print the file.

REDIRECTING *stdout* TO A FILE

Redirecting **stdout** to a file requires adding on the command line, after the name of the executable file, the output redirection symbol (>) followed by the name of the output file. If the output file does not already exist, it will be created; if it does already exist, it will be overwritten. Example V-2 shows how to redirect **stdout** to a file.

EXAMPLE V-2

Let's assume the output file is to be called **a5.out** and is to go to the same drive and subdirectory as the executable file. To redirect **stdout** to **a5.out**, type on the command line whichever of the following is appropriate for your system:

```
DOS: app5 > a5.out        Unix: a.out > a5.out
```

When **stdout** is redirected to a file **a5.out**, the general diagram shown in Figure V-1 changes to the more specific one shown in Figure V-3.

REDIRECTING INPUT

Input can also be redirected. Specifically, we can tell the program to redirect the program's input to come from a data file on a disk, rather than from the keyboard. Appendix VI begins with a brief introduction to files, which includes a section on creating a data file and another on the advantages of using data files. You might wish to read that now.

FIGURE V-3 Program with **stdout** redirected to a file

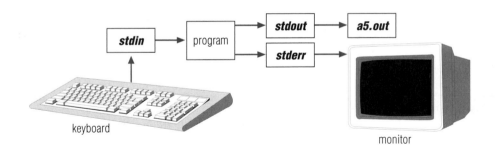

Reading from a data file can be done directly, by using file I/O functions (see Appendix VI), or indirectly, by using redirection.

REDIRECTION OF *stdin*

Redirecting **stdin** to come from a file requires adding, after the name of the executable file, the input redirection symbol (<) followed by the name of the input file. The input file must exist or you get an error message from the operating system. Example V-3 shows how to redirect **stdin**.

EXAMPLE V-3   Assume that program **app5.c** is to read input from a file **a5.dat**. To redirect **stdin** to come from **a5.dat**, which is on the same drive and subdirectory as the executable file, type on the command line whichever of the following is appropriate for your system:

  DOS: `app5 < a5.dat`   *Unix:* `a.out < a5.dat`

If the data file is on a different drive or directory, you must provide the complete path name for the file. In DOS and Windows, if your data file is on a disk in drive a:, you would type the following:

  DOS: `app5 < a:a5.dat`

When **stdin** is redirected to come from **a5.dat**, the general diagram shown in Figure V-1 changes to the more specific one shown in Figure V-4.

REDIRECTING BOTH *stdin* AND *stdout*

Redirecting both **stdin** and **stdout** requires adding two things after the name of the executable file: (1) the input direction symbol (<) followed by the name of the input file, and (2) the output redirection symbol (>) followed by the name of the output file. The order of (1) and (2) does not matter. Example V-4 shows how to redirect both **stdin** and **stdout**.

EXAMPLE V-4   Assume that program **app5.c** is to read input from a file **a5.data** and is to send output to file **a5.out**. Typing either one of the following on the command line redirects **stdin** to come from **a5.dat** and sends the output to **a5.out**.

  DOS: `app5 < a5.dat > a5.out`   *Unix:* `a.out < a5.dat > a5.out`

FIGURE V-4   Program with input redirection

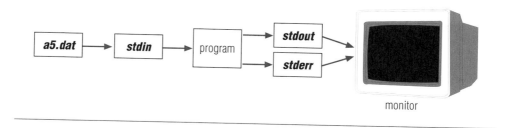

When both *stdin* and *stdout* are redirected as in Example V-4, the general diagram shown in Figure V-1 changes to the more specific one shown in Figure V-5.

WHY USE I/O REDIRECTION?

Typically, I/O redirection is used for several reasons. Simplicity is the primary reason for introducing I/O redirection to beginning programmers.

1. You don't have to use any extra statements or even know anything about files or file I/O functions.

2. You can switch the I/O from using standard streams to using files without changing anything in the program. Instead, you can just change the way you run the program:

   ◆ If the output scrolls off the screen, or if you need to examine it more carefully, you can redirect *stdout* to a file.

   ◆ If the data set is too long to enter from the keyboard, you can prepare it in advance, type it into a file, redirect *stdin* to come from the file, and read the data from the file.

In addition, redirection can be useful in program testing. Before hard-coding a program to read from specific input files, a programmer may wish to test the program on several files of various types: long ones, short ones, empty ones. With redirection, this is easily

FIGURE V-5   Program with input and output redirection

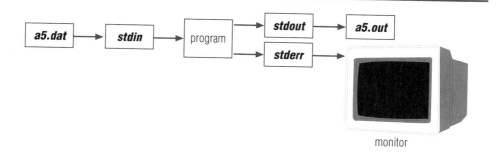

done. Once a program works, the programmer can change the I/O statements so that the program reads from the appropriate files.

STYLE WORKSHOP Although in theory no changes in the program have to be made to use I/O redirection, in practice, prompts are not necessary when input comes from a file. If all input is to come from files, it is best to remove the prompts entirely, as they simply clutter the screen.

WHAT APPEARS ON THE SCREEN?

An advantage of redirecting *stdin* and *stdout* is that fewer things appear on your screen. Normally anything typed on the keyboard (*stdin*) also appears on the screen; we say the input is **echoed** to the screen. Anything sent to *stdout* normally goes directly to the screen. However, if *stdin* is redirected to come from a file, none of the program's input echoes to the screen; if *stdout* is redirected to go to a file or to the printer, none of the program's output to *stdout* appears on the screen. Only messages sent to *stderr* still go to the screen, as illustrated in Example V-5.

EXAMPLE V-5   Suppose we have the following I/O statements in program *app5*:

```
printf("%d\n",123);
scanf("%d",&num);
```

Normally, *stdout* goes to the screen, and *stdin* comes from the keyboard (with an echo sent to the screen), so the screen looks like Figure V-6A. Figure V-6B illustrates that there is no echo when *stdin* is redirected. Figure V-6C shows what the screen looks like if *stdout* is redirected. Figure V-6D shows what happens to the screen when both *stdout* and *stdin* are redirected.

REDIRECTION USING *fprintf* AND *fscanf*; APPLICATION TO PROGRAM 3

The next few sections are slightly more complicated than the previous sections; they cover topics which are discussed in more detail in Appendix VI. Unlike the presentation in Appendix VI, this material can be used as early as Chapter 3. It introduces a solution to the problem of printing neat output for the program from Chapter 3.

USING *stderr* TO SPLIT OUTPUT: I/O STREAMS AND *fprintf*

There are times when a program should send some output to the monitor and other output to the printer. For example, in Chapter 3, the program issues prompts, which should go to the screen, but it also produces output that should go to the printer. However, all output from *printf* goes to the same place: to the screen (by default), to the printer (by using redirection or piping), or to a file (also by redirection).

By replacing all calls to *printf* with calls to *fprintf*, separating the output between *stdout* and *stderr*, and using redirection, a program can send output to two destinations, as explained on the next page.

FIGURE V-6 *A*, screen shows both ***stdout*** and echo of ***stdin***; *B*, ***stdin*** is redirected; screen shows ***stdout***; *C*, ***stdout*** is redirected; screen echoes ***stdin***; *D*, ***stdout*** and ***stdin*** are redirected; screen shows nothing.

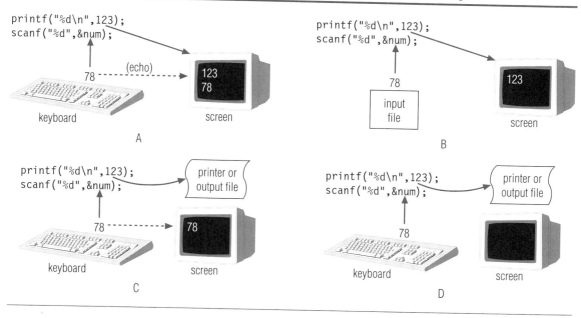

USING *fprintf*

While ***printf*** sends output only to ***stdout***, C has another output function, ***fprintf***, which can send output to many different places. (Appendix VI explains ***fprintf*** in more detail.) By using ***fprintf***, we can separate the output of a program between the two streams, ***stdout*** and ***stderr***.

A call to ***fprintf*** looks exactly like a call to ***printf***, except that ***fprintf*** requires the programmer to specify, as the first item inside the parentheses, the destination of the output. When the destination of a call to ***fprintf*** is ***stdout***, it means exactly the same thing as the corresponding call to ***printf***. Thus the two lines below are exactly equivalent:

```
fprintf(stdout,"%d\n",num);     is equivalent to   printf("%d\n",num);
```

To divide the output between the printer and the screen, first change each ***printf*** in the program to ***fprintf***. Then specify the destination of each call to ***fprintf***. Example V-6 shows how to use ***fprintf*** to send output to two different destinations.

EXAMPLE V-6 The following code issues a prompt, sending it to ***stderr***. It reads in a number, doubles it, and sends the computed result to ***stdout***.

```
int num;

fprintf(stderr,"Enter a number> ");
scanf("%d",&num);
fprintf(stdout,"The result is %d",2*num);
```

STYLE WORKSHOP You may wonder why prompts, which are not errors, are sent to *stderr*. Despite its name, *stderr* is simply a second available output stream; it is typically used for error messages, but it can be used for any output which should always go to the screen.

REDIRECTION OF *stdout* WHILE USING *stderr*

Since *stdout* goes to the screen, and so does *stderr*, their output is normally mixed together. Unless you redirect the output of your program, you won't see any difference between sending output to *stdout* and sending output to *stderr*, as shown in Figure V-7A. However, when you redirect the output of a program, you are redirecting *stdout*; in other words, anything sent to *stdout* goes to the new location. Redirection does not affect *stderr*, which still goes to the screen, as shown in Figure V-7B.

By sending some output to *stdout*, other output to *stderr*, and redirecting *stdout*, a program can split its output, sending prompts or error messages to the screen, and computed output to the printer or to a file. This technique is simpler than using files directly (which is done in Appendix VI).

USING *fscanf*

While *scanf* reads input only from *stdin*, C has another input function, *fscanf*, which reads input either from *stdin* or from a file.

A call to *fscanf* looks exactly like a call to *scanf*, except that *fscanf* requires the programmer to specify, as the first item inside the parentheses, the source of its input. When the source of *fscanf* is *stdin*, it means exactly the same thing as the corresponding *scanf*. Thus the two lines below are exactly equivalent:

  `fscanf(stdin,"%d",&num);` *is equivalent to* `scanf("%d",&num);`

This function is discussed in more detail in Appendix VI.

WHAT APPEARS ON THE SCREEN USING REDIRECTION, REVISITED

What happens if a program that writes to both *stdout* and *stderr* redirects *stdout*? When *stdout* is redirected, *stderr* continues to go to the screen, but *stdout* does not. Similarly, if

FIGURE V-7 *A*, **stdout** and **stderr**, without redirection; *B*, **stdout** and **stderr**, with redirection of **stdout**.

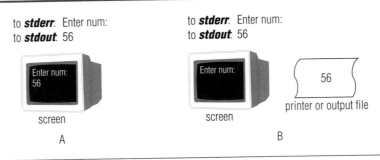

to **stderr**: Enter num:
to **stdout**: 56

to **stderr**: Enter num:
to **stdout**: 56

Enter num:
56

Enter num:
56

56

printer or output file

screen

screen

A

B

a program redirects *stdin*, no echo of the input appears on the screen. Example V-7 illustrates this.

EXAMPLE V-7   Suppose we have the following I/O statements:

```
fprintf(stdout,"%d\n",123);
fprintf(stderr,"Error\n");
fscanf(stdin,"%d",&num);
```

Normally, *stdout* and *stderr* go to the screen, and *stdin* comes from the keyboard (with an echo to the screen), so the screen looks like Figure V-8A. Figure V-8B illustrates what happens when *stdin* is redirected. Figure V-8C illustrates the separation of the output streams when *stdout* is redirected to a file or a printer. Finally, Figure V-8D illustrates what happens when both *stdout* and *stdin* are redirected.

FIGURE V-8   *A*, screen shows ***stdout***, ***stderr***, and echo of ***stdin***; *B*, ***stdin*** is redirected; screen shows ***stdout*** and ***stderr***; *C*, ***stdout*** is redirected; screen shows ***stderr*** and echoes ***stdin***; *D*, ***stdout*** and ***stdin*** are redirected; screen shows ***stderr***.

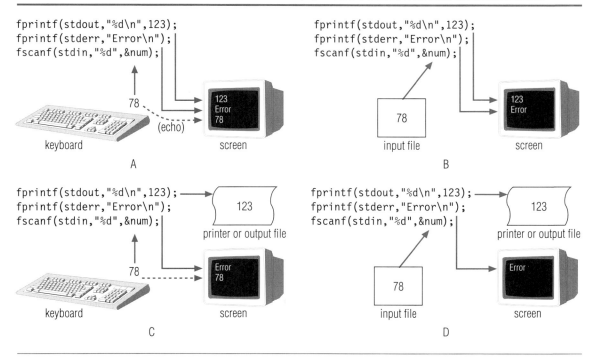

USING FILES—*fopen, fclose, fprintf, fscanf*; COMMAND-LINE PARAMETERS; *atoi*

C has a number of I/O functions—*printf, scanf, putchar, getchar, puts,* and *gets*—which automatically take input from or send output to the standard I/O streams. These functions are used so that a beginning programmer doesn't have to learn about files. However, each has an equivalent function which allows the programmer to specify a file as the source of the input or the destination of the output.

WHAT IS A FILE?

A **file** is a collection of data stored on disk. An **input file** (also called a **data file**) contains the same items you might have typed in from the keyboard during interactive data entry. An **output file** contains the same information that might have been sent to the screen as the output from your program.

USING FILES FOR INPUT

Input done with the functions *scanf, getchar,* and *gets* is very limited because these functions read only from the keyboard. Typing in data can be time consuming and can lead to careless errors. Furthermore, the keyboard is the program's sole source of input. While redirection (see Appendix V) allows a program to receive its input from a file rather than from the keyboard, the input must still come from a single source.

In contrast, by explicitly specifying input files, a program can read data from several sources. The program from Chapter 9, for example, can read in the original letter from one file and the changes from another file.[1] It is not necessary either to enter the data from the keyboard or to hard-code the data into the program.[2]

---

[1] A program on your disk, *prog9f.c*, includes modifications which allow it to use files; the I/O statements it uses are discussed in Appendix VII.

[2] **Hard-coding** means using assignment statements to give specific values to the variables. More generally, hard-coding refers to writing any kind of values directly into the code instead of using some more flexible method such as sending values as parameters or reading them in.

CREATING A DATA FILE

An input or data file is created the same way a C program file is created, by typing data in at the keyboard with a text editor (like the Turbo editor or *vi*). This file can then be given a name that associates it with the program. For example, if the program is called *app6.c*, the data file might be called *inapp6.dat*, *data6*, or *a6.dat* (see Figure VI-1).

CAUTION In DOS, be careful not to give a data file (or an output file) the same file name as your program. Each time a file is saved, Turbo C creates a backup file with the same file name, followed by the file extension *.bak*. If two files have the same name except for the extension—*app6.c* and *app6.dat*—their backup files are given the same name—*app6.bak*—and one or the other backup is lost. This is not a problem under Unix, which does not create backup files.

THE ADVANTAGES OF CREATING AND USING A DATA FILE

For several reasons, it is usually more convenient to read input from a data file than to enter data interactively.

First, the values must be typed in only once, when you create the file. You can correct the data values as you enter them. Once you have created and saved a data file, the data values are permanently stored on the disk.

Second, once a program is debugged, it is usually necessary to test the program on many different sets of data values to make sure that the program works in all cases. Reading the sets of data values from files guarantees that each modification of the program is tested on the same sets.

Third, in commercial programs, data sets are much too large for the values to be entered one at a time. Additionally, using an input file allows the output from one program to be the input for another. Finally, and perhaps more important, if a program reads from a file, no one needs to be present when the program is run; the program itself can locate and use the data.

FIGURE VI-1 A program file and a data file

```
/* app6.c */
#include <stdio.h>
main()
{
    int  i,num;

    for (i = 0;i <= 2; i++)
        scanf("%d",&num);
}
```

file *app6.c*

```
12
7
5
```

file *a6.dat*

USING FILES FOR OUTPUT

The functions *printf*, *putchar*, and *puts* are limited to sending output only to the screen. Without redirection, these functions provide no way to view long output, save the output from a program, or print it. Even with redirection, a program is limited: it can split output between only two destinations.

The use of files allows us to solve all these problems easily: a program can send output to several destinations. It can send error messages and prompts to the screen, so that the user can see them immediately; it can send some results to the printer and other results to one or more files on disk.

Each type of output can be directed to its own file and does not interfere with output sent to another file. Once in a file, output can later be checked for errors, edited, printed, or read into another program as data.

DATA TYPE *FILE* *

A **file pointer** is used to address the file from within a C program. A file pointer has data type *FILE* *, which means "pointer to a file." Note that data type *FILE* is defined in *stdio.h* using capital letters.

EXAMPLE VI-1

Here is a declaration for three file pointers. The first two are intended to point to two different input files, and the third is intended to point to an output file. (Note, however, that nothing in the declaration specifies how they are to be used.)

```
FILE *infile,*changes,*outfile;
```

OPENING AND CLOSING FILES

Before using a file, a C program must open it. Opening a file tells the operating system to look for a file by the specified name, or, if the file does not exist, to create a file with the specified name. In addition, it tells the operating system to prepare to read from or write to the beginning of the file.

After using a file, a C program must close it. Closing the file saves the file and any changes made to it. Between opening and closing a file, the program must specify in its I/O statements which file is to be used. It is not necessary to open or close standard I/O streams.

OPENING A FILE

Opening a file is done by a call to the function *fopen*, which tells the operating system the name of the file and whether the file is to be opened for reading (input) or for writing (output). The function *fopen* associates a file with a stream and returns a pointer to that stream; the pointer is the name by which the stream is known in the program.

General Form of a Call to *fopen*

```
filepointer = fopen(filename,mode);
```

The function *fopen* takes two parameters, both of which are strings. The parameter *file-name* is the name of the disk file to be opened. If the file is not in the default directory, a full path name must be provided. Parameter *mode* defines the way the file is to be opened; the most common modes are shown below. Notice that the mode is a string, not a character, and must be enclosed in double quotation marks. Here is an explanation of these modes:

◆   If *mode* is "r", the program will read from the file. The file should already exist.

◆   If *mode* is "w", the program will write to the file. If the file does not exist, it will be created. It the file does exist, it will be overwritten.

◆   If *mode* is "a", the program will append new output to the end of the file. If the file does not exist, it will be created.

The function *fopen* returns a value of type *FILE* *, either a pointer to the file or *NULL* if there is an error.[3]

EXAMPLE VI-2

This example shows three calls to *fopen*; the first two open files *letter.dat* and *changes* for input, and the third opens file *newfile.out* for output. The calls to *fopen* do not specify directory paths, so the system assumes that the files are in the default directory.

```
FILE *infile,*changes,*outfile;

infile = fopen("letter.dat","r");
changes = fopen("changes","r");
outfile = fopen("newfile.out","w");
```

Notice that the name of the file and its file pointer can be the same, but this is not necessary.

CAUTION If the file to be opened is in a subdirectory, C requires the file's full path name in order to open the file. If a file called *p6.dat* is in the subdirectory *hw* on the *c:* drive, DOS would call this file *c:\hw\p6.dat*. However, C does not correctly interpret the \ symbol as a path separator since the \ symbol is the escape character. To use \ in a file name, place the escape character \ in front of each \ in the path name. To open file *c:\hw\p6.dat* in a DOS C program, write the following:

```
cfile = fopen("c:\\hw\\pa6.dat","r");
```

This problem does not occur in Unix, which uses the / character for directory paths.

STYLE WORKSHOP Because an error might prevent opening the input file, it is customary to check the return value from *fopen* by comparing the file pointer with *NULL*.

Example VI-3 shows how to check for an error in opening a file.

EXAMPLE VI-3

```
FILE *infile;

infile = fopen("letter.dat","r");
if (infile == NULL) {
    printf("error in opening file letter.dat\n");
    exit(1);
}
```

---

[3]The identifier *NULL* is predefined in *stdio.h*. A pointer with value *NULL* points to nothing.

A failure to open file *letter.dat* causes the program to display an error message and to call the function *exit* with a non-zero exit code, indicating an error. In Example VI-6, we show how to send this error message to *stderr*.

CLOSING A FILE

After a file has been used, it must be closed. This is done by a call to the function *fclose*. The *fclose* function breaks the connection between the stream and the file. (C does this automatically when the program terminates, but it is good practice to closes all files explicitly, in case the program crashes.)

General Form of a Call to *fclose*

```
fclose(filepointer);
```

The function *fclose* takes one parameter, which is a pointer to a file. If there is an error, such as trying to close a file that is not open, the function returns *EOF*; otherwise it returns 0. This return value is usually not checked.

EXAMPLE VI-4

This example shows three calls to *fclose*.

```
FILE *infile,*changes,*outfile;

fclose(infile);
fclose(changes);
fclose(outfile);
```

Between opening and closing a file, we use file I/O functions to read from or write to the file. In this appendix, we discuss the file I/O functions *fscanf* and *fprintf*. In Appendix VII, we discuss *fgets* and *fputs*, the file I/O functions for strings, as well as *fgetc* and *fputc*, the file I/O functions for characters.

OUTPUT USING *fprintf*

While *printf* sends output only to *stdout*, the corresponding function *fprintf* allows a program to send output to many different places: the screen, the printer, or a file on a disk.

A call to *fprintf* looks exactly like a call to *printf*, except that the program must specify, as the first parameter, the destination of the output. This destination can be an I/O stream—*stdout* or *stderr*—or it can be a file.

General Form of a Call to *fprintf*

```
fprintf(destfile,"format string",list of variables);
```

In this call, ***destfile*** is the name of an output stream (***stdout*** or ***stderr***) or a pointer to a file which has already been opened. The format string and list of variables are the same as those in a call to ***printf***.

SENDING OUTPUT TO A STANDARD OUTPUT STREAM

When the destination of a call to *fprintf* is *stdout*, the call means exactly the same thing as a call to *printf*. Example VI-5 compares a call to *fprintf* with a call to *printf*.

EXAMPLE VI-5

The two statements below are exactly equivalent:

```
fprintf(stdout,"%d\n",num);    and    printf("%d\n",num);
```

It is also possible to send output to *stderr*, the other output stream whose destination is the screen. An error message or diagnostic message is generally sent to *stderr*. Example VI-6 shows a call to *fprintf* which sends output to *stderr*.

EXAMPLE VI-6

This example rewrites Example VI-3 to direct the error message to *stderr* rather than to *stdout*:

```
FILE *infile;

infile = fopen("letter.dat","r");
if (infile == NULL) {
    fprintf(stderr,"error in opening file letter.dat\n");
    exit(1);
}
```

In this example, no matter where *stdout* goes, or where other output is directed, *stderr* sends its output to the screen to alert the programmer to the error.

IN DEPTH

Although we do not show how, it is possible to redirect *stderr*. In a commercial program, *stderr* might be redirected to send output to a journal, a log, or the operating system, instead of to the screen. This can protect the end user from getting incomprehensible error messages.

SENDING OUTPUT TO A FILE

A call to *fprintf* can specify a file rather than a standard I/O stream. In this case, the first parameter in the function call must be a file pointer, as shown in Example VI-7.

EXAMPLE VI-7

```
FILE *fileout;

fileout = fopen("pa6.out","w");
fprintf(fileout,"%d\n",num);
```

INPUT USING *fscanf*

While the *scanf* function reads input only from *stdin*, the keyboard, the corresponding function *fscanf* allows a program to receive input from either the keyboard or a file.

A call to *fscanf* looks exactly like a call to *scanf*, except that the programmer must specify, as the first parameter, the source of the input. This source can be *stdin* or it can be a file.

General Form of a Call to *fscanf*

```
fscanf(sourcefile,"format string",list of variables);
```

In this call, *sourcefile* is *stdin* or a pointer to a file which has already been opened. The format string and list of variables are the same as those in a call to *scanf*. Like *scanf*, *fscanf* returns *EOF* if it attempts to read at end-of-file; otherwise it returns the number of items read in and successfully converted.

RECEIVING INPUT FROM *stdin*

When the source file for a call to *fscanf* is *stdin*, the call means exactly the same thing as a call to *scanf*. Example VI-8 compares a call to *fscanf* with a call to *scanf*.

EXAMPLE VI-8   The two statements below are exactly equivalent:

```
fscanf(stdin,"%d",&num);        and        scanf("%d",&num);
```

RECEIVING INPUT FROM A FILE

A call to *fscanf* can specify a file rather than a standard I/O stream. In this case, the first parameter in the call must be a file pointer, as shown in Example VI-9.

EXAMPLE VI-9
```
FILE *filein;
int  num;

filein = fopen("p6in.dat","r");
fscanf(filein,"%d",&num);
```

ERROR CHECKING

It is customary to check the results of *fscanf*, just as we check the results of *scanf*. Example VI-10 checks the result of *fopen* as well as the result of *fscanf*.

EXAMPLE VI-10   Here is a section of code which opens file *p6in.dat* for input, reads in a series of numbers until end-of-file, and displays each number on the monitor.

```
FILE *filein;
int  num;

filein = fopen("p6in.dat","r");
if (filein == NULL) {
    fprintf(stderr,"error in opening file p6in.dat\n");
    exit(1);
}
while (fscanf(filein,"%d",&num) > 0)
    fprintf(stdout,"%d\n",num);
fclose(filein);
```

If the file does not exist, the program section prints an error message to ***stderr*** and terminates with a non-zero exit code, indicating error. If the file exists, the program reads numbers from the file. Each time it reads a number, ***fscanf*** returns 1, as well as storing the value in ***num***. The call to ***fprintf*** inside the ***while*** loop prints the number. If there are no numbers in the file, or if it has read the last number, ***fscanf*** returns ***EOF***, which causes the loop to terminate. At that point, the program closes the file.

READING IN FILE NAMES

Writing the names of specific files directly in the program (hard-coding the names of the files) is sometimes very limiting. A program should be able to read from many different files or write to several different destinations. If the file name is hard-coded, changing it means physically changing the program code, recompiling the program, and then rerunning it. As we have said throughout the book, a programmer does not want to change a working program.

There are several solutions to this problem. One solution is to read in file names, as shown in Example VI-11.

EXAMPLE VI-11

```
FILE *fin, *fout;
char infile[30],outfile[30];

fprintf(stdout,"Enter the name of the input file\n");
fscanf(stdin,"%s",infile);
fprintf(stdout,"Enter the name of the output file\n");
fscanf(stdin,"%s",outfile);

fin = fopen(infile,"r");
fout = fopen(outfile,"w");
```

The program prompts the user to enter the file names, and then reads them into ***infile*** and ***outfile***. The file names entered are strings, suitable to be used as parameters to the ***fopen*** function.[4] (Don't type quotation marks as part of the file name.)

The method shown above is the only way of entering file names in many computer languages. C, however, has an even better method of supplying file names.

COMMAND-LINE PARAMETERS

C allows passing values to a program from the command line. (Appendix V explains how to run a program from the command line.) The values are called **command-line parameters**. All command-line parameters are strings; how they are interpreted is dependent on how they are used in the program. One common use of command-line parameters is to specify the files on which a program should operate. Example VI-12 shows how to run a program that uses command-line parameters.

---

[4]In DOS, any backslash used in a file name (even when entered as data) must still be preceded by the escape character (\): for example, "c:\\hw\\p6in.dat".

EXAMPLE VI-12 Each line below runs a program and sends it one or more parameters. In each case, the first word on the line is the name of the executable file (the program): everything else on the line is a parameter to the program.

DOS and Windows: (when running from the command line)

```
add 2 6
classify December 31
modify a:letter.dat c:changes.txt a:revision.txt
```

Unix: (The last two examples assume **a.out** has been renamed.)

```
a.out 4
classify June 6
replace letter.dat changes revision
```

Some of these command-line parameters will be used as numbers, some as strings, and some as file names.

 CAUTION No blanks are permitted within a single parameter; a blank indicates that the parameter has ended and another has started.

FOR TURBO C USERS

In Turbo C, a program that uses command-line parameters must be run in one of two ways.

◆ One way is to run it from the command line, as explained at the end of Appendix V. In this case, command-line parameters are supplied as shown in Example VI-12.

◆ A second way is to run the program from within the integrated environment, supplying command-line parameters by using the pull-down menus. Pull down the Run menu (ALT-R), and select *A*; this opens a window containing a dialog box labeled *Arguments*. Type the command-line arguments in this box, just as they appear in Example VI-12 (but omit the name of the program), and press ENTER. Then run the program as usual.

FOR USERS OF TURBO C++ FOR WINDOWS

In Turbo C++ for Windows, running from the command line is done through Program Manager. First, compile and link the program, without running it, by clicking on the icon immediately to the left of the Run icon. In Program Manager, choose File|Run. A Run window will open with an input box labeled *Command Line*. In this box, type the name of the file, followed by the command-line parameters, and then click on OK.

INCLUDING COMMAND-LINE PARAMETERS IN THE MAIN FUNCTION HEADER

It is necessary to change the main function header to indicate that the main program receives command-line parameters. We finally get a use for those parentheses we've been typing after the word **main**. Here is an example:

```
main (int argc, char *argv[])                        /* main program header */
```

Although it may seem strange to use empty brackets for an array (*argv[]*) in the main program, this is legal because, technically, the main program is a function, called by the operating system. The main program header now looks like a typical function header, but without the return value.

argc AND *argv*

The variables *argc* and *argv*, which are parameters to *main*, get their values from the command line when the program is run. Since the variables get their values at the very beginning of execution, they can be used anywhere in the program. One important difference between these parameters and ordinary parameters to functions is that command-line parameters do not get their values by a simple match-up of actual and formal parameters.

The first variable, *argc*, is given an integer value representing the number of items on the command line, *including* the name by which the program was invoked. In Example VI-12, the value of *argc* is 3 for *add*, 3 for *classify*, 4 for *modify*, 2 for *a.out*, and 4 for *replace*.

The second variable, *argv*, is an array of character strings. One element of the array is filled for each of the items on the command line. Thus if there are three items on the command line, *argc* has the value 3, and *argv[0]*, *argv[1]*, and *argv[2]* have values. In every case, *argv[0]* contains the name of the program. Each successive element in *argv* contains the next item on the command line.

A program can have any number of command-line parameters. Because *argv* is an array, the same header is used regardless of how many command-line parameters are sent to the program. If the user enters more parameters than the program uses, the extra parameters are ignored. However, in most cases, too few parameters cause an error.

The variable names *argc* and *argv* stand for *argument-count* and *argument-variables*. In your programs, you can use whatever names you like for these variables.

EXAMPLE VI-13A (DOS and Windows)

Suppose the following line is typed at the command prompt to run a program called *find*:

```
find Smith Johnson letter.txt
```

When the program starts to execute, the command-line parameters have the following values:

argc	*has the value*	4
argv[0]	*has the value*	"find"
argv[1]	*has the value*	"Smith"
argv[2]	*has the value*	"Johnson"
argv[3]	*has the value*	"letter.txt"

The same values will be placed in *argc* and *argv* if the parameters are entered from the Run menu (Turbo C) or if the program is run from Program Manager (Turbo C++ for Windows).

EXAMPLE VI-13B (Unix)

Suppose the following line is typed in Unix at the command prompt to run a program called *a.out*:

```
a.out Smith Johnson letter
```

When the program starts to execute, the command-line parameters have the following values:

argc	*has the value*	4
argv[0]	*has the value*	"a.out"
argv[1]	*has the value*	"Smith"
argv[2]	*has the value*	"Johnson"
argv[3]	*has the value*	"letter"

USING *argc*

It is important to make sure that the user has entered the correct number of values on the command line. Checking the value of *argc* lets you tell whether the parameters are all there and the program can proceed, or whether some parameters are missing and the program should stop.

Example VI-14 shows a program *gettwo* that checks to see whether it has received the correct number of parameters.

EXAMPLE VI-14 The program tests *argc* to make sure that the correct number of parameters has been received. It terminates if the number is too small; however, extra parameters are simply ignored.

```
/*
 * gettwo accepts two command-line parameters, and
 * terminates if there are fewer than two
 */
#include <stdio.h>
#include <stdlib.h>
main(int argc,char *argv[])
{
    ...

    if (argc < 3) {
        fprintf(stderr,"missing one or more parameters\n");
        fprintf(stderr,"correct format is: ");
        fprintf(stderr,"pgmname value1 value2\n");
        exit(1);
    }

    continue processing
}
```

The program checks for three parameters since the name of the program is counted as one of the parameters.

A programmer may want to allow a variable number of command-line parameters. In this case, the program can use *argc* to control a loop, as shown in Example VI-15.

EXAMPLE VI-15 This program simply prints each of a variable number of command-line parameters.

```
/*
 * uses a loop to print a variable number of command-line parameters
 */
```

```
#include <stdio.h>
main(int argc,char *argv[])
{
    int i=1;

    while (i < argc) {
        printf("%s\n",argv[i]);
        i++;
    }
}
```

The counter *i* starts at 1 because *argv[0]* is the name of the program; in the special case where *argc* is 1, there are no other parameters, and the loop is not entered.

Example VI-16 shows how to use a string entered as a command-line parameter.

EXAMPLE VI-16

Below is a program called **guess.c**, which asks the user to guess a word by entering it as a command-line parameter—for example, **guess banana**. The program checks to see whether the word entered as a command-line parameter matches the secret word in the program.

```
/*
 * lets user guess the secret word as a command-line parameter
 */
#include <stdio.h>
#include <string.h>
#include <stdlib.h>
main(int argc,char *argv[])
{
    char name[20] = "apple";

    if (argc < 2)
        exit(1);

    if (strcmp(name,argv[1]) == 0)
        printf("your guess—%s—matches the secret word\n",argv[1]);
    else
        printf("your guess—%s—isn't a match\n",argv[1]);
}
```

Suppose the program is executed twice by typing the following:

DOS and Windows:	Unix:
guess orange	a.out orange
guess apple	a.out apple

The first run causes the program to print the following:

```
your guess--orange--isn't a match
```

The second run causes the program to print the following:

```
your guess--apple--matches the secret word
```

CONVERTING NUMBERS ENTERED ON THE COMMAND LINE

The values of *argv* are always strings, even if the value entered on the command-line is something like 4 or 17. If the program expects numbers as data, it has to convert the command-line strings to numbers.

EXAMPLE VI-17A

Suppose we write a program, *trytosum*, which receives any number of command-line parameters and sums them, displaying the result on the screen. The program can be invoked by typing the following:

DOS and Windows: *Unix:*
trytosum 16 25   a.out 16 25

For these parameters, we want the program to display 41.

The following version does *not* work because the values typed on the command line are strings, not integers.

```
/*
 * trytosum accepts a variable number of numbers as command-line parameters,
 * tries to sum them and display the result
 */
#include <stdio.h>
#include <stdlib.h>
main(int argc,char *argv[])
{
    int result=0,i=1;

    while (i < argc) {
        result += argv[i];                          /* incorrect */
        i++;
    }
    printf("%d\n",result);
}
```

The attempt to add *argv[i]* to *result* causes a compilation error.

THE *atoi* FUNCTION

The *atoi* function can be used to convert command-line parameters from strings to integers. (The function name, pronounced *a to i*, means "convert ascii to integer"). The *atoi* function receives one parameter, which is a string, and returns the corresponding integer value.

General Form of a Call to *atoi*

```
intval = atoi(strval);
```

The parameter *strval* is a string, while *intval* is an integer. If possible, the *atoi* function converts the string to the corresponding integer value and returns that integer value. The function *atoi* can successfully convert strings like "–9845" or " 123" or "476", but it converts "4.5" to 4, since any non-digit following a string of digits stops the conversion process. In the case of strings like "abc" or "c3po", which *atoi* cannot convert to an integer, it returns 0.

The function *atoi* is defined in *stdlib.h*; this header file should be included in any program that uses *atoi*. Actually, the *atoi* function can be used to convert any string, not just a command-line parameter, to an integer.[5]

Example VI-17B revises the *trytosum* program from Example VI-17A, using *atoi* to make it work correctly.

EXAMPLE VI-17B Program *sum* uses *atoi* to convert the command-line parameters.

```
/*
 * sum accepts a variable number of numbers as command-line parameters,
 * sums them and displays the result
 */
#include <stdio.h>
#include <stdlib.h>
main(int argc,char *argv[])
{
    int result=0,i=1;

    while (i < argc) {
        result += atoi(argv[i]);                        /* correct */
        i++;
    }
    printf("%d\n",result);
}
```

The first time *atoi* is called, it receives the string "16" as a parameter and returns 16; the second time *atoi* is called, it receives the string "25" as a parameter and returns 25. The main program adds each of the returned values to *result*, producing 41.

FILE NAMES AS COMMAND-LINE PARAMETERS; ERROR CHECKING

As we have shown in Examples VI-12 and VI-13, you can specify a file name as a command-line parameter. The file name can match DOS or Unix file-naming conventions (with \\ for \ in DOS). You do not put quotation marks around the name, but simply type it following the name of the program.

Example VI-18 shows a program *testfile* that receives two file names as parameters.

EXAMPLE VI-18 To run *testfile*, type one of the following on the command line.

> *DOS and Windows:* `testfile intest outtest`
> *Unix:*   `a.out intest outtest`

---

[5]Other functions—*atof* and *atol*—permit conversion from ASCII to *double* and *long*, respectively.

```
/*
 * testfile accepts two file names as command-line parameters,
 * terminates if there are fewer than two; otherwise, opens the files
 */
#include <stdio.h>
#include <stdio.h>
main(int argc,char *argv[])
{
      FILE *infile,*outfile;

      if (argc < 3) {
          fprintf(stderr,"missing one or more parameters\n");
          fprintf(stderr,"correct format is: ");
          fprintf(stderr,"pgmname infile outfile\n");
          exit(1);
      }
      infile = fopen(argv[1],"r");
      outfile = fopen(argv[2],"w");
      ...
}
```

If two file names are entered on the command line, this program opens the files specified and continues execution. However, if any file name is missing, the program terminates with an error message.

Using the values shown on the command line just above, **infile** is "intest" and **outfile** is "outtest".

The name of an I/O stream (**stdout**, **stdin**, or **stderr**) can be sent as a command-line parameter, but you must be careful how you use a stream specified in this manner. If you attempt to open a file called *stdout*, C opens a disk file with that name, rather than opening the output stream. Example VI-19A shows one way to handle a stream specified as a command-line parameter.

EXAMPLE VI-19A The program **testream** can receive file names or streams as command-line parameters. It can be run by typing one of the following (or a combination) on the command line:

DOS and Windows:	Unix:
testream intest outtest	a.out intest outtest
testream stdin stdout	a.out stdin stdout

Given these command-line parameters, **argv[1]** is either "intest" or "stdin", while **argv[2]** is either "outtest" or "stdout". The string "stdin" is not the same as the constant **stdin**, meaning the input stream, nor is "stdout" the same as **stdout**, and the program must allow for this.

```
/* testream checks whether command-line parameters are files or streams */
#include <stdio.h>
#include <string.h>
#include <stdlib.h>
main(int argc,char *argv[])
{
```

```
        FILE *infile,*outfile;

        if (argc < 3) {
            fprintf(stderr,"missing one or more parameters\n");
            ...
            exit(1);
        }
        if (strcmp(argv[1],"stdin") != 0)
            infile = fopen(argv[1],"r");
        else
            infile = stdin;

        if (strcmp(argv[2],"stdout") != 0)
            outfile = fopen(argv[2],"w");
        else
            outfile = stdout;
        ...
    }
```

The program checks each of the command-line parameters. If any one is the name of a standard I/O stream, the program does not attempt to use the command-line string directly (which would open a disk file called *stdin* or *stdout*); instead it uses the stream **stdin** or **stdout**, as specified.

A UNIX CONVENTION

By convention in Unix, when it is necessary to specify **stdin** or **stdout** as a command-line parameter, a single hyphen is used instead. This convention frees the programmer to use *stdin* or *stdout* as a file name. Using this convention, the program from Example VI-19A can be modified as shown in Example VI-19B.

EXAMPLE VI-19B To specify that the program reads from **stdin** and writes to **stdout**, a Unix programmer types

```
        a.out - -
```

The heart of the code can change to the following:

```
        infile = strcmp(argv[1],"-") ? fopen(argv[1],"r") : stdin;
        outfile = strcmp(argv[2],"-") ? fopen(argv[2],"w") : stdout;
```

This code is particularly idiomatic. The result of the **strcmp** function is used with the conditional operator. If **strcmp** returns 0 (meaning the strings are equal), the condition is false, and **stdin** is assigned to **infile**. If **strcmp** returns anything but 0 (meaning the strings are not equal), the condition is true, the file named in the command-line parameter is opened, and a pointer to that file is assigned to **infile**.

COMBINING COMMAND-LINE PARAMETERS WITH REDIRECTION

Command-line parameters go on the command line following the name of the program, but so do redirection and piping symbols. They can be used together as shown in Example VI-20.

EXAMPLE VI-20   To run a program *test* using one command-line parameter (the string "param") plus redirection of both input and output, we can put the command line parameters and the redirection information in any order; here are a few samples:

DOS:	Unix:
`test param < infile > outfile`	`a.out param < infile > outfile`
`test < infile > outfile param`	`a.out < infile > outfile param`
`test < infile param > outfile`	`a.out < infile param > outfile`
`test > outfile < infile param`	`a.out > outfile < infile param`

Since sending output to the printer in DOS is done through redirection, *prn* can be substituted for *outfile* in any of the cases in Example VI-20. However, in Unix, where output is piped to the printer, **|** *lpr* must be the last item on the command line; for example,

```
a.out < infile param | lpr
```

FILE I/O FUNCTIONS FOR STRINGS AND CHARACTERS— *fgets, fputs, fgetc, fputc*

This appendix assumes that you have read Chapter 9.

PROBLEMS WITH *gets*

As we mentioned in Chapter 9, Section 3, the *gets* function doesn't check to see whether there is room in the input area for the string which is being read in. Therefore, even a successful call to *gets* may overwrite and destroy other variables in the program. Example 9-26 shows how this can happen.

STRING INPUT FROM A FILE: *fgets*

The *fgets* function eliminates the problem of overwriting. It reads characters from a file, up to the maximum number of characters, which is specified as a parameter. This function requires specifying the source of its input. As a special case, *stdin* may be that source.

General Form of a Call to *fgets*

```
strptr = fgets(inputarea,n,source);
```

The *fgets* function takes three parameters and returns a value of type *char **, a pointer to the value read in; in this case, that value is assigned to *strptr*. The parameter *inputarea* is the name of the character array which is to get the data; *n* is an integer representing the size of the input field, which is one more than the maximum number of characters to be read in; *source* identifies the file from which to read. It can be *stdin* or a pointer to a file. If it is a pointer to a file, the file should already be open.

The *fgets* function continues to read from *source* until it has read *n-1* characters or a newline character, whichever comes first. If it reads a newline character, it retains the newline character as part of the string and appends a null character. If it does not read a newline character, it appends a null character to the end of what it reads in. If successful, it returns a pointer to the string read in; otherwise it returns *NULL*.

CAUTION The programmer is responsible for sending the correct value for the second parameter to *fgets*. If the value is *n*, the *fgets* function reads up to *n-1* characters; if the value of *n* is too large, the *fgets* function can read in too many characters and cause the same kind of problem as *gets*.

Example VII-1 shows how to read a line of data from *stdin* using *fgets*.

EXAMPLE VII-1

```
char inarea[15];
char *instring;

instring = fgets(inarea,15,stdin);
if (instring != NULL)
       . . .
```

If the call to *fgets* is successful, *inarea* contains the string read in (but no more than 14 characters), and *instring* points to it. The *if* statement checks the return value of *fgets* to see if the call was successful.

STYLE WORKSHOP   After the data value has been read into the string, the programmer can process the string by referring to the array name (*inarea*, in Example VII-1) or the pointer name (*instring*). Although the two names are interchangeable after the call to *fgets*, it is common to use the pointer name with pointer notation, and the array name with subscript notation.

READING STRING DATA FROM A FILE

To read data from a file, the call to *fgets* must specify a file pointer as its third parameter. Example VII-2 shows how this is done.

EXAMPLE VII-2

```
#define MAX 15

char inarea[MAX];
char *instring;
FILE *filein;

filein = fopen("a7in.dat","r");
if (filein != NULL) {
     instring = fgets(inarea,MAX,filein);
     if (instring != NULL)
           . . .
}
```

In this example, there are two kinds of pointers. The variable *filein* is a file pointer, pointing to the input file. Each call to *fgets* read up to *MAX-1* or 14 characters from *filein*, which means it reads from file *a7in.dat*. The variable *instring* is a pointer to *char*; it points to *inarea*, the area which holds the string value.

THE FUNCTION *fgets* AND THE NEWLINE CHARACTER

Let's look at the value stored as a result of the calls to *fgets* in Examples VII-1 and VII-2. (The difference between the two examples is simply the source of the data.)

If the line of data consists of "here we are" (ENTER), *inarea* gets the value shown in Figure VII-1A. Notice that the newline character is stored in position 11 of *inarea*, followed by the null character in position 12. In contrast, if the line of data consists of "here we are a-wandering" (ENTER), *inarea* gets the value shown in Figure VII-1B.

In Figure VII-1B, the newline character is not stored in the string, since it comes after *fgets* has already read in 14 characters. The *fgets* function simply appends the null character to what it has read in.

CAUTION Those extra characters that go past the length of *inarea* (the characters "wandering") are stored in the input buffer. They are read the next time any function uses the same source of input. Because of this, make sure that the line of data is shorter than the variable into which it is being read.

STRING OUTPUT TO A FILE: THE *fputs* FUNCTION

There is also a string output function, *fputs*, designed to print a string.

General Form of a Call to *fputs*

```
fputs(string,destfile);
```

The *fputs* function takes two parameters: a pointer to a string, and the destination of the output: either an output stream (*stdout* or *stderr*) or a pointer to a file. The *fputs* function sends the string to the output destination. If the destination is a pointer to a file, the file should already be open. Unlike *puts*, *fputs* does not automatically write a new line to the file after displaying a string; it writes a new line only if the output string contains a newline character.

Example VII-3A shows a loop that reads in lines of data from *stdin* using *fgets* and then displays them using *fputs*.

FIGURE VII-1 *A, **inarea**, filled by **fgets** from data "here we are"; B, **inarea**, filled by **fgets** from data "here we are a-wandering".*

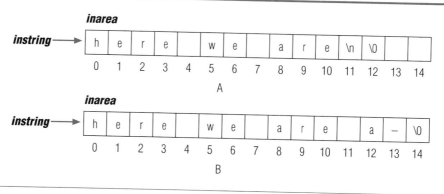

EXAMPLE VII-3A

```
char inarea[80];
char *instring;

instring = fgets(inarea,80,stdin);
while (instring != NULL) {
     fputs(instring,stdout);
     instring = fgets(inarea,80,stdin);
}
```

Each string read in from **stdin** is sent to **stdout**.

Example VII-3B modifies Example VII-3A, incorporating the input statement in the header of the **while** loop. This header uses side effects (see Chapter 12, Section 4).

EXAMPLE VII-3B

```
char inarea[80];
char *instring;

while ((instring = fgets(inarea,80,stdin)) != NULL)
     fputs(instring,stdout);
```

The two calls to **fgets** are combined into one in the header of the loop. This loop header reads a value into **inarea** and sets **instring** to point to it. As a side effect, the value of the assignment statement is the value returned by **fgets**; this value is compared with **NULL** to control the loop.

USING **fputs** TO WRITE TO A FILE

The **fputs** function allows a program to write to one or more files. Example VII-4 reads input from a file and writes output to three different files, depending on the first letter of each input line.

EXAMPLE VII-4

```
char buffer[80];
char *instring;
FILE *filein,*filea,*fileb;

filein = fopen("instuff","r");
filea = fopen("outone","w");
fileb = fopen("outtwo","w");
while ((instring = fgets(buffer,80,filein)) != NULL)
     if (*instring == 'a')
          fputs(instring,filea);
     else if (*instring == 'b')
               fputs(instring,fileb);
          else
               fputs(instring,stdout);
```

Suppose file ***instuff*** contains the following:

a Twinkle, twinkle, little star
b Mary had a little lamb
b Its fleece was white as snow
c Freres Jacques, freres Jacques
a How I wonder what you are
a Up above the roof so high
b And everywhere that Mary went
c Dormez vous, dormez vous
b The lamb was sure to go
c Sonnez les matines, sonnez les matines
a Like a diamond in the sky
c Ding dang dong, ding dang dong

Then the output from this program would be the following:

file *outone*

```
a Twinkle, twinkle, little star
a How I wonder what you are
a Up above the roof so high
a Like a diamond in the sky
```

file *outtwo*

```
b Mary had a little lamb
b Its fleece was white as snow
b And everywhere that Mary went
b The lamb was sure to go
```

stdout (the screen)

```
c Freres Jacques, freres Jacques
c Dormez vous, dormez vous
c Sonnez les matines, sonnez les matines
c Ding dang dong, ding dang dong
```

ELIMINATING THE NEWLINE CHARACTER READ BY *fgets*

There is another difference between ***fgets*** and ***gets***. Either one may read in a newline character as the last character of the input (***gets*** always does; ***fgets*** does if the input string is short enough). However, ***gets*** replaces the newline character at the end of the string with the null character; if ***fgets*** reads a newline character, it keeps the newline character and appends a null character.

To see the difference, compare the strings shown in figures VII-2A and VII-2B. These two strings are different in position 11. The value read in by ***gets*** will be equal to "here we are", while the value read in by ***fgets*** will not.

A program must explicitly strip the newline character from a string read in by ***fgets*** before processing the string (for example, before doing a string comparison).

THE FUNCTION *getstring*

To make ***fgets*** more useful, we can write a function ***getstring*** that acts as an intermediary between ***fgets*** and the calling program. It calls ***fgets***, strips the newline character from the string read in, and returns the modified string. Example VII-5 shows the function ***getstring***.

FIGURE VII-2   *A,* ***str1****,* as read in by ***gets****; B,* ***str1****,* as read in by ***fgets****.*

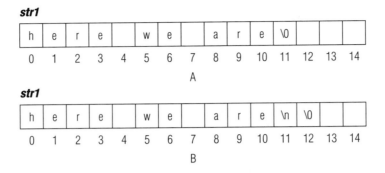

EXAMPLE VII-5 The **getstring** function receives the same three parameters as **fgets**: **buffer**, **num**, and **infile**. First it calls **fgets** to read a string of **num-1** characters into **buffer** from file **infile**. If there is a newline character in the string, **getstring** replaces it with the null character. It returns a pointer to the modified string, or **NULL** if there is no string in the input.

```
/*
 * getstring reads a string using fgets; strips off any newline character
 *    returns a pointer to the string buffer; if no string, returns NULL
 */
char *getstring(char *buffer,int num,FILE *infile)
{
    char *outstr;
    int  len;

    outstr = fgets(buffer,num,infile);
    if (outstr != NULL) {
        len = strlen(outstr);
        if (outstr[len-1] == '\n')
            outstr[len-1] = '\0';
    }
    return outstr;
}
```

If **fgets** successfully reads in a string (**outstr** does not equal **NULL**), **getstring** calls **strlen**, which returns the number of characters in the string, excluding the null character. If the string is "jump\n\0", **strlen** returns 5. The value assigned to **len** is thus the position of the null character. Any newline character must be in the position before **len**, or **len-1**, and **getstring** replaces it with the null character.

A CALL TO *getstring*

The call to **getstring** looks like a call to **fgets**. We send three parameters: a string array to fill, the maximum number of characters to read in, and the pointer to the file from which to read. Here is a call to **getstring**:

```
char inarea[15];
char *instring;
FILE *filein;

filein = fopen("file1","r");
instring = getstring(inarea,15,filein);
```

If the program goes on to print the string read in by ***getstring***, it must explicitly print a newline character, since ***getstring*** stripped off the one read in by ***fgets***.

FILE I/O FOR CHARACTERS: *fgetc* AND *fputc*

The file I/O functions equivalent to ***getchar*** and ***putchar*** are ***fgetc*** and ***fputc***.

General Form of a Call to *fgetc*

```
ch = fgetc(source);
```

The ***fgetc*** function reads a character from ***source***, which is ***stdin*** or a pointer to a file. If ***source*** is a pointer to a file, the file should already be open. The function returns the character read in, converted to ***int***. On end-of-file, ***fgetc*** returns ***EOF***.

General Form of a Call to *fputc*

```
fputc(ch,destfile);
```

The ***fputc*** function takes two parameters: a character, and the destination of the output: either an output stream (***stdout*** or ***stderr***) or a pointer to a file. The ***fputc*** function sends the character to the output destination. If the destination is a pointer to a file, the file should already be open.

Example VII-6 illustrates using ***fgetc*** and ***fputc*** to read characters from ***stdin*** and write them to a file. When entering data interactively, the end of input for ***fgetc*** is signaled by pressing CTRL-Z in DOS or CTRL-D in Unix.

EXAMPLE VII-6

```
int  ch;
FILE *fp;

fp = fopen("a7.out","w");
ch = fgetc(stdin);
while (ch != EOF) {
     fputc(ch,fp);
     ch = fgetc(stdin);
}
fclose(fp);
```

Here is another way of writing this loop, using side effects (see Chapter 12, Section 4):

```
while ((ch = fgetc(stdin)) != EOF)
     fputc(ch,fp);
```

SELF-CHECK ANSWERS

SELF-CHECK 0-1

1. a program
2. high-level languages—C, Fortran, and Pascal; natural languages—Chinese, English, French, Russian, and Spanish
3. C—in commercial and scientific applications, and in education

SELF-CHECK 0-2

1. CPU (central processing unit) and the main memory
2. input—keyboard, mouse, scanner, and microphone; output—monitor (or screen), printer, plotter, and speakers
3. megabyte, approximately one million bytes

SELF-CHECK 0-3

1. braces ({ and })
2. line 5, the *printf*
3. prints "Welcome to computer programming!" on the screen

SELF-CHECK 1-1

1. an intermediate step in translating a problem description to a computer program; a mixture of English and C
2. often too difficult to translate a problem statement directly into C; pseudocode simplifies this process
3. a precise method of solving a problem which can be expressed in pseudocode and then a program

SELF-CHECK 1-2

1. to explain the program to a person reading it; begins with /*, ends with */
2. `#include <stdio.h>`
3. `#include <stdio.h>` *and* `main()`

SELF-CHECK 1-3

1. a physical location within the computer which holds a value used in a program
2. *number* is shorter and easier to type than *numbersfrom4to9*, more mnemonic than *n*
3. a data type

734

SELF-CHECK 1-4

1. one value, which can change; old value is replaced by the new
2. to print output
3. screen (default) and printer

SELF-CHECK 1-5

1. the closing brace (})
2. no
3. the two values would print next to each other, with no space

SELF-CHECK 1-6

1. adding some number (usually 1) to its value; $x = x + 1$
2. + for addition, * for multiplication
3. a loop

SELF-CHECK 1-7

1. three; the first is normally initialization; the second is a test to determine whether to continue the loop; the third is normally an increment
2. one; a pair of braces is used to combine several statements into a single compound statement
3. empty; the *printf* follows the *for* loop; indenting is ignored

SELF-CHECK 1-8

1. *vi*; Turbo C has a built-in editor
2. the line does not end in a semicolon
3. compiling means translating into machine language; running means having the computer follow the instructions of the program

SELF-CHECK 1-9

1. problem statement, analysis, write pseudocode, write program, compile program (and correct errors), run and test program (and correct errors), submit program (and correct errors)
2. the first four steps
3. the remaining steps, starting from compiling the program

SELF-CHECK 1-10

1.
   a. 2
   b. 1
   c. 0
   d. 1
   e. 1.5
   f. 1.99

2.
   a. 0
   b. 2
   c. 5
   d. 99
   e. 0
   f. 1

SELF-CHECK 1-11

1. must start with a letter (lowercase, uppercase, or the underbar); the remaining symbols must be letters or digits (0–9); some compilers may have additional length restrictions
2. keyword—has a special meaning in C and cannot be used for any other purpose (e.g., *for* or *int*); standard identifier—has a special meaning, but a programmer is allowed to override it (e.g., *printf*); a programmer-defined identifier—a name given an explicit declaration in a program (e.g., *number* or *sqnumber*)
3. lowercase

SELF-CHECK 1-12

1. decreased by some value
2. any number in the initialization or update portion; only one expression in the test portion

3. *i++* and *++i* both increment the value of *i* by 1; *i--* decrements the value of *i* by 1 (*i* = *i* − *1*)

SELF-CHECK 2-1

1. yes, but that would be misleading
2. *gpa++* adds 1 to the value of *gpa*, but we want to add 0.5

3. 2.500000   −4.76000

SELF-CHECK 2-2

1. first prints 3, the value of a variable named **help**; second prints the word "help"
2. to choose one of two alternatives

3. missing parentheses around the *if* condition *x* < 7

SELF-CHECK 2-3

1. order in which C executes operations within an expression
2. C follows the rules for associativity; in most cases, left to right; a few (e.g., ++) go right to left

3. parentheses

SELF-CHECK 2-4

1. a. subtractions inside parentheses first, then addition; −5
   b. plus inside parentheses first, then *, then −; −46

2. (c) and (d) are correct, but (d) has extraneous parentheses, so (c) is preferred

SELF-CHECK 2-5

1. comment is part of the program listing, seen by those who look at the program; heading is part of the output, seen by those who look at the output

2. output is usually neater if things align under column headings
3. include \n as the first item within the **printf** control string

SELF-CHECK 2-6

1. combination of two or more symbols starting with \ used to represent a special character

2. \
3. %

SELF-CHECK 2-7

1. a. >   b. !=   c. <   d. >=
2. condition is *x* = *4*, but it should be *x* == *4*

3. a. `sum += num;`   d. `numleft -= 1;`
   b. `count += 1;`   e. cannot be done
   c. `result %= 4;`   f. `result *= 2;`

SELF-CHECK 2-8

1. *float* and *double*; *double* is used in the text
2. 2.5475×10^2 25.475×10^1 2547.5×10^{-1}
3. 2.547500e+02, 254.750000

SELF-CHECK 2-9

1. computes the square root of whatever value is sent to it
2. allows a program to use the standard library functions whose headers are in *math.h*
3.
   a. *double*   c. *double*
   b. *char*   d. *int*

SELF-CHECK 2-10

1. compilation error is an error caught by the compiler as it is translating into machine language—misspelled keyword, missing semicolon, undeclared variable
2. execution error is caught as the program is running—attempt to divide by a variable whose value is 0
3. an error in a program; process of finding and removing bugs

SELF-CHECK 3-1

1. makes it easier to see which statements are in the body of a loop
2. information supplied to a program during execution; can be used by the program to compute results
3. repeat …

SELF-CHECK 3-2

1. a. true   b. false
2. a. body of loop is never executed
   b. body of loop is executed "forever" (infinite loop)
3. signals the set of data values is complete

SELF-CHECK 3-3

1. to read in data
2. a. missing an ampersand (&) before the variable name
   b. format specification should be *%lf* rather than *%f*
3. more flexibility—as the data values change, the results computed by the program can also change; not necessary to change the instructions in a program to compute different things; person typing in the data can decide at that time what values to enter, instead of having to make this decision in advance

SELF-CHECK 3-4

1. no
2. that value may be the trailer which signals the end of the set of data
3. at that point, we have processed 0 employees; if something has been done 10 times, it may make sense to start counting at 10

SELF-CHECK 3-5

1. to know what data value to enter next
2. no prompt appears—the person entering data has to remember what to do
3. a prompt appears, but there is no chance for a data value to be read in

SELF-CHECK 3-6

1. a. %4.1f   b. %7.2f   2. a. %6.3f   b. %8.6f

SELF-CHECK 3-7

1. *while* condition is initially false; body of the loop is never executed
2. it will be computed based on values of *hours* and *rate*

3. you might make a mistake in the changed portion or some other inadvertent change

SELF-CHECK 3-8

1. y = 8
2. semicolon immediately after the *if* condition, missing semicolon before *else*

```
if (x < y)
    z = x + 1;
else
    z = x + 2;
```

3. 18

SELF-CHECK 3-9

1. no, can be used as part of a larger expression
2. a. expression to be tested
   b. value of the conditional if expression is true
   c. value if the expression is false

3. a. 10   b. 0   c. 1

SELF-CHECK 4-1

1. serves as a starting point for stepwise-refinement; divide the tasks shown into simpler subtasks

2. 0 for a sum, 1 for a product

SELF-CHECK 4-2

1. can use any refinement (they all represent the same process)
2. last, which is the most precise and closest to C

3. square of an integer is an integer, as is the sum of two integers

SELF-CHECK 4-3

1. capital letters
2. associates a name with a specific value

3. change the value specified in the constant definition; the program has been changed, so it must be recompiled

SELF-CHECK 4-4

1. gives a program additional flexibility over using a constant; no

2. no
3. run the program again, then type in the new data value

SELF-CHECK 4-5

1. yes, but the program will not work in the intended way; no

2. the *m2 for* loop, plus the calls to *printf* surrounding it
3. `printf("%5d",m1 * m2)`

SELF-CHECK 4-6

1. 1, 2, 3, 4, 5
2. when *i* is 1, *j* has the values from 1 to 4; similarly, when *i* is 2, 3, 4, and 5, *j* has the values from 1 to 4
3. next iteration of the outer loop begins after the increment and test steps are performed; entire nested loop is complete

SELF-CHECK 4-7

1. general set of rules governing style of programming
2. spacing, blank lines, aligning and indenting, proper use of comments
3. statement of the problem, pseudocode, program listing, set of instructions describing how to use the program, and complete set of test cases with sample output

SELF-CHECK 5-1

1. statement which tells the computer to switch control to the function; information specified in the function call which will be used by the function
2. once; any number of times
3. separating the details of how to do something from its use, specifying the details just once but using them many times

SELF-CHECK 5-2

1. expression giving a value that is sent to the function; variable in the function that receives the value of the actual parameter
2. always returns to the point at which it was called
3. `ceil;   v;   z`

SELF-CHECK 5-3

1. `int`
2. `numb;   int`
3. variable *a*, variable *numb*, expression *a−1*, constant 4, variable *a*; in each case, data type *int*

SELF-CHECK 5-4

1. give the compiler information about the function before the function definition is seen
2. type of answer returned, name of the function, and, inside a set of parentheses, the data type of each formal parameter
3. prototype must end in a semicolon, while header does not; header must specify a name and a data type for each formal parameter, but the prototype can omit the name

SELF-CHECK 5-5

1. variable declared within a function; no
2. yes; can return only one value on a single call
3. because the value of *x* must be exactly one of the following: positive, negative, or zero

SELF-CHECK 5-6

1. yes; matched in order to the actual parameters
2. call to *f2*
3. 8

SELF-CHECK 5-7

1. either before or after the main program, or the function can be compiled in a separate file

2. prototype should occur before the function call
3. compiled in separate files

SELF-CHECK 5-8

1. issue a series of function calls covering all possible test cases

2. main program designed to test a function
3. no; must use a complete set of test data

SELF-CHECK 5-9

1. function which does not return a value
2. return type is *void*; *return* statement does not specify value to return (which can be omitted or simply *return*)

3. prototype starts with *void*

SELF-CHECK 5-10

1. `funcname(void)` *or* `funcname()`
2. `funcname()`

3. yes

SELF-CHECK 5-11

1. a. return the value of the largest
   b., c., d. void function
2. a. `int largest (int x,int y,int z)`
   b. `void printlargest(int x,int y,int z)`

   c. `void printdirections(void)`
   d. `void printname(void)`
3. yes, command-line parameters or arguments

SELF-CHECK 5-12

1. *I*—possible forms of input to a function, usually parameters or values read in by the function
2. *P*—process, the task performed by the function

3. *O*—possible forms of output from a function, usually printed on the screen or returned by the function

SELF-CHECK 5-13

1. doesn't need parameters to perform its task
2. it needs to know which row of the table to print

3. *printrow* doesn't return an answer; nothing can be stored in *z*

SELF-CHECK 5-14

1. a. 11
   b. 12 (including the newline character)
2. a. 1 if a value is read in and converted; 0 if a value is read in but it could not be converted to an

   integer; and *EOF* if no value is read in; we do not know what the input is
   b. 2 if two values are read in and converted to integers, plus any of those described in part (a)

SELF-CHECK 5-15

1. function can return only one value
2. first two are not pointers

3. `void settolarger(int *x, int *y)`

SELF-CHECK 6-1

1. classify the month value (***month***) into a season within the year and the day value (***day***) into a week within the month

2. classify ***month*** into a season; classify ***day*** into a week
3. simplifies the main program, making testing and debugging much easier

SELF-CHECK 6-2

1. it doesn't return an answer
2. include **\n\n** at the beginning of the control string

3. answer can be tested in a ***while*** or ***do-while*** condition

SELF-CHECK 6-3

1. at the bottom of the loop
2. only one statement (which can be a compound statement)

3. no, unless the body is a compound statement

SELF-CHECK 6-4

1. ***f1***—calling function, ***f2***—called function
2. returns to ***f2***

3. ||

SELF-CHECK 6-5

1. space a number of positions on the output line
2. &&

3. ***translate*** and ***whichseason***—value outside the range 1-12, ***whichweek***—value outside the range 1-31

SELF-CHECK 6-6

1. yes
2. a complete set, with both bad data and correct data

3. no, users make mistakes or misinterpret directions

SELF-CHECK 6-7

1. first one tested
2. four individual ***if*** statements, three conditions

3. Figure 6-5B

SELF-CHECK 6-8

1. no
2. the program falls through from one group to the next; for 2, even prime number, even nonprime, an odd prime, and an odd nonprime, then the message from

the default clause print; for 6, even nonprime, both messages about odd numbers, plus the default message; for 5, both messages about odd numbers and the default message; none is correct.
3. entire program halts

SELF-CHECK 6-9

1. at least one false; both true

2. both false; at least one true

SELF-CHECK 7-1

1. 4 is parameter value, specifying 4 data values will follow

2. no
3. `count <= n` *or* `count < n + 1`

SELF-CHECK 7-2

1. dividing by 0—an execution error.
2. n

3. value of ***count*** always matches the number of values read in

SELF-CHECK 7-3

1. group a series of related values together
2. a. array for sets, with each element holding number of games won in that set
   b. array for frames, with each element holding number of pins scored up to and including that frame

   c. no
   d. array for innings, with each element holding number of runs scored in that inning
3. a. 7   b. 12

SELF-CHECK 7-4

1. a. `double numbs[50];`
   b. `char str[26];`
2. a. 25
   b. lower bound 0 (as in every array), upper bound 24

3. can sometimes be treated as a single unit (called a string)

SELF-CHECK 7-5

1. a. `item[5]`
   b. `amount[25]`
      (beyond the array upper bound)

2. `for (i=0; i < 25; i++)`
   `    item[i] = i + 1;`
3. these arrays don't hold the same type of data

SELF-CHECK 7-6

1. a. all data values are available for later processing, modularity
   b. declaration for ***mark*** must change, each reference to ***mark*** must include a subscript

2. yes
3. a simple variable

SELF-CHECK 7-7

1. a. an average should with decimal places
   b. ***avgarray*** calls ***sumarray***
2. brackets after the data type (***int []***)

3. size will be determined from the size of the actual parameter
4. the function reads values into the elements, and the main program can access these values

SELF-CHECK 7-8

1. person may check the list and pick the largest haphazardly, but the computer uses a precise algorithm
2. −1 is largest value (even though it is not in the array)

3. smallest uses same algorithm as largest, substituting < for >; second largest uses two passes, first, finding largest, then finding largest of remaining values; ties use two passes first finding largest and then all equal values

SELF-CHECK 7-9

1. 0 data values are read in; ***avgarray*** divides by 0, causing an execution error
2. to make sure that all possible paths through the program are tested
3. easier to write a program in the first place (individual modules are simple), easier to debug, and easier to reuse pieces in later programs

SELF-CHECK 7-10

1. 25, 5
2. `double labdata[10][5];`
3. `labdata[0][1]`   `labdata[3][2]`

SELF-CHECK 7-11

1. number of columns
2. `double sales [5][12][3];`

SELF-CHECK 7-12

1. integer
2. by typing the end-of-file character ([CTRL]-[Z] in DOS or [CTRL]-[D] in Unix)
3. trailer value, user-response, header value, ***EOF***

SELF-CHECK 8-1

1. 0 or 1; 256 possible values; on a PC, two; on a Sun, four
2. addresses cannot be the same, but values can
3. first two incorrect because they attempt to store values of type ***double*** or ***int*** in a pointer; third incorrect because it stores the address of a variable of type ***double*** instead of type ***int***; fourth is correct (stores the address of an integer)

SELF-CHECK 8-2

1. a. %d   b. %u *or* %p   c. %d
2. address of ***a***
3. stores the value of ***a*** at the location whose address is stored in ***p***

SELF-CHECK 8-3

1. initially, 5, then changes to 6; actual parameter stays at 5
2. address of ***k*** which does not change; the value stored in ***k*** changes to 6
3. first call sends an integer rather than an address; second call uses the * operator on an integer rather than an address

SELF-CHECK 8-4

1.
```
double temp;

temp = d1;
d1 = d2;
d2 = temp;
```

2. next step must put the value of ***a*** into ***b***, otherwise the value of ***a*** is lost; final step must move the value stored in ***temp*** into ***a***
3. compiler will not recognize this as an error; it may generate an error during execution; it will definitely not read a value into the variable

SELF-CHECK 8-5

1. `void arraywork(double *values)`
2. `void twochars(char *s1, char *s2)`

3. `ans = sumarray(x+6,10);`

SELF-CHECK 8-6

1. *n* is a pointer which holds an address, so an ampersand is not necessary
2. only change needed is a change in the conditional from > to <; preferable to change the variable name
3. `*largest = 0;`
   `*smallest = 0;`

```
for (...) {
    if (*largest < num[count])
        *largest = num[count];
    if (*smallest < num[count])
        *smallest = num[count];
}
return;
```

SELF-CHECK 8-7

1. call to *printf* uses * to refer to the value at a specific address; call to *scanf* uses the address itself
2. first (*int *num*) uses pointer notation for the array *num*; the * before *largest* and *smallest* says these variables are pointers

3.
```
void readdata(int [], int);
int sumarray(int [], int);
double avgarray(int [], int);
void findlimits(int [], int *, int *);
void countmarks(int [], int, double, int
    *, int *, int *);
```

SELF-CHECK 9-1

1. a. number specified in the declaration inside *[]*
   b. current number of characters stored up to but not including the '\0'
   c. size includes room for '*\0*', but the length does not

2. to signal the end of the string
3.
```
char student[50] = {'j','a','c','k','
    ','l','u','m','\0'};
char student[50] = "julia prutchenko";
```

SELF-CHECK 9-2

1. name of the variable is already an address
2.
```
char str[10] =
    {'a','n','i','m','a','l','\0'};
char str[10] = "animal";
str[0] = 'a';
str[1] = 'n';         etc.
```

3. a. (1) "cityscape\0" (3) "thingamaji" (no '*\0*') (2) "New\0" (4) nothing is read in
   b. (3) and (4) may cause unpredictable results

SELF-CHECK 9-3

1. a. `strcpy(str,"toad");`
   b. `strcpy(input,str);`
2. *sizeof*: a. 5   b. 80
   strlen: a. 4   b. 4

3. a. negative
   b. positive, negative
   c. negative

SELF-CHECK 9-4

1. a. ***big*** holds "a sunny daywas\0"
   b. ***little*** holds "wasin" (without '**\0**'); remaining characters from ***middle*** destroy another variable
   c. ***big*** holds "a sunny dayin the park\0"
2. a. negative   b. negative

3. a.
```
strncpy(dest,big+11,3);
dest[3] = '\0';
```
   b.
```
strncpy(dest,big,3);
dest[3] = '\0';
```

SELF-CHECK 9-5

1. ***gets*** reads in an entire line, including blanks; ***scanf*** stops at the first blank

2. (b), (e), and (f) are illegal because there is an extra parameter; (c) is illegal because ***num*** is not a string; (a) and (d) are legal

SELF-CHECK 9-6

1. `char *twostr(char *, char *);`
2. it searches for the null character

3. `return !found ? -1 : i;`

SELF-CHECK 9-7

1. the character can occur in position 0 of the array
2. value of ***p*** is initially –1, and the inner ***while*** loop is never executed

3. yes

SELF-CHECK 9-8

1. to read in a single character
2. ***getchar*** can return ***EOF***, a value outside the range of type ***char***

3. prints the newline character, moving the cursor to the next line

SELF-CHECK 9-9

1. a. 0   c. 0   e. '*P*'   g. '*m*'
   b. 1   d. 1   f. '*J*'   h. 1

2. not able to access the library function with the same name

SELF-CHECK 9-10

1. a. `char courses[20][30];`
   b. `char lines[50][80];`
2. each of the 10 strings holds up to three characters, but initial values are much larger (subscripts are reversed)

3. 10 strings in the array (each of size 15), but ***for*** loop tries to print 15 strings (subscripts are reversed)

SELF-CHECK 10-1

1. it must win that later competition
2. 4, 55, ***n–1***; one for each pass but the last pass does two

3. easy for three, increasingly more difficult for four or five, much harder past five

SELF-CHECK 10-2

1. first pass—20 is compared to 100 and then –12, causing a switch; second pass—100 switches with 20, then 20 and 5 switch; third pass—100 and 5 switch

2. *pass* loop—run through the various array positions; *cand* loop—run through each position's candidates

3. no

SELF-CHECK 10-3

1. on the first pass, 20 and 0 switch, then 20 and –2 switch, then 20 and 15 switch; on the second pass, 0 and –2 switch, but no others; on the third pass, no switches

2. yes, as shown: `for (pos = 0, swapped = 0; pos < n - 1; pos++)`

3. cannot continue to have swaps on every pass; eventually, every element must be correct

SELF-CHECK 10-4

1. an item could be found in position 0 of the array
2. function must always return the same type of answer

3. a. 4 in pos. 2, 1 not found
   b. 5 not found, 20 in pos. 1

SELF-CHECK 10-5

1. 1, in case the user types *n* the first time; no upper limit
2. values returned are: a.   2, –1, 0, 6, 8, 2, –1
                    b.   –1, 1, –1, 5, –1

3. only difference is in the header: `void locatevalues(int *numb, int n)`

SELF-CHECK 10-6

1. yes, but it is wasteful
2. we search for a series of values using the loop in *locatevalues*

3. in bottom-up, the details of the main program are last; in top-down, the details of the functions are last

SELF-CHECK 10-7

1. left to the reader
2. `void linearsort(int *, int);`
   `void linearsearch(int *,int, int);`
   no difference

3. need prototype for *bubblesort*, main program calls *bubblesort* (with same parameters), and body of *bubblesort* included

SELF-CHECK 10-8

1. on first pass, 50.1 and 6.3 switch, as do 6.3 and 4.4; on second pass, 50.1 and 6.3 switch, as do 6.3 and the second 4.4; remaining passes left to the reader
2. function *swap* declares a local variable

3. use following lines in the body of the *for* loop:
   ```
   if (numb[pos] > numb[pos+1]) {
       swapped = 1;
       swap(&numb[pos],&numb[pos+1]);
   }
   ```

SELF-CHECK 10-9

1. binary search can reject half of the remaining portion of the array because the elements in the array are in order

2. values returned are: a.   3, –1, 5, –1
                          b.   1, –1, –1

3. roughly 22 guesses (two more than for one million)

SELF-CHECK 11-1

1. not possible to store all values in a single array because they have different data types; parallel arrays (one for names, ones for ages, etc.) will work

2. *readdata* can call *prettyprint*; transfer the loop shown in main to a function; *selecttrait* (and the other functions) can call *printmenu* or print the menu itself

SELF-CHECK 11-2

1. can use heterogeneous data types and can impose a logical hierarchy on a collection of items

2.
```
struct bus {
    char    name[5];
    int     frequency;
    char    startpt[15], endpt[15];
    double  fare;
};
```

3.
```
struct bus {
    ...
} busvar1;
struct bus busvar2;
```

SELF-CHECK 11-3

1. pieces of information have different data types

2.
```
strcpy(class.department,"Geology");
class.courseinfo.coursenumber = 23;
class.courseinfo.num_credits = 4.5;
class.courseinfo.class_size = 35;
```

3. can define one structure as part of another, larger structure, reflecting the hierarchal relationships within a set of data

SELF-CHECK 11-4

1.
```
strcpy(pet[0].species,"cat");
pet[0].sex = 'F';
pet[0].age = 2;
strcpy(pet[0].name,"Diva");
```

2.
```
struct petinfo *petptr;
```
3.
```
petptr -> age, petptr -> name
```
   or   `(*petptr).age, (*petptr).name`

SELF-CHECK 11-5

1.
```
void fillstudent(struct stud *stuptr)
```

2.
```
struct class *findtop(struct class
section[], int numclasses)
```

SELF-CHECK 11-6

1. seven arrays, one per each member in the structure

2. some (*prettyprint*) need all of the arrays, some (*findage*) need only one or two

SELF-CHECK 11-7

1. at the beginning of the file, above the main program

2. `struct part inventory[100];`
   or `part_type inventory[100];`

SELF-CHECK 11-8

1. union—one alternative exists at a given time; structure—all members are allocated space

2. programmer's responsibility, usually done using another variable or constant

3. space is allocated for the largest alternative

SELF-CHECK 12-1

1. to allow the recursion to end
2. body of the function contains a call to that same function (or it forms a recursive chain)

3. `if (n == 1)` *function* `fact`
   `if (k <= 1)` *function* `reverse`
   `if (n == 0 || n == 1)`   *function* `fib`

SELF-CHECK 12-2

1. variable declared in a file before the functions (including **main**)

2. can be used if it represents a major data structure; should not be used for simple variables or in general-purpose functions

3. automatic

SELF-CHECK 12-3

1. allows a program to declare only those locations it needs

2. **malloc**—block of storage of a certain size is allocated; **free**—block of storage pointed to by a pointer is freed

3. signals the end of the list

SELF-CHECK 12-4

1. a. M (but **c** now holds 'N')
   b. N (which is the current value stored in **c**)
   c. 100 (but **i** now holds 99)
   d. 99 (which is the current value stored in **i**)

2. a. **y** is set to 5, and **x** to 8
   b. **y** is set to 8, and **x** to 8
   c. same as (b)
   d. **x** is set to 3, and **y** is unchanged

INDEX

Note: Page references in boldface type mark the most important entries or places where an indexed term is defined.

/* */ 18, 53
< > 19
( ) 19, 74, 75
{ }. *See* braces
" " 26–27, 70, 95
' ' 95
[ ] 345
; 21, 39, 53, 70
= 22, 54, 87, 100
+ 23, 54, 73, 100
* (multiplication) 24, 54, 100
* (dereferencing) 252, **255–56**, **406**, **409–11**
– (minus) 46, 54, 73, 100
– (alignment) 135, 152
% (modulus) 46, 54, 60, 100
% (in conversion specification) 78, 86
/ 46, 54, 60, 100
++. *See* increment operator
––. *See* decrement operator
+=. *See* compound assignment operator
–=. *See* compound assignment operator
*=. *See* compound assignment operator
/=. *See* compound assignment operator
%=. *See* compound assignment operator
\ **85–86**, 100. *See also* escape character
n. *See* character, newline
t. *See* character, tab
0. *See* character, null
>. *See* relational operator; redirection, output
<. *See* relational operator; redirection, input
>=. *See* relational operator
<=. *See* relational operator
==. *See* relational operator
!=. *See* relational operator
& (address) 118–19, 153, **256**, **405–06**, 443
& (bitwise and) 695
! (not). *See* logical operation, not
! (factorial) 203–04

| (bitwise or) 695
| (pipe). *See* piping
?:. *See* conditional operator
||. *See* logical operation, or
&&. *See* logical operation, and
. (dot) **594**, 641, 643. *See also* structure, dot operator
-> **608–09**, 643. *See also* structure, arrow operator
19, 180–81, 197
#define directive 180–81, 197, 633
    compared with **typedef** 633
#include directive 19, 53, 94, 219, 468, 510

abs function 93, 101
absolute value 93
action portion of program 19
address **404–06**, 443
    operator. *See* operator, address
algorithm **17**, 53, 175
alignment 35, 53
ampersand 118–19, **405**, **407–08**, 413–14, 443
ANSI C **3–4**, 38, 52, 693
argc. *See* function, parameters, command-line
argument. *See* function, parameters
argv. *See* function, parameters, command-line
arithmetic
    associativity **73**
    conversion
        automatic type 92
        casting 342
        forcing 341–42
    expression **24**
    mixed mode **92**, 341–42
    operations 23–24, **45–47**, 54, 60
    operators 45–46, 54, 73
    precedence **72–74**, **695**

array **344–83**, **426–34**
    advantages **372–73**, 386
    brackets 345
    bounds **347**, 386
        selecting **354**
    changing value in a function **361–63**, 426–34, 445
    of **char**. *See* **char**, array of
    compared with a structure 592, 597–98, 641
    declaration **347–48**
    dimension **347**
    disadvantages **372–73**, 387
    elements 345–46, 353–54
    finding the largest element **365–68**, 387
    finding the smallest element **534**
    in a **for** loop 347
    in a function **359–64**, 387, **426–34**, 438, 445
    index **345**. *See also* array, subscript
    initialization 348
    one-dimensional **344–74**
    multidimensional **382**, 388
    parallel **353**
    pointer notation **432–33**, 438, 445
    of pointers **674**, 686
    restrictions 592, 641
    size **347**, 355, 386
    subscript **345**, 347–48, 351–52, 354, 356, 386, 432–33, 445
    two-dimensional **374–83**, 387–88
arrow operator. *See* structure, arrow operator
ASCII code **95**, **472**, 507, 519, **562**, **694**
assembly language **2–3**
assignment statement **22–24**, 54, 87, 680–81, 684
    as an expression 680–81
    side effects 680–81
    value of 681